The Milken Institute Series on Financial Innovation and Economic Growth

Volume 8

Series Editors

James R. Barth
Milken Institute, Santa Monica, CA, USA
and
Auburn University, Auburn, AL, USA

Glenn Yago
Milken Institute, Santa Monica, CA, USA

For further volumes:
http://www.springer.com/series/6290

James R. Barth · John A. Tatom · Glenn Yago
Editors

China's Emerging Financial Markets

Challenges and Opportunities

Springer

Editors
James R. Barth
Milken Institute
Senior Fellow
1250 Fourth Street
Santa Monica, CA, 90401
USA
jbarth@milkeninstitute.org

John A. Tatom
Networks Financial Institute
2902 N. Meridian St.
Indianapolis, IN, 46208
USA
john.tatom@isunetworks.org

Glenn Yago
Milken Institute
Director of Capital Studies
1250 Fourth Street
Santa Monica, CA 90401
USA
gyago@milkeninstitue.org

ISBN 978-0-387-93768-7 e-ISBN 978-0-387-93769-4
DOI 10.1007/978-0-387-93769-4
Springer New York Dordrecht Heidelberg London

Library of Congress Control Number: 2008942365

Printed on acid-free paper

Springer is part of Springer Science + Business Media (www.springer.com)

About the Editors

James R. Barth is a Senior Finance Fellow at the Milken Institute and the Lowder Eminent Scholar in Finance at Auburn University. His research has focused on financial institutions and capital markets, both domestic and global, with special emphasis on regulatory issues. Recently he served as leader of an international team advising the People's Bank of China on banking reform.

Barth was an appointee of Presidents Ronald Reagan and George H.W. Bush as chief economist of the Office of Thrift Supervision and previously chief economist of the Federal Home Loan Bank Board. He has also held the positions of professor of economics at George Washington University, associate director of the economics program at the National Science Foundation and Shaw Foundation Professor of Banking and Finance at Nanyang Technological University. He has been a visiting scholar at the U.S. Congressional Budget Office, Federal Reserve Bank of Atlanta, Office of the Comptroller of the Currency and the World Bank. He is a member of the Advisory Council of George Washington University's Financial Services Research Program.

Barth's expertise in financial institution and capital market issues has led him to testify before the U.S. House and Senate banking committees on several occasions. He has authored more than 200 articles in professional journals and has written and edited several books, including *The Great Savings and Loan Debacle* (American Enterprise Press) and *The Reform of Federal Deposit Insurance* (HarperBusiness). His most recent books are *The Rise and Fall of the U.S. Mortgage and Credit Markets* (John Wiley & Sons, 2009), *Rethinking Bank Regulation: Till Angels Govern*, with Jerry Caprio and Ross Levine, (Cambridge University Press, 2006) and *Financial Restructuring and Reform in Post-WTO China*, with Zhongfei Zhou, Douglas Arner, Berry Hsu and Wei Wang (Kluwer Law International, 2007). He is the overseas associate editor of *The Chinese Banker* and has been quoted in publications ranging from the *New York Times* and *Wall Street Journal* to *Time* and *Newsweek*.

Barth serves on several editorial boards and is included in Who's *Who in Economics: A Biographical Dictionary of Major Economists, 1700 to 1995*.

Barth received a Ph.D. in economics from Ohio State University.

John A. Tatom is the Director of Research at Networks Financial Institute, part of Indiana State University, and Associate Professor of Finance at Indiana State University. He has held both positions since June 2005. Previously, he was an adjunct professor in the Economics Department at DePaul University in Chicago from 2000 until 2005. In 2003-2004, he was also a senior fellow at the Tax Foundation in Washington, D.C.

Tatom served from 1995 to 2000 in various capacities for UBS in Zurich, including chief U.S. economist in the Asset Allocation and Currency Group at UBS Asset Management in Chicago; executive director and head of country research and limit control in Zurich; and chief economist for emerging market and developing countries in Zurich. From 1976 to 1995, he served as assistant vice president and policy adviser in the Research Department of the Federal Reserve Bank of St. Louis. He has taught at several other colleges and universities. He holds a Ph.D. from Texas A&M University.

He has published widely on international and domestic monetary and fiscal policy issues, inflation, capital formation, productivity and growth, energy price shocks, and other macroeconomic and international topics. His focus at Networks Financial Institute is on financial sector performance and regulatory reform, the link between the financial sector and economic growth, and financial literacy. He has edited *In Search of Effective Corporate Governance*, (November 2007), *The Health Care Financing Bomb: Where's the Money (or the Solution)?* (August 2006), *Assessing Adult Financial Literacy* (March 2006), *Is Your Bubble About to Burst?* (October 2005), *The Social Security Dilemma* (September 2005) for Networks Financial Institute, and (with Costa Vayenas and Heinrich Siegmann) *The UBS Guide to the Emerging Markets*, Bloomsbury (1997).

Glenn Yago is Director of Capital Studies at the Milken Institute and a leading authority on financial innovations, capital markets, emerging markets, and environmental finance. He is also a Senior Koret Fellow, directing postgraduate research on economic and financial reform in Israel. Yago focuses on the innovative use of financial instruments to solve long-standing economic development, social, and environmental challenges. His work has contributed to policy innovations fostering the democratization of capital to traditionally underserved markets and entrepreneurs in the United States and around the world. Prior to joining the Institute, Yago served as a professor at the State University of New York-Stony Brook and City University of New York Graduate Center. He has also taught at Tel-Aviv University and the Interdisciplinary Center-Herzliya. He is the author of multiple books, including *The Rise and Fall of the U.S. Mortgage and Credit Markets* (John Wiley & Sons, 2009), *Global Edge* (Harvard Business School Press), *Restructuring Regulation and Financial Institutions* (Kluwer) and *Beyond Junk Bonds* (Oxford University Press), and co-editor of the *Milken Institute Series on Financial Innovation and Economic Growth* (Springer). Yago created the Milken Institute's *Capital Access Index*, an annual survey measuring access to capital for entrepreneurs across countries, and co-created the *Opacity Index*, measuring financial risks associated with corruption, legal, enforcement, accounting, and regulatory practices internationally. His opinions have appeared in *The Los Angeles Times* and *The Wall Street Journal.* Yago is a recipient of the 2002 Gleitsman Foundation Award of Achievement for social change. He earned a Ph.D. at the University of Wisconsin, Madison.

Preface

China's emerging financial markets reflect the usual contrast between the country's measured approach toward policy, regulatory, and market reform, and the dynamic pace of rapid economic growth and development. But they also offer unusual challenges and opportunities. In the past five years, the pace of opening and reform has accelerated sharply. Recapitalization and partial privatization of the largest banks, and the allowance of some joint venture and branch operations for foreign financial institutions, are making rapid headway in developing and expanding financial services and improving access to domestic business and households.

This book provides the most extensive look available at the evolving Chinese financial system. It begins with alternative perspectives on the evolution of the financial system and the broad outlines of its prospects and potential contribution to economic growth.

Three articles review broad aspects of the financial system. Franklin Allen, Jun "QJ" Qian, Meijun Qian, and Mengxin Zhao lead off with overviews of the banking system and performance of the equity market and other institutions. They highlight the importance of alternative financing channels, governance mechanisms, and financial institutions and take note of the differences between this "non-traditional" sector and its more established western counterparts. Co-editor James Barth and contributors Gerard Caprio Jr., and Triphon Phumiwasana describe the growth and financial reform record of China and the sources of growth and its unbalanced nature; they also provide a history of the changing role of the financial system in promoting growth. In his essay, Albert Keidel emphasizes the dual financial system—the state-owned sector and the private sector; he explores how it has operated in the past, and the convergence problems it confronts as it transitions to a largely private approach to organizing financial firms and activity. In his view, the state-sector will remain important for at least twenty to thirty years.

In Part II, we turn to monetary policy and the foreign exchange market, with two articles on monetary policy and five on the foreign exchange market. Bernard Laurens and Rodolfo Maino from the International Monetary Fund describe the monetary policy procedures followed by the People's Bank of China and its evolution. They also provide an analysis of the direction of future monetary and exchange rate policies. Jonathan Anderson, meanwhile, provides a sweeping overview of monetary policy, how policy is organized, the quantitative procedures employed, and the relationship of the central bank to financial markets and the future direction of monetary policy. Though similarities exist in the topical coverage of the first two articles, the different perspectives of IMF economists and Anderson, a global bank economist, generate a greater depth of understanding.

No discussion of the financial system would be complete without attention to the evolving foreign exchange regime and a discussion of the rationale for a slow approach to exiting a fixed exchange rate regime and the special problems of the current managed float. Following up on the monetary policy chapters, Priscilla Liang, Alice Ouyang, and Thomas D. Willett; co-editor John A. Tatom (two chapters); Jeffrey A. Frankel; and Jie Li, Jing Chen, and Liqing Zhang provide five analyses of China's controversial exchange rate policies and recent changes. All five chapters bear on the rationale for China's pace of rapid foreign exchange accumulation and the connection between financial opening and the freeing of the foreign exchange market. They also examine the difficulties of achieving fixed or managed exchange rates, while applying independent monetary policies and moving toward greater capital mobility. Liang, Ouyang, and Willett argue that China's currency remains substantially undervalued and that further appreciation is in the longer-run interests of both China and the rest of the world. However, they also point out that short-term and special interests provide major obstacles to needed adjustments. They note that exchange rate adjustments alone will not be sufficient to restore global balance but are an important part of the lowest-cost policy mix for doing so. Tatom focuses on the role of exchange rate stability in providing a nominal anchor to monetary policy. He argues that the exchange rate is not undervalued—but if it were, it could be corrected by inflation, without taking the risk of currency appreciation, capital inflows, and reversals. Frankel provides a useful new method to assess the changing exchange rate regime. He simultaneously estimates weights in a currency basket and a changing degree of flexibility of an exchange rate with a single currency anchor. He argues that, since mid-2007, the appreciation of the yuan against the dollar does not reflect new flexibility or an upward trend of the currency against its basket but rather an increasing weight of the euro in the Chinese currency basket. Thus, appreciation against the dollar reflects the appreciation of the euro against the dollar. In his second chapter, Tatom notes the role of capital outflow restrictions in preventing a managed exchange rate regime without creating inflation, financial repression, and banking sector losses. Li, Chen and Zhang trace the origins of pressures on China to build relatively large foreign exchange position, especially the role of the 1997–1998 Asian financial crisis. They explain the response of reserve hoarding and managed appreciation as responses to the demand for a new international financial architecture, and attempt to determine the criteria for establishing an appropriate reserve level or for determining when reserves are truly excessive.

Part III presents six chapters on banking and bank regulation, including a review of the prospects for a regulatory approach to ensure access to banking services for such a large and diverse population and geography. The section leads off with a chapter by Allen Berger, Iftekhar Hasan, and Mingming Zhou, who examine the increasingly important role of minority foreign ownership of banking firms in China, and the importance for diversification, efficiency, and profitability of Chinese banks. They highlight the structural change in ownership patterns and its permanence, as well as the contribution of the new regulatory strategy to banking sector development. Tong Li reviews the current state of non-performing loans in China and the prospects for improvement in banking performance. The state created detailed mechanisms to deal with this problem in 1999, but problem loans did not end then. Moreover, the process of trying to deal with "toxic assets" is continuing. Richard C. K. Burdekin and Ran Tao provide an analysis of the bank loan growth, lending patterns, and performance among the largest state-owned banks, both before and after their initial public offerings in 2005–2006. Chung-Hua Shen, Qi Liang, and Xiang-Chao Hao study the determinants of location choice of foreign banks, in particular the role of market opportunity, labor cost and IT infrastructure. Perry Wong and Diehang Zheng review the impact of bank lending on housing prices, which is a widely noted linkage in developed and other developing countries. China has experienced some booms in housing prices in selected areas, and Wong and Zheng find that the link to bank lending is also critical in influencing these developments in China. Yufeng Gong and Zhongfei Zhou examine the role of regulations in improving access to banking services in China. They discuss the efforts of regulators to improve financial services for low-income and rural populations as part of a decades-long agenda of reducing poverty. A common theme of these chapters is the assessment of the inefficiencies of past and current bank regulation and the prospects for reform as China moves toward taking up its role as a global competitor in financial services with a strong, stable, and predictable currency.

Part IV provides a detailed look at the bond and equity markets. Haizhou Huang and Ning Zhu take a close look at the development of China's modern bond market, and its prospects for success. Chung-Hsing Chen of Xinhua Finance provides an update on the Chinese capital markets, focusing on developments in the securities market. Chen describes the state of securitization on China and its prospects and current constraints. His update is followed by Jie Gan's look at the development of privatization of state-owned companies and how that has proceeded in equity markets. Chen Lin, Clement Chun-Yau Shum, and Sonia Man-Lai Wong explain the importance and emergence of shareholder protection on China, and the prospects for further enhancement of shareholder rights. In the fifth chapter in this section, Honghui (David) Cao and Huazhao Liu examine the issues of segmented share markets and the impact of reform on the market behavior of large shareholders.

In the final chapter in the book, co-editor Tatom returns to the issue of growth and global convergence in China. A common theme throughout this book is the role of institutions in promoting efficiency, competitiveness, and growth in financial markets, and in the overall economy. Policy makers and market efforts to improve the functioning of markets will be key to China's leadership in the world economy and in its financial markets. China is the second largest economy in Asia and the largest of the emerging markets in Asia or the rest of the world. The country's recent progress and its continuing economic development suggest that China, and Shanghai in particular, could rival Asia's other financial centers within a decade or so—and could become the dominant financial center in Asia, perhaps rivaling the top tier of the world's leading financial centers. The analysis of the current state of the Chinese financial market and of the challenges and opportunities facing policy makers and industry leaders frame the issue of these possibilities.

This book is the eighth in the Milken Institute Series on Financial Innovation and Economic Growth. It is an outgrowth of a conference, "China: A Two-way Street," jointly sponsored by Indiana State University, Liaoning University, and Networks Financial Institute on January 24–25, 2007. The volume includes three updated papers by two of the co-editors, and a paper by Albert Keidel, that were presented at the conference or written for it. As a result of the success of the conference, the editors agreed that a more comprehensive look at China's financial markets was necessary and would be valuable to scholars, students, and policy makers in assessing the unique features of the Chinese financial system, the challenges it faces, and the opportunities that financial sector development present. The result brings together the ideas and analyses of 41 financial and policy experts, including scholars, industry and government advisers and leaders, and experts from international institutions. More than half of the contributors are Chinese and have had the advantage of front-row seats in the emerging Chinese financial markets and an understanding of the players and the process of change that is more difficult for outside analysts to obtain.

The editors are extremely grateful for the excellent assistance provided by Wenling Lu in the preparation of this book.

Santa Monica, CA — James R. Barth
Indianapolis, IN — John A. Tatom
Santa Monica, CA — Glenn Yago

Contents

About the Milken Institute

The Milken Institute is an independent economic think tank whose mission is to improve the lives and economic conditions of diverse populations in the United States and around the world by helping business and public policy leaders identify and implement innovative ideas for creating broad-based prosperity. We put research to work with the goal of revitalizing regions and finding new ways to generate capital for people with original ideas.

We focus on:
human capital: the talent, knowledge, and experience of people, and their value to organizations, economies, and society;

financial capital: innovations that allocate financial resources efficiently, especially to those who ordinarily would not have access to them, but who can best use them to build companies, create jobs, accelerate life-saving medical research, and solve long-standing social and economic problems; and

social capital: the bonds of society that underlie economic advancement, including schools, health care, cultural institutions, and government services.

By creating ways to spread the benefits of human, financial, and social capital to as many people as possible—by *democratizing* capital—we hope to contribute to prosperity and freedom in all corners of the globe.

We are nonprofit, nonpartisan, and publicly supported.

Contributors

Franklin Allen Wharton School, University of Pennsylvania, Philadelphia, PA, USA, allenf@wharton.upenn.edu

Jonathan Anderson UBS, Hong Kong, China, jonathan.anderson@ubs.com

James R. Barth Milken Institute, Santa Monica, CA, USA; Auburn University, Auburn, AL, USA, jbarth@milkeninstitute.org

Allen N. Berger Moore School of Business, University of South Carolina, Columbia, SC, USA; Wharton Financial Institutions Center, Philadelphia, PA, USA, aberger@moore.sc.edu

Richard C.K. Burdekin Claremont McKenna College, Claremont, CA, USA, richard.burdekin@claremontmckenna.edu

Honghui Cao Institute of Finance and Banking, Chinese Academy of Social Sciences, Beijing, China, davidcao@163.com

Gerard Caprio Jr. Williams College, Williamstown, MA, USA, gerard.caprio@williams.edu

Jing Chen Central University of Finance and Economics, Beijing, China, chenjingcafd@gmail.com

Chung-Hsing Chen Xinhua Finance, Shanghai, China, ch.chen@xinhuafinance.com

Jeffrey A. Frankel Kennedy School of Government, Harvard University, Cambridge, MA, USA, jeffrey_frankel@harvard.edu

Jie Gan Hong Kong University of Science and Technology, Hong Kong, China, jgan@ust.hk

Yufeng Gong Shanghai University of Finance and Economics, Shanghai, China, florayufeng@yahoo.com.cn

Xiang-Chao Hao Research Center of Corporate Governance, Nankai University, Tianjin, China, haoxiangchao@163.com

Iftekhar Hasan Lally School of Management and Technology, Rensselaer Polytechnic Institute, Troy, NY, hasan@rpi.edu

Haizhou Huang China International Capital Corporation, Beijing, China, huanghz2@cicc.com.cn

Albert Keidel Carnegie Endowment for International Peace, Washington, D.C., USA, akeidel@carnegieendowment.org

Bernard J. Laurens International Monetary Fund, Washington D.C., USA, blaurens@imf.org

Jie Li Central University of Finance and Economics, Beijing, China, jieli.cn@gmail.com

Tong Li Milken Institute, Santa Monica, CA, USA, cli@milkeninstitute.org

Priscilla Liang California State University, Channel Islands, Camarillo, CA, USA, priscilla.liang@csuci.edu

Qi Liang School of Economics, Nankai University, Tianjin, China, liangqi@nankai.edu.cn

Chen Lin City University of Hong Kong, Hong Kong, China, chenlin@cityu.edu.hk

Huazhao Liu Graduate School of Chinese Academy of Social Sciences, Beijing, China, caohonghui@gmail.com

Rodolfo Maino International Monetary Fund, Washington, D.C., USA, rmaino@imf.org

Alice Ouyang Central University of Finance and Economics, Beijing, China, alice.ouyang@gmail.com

Triphon Phumiwasana Milken Institute, Santa Monica, CA, USA

Jun "QJ" Qian Carroll School of Management, Boston College, Chestnut Hill, MA, USA, qianju@bc.edu

Meijun Qian NUS Business School, National University of Singapore, Singapore, bizqmj@nus.edu.sg

Chung-Hua Shen National Taiwan University, Taipei, Taiwan, China, chshen01@ntu.edu.tw

Clement Chun-Yau Shum Lingnan University, Hong Kong, China, clement@ln.edu.hk

Ran Tao Claremont Graduate University, Claremont, CA, USA, nancy.tao@cgu.edu

John A. Tatom Networks Financial Institute at Indiana State University, Indianapolis, IN, USA, john.tatom@isunetworks.org

Thomas D. Willett Claremont Institute for Economic Policy Studies, Claremont Graduate University, Claremont, CA, USA, tom.willett@cgu.edu

Perry Wong Milken Institute, Santa Monica, CA, USA, pwong@milkeninstitute.org

Sonia Man-Lai Wong Lingnan University, Hong Kong, China, soniawong@ln.edu.hk

Liqing Zhang Central University of Finance and Economics, Beijing, China, zhlq@cufe.edu.cn

Mengxin Zhao School of Business, University of Alberta, Edmonton, AB, Canada, mengxin1@ualberta.ca

Diehang Zheng University of Southern California, Los Angeles, CA, USA, zhengdh37@hotmail.com

Mingming Zhou School of Management, University of Alaska Fairbanks, Fairbanks, AK, USA, m.zhou@uaf.edu

Zhongfei Zhou Shanghai University of Finance and Economics, Shanghai, China, zhongfeizhou@yahoo.cn

Ning Zhu UC Davis and Lehman Brothers, ningzhu@lehman.com

Part I
Overview of the Chinese Financial System

A Review of China's Financial System and Initiatives for the Future

Franklin Allen, Jun "QJ" Qian, Meijun Qian, and Mengxin Zhao

Abstract We provide a comprehensive review of China's financial system and explore directions of future development. First, the current financial system is dominated by a large banking sector. In recent years, banks have made considerable progress in reducing the amount of non-performing loans and improving their efficiency. It is important that these efforts are continued. Second, the role of the stock market in allocating resources in the economy has been limited and ineffective. Further development of China's stock market and other financial markets is the most important task in the long term. Third, the most successful part of the financial system, in terms of supporting the growth of the overall economy, is a non-standard sector that consists of alternative financing channels, governance mechanisms, and institutions. This sector should co-exist with banks and markets in the future in order to continue to support the growth of the Hybrid Sector (non-state, non-listed firms). Finally, in order to sustain stable economic growth, China should aim to prevent and halt damaging financial crises, including a banking sector crisis, a real estate or stock market crash, and a "twin crisis" in the currency market and banking sector.

Keywords Banks · Non-performing loans · Markets · Corporate governance · Hybrid sector · Financial crisis

1 Introduction

In this paper, we provide a comprehensive review of China's financial system and extensive comparisons with other countries. Almost every functioning financial system includes financial markets and intermediaries (e.g., a banking sector), but how these two standard financial sectors contribute to the entire

F. Allen (✉)
Wharton School, University of Pennsylvania, Philadelphia, PA, USA
e-mail: allenf@wharton.upenn.edu

J.R. Barth et al. (eds.), *China's Emerging Financial Markets*,
The Milken Institute Series on Financial Innovation and Economic Growth 8,
DOI 10.1007/978-0-387-93769-4_1,

financial system and economy differs significantly across different countries. In this regard, we discuss what has worked and what remains to be done within the two sectors and examine how further development can better serve the entire economy. We also examine a non-standard financial sector, which operates outside the markets and banking sectors and consists of alternative financing channels, governance mechanisms, and institutions. Finally, we provide guidelines for future research and policy making on several important unresolved issues, including how China's financial system should integrate into the world's markets and economy without being interrupted by damaging financial crises. Although there is no consensus regarding the prospects for China's future economic growth, a prevailing view on China's financial system speculates that it is one of the weakest links in the economy, and it will hamper future economic growth.

We draw four main conclusions about China's financial system and its future development.

First, when we examine and compare China's banking system and financial markets with those of both developed and emerging countries, we find China's financial system is currently dominated by a large but underdeveloped banking system. Even with the entrance and growth of many domestic and foreign banks and financial institutions in recent years, China's banking system is still mainly controlled by the four largest state-owned banks. Three of the "big four" banks have recently become publicly listed and traded companies, with the government being the largest shareholder and retaining control. The continuation of the effort to improve the banking system, in particular, to reduce the amount of NPLs of the major banks and to improve their efficiency, is the most important aspect of reforming China's financial system in the short run.

Our second conclusion concerns China's financial markets. Two domestic stock exchanges, the Shanghai Stock Exchange (SHSE hereafter) and Shenzhen Stock Exchange (SZSE), were established in 1990. Their scale and importance are not comparable to the banking sector; and they have not been effective in allocating resources in the economy, in that they are highly speculative and driven by insider trading. Going forward, however, financial markets are likely to play an increasingly important role in the economy, and their further development is the most important long-term task for China's financial system. We propose several measures that can increase their size and scope and help improve the efficiency of the markets.

Third, in an earlier paper, Allen, Qian and Qian (2005a, AQQ hereafter), we find that the most successful part of the financial system, in terms of supporting the growth of the overall economy, is not the banking sector or financial markets but rather a sector of alternative financing channels, such as informal financial intermediaries, internal financing and trade credits, and coalitions of various forms among firms, investors, and local governments. Many of these financing channels rely on alternative governance mechanisms, such as competition in product and input markets, and trust, reputation, and relationships. Together, these mechanisms of financing and governance have supported the growth of a "Hybrid Sector" of non-state, non-listed firms with various types of ownership structures. It is important to point out at the outset that our definition of the Hybrid Sector is broader than privately or individually owned firms, which are only part of this sector. In particular, firms that are partially owned by *local* governments (e.g., Township Village Enterprises or TVEs) are also included in the Hybrid Sector. This is done for two reasons. First, despite the ownership stake of local governments, and the sometimes ambiguous ownership structure and property rights, the operation of these firms resembles more closely that of a for-profit, privately owned firm than that of a state-owned firm. Second, the ownership stake of local governments in many of these firms has been privatized.[1] The growth of the Hybrid Sector has been much higher than that of the State Sector (state-owned enterprises or SOEs, and all firms where the central government has ultimate control) and the Listed Sector (publicly listed and traded firms with most of them converted from the State Sector) and contributes to most of the economic growth. We believe that these alternative channels and mechanisms should be encouraged going forward. They can co-exist with banks and markets, while continuing to fuel the growth of the Hybrid Sector.

Finally, in our view, a significant challenge for China's financial system is to avoid damaging financial crises that can severely disrupt the economy and social stability. China needs to guard against traditional financial crises, including a banking sector crisis stemming from continuing accumulation of NPLs and a sudden drop in banks' profits, or a crisis/crash resulting from speculative asset bubbles in the real estate market or stock market. China also needs to guard against new types of financial crises, such as a "twin crisis" (simultaneous foreign exchange and banking/stock market crises) that struck many Asian economies in the late 1990s. The entrance of China into the World Trade Organization (WTO) introduced cheap foreign capital and technology, but large-scale and sudden capital flows and foreign speculation increased the likelihood of a twin crisis. At the end of 2007, China's foreign currency reserves surpassed US $1.5 trillion, the largest in the world; it increased to US $1.68 trillion as of March 2008. The rapid increase in China's foreign exchange reserves suggests that there is a large amount of speculative, "hot" money in China in anticipation of a continuing (possibly considerable) appreciation of the RMB, China's currency, relative to all other major currencies, especially the US dollar. Depending on how the government and the central bank handle the process of revaluation, there could be a classic currency crisis as the government

---

[1] The Hybrid Sector comprises all the firms that are not state-owned or publicly listed, and more specifically, it includes the following types of firms: (1) privately owned companies (but *not* publicly listed and traded); controlling owners can be Chinese citizens, investors (or companies) from Taiwan or Hong Kong, or foreign investors (or companies); (2) collectively and jointly owned companies, where joint ownership among local government, communities, employees, and institutions is forged.

and central bank try to defend the partial currency peg, which in turn may trigger a banking crisis, if there are large withdrawals from banks.

The remaining sections are organized as follows. In Section 2, we briefly review the history of China's financial system development, present aggregate evidence on China's financial system and compare them to those of developed and other developing countries. In Section 3, we examine China's banking system and the problem of NPLs and reforms. In Section 4, we examine the growth and irregularities of financial markets, including the stock market, real estate market, and listed firms, and propose several initiatives to develop new markets and further develop existing markets, as well as measures to improve corporate governance among listed firms. In Section 5, we examine the non-standard financial sector, including alternative financial channels and governance mechanisms. Motivated by the success of this financial sector and firms in the Hybrid Sector, we also compare the advantages and disadvantages of using the law as the basis of finance and commerce. In Section 6, we then examine different types of financial crises and how China's financial system can be better prepared for these crises, Finally, Section 7 concludes the paper. In terms of converting RMB into US dollars, we use the exchange rate of US $1 = RMB 8.28 (*yuan*) for transactions and events occurring before 2005, and the spot rate at the end of each year for those activities during and after 2005 (Fig. 8 provides a graph of the exchange rates).

2 Overview of China's Financial System

In this section, we examine China's financial system, focusing on both the banking sector and financial markets, as well as firms' financing channels at the aggregate level, including non-bank and non-market channels.

2.1 A Brief Review of the History of China's Financial System

China's financial system was well developed before 1949.[2] One key finding in reviewing the history of this period, including the rise of Shanghai as one of the financial centers of Asia during the first half of the twentieth century, is that the development of China's commerce and financial system as a whole was by and large *outside* the formal legal system. For example, despite the entrance of Western-style courts in Shanghai and other major coastal cities in the early 1900s, most business-related disputes were resolved through mechanisms outside courts, including guilds (merchant coalitions), families, and local notables.

[2] For more descriptions of the pre-1949 history of China's financial system, see a companion paper of this chapter, AQQ (2005b); for more anecdotal evidence on the development of China's financial system in the same period, see, for example, Kirby (1995) and Lee (1993).

In Section 5.3 below, we argue that modern equivalents of these dispute resolution and corporate governance mechanisms are behind the success of Hybrid Sector firms in the same areas in the 1980s and 1990s and that these alternative mechanisms may be superior to the law and legal institutions in adapting to changes in a fast-growing economy like China.

After the foundation of the People's Republic of China in 1949, all the pre-1949 capitalist companies and institutions were nationalized by 1950. Between 1950 and 1978, China's financial system consisted of a single bank – the People's Bank of China (PBOC), a central government-owned and controlled bank under the Ministry of Finance, which served as both the central bank and a commercial bank, controlling about 93% of the total financial assets of the country and handling almost all financial transactions. With its main role of financing the physical production plans, the PBOC used both a "cash-plan" and a "credit-plan" to control the cash flows in consumer markets and transfer flows between branches.

The first main structural change began in 1978 and ended in 1984. By the end of 1979, the PBOC departed the Ministry and became a separate entity, while three state-owned banks took over some of its commercial banking businesses: The Bank of China[3] (BOC) was given the mandate to specialize in transactions related to foreign trade and investment; the People's Construction Bank of China (PCBC), originally formed in 1954, was set up to handle transactions related to fixed investment (especially in manufacturing); the Agriculture Bank of China (ABC) was set up (in 1979) to deal with all banking business in rural areas; and the PBOC was formally established as China's central bank, and a two-tier banking system was formed. Finally, the fourth state-owned commercial bank, the Industrial and Commercial Bank of China (ICBC) was formed in 1984, and took over the rest of the commercial transactions of the PBOC.

For most of the 1980s, the development of the financial system was characterized by the fast growth of financial intermediaries outside the "Big Four" banks. Regional banks (partially owned by local governments) were formed in the Special Economic Zones (SEZs) in the coastal areas; in rural areas, a network of Rural Credit Cooperatives (RCCs; similar to credit unions in the United States) was set up under the supervision of the ABC, while Urban Credit Cooperatives (UCCs), counterparts of the RCCs in the urban areas, were also founded. Non-bank financial intermediaries, such as the Trust and Investment Corporations (TICs; operating in selected banking and non-banking services with restrictions on both deposits and loans), emerged and proliferated in this period.

The most significant event for China's financial system in the 1990s was the inception and growth of China's stock market. Two domestic stock exchanges (SHSE and SZSE) were established in 1990 and grew very fast during most of

[3] BOC, among the oldest banks currently in operation, was originally established in 1912 as a private bank and specialized in foreign currency-related transactions.

the 1990s and in recent years in terms of the size and trading volume. In parallel with the development of the stock market, the real estate market also went from nonexistent in the early 1990s to one that is currently comparable in size with the stock market.[4] Both the stock and real estate markets have experienced several major corrections during the past decade and are characterized by high volatilities and speculative short-term behaviors by many investors.

These patterns are in part due to the fact that the development of a supportive legal framework and institutions has been lagging behind that of the markets. For example, on a trial basis, China's first bankruptcy law was passed in 1986 (governing SOEs), but the formal company law was not effective until the end of 1999. This version of the company law governs all corporations with limited liability, publicly listed and traded companies, and branches or divisions of foreign companies, as well as their organizational structure, securities issuance and trading, accounting, bankruptcy, and mergers and acquisitions (for details, see the Web site of China Securities Regulatory Commission, or CSRC, http://www.csrc.gov.cn/). In August 2006, a new bankruptcy law was enacted, and it became effective June 1, 2007. We provide a detailed analysis of the status and problems of the stock market and real estate market in Section 4 below.

Following the Asian Financial Crisis in 1997, the financial sector reform has focused on state-owned banks and especially the problem of NPLs (the China Banking Regulation Committee was also established to oversee the banking industry). We will further discuss this issue in Section 3. China's entry into the WTO in December 2001 marked the beginning of a new era, as we continue to observe increasing competition from foreign financial institutions and more frequent and larger scale capital flows. While increasingly larger inflows of foreign capital and the presence of foreign institutions will continue to drive further growth of the financial system and economy, larger scale capital flows can also increase the likelihood of damaging financial crises. We will discuss these issues in Sections 4 and 6.

A developed financial system is characterized by, among other factors, the important role played by institutional investors. In China, institutional investors began to emerge in the late 1990s: The first closed-end fund, in which investors cannot withdraw capital after initial investment, was set up in 1997, and the first open-end fund, in which investors can freely withdraw capital (subject to share redemption restrictions), was established in 2001. By the end of 2006, there were 58 fund companies managing 307 funds with 254 open-ended funds and the rest close-ended. The total net asset value (NAV) increased from RMB 11 billion (or US $ 1.3 billion) in 1998 to RMB 2,579 billion (or US $322 billion) in May 2008, which is still small compared to the assets within the banking sector. In 2003, a few qualified foreign institutional investors (QFII) entered China's asset management industry, and they have been operating by

[4] At the end of 2007, the total market capitalization of the two domestic exchanges (SHSE and SZSE) is around $4.5 trillion, whereas total investment in the real estate market is around $2.53 trillion.

forming joint ventures with Chinese companies. On the other hand, China allowed Qualified Domestic Institutional Investors (QDII) to invest in overseas markets beginning in July 2006. As of early 2008, 10 fund companies have obtained the license to launch QDII with a total investment quota of US $42.17 billion, and five QDII funds have been set up.

Endowed with limited capital and problems with the administration of the pension system, pension funds have not played an important role in the stock or bond market.[5] With a fast-aging population and the growth of households' disposable income, further development of a multi-pillar pension system, including individual accounts with employees' self-contributed (tax exempt) funds that can be directly invested in the financial markets, is important for the development of both the financial and fiscal systems, as well as for social stability. Finally, there is no hedge fund that implements "long-short" strategies at present time, as short selling is prohibited.

Figure 1 depicts the current structure of the entire financial system. In what follows, we will describe and examine each of the major sectors of the financial system. In addition to the standard sectors of banking and intermediation and financial markets, we will document the importance of the non-standard financial sector. Due to space limitation, we do not cover China's "foreign sectors" in this chapter; for discussions on the history and the role of these sectors in supporting the growth of the economy, see, for example, AQQ (2005b), and Prasad and Wei (2005) for a review on foreign direct investment (FDI).

2.2 *Size and Efficiency of the Financial System: Banks, Markets, and Alternative Finance*

For a comparison of countries, we follow the law and finance literature and, in particular, the sample of countries studied in La Porta, Lopez-de-Silanes, Shleifer, and Vishny (1997a, 1998, hereafter LLSV). They classify most of the countries by their legal origin; countries with the English common-law (French civil-law) origin provide the strongest (weakest) legal protection to investors, and strong legal protection is also associated with better economic and financial "outcomes." In Table 1A, we compare China's financial system to those of LLSV sample countries (as of 2005), with measures for the size and efficiency of banks and markets taken from Levine (2002) and Demirgüç-Kunt and Levine (2001). For definitions of all the variables used in the tables and figures, see, for example, AQQ (2005a,b).

[5] While there is a nationwide, government-run pension system (financed mainly through taxes on employers and employees), the coverage ratio of the pension system varies significantly across regions and is particularly low in rural areas. Moreover, there is a very limited amount of capital in individual accounts, and most of the capital has been invested in banks and government projects with low returns. See, for example, Feldstein (1999, 2003) and Feldstein and Liebman (2006), for more details on China's pension system.

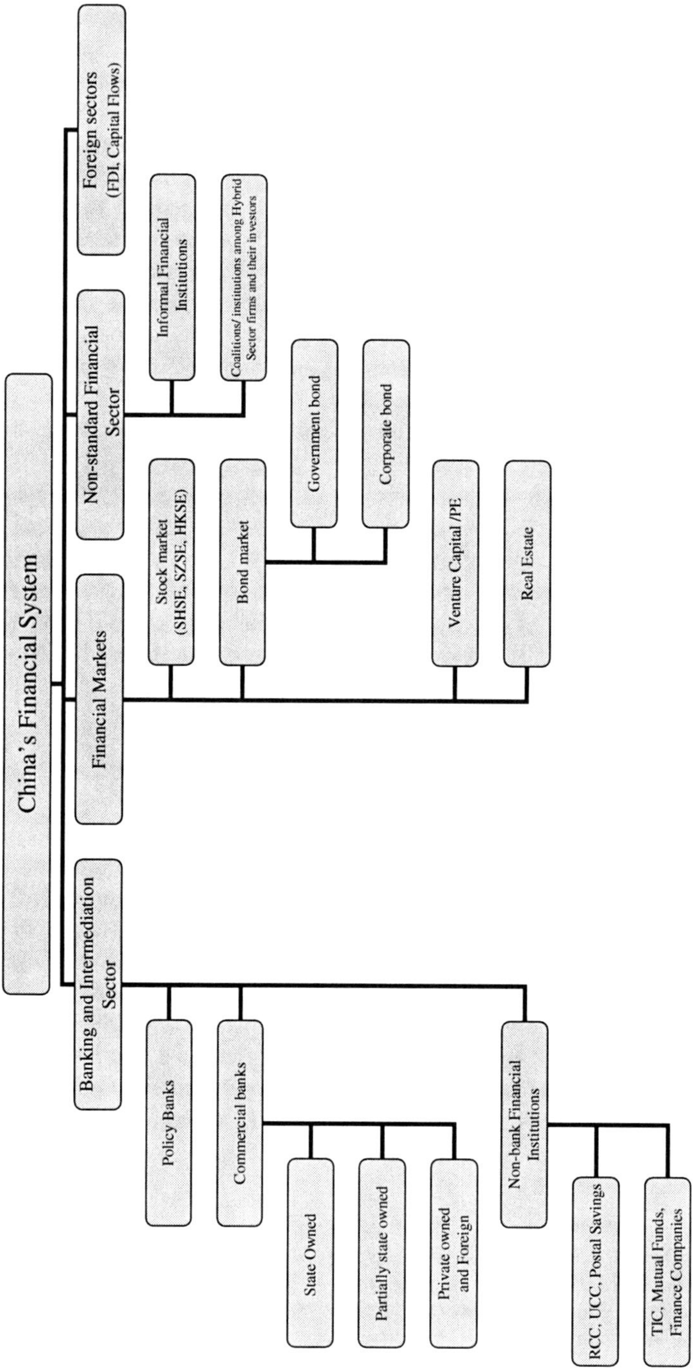

Fig. 1 Overview of China's financial system

We first compare the *size* of a country's banks and equity markets relative to that country's gross domestic product (GDP) (first four columns of Table 1). In terms of total market capitalization, China's stock market, 32% of its GDP in 2005, is much smaller than that of most of the LLSV sample countries (Panel A) with a weighted (by each country's GDP) average of 102% of GDP; it is also smaller than that of most other major emerging economies (see Panel B) with a weighted average of 65% of GDP. "Value Traded" is perhaps a better measure of the actual size of the market than "market capitalization," because the latter includes non-tradable shares or tradable shares that are rarely traded. In this regard, the size of China's stock market (26% of GDP) is even smaller than those of LLSV countries (with a weighted average of 117% of GDP) and emerging economies (with an average of 62% of GDP) as of 2005. Similarly, the size of China's banking system, in terms of total bank credit to non-state sectors, is 31% of its GDP in 2005, much smaller than that of most of LLSV country groups (with a weighted average of 78% of GDP) and not very different from the average of other major emerging economies (with a weighted average of 32% of GDP).[6] In terms of the ratio of overhead costs to total assets (1%), China's banking sector is quite efficient compared to that of most other countries, but this is perhaps due to different methods of measuring costs.

The next two columns of Table 1 ("Structure indices") compare the relative importance of financial markets vs. banks, with a lower score indicating that banks are more important relative to markets. China's scores for both "Structure Activity" (Log of the ratio of Float supply of market cap/Total Private Bank Credit) and "Structure size" (Log of the ratio of Market Capitalization/Total Private Bank Credit) are smaller than the sample averages of LLSV countries, and its score on "Structure size" is also smaller than the average of other emerging economies. These numbers suggest that China's financial system is bank-dominated, and more so than many other developing and developed countries. In terms of "Structure efficiency" (Log of product (Market capitalization/GDP) × (bank overhead cost/bank total assets)), which denotes the relative efficiency of markets vs. banks, China has a lower score than most other countries, suggesting that its banks are relatively more efficient than markets compared to other countries. "Structure regulatory" measures the extent to which commercial banks are restricted to participate in activities outside commercial lending, and China's score of 16 is higher than that of most other countries, suggesting that by law commercial banks in China face tight restrictions to operate in other areas.

---

[6] If we look at total bank credit, including loans to state sectors, the ratio of China's bank credit to GDP rises to 1.10, higher than even the German-origin countries (with a weighted average of 1.06). The difference between total bank credit and private credit suggests that most of the bank credit is issued to companies that are ultimately owned by the state.

Table 1 Comparing financial systems: banks and markets in 2005

	Size of banks and markets				Structure indices: markets vs. banks**					Financial development*** (banking and market sectors)	
Measures	Bank credit/ GDP	Bank over-head cost/ Bank assets	Value traded/ GDP	Market cap./ GDP	Structure activity	Structure size	Structure efficiency	Structure regulatory	Finance activity	Finance size	Finance efficiency
Panel A China and LLSV Country Groups											
China	0.31[a]	0.01	0.26	0.32	–0.16	0.03	–5.87	16	–2.51	–2.31	3.19
English origin*	0.66	0.04	1.53	1.31	0.87	0.76	–3.05	2.26	–0.21	–0.14	3.71
French origin*	0.77	0.04	0.60	0.66	–0.43	–0.05	–4.02	8.50	–1.45	–1.08	2.50
German origin*	1.06	0.02	1.05	0.82	–0.16	–0.37	–4.01	9.65	–0.08	–0.27	3.90
Nordic origin*	1.05	0.02	0.99	0.85	–0.07	–0.20	–3.86	7.74	–0.08	–0.21	3.71
Sample Ave.	0.78	0.03	1.17	1.02	0.28	0.28	–3.55	8.53	–0.50	–0.50	3.48
Panel B Other Large Emerging Markets (EMs)											
Argentina (F)	0.10	0.08	0.09	0.30	–0.12	1.07	–4.95	7	–4.70	–3.51	0.13
Brazil (F)	0.29	0.08	0.19	0.51	–0.40	0.56	–4.20	10	–2.88	–1.91	0.93
Egypt (F)	0.45	0.02	0.28	0.66	–0.45	0.39	–5.13	13	–2.06	–1.22	2.61
India (E)	0.37	0.02	0.56	0.60	0.43	0.49	–4.44	10	–1.57	–1.51	3.30
Indonesia (F)	0.22	0.03	0.15	0.27	–0.40	0.22	–5.48	Na	–3.45	–2.83	1.63
Korea (G)	Na	0.02	1.53	0.73	Na	Na	–3.73	Na	Na	Na	4.57
Malaysia (E)	1.03	0.01	0.38	1.44	–0.99	0.33	–5.22	10	–0.93	0.39	3.30
Mexico (F)	0.15	Na	0.07	0.27	–0.75	0.61	Na	12	–4.60	–3.24	Na
Pakistan (E)	0.27	0.02	1.27	0.34	1.56	0.24	–3.58	10	–1.08	–2.40	4.06

Table 1 (continued)

Measures	Size of banks and markets				Structure indices: markets vs. banks**					Financial development*** (banking and market sectors)	
	Bank credit/ GDP	Bank over-head cost/ Bank assets	Value traded/ GDP	Market cap./ GDP	Structure activity	Structure size	Structure efficiency	Structure regulatory	Finance activity	Finance size	Finance efficiency
Peru (F)	0.18	0.07	0.03	0.36	–1.93	0.70	–6.35	8	–5.39	–2.75	–0.98
Philippines (F)	0.26	0.06	0.07	0.35	–1.32	0.29	–5.51	7	–3.98	–2.37	0.21
S. Africa (E)	0.80	0.05	0.84	2.14	0.04	0.98	–3.12	8	–0.40	0.54	2.76
Sri Lanka (E)	0.30	0.04	0.05	0.20	–1.81	–0.40	–6.22	7	–4.24	–2.82	0.16
Taiwan (G)	Na	0.02	1.79	1.35	Na	Na	–3.62	12	Na	Na	4.78
Thailand (E)	0.73	0.02	0.51	0.68	–0.37	–0.07	–4.72	9	–0.99	–0.70	3.36
Turkey (F)	0.21	0.06	0.55	0.36	0.96	0.52	–3.40	12	–2.14	–2.57	2.21
Ave. for EMs	0.32	0.04	0.62	0.65	–0.32	0.53	–4.19	7.97	–3.00	–2.15	2.55

* the numerical results for countries of each legal origin group are calculated based on a value- (GDP of each country) weighted approach;
** Structure indices measure whether a country's financial system is market- or bank-dominated; the higher the measure, the greater the domination of the system by markets. Specifically, "structure activity" is equal to log(value traded/bank credit) and measures size of bank credit relative to trading volume of markets; "structure size" is equal to log(market cap/bank credit) and measures the size of markets relative to banks; "structure efficiency" is equal to log(market cap ratio × overhead cost ratio) and measures the relative efficiency of markets vs. banks; finally, "structure regulatory" is the sum of the four categories in regulatory restriction or the degree to which commercial banks are allowed to engage in security, firm operation, insurance, and real estate: (1) unrestricted; (2) permit to conduct through subsidiary; (3) full range not permitted in subsidiaries; and (4) strictly prohibited;
*** Financial development variables measure the entire financial system (banking and market sectors combined), and the higher the measure, the larger or more efficient the financial system. Specifically, "finance activity" is equal to log (total value traded ratio × private credit ratio), "finance size" is equal to log (market cap ratio × bank private credit ratio), and "finance efficiency" is equal to log (total value traded ratio/bank overhead cost).

This table compares various aspects of financial markets and banking sector of the Indian financial system with those of other emerging countries and LLSV country groups (sorted by legal origins). All the measures are taken from Levine (2002) or calculated from the World Bank Financial Database using the definitions in Levine (2002). We use 2005 figures for all countries.

We also compare the development of the financial system ("Financial Development"), including both banks and markets (the last three columns of Table 1). China's overall financial market size, in terms of both "Finance Activity" (Log of product of (Float supply of market/GDP) × (Private credit/GDP)) and "Finance Size" (Log of product of (Market capitalization/GDP) + (Private credit/GDP)), is smaller than the LLSV sample average level and each of the four subsamples and not very different from the averages of other emerging countries. In terms of "Finance Efficiency" (Log of (Total floating supply/GDP)/Overhead cost), China's measure is below the average of LLSV countries and only slightly higher than the average of other emerging countries. Based on the above evidence, we can conclude that China's banks and markets, or the formal sectors of the financial system, are small compared to its economy. Moreover, the banking sector does not lend much to the Hybrid Sector, which as we will see in Section 5, is the dynamic part of the economy.

If banks and markets are small relative to the overall economy of China, then where do most firms get the capital and funds? As shown in AQQ (2005b, 2008a), the four most important financing sources for all firms in China, in terms of firms' *fixed asset investments*, are (domestic) bank loans, firms' self-fundraising, the state budget, and FDI, with self-fundraising and bank loans carrying most of the weight. Self-fundraising, falling into the category of alternative finance (non-bank, non-market finance), includes proceeds from capital raised from *local* governments (beyond the state budget), communities and other investors, internal financing channels such as retained earnings, and all other funds raised domestically by the firms. The size of total self-fundraising of all firms has been growing at an average annual rate of 17.8% over the period 1994–2006 and reached US $665.5 billion at the end of 2006, compared to a total of US $364.8 billion for domestic bank loans for the same year. It is important to point out that equity and bond issuance, which are included in self-fundraising (but falls into the category of formal external finance), apply only to the Listed Sector and account for a small fraction of this category.

While the Listed Sector has been growing fast, SOEs are on a downward trend, as privatization of these firms is still in progress. Around 30% of publicly traded companies' funding comes from bank loans, and this ratio has been very stable. Around 45% of the Listed Sector's total funding comes from self-fundraising, including internal financing and proceeds from equity and bond issuance. Moreover, equity and bond sales, which rely on the use of external markets, only constitute a small fraction of total funds raised in comparison to internal financing and other forms of fundraising. Combined with the fact that self-fundraising is also the most important source of financing for the State Sector (45–65%), we can conclude that alternative channels of financing are important even for the State and Listed Sectors.

Not surprisingly, self-fundraising plays an even more important role for firms in the Hybrid Sector, accounting for close to 60% of total funds raised, while individually owned companies, a subset of the Hybrid Sector, rely on self-fundraising for 90% of total financing. Self-fundraising here includes all forms of internal finance, capital raised from family and friends of the founders and managers, and funds raised in the form of private equity and loans. Since firms in this sector operate in an environment with legal and financial mechanisms and regulations that are probably poorer than those available for firms in the State and Listed Sectors, financing sources may work differently from how they work in the State and Listed Sectors and those in developed countries. In Allen, Chakrabarti, De, Qian and Qian (ACDQQ, 2008c), the authors argue that alternative finance channels substitute for formal financing channels through banks and markets and expand the capacity of financial systems in emerging countries such as China and India.

3 The Banking and Intermediation Sector

In this section, we examine the status of China's banking and intermediation sector. After reviewing aggregate evidence on bank deposits and loans, we analyze the problem of NPLs in the banking sector as well as assess solutions to this problem. Finally, we review evidence on the growth of non-state banks and financial intermediaries.

3.1 Aggregate Evidence on Bank Deposits and Loans

As in other Asian countries, China's household savings rates have been high throughout the reform era. Given the growth of the economy, the sharp increase in personal income, and limited investment opportunities, it is not surprising that total bank deposits from individuals have been growing fast since the mid-1980s, with the 2007 figure approaching RMB 13 trillion ($1.6 trillion). Figure 3A shows that residents in metropolitan areas contribute the most to total deposits beginning in the late 1980s (roughly 50%), while deposits from enterprises (including firms from all three sectors) provide the second most important source. The role of deposits from government agencies and organizations (including non-profit and for-profit organizations, not shown in the figure) has steadily decreased over time.

Table 2A compares total savings and bank deposits across China, Japan, South Korea, and India during the period 1997–2005. In terms of the ratio of Time and Savings Deposits/GDP, China maintains the highest or second highest level (an average of over 90% in recent years), while Japan leads the group in terms of total amount. Figure 2A shows the breakdown of bank deposits, in which interest-bearing "savings deposits" are by far the most important form of deposits in China, providing a good source for bank loans and other forms of

Table 2A Comparisons of total savings and deposits (in US$ billions)

	1997	1998	1999	2000	2001	2002	2003	2004	2005
China									
Demand deposits[a]	298	335	391	465	534	647	777	900	1005
Savings deposits[b]	559	645	720	777	891	1050	1251	1444	1704
Time deposits[c]	81	100	114	136	171	198	253	307	400
Time & Savings Deposits /GDP	67%	73%	77%	76%	80%	86%	92%	91%	95%
Japan									
Demand deposits[a]		1151	1465	1447	1543	1969	2154	2264	2601
Time & Savings deposits[b]		4805	5339	5062	4314	3736	3792	3771	3977
Time & Savings Deposits /GDP		125%	122%	109%	105%	95%	89%	82%	87%
South Korea									
Demand deposits[a]		23	29	30	36	45	50	56	71
Time & Savings deposits[b]		170	210	242	252	294	322	350	397
Time & Savings Deposits /GDP		49%	47%	47%	52%	54%	53%	51%	50%
India									
Demand deposits[a]	28	29	32	34	36	40	46	58	79
Time & Savings deposits[b]	145	162	182	194	217	257	288	343	418
Time & Savings Deposits/GDP	35%	39%	41%	42%	46%	52%	50%	51%	54%

[a] Demand deposits, balance of the accounts can be withdrawn on demand of customers (e.g., check-writing);
[b] Savings deposits, interest-bearing accounts that can be withdrawn but cannot be used as Money (e.g., no checking writing);
[c] Time deposits, savings accounts or CD with a fixed term.
Source: Statistical Bureau of China, People's Bank of China, Statistical Bureau of Japan, Bank of Korea, Ministry of Finance, India, Ministry of Finance, Korea, Korean Statistical Information System.

investment. Figure 2B compares total (non-state) bank credit (over GNP) extended to Hybrid Sector firms in China and privately owned firms (including those publicly listed and traded) in Taiwan and South Korea. For South Korea, we also plot the bank credit ratios during its high economic growth period of the 1970s and 1980s (each year appearing on the horizontal axis indicates the time period for China, while a particular year *minus* 20 indicates the time period for South Korea). We can see that the scale and growth of China's "hybrid" bank credit during 1997–2006 are far below those (of private bank credit) of Taiwan and South Korea in the same period but are similar to those of South Korea 20 years ago. Consistent with the aggregate evidence from Section 2 above and our firm-level evidence below, we find that bank

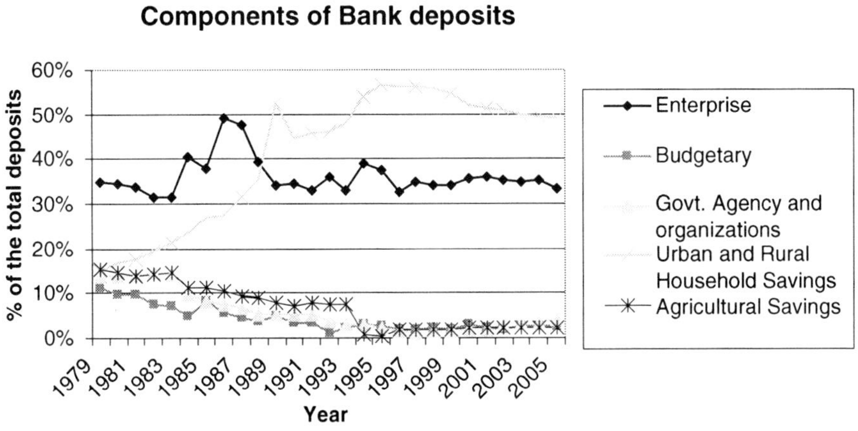

Fig. 2A Sources for bank deposits in China

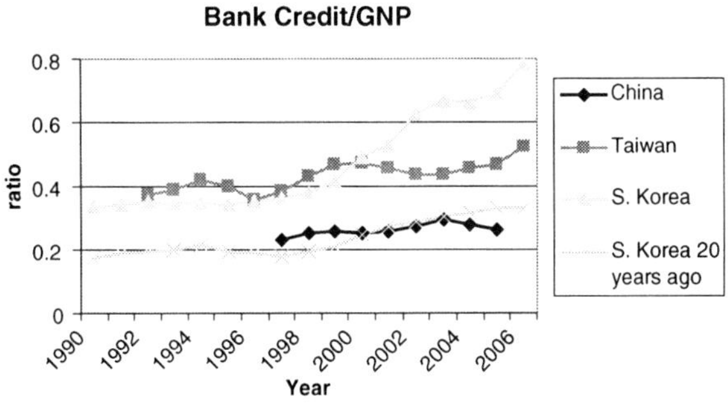

Fig. 2B Comparing total bank credit

loans were one of the most important financing sources for Hybrid Sector firms but started to increase the influence.

Table 2B breaks down China's bank loans by maturities, loan purposes, and borrower types during the period 1994–2006. While there has been a shift from short-term to long-term loans (first two columns), the majority of loans goes to SOEs in manufacturing industries ("Industrial Loans" and "Commercial Loans"). Most of the "Infrastructure/Construction Loans" (a small component of total loans) fund government-sponsored projects, while the size of "Agricultural Loans" is much smaller. More importantly, the size of loans made to TVEs, privately and collectively owned firms, and joint ventures (last three columns), which all belong to the Hybrid Sector, is also much smaller. Researchers have argued that the imbalance between loans made to the State Sector and the Hybrid Sector reflects the government's policies of wealth transfer from the Hybrid Sector to the State Sector via state-owned banks (e.g., Brandt and Zhu, 2000).

Table 2B Breakdown of bank loans (end-of-year figures in RMB billions)

Year	Total loans	Short-term loans	Industrial loans	Commercial loans	Infrastructure construction loans	Agricultural loans	Loans to TVEs	1	Joint ventures & cooperative firms
1994	3,997.60	2,694.87	994.83	1,050.98	61.72	114.39	200.24	15.59	79.23
1995	5,054.41	3,337.20	1,177.47	1,283.71	79.93	154.48	251.49	19.62	99.91
1996	6,115.66	4,021.00	1,421.33	1,533.26	97.38	191.91	282.19	27.98	134.63
1997	7,491.41	5,541.83	1,652.66	1,835.66	159.11	331.46	503.58	38.67	189.10
1998	8,652.41	6,061.32	1,782.15	1,975.24	162.87	444.42	558.00	47.16	248.75
1999	9,373.43	6,388.76	1,794.89	1,989.09	147.69	479.24	616.13	57.91	298.58
2000	9,937.11	6,574.81	1,701.93	1,786.85	161.71	488.90	606.08	65.46	304.98
2001	11,231.47	6,732.72	1,863.67	1,856.34	209.96	571.15	641.30	91.80	326.35
2002	13,129.39	7,424.79	2,019.05	1,797.31	274.80	688.46	681.23	105.88	269.74
2003	15,899.62	8,366.12	2,275.60	1,799.44	300.21	841.14	766.16	146.16	256.94
2004	17,819.78	8,684.06	2,389.66	1,707.41	278.01	984.31	806.92	208.16	219.84
2005	30,204.28	8,744.92	2,251.67	1,644.76	298.37	1,152.99	790.18	218.08	197.53
2006	36,523.01	9,853.44	2,865.4	1,667.15	361.26	1,320.82	6,222.0	266.76	183.27

Source: Statistical Yearbooks of China (1985–2007).

3.2 The Problem of NPLs and Possible Solutions

China's banking sector is dominated by large state-owned banks, namely, the "Big Four" banks of ICBC, BOC, PCBC, and ABC.[7] The dominance of the Big Four banks also implies that the degree of competition within the banking sector has been low. For example, Demirgüç-Kunt and Levine (2001) compare the five-bank concentration (share of the assets of the five largest banks in total banking assets) and find that China's concentration ratio of 91% at the end of 1997 (and for much of 1990s) is one of the highest in the world. However, China's concentration ratio has been falling sharply since 1997 with the entrance of many non-state banks and intermediaries.

The most significant problem for China's banking sector, and for the entire financial system in recent years, has been the amount of NPLs within state-owned banks, and in particular, among the Big Four banks. Reducing the amount of NPLs to normal levels was the most important task for China's financial system in the short term. The main obstacle when we analyze the NPLs is the lack of comprehensive and objective data on banks' profitability (aggregate and bank-level) and NPLs. We mainly rely on official sources for our analysis on NPLs, but we also speculate based on data from non-government sources, including case studies from particular regions or banks. Some of these data and speculations paint a much gloomier picture of the NPLs and China's state-owned banks than the official data suggest. Since without objective and accurate bank-level data we cannot determine the exact amount of NPLs, we present both an optimistic view and a pessimistic view when discussing these issues.

3.2.1 Comparing NPLs

In Panel A of Table 3A, we compare NPLs in China, the United States, and other major Asian economies during 1998–2006 based on official figures. NPLs are measured by their size (in US $ billion) and as a percentage of GDPs in the same year (shown in brackets). Measured as a fraction of GDPs, China's NPLs are the highest in the group from 2000 to 2006 and as high as 20–22.5% of GDP (in 2000 and 2001). Notice that the official information on China's NPLs first became available in 1998, but the figures in 1998 and 1999 in Table 3A probably significantly underestimate the actual size of NPLs; this also explains the jump in the size of China's NPLs from 1999 to 2000. The cross-country comparison on NPLs includes the period during which Asian countries recovered from the

---

[7] La Porta, Lopez-de-Silanes and Shleifer (2002) show that the government owned 99.45% of the assets of the 10 largest commercial banks in China in 1995, one of the highest in their sample of 92 countries. Moreover, their result on the negative relationship between government ownership of banks and the growth of a country's economy seems to apply to China's State Sector and the banking sector. However, we show that the high government ownership of banks has not slowed down the growth of the Hybrid Sector.

Table 3A A comparison of non-performing loans (NPLs) and government debt

Year	China	US	Japan	S. Korea	India	Indonesia	Taiwan
Panel A: Size of NPLs: In US$ billion and as percentage of GDPs in the same year (in brackets)							
1997	–	66.9 (0.8%)	217.4 (5.1%)	16.2 (3.1%)	–	0.2 (0.1%)	19.6 (6.5%)
1998	20.5 (2.0%)	71.3 (0.8%)	489.7 (12.7%)	23.2 (6.7%)	12.7 (3.1%)	5.5 (5.2%)	21.8 (7.9%)
1999	105.1 (9.7%)	72.2 (0.8%)	547.6 (12.6%)	54.4 (12.2%)	14.0 (3.2%)	3.1 (3.8%)	27.2 (9.1%)
2000	269.3 (22.5%)	90.1 (0.9%)	515.4 (11.1%)	35.5 (6.9%)	12.9 (2.8%)	6.3 (2.7%)	33.2 (10.3%)
2001	265.3 (20.0%)	108.4 (1.1%)	640.1 (15.6%)	12.2 (2.5%)	13.2 (2.8%)	4.3 (1.7%)	37.9 (13.0%)
2002	188.4 (13.0%)	107.8 (1.0%)	552.5 (14.1%)	9.9 (1.8%)	14.8 (3.0%)	3.3 (2.0%)	30.7 (10.4%)
2003	181.2 (11.0%)	95.9 (1.0%)	480.1 (11.3%)	11.7 (1.9%)	14.6 (2.5%)	4.7 (1.5%)	23.1 (7.7%)
2004	207.4 (10.7%)	81.3 (0.9%)	334.8 (7.3%)	10.0 (1.5%)	14.4 (2.2%)	3.8 (2.1%)	16.4 (5.1%)
2005	164.2 (7.3%)	84.6 (0.7%)	183.3 (4.0%)	7.6 (1.0%)	13.4 (1.7%)	6.0 (1.5%)	11.2 (3.2%)
2006 (Q2)	160.3 (6.3%)	88.8 (0.7%)	108.2 (2.4%)	7.4 (0.8%)	11.8 (1.4%)	7.3 (2.1%)	–
Panel B: Outstanding government debt ($ billion)							
	Outstanding government bond	Total government debt	Total government debt	Outstanding treasury bonds	Total public debt	Outstanding government bond	Outstanding government bond
1997	66.5	5,802.8	4254.0	5.3	–	–	–
1998	93.8	5,788.8	4858.0	14.4	178.4	–	–
1999	127.3	5,822.7	6053.1	28.5	260.2	34.1	46.5
2000	165.1	5,612.7	6209.8	32.7	232.4	45.1	45.5
2001	188.6	5,734.4	6036.0	39.8	225.4	43.5	58.7
2002	233.5	6,169.4	6321.3	45.2	250.2	42.1	77.7
2003	273.0	6,789.7	6852.9	67.9	259.7	48.0	75.7
2004	311.3	7,335.6	7446.6	107.0	299.6	44.7	85.2
2005	350.0	7,809.5	8299.5	165.5	347.1	39.9	–
2006	–	8,289.1	7880.5	209.1	378.9	44.8	–

Table 3A (continued)

Year	China	US	Japan	S. Korea	India	Indonesia	Taiwan
Panel C: (NPLs + Outstanding government debt)/GDP							
1997	–	0.71 (0.54)	1.05 (0.40)	0.04	–	–	–
1998	0.11 (0.13)	0.67 (0.50)	1.39 (0.63)	0.11	0.46	–	–
1999	0.21 (0.31)	0.64 (0.45)	1.51 (0.64)	0.19	0.62	0.24	0.25
2000	0.36 (0.59)	0.58 (0.40)	1.45 (0.65)	0.13	0.53	0.31	0.24
2001	0.34 (0.54)	0.58 (0.39)	1.63 (0.83)	0.11	0.50	0.30	0.33
2002	0.29 (0.42)	0.60 (0.42)	1.76 (0.90)	0.10	0.54	0.23	0.37
2003	0.28 (0.39)	0.63 (0.45)	1.73 (0.86)	0.13	0.48	0.22	0.33
2004	0.27 (0.38)	0.63 (0.46)	1.70 (0.81)	0.17	0.47	0.19	0.32
2005	0.23 (0.30)	0.63 (0.47)	1.86 (0.84)	0.22	0.47	0.16	–
2006	–	0.63 (0.47)	1.79 (0.89)	0.25	0.46	0.15	–

This table compares total outstanding NPLs within the banking system, government debt, and the ratio of (NPLs + Government Debt)/GDP among China, the US, and other major Asian countries for the period 1997–2006. Panel A presents the size of the NPLs, as measured by US$ billion and as the percentage of GDPs in the same year. NPLs in the US measure the outstanding "delinquency loan"; NPLs in Japan measure the "risk management loans" (or loans disclosed under the Financial Reconstructed Law and/or loans subject to self-assessment). In Panel B, outstanding government debt is measured at the end of each year; for the US and Japan, total government debt includes domestic and foreign debt. In Panel C, the ratios for China include using the official NPL numbers and using doubled official NPLs (i.e., the ratios in the brackets are (doubled NPLs + government debt)/GDP); the ratios in the brackets for the US and Japan are (net government debt + NPLs)/GDP, where net government debt is the difference between government borrowing (stock measure) and government lending (flow measure). All figures are converted into US dollars using the average exchange rate within the observation year.

Sources: Statistical Bureau of China, the People's Bank of China, Chinese Banking Regulatory Commission; Board of Governors of the Federal Reserve Bank, Statistical Abstracts of the US, the Statistical Bureau of Japan; Ministry of Finance, Korea, the Bank of Korea, Korean Statistical Information System; IMF, World Bank; Bank Indonesia; Ministry of Finance, India; National Statistical Bureau of Taiwan.

1997 financial crisis (e.g., the size of NPLs in South Korea exceeded 12% of GDP in 1999, but it was reduced to below 3% 2 years later) and the period during which the Japanese banking system was disturbed by the prolonged NPL problem (the size of Japan's NPLs is the largest of the group throughout the time period except for 2006; the ratio of NPLs over GDP reached 15.6% in 2001 but was reduced to below 5% by the end of 2005).

As bad as the numbers in Panel A of Table 3A appear, they may still significantly underestimate the amount of NPLs within China's banking system according to the pessimistic view. First, the official figures on outstanding NPLs (cumulated within all commercial banks in China) do not include the bad loans that have been transferred from banks to four state-owned asset management companies (AMCs), with the purpose of AMCs liquidating these bad loans. For example, if we add the NPLs held by the four AMCs (book value of RMB 866 billion, or US $108 billion, shown in the last row of Table 3B) in the first quarter of 2006 to the mix of NPLs shown in Panel A of Table 3A, the total amount of China's NPLs would increase by two-thirds. Second, the classification of NPLs has been problematic in China. The Basle Committee for Bank Supervision classifies a loan as "doubtful" or bad when any *interest* payment is overdue by 180 days or more (in the United States it is 90 days); whereas in China, this step has not typically been taken until the *principal* payment is delayed beyond the loan maturity date or an extended due date, and in many cases, until the borrower has declared bankruptcy and/or has gone through liquidation. Qiu et al. (2000) estimate that the ratio of loan interest

Table 3B Liquidation of NPLs by four asset management companies (RMB billion)

	Book value of assets (accumulated)	Assets recovered	Cash recovered	Asset recovery rate (%)	Cash recovery rate (%)
2001					
Hua Rong	23.21	12.54	7.55	54.0	32.5
Great Wall	53.11	6.30	3.69	11.9	6.9
Oriental	18.29	8.51	4.42	46.5	24.2
Xin Da	29.90	22.50	10.49	75.3	35.1
Total	124.51	49.86	26.15	40.0	21.0
2002					
Hua Rong	32.04	11.43	10.20	35.7	31.8
Great Wall	45.48	7.94	5.47	17.5	12.0
Oriental	22.10	10.60	5.57	47.9	25.2
Xin Da	33.10	17.46	10.51	52.7	31.8
Total	132.73	47.43	31.75	35.7	23.9
2004					
	Accumulated disposal[1]	Cash recovered	Disposal ratio (%)[2]	Asset recovery ratio (%)[3]	Cash recovery ratio (%)[4]
Hua Rong	209.54	41.34	59.77	25.29	19.73
Great Wall	209.91	21.57	61.91	14.43	10.27
Oriental	104.55	23.29	41.42	29.50	22.27
Xin Da	151.06	50.81	48.90	38.29	33.64
Total	675.06	137.00	53.96	25.48	20.29

Table 3B (continued)

	Book value of assets (accumulated)	Assets recovered	Cash recovered	Asset recovery rate (%)	Cash recovery rate (%)
2005					
Hua Rong	243.38	54.39	69.17	26.92	22.35
Great Wall	263.39	27.35	77.88	12.90	10.39
Oriental	131.76	32.01	52.08	28.73	24.30
Xin Da	201.21	62.84	63.82	34.30	31.23
Total	839.75	176.60	66.74	24.58	21.03
2006 (Q1)					
Hua Rong	246.80	54.66	70.11	26.50	22.15
Great Wall	270.78	27.83	80.11	12.70	10.28
Oriental	141.99	32.81	56.13	27.16	23.11
Xin Da	206.77	65.26	64.69	34.46	31.56
Total	866.34	180.56	68.61	24.20	20.84

[1] Accumulated Disposal refers to the accumulated amount of cash and non-cash assets recovered, as well as loss incurred by the end of the reporting period.
[2] Disposal Ratio = Accumulated Disposal/Total NPLs purchased.
[3] Asset Recovery Ratio = Total Assets Recovered/Accumulated Disposal.
[4] Cash Recovery Ratio = Cash Recovered/Accumulated Disposal.
This table presents results on the liquidation of NPLs by four state-owned asset management companies in China during the period 2001 to the 1st quarter of 2006. These asset management companies were set up to specifically deal with NPLs accumulated in the 'Big Four' state-owned banks.
Source: Almanac of China's Finance and Banking 2002–2005, and the reports of China Banking Regulatory Commission 2004–2006.

paid to *state-owned* banks over loan interest owed is on average less than 50% in 1999, suggesting that the actual ratio of NPLs over total loans made can be higher than 50% in 1999. This piece of evidence, along with others, suggests that the amount of NPLs (and as percentage of GDP) could be twice as large as the official figures reported in Panel A of Table 3A.[8]

Since a large fraction of the NPLs among state-owned banks, and in particular, the Big Four banks, resulted from poor lending decisions made for SOEs, some of which were due to political or other non-economic reasons, in our view the government should bear the burden of reducing the NPLs. This view of essentially treating NPLs as a fiscal problem implies that the ultimate source of eliminating NPLs lies in China's overall economic growth.[9] As long as the economy maintains its strong growth momentum so that tax receipts also increase, the government can always assume the remainder of the NPLs without significantly affecting the economy. In this regard, Panel B of Table 3A compares total outstanding government debt, and Panel C presents a comparison of the ratio of (NPLs + Government Debt)/GDP across countries, with the sum of NPLs and government debt indicating total burden of the government. Depending on data availability, total government debt is either measured by

[8] Consistent with this view, Lardy (1998) argues that, if using international standards on bad loans, the existing NPLs within China's state-owned banks as of the mid-1990s would make these banks' total net worth negative, so that the entire network of state banks would be insolvent.

[9] See, for example, Perkins and Rawski (2008) for a review and projections on the prospects of long-running economic growth and statistics in China.

the sum of all types of domestic and foreign debt (the United States, Japan, and India) or by the level of outstanding government bonds (all other countries) in a given year.

Unlike the severity of its NPL problem, the Chinese government does not carry a large amount of debt, with total outstanding government bonds growing from only 9% of GDP in 1998 to around 15% of GDP in 2007. By contrast, countries such as the United States and India have a large amount of government debt even though their banking sectors are healthy (as measured by low levels of NPLs). Japan is the only country in the group that has large amount of NPLs *and* government debt. When we combine the results from Panels A and B and compare total government burden in Panel C, we use two sets of ratios for China: the first set of ratios are based on official NPLs numbers presented in Panel A, while the second set (presented in brackets) is based on doubling the size of official NPLs. For the United States and Japan, we also present two sets of ratios. In addition to using total outstanding government debt, we also use ratios (in the brackets) based on the sum of *net* government debt and NPLs, where net government debt is the difference between government borrowing (a "stock" measure) and government lending (also a stock measure); not surprisingly, these ratios are much lower than using the gross figures.

From Panel C, China's total government burden is in the middle of the pack: the ratios of total government burden over GDP (using the official NPL figures) are lower than those in the United States, India, and Japan, are comparable with those of Taiwan, and are higher than Indonesia and Korea. China's ratios are much higher if NPL figures are doubled, but total government burden in that case is still comparable with or lower than that of the United States (using gross or net government debt) and much lower than Japan. Based on these crude comparisons, it seems that the NPLs will not be a particularly arduous burden for the Chinese government due to its small size of debt, while the same cannot be said for Japan. Caution is again needed for this conclusion: first, new NPLs in China may grow much faster than in other countries; and second, China's currently small government debt may experience a sharp increase in the near future given the need for higher fiscal spending in areas such as pension plans and other social welfare programs.

Recognizing the importance of and its responsibility in reducing NPLs in the Big Four banks, the Chinese government has injected foreign currency reserves (mostly in the form of US dollars, T-bills, Euros, and Yen) into these banks to improve their balance sheets in preparation for going public. This process began at the end of 2003, with the establishment of the Central Huijin Investment Company, through which the PBOC injected US $45 billion of reserves into the BOC and PCBC, while ICBC (the largest commercial bank in China and one of the largest in the world in terms of assets) received US $15 billion during the first half of 2005 (e.g., *Financial Times*, 01/09/2004, 04/21/2005; *Asia Wall Street Journal*, 01/13/2004). All three banks have since become publicly listed and traded in either the HKSE and/or the SHSE. Given that China's total foreign exchange reserve reached US $1.68 trillion as of March 2008, the largest in the world, while the total amount of NPLs is around US $160 billion at the end of 2007, the foreign reserve itself should be more than enough to remove all the existing NPLs off the books of all the banks in China.

However, the injection plan will not prevent new NPLs from originating in the banking system. In fact, it may create perverse incentives for state-owned banks, in that if these banks (that have received or will receive the cash/assets injection) believe that there will be a "bailout" whenever they run into future financial distress, they lose the incentive to improve efficiency while an incentive to take on risky, negative-NPV projects surfaces. This moral hazard problem can thwart the government's efforts in keeping the NPLs in check, while similar problems occurred during and after the government bailout of the S&L crisis in the United States in the 1980s (e.g., Kane 1989, 2003). Hence, it is important for the government to credibly commit that the injection plan is a one-time measure to boost the capital adequacy of these banks and that there will be no bailout plans in the future, especially after they become listed companies. The second problem arises because the significant increase in foreign reserves is in part due to the presence of large amounts of speculative foreign currencies in anticipation of an RMB appreciation relative to major international currencies. Depending on how the government and the central bank allow the flexible RMB exchange rate mechanism introduced in July 2005 to operate, large movements of the speculative currencies may cause a twin crisis in the currency market and the banking sector. We further discuss this issue in Section 6 below.

3.2.2 Reducing NPLs and Improving the Efficiency of State-Owned Banks

In recent years, the Chinese government has taken active measures to reduce the NPLs and improve the efficiency of the banking sector. First, as mentioned above, four state-owned AMCs were formed with the goal of assuming the NPLs (and offering debt-for-equity swaps to the banks) accumulated in each of the Big Four banks and liquidating them. The liquidation process includes asset sales, tranching, securitization, and resale of loans to investors.[10] Table 3B shows that *cash* recovery on the bad loans processed by the AMCs ranges from 6.9 to 35% between 2001 and 2006 (first quarter), while the asset recovery rates are slightly higher. A critical issue that affects the effectiveness of the liquidation process is the relationship among AMCs, banks, and distressed or bankrupt firms. Since both the AMCs and the banks are state-owned, it is not likely that the AMCs would force the banks to cut off (credit) ties with defaulted borrowers (SOEs or former SOEs) as a privately owned bank would do. Thus, as the old NPLs are liquidated, new NPLs from the same borrowers continue to surface.

---

[10] The sale of tranches of securitized NPLs to foreign investors first occurred in 2002. The deal was struck between Huarong, one of the four AMCs, and a consortium of US investment banks led by Morgan Stanley (and including Lehman Brothers and Salomon Smith Barney) and was approved by the Chinese government in early 2003 (*Financial Times*, 05/2003).

Second, state-owned banks have diversified and improved their loan structure by increasing consumer-related loans while being more active in risk management and monitoring of loans made to SOEs. For example, the ratio of consumer lending to total loans made for the four state-owned banks increased from 1% in 1998 to 10% in 2002; by the end of 2004, 10% of all outstanding bank loans (RMB 2 trillion or US $250 billion) were extended to consumers. The size of mortgages, now the largest component (almost 90%) of consumer credit, grew 100 times between 1997 and 2006, reaching a total of RMB 2 trillion (US $250 billion) (*Xinhua News*). One problem with the massive expansion of consumer credit is that China lacks a national consumer-credit database to spot overstretching debtors, although a pilot system linking seven cities was set up in late 2004. The deficiency in the knowledge and training of credit risk and diligence of loan officers from state-owned banks is another significant factor in credit expansion, which can lead to high default rates and a large amount of new NPLs if the growth of the economy and personal income slows down. Accompanying the rapidly expanding automobile industry, the other fast growing category of individual-based loans is automobile loans, most of which are made by state-owned banks. The total balance of all China's individual auto loans rocketed from RMB 400 million (US $50 million) in 1998 to RMB 200 billion (US $25 billion) at the end of 2003, and as much as 30% of all auto sales were financed by loans during this period (*Financial Times*, 05/25/2005). The growth in both auto sales and loans slowed down significantly since 2004 in part due to the high default rates. Shanghai and Beijing have the largest number of car sales and loans. As many as 50% of debtors defaulted on their car loans in these cities. There are examples in which loan applications were approved based solely on applicants' description of their personal income without any auditing (*Barron's*, 12/06/2004). However, the slowdown of the auto loan market was temporary and it quickly resumed its fast pace of growth, in part due to the tremendous potential of the market. In aggregate auto loans amount to 10–20% of the total amount spent on autos. Most loans mature in 3–5 years.[11]

The above examples on auto loans and consumer credit illustrate the importance of reforming state-owned banks in solving the problems of NPLs and improving the entire banking sector. A central question in reforming the state-owned banks is the ongoing privatization process. There are two imminent issues. First, more competition in the banking and intermediation sector, including the entrance of more non-state (domestic and foreign) banks and intermediaries, is good for improving the efficiency of both the Big Four banks and the entire banking sector.[12] Another issue is the government's dual role as

---

[11] A few foreign lenders (e.g., GM and Ford) were approved to enter China's auto loan market by forming joint ventures with Chinese automakers (*Financial Times*, 05/27/2005).

[12] For example, Park et al. (2003) find that competition among banks and intermediaries leads to better effort of the banks (especially state-owned banks) and better loan decisions in China's rural areas.

regulator and as majority owner. These potentially conflicting roles diminish the effectiveness in each of the two roles that the government intends to carry out. In Section 4 below, we argue that the ongoing process of floating non-tradable government shares in many listed companies should also be applied to the privatization process of state-owned banks. Only after these banks are (majority) owned by non-government entities and individuals can they unconditionally implement all profit- and efficiency-enhancing measures. In fact, with a sample of both state- and non-state-owned banks, Berger et al. (2006) show that the addition of foreign ownership stakes into banks' ownership structure is associated with significant improvement of bank efficiency.

Table 4A presents the performance of IPOs of three of the Big Four banks (ABC remains in the State Sector) and that of the Bank of Communications (BComm). The most notable case is the IPO of ICBC. Simultaneously carried out in the HKSE and SHSE on October 27, 2006, ICBC raised over US $20 billion, making it the largest IPO up to that date in the world. The first day (and first week cumulative) return, measured by the net percentage return of the closing price on the first (fifth) trading day over offer price, was almost 15%, suggesting high demand for ICBC's H shares among (foreign) investors. At the end of 2007, by market capitalization ICBC exceeded Citibank and become the largest bank in the world, but only 22% of the market cap is "free float" or tradable. The largest foreign shareholder is Goldman Sachs with its 5.8% ownership stake negotiated before the IPO. While the IPOs of the other three large state-owned have not grabbed as much attention, they are also successful in terms of total proceeds raised, and they have all attracted significant foreign ownership at the IPO date. Allen, Qian and Zhao (2008b) provide more information on the IPO process of ICBC and other large Chinese banks. On the other hand (from the *Chinese Banking Regulatory Commission*), Moody's ratings on these publicly listed banks (on both deposits and loans) range from A to Baa (highest rating is Aaa); while S&P rates these banks' outstanding bonds between A and BBB (highest rating is AAA).

Table 4A Performance of Chinese banks' IPOs

	ICBC HKSE (HK$)	SHSE (RMB)	BOC HKSE (HK$)	SHSE (RMB)	PCBC HKSE (HK$)	BComm HKSE (HK$)
IPO date	10/27/2006	10/27/2006	6/01/2006	7/05/2006	10/27/2005	6/23/2005
Offer price (per share)	3.07	3.12	2.95	3.08	2.35	2.5
IPO proceeds (amount)	124.95B	46.64B	82.86B	20.00B	59.94B	14.64B
1st day return	14.66%	5.13%	14.41%	22.73%	0.00%	13.00%
1st week return	16.94%	4.81%	19.49%	19.16%	−1.06%	13.00%
Foreign ownership	7.28%	–	14.40%	–	14.39%	18.33%

This table presents information on the IPOs of three of the Big Four banks and that of Bank of Communications (BComm). ICBC went IPO in both the HKSE (HK dollar) and SHSE (RMB), while PCBC and BComm only listed shares on the HKSE. First day (first week) return is percentage return of closing price of first day (fifth trading day) over offer price. Foreign ownership indicates size of ownership stakes of foreign institutions and investors at the date of IPOs.

Source: IPO prospectuses submitted to SHSE and HKSE; SHSE and HKSE.

To summarize, the optimistic view points out that NPLs have been considerably reduced in recent years. The reform of state-owned banks and development of the banking sector have been effective in reducing NPLs, which is why NPLs have been falling (2000–2006; Panel A of Table 3A). Given that the economy will probably maintain its current pace of growth, the government can always write off a large fraction of the rest of the NPLs to avert any serious problems for China. However, the pessimistic view believes that NPLs are bigger than the official statistics suggest to begin with, and that a substantial amount of new NPLs will continue to arise within state-owned banks. Moreover, the reform of the banking sector will not be effective because it will take a long time before the government relinquishes majority control of state-owned banks. During this period, if the growth of the economy significantly slows down, while the accumulation of NPLs continues, the banking sector problems could lead to a financial crisis. This could spill over into other sectors of the economy and cause a slowdown in growth or a recession. In this view, the NPL problem poses the most serious problem to China's continued prosperity.

3.3 Growth of Non-state Financial Intermediaries

The development of both non-state banks and other (state and non-state) financial institutions is crucial for China to have a stable and functioning banking system in the future. In addition to boosting the overall efficiency of the banking system and alleviating the problems of NPLs, these financial institutions provide funding to support the growth of the Hybrid Sector.

First, we examine and compare China's insurance market to other Asian economies (South Korea, Taiwan, and Singapore). In terms of the ratio of total assets managed by insurance companies over GDP (Fig. 2C), China's insurance market is significantly smaller than that of other economies. At the end of 2006 total assets managed were still less than 10% of GDP (while this ratio for the other three economies is over 30%). It is clear that the insurance industry is also significantly undersized compared to China's banking industry, and property insurance is particularly underdeveloped due to the fact that the private real

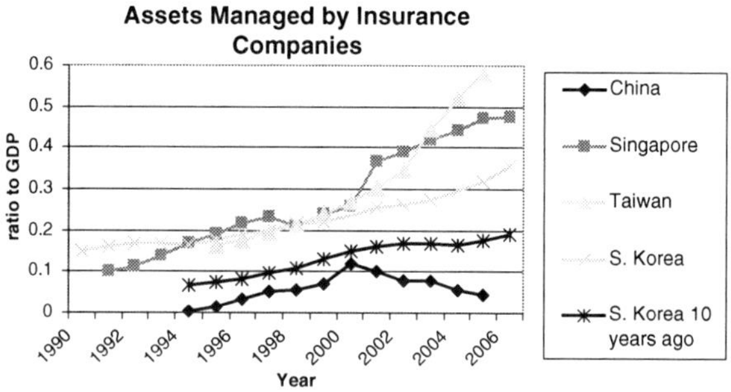

Fig. 2C A comparison of assets under management of insurance companies

estate market was only recently established (in the past most housing was allocated by employers or the government). Despite the fast growth of insurance coverage and premium income, only 4% of the total population was covered by life insurance, the insurance premium was only 2.9% of GDP in 2007, ranking 49th in the world (a per capita premium was about RMB 273 per year in 2006); coverage ratios for property insurance are even lower (according to the reports by KPMG and Swiss Re). The encouraging news is that coverage ratios have been growing steadily at an average annual rate of 6% between 1998 and 2005 (*XinHua News*).

Table 4B provides a (partial) breakdown of the different types of banks. During the period of 2001–2004, although the Big Four banks dominate in every aspect of the banking sector, the role of the non-Big Four banks in the entire banking sector cannot be ignored. As of 2004, other banks and credit

Table 4B State-owned and private banks in China (RMB billion)

Types of banks	Total assets	Total deposits	Outstanding loans	Profit	NPL rate (%)
2004					
Big four banks	16,932.1	14,412.3	10,086.1		15.57
Other commercial banks	4,697.2	4,059.9	2,885.9	50.7	4.93
1) Joint equity					
2) City commercial banks	1,693.8	1,434.1	904.5		11.73
Foreign banks	515.9	126.4	255.8	18.8	1.34
Urban credit cooperatives	171.5	154.9	97.9		
Rural credit cooperatives	3,101.3	2,734.8	1,974.8	9.65	
2003					
Big four banks	16,275.1	13,071.9	9,950.1	196.5	19.74
Other commercial banks	3,816.8	3,286.5	2,368.2		7.92
1) Joint equity					
2) City commercial banks	1,465.4	1,174.7	774.4	5.4	14.94
Foreign banks	333.1	90.7	147.6	18.1	2.87
Urban credit cooperatives	148.7	127.1	85.6	0.01	
Rural credit cooperatives	2,674.6	2,376.5	1,775.9	4.4	
2002					
Big four banks	14,450.0	11,840.0	8,460.0	71.0	26.1
Other commercial banks	4,160.0	3,390.0	2,290.0	–	–
1) Joint equity	2,990.0	–	–	–	9.5
2) City commercial banks	1,170.0	–	–	–	17.7
Foreign banks	324.2	–	154.0	15.2	–

Table 4B (continued)

Types of banks	Total assets	Total deposits	Outstanding loans	Profit	NPL rate (%)
Urban credit cooperatives	119.0	101.0	66.4	–	–
Rural credit cooperatives	–	1,987.0	1,393.0	–	–
2001					
Big four banks	13,000.0	10,770.0	7,400.0	23.0	25.37
Other commercial banks	3,259.0	2,530.7	1,649.8	12.9	–
1) Joint equity	2,386.0	1,849.0	1,224.0	10.5	12.94
2) City commercial banks	873.0	681.7	425.8	2.4	–
Foreign banks	373.4	–	153.2	1.7	–
Urban credit cooperatives	128.7	107.1	72.5	2.6	–
Rural credit cooperatives	–	1,729.8	1,197.0	–	–

Source: Almanac of China's Finance and Banking 2000–2005.

cooperatives' total assets compose close to 50% of the Big Four (the actual fraction is likely to be higher due to incomplete information on all types of deposit-taking institutions); similar comparisons can be made for outstanding loans. In addition, these banks have less NPLs than the Big Four banks. Table 4C provides evidence on the growth of non-bank intermediaries. Overall, the growth of these non-bank intermediaries has been impressive since the late 1990s. In terms of combined total assets held or managed, the size of all the banks and intermediaries outside of the Big Four banks (first column in Table 4B) is about 49% of the Big Four banks at the end of 2007. Among them, "other commercial banks" (many of them are state-owned), RCCs, and TICs hold the largest amount of assets; the size of foreign banks and mutual funds (not listed in the table) is minuscule, and these are likely to be the focus of development in the near future.[13] Finally, our coverage of non-bank financial institutions excludes various forms of informal financial intermediaries, some of which are deemed illegal but overall provide important financing to firms in the Hybrid Sector.

4 Financial Markets

In this section, we examine China's financial markets, including both the stock and real estate markets, and the recent addition of venture capital and private equity markets, as well as asset management industries. We also compare, at the

[13] Postal savings (deposit-taking institutions affiliated with local post offices) is another form of non-bank intermediation that is not reported in Table 4B due to lack of time series data. However, at the end of 1999, total deposits within the postal savings system exceeded RMB 380 billion, or 6.4% of all deposits in China.

Table 4C Comparison of assets held by China's non-bank intermediaries (RMB billion)

Year	State-owned banks	RCCs	UCCs	Insurance companies	TICs	Non-deposit intermediaries	Other commercial banks	Foreign banks
1995	5,373.34	679.10	303.92	–	458.60	48.97	536.91	42.90
1996	6,582.74	870.66	374.78	–	563.70	82.02	769.98	55.30
1997	7,914.41	1,012.20	498.94	–	636.40	100.42	948.61	75.80
1998	8,860.93	1,143.11	560.63	–	802.50	120.97	1,128.18	118.40
1999	9,970.63	1,239.24	630.15	260.41	907.50	137.08	1,376.89	191.40
2000	10,793.73	1,393.06	678.49	337.39	975.90	160.82	1,828.26	379.20
2001	11,188.22	1,610.80	780.02	459.13	1,088.30	223.67	2,255.70	341.80
2002	13,549.60	2,205.21	119.23	649.41	1,544.10	408.10	2,997.72	317.90
2003	16,275.10	2,674.62	148.72	912.28	–	495.58	3,816.80	331.10
2004	16,932.10	3,103.30	171.50	933.41	–	–	4,697.20	515.90

This table compares *total assets* held by banks and non-bank intermediaries during the period 1995–2004.
Source: Aggregate Statistics from the People's Bank of China (China's Central Bank), 2000–2006.

aggregate level, how firms raise funds in China and in other emerging economies through external markets in order to determine whether China's experience in terms of a firm's fund raising is unique. We then focus on publicly traded companies and examine their financing and investment decisions. Finally, we discuss how to further develop financial markets as well as improve corporate governance and the performance of listed firms.

4.1 Stock Exchanges and Market Inefficiencies

After the inception of China's domestic stock exchanges, the SHSE and SZSE, in 1990, they initially grew quickly. The high growth rates continued in most of the 1990s and the market reached a peak by the end of 2000. As shown in Fig. 3, the momentum of the market, indicated by the SSE Index, then reversed during the next 5 years as it went through a major correction with half of the market capitalization lost. Interestingly, most of the losses were recovered by the end of 2006, and the market had reached new heights during the first half of 2007. However, following a string of negative news worldwide (including the subprime loans crisis in the United States) and domestically (including high levels of inflation), as of June 30, 2008, China's stock market has fallen back to the level in 2006. Figure 3 compares the performance of some of the major stock exchanges around the world, as measured by the "buy-and-hold" return in the period 1992–2007 (gross return at the end of 2007 with $1 invested in each of the valued-weighted stock indexes at the end of 1992). While the performance of the value-weighted SHSE index (the calculation for the SZSE is very similar) is better than that of the FTSE (London) and the Nikkei Index, whose poor

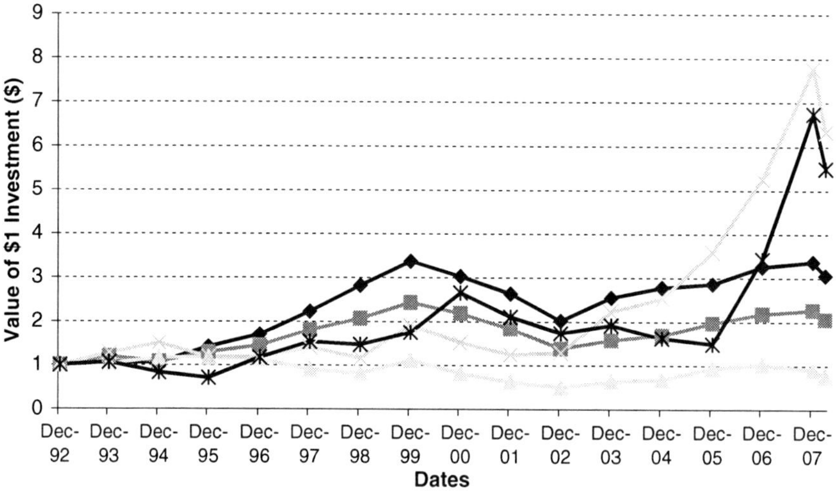

Fig. 3A Comparison of performance of major stock indexes (Buy-and-hold returns of $1 between Dec. 1992 and Dec. 2007)

performance was caused by the prolonged recession of the Japanese economy in the 1990s, the SHSE underperforms the S&P 500 (during 1992–2006) and the SBE (India), the best performing market index of the group. Since China's economy was growing at much higher rates than the United States during 1992–2006 (10.1% per annum for China vs. 3.0% for the United States in real terms), the fact that the SHSE index under-performed the S&P index suggests that listed firms are among the low-quality firms in China.

As Table 5A indicated, at the end of 2007, the SHSE is ranked the sixth largest market in the world in terms of market capitalization, while the SZSE is ranked the twentieth largest. China's total market capitalization (SHSE and SZSE) is around $4.48 trillion (excluding Hong Kong), the second largest country in the world behind only the United States; the Hong Kong Stock Exchange (HKSE), where selected firms from Mainland China have been listed and traded, is ranked the seventh largest in the world. Needless to say, the Chinese financial markets will play an increasingly more important role in

Table 5A A comparison of the largest stock markets in the world (01/01–12/31, 2007)

Rank	Stock exchange	Total market cap (US$ million)	Concentration (%)	Turnover velocity (%)
1	NYSE group	15,650,832.5	57.2	167.1
2	Tokyo SE group	4,330,921.9	62.1	138.4
3	Euronext	4,222,679.8	68.1	136.9
4	Nasdaq	4,013,650.3	65.1	303.6
5	London SE	3,851,705.9	86.0	154.2
6	Shanghai SE	3,694,348.0	73.6	211.0
7	Hong Kong exchanges	2,654,416.1	74.4	94.1
8	TSX group (Canada)	2,186,550.2	62.1	83.7
9	Deutsche Börse	2,105,197.8	78.5	208.4
10	Bombay SE	1,819,100.5	87.0	29.4
11	BME Spanish exchanges	1,799,834.0	–	191.9
12	National stock exchange India	1,660,096.9	68.5	67.7
13	Sao Paulo SE	1,369,711.3	65.7	57.1
14	Australian SE	1,298,315.0	87.4	101.6
15	Swiss exchange	1,271,047.7	71.4	133.9
16	OMX Nordic exchange	1,242,577.9	68.5	137.0
17	Korea exchange	1,122,606.3	81.8	192.6
18	Borsa Italiana	1,072,534.7	66.5	204.1
19	JSE (South Africa)	828,185.3	33.8	52.5
20	Shenzhen SE	784,518.6	38.7	389.2%

All figures are from http://www.world-exchanges.org, the Web site of the international organization of stock exchanges. Concentration is the fraction of total turnover of an exchange within a year coming from the turnover of the companies with the largest market cap (top 5%). Turnover velocity is the total turnover for the year expressed as a percentage of the total market capitalization.

world financial markets. Also from Table 5A, "Concentration" is the fraction of total turnover of an exchange within a year coming from the turnover of the companies with the largest market cap (top 5%), and SZSE (38.7%) has one of the lowest concentration ratios among the largest exchanges, indicating that there is a large amount of trading of small- and medium-cap stocks. "Turnover velocity" is the (annual) total turnover for all the listed firms expressed as a percentage of the total market capitalization, and the figures for both SHSE and SZSE are among the highest among the largest exchanges, with SZSE having the highest turnover ratio. These results show that there is a large amount of speculative trading especially among small- and medium-cap stocks (as these are more easily manipulated than large-cap stocks) in the Chinese markets.

There are two other markets established to complement the two main exchanges. First, a fully electronically operated market ("*Er Ban Shi Chang*" or "second-tier market," similar to the NASDAQ) for small and medium enterprises (SMEs) was opened in June 2004. It was designed to lower the entry barriers for SME firms, especially newly established firms in the high-tech industries. By the end of February 2007, there were 119 firms listed in this market. Second, a "third-tier market" ("*San Ban Shi Chang*," or "third-tier market") was established to deal primarily with de-listing firms and other over-the-counter (OTC) transactions. Since 2001, some publicly listed firms on both SHSE and SZSE that do not meet the listing standards have been de-listed and the trading of their shares shifted to this market.

In addition to the evidence presented in Table 5A, there is abundant evidence showing that China's stock markets are not efficient in that prices and investors' behavior are not necessarily driven by fundamental values of listed firms. For example, Morck et al. (2000) find that stock prices are more "synchronous" (stock prices move up and down together) in emerging countries, including China, than in developed countries. They attribute this phenomenon to poor minority investor protection and imperfect regulation of markets in emerging markets. With a large data set of individual trading, Feng and Seasholes (2004) find that buy-and-sell trades are highly correlated (occur at the same time period, such as in the same day) in China, especially among investors who conduct their trades near one of the two stock exchanges or near firms' headquarters.

In addition, there have been numerous lawsuits against insider trading and manipulation.[14] In many cases, unlike Enron and other well-known companies

---

[14] An example is Guangxia Industry Co., Ltd., dubbed as "China's Enron." Located in Ningxia Province, one of the poorest areas of China, Guangxia was listed on the SZSE in 1994 as a manufacturer of floppy disks. After experiencing poor performance for the first five years, the company reported unprecedented high EPS (earnings per share) at the end of 1999 and claimed that they had mastered the techniques of CO_2 fluid extraction. The company's stock price shot up from RMB 14 to 76 in one year. A CSRC investigation later revealed that the reported earnings and sales records were fabricated, and the company continued losing money in their original line of businesses. The company's top executives were criminally charged, and its auditors lost their licenses, while shareholders' lawsuits were eventually processed by courts for the first time in China. For more details on this case and other cases, see, for example, AQQ (2005b).

in developed markets stricken by corporate scandals, managers and other insiders from the Chinese companies did not use any sophisticated accounting and finance maneuvers to hide their losses (even by China's standards). These cases reveal that the inefficiencies in the Chinese stock markets can be (partially) attributed to poor and ineffective regulation. The current process of listing companies fosters both a problem of adverse selection among firms seeking an initial public offering (IPO) and a moral hazard problem among listed firms. First, even though there is no explicit regulation or law against the listing of firms from the Hybrid Sector, the going public process strongly favors former SOEs with connections with government officials. For example, until recently each candidate firm had to apply and obtain listing quota/permission from the government; all candidate firms have to (and still do) disclose financial and accounting information and are subject to a lengthy evaluation process. The process is inefficient due to bureaucracy, fraudulent disclosure, and lack of independent auditing. As a result, most of the listed firms are indeed former SOEs. Second, once listed, managers in firms with severe agency problems do not have an incentive to manage assets to grow but rather to rely on the external capital markets to raise funds – mainly through mergers and acquisitions and seasoned offerings of securities – to pursue private benefits.[15]

4.2 Overview of Bond Markets

Table 5B provides information on China's bond markets. The government bond market had an annual growth rate of 26.9% during the period 1990–2005 in terms of newly issued bonds, while total outstanding bonds reached RMB 3,144.9 billion (or US $393 billion) at the end of 2006.[16] The second largest component of the bond market is called "policy financial bonds" (total outstanding amount RMB 2,283.5 billion (or US $285 billion) at the end of 2006). These bonds are issued by "policy banks," which operate under the supervision of the Ministry of Finance, and the proceeds of bond issuance are invested in government-run projects and industries such as infrastructure construction (similar to municipal bonds in the United States). Compared to government-issued bonds, the size of the corporate bond market is minuscule:

[15] For example, Du et al. (2008) find that many private, non-listed firms use acquisition of blocks of shares of listed firms as a means to gain access to financial markets (without improving operating performance), as indicated by the frequent fundraising activities such as SEO followed acquisition.

[16] During most of the period 1988–2003, Moody's rated China's government bonds (foreign currency) A2 or A3 (lower than Aa3 and A1 but higher than Baa1; highest rating is Aaa) with a "positive" or "stable" outlook, while the rating on bank deposits (foreign currency ceilings) was Baa, at or above the "investment" grade. These ratings are better or comparable than Moody's ratings on government bonds from most emerging economies.

Table 5B China's bond markets: 1990–2006 (Amount in RMB billion)

	Treasury bonds			Policy financial bonds			Corporate bonds		
Year	Amount issued	Redemption amount	Balance	Amount issued	Amounts redemption	Balance	Amounts issued	Amounts redemption	Balance
1990	19.72	7.62	89.03	6.44	5.01	8.49	12.4	7.73	19.54
1991	28.13	11.16	106.00	6.69	3.37	11.81	24.9	11.43	33.11
1992	46.08	23.81	128.27	5.50	3.00	14.31	68.37	19.28	82.20
1993	38.13	12.33	154.07	0.00	3.43	10.88	23.58	25.55	80.24
1994	113.76	39.19	228.64	0.00	1.35	9.53	16.18	28.20	68.21
1995	151.09	49.70	330.03	–	–	170.85	30.08	33.63	64.66
1996	184.78	78.66	436.14	105.56	25.45	250.96	26.89	31.78	59.77
1997	241.18	126.43	550.89	143.15	31.23	362.88	25.52	21.98	52.10
1998	380.88	206.09	776.57	195.02	32.04	512.11	15.00	10.53	67.69
1999	401.50	123.87	1,054.20	180.09	47.32	644.75	15.82	5.65	77.86
2000	465.70	152.50	1,367.40	164.50	70.92	738.33	8.30	0.00	86.16
2001	488.40	228.60	1,561.80	259.00	143.88	853.45	14.70	0.00	100.86
2002	593.43	226.12	1,933.60	307.50	155.57	1,005.41	32.50	0.00	133.36
2003	628.01	275.58	2,260.36	456.14	250.53	1,165.00	35.80	0.00	169.16
2004	692.39	374.99	2,577.76	414.80	177.87	1,401.93	32.70	0.00	201.86
2005	704.20	104.55	2,877.40	585.17	205.30	1,781.80	204.65	3.70	401.81
2006	888.33	620.86	3144.87	908.0	379.0	2283.5	393.83	167.24	553.29
Growthrate	26.87%	16.35%	24.96%	36.24%	31.05%	42.86%	24.13%	21.18%	23.24%

This table presents the development of China's bond markets. "Policy Financial Bonds" are issued by "policy banks," which belong to the Treasury Department, and the proceeds of bond issuance are invested in government run projects and industries such as infrastructure construction (similar to municipal bonds in the US).

Source: Aggregate Statistics from the People's Bank of China (China's Central Bank) 2000–2007 and the Statistical Yearbook of China 2000–2007.

In terms of the amount of outstanding bonds at the end of 2006, the corporate bond market was less than one-tenth of the size of the government bond market.

In fact, the underdevelopment of the bond market, especially the corporate bond market, relative to the stock market, is common among Asian countries. AQQ (2008) compares different components (bank loans to private sectors or the Hybrid Sector of China; stock market capitalization; public/government and private/corporate bond markets) of the financial markets around the world at the end of 2003. Compared to Europe and the United States, they find that the size of both the government (public) and corporate (private) bond markets is smaller in Asia excluding Japan (Hong Kong, South Korea, Malaysia, Taiwan, Singapore, Indonesia, Philippines, and Thailand); even in Japan, the size of the corporate bond market is much smaller compared with its government bond market. They also find that the size of all four components of China's financial markets is small relative to that of other regions and countries, including bank loans made to the Hybrid Sector (private sector) in China (other countries). Moreover, the most underdeveloped component of China's financial markets is the corporate bond market (labeled "private" bond market).

There are a number of reasons for the underdevelopment in bond markets in China and other parts of Asia (see, e.g., Herring and Chatusripitak 2000). Lack of sound accounting/auditing system and high-quality bond-rating agencies is an important factor. Given low creditor protection and court inefficiency (in China and most other emerging economies) the recovery rates for bondholders during default are low, which in turn leads to underinvestment in the market (by domestic and foreign investors). Lack of a well-constructed yield curve is another important factor in China. Given the small size of the publicly traded treasury bond market and lack of historical prices, we can only plot "snapshots" of a partial yield curve (maturities range from 1 month to 1 year only) based on pricing data of treasury bonds in the national interbank market. This is far from the standard yield curve covering interest rates on bond maturities ranging from 1 month to 10 years. The deficiencies in the term structure of interest rates hamper the development of derivatives markets that enable firms and investors to manage risk, as well as the effectiveness of the government's macroeconomic policies. Therefore, it is important that China develop its bond markets in the near future along with its legal system and related institutions.

Before we close this subsection, we compare, at the aggregate level, external financing (i.e. financing from outside the firm) in China and other major emerging economies. We also relate the aggregate financing channels with the growth of the economy during different periods, in order to determine whether the Chinese experience in financing is unique. First, Fig. 4A compares the development of stock markets at the aggregate level, while Fig. 4B compares the growth rates of (PPP-adjusted) GDP. Both Taiwan and South Korea experienced high GDP growth in the 1970s and early 1980s, while the total market capitalization of their respective stock markets accounted for less than 20% of their GNPs during the same period, and the growth of stock markets did not take off until the mid- to late-1980s. Figure 4C compares the growth of

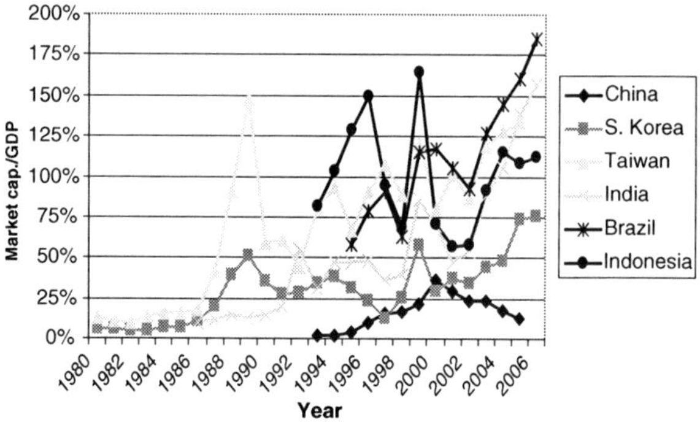

Fig. 4A Market cap/GNP ratios

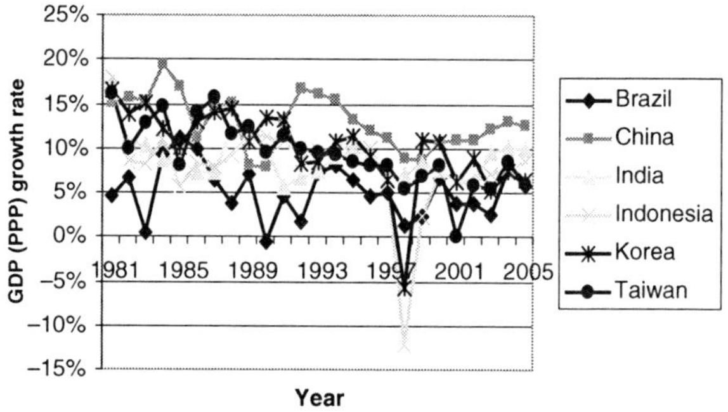

Fig. 4B GDP growth rates

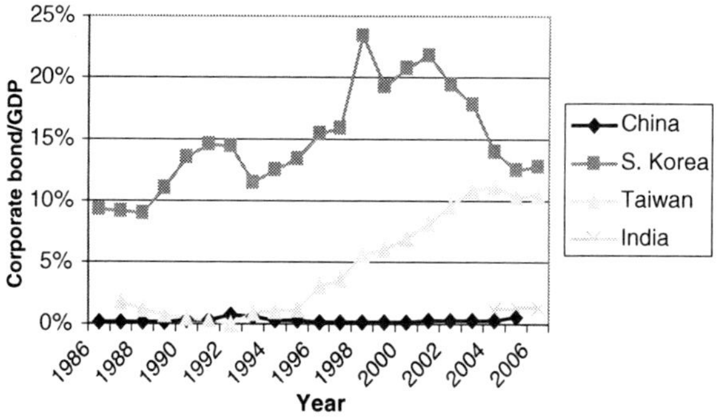

Fig. 4C Corporate bond market

corporate bond markets: South Korea having the fastest growth path, while in Taiwan and China the corporate bond markets seem to lag the development of stock markets. Finally, Fig. 4D compares total equity issuance including IPOs and seasoned equity offerings (SEOs). With the exception of South Korea, China seems to be on a similar pace in terms of size of equity issuance (as fraction of GNP in a given year) with Taiwan, India, and Brazil.

From the above comparisons, it is clear that the development of China's external markets relative to its overall economic growth is not dramatically

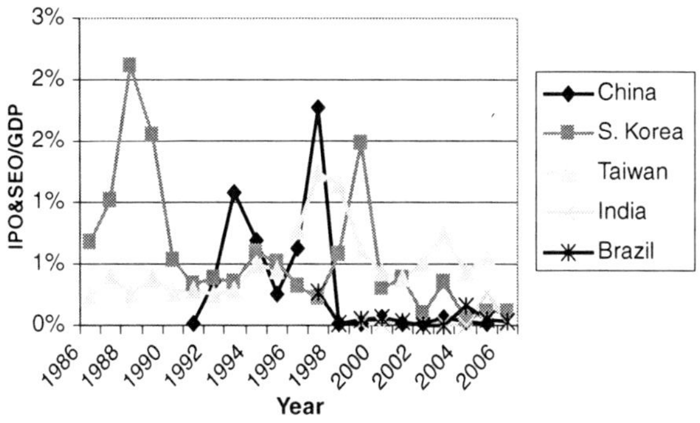

Fig. 4D Equity issuance
Figure 4A compares the time series of stock market capitalization/GDP ratios across six emerging economies. Figure 4B compares time series of the growth rates of GDP, and the growth rates are calculated using PPP-adjusted GDP figures in order to avoid biases caused by different currency policies. Figure 4C presents the time series of the ratios of the amount of corporate bonds outstanding/GNP, while Fig. 4D presents the time series of IPO and SEO (in a given year)/GDP. The calculations for all the ratios in Figs. 4A, C, and D are based on local currencies of a country in a given year.

different from that of other emerging countries. One of the common patterns is that the development of external markets trails that of the growth of the overall economy. During the early stages of economic growth, alternative institutions and mechanisms can support the growth of firms and the overall economy, as is the case for China based on our evidence. Perhaps similar institutions have worked well in other emerging and developed economies as well.

4.3 Evidence on the Listed Sector

In this section, we examine publicly listed and traded companies in China. It is worthwhile to first clarify whether firms from the Hybrid Sector can be listed and publicly traded. Regulations and laws (the 1986 trial version of the bankruptcy law and the 1999 version of the company law) never prohibit the listing of Hybrid Sector firms; and selected firms from the Hybrid Sector enter the Listed Sector through an IPO or by acquiring a listed firm from the inception of SHSE and SZSE. However, the accessibility of equity markets for these firms has been much lower than for former SOEs in practice due to the enforcement of the listing standards and process. As a result, AQQ (2005a) find that 80% of their sample of more than 1,100 listed firms are converted from former SOEs. In recent years, the government has attempted to change the composition of listed firms by relaxing regulations toward Hybrid Sector firms.

Until the recent share reform, listed firms in China issued both tradable and non-tradable shares (Table 6A). The non-tradable shares were either held by the

Table 6A Types of common stock issued in China

Tradable?		Definition
No (Private block transfer possible)	State-owned shares* (G shares after recent reform and tradable)	Shares that are controlled by the central government during the process when firms are converted into a limited liability corporation but before listing. These shares are either managed and represented by the Bureau of National Assets Management or held by other state-owned companies, both of which also appoint firms' board members. After reforms announced in 2005 and implemented in 2006–2007 state shares became G shares and are tradable.
	Entrepreneur's shares	Shares reserved for firms' founders during the same process described above; different from shares that founders can purchase and sell in the markets.
	Foreign owners	Shares owned by foreign industrial investors during the same process
	Legal entity holders	Shares sold to legal identities (such as other companies, listed or non-listed) during the same process.
	Employee shares	Shares sold to firm's employees during the same process.
Yes (Newly issued shares)	A Shares	Shares issued by Chinese companies that are listed and traded in the Shanghai or Shenzhen Stock Exchange; most of these shares are sold to and held by Chinese (citizen) investors.
	B Shares	Shares issued by Chinese companies that are listed and traded in the Shanghai or Shenzhen Stock Exchange; these shares are sold to and held by foreign investors; starting in 2001, Chinese investors can also trade these shares.
	H Shares	Shares issued by selected Chinese companies listed and traded in the Hong Kong Stock Exchange; these shares can only be traded on the HK Exchange but can be held by anyone.

* There are sub-categories under this definition

government or by other state-owned legal entities (i.e., other listed or non-listed firms or organizations). Table 6B demonstrates that, as of the first half of 2006, non-tradable shares constituted a majority of all shares, and most of these shares were held by the state, while the majority of tradable shares were A shares. Among the tradable shares, Classes A and B shares were listed and traded in either the SHSE or SZSE, while Class A(B) shares were issued to and traded by Chinese investors (foreign investors including those from Taiwan and

Table 6B Tradable vs. Non-tradable shares for China's listed companies

Year	State/total shares	Non-tradable°/ total shares	Tradable/ total shares	A/total shares	A/Tradable shares*
1992	0.41	0.69	0.31	0.16	0.52
1993	0.49	0.72	0.28	0.16	0.57
1994	0.43	0.67	0.33	0.21	0.64
1995	0.39	0.64	0.36	0.21	0.60
1996	0.35	0.65	0.35	0.22	0.62
1997	0.32	0.65	0.35	0.23	0.66
1998	0.34	0.66	0.34	0.24	0.71
1999	0.36	0.65	0.35	0.26	0.75
2000	0.39	0.64	0.36	0.28	0.80
2001	0.39	0.64	0.36	0.29	0.80
2002	N/a	0.65	0.35	0.26	0.74
2003	N/a	0.64	0.35	0.27	0.76
2004	N/a	0.64	0.36	0.28	0.77
2005	N/a	0.62	0.38	0.30	0.78
2006 (June)	N/a	0.57	0.43	0.35	0.81

^ Non-tradable shares include "state-owned" and "shares owned by legal entities";
* tradable shares include A, B, and H shares;
Source: China Security Regulation Committee Reports (2000–2006) and http://www.csrc.gov.cn

Hong Kong and QFIIs). While the two share classes issued by the same firm are identical in terms of shareholder rights (e.g., voting and dividend), B shares are traded at a significant discount relative to A shares and are traded less frequently than A shares.[17] The "B share discount" has been reduced significantly since the CSRC allowed Chinese citizens to trade B shares (with foreign currency accounts) in 2001. In addition, Class H shares, issued by selected "Red Chip" Chinese companies, are listed and traded on the HKSE. Finally, there are N shares and S shares for firms listed in the United States and Singapore but operating in China (we omit discussions on these shares since they are not listed on the domestic exchanges). After the share reforms discussed below in Section 4.6, government shares became G shares and are tradable.

We next describe standard corporate governance mechanisms in the Listed Sector. First, according to the (2005) Company Law, listed firms in China have a two-tier board structure – the Board of Directors (five to nineteen members) and the Board of Supervisors (at least three members), with supervisors ranking above directors. The main duty of the Board of Supervisors is to monitor firms'

[17] Explanations of the B share discount include (1) Foreign investors face higher information asymmetry than domestic investors, (2) lower B share prices compensation for the lack of liquidity (due to low trading volume), and (3) the A share premium reflects a speculative bubble component among domestic investors. See Chan et al. (2007) and Mei et al. (2003) for more details.

operations as well as top managers and directors; it consists of representatives of shareholders and employees, with the rest being either officials chosen from government branches or executives from the parent companies; directors and top managers of the firms cannot hold positions as supervisors. The Board of Directors perform similar duties as their counterparts in the United States, including appointing and terminating CEOs. According to the "one-share, one-vote" scheme adopted by firms in the Listed Sector, shareholders including the state and legal person shareholders (that typically own the majority of shares) appoint the board members. Specifically, the Chairman (one person) and Vice Chairman (one or two) of the Board are elected by all directors (majority votes); at the approval of the Board, the CEO and other top managers can become members of the Board. The CSRC requires at least one-third (a minimum of two people) of the Board to be independent.

Since the law does not specify that every member of the Board must be elected by shareholders during general shareholder meetings, in practice some directors are nominated and appointed by the firms' parent companies, and the nomination process is usually kept secret, in particular for former SOEs. Since not all members of either board are elected by shareholders, a major problem with the board structure is the appointment of and contracting with the CEOs. Fan et al. (2007) find that almost one-third of their sample of 625 listed companies' CEOs are either current or former government bureaucrats; the performance of these firms is significantly worse than other firms without politically connected CEOs. Based on firm-level compensation data (available since 1998 due to disclosure requirements), Fung et al. (2003) and Kato and Long (2004) find that no listed firms grant stock options to CEOs or board members, while the cash-based compensation level for CEOs is much lower than their counterparts in developed countries, and the consumption of perks, such as company cars, is prevalent.

Second, the existing ownership structure, characterized by the large amount of non-tradable shares including cross-holdings of shares among listed companies and institutions, makes it difficult for value-increasing M&As. According to the *China Mergers and Acquisitions Yearbook* (2006), there are 1,396 M&As involving listed firms in 2005 totaling US $40 billion, a small fraction of the total market capitalization. In many deals, a Hybrid Sector firm (non-listed) acquires a listed firm that is converted from an SOE, but the large amount of non-tradable shares held by the state remains intact after the transaction.[18] Such an acquisition can be the means through which low-quality,

[18] If we include the cross-border M&As and transactions between parent companies and subsidiaries, the total amount increases to US$47 billion in 2000, $14 billion in 2001, $29 billion in 2002, and $24 billion in the first three quarters of 2003. Sixty-eight percent of all M&A deals (66% in terms of dollar deal amount) are initiated by Hybrid Sector firms, while former SOEs and foreign firms initiate 29 and 3% of the rest, respectively (27 and 7% in deal amount). M&As are most active in coastal regions, and in industries such as machinery, information technology, retail, and gas and oil.

non-listed companies bypass listing standards and access financial markets (e.g., Du et al. 2008).

Third, an important factor contributing to the occurrence of corporate scandals is the lack of institutional investors (including non-depository financial intermediaries) as they are a very recent addition to the set of financial institutions in China. Professional investors would perhaps not be so easily taken in by simple deceptions. Another factor is that the enforcement of laws is questionable due to the lack of legal professionals and institutions. For example, ineffective bankruptcy implementation makes the threat and penalty for bad firm performance non-credible.[19] As mentioned above, the new Bankruptcy Law introduces the role of trustees in the bankruptcy procedure, along with other provisions enhancing creditor rights and facilitating the corporate bankruptcy procedure. It is a step toward establishing a comprehensive and modern bankruptcy system in accordance with international standards.[20]

Fourth, the government plays the dual roles of regulator and blockholder for many listed firms, including banks and financial services companies. The main role of the CSRC (counterpart of the SEC in the United States) is to monitor and regulate stock exchanges and listed companies. The government exercises its shareholder control rights in listed firms through the Bureau of National Assets Management, which holds large fractions of non-tradable shares, or other SOEs (with their holdings of non-tradable shares). However, since the top officials of the bureau are government officials, it is doubtful that they will pursue their fiduciary role as control shareholders diligently. Moreover, the government's dual roles can lead to conflicting goals (maximizing profits as shareholder vs. maximizing social welfare as regulator or social planner) in dealing with listed firms, which in turn weaken the effectiveness of both roles.[21] There are cases in which the government, aiming to achieve certain social goals, influenced the markets through state-owned institutional investors (e.g., asset management companies) but created unintended adverse effects.

Overall, internal and external governance for the Listed Sector is weak, and further development of governance mechanisms is one of the main objectives

---

[19] Cross-country information on the efficiency of bankruptcy procedures, based on surveys of lawyers and bankruptcy judges around the world, is available from World Bank (http://rru.worldbank.org/Doingbusiness). Among 108 countries, China's "goals of insolvency" index is equal to the median of the sample.

[20] With a large sample of syndicated loans around the globe, Qian and Strahan (2007) show that strong creditor protection (in borrower countries) enhances loan availability as lenders are more willing to provide credit on favorable terms (e.g., longer maturities and lower interest rates).

[21] Gordon and Li (2003) show that the ownership structure (with large state ownership stakes) can be attributed to government collecting monopoly rents from investors and subsidizing listed firms that were formerly SOEs. However, they argue that this behavior is not as efficient as explicit taxes on investors.

for this sector going forward. In Section 4.7 below, we provide some general suggestions. In addition, AQQ (2005a) show that the dividend ratio, valuation (Tobin's Q), and post-IPO performance of listed firms in China are much lower or worse compared to similar firms operating in countries with stronger investor protections. In summary, the overall evidence on the comparison of China and other countries' external markets and listed firms is consistent with LLSV (1997a, 1998) predictions: With an underdeveloped legal system and weak investor (both shareholder and creditor) protection, China's small markets for finance from outside the firm and low-quality of listed firms come as no surprise.

4.4 Real Estate Market

Like other economic sectors, China's real estate market has long been operating under the "dual tracks" of both central planning and market-oriented systems. Prior to 1998, government control was dominant with the market only playing a secondary role, and mortgages were not designated for retail customers and households. Chinese citizens working for the government and government-owned companies and organizations could purchase properties at prices significantly below market prices, with the subsidies coming from their employers. The reform policies introduced in 1998 aimed to end the distribution of properties by employers and establish new housing finance and market systems. Provinces and autonomous regions have established programs to sell properties (e.g., apartments in urban areas) to individuals instead of allocating residency as part of the employment benefits.

Since 1998, the residential housing reform and the development of individual mortgages, along with rising household income and demand for quality housing, had stimulated the fast growth of the real estate market. According to the National Bureau of Statistics, from March 1998 to the end of 2006, the residential property price index climbed from 101.30 to 140, a total 40% increase or an annual growth of 4.3%. Some metropolitan areas such as Beijing, Shanghai, Shenzen, and Guangzhou had much higher growth rates than the national average. Figure 5A shows the total real estate investments and their funding sources over time. Total investment increased from 321 billion RMB in 1996, or 12% of the national fixed assets investments, to 2.5 trillion RMB in 2007 or 25% of the national fixed assets investments. Most of the investment funds have come from domestic sources. China's continuing economic growth, especially in private sectors, urbanization and industrialization, limited land supply, increasing foreign direct investments and institutional investments, will further enhance the liquidity and long-term prospects of China's real estate assets.

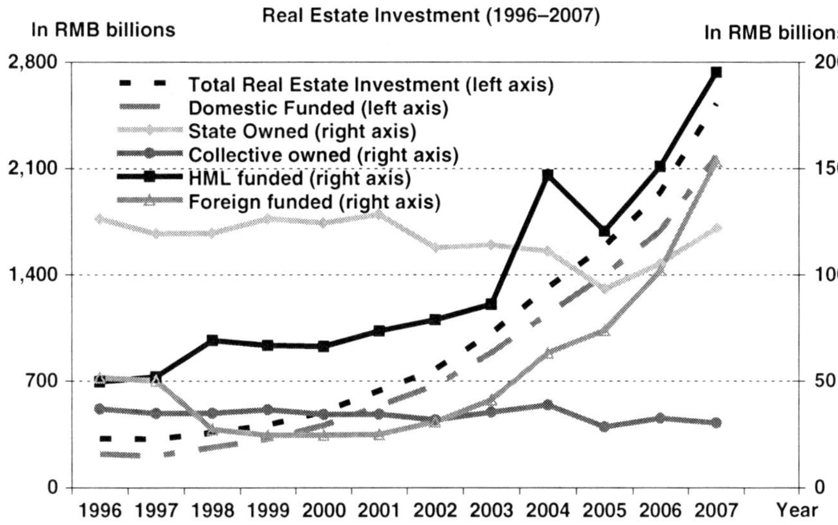

Fig. 5A Total real estate investments and their sources (1996–2007)

As the real estate sector gains more weight in the economy, its impact on other industries, especially financial and banking industries, has also increased considerably. Bank loans are the most important source of real estate financing. With the expansion of the real estate market, banks and other financial institutions lent more to keep up with the demand for financing; when the fast expansion could not be sustained by economic growth and household income, inflated demand led to hikes in property prices and a real estate bubble surfaced. Some metropolitan areas have experienced annual price increases as high as 20% or more and subsequent crashes of the market. The government has been taking aggressive fiscal measures to control property prices; since 2004, it has issued new policies in order to suppress speculative activities. Another policy measure to control the growth of the real estate market is through the PBOC's required reserve deposit ratio. We analyze the formation, bursting, and economic consequences of real estate and other market bubbles in Section 5 below.

Despite the significant rise of residential property price, the overall price trend in mainland appears to be in line with the pace of China's economic growth. According to the PBOC, the property price to income ratio is the price per unit squared meter multiplied by the area of a property sold and then divided by an urban family's average annual disposable income (the average household income equals annual income per person multiplied by average number of persons per family). Data on the price–income ratios show that the ratio has remained stable since 1998, ranging between 6.2 and 6.9 (for more details, see Cao (2008)). There are two real estate indices

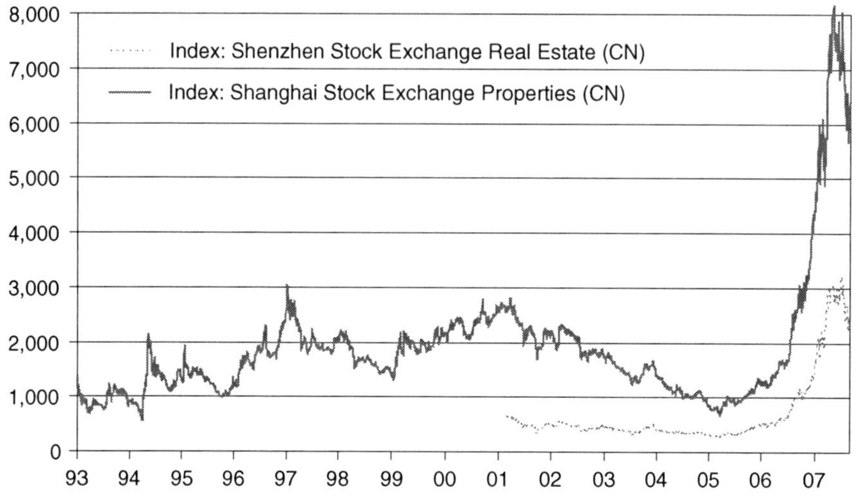

Fig. 5B Performance of real estate indexes (Dec. 1993–Dec. 2007)

in China tracking the stock performance of top real estate developers, with the initial recording on April 30, 1993 for the SHSE and July 2, 2001 for the SZSE. Figure 5B shows the trends of these indexes. Based on the trend of the Shanghai Index, we can observe the effects of a few fiscal tightening policies, one in mid-1996 prior to the Asia Financial Crisis and another in late 2006. The fiscal tightening in late 2006 was much more dramatic due to the fast pace of real estate growth in the previous few years. This coincided with the appreciation of the RMB in August 2005. With the continuing appreciation of RMB and the robust prospects of economic growth, it is conceivable that RMB-denominated real estate assets will become more enticing to foreign investors in the future.

4.5 Private Equity/Venture Capital and the Funding of New Industries

Allen and Gale (1999, 2000a) have suggested that stock market-based economies, such as the United Kingdom in the nineteenth century and the United States in the twentieth century, have been more successful in developing *new* industries than intermediary-based economies such as Germany and Japan. They argue that markets are better than banks for funding new industries, because evaluation of these industries based on experience is difficult, and there is a wide diversity of opinion. Stock market-based economies such as the United States and United Kingdom also tend to have well-developed systems for the acquisition and distribution of information, so the cost of information to investors is low. Markets then work well because investors can gather information at low costs and those that anticipate high profits can provide the finance to the firms operating in the new industries.

An important part of this process is the private equity/venture capital sector (see, e.g., Kortum and Lerner 2000). Venture capitalists are able to raise large amounts of funds in the United States because of the prospect that successful firms will be able to undertake an IPO. With data from 21 countries, Jeng and Wells (2000) find that venture capital is less important in other countries, while the existence of an active IPO market is the critical determinant of the importance of venture capital in a country. This is consistent with the finding of Black and Gilson (1998) in a comparison of the United States and Germany that the primary reason venture capital is relatively successful in the United States is the active IPO market that exists there. AQQ (2005b) provide detailed information on the fast-growing private equity/venture capital sector in China.

The reason that China should develop active venture capital and private equity markets is to provide financing for new industries. What is unusual about China (perhaps along with India) is that it currently has the ability to develop both traditional industries, such as manufacturing, and in the near future new, high-tech industries, such as aerospace, computer software, semiconductors, and bio-genetics. This is different from the experience of South Korea and Taiwan in the 1970s, and that of most other emerging economies in the 1990s, as all these other countries focused on developing manufacturing industries first. In terms of developing traditional industries (e.g., Korea and Taiwan in the 1970s), China has already followed suit in first introducing advanced (relative to domestic companies) but not the most advanced technologies from developed countries and "nationalizing" these technologies within designated companies before moving toward the more advanced technologies. Allen and Gale (1999, 2000a) argue that banks are better than financial markets for funding mature industries because there is wide agreement on how they should be managed, so the delegation of the investment decision to a bank works well. This delegation process, and the economies of scale in information acquisition through delegation, makes bank-based systems more efficient in terms of financing the growth in these industries. Therefore, the banking system can contribute more in supporting the growth and development of these industries than markets.

4.6 Asset Management Industries

The mutual fund industry in China has gone through three stages of development. The first stage is between 1992, when China's first fund (*LiuBo*) was established, and 1997, when the first version of the mutual fund regulation was drafted and passed by the CSRC. The *LiuBo* Fund was a close-end fund with NAV RMB 100 million (US $12.5 million) and began to trade at the SHSE in

1993. While the industry experienced fast growth in the few years after 1992, lack of regulation and problems associated with fund trading hampered the further development of the industry. The first open-end fund was established in September 2001 (*Hua An Chuangxin*), following the announcement of the proposal for open-end fund investment by the CSRC, a milestone for China's mutual fund industry.

Figure 6 shows the development of the mutual fund industry in China. With only a handful of funds in 1998, China had 58 fund companies managing 307 different funds by the end of 2006. The total fund value increased from RMB 11 billion (or $1.3 billion) in 1998 to about RMB 2.58 trillion (or $322 billion) in May 2008 (this figure was much higher in the second half of 2007 before the market went down). In 2001, the NAV of all funds was about 0.8% of GDP and 1.19% of total national savings; these figures rose to 4.09% of GDP and 5.30% of total savings in 2006. The growth of open-end funds contributed to most of the growth in the industry. At the end of 2006, 254 funds were open-ended and 53 were close-ended, with 81% of the total fund value managed by open-end funds; this percentage of fund value increased to 91% by the end of May 2008. The most popular investment style is actively managed (domestic) equity, with only a few index funds and exchange traded funds (ETFs).

Many mutual fund companies are owned by securities and other financial services companies. Like their counterparts in the United States, management

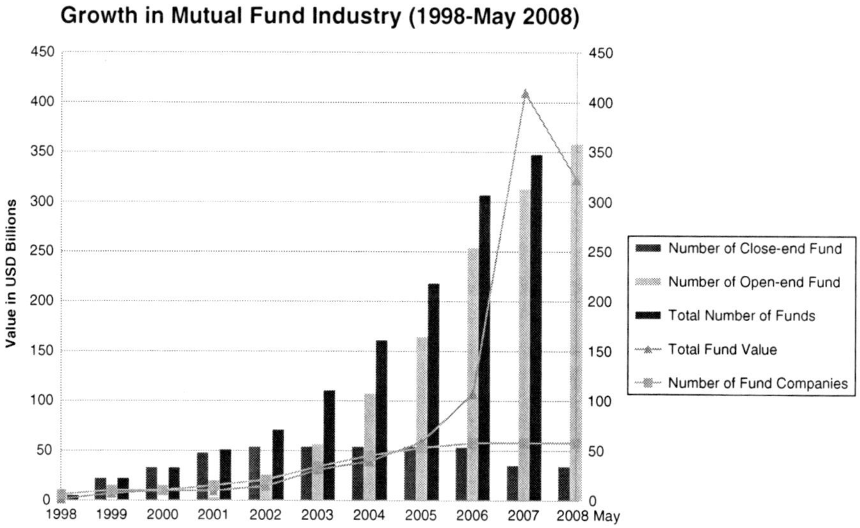

Fig. 6 Growth in China's mutual fund industry (1998–2008)

fee is the major source of income for fund companies, accounting for about 80% of total income. Administration fees account for 9% of total income, and the rest of the income comes from investment and other incomes. More than half of the fund managers have a master-level or higher academic degree, and the majority of them are 36–45 years old. Investment capital from institutional investors was about the same as that from individual investors in 2005, but in 2006 individual investors accounted for 70% of the total mutual fund investment.

The first fund managed by a qualified foreign institutional investor (QFII) was set up in 2002. The State Administration of Foreign Exchange (SAFE) is the government agent that regulates the QFII funds. The QFII Act allows foreign investors to invest in Chinese securities, with the intention of introducing sophisticated foreign investors to the Chinese market with the hope that their presence would improve market efficiency. In addition, with the exercise of their shareholder rights, their presence could also help improve corporate governance of the Listed Sector. However, the original QFII rules imposed restrictions on foreign investors, such as a capital lock-up period of 1–3 years, limiting capital withdrawal (and leaving China) and other operating restrictions. In August 2006, CSRC revised QFII rules to promote more participation from foreign investors. Under the new rules, there has been a significant increase in applications from foreign investors for QFII quotas.

Most of the first group of QFII applicants were securities companies and investment banks, with other financial services companies such as insurance companies and pension fund companies also on the list. By the end of July 2006, China had approved a total of $7.495 billion foreign investment capital (quota) from 45 QFIIs, or three quarters of the then ceiling of $10 billion capital inflow through QFIIs. In December 2007, the investment quota/ceiling was tripled, from $10 billion to $30 billion. Some analysts believe that the move to increase the QFII quota was also intended to prepare for the large amount of floating of non-tradable shares. If the holders of the newly floated shares rush to sell, QFII funds might be an important stabilizing source of the market. As of April 2008, there are a total 54 of QFIIs operating in China.

The approval of qualified domestic institutional investors (QDII) to invest in overseas markets came after QFII, in July 2006. The QDII funds were invested in stocks, bonds, real estate investment trusts, and other mainstream financial products in markets such as New York, London, Tokyo,, and Hong Kong. Similarly to the QFII scheme, it is a transitional arrangement that provides limited opportunities for domestic investors to access foreign markets at a stage in which a country/territory's currency is not freely convertible and capital flows are restricted. As of early 2008, 10 fund companies have obtained the approval to launch QDII; five QDII funds have been launched by January 2008. At the end of September 2007, QDIIs had received investment quotas of $42.17 billion, with an actual outflow of $10.86 billion. Given the recent turmoil in the global financial markets, including the impact of the subprime loans crisis, the performance of the QDII funds has been less than stellar. Going forward, the probable continuing appreciation of the RMB against major international currencies including the dollar is a major concern for QDII investors.

China's asset management industry is expected to continue their growth in the near future. In the United States, mutual funds became the largest financial intermediary in financial markets in 1999, holding 29% of all financial assets. By contrast, mutual funds in China only hold around 1.5% of all financial assets. The further growth of the economy and continuing reform of the pension system will generate both demand and supply of capital for the industry. If the trend of opening up domestic markets to foreign investors continues, there will be greater inflow of QFIIs.

4.7 Further Development of Financial Markets

As documented, the financial markets in China do not currently play nearly as important a role as banks. Going forward, if China wishes to develop high-technology industries as discussed in Section 4.5, then it is important that it improves its financial markets. In addition, if it is to enlarge risk management possibilities for its financial institutions and firms, it needs to develop new financial products and markets. Finally, if there is to be an alternative to banks for raising large amounts of capital, then China needs deep and efficient markets.

In recent years, the performance of the stock markets has been volatile. This is somewhat surprising given the robust performance of the real economy. We attribute this (relatively) poor performance to a number of factors, including the following:

(i) Limited self-regulation and formal regulation.
(ii) The large overhang of shares owned by government entities.
(iii) The lack of listed firms originating in the Hybrid Sector.
(iv) The lack of trained professionals.
(v) The lack of institutional investors.
(vi) Limited financial markets and products.

It is important that these weaknesses be overcome. However, some of these are problems that must be tackled over the long run. They cannot be solved in a few years. We discuss each in turn.

4.7.1 Improve Regulations

There are two ways in which markets are regulated in practice, and each has advantages and disadvantages: First, market forces and self-regulation, and second, government regulation.

A good example of regulation through market forces and self-regulation is provided by the capital markets in the UK in the nineteenth and early twentieth century (Michie 1987). The role of government regulation and intervention was minimal. Despite this, the markets did extremely well and London became the financial capital of the world. Many firms and countries from all over the world raised large amounts of funds. Reputation and trust were an important factor in the smooth operation of these markets. For example, in an important paper Franks et al. (2003) compare the early twentieth century capital markets with those in the mid-twentieth century. Despite extensive changes in the laws protecting minority shareholders, there was very little change in the ways in which the market operated. The authors attribute this to the importance of trust.

We argue below that China's Hybrid sector is another example of a situation where market forces are effective. Formal regulation and legal protections do not play much of a role, and yet financing and governance mechanisms are quite effective. In this case, as we shall see, it appears that competition as well as reputation and trust work well.

In contrast, the examples of fraud and other problems of manipulation and the inefficiency of markets pointed to in Section 4.1 suggest that in China's formal financial markets these alternative mechanisms do not work well. Although such mechanisms may develop in the long run as in the nineteenth and early twentieth century UK, it seems that in the short run at least it is likely to require formal government regulation of the type developed in the United States in the 1930s and subsequently as a response to the stock market collapse that started in 1929 and the Great Depression. There is evidence from many countries that this type of formal regulation is effective. For example, based on a study of securities laws with the focus on the public issuance of new equity in 49 countries (China is not included), LLS (2006) find that disclosure and liability rules help to promote stock market development.

4.7.2 Sale of Government Shares in Listed Firms

One of the major problems Chinese stock markets have faced in recent years has been caused by the large amount of shares in listed companies owned by the government and government entities shown in Table 6B. The Chinese government attempted sales of state shares of selected firms in 1999 and 2001 but halted the process both times after share prices plunged and investors grew panicky about the value of the entire market. This overhang created great uncertainty about the quantity of shares that would come onto the market going forward. This uncertainty was probably in part responsible for the stagnation of share prices between 2002 and 2005 despite the very high levels of growth in the economy.

In 2005, the government announced a new plan of "fully floating" state shares. Under the new plan, the remaining state shares among listed firms are converted to "G" shares. The CSRC outlines the format for compensating existing shareholders and also imposes lockups and restrictions on the amount of G shares that can be sold immediately after they become tradable. More specifically, the new plan stipulates that G shares are not to be traded or transferred within 12 months after the implementation of the share structure reform. Shareholders owning more than 5% of the original non-tradable shares can only trade less than 5% of the total shares outstanding within one year and less than 10% within 2 years. These restrictions of G share sales are intended to reduce the downward pressure on the stock price, maintain market stability, and protect the interests of public investors. The details of the "fully floating plan" for a firm, including the number of G shares to be granted to each Class A shareholder and the time window (e.g., 1–3 years) of G shares become fully floating, must be approved by two thirds of Class A shareholders of the firm.

Three remarks for the reform are in order. First, the government's commitment to the plan is superior to a series of partially unanticipated trials that are subject to termination, if a significantly negative market reaction is observed. Second, while under the current plan, the full floating of all G shares may only take a few years (if this is what the majority of shareholders of all firms desire) and hence may trigger some volatility, the plan does compensate Class A shareholders for the negative price impact and allow them to decide on the timing of the floating. Third, there is some uncertainty as to whether firms will sell at the same time or not. If they do sell simultaneously then there may be a lack of overall liquidity, and this may induce volatility in the markets. The recent run of bearish markets in China can be in part attributed to the significant increase in supply of shares of many listed firms. Share reforms began with a pilot program with only four companies participating in April 2005. By the end of 2006, 96% of all the listed companies had completed share reforms; by the end of 2007, there were only a few companies that had not reached an agreement with their shareholders on the terms of the reform.[22]

4.7.3 Encourage Listing of Firms from the Hybrid Sector

One of the major problems of the stock exchanges is that most of the firms listed are former SOEs. Relatively few are firms from the more dynamic Hybrid Sector. A high priority for reform for the markets is changing of listing requirements to make it advantageous for dynamic and successful companies to be listed on the exchanges.

4.7.4 Train More Professionals

This is the most important factor in terms of improving the enforcement of laws and contracts. First, an independent and efficient judicial system requires a

[22] Huang et al. (2008) document that share reform increases turnovers, especially for firms with low liquidity prior to the reform, and reduces speculative trading. Although share prices drop significantly on the day share supply increases, shareholder wealth increases by 15% overall. Beltratti and Bortolotti (2006) document 8% abnormal return around the date of share reform announcement. Liao and Liu (2008) show that market reactions to share reforms are positively associated with the quality of the listed firms (as measured by firm disclosure), providing evidence of improved market efficiency.

sufficient supply of qualified legal professionals. The Ministry of Justice of China states that there are 114,000 lawyers and 11,691 law firms as of 2005, while Orts (2001) estimates that there are 150,000 lawyers in China, roughly the same number of licensed attorneys as in the state of California. Two hundred and six of China's 2,000 counties still do not have lawyers. Lawyers represent only 10–25% of all clients in civil and business cases, and even in criminal prosecutions, lawyers represent defendants in only half of the cases. Among the approximately five million business enterprises in China, only 4% of them currently have regular legal advisers. Moreover, only one-fifth of all lawyers in China have law degrees, and even a lower fraction of judges have formally studied law at a university or college. As mentioned before, a similar situation exists for auditors and accounting professionals.

4.7.5 Encourage the Development of Institutional Investors

In most developed stock markets, institutional investors, such as insurance companies, pension funds, mutual funds, and hedge funds, play an important role. They employ well-trained professionals who are able to evaluate companies well. This causes markets to have a higher degree of efficiency than if they are dominated by individual investors. In addition, there can be advantages in terms of corporate governance, if institutional investors actively participate in the monitoring of firms' managers and are directly involved in firms' decision-making process as blockholders of stocks. For example, in the United States, pension funds such as CALPERS have become the symbol of shareholder activism that strengthens corporate governance, while in Japan and Germany, financial intermediaries serve similar purposes. For China, an effective way to improve the efficiency of China's stock markets, as well as corporate governance of listed firms, is to encourage further development of domestic financial intermediaries that can act as institutional investors. With their large-scale capital and expertise in all relevant areas of business, financial intermediaries can provide a level of stability and professionalism that is sorely lacking in China's financial markets.

Currently institutional investors such as insurance companies, mutual funds, and pension funds are relatively small in terms of assets held given their early stage in the development. However, they are expanding dramatically. For example, the sum of all mutual funds' NAVs reached RMB 32.8 trillion (or US $4.1 trillion) at the end of 2007. One way to further encourage the development of such intermediaries is to give tax advantages to various types of products such as life insurance and pension-related savings and investments.

4.7.6 Develop More Financial Products and Markets

Another issue is to develop more financial products so that investors can form diversified portfolios with more than just stocks. First, corporate bond markets should be developed, along with better enforcement of bankruptcy laws and bond-rating agencies. Second, more derivative securities such as forwards, futures, and options on commodities (already in place and trading), as well as on other securities, should be introduced to the market so that investors and firms have more tools for risk management. Third, insurance companies should expand their coverage and offer more products in property and auto insurance, as well as life and medical insurance, while other financial services companies should develop the market for asset-backed securities.

5 The Non-standard Financial Sector and Evidence on Hybrid Sector Firms

In this section, we study how the non-standard financial sector supports firms in the Hybrid Sector to raise funds and to grow from start-ups to successful industry leaders. We also examine the alternative governance mechanisms employed by investors and firms that can substitute for formal corporate governance mechanisms. Due to data limitations, much of this evidence is by necessity anecdotal or by survey.[23]

We first compare the Hybrid Sector with the State and Listed Sectors to highlight the importance of its status in the entire economy in Section 5.1. Second, we consider survey evidence in Section 5.2. Finally, Section 5.3 provides discussions and comparisons of alternative financing channels and governance mechanisms that support the growth of the Hybrid Sector versus formal financing channels (through banks and markets) and governance mechanisms (laws and courts).

5.1 Comparison of Hybrid Sector vs. State and Listed Sectors

Figure 7A compares the level and growth of *industrial output* produced in the State and Listed Sectors combined vs. that of the Hybrid Sector from 1990 to 2006. The output from the Hybrid Sector has been steadily increasing during this period and exceeded that of the other two sectors in 1998. The total output in 2006 is close to US $2,091 billion for the Hybrid Sector, while it is around US $1,236 billion in the State and Listed Sectors combined.[24] The Hybrid Sector

---

[23] All firms, including Hybrid Sector firms, must disclose accounting and financial information to the local Bureau of Commerce and Industry, and most of the reports are audited. However, these data are then aggregated into the Statistical Yearbook without any firm-level publications.

[24] Due to data limitations, our calculations underestimate the output of the State and Listed Sectors. We use the output produced by SOEs and listed firms in which the state has at least a 50% ownership stake as the total output for these sectors, but this calculation excludes output from listed firms that are *not* majority-owned by the state; the output for the Hybrid Sector is the difference between the total output and the total for the other two sectors. However, as mentioned above, only around 20% of all listed firms do not have the state as the largest owner, hence the total output of these firms is not likely to change our overall conclusion on the dominance of the Hybrid Sector over the other two sectors.

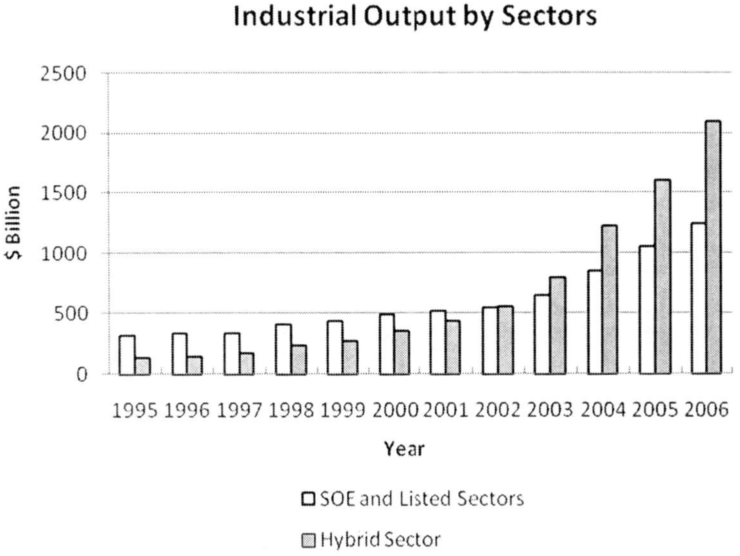

Fig. 7A Comparing the sectors – industrial output
In this figure we plot total "industrial output" for State (SOEs) and Listed (publicly listed and traded firms) Sectors combined and for the Hybrid Sector (all the rest of the firms) during 1990–2006. Data source for this table is the Chinese Statistical Yearbook (1998–2007).

grew at an annual rate of over 14% between 1990 and 2004, while the State and Listed Sectors combined grew at around 5% during the same period.[25] In addition, the growth rates for investment in fixed assets of these sectors are comparable (*China Statistics Yearbooks*; and AQQ (2005a)), which implies that the Hybrid Sector is more productive than the State and Listed Sectors. In fact, with large samples of firms (from sources) with various ownership structures, Liu (2007) and Dollar and Wei (2007) find that the returns to capital is much higher in non-state sectors than the State Sector and that a capital reallocation from state to private sectors will generate more growth in the economy. Fan et al. (2006) and Li et al. (2007) find that state-owned firms in China have a much easier access to the debt market and accordingly higher leverage than non-state firms. One reason for the differences is that due to government protection (for economic and social/political reasons) the costs for bankruptcy and financial distress are much lower for state-owned firms. These firms also have easier access to bank loans, especially credit extended by state-owned banks.

[25] There is an ongoing process of privatizing SOEs. Potentially this may bias the growth rate of the Hybrid Sector higher, as there are firms shifting from the State Sector to the Hybrid Sector. However, the overwhelming majority of SOEs are transformed into the Listed Sector (the main channel through which SOEs were partially privatized prior to 2004); thus this process is unlikely to change the validity of the results above.

All the above facts make the growth of the Hybrid Sector even more impressive. Not surprisingly, there has been a fundamental change among the State, Listed, and Hybrid Sectors in terms of their contribution to the entire economy: the State Sector contributed more than two thirds of China's GDP in 1980, but in 2004 it contributed less than one-third of GDP; in 1980, (non-agricultural) privately owned firms, a type of Hybrid Sector firm, were negligible, but in 2001 they contributed 33% of GDP after growing at an average rate of 20% during this period (*China Statistical Yearbook*, 1998–2002). The above trend of the Hybrid Sector replacing the State Sector will continue in the near future.

Figure 7B presents the number and growth of non-agricultural employees in the three sectors. The Hybrid Sector is a much more important source for employment opportunities than the State and Listed Sectors. Over the period from 1990 to 2006, the Hybrid Sector employed an average of over 70% of all non-agricultural workers; the TVEs (part of the Hybrid Sector) have been the most important employers providing (non-agricultural) jobs for residents in the rural areas, while (non-agricultural) privately owned firms employed more than 40% of the workforce in the urban areas. Moreover, the number of employees working in the Hybrid Sector has been growing at 1.5% over this period, while the labor force in the State and Listed Sectors has been shrinking.[26] These patterns are particularly important for China, given its vast population and potential problem of unemployment.

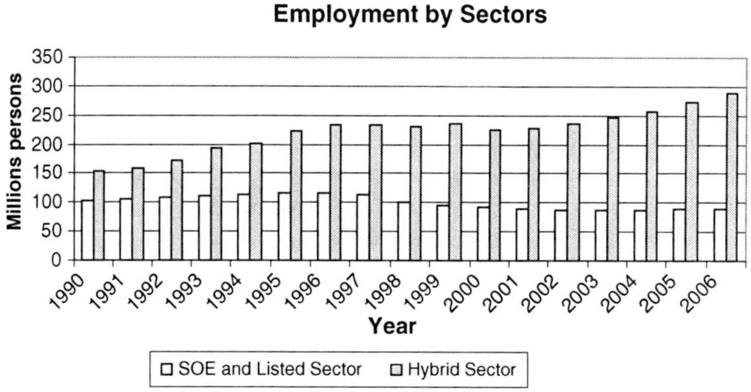

Fig. 7B Comparing the sectors – employment
In this figure we plot total number of workers employed by the State (SOEs) and Listed (publicly listed and traded firms) Sectors combined and by the Hybrid Sector (all the rest of the firms) during 1990–2006. Data source for this table is the Chinese Statistical Yearbook (1998–2007).

[26] Our calculations of the total number of workers employed by the Hybrid Sector actually underestimate the actual work force in the sector, because the Statistics Yearbooks do not provide employment data for all types of firms (by ownership structure) in the Hybrid Sector.

5.2 Survey Evidence

Much of the information concerning the Hybrid Sector comes from surveys. We focus on evidence in AQQ (2005a) and Cull and Xu (2005). The most important findings of these surveys regarding financing channels are the following. First, during the startup stage, funds from founders' family and friends are an important source of financing. Banks can also play an important role. Second, internal financing, in the form of retained earnings, is also important. During their growth period financing from private credit agencies (PCAs), instead of banks, as well as trade credits are important channels for firms in AQQ's sample. As documented by Tsai (2002), PCAs take on many forms, from shareholding cooperative enterprises run by professional money brokers, lenders, and middlemen to credit associations operated by a group of entrepreneurs (raising money from group members and from outsiders to fund firms; *zijin huzushe*), and from pawnshops to underground private money houses.

As far as corporate governance is concerned, when asked about what type of losses concern them the most if the firm failed, every firm's founders/executives (100%) included in the AQQ study said reputation loss is a major concern, while only 60% of them said economic losses are of major concern. Competition also appears to be an important factor ensuring firms are well run.

Cull and Xu (2005) find that firms in most regions and cities rely on courts to resolve less than 10% of business-related disputes (the highest percentage is 20%), with a higher reliance on courts in coastal and more developed areas. One reason that firms go to courts to resolve a dispute is because the courts are authoritative so that the dispute would be resolved even though the resolution may not be fair (e.g., Clarke et al. 2008).

5.3 Discussion on How the Non-standard Financial Sector Works

In this subsection, we first discuss mechanisms within the non-standard financial sector in supporting the growth of the Hybrid Sector. We then compare these alternative institutions that operate outside the legal system with the law and legal institutions that have been widely regarded as the basis for conducting finance and commerce. There are two important aspects to alternative financing channels in the Hybrid Sector. The first is the way in which investment is financed. The second is corporate governance. We consider each in turn.

Once a firm is established and doing well, internal finance can provide the funds necessary for growth. AQQ (2005a) find that about 60% of the funds raised by the Hybrid Sector are generated internally. Of course, internal finance is fine once a firm is established, but this raises the issue of how firms in the Hybrid Sector acquire their "seed" capital, perhaps the most crucial financing during a firm's life cycle. AQQ present evidence on the importance of alternative and informal channels, including funds from family and friends and loans from private (unofficial) credit agencies (see also Tsai 2002). There is also evidence that financing through illegal channels, such as smuggling, bribery, insider trading, and speculations during early stages of the development of financial markets and real estate market, and other underground or unofficial businesses also play an important role in the accumulation of seed capital. Though a controversial issue for the government, our view, based on similar episodes in the history of other developing countries, is that depending on the precise nature of the activity, and as long as the purpose of money making is to invest in a legitimate company, it may be more productive for the government to provide incentives for investment rather than to expend costs discovering and punishing these activities.

Perhaps the most important corporate governance mechanism is competition in product and input markets, which has worked well in both developed and developing countries (e.g., McMillan 1995, 1997; Allen and Gale 2000b). What we see from the success of Hybrid Sector firms in WenZhou and other surveyed firms recounted in AQQ suggest that it is only those firms that have the strongest comparative advantage in an industry (of the area) that survived and thrived. A relevant factor for competition in an industry is entry barriers for new firms, as lower entry barriers foster competition. Djankov, La Porta, Lopez-de-Silanes, and Shleifer (2002, DLLS hereafter) examine entry barriers across 85 countries and find that countries with heavier (lighter) regulation of entry have higher government corruption (more democratic and limited governments) and larger unofficial economies. With much lower barriers to entry compared to other countries with similar (low) per capita GDP, China is once again an "outlier" in the DLLS sample given that China is one of the least democratic countries, and such countries tend to have high barriers to entry. Survey evidence from AQQ (2005a) reveals that there exist non-standard methods to remove entry barriers in China, which can reconcile these seemingly contradictory facts.

Another important mechanism is reputation, trust, and relationships. Greif (1989, 1993) argues that certain traders' organizations in the eleventh century were able to overcome problems of asymmetric information and the lack of legal and contract enforcement mechanisms, because they had developed institutions based on reputation, implicit contractual relations, and coalitions. Certain aspects of the growth of these institutions resemble what worked to promote commerce and the financial system in China prior to 1949 (e.g., Kirby 1995) and the operation of the non-standard financial sector today (AQQ (2005a)), in terms of how firms raise funds and contract with investors and business partners. In addition, Greif (1993) and Stulz and Williamson (2003) point out the importance of cultural and religious beliefs for the development of institutions, legal origins, and investor protections.

The above factors are of particular relevance and importance to China's development of institutions. Without a dominant religion, some argue that the most important force in shaping China's social values and institutions is the set of beliefs first developed and formalized by *Kongzi*(Confucius). This set of beliefs clearly defines family and social orders, which are very different from Western beliefs on how legal codes should be formulated. Using the World Values Survey conducted in the early 1990s, LLSV (1997b) find that China has one of the highest levels of social trust among a group of 40 developed and developing countries.[27] We interpret high social trust in China as being influenced by Confucian beliefs. Throughout this chapter and AQQ (2005a,b, 2008), we have presented evidence that reputation and relationships make many financing channels and governance mechanisms work in China's Hybrid Sector.

There are other effective corporate governance mechanisms. First, Burkart et al. (2003) link the degree of separation of ownership and control to different legal environments and show that *family-run* firms will emerge as the dominant form of ownership structure in countries with weak minority shareholder protections, whereas professionally managed firms are the optimal form in countries with strong protection. Survey evidence on the Hybrid Sector in AQQ and empirical results on the Listed Sector, along with evidence in Claessens et al. (2000, 2002) and ACDQQ (2008c), suggests that family firms are a norm in China and other Asian countries, and these firms have performed well. Second, Allen and Gale (2000a) show that, if cooperation among different suppliers of inputs is necessary, and all suppliers benefit from the firm doing well, then a good equilibrium with no external governance is possible, as internal, mutual monitoring can ensure the optimal outcome. AQQ (2005a) and ACDQQ (2008c) present evidence on the importance of trade credits as a form of financing for firms in the Hybrid Sector. Cooperation and mutual monitoring can ensure payments (as long as funds are available) among business partners despite the lack of external monitoring and contract enforcement. The importance of trade credits is also found in other emerging economies (e.g., ACDQQ 2008c on India) as well as in developed countries (Burkart et al. 2007) on the United States).

It is worth mentioning how entrepreneurs and investors alleviate and overcome problems associated with government corruption. According to proponents of institutional development (e.g., Rajan and Zingales 2003b; Acemoglu and Johnson 2005), poor institutions, weak government, and powerful elites should severely hinder China's long-running economic growth. However, our evidence shows that corruption has not prevented a high rate of growth for China's firms, in particular, firms in the Hybrid Sector, where legal protection is perhaps weaker and problems of corruption worse compared to firms in the State and Listed sectors. A potentially effective solution for corruption is competition among local governments/bureaucrats from different regions within the same country. Entrepreneurs can move from region to region to find the most supportive government officials for their private firms, which in turn motivates officials to lend "helping hands" rather than "grabbing hands" in the provision of public goods or services (e.g., granting of licenses to start-up

[27] Interestingly, the same survey, used in LLSV (1997b), finds that Chinese citizens have a low tendency to participate in civil activities. However, our evidence shows that, with effective alternative mechanisms in place citizens in the developed regions of China have a strong incentive to participate in business/economic activities.

firms), or else there will be an outflow of profitable private businesses from the region (Allen and Qian 2007). This remedy should be typically available in a large country with diverse regions like China.[28]

To summarize, the extraordinary economic performance of China in recent decades, especially that of the Hybrid Sector, raises questions about the conventional wisdom of using the legal system as the basis of commerce. Most observers would characterize the economic performance in China and India as "successful *despite* the lack of western-style institutions," and the failure to adopt Western institutions' style will be one of the main factors to halt the long-running economic growth. By contrast, Allen and Qian (2008) argue that China's economy has been successful *because of* this lack of Western-style institutions – in that conducting business outside the legal system in fast-growing economies such as China can actually be superior to using the law as the basis for finance and commerce.

Focusing on dispute resolution and contract enforcement mechanisms based on the law and courts vs. alternative mechanisms operating outside the legal system, Allen and Qian (2008) argue that despite many well-known advantages, there are disadvantages in using legal institutions. First, recent research on political economy factors, and in particular, work by Rajan and Zingales (2003a,b) shows that rent-seeking behaviors by vested interest groups can turn legal institutions into barriers to changes. We expect these problems to be much more severe in developing countries, and the costs of building good institutions can be enormous.[29] One way to solve this problem is *not* to use the law as the basis for commerce but instead to use alternative mechanisms *outside* the legal system. Evidence presented in this chapter and other related work on China and other emerging economies (e.g., ACDQQ 2008c on India) suggests that these alternative mechanisms can be quite effective.

Second, in democracies there can be a lengthy political process before significant changes can be approved (by the majority of the population and/or legislature), and the people in charge of revising the law (e.g., politicians and judges) may lack the expertise of business transactions and have limited

[28] Another effective solution for corruption is the common goal of sharing high prospective profits, which aligns interests of government officials with those of entrepreneurs and investors. Under this common goal in a multi-period setting, implicit contractual agreements and reputation can act as enforcement mechanisms to ensure that all parties, including government officials, fulfill their roles to make the firm successful.

[29] A frequently talked about and controversial topic is intellectual property rights, including patents and copyrights. The practice of enforcing intellectual property rights by courts is much more vigilant and prevalent in developed countries than in developing countries such as China. An extensive literature in economics has found mixed evidence on the relationship between patent/copyright protection and the pace of innovations. While exclusive property rights provide strong incentives for innovations and do lead to more innovations in a few industries such as chemicals and pharmaceuticals, excessive protection deters competition, which is another important factor in spurring innovations.

capacity (time and effort) to examine the proposed changes.[30] In the context of a fast-growing economy with frequent changes such as China, Allen and Qian show that there is an additional advantage of using alternative institutions because this type of system can adapt and change much more quickly than when the law is used. In particular, competition can ensure the most efficient mechanism prevails, and this process does not require persuading the legislature and the electorate to revise the law when circumstances change.

To conclude, we argue that while legal institutions along with formal financing channels are an important part of developed economies' institutions, alternative mechanisms and financing channels play a much more prominent role in emerging economies and can be superior to legal mechanisms in supporting business transactions in certain industries or entire economies. Therefore, our main policy implication is that in emerging economies alternative dispute resolution and contract enforcement mechanisms should be encouraged and developed alongside the development of legal and other formal institutions. The coexistence of and competition between alternative and legal mechanisms can also exert positive impact on the development of legal institutions so that they are less likely to be captured by interest groups and become more efficient in adapting to changes.

6 Financial Crises

Financial crises often accompany the development of a financial system. Conventional wisdom says that financial crises are bad. Often they are very bad, as they disrupt production and lower social welfare as in the Great Depression in the United States. Hoggarth et al. (2002) carefully measure the costs of a wide range of recent financial crises and find that these costs are on average roughly 15–20% of GDP. It is these large costs that make policy makers so averse to financial crises.

It is important to point out, however, that financial crises may be welfare improving for an economy. One possible example is late-nineteenth-century United States, which experienced many crises but at the same time had a high long-running growth rate. In fact, Ranciere et al. (2003) report an empirical observation that countries which have experienced occasional crises have

[30] A good example is the US payment system. At the beginning of the twenty-first century the US had a nineteenth-century system: Checks had to be physically transported from where they were deposited to a central operations center, then to the clearer and then back to the banks they were drawn on. Despite repeated calls for changes from the banks and businesses, the US Congress did not act on this simple yet costly problem, until September 11, 2001. After the terrorist attack all commercial flights in the were grounded for several days, completely halting the check-clearing process. The check clearing for the 21st Century Act was signed in October 2003, allowing electronic images to be a substitute for the original checks, and thus the clearing process is no longer dependent on the mail and transportation system.

grown on average faster than countries without crises. They develop an endogenous growth model and show theoretically that an economy may be able to attain higher growth when firms are encouraged by a limited bailout policy to take more credit risk in the form of currency mismatch, even though the country may experience occasional crises (see Allen and Oura (2004) for a review of the growth and crises literature, see Allen and Gale (2004a) who show that crises can be optimal, and Allen and Gale (2007) for a review of the crises literature).

In this section, we consider financial crises in China. Given China's current situation with limited currency mismatches, any crisis that occurs is likely to be a classic banking, currency, or twin crisis. It is perhaps more likely to be of the damaging type that disrupts the economy and social stability than of the more benign type that aids growth. The desirability of preventing crises thus needs to be taken into account when considering reforms of China's financial system. First, we examine how China can prevent traditional financial crises, including a banking sector crisis and a stock market, or real estate crisis/crash. We then discuss how China should be better prepared for new types of financial crises, such as the "twin crisis" (simultaneous foreign exchange and banking/stock market crises) that occurred in many Asian economies in the late 1990s.

6.1 Banking Crises and Market Crashes

Among traditional financial crises, banking panics, arising from the banks' lack of liquid assets to meet total withdrawal demands (anticipated and unanticipated), were often particularly disruptive. Over time, one of the most important roles of central banks was the elimination of banking panics and the maintenance of financial stability. To a large degree, central banks in different countries performed well in this regard in the period following the Second World War. However, in recent years, banking crises are often preceded by abnormal price rises ("bubbles") in the real estate or stock markets. At some point, the bubble bursts and assets markets collapse. In many cases banks and other intermediaries are overexposed to the equity and real estate markets, and following the collapse of asset markets a banking crisis ensues. Allen and Gale (2000c) provide a theory of bubbles and crises based on the existence of an agency problem. Many investors in real estate and stock markets obtain their investment funds from external sources. If the providers of the funds are unable to observe the characteristics of the investment, and because of the investors' limited liability, there is a classic risk-shifting problem (Jensen and Meckling 1976). Risk shifting increases the return to risky assets and causes investors to bid up asset prices above their fundamental values. A crucial determinant for asset prices is the amount of credit that is provided for speculative investment. Financial liberalization, by expanding the volume of credit, can interact with the agency problem and lead to a bubble in asset prices.

As discussed above in Section 3, if NPLs continue to accumulate and/or if growth slows significantly then there may be a banking crisis in China. This may involve withdrawal of funds from banks. However, given the government's strong position regarding the low level of debt (Table 3A), it should be feasible for the government to prevent this situation from getting out of control. Since the real estate markets in Shanghai and Shenzhen (largest volume and most developed) and other major cities have already experienced bubbles and crashes (see *China Industry Report*, http://www.cei.gov.cn, http://house.focus.cn and Cao (2008) for more details), it is quite possible that similar episodes in the future could cause a banking crisis that will be more damaging to the real economy. With booming real estate markets, there will be more speculative money poured into properties with a large amount coming from banks. The agency problem in real estate lending and investment mentioned above worsens this problem. If the real estate market falls significantly within a short period of time, defaults on bank loans could be large enough to trigger a banking panic and crisis. The size of the stock market during the first decade of its existence was small relative to the banking sector and the overall economy, and hence a crash in the market could hardly put a dent in the real economy. However, given the quick growth of the stock market (as shown in Table 5A), and the fact that large and small investors may borrow (from banks) to finance their investment, especially during a bubble period, a future market crash will have much more serious consequences. Overall, a banking crisis triggered by crashes in the stock and/or real estate markets represents the most serious risk of a financial crisis in China.

6.2 Capital Account Liberalization, Currency Float, and Twin Crisis

After the collapse of the Bretton Woods system in the early 1970s, a new breed of financial crisis emerged. Lindgren et al. (1996) found that three-quarters of the IMF's member countries suffered some form of banking crisis between 1980 and 1996, and their study did not include the subsequent Asian financial crisis in 1997. In many of these crises, banking panics in the traditional sense were avoided either by central bank intervention or by explicit or implicit government guarantees. But as Kaminsky and Reinhart (1999) find, the advent of financial liberalization in many economies in the 1980s, in which free capital inflows and outflows, and the entrance and competition from foreign investors and financial institutions follow in the home country, has often led to "twin" banking and currency crises. A common precursor to these crises was financial liberalization and significant credit expansion and subsequent stock market crashes and banking crises. In emerging markets, this is often then accompanied by an exchange rate crisis as governments choose between lowering interest rates to ease the banking crises or raising them to defend the home currency.

Finally, a significant fall in output occurs and the economies enter recessions (Fig. 8).

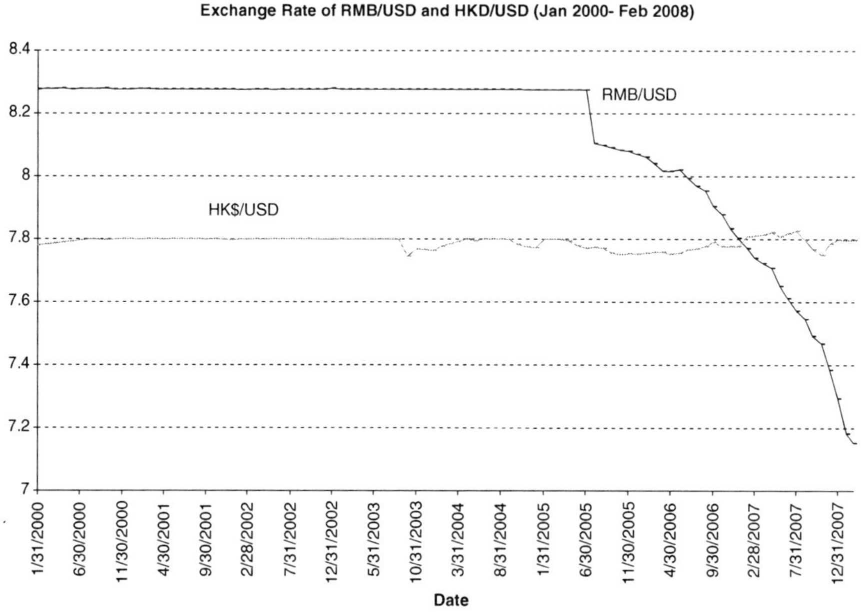

Fig. 8 Trends of exchange rates (US$, RMB, and HK$)

6.2.1 Liberalization of the Capital Account and Financial Sector

Capital account liberation can attract more foreign capital, but large-scale and sudden capital flows and foreign speculation significantly increase the likelihood of a twin crisis. The first key question is, when and to what extent should a country open its capital account and financial sector to foreign capital and foreign financial institutions? The prevailing view, expressed by McKinnon (1991), Dornbusch (1998), and Fischer (1998), is that success or failure of this policy hinges on the efficiency of domestic financial institutions and that reforming the financial sector should be a pre-condition to liberalizing. This latter view assumes that financial liberalization does not alter the efficiency of domestic financial institutions. But this policy change affects both the supply and price of capital, two important determinants of lending contracts. With a model of endogenous financial intermediation, Alessandria and Qian (2005) demonstrate that an efficient financial sector prior to liberalization is neither necessary nor sufficient for a successful financial liberalization.

Applying these ideas to China, even though the overall efficiency of China's banking sector (especially state-owned banks) is still low compared to international standards, banks can have a stronger incentive to limit the moral hazard concerning borrowers' choices of investment projects through monitoring and designing of loan contracts (e.g., adjusting interest rates and/or maturities) following a capital account liberalization. Therefore, the efficiency of the banking sector improves, and the liberalization can generate a large welfare increase, since it leads to both a larger scale of investment *and* a better composition of investment projects. This is more likely to occur with low interest rates in international markets (so that cost of capital for domestic banks is also low). A financial sector liberalization, which allows foreign financial institutions to enter China's lending markets, can further improve welfare as more competition provides stronger incentives for all banks to further discourage moral hazard in investment. As long as the adverse selection problem (entrance of borrowers with negative-NPV projects in the markets can become worse with more competition in the banking sector) is not severe, financial sector liberalization will further improve welfare. Overall, we conclude that a liberalization of the capital account is likely to be beneficial for China as long as the (post-liberalization) cost of capital for Chinese banks does not rise sharply.

6.2.2 Currency Crisis and Banking Crisis (A Twin Crisis)

A currency crisis that may trigger a banking crisis is a possibility. The rapid increase in foreign exchange reserves in recent years suggests that there is a lot of speculative money in China in anticipation of an RMB revaluation. If there is a significant future revaluation, or if after some time it becomes clear that there will not be one, then much of this money may be withdrawn. What happens then will depend on how the government and central bank respond. If they allow the currency to float so that they do not use up the exchange reserves, then any falls in the value of the RMB may occur quickly, and this may limit further outflows. If they try to limit the exchange rate movement, then there may be a classic currency crisis. This in turn may trigger a banking crisis, if there are large withdrawals from banks as a result. Quickly adopting a full float and avoiding a twin crisis would be preferable.[31]

6.2.3 Financial Contagion

Another phenomenon that has been important in many recent crises (e.g., the 1997 Asian crisis) is that financial crises are contagious. A small shock that initially affects only a particular region or sector can spread by contagion within the banking system or asset markets to the rest of the financial sector, then to the entire economy and possibly other economies. Contagion can occur in a number of ways. In the Chinese context where financial markets are relatively

---

[31] Chang and Velasco (2001) develop a model of twin crisis based on the Diamond and Dybvig (1983) model of bank runs. Money enters agents' utility function, and the central bank controls the ratio of currency to consumption. In some regimes, there exists both a "good" equilibrium in which early (late) consumers receive the proceeds from short-term (long-term) assets and a "bad" equilibrium in which everybody believes a crisis will occur, and these beliefs are self-fulfilling. If the bad equilibrium occurs, there is a twin crisis.

unimportant, it is most likely they will occur either from contractually interconnected financial institutions or large asset price movements that cause spillovers to financial institutions.

Allen and Gale (2000d) focus on the channel of contagion that arises from the overlapping claims that different regions or sectors of the banking system have on one another through interbank markets. When one region suffers a banking crisis, the other regions suffer a loss, because their claims on the troubled region fall in value. If this spillover effect is strong enough, it can cause a crisis in the adjacent regions, and a contagion can occur which brings down the entire financial system. Allen and Gale (2004b) show how large price falls can come about as a result of forced liquidations when there is a limited supply of liquidity in the market. Cifuentes et al. (2005) show that contagion is likely to be particularly severe when these two factors interact.

Given China's current financial system, what is the likelihood of financial contagion caused by contractual interlinkages as in the interbank market or because of a meltdown in asset prices if there are forced sales? China's interbank market grew very quickly since its inception in 1981; in fact, the growth of this market was so fast, with the participation of many unregulated financial institutions and with large amount of flows of funds through this market to fixed asset investment, that it exacerbated high inflation in the late 1980s. Since then the government and PBOC increased their regulation by limiting participation of non-bank financial institutions and by imposing restrictions on interest rate movements. In 1996 a nationwide, uniform system of interbank markets was set up. It contains two connected levels: the primary network, which includes the largest PBOC branches, large commercial banks, and a few large non-bank financial institutions, and the secondary network that includes many banks and non-bank institutions and their local branches (see *China Interbank Market Annual Reports* for more details). Table 7 documents the growth of the interbank market during 2001–2006: while the trading volume of long maturity contracts (20 days or longer) is low, the volume of short-term contracts (overnight and week-long) has been high (reaching RMB 1 trillion to 2 trillion, or $125 billion to $250 billion). Therefore, the increasing interlinkages can potentially create a contagion should a crisis develop in one area or sector.

Table 7 Trading volume of national interbank market (RMB billion)

Maturity	Overnight	7 days	20 days	30 days	60 days	90 days	120 days
2001	103.88	560.69	93.35	35.28	9.40	4.73	0.87
2002	1,059.33	2,086.47	77.69	56.29	13.28	15.45	3.94
2003	641.89	1,456.31	56.60	44.11	10.14	10.18	2.81
2004	641.89	1,456.31	56.60	44.11	10.14	10.18	2.81
2005	223.03	896.26	60.42	29.91	7.51	14.09	1.54
2006 (Jan.–Sept.)	376.51	842.28	30.79	14.29	10.05	2..31	0.90

Source: China Interbank Market Annual Reports (1999–2006).

With regard to a meltdown of asset prices, this can happen because of a limited supply of liquidity, if there is a rapid liquidation of assets. It seems unlikely that this can occur and cause a serious problem in China's securities markets. A more serious threat is real estate markets if there are bankruptcies and forced selling. This could potentially interact with bank interlinkages and cause a systemic problem. As mentioned above, a crash in real estate and/or stock markets is very likely the cause of a financial crisis in China.

7 Summary and Concluding Remarks

One of the most frequently asked questions about China's financial system is whether it will stimulate or hamper its economic growth. Our answer to this question, based on examining the history and current status of the financial system and comparing them to those of other countries, is in four parts. First, the large banking sector dominated by state-owned banks has played a much more important role in funding the growth of many types of firms than financial markets. While the problem of NPLs has been under control in recent years, continuing the improvement of the efficiency of major banks toward international standards remains a top priority. Second, the stock market has been growing fast since 1990 but has played a relatively limited role in supporting the growth of the economy. However, with rapid growth that will be sustained in the near future, the role of the financial markets in the economy will become increasingly more important. In our view, further development of China's stock market and other financial markets is the most important task in the long term.

If we can summarize that the role of the banking sector and financial markets has not done enough *not* to slow down the growth of the economy, our third conclusion is that alternative financing channels have had great success in supporting the growth of the Hybrid Sector, which contributes to most of the economic growth compared to the State and Listed Sectors. The non-standard financial sector relies on alternative financing channels, including internal finance, and on alternative governance mechanisms, such as those based on trust, reputation, and relationships, and competition to support the growth of the Hybrid Sector. It is possible that these alternative institutions are superior to Western-style legal institutions in supporting a fast-growing economy as is the case in China. Going forward, we believe that these alternative financing channels and governance mechanisms should be encouraged rather than replaced. They should be allowed to co-exist with the banks and markets and continue to fuel the growth of the Hybrid Sector.

We conclude by pointing out the most significant challenge for improving China's financial system: Economic stability is crucial for the continuing development of the Chinese economy, and the stability of the financial system relates to economic stability in three dimensions. The continuing effort to reduce NPLs and improve efficiency is important in avoiding a banking crisis, while the effort to improve the regulatory environment surrounding the financial markets (including governance and accounting standards) can certainly help prevent a crash/crisis in the stock and/or real estate market. If China further opens the capital account, there will be a large inflow of foreign capital, but large-scale capital flows and speculations also bring the risk of a twin crisis (foreign exchange and banking/stock market crisis), which severely damaged emerging economies in Asia in 1997. In order to guard against such a crisis, policies toward improving the financial system must be made along with supportive fiscal and trade policies.

Acknowledgments We wish to thank Bibo Liu and Zhenrui Tang for their excellent research assistance, Yingxue Cao for sharing data and information on China's real estate markets, and Boston College and the Wharton Financial Institutions Center for financial support. The authors are responsible for the remaining errors.

References

Acemoglu, Daron and Simon Johnson, 2005. "Unbundling Institutions," *Journal of Political Economy* 113(5), 949–995.

Alessandria, George, and Jun Qian, 2005. "Endogenous Financial Intermediation and Real Effects of Capital Account Liberalization," *Journal of International Economics* 67, 97–128.

Allen, Franklin, and Douglas Gale, 1999. "Diversity of Opinion and Financing of New Technologies," *Journal of Financial Intermediation* 8, 68–89.

Allen, Franklin, and Douglas Gale, 2000a. *Comparing Financial Systems*, MIT Press, Cambridge, MA.

Allen, Franklin, and Douglas Gale, 2000b. "Corporate Governance and Competition," in *Corporate Governance: Theoretical and Empirical Perspectives*, Xavier Vives, Ed., Cambridge University Press, London, pp. 23–94.

Allen, Franklin, and Douglas Gale, 2000c. "Bubbles and Crises," *Economic Journal* 110, 236–255.

Allen, Franklin, and Douglas Gale, 2000d. "Financial Contagion," *Journal of Political Economy* 108, 1–33.

Allen, Franklin, and Douglas Gale, 2004a, "Financial Intermediaries and Markets" (with D. Gale), *Econometrica* 72, 1023–1061.

Allen, Franklin, and Douglas Gale, 2004b, "Financial Fragility, Liquidity and Asset Prices" (with D. Gale), *Journal of the European Economic Association* 2, 1015–1048.

Allen, Franklin, and Douglas Gale, 2007, *Understanding Financial Crises*, Clarendon Lectures in Finance, Oxford University Press, Oxford and New York.

Allen, Franklin, and Hiroko Oura, 2004. "Sustained Economic Growth and the Financial System," *Monetary and Economic Studies, Bank of Japan*, 22(S-1), 95–119.

Allen, Franklin, and Jun Qian, 2007."Corruption and Competition," working paper, University of Pennsylvania.

Allen, Franklin, and Jun Qian, 2008."Comparing Legal and Alternative Institutions in Commerce," working paper, University of Pennsylvania.

Allen, Franklin, Michael Chui, and Angela Maddaloni, 2004. "Financial Systems in Europe, the USA, and Asia," *Oxford Review of Economic Policy* 20, 490–508.

Allen, Franklin, Jun Qian, and Meijun Qian, 2005a. "Law, Finance, and Economic Growth in China," *Journal of Financial Economics* 77, 57–116.

Allen, Franklin, Jun Qian, and Meijun Qian, 2005b. "China's Financial System: Past, Present, and Future," Wharton Financial Institutions Center Working Paper No. 05-17.

Allen, Franklin, Jun Qian, and Meijun Qian, 2008a. "China's Financial System: Past, Present, and Future," Chapter 14 in *China's Great Economic Transformation*, L. Brandt and T. Rawski, Eds., Cambridge University Press, Cambridge.

Allen, Franklin, Jun Qian, and Mengxin Zhao, 2008b. "ICBC's IPO and the Reform of China's Banking Sector," working paper, Wharton Financial Institutions.

Allen, Franklin, Rajesh Chakrabarti, Sankar De, Jun Qian, and Meijun Qian, 2008c. "The Financial System Capacities of China and India," working paper, Wharton School, University of Pennsylvania.

Beltratti, Andrea and Bernardo Bortolotti, 2006. "The Nontradable Share Reform in the Chinese Stock Market," Fondazione Eni Enrico Mattei Note di Lavoro Series Index, 15.

Berger, Allen, Iftekhar Hasan, and Mingming Zhou, 2006. "Bank Ownership and Efficiency in China: What will Happen in the World's Largest Nation?", *Journal of Banking and Finance* (forthcoming).

Black, Bernard S., and Ronald J. Gilson, 1998. "Venture Capital and the Structure of Capital Markets: Bank versus Stock Markets," *Journal of Financial Economics* 47, 243–277.

Brandt, Loren, and Xiaodong Zhu, 2000. "Redistribution in a Decentralized Economy: Growth and Inflation in China under Reform," *Journal of Political Economy* 108, 422–439.

Burkart, Mike, Fausto Panunzi, and Andrei Shleifer, 2003. "Family Firms," *Journal of Finance* 58, 2167–2201.

Burkart, Mike, Tore Elligensen, and Mariassunta Giannetti, 2007. "What You Sell is What you Lend? Explaining Trade Credits Contracts," *Review of Financial Studies* (forthcoming).

Cao, Yingxue, 2008. Ph.D. dissertation, Tsinghua University.

Chan, Kalok, Albert Menkveld, and Zhishu Yang, 2007. "Information Asymmetry and Asset Prices: Evidence from the China Foreign Share Discount," *Journal of Finance* (forthcoming).

Chang, Roberto, and Andres Velasco, 2001. "A Model of Financial Crises in Emerging Markets," *Quarterly Journal of Economics* 116, 489–518.

Che, Jiahua, and Yingyi Qian, 1998. "Insecure Property Rights and Government Ownership of Firms," *Quarterly Journal of Economics* 113, 467–496.

Cifuentes, Rodrigo, Gianluigi Ferrucci, and Hyun Song Shin, 2005, "Liquidity Risk and Contagion," *Journal of the European Economic Association* 3, 556–566.

Claessens, Stijn, Simeon Djankov, and Larry Lang, 2000. "The Separation of Ownership and Control in East Asian Corporations," *Journal of Financial Economics* 58, 81–112.

Claessens, Stijn, Simeon Djankov, Joseph Fan, and Larry Lang, 2002. "Expropriation of Minority Shareholders in East Asia," *Journal of Finance* 57, 2741–2771.

Clarke, Donald, Peter Murrell, and Susan Whiting, 2008. "Law, Property Rights and Institutions," Chapter 11 in *China's Great Economic Transformation*, L. Brandt and T. Rawski, Eds., Cambridge University Press, Cambridge.

Cull, Robert, and Colin Xu, 2005. "Institutions, Ownership, and Finance: The Determinants of Reinvestments of Profit among Chinese Firms," *Journal of Financial Economics* 77, 117–146.

Demirgüç-Kunt, Asli, and Ross Levine, 2001. *Financial Structure and Economic Growth: Cross-country Comparisons of Banks, Markets, and Development*, MIT Press, Cambridge, Massachusetts.

Diamond, Douglas, and Philip Dybvig, 1983. "Bank Runs, Deposit Insurance, and Liquidity," *Journal of Political Economy* 91, 401–419.

Djankov, Simeon, Rafael La Porta, Florencio Lopez-de-Silanes, and Andrei Shleifer, 2002. "The Regulation of Entry," *Quarterly Journal of Economics* 117, 1–37.

Dollar, David, and Shang-jin Wei, 2007. "Das (Wasted) Kapital: Firm Ownership and Investment Efficiency in China," working paper, IMF.

Dornbusch, Rudiger, 1998. "Capital Controls: An Idea Whose Time is Past," *Princeton Essays in International Finance* No. 207.

Du, Julan, Oliver Rui, and Sonia Wong, 2008. "Financing Motivated Takeovers: The Case of China," working paper, Chinese University of Hong Kong.

Fan, Joseph, Oliver Rui, and Mengxin Zhao, 2006. "Rent Seeking and Corporate Finance: Evidence from Corruption," working paper, Chinese University of Hong Kong.

Fan, Joseph, T.J. Wong, and Tianyu Zhang, 2007. "Politically-connected CEOs, Corporate Governance and Post-IPO Performance of China's Partially Privatized Firms," *Journal of Financial Economics* (forthcoming).

Feldstein, Martin, 1999. "Social Security Pension Reform in China," *China Economic Review* 10, 99–107.

Feldstein, Martin, 2003. "Banking, Budgets, and Pensions: Some Priorities for Chinese Policy," mimeo, Harvard University, Cambridge.

Feldstein, Martin, and Jeffrey Liebman, 2006. "Realizing the Potential of China's Social Security Pension System," *China Economic Review* 17.

Feng, Lei, and Mark Seasholes, 2004. "Correlated Trading and Location," *Journal of Finance* 59, 2117–2144.

Fischer, Stanley. 1998. "Capital Account Liberalization and the Role of the IMF," *Princeton Essays on International Finance* No. 207.

Franks, Julian, Colin Mayer, and Stefano Rossi, 2003. "Ownership: Evolution and Regulation," working paper, London Business School.

Fung, Peter, Michael Firth, and Oliver Rui, 2003. "Corporate Governance and CEO Compensation in China," working paper, Chinese University of Hong Kong.

Gordon, Roger, and Wei Li, 2003. "Government as Discriminating Monopolist in the Financial Market: The Case of China," *Journal of Public Economics* 87, 283–312.

Greif, Avner, 1989. "Reputation and Coalitions in Medieval Trade: Evidence on the Maghribi Traders," *Journal of Economic History* 49, 857–882.

Greif, Avner, 1993. "Contract Enforceability and Economic Institutions in Early Trade: The Maghribi Traders' Coalition," *American Economic Review* 83, 525–548.

Herring, Richard, and Nathporn Chatusripitak, 2000. "The Case of the Missing Market: The Bond Market and Why it Matters for Financial Development," working paper, Wharton Financial Institutions Center.

Hoggarth, Glenn, Ricardo Reis, and Victoria Saporta, 2002. "Costs of Banking System Instability: Some Empirical Evidence," *Journal of Banking and Finance* 26, 825–855.

Jeng, Leslie A., and Philippe C. Wells, 2000. "The Determinants of Venture Capital Funding: Evidence across Countries," *Journal of Corporate Finance* 6, 241–289.

Jensen, Michael, and William Meckling, 1976. "Theory of the Firm: Managerial Behavior, Agency Costs, and Ownership Structure," *Journal of Financial Economics* 3, 305–360.

Kaminsky, Graciela, and Carmen Reinhart, 1999. "The Twin Crises: The Causes of Banking and Balance-of-payments Problems," *American Economic Review* 89, 473–500.

Kane, Edward, 1989. *The S&L Mess: How Did It Happen?* The Urban Institute Press, Washington, DC.

Kane, Edward, 2003. "What Economic Principles Should Policymakers in Other Countries Have Learned from the S&L Mess?" *Business Economics* 38, 21–30.

Kato, Takao, and Cheryl Long, 2004. "Executive Compensation and Corporate Governance in China," William Davidson Institute Working Paper No. 690.

Kirby, William, 1995. "China Unincorporated: Company Law and Business Enterprise in Twentieth-Century China," *Journal of Asian Studies* 54, 43–63.

Kortum, Samuel, and Josh Lerner, 2000. "Assessing the Contribution of Venture Capital on Innovation," *RAND Journal of Economics* 31, 674–692.

La Porta, Rafael, Florencio Lopez-de-Silanes, Andrei Shleifer, and Robert Vishny, 1997a. "Legal Determinants of External Finance," *Journal of Finance* 52, 1131–1150.

La Porta, Rafael, Florencio Lopez-de-Silanes, Andrei Shleifer, and Robert Vishny, 1997b. "Trust in Large Organizations," *American Economic Review* 87, 333–338.

La Porta, Rafael, Florencio Lopez-de-Silanes, Andrei Shleifer, and Robert Vishny, 1998, "Law and Finance," *Journal of Political Economy* 106, 1113–1155.

La Porta, Rafael, Florencio Lopez-de-Silanes, Andrei Shleifer, and Robert Vishny, 1999. "The Quality of Government," *Journal of Law, Economics, and Organization* 15, 222–279.

La Porta, Rafael, Florencio Lopez-de-Silanes, Andrei Shleifer, and Robert Vishny, 2000a, "Investor Protection and Corporate Governance," *Journal of Financial Economics* 58, 141–186.

La Porta, Rafael, Florencio Lopez-de-Silanes, Andrei Shleifer, and Robert Vishny, 2000b, "Agency Problems and Dividend Policy around the World," *Journal of Finance* 55, 1–34.

La Porta, Rafael, Florencio Lopez-de-Silanes, and Andrei Shleifer, 2002. "Government Ownership of Banks," *Journal of Finance* 57, 265–302.

La Porta, Rafael, Florencio Lopez-de-Silanes, Andrei Shleifer, and Robert Vishny, 2002. "Investor Protection and Corporate Valuation," *Journal of Finance* 57, 1147–1170.

La Porta, Rafael, Florencio Lopez-de-Silanes, and Andrei Shleifer, 2006. "What Works in Securities Laws?" *Journal of Finance* 61, 1–32.

Lardy, Nicholas R., 1998. *China's Unfinished Economic Revolution*, Brookings Institution Press, Washington, DC.

Lau, Lawrence, Yingyi Qian, and Gerard Roland, 2000. "Reform without Losers: An Interpretation of China's Dual-Track Approach to Transition," *Journal of Political Economy* 108, 120–143.

Lee, Tahirih V., 1993. "Risky Business: Courts, Culture, and the Marketplace," *University of Miami Law Review* 47, 1335–1414.

Levine, Ross, 2002. "Bank-based or Market-based Financial Systems: Which is Better?" *Journal of Financial Intermediation* 11, 1–30.

Li, David, 1996. "A Theory of Ambiguous Property Rights: The Case of the Chinese Non-state Sector," *Journal of Comparative Economics* 23, 1–19.

Li, David, 1998. "Changing Incentives of the Chinese Bureaucracy," *American Economic Review* 88, 393–397.

Li, Kai, Heng Yue, and Longkai Zhao, 2007. "Ownership, Institutions, and Capital Structure: Evidence from Non-listed Chinese Firms," working paper, University of British Columbia.

Liao, Li, and Bibo Liu, 2008. "Moral Hazard, Information Disclosure and Market Efficiency: Evidence from China's Share Reform," working paper, Tsinghua University.

Lindgren, Carl-Johan, Gillian Garcia, and Matthew I. Saal, 1996. *Bank Soundness and Macroeconomic Policy*, International Monetary Fund, Washington, DC.

Liu, Qiao, 2007. "Institutions, Financial Development, and Corporate Investment: Evidence from an Implied Return on Capital in China," working paper, University of Hong Kong.

McKinnon, Ronald I., 1991. *The Order of Economic Liberalization*, Johns Hopkins University Press, Baltimore, Maryland.

McMillan, John, 1995. "China's Nonconformist Reform," *Economic Transition in Eastern Europe and Russia: Realities of Reform*, Edward Lazear, Ed., Hoover Institution Press, Stanford, pp. 419–433.

McMillan, John, 1997. "Markets in Transition," Chapter 6 in *Advances in Economics and Econometrics*, Vol. 2, David M. Kreps and Kenneth F. Wallis, Eds., Cambridge University Press, Cambridge, pp. 210–239.

McMillan, John, and Barry Naughton, 1992. "How to Reform a Planned Economy: Lessons from China," *Oxford Review of Economic Policy* 8, 130–143.

Mei, Jianping, Jose Scheinkman, and Wei Xiong, 2003. "Speculative Trading and Stock Prices: An Analysis of Chinese A-B Share Premia," working paper, Princeton University.

Michie, Ranald C, 1987. *The London and New York Stock Exchanges 1850–1914*, Allen & Unwin, London.

Morck, Randall, Bernard Yeung, and Wayne Yu, 2000. "The Information Content of Stock Markets: Why do Emerging Markets Have Synchronous Stock Price Movement?" *Journal of Financial Economics* 58, 215–260.

Orts, Eric, 2001. "The Rule of Law in China," *Vanderbilt Journal of Transitional Law* 34, 43–115.

Park, Albert, Loren Brandt, and John Giles, 2003. "Competition under Credit Rationing: Theory and Evidence from Rural China," *Journal of Development Economics* 71, 463–495.

Perkins, Dwight, and Thomas Rawski, 2008. "Forecasting China's Economic Growth to 2025," Chapter 20 in *China's Great Economic Transformation*, L. Brandt and T. Rawski, Eds., Cambridge University Press, Cambridge.

Prasad, Eswar, and Shang-Jin Wei, 2005. "The Chinese Approach to Capital Flows: Patterns and Possible Explanations," in *Capital Controls and Capital Flows in Emerging Economies*, Sebastian Edwards, Ed., University of Chicago Press, Chicago (forthcoming).

Qian, Jun, and Philip Strahan, 2007. "How Laws and Institutions Shape Financial Contracts: The Case of Bank Loans," *Journal of Finance* 62, 2803–2834.

Qiu, Yuemin, Bing Li, and Youcai Cai, 2000. "Losses of State-Owned Commercial Banks: Reasons and Policy Response," *Jingji gongzuozhe xuexi ziliao* [Study Materials for Economic Workers], no. 44.

Rajan, Raghuram, and Luigi Zingales, 2003a. "The Great Reversals: The Politics of Financial Development in the Twentieth Century," *Journal of Financial Economics* 69, 5–50.

Rajan, Raghuram, and Luigi Zingales, 2003b. *Saving Capitalism from Capitalists: Unleashing the Power of Financial Markets to Create Wealth and Spread Opportunity*, Random House, New York.

Ranciere, Romain, Aaron Tornell, and Frank Westermann, 2003. "Crises and Growth: A Re-evaluation," NBER Working Paper 10073.

Schipani, Cindy, and Junhai Liu, 2002. "Corporate Governance in China: Then and Now," *Columbia Business Law Review*, Vol. 2002, 1–69.

Stulz, Rene, and Rohan Williamson, 2003. "Culture, Openness, and Finance," *Journal of Financial Economics* 70, 261–300.

Tsai, Kellee, 2002. *Back-alley Banking*, Cornell University Press, Ithaca, NY.

The Transformation of China from an Emerging Economy to a Global Powerhouse

James R. Barth, Gerard Caprio Jr., and Triphon Phumiwasana

Abstract Throughout the past three decades of fast growth, China has undergone tremendous structural changes in its economy and financial system. This chapter examines China's evolving financial landscape so as to assess whether it can catch up with or even drive economic growth. China has achieved remarkable growth over the past quarter of a century despite a relatively inefficient financial system. Just as the public sector around the world has not proved to be an efficient manager of enterprises, it also has not been an efficient manager of banks. A solution that would seem to work in theory would be to grow the private sector's role in the banking system, using banks that operate on market principles as a way to continually starve inefficient enterprises of credit, while supplying credit to the productive enterprises. Finding a way to make this work in practice will require both finesse and good fortune on a scale commensurate with China's growing importance in the world economy.

Keywords Bank · Banking sector · Financial market · Big Four · GDP · Economic growth · Financial system · Trade · Renminbi · Exchange rate · India · Foreign exchange reserve · Non-performing loan

1 Introduction

China has captured the attention of the world with its unprecedented growth for such a big country during the past 30 years. At an average rate of 9.7%, China's GDP has grown almost three times the world average. In 2007, China was the fourth largest country in the world, behind only the United States, Japan, and Germany.[1]

---

[1] China ranks fourth when GDP is measured on the basis of exchange rates but second on a purchasing-power basis.

J.R. Barth (✉)
Milken Institute, Santa Monica, CA, USA; Auburn University, Auburn, AL, USA
e-mail: jbarth@milkeninstitute.org; barthjr@auburn.edu

J.R. Barth et al. (eds.), *China's Emerging Financial Markets*,
The Milken Institute Series on Financial Innovation and Economic Growth 8,
DOI 10.1007/978-0-387-93769-4_2,

If such rapid growth continues, China's GDP will be larger than that of the top three countries in the not-too-distant future. The pace of economic growth coupled with limits on population growth, moreover, has enabled China to double its GDP per capita three times since 1978. This was the year Vice Premier Deng Xiaoping initiated China's transition from a centrally planned economy to a socialist market economy, 2 years after the death of Chairman Mao Zedong.

Throughout the past three decades of fast growth, China has undergone tremendous structural changes in its economy. There has been significant and continuing industrialization, urbanization, and integration into the world economy. The financial system has also undergone major changes, with the People's Bank of China (PBOC) ending its monopoly of the banking sector and being recast as the nation's central bank in the late 1970s and early 1980s. At the same time, four state-owned commercial banks (SOCB) (the so-called Big Four)[2] were established to take over the role of the PBOC in allocating credit throughout the economy. In the mid-1990s, three policy development banks were established to relieve the Big Four of the responsibility of making loans to implement the policies of the government, thereby enabling them to operate more fully as true commercial banks.

Beginning in the late 1990s, still further changes in the financial system occurred. The Big Four had accumulated enormous non-performing loans (NPLs) as a result of their earlier policy-directed lending, so the government undertook a series of actions to address this problem. These actions became more urgent when China became a member of the World Trade Organization (WTO) in December 2001 and committed to fully opening up its banking sector to foreign firms by December 2006. The actions taken over several years sufficiently improved the financial condition of three of the Big Four for them to go public in 2005 and 2006, with the last bank doing so being the biggest initial public offering (IPO) in history up to that time.

Other changes in the financial system took place as well. In the early 1990s, two stock exchanges were established: one in Shanghai and the other in Shenzhen. Laws were also enacted establishing three new financial regulatory agencies in the 1990s and early 2000s: one each to oversee the banking, securities, and insurance industries. This frees the PBOC of the responsibility to supervise these financial sectors so that it can focus on monetary policy. While still more changes will take place, China has already implemented many reforms to improve the functioning of the overall financial system in an attempt to promote continued and sustained growth in the economy.

The purpose of this chapter is to examine China's evolving financial landscape so as to assess whether it can catch up with or even drive economic growth. China has achieved remarkable growth over the past quarter of a

---

[2] The Big Four refers to the Industrial and Commercial Bank of China (ICBC), the Agricultural Bank of China (ABC), the Bank of China (BOC), and the China Construction Bank (CCB). In 2007, China Banking Regulatory Commission (CBRC) began including the Bank of Communications (BOCOM), the fifth largest bank, among state-owned commercial banks (SOCBs) in their statistical reports.

century despite a relatively inefficient financial system. The allocation of credit has not yet been based primarily on the basis of risk-and-return trade-offs despite the shift away from a command and control economy to a more market-oriented economy. The financial system, moreover, is imbalanced in the sense that it is dominated by the banking sector, which to a large degree means the Big Four, with the bond and stock markets still relatively under-developed. Firms are, therefore, mainly dependent on bank loans and retained earnings to finance working capital and investment. At the same time, economic growth is also imbalanced in the sense that it is driven largely by investment and exports, with consumption playing a fairly modest role.

These imbalances in the real and financial sectors are interrelated insofar as the growth in exports has resulted in current account surpluses that have led to substantial foreign currency inflows. This, in turn, has contributed to rapid growth in the money supply and bank credit as the foreign currency is exchanged for domestic currency. This growth has been limited to some extent by sterilization actions in which the PBOC has sold relatively low-yielding bonds of its own to the banks. To lessen the need for those actions, China could allow its currency to appreciate far more than it has done recently to reduce exports. A side benefit of doing this would be the need to sell fewer bonds to banks which would improve their net interest margins because the interest rate on the PBOC bonds is significantly lower than the rate on loans. However, such an appreciation could seriously weaken exporting firms and thereby lead to unemployment and more NPLs for banks that had lent to these firms. A still bigger and related problem is the build-up in investment that is the number one driver in growth. There are already concerns that there is an investment "boom" that may soon collapse into a "bust," which if it happens will reduce economic growth and create even more NPLs at banks. All these issues will be explored in this chapter.

The plan of the remainder of this chapter is as follows. The second section provides a brief overview of China's role in the world economy compared to other select countries. The third section examines the sources of China's economic growth and the unbalanced nature of that growth. The fourth section discusses the opening of China's economy to the world both in terms of the current account and the capital account, including the implications of the recent and substantial cross-border inflow of funds with a relatively pegged exchange rate regime. The fifth section focuses on the financial system, with special emphasis on the banking sector and the potential problems it presents for sustaining China's economic growth. The last section provides a summary and conclusions.

2 An Overview of China's Economy and Financial System

All the talk about China being the fastest-growing economy today, while certainly true, requires a somewhat broader historical perspective. As Table 1 shows, in 1820 China was not only the biggest country in terms of population but also the biggest in terms of GDP. At that time, India was the second biggest

Table 1 Top 10 leading economies, 1820 and 2007

1820, share of world total			2007, share of world total		
(In percent)	GDP	Population	(In percent)	GDP	Population
China	28.7	35.7	United States	24.5	4.6
India	16.0	19.6	Japan	7.8	2.0
France	5.4	2.9	Germany	5.9	1.3
U.K.	5.2	2.0	China	5.8	20.3
Prussia	4.9	4.2	U.K.	4.9	0.9
Japan	3.1	2.9	France	4.5	0.9
Austria/ Hungary	1.9	1.3	Italy	3.7	0.9
Spain	1.9	1.1	Spain	2.6	0.7
US	1.8	0.9	Canada	2.5	0.5
Russia	1.7	1.1	Brazil	2.3	2.9
			India (12th)	1.9	17.3
Top ten total	70.6	71.7	Top ten total	64.6	35.1

Source: International Monetary Fund for 2007 data and Angus Maddison, *The World Economy: Volume 1: Millennial Perspective* and *Volume 2: Historical Statistics*, OECD, 2001 and 2003, for 1820 data.

country in terms of both population and GDP. More generally, in the early 1800s there was a positive correlation between the shares of world population and shares of world GDP accounted for by countries. This was mainly due to the agricultural sector being the major contributor to employment and GDP as a result of the still rudimentary state of technological development. The industrial revolution changed things quite dramatically for countries around the world. By 2007, India, the largest democracy in the world, was in twelfth place and China, the largest communist country in the world, was in fourth place. The shake-up in rankings reflected the shift to services and manufacturing from agriculture as the major contributors to growth. This was made possible by advances in engineering and production technology and improved human capital that created a change in the composition of GDP for many countries and thereby made population per se less crucial in determining the size of a country's GDP. These developments have enabled countries with relatively small populations to achieve high levels of GDP per capita. Indeed, both China's and India's GDP per capita are far less than those of the other top ten leading economies listed in Table 1 even though the two Asian Giants account for about 40% of the world's population.

Nevertheless, as Chart 1 shows, the recent rapid growth rates in China and India have enabled them to double their GDP per capita in fewer years than it took both the United Kingdom and the United State to do so.[3] If the rapid growth continues in these countries, their GDPs will exceed today's rich countries in the not-too-distant future.[4] A projection by Goldman Sachs as to exactly when this will happen is provided in Table 2, with projections included

[3] China adopted a one-child policy in 1979, which has contributed to the more than eight-fold increase in GDP per capita in just less than 30 years.

[4] GDP doubles every decade at a growth rate of 7%.

Chart 1 Pace of economic growth, number of years to double per capita GDP
Source: Milken Institute.

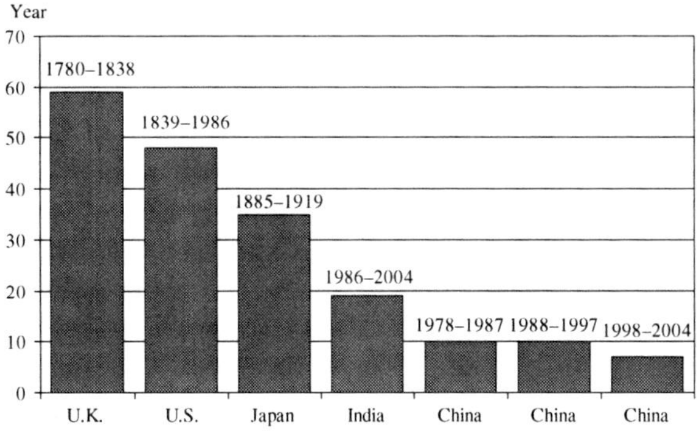

Table 2 When will the BRICs grow larger than large developed countries of the world?

	France	Germany	Italy	Japan	UK	US
Brazil (B)	2031	2036	2024	Beyond 2050	2036	Beyond 2050
China (C)	Passed in 2003	2007	Passed in 2001	2016	2005	2042
India (I)	2019	2023	2016	2032	2022	Beyond 2050
Russia (R)	2023	2028	2018	Beyond 2050	2028	Beyond 2050

Source: Authors' calculation based on Goldman Sachs projections.

for Brazil and Russia.[5] As may be seen, China is expected to pass the United States in 2042 and India to pass Japan in 2030. Furthermore, China ranks second and India ranks ninth among the top ten contributors to world GDP growth from 1997 to 2007 (see Chart 2). Remarkably, at the market exchange rate in 2007, China contributed to world GDP growth more than the United States. Of course, starting from a fairly low level of GDP with underutilized or surplus natural and human resources enables a country to grow much faster

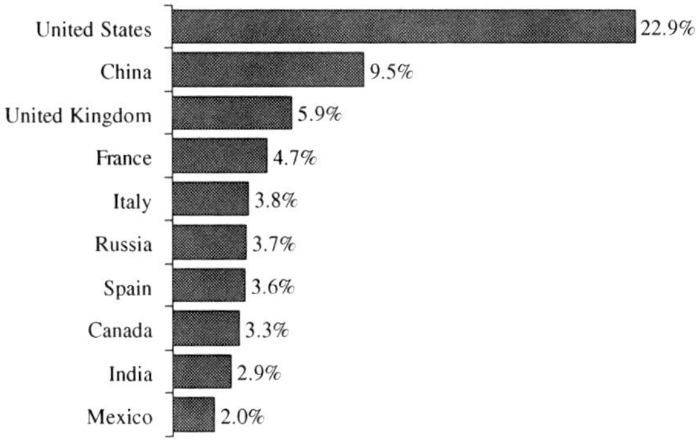

Chart 2 Major contributors to world GDP growth 1997–2007
Source: International Monetary Fund.

[5] Dekle and Vandenbroucke (2006) project GDP growth at about 5.8% a year between now and 2040.

than advanced countries. This is not to belittle each of these country's recent accomplishments, however, given the lack of similar growth in many other countries with low levels of GDP and less than fully utilized resources.

Table 3 provides a broader perspective of China by comparing it to select countries in terms of shares of world population, GDP, and total financial assets (including bank assets, bonds outstanding, and stock market capitalization). It is clear that the world's income and financial assets are not distributed among these countries based on their shares of the world's population. Indeed, China accounts for 20.4% of the world's population but only 5.5% of the world's GDP and 3.8% of the world's financial assets. India is in an even worse comparative position, accounting for 17.3% of the world's population but less than 2% of the world's GDP and less than 1% of the world's financial assets. In sharp contrast, the United States accounts for less than 5% of the world's population but nearly 30% of the world's GDP and the world's financial assets. It is also clear from the figures that in the case of Japan, the European Union's (EU) 27 member countries,[6] and the United States that each country's share of total financial assets is slightly more than its share of world GDP. In the case of China and India, however, their financial asset shares are only two-thirds and one-half of their GDP shares. This reflects the fact that both countries still have relatively underdeveloped financial systems. Furthermore, in China bank assets are twice as large as equities and bonds, whereas in the advanced countries the situation is the reverse. India simply has an underdeveloped banking sector which produces a financial system composition that more closely approximates that of the advanced countries.

Table 3 Distribution of world's population, GDP and financial assets

		Percent accounted for by				
2006		China	India	US	Japan	EU27
GDP	$48 trillion	5.5	1.8	27.5	9.1	30.1
Population	6.4 billion	20.4	17.3	4.6	2.0	7.6
Bank assets	$87.2 trillion	5.1	0.7	15.9	11.8	51.1
Equity market	$53.4 trillion	4.5	1.5	36.3	8.8	24.0
Bond market	$68.1 trillion	1.7	0.5	39.2	12.8	34.6
Total financial assets	$208.8 trillion	3.8	0.8	28.7	11.4	38.8

Source: International Monetary Fund, World Federation of Exchanges, Standard and Poor's, and Bank for International Settlements.

The relative size and composition of financial systems is important because the overwhelming evidence to date indicates that more developed and balanced financial systems promote economic growth and development.[7] Both China and India have ample room to expand the size of their financial systems,

[6] This excludes Romania and Bulgaria which became member countries in early 2007, which enlarged the EU to 27 members.

[7] See Levine (1997, 2005).

including the banking sector and the capital markets, to facilitate continued economic growth and development.[8] The development of a broader and more diversified financial system, however, should be accompanied by reforms to ensure that savings are allocated to investment projects on the basis of risk and return considerations rather than political connections or cronyism.

3 Contributors to China's Economic Growth

China achieved a remarkable growth rate of 11.5% in 2007. This marked the fifth consecutive year of double digit growth and was the fastest pace of expansion in 13 years despite government efforts to slow somewhat its rapidly growing economy. Table 4 compares the basic contributors to the economic growth of China and India in 2006.[9] There are several comments about the information in this table. First, China's growth is imbalanced in the sense that it depends heavily on investment and exports and much less than one might expect on consumption. As may be seen, the situation is nearly reversed in the case of India, with consumption being the major contributor to growth. Corresponding to the low consumption rate is a high saving rate in China. Both households and businesses have high saving rates, at 20 and 23%, respectively.[10] This means that China is

Table 4 Contributors to China's and India's recent real GDP growth, 2006

	Shares of real GDP 2006		Component contribution to 2006 real GDP growth	
In percent	China	India	China	India
Consumption	36	58	3.7	3.9
Government spending	14	12	–1.4	1.1
Investment	43	33	5.7	4.5
Exports	37	24	8.7	4.8
Imports	–30	–27	–5.6	–5.0
GDP	100	100		
GDP growth			11.1	9.3

Note: Real GDP and its components are estimated based on nominal figures deflated by price indices in the case of China because it does not publish real expenditure-side GDP.
Source: International Monetary Fund and Milken Institute estimates.

---

[8] See Appendix 1 for a comparison of China's and India's financial systems to several other countries'.

[9] As of this writing, China's GDP components in 2007 still have not been released. The issue of reliability of China's national account data is an ongoing concern. In December 2005, China substantially revised its historical GDP data upward, showing that real growth in 2004 was 10.1% instead of 9.5%. The 2004 nominal GDP was revised upward by 2.3 trillion yuan to 15.99 trillion yuan, an increase of 16.8%.

[10] Many attribute the high household saving rate to the lack of adequate health and pension plans. According to *China Money* (November 7–13, 2005), only 15% of the population is covered by the country's pension system. More generally, see Kuijs (2005) for more detailed information on investment and saving in China.

able to finance its investment with internally generated funds, rather than being a net borrower from abroad, which is the more typical case for a developing country. At the same time, as will be discussed more fully below, most household saving flows into the banks, given the underdeveloped capital markets and the relatively strict capital controls that limit the amount of funds that may flow abroad. The savings or retained earnings of firms also tend to stay mainly within the country and to be used to fund further expansion. The saving rate of the state-owned enterprises (SOEs) in particular is quite high because they are not required to pay dividends to their capital owners, namely, the government.

Second, investment is clearly the main driver in China's rapid economic growth. It is funded mainly with the retained earnings of firms and loans from banks, with the issuance of stock and bonds playing a relatively minor role, though one that has become more important recently for a growing number of firms. Accounting for a 43% share of real GDP in 2006 and still seemingly growing fairly rapidly, there are concerns that investment has led to excess capacity in some sectors of the economy. Indeed, China's Prime Minister Wen recently stated:

> ...Beijing is increasingly concerned about the quality of growth. He admitted that it had failed to adequately control investment in fixed assets such as factories and machinery. Overinvestment is among the biggest threats to the economy, as it leads to production gluts and can wipe out corporate profits, causing bankruptcies and a jump in bad loans. 'The problem of excess production is getting worse, corporate profits are down and losses are increasing, causing greater potential financial risks' (*Wall Street Journal*, March 6, 2006).

Underscoring the concern about overinvestment, Chart 3 shows the relationship between the ratio of investment to GDP and real GDP growth in China over the period 1980–2006. As may be seen, whenever the investment-to-GDP ratio reached a peak and then fell, real GDP growth subsequently declined. The chart also shows that in 2005, the ratio was at the highest level in 25 years and only reduced slightly in the following year, which reinforces concerns about an investment boom and then a bust, with adverse consequences for economic growth, employment, and banks (i.e., NPLs).[11]

Third, the export sector has also been an important contributor to China's growth. Indeed, as Table 3 shows, exports are second only to investment in terms of the contribution made to real GDP growth in 2006. Moreover, exports have exceeded imports every year over the past decade, which only serves to underscore the important role exports have played in China's growth story. Indeed, this fact leads some to refer to China as "Wal-Mart with an army." The contribution of exports to growth and employment has led to tremendous development and urbanization in the eastern coastal areas of China. This situation has created a widening income gap between those working in these

---

[11] Liang (2006, p. 22), however, considers investment spending to be overstated and consumption understated. He therefore considers "China's investment cycle [to be] ... profitable and sustainable."

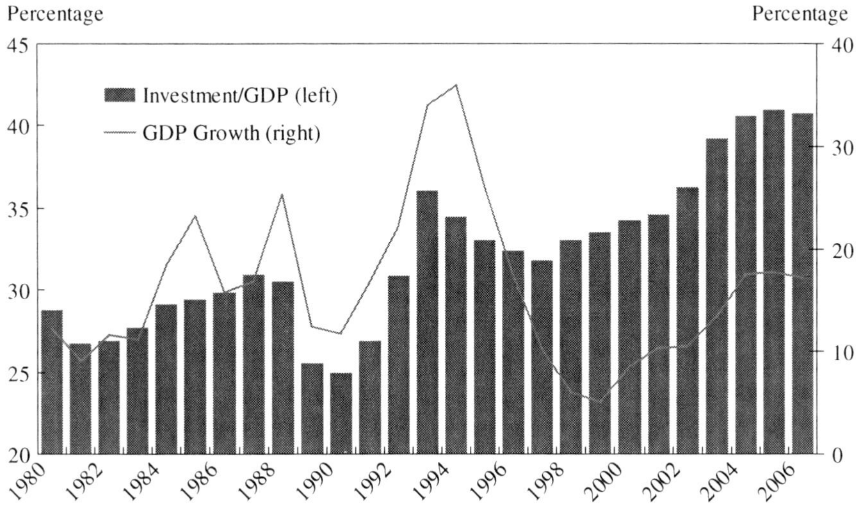

Chart 3 Investment's contribution to China's GDP growth, 1980–2006
Source: International Monetary Fund.

areas and those located in the interior.[12] While the government tries to improve economic conditions in the inland regions of the country, it is also careful to avoid taking any precipitous actions that would adversely affect growth and employment in the export sector, including allowing too much flexibility in its exchange rate too quickly, as will be discussed in the next section.

4 China's Integration into the World Economy

China made a major decision to begin the process of opening its economy to the world in the late 1970s. Chart 4 shows the tremendous strides it has made since then. Indeed, both China's exports and imports exploded over the past 27 years, increasing more than 5,000 and 3,500%, respectively. This is in sharp contrast to the progress that India has made on this score, as the chart shows. The growth, moreover, has far surpassed the growth in world exports and imports over this same period. As a result of this growth, China is now the third largest trading nation in the world when measured by the sum of exports and imports, behind only the Euro area and the United States (see Table 5).[13] China, moreover, is far more "open" than the United States when openness is measured by the ratio of exports plus imports to GDP. Furthermore, Chart 5 shows that

---

[12] The eastern coastal areas account for about two-thirds of GDP and have a GDP per capita that is about twice the national average, according to the China Statistical Yearbook. For more information on these disparities, see Catin et al. (2005).

[13] For purposes of comparison, India ranks 18.

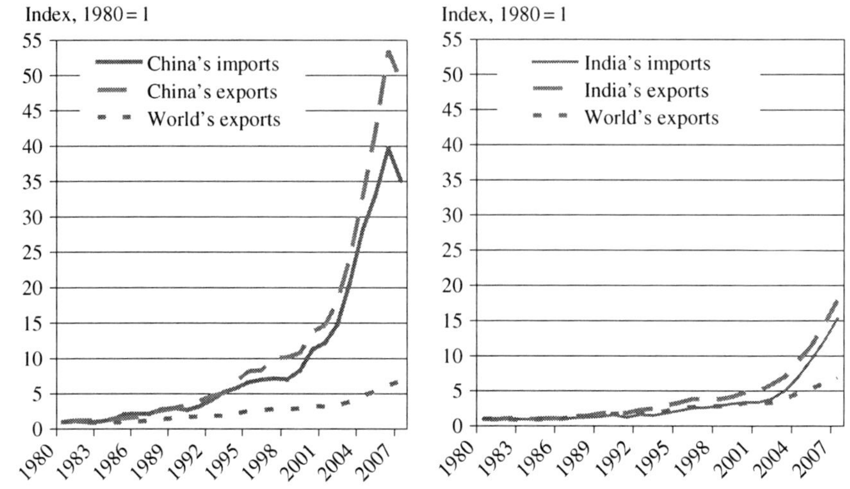

Chart 4 Growth in trade: China vs. India
Source: International Monetary Fund.

Table 5 Top global trading nations, 2007

		Trade (US$ billions)	GDP (US$ billions)	Trade/GDP (%)
1	Euro area	5,334	12,158	44
2	United States	1,535	13,844	11
3	China	1,180	3,251	36
4	Germany	1,170	3,322	35
5	Japan	666	4,384	15
6	France	601	2,560	23
7	United Kingdom	534	2,773	19
8	Netherlands	501	769	65
9	Italy	494	2,105	23
10	Canada	399	1,432	28
21	India	164	1,099	15

Source: International Monetary Fund.

there is a fairly close and positive relationship between the growth in China's share of world trade and the growth in its share of world GDP. Once again, in sharp contrast, India's share of world trade has remained relative flat over the past 27 years and so too has its share of world GDP until the last 3 years.

At the same time that China had been rapidly integrating into the world economy through trade, it had been running a trade surplus for every year since 1990, except for 1993. The surpluses, moreover, have been increasing over time, reaching a record $270 billion in 2007. This, of course, means that some other countries have been running trade deficits with China. The US official figure for

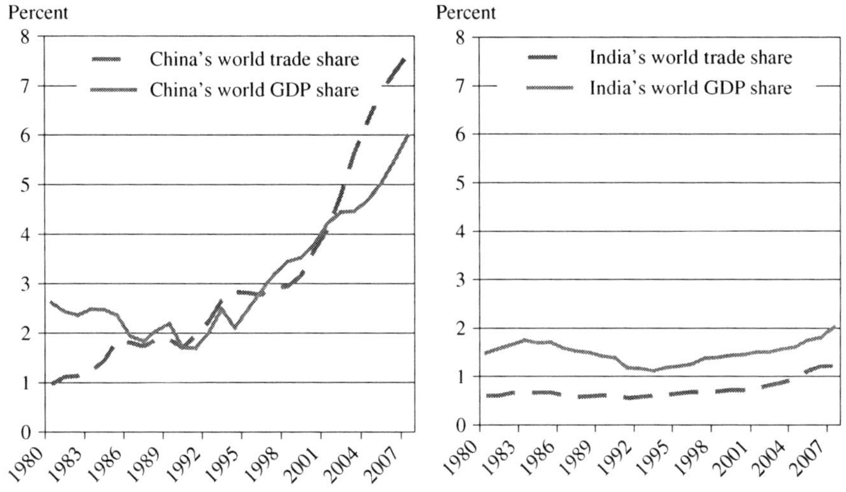

Chart 5 World trade and GDP shares: China vs. India
Source: International Monetary Fund.

the US trade deficit reached a record $274 billion in 2007.[14] To reduce this deficit, the United States has been pressuring China to allow its currency, the yuan or renminbi (RMB), to fluctuate to a far greater degree than China has so far allowed.[15] The pressure being applied is based on the reasonable assumption that market forces would cause a significant appreciation of the RMB against the US dollar and thereby help reduce the US trade deficit. Chart 6 shows that China had pegged the RMB to the US dollar from 1995 until July 21, 2005, when it revalued its currency against the US dollar by 2.1%. (For purposes of comparison, Chart 6 also shows that India has not pegged its currency to the US dollar.) China also put in place a band within which it would allow the RMB to fluctuate on a daily basis with respect to the US dollar and a slightly wider band within which its currency could fluctuate against a basket of currencies. From July 20, 2005, to June 20, 2008, the RMB had appreciated with respect to the US dollar by about 15.2%. Even with this rate of RMB appreciation, foreign exchange reserves have still accumulated at a very fast pace, growing 30 and 46% in 2006 and 2007, respectively (Chart 7). In the first half of 2008, reserves grew more than 18%. With this growth pace, by the end of 2008, China's foreign exchange reserves will exceed US$2 trillion.

---

[14] The total US trade deficit, however, was $854 billion. The Chinese government reported that trade surpluses with the US and the world are $167 billion and $270 billion in 2007, respectively.

[15] In addition, the United States filed a compliant with the WTO in early February 2007 charging China with unfairly subsidizing exports by Chinese companies.

Chart 6 Exchange rates: China vs. India
Source: International Monetary Fund.

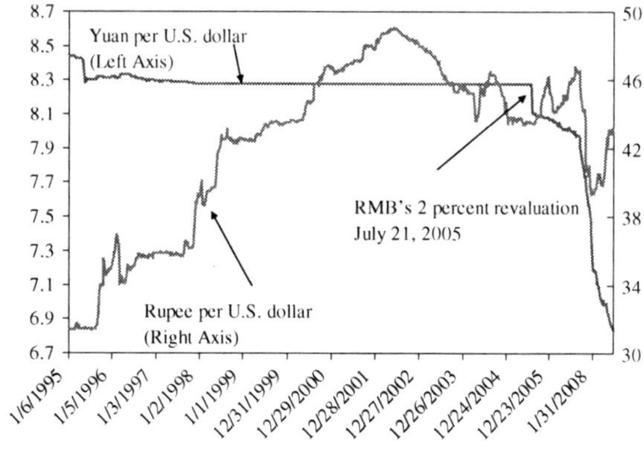

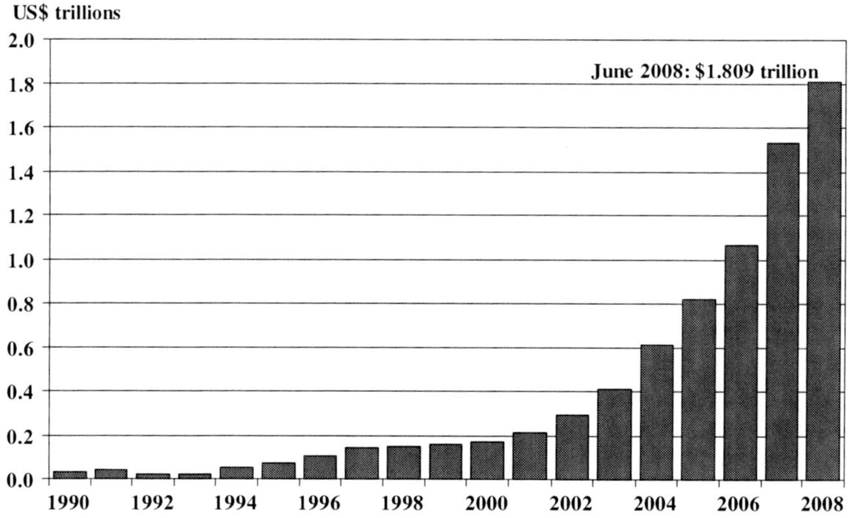

Chart 7 China's rapidly growing foreign exchange reserves
Source: International Monetary Fund and State Administration of Foreign Exchange.

In addition to the current account surpluses, China has been running surpluses on its capital account. As Chart 8 shows, the most important and stable source of private net capital flows to China from 1982 to 2006 has been foreign direct investment (FDI). Its share of world foreign direct investment inflows increased to 5.3% in 2006 from only 0.1% in 1980. In 2006, about 20% of all FDI inflows into developing countries went to China.[16] In 2007, China received FDI inflows of $82.6 billion and accumulatively the total reached $742 billion at year-end 2007. During the first half of 2008, China had already received $52.4

[16] *World Investment Report* 2007, UNCTAD.

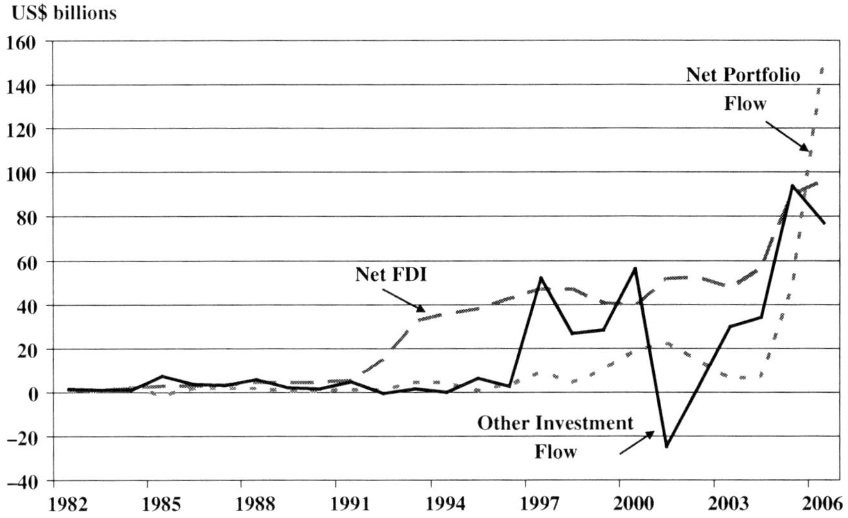

Chart 8 Net private capital flows to China
Source: International Monetary Fund.

billion in FDI.[17] In this regard, Whalley and Xin (2006) point out that foreign companies supplying foreign direct investment often form joint ventures with Chinese enterprises supplying land and labor; see Table 6. This is important because they indicate that these Foreign Invested Enterprises (FIEs) account for over 50% of exports and 60% of imports. Furthermore, Walley and Xin estimate that China's FIEs contributed over 40% of China's economic growth in 2003 and 2004, and that without this inward FDI, China's overall GDP growth rate would have been 3.4 percentage points lower.

Table 6 Foreign direct investment by type of enterprise

	FDI	Joint ventures and cooperative ventures	Foreign enterprises and foreign invested shareholding enterprises	Others
	US$ billions	Share of total FDI		
2000	40.7	51.4	47.6	0.9
2001	46.9	46.8	52.1	1.1
2002	52.7	38.0	61.5	0.5
2003	53.5	35.9	63.0	1.1
2004	60.6	32.2	67.6	0.2
2005	72.4	22.7	60.6	16.7
2006	72.6	23.2	67.5	8.9
2007	82.7	20.6	69.9	9.5

Source: CEIC Database.

[17] China's Ministry of Commerce.

In the past several years, outward direct investment from China has become increasingly important as a tool for reducing appreciation pressure on the RMB as well as increasing the supply of natural resources, both of which are necessary for manufacturing export-driven growth. According to the "10th Five-Year Plan for National Economic and Social Development," China will "proactively make use of overseas natural resources, establish overseas supply bases for both oil and gas, diversify oil imports, build up a strategic petroleum reserve and maintain national energy security" (Pamlin and Long, 2007). Chart 9 shows the number and deal value of Chinese companies that are expanding abroad. Both the value and number of deals have increased sharply since 2005.

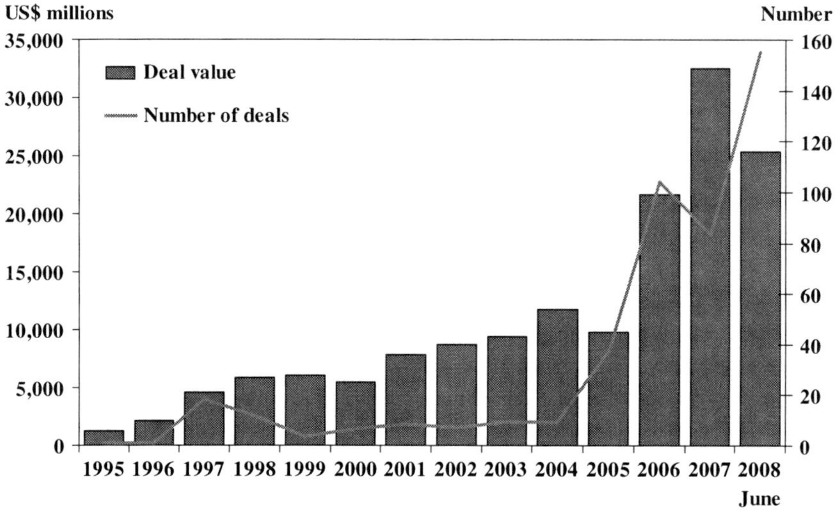

Chart 9 Completed M&As abroad by Chinese companies
Source: Dealogic.

Comparing outward direct investment of China with those of other countries (Chart 10) shows that not only is China a relatively new player in the outward direct investment market, but it is still a relatively small player compared to developed countries, like the Netherlands, France, and the United Kingdom, all of which had more than $100 billion in outward investment in 2006. Given China's need to support its manufacturing and export sectors, it is not surprising that most of the outward direct investment recently has involved energy and other natural resources (see Chart 11).

Although China has more recently relaxed direct investment inflow and outflow restrictions, other types of capital inflows have been more strictly limited and outflows of capital have also been even more restricted.[18] China

[18] The QFIIs are allowed to invest in A shares (shares denominated in renminbi). There are also B shares (shares denominated in US or HK dollars) that are available to domestic (since

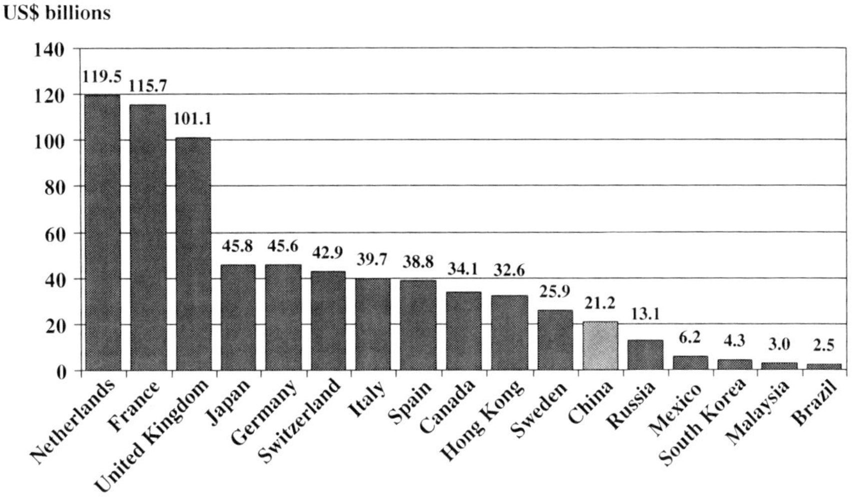

Chart 10 Ranking countries' outward direct investment by amount, 2006
Source: UNCTAD.

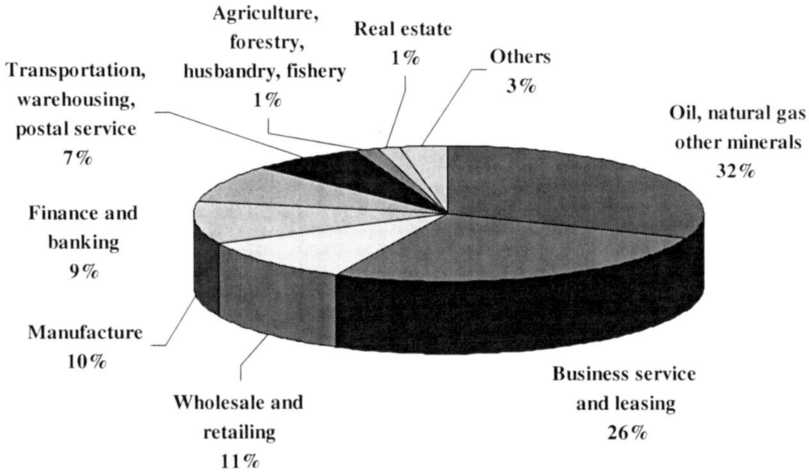

Chart 11 China's outward direct investment by industry: Cumulative flows, 2004–2006
Source: Dealogic.

did, however, establish a qualified foreign institutional investor (QFII) program in December 2002 and a qualified domestic institutional investor (QDII) program in April 2006, which allow portfolio inflow and outflow investments, respectively, through licensed banks, insurance companies, and fund managers

2002) and foreign (since 1992) investors in China's two stock exchanges. H shares, N shares, and S shares are shares of Chinese companies listed in Hong Kong, New York, or Singapore, respectively.

to the level permitted by quotas. As of May 2008, China Securities Regulatory Commission had approved $10.3 billon QFII quotas to 54 foreign institutions and $48.2 billion QDII to 52 domestic institutions.

Along with the QDII program, China also employs other administrative measures to ease capital outflow restrictions. In April 2006, Chinese firms and residents were allowed to buy only fixed-income foreign assets. A year later, China allowed outward investment in equities. Furthermore, in 2006 China allowed individuals to convert RMB to dollar up to $20,000 per year to take out of China.[19] The amount has been expanded to $50,000 in 2007. China has initially chosen to liberalize primarily its capital controls with respect to foreign direct investment inflows, which not only provide funds for investment projects but also much needed technology and managerial skills that can spread to domestic firms throughout the country.[20]

The reason China has retained fairly rigid capital controls with a pegged exchange rate regime is attributable to the events that occurred in East Asia in the summer of 1997. The collapse of the Thai baht in July was followed by a financial crisis in the region. Countries with weak financial systems tried to defend the currency pegs that existed at the time through contractionary measures rather than abandoning them, even when the pegs became unsustainable and foreign currency reserves were being depleted. As Chart 12 shows, several countries in East Asia suffered severe recessions due to the crisis, but China did not. A difference is that these other countries had not only adopted pegged exchange rate regimes but also had liberalized their capital controls. Although this allowed a surge in capital inflows to finance investment, it made the countries vulnerable to sudden and large financial outflows when investors decided that their financial systems were weak and the currency pegs were not sustainable. In view of what happened, China has proceeded quite cautiously with respect to removing the controls it has placed on the flow of capital funds into and out of the country while it still retains a fairly tightly pegged exchange rate regime.

As result of its exchange rate policy and capital controls, unlike other countries at the same stage of economic development, China has been running surpluses on both its current and capital accounts.[21] This has enabled China to accumulate an enormous amount of foreign exchange reserves, about $1.8 trillion in June 2008, replacing Japan as the world's top holder of such reserves.[22] Once China allows the RMB to be fully convertible on the capital account, its large reserve holdings

---

[19] See US Treasury Department (2006).

[20] World Investment Report, 2007, shows that China ranks 58th out of 141 countries in terms of outward FDI over 2004–2006. This situation may change if China redeploys its huge foreign exchange reserves away from its substantial holdings of US securities.

[21] China allowed fully convertibility on the current account in 1996.

[22] This is more than ten times the amount in 2000, which was $168 billion. Interestingly, Frankel (2006, p. 658), in a comment on a paper by Dooley et al. (2003), points out that in their view: "China is piling up dollars. . .as part of an export-led development strategy that is rational given China's need to import workable systems of finance and corporate governance."

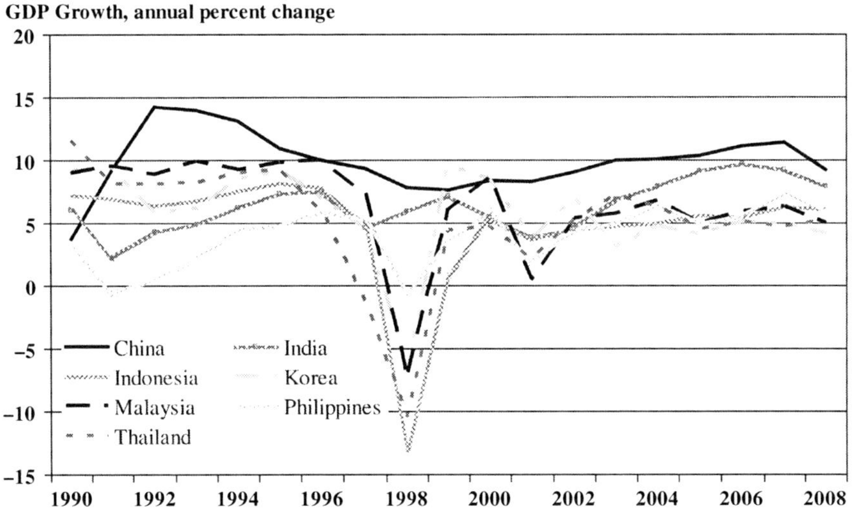

Chart 12 China and India avoid Asian financial crisis
Sources: World Economic Outlook and International Financial Statistics, the International Monetary Fund.

can help assure foreign investors that the country can withstand an attack on its currency, thereby preventing what happened in East Asia in 1997–1998.[23]

China is now the largest exporter of capital in the world, while the United States is the largest importer of capital.[24] A large portion of China's foreign exchange reserves are invested in US bonds, which has helped keep US interest rates lower than otherwise. To the extent that shifts in the composition of its portfolio are away from bonds to equities, and away from U.S. securities to EU securities, prices in world securities markets may undergo significant changes. At the moment, the securities that China has been accumulating with its growing stock of foreign exchange reserves are assets on the balance sheet of the PBOC. By shifting the composition of the portfolio to higher yielding investments, the PBOC could increase the earnings on its assets. The risk of such a newly rebalanced portfolio, however, would also increase. To the extent that another institution is used to invest a portion of the foreign exchange reserves in higher yielding assets, the risk of sizable capital losses on the balance sheet of the PBOC is correspondingly reduced. In this regard, in September 2007, the China Investment Corporation (CIC) was established as a state-owned investment company with an initial capital of $200 billion. The CIC invests in domestic financial institutions as well as other projects abroad. The CIC spent about $67 billion to acquire Central Huijin Investment Company Limited, an investment arm

---

[23] China's current foreign exchange reserves are 160% of its annual imports in 2007.

[24] See Dollar and Kraay (2005) for an analysis of this issue with respect to China. Also, see Appendix 2 for a comparison China and India's international investment positions.

of the PBOC that holds shares of the Big Four. The CIC also has acquired ownership stakes in three large international finance companies: $2 billion in Blackstone Group, $5 billion in Morgan Stanley, and $100 million in VISA.

The buildup in foreign exchange reserves at the PBOC has resulted from sterilization actions taken by the government. To prevent excessive growth in the money supply that would worsen inflation and bank credit that would contribute to overinvestment as foreign currency is exchanged for RMB, the PBOC has been selling bonds paying relatively low interest rates to banks, rates lower than those charged on loans made by banks. This type of operation enables the PBOC to earn profits insofar as the interest earnings on its assets exceeds the interest paid on its liabilities, including the bonds it issues to sterilize foreign currency inflows and the reserves it requires banks to deposit with it.[25] Indeed, it is reported that the PBOC had gross earnings of $44 billion in interest payments in 2006 on its foreign exchange investments, while it had expenses of $11.5 billion in interest payments on its debt and on interest for the reserves of commercial banks it holds.[26]

The problem that arises in this situation is that the PBOC is increasing its profits at the expense of the banks; truly commercial banks would not endure this arrangement for long.[27] The central bank is in essence serving as a financial intermediary insofar as it is channeling a large portion of the savings of the public through the banks into investment, but foreign investment is largely not available to the banks or the public due to capital controls. Table 7 provides an example of the effect of this situation by examining the financial statements reported by China Construction Bank as of December 2007. As may be seen, deposits fund 81% of total assets and depositors are paid an average rate of 1.57%. Yet, loans and advances account for only 48% of total assets, while investments in debt securities account for 33%, which includes the PBOC

Table 7 China Construction Bank, December 2007

Average annualized cost of deposits from customers	1.57%	Deposits from customers/ total assets	80.94%
Average annualized yield on loans and advances from customers	6.31%	Loans and advances/total assets	48.24%
Average yield on Investment in debt securities	3.29%	Investment in debt securities/total assets	32.92%
Net interest margin	3.18%		
Non-interest income/total income	12.66%		

Source: China Construction Bank.

[25] The PBOC also increased reserve requirements for banks several times in recent years to help curtail growth in money and credit. In the mid-2008, the reserve requirement was 17.5%.

[26] Ye Xie, "Chinese central bank seen making a profit," *International Herald Tribune*, January 7, 2007.

[27] For example, it was the rebellion by Japanese banks against the practice of forcing them to take up government debt with below-market interest rates that helped set off the deregulation of the Japanese banking system in the early 1980s.

securities issued for sterilization purposes. The average yield on loans is 6.31%, whereas the average yield on investments is a much lower 3.29%. The result is a net interest margin of 3.18%. This situation means that Chinese banks are vulnerable to any slowing in loan growth because they derive most of their income from the net interest margin.[28]

The huge amount of foreign exchange reserves that are denominated in US dollars poses a problem for China. Assume for purposes of illustration that 70% of the $1.8 trillion in reserves are denominated in US dollars. This means that there is a 15.3% appreciation of the RMB against the US dollar since the initial revaluation results in an unrealized capital loss of $191 billion. Of course, total reserves were not this high since China allowed its currency to appreciate against the US dollar in July 2005. Also, the remaining 30% of the reserves are denominated in other foreign currencies against which the RMB may have depreciated. Nevertheless, depending on the degree to which the reserves are hedged, the fact that the RMB is most tightly pegged to the US dollar means that any appreciation creates unrealized capital losses for the PBOC. It also creates potential problems for exporting firms that receive revenue in US dollars and that have outstanding bank loans in RMB, unless such exchange rate risk has been properly hedged. The banking sector, however, is less exposed to this exchange rate risk because it has less than 5% of its assets, and about the same percentage of its liabilities, denominated in foreign currencies. Furthermore, the expectation of further appreciation has contributed to "hot money" flows into China, particularly into the real estate sector with a view toward selling the real estate and reaping both capital gains and exchange rate gains after a significant degree of appreciation occurs.

Chinese officials are well aware of the problems resulting from current and capital account surpluses with its currency pegged within a trading range. But they are also acutely aware of the risk of any major changes in relaxing capital controls and further widening the trading band for the RMB and are attempting the difficult task of pursuing sustainable economic growth without the ability to use macro-monetary tools to prevent excessive growth in both money and credit. Instead, China is relying on various micro-monetary tools to prevent serious disruptions to investment and export growth that would worsen unemployment until more balanced growth can occur. Given the crucial role that banks play in this "balancing act," the next section examines in greater detail their position in the overall financial system and their recent condition and current prospects as drivers of growth.

---

[28] Unlike banks in the United States, Chinese banks earn relatively little of their total income from non-interest revenue. This trend, however, is changing rapidly; in the case of China Construction Bank, the increase was only 14.2% in 2007, from 8.95% in 2006.

5 The Structure, Performance, and Risks of China's Financial System[29]

China has a bank-centered financial [29]system, much more so than either India or the United States, as Chart 13 shows. Indeed, operating in a capital markets-oriented financial system, firms in the United States have a greater opportunity to access external funds by selling stocks and bonds, thereby significantly lessening the need to rely on credit from banks.[30] This difference in the development of the financial system is not surprising: arms-length finance, such as corporate debt and equity, requires a much more sophisticated, timely, and reliable information network, compared with bank finance. As a result, these parts of the financial system usually develop later, leaving most developing economies with a heavy bank-based system. Yet a balanced financial system is desirable. Most importantly, when the financial condition of banks deteriorates and loan growth is curtailed, firms are more easily able to obtain alternative funding in a more balanced financial system than the one that currently exists in China. Indeed, in 2006, the China non-financial sector raised about $500 billion, of which 82% was from bank loans, 5.6% from stocks, 5.7% from corporate bonds, and 6.7% from government bonds.[31]

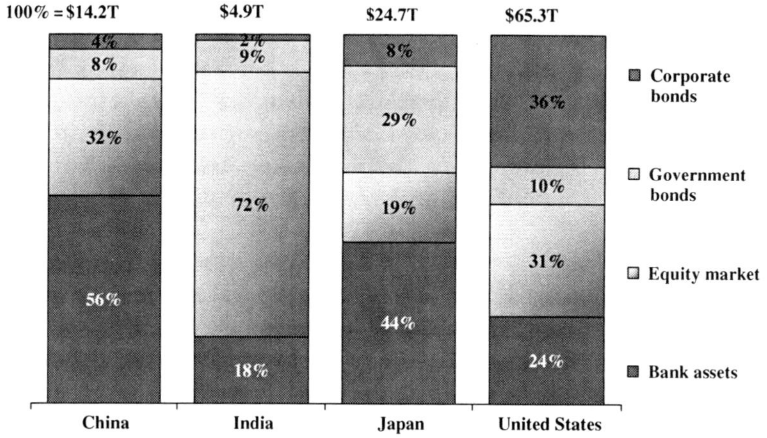

Chart 13 Financial system composition, 2007
Source: International Financial Statistics, International Monetary Fund, Standard and Poor's, Bank for International Settlements, and China Banking Regulatory Commission.

[29] For current and detailed information on the laws and regulations pertaining to the financial restructuring and reform that has taken place in China, see Barth et al. (2007).

[30] Of course, in most countries, including in the United States, small and medium size enterprises (SMEs) typically encounter problems when trying to obtain external funding. Venture capital funds can provide the same, albeit limited, assistance in this regard.

[31] *Financial Stability Report 2007*, People's Bank of China.

The Chinese government recognizes this situation and has taken action to facilitate further development of its capital markets. For example, revisions were made to the Company Law and Securities Law, which became effective January 1, 2006, that strengthen minority shareholder rights, and beginning April 2005 all non-tradable shares in SOEs listed on China's two stock exchanges were required to be converted into tradable shares, which will eliminate the problem of the overhang of state-owned shares. The SOEs constitute about 70% of the 1,400 listed companies in China. As of January 2006, the share conversion process had been completed in companies that account for about 50% of the total market capitalization of the domestic stock exchanges. Also, on February 15, 2006, the Ministry of Finance issued new accounting practices that will bring Chinese accounting practices largely in line with International Financial Reporting Standards (IFRS).[32] Furthermore, the development of the corporate bond market, as well as banks, will benefit by better protecting the rights of creditors. Specifically, a new Enterprise Bankruptcy Law was approved by the National People's Congress. The importance of the law is as follows:

> The law, to take effect June 1, 2006, will replace rules issued in 1986 that applied only to state-owned enterprises. China's bankruptcy rules require insolvent companies to pay off obligations to employees before they address creditors' claims. The new law, which governs state-owned and privately owned companies, requires companies that go bankrupt to pay guarantees to creditors first, with employee salaries and other obligations paid out of what remains, the official Xinhua news agency said. Experts have long complained that China's rules offered scant protection for creditors and give little guidance for dealing with insolvent companies in an increasingly market-driven economy (*Wall Street Journal*, August 28, 2006-A4).

Although banks account for 56% of the total financial assets in China (see Chart 9), the top five SOCBs account for roughly 52% of total bank assets, or just under half of all financial assets. Chart 14 shows the different shares of total assets of all financial institutions in China by type of institution.[33] The five SOCBs clearly dominate in terms of total assets, total loans, and total deposits, at shares of 52, 47, and 56%, respectively. The concentration of financial assets in just five institutions underscores all the attention they receive because in a way they provide a major indicator of the health of the entire financial system and, more broadly, the economy.

Between the formation of the People's Republic of China in 1949 and late 1970, the PBOC functioned as both a central bank and as the primary commercial bank. It engaged in deposit-taking and lending activities in accordance with the central plan of the government. This "monopoly" of the banking sector ended in 1979 when the PBOC gave up part of its commercial operations with the formation of the Agricultural Bank of China (ABC) and the Bank of China (BOC). This was followed by giving up the remainder of its

---

[32] See Institute of International Finance (2006).

[33] In 2007, there were roughly 8,877 financial institutions in China, with about 8,348 being rural credit cooperatives. There were 5 state-owned commercial banks (Big Four), 3 policy-development banks, 12 joint-stock commercial banks, 124 city commercial banks, and 42 urban credit cooperatives, among other financial institutions.

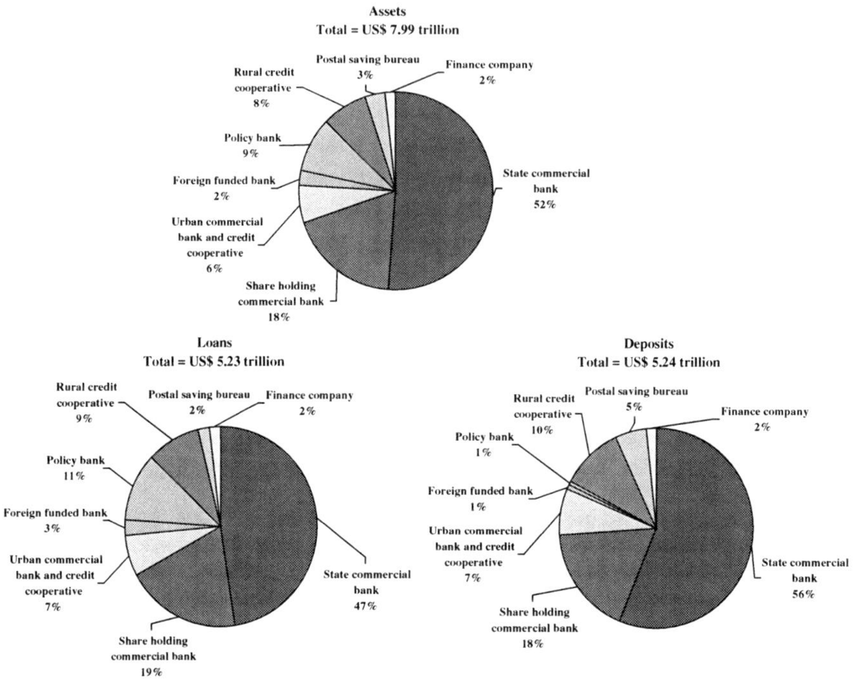

Chart 14 Distribution of assets, deposits and loans by type of Financial Institution in China, March 2008
Note: State-owned commercial banks include Big Four and Bank of Communications.
Source: CEIC.

commercial banking operations with the formation of China Construction Bank (CBC) and the Industrial and Commercial Bank of China (ICBC) in 1983. These four institutions, the Big Four, simply continued providing the commercial banking functions previously provided by the PBOC, with ABC specializing in agricultural financing, BOC specializing in foreign exchange and trade financing, CBC specializing in construction and infrastructure financing, and ICBC specializing in urban commercial financing. The PBOC was designated by the State Council as the nation's central bank and the regulator and supervisor of the banking system.

To improve the commercialization of the banking industry in the 1980s, the Big Four were allowed to expand into new commercial banking businesses beyond those in which they had specialized. New commercial banks and other nonbank financial institutions were established beginning in the late 1980s to develop a more modern financial system. This included joint-stock commercial banks with nationwide banking licenses and urban commercial banks with licenses to engage in commercial banking activities within their designated geographic areas.[34] Then,

[34] Prior to China becoming a member of the WTO, foreign banks were allowed to set up representative offices in China since 1979, and foreign banks were approved to establish branches

in 1994, three policy development banks, the China Development Bank, the Export-Import Bank of China, and the Agricultural Development Bank of China, were established to take over the policy lending functions of the Big Four.[35] In 1995, the National People's Congress passed the Commercial Banking Law, which enabled the Big Four to operate more like genuine commercial banks and segregated the business operations of banks, securities firms, and insurance companies. This separation subsequently led to the establishment of three separate regulatory agencies to oversee each industry. The China Securities Regulatory Commission (CSRS) was established in 1992 initially to oversee the two stock exchanges but also given supervisory responsibility of the securities market in 1998. The China Insurance Regulatory Commission (CIRC) was established in 1998 to oversee the insurance industry. Lastly, the China Banking Regulatory Commission (CBRC) was established in 2003 to oversee the banking industry. These three agencies assumed the majority of the regulatory and supervisory functions of the PBOC over financial institutions.[36] Figure 1 shows the regulatory structure of China's financial sector.

If the transition from a centrally planned economy to a socialist market economy was to be successful, the banking sector had to be relived of the burden of holding large amounts of NPLs that had accumulated over the years. The Big Four in particular had historically been collecting deposits and then using them to fund projects as directed by the government. Credit was not allocated on the basis of risk and return considerations, which are crucial in a market-oriented economy to ensure the efficient allocation of credit. To put the Big Four in a position to pay greater attention to risk and return trade-offs required that their balance sheets be strengthened by removing NPLs that represented a legacy of past practices and simultaneously by increasing their capital. Strengthening the financial condition of the Big Four became especially important once China became a member of the World Trade Organization (WTO) on December 11, 2001 and committed to open up its banking sector in phases over a 5-year period that ended on December 11, 2006 (see Table 8).[37] By removing bad loans and

---

in 1981. In December 1996 and August 1998, qualified branches of foreign banks were allowed to offer RMB products. Zhu Xinqing, "Development of China Banking Industry and Restructuring Practices of BOC," PowerPoint presentation, Chicago, IL November 4–5, 2004.

[35] Also, beginning in 1994, the government was precluded from borrowing from the PBOC to finance any budget deficits. This helped stimulate growth in the bond market. It is reported, moreover, that China Development Bank is being considered by the government for conversion into a commercial bank. (*XFN News,* January 8, 2007).

[36] For detailed information on China's laws and regulations pertaining to the financial sector, see Barth et al. (2007).

[37] In November 2006, China said it would fulfill its WTO commitment of giving foreign banks full access to its banking market if they incorporated their China operations locally (*Wall Street Journal*, February 8, 2007, p. C4). This requirement is related to the plan by the Chinese government to introduce a system of deposit insurance insofar as deposits in branches outside a bank's home country can be uninsured, which is the case for branches of a US bank located outside the country.

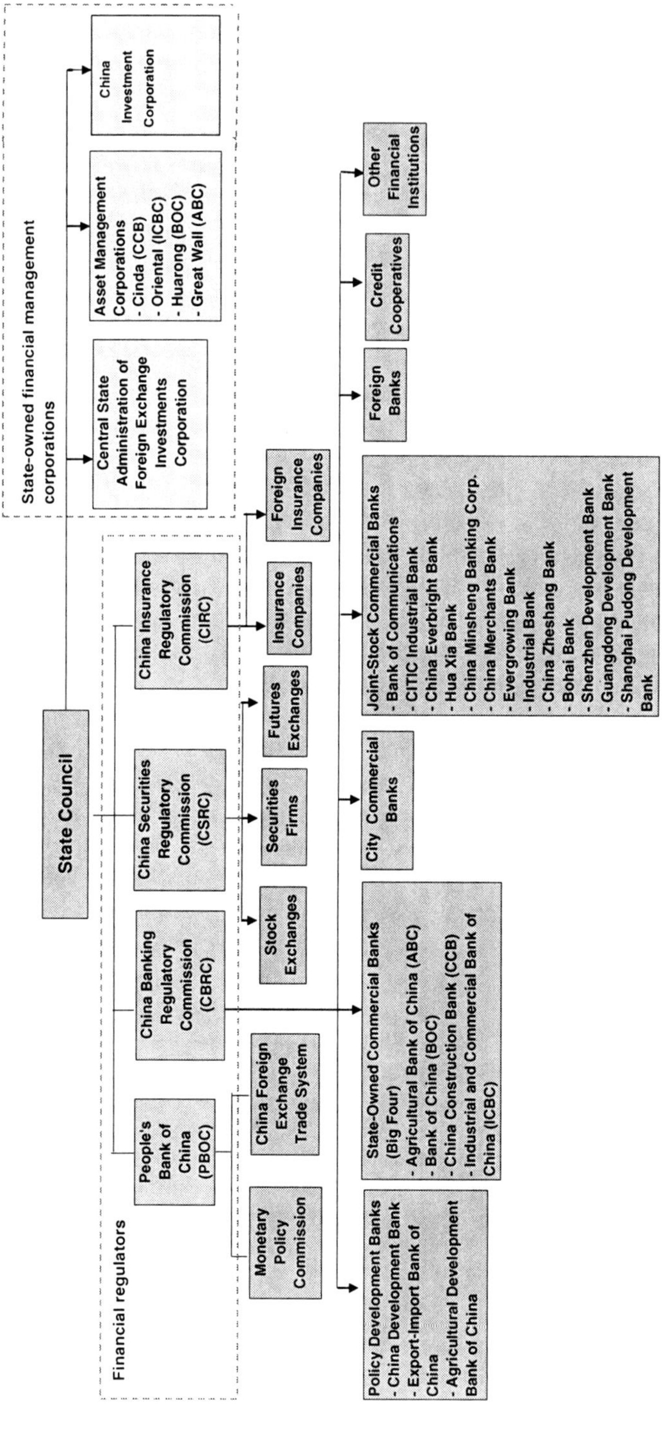

Fig. 1 The financial regulatory structure in China

Table 8 China's WTO commitments: Banking

Time	Form of establishment	Regions	Clients
Entry	Subsidiary or branches subject to certain (prudential) requirements	No restrictions for foreign currency business RMB business: Shanghai, Shenzhen, Tianjin, Dalian	Foreign currency business: All types of clients
By 11 Dec. 2002		RMB business: Guangzhou, Zhuhai, Qingdao, Nanjing, Wuhan	
By 11 Dec. 2003		RMB business: Jinan, Fuzhou, Chengdu, Chongqing	RMB business: only to Chinese enterprises
By 11 Dec. 2004		RMB business: Kunming, Beijing, Xiamen	
By 11 Dec. 2005		RMB business: shantou, Ningbo, Xi'an	
By 11 Dec. 2006		RMB business: no geographic restrictions	RMB business: to all Chinese clients

increasing capital, the goal of the government has been to enable the Big Four to become internationally competitive banks.

To assist in addressing the loan problems of the Big Four, four asset management companies (AMCs)—Cinda, Oriental, Great Wall, and Huarong—were established in 1999, one initially designated for each of the four state-owned banks. At that time \$169 billion NPLs were transferred from the Big Four to the AMCs in exchange for 10-year bonds with an annual interest rate of 2.25%.[38] Overall, \$200 billion in NPLs was transferred to the AMCs or sold to other entities from 1999 to 2006. In addition, \$80 billion in capital was injected into the Big Four from 1998 to 2006, with \$45 billion to BOC and CCB in 2005 and \$15 billion to ICBC in 2005.[39] As a result of these efforts, the NPL ratios (i.e., non-performing loans to total loans) of each of the Big Four declined sharply from 2002 to 2007, as may be seen in Table 9.[40] However, it is obvious

[38] The AMCs had a mandate when established to clean up all the NPLs they acquired within 10 years (i.e., 2008). The NPLs transferred in 1999 were made prior to 1996, and classified under the four-tier category system as being overdue for more than one year.

[39] Foreign firms have also injected capital into Chinese banks through the acquisition of ownership shares, although the total foreign ownership in a bank is limited to less than 20% for a single investor and to less than 25% for all foreign investors.

[40] In January 2002, a new five-category loan classification system was introduced. Under this system, commercial banks are required to classify their loans into the following 5 categories: "pass," "special mentioned," "sub-standard," "doubtful," and "loss". A loan is classified as a "non-performing loan" if it is classified as "sub-standard", "doubtful," or "loss." Also, a new provisioning

Table 9 Non-performing loans to total loans of the Big Four

Percentages, end of year	2002	2003	2004	2005	2006	2007
Agricultural Bank of China	36.7	30.7	26.8	26.3	23.7	23.5
Industrial and Commercial Bank of China	25.5	21.3	19.1	4.7	3.8	2.7
Bank of China	22.4	15.9	5.1	4.6	4.0	3.1
China Construction Bank	15.4	9.1	3.7	3.8	3.4	2.6
Aggregate of the Big Four	23.1	17.8	15.6	10.5	9.1	8.9

Source: People's Bank of China and China Banking Regulatory Commission.

that while three of the banks have seen their ratios fall to around 3% in 2007, the fourth, ABC, still has a high ratio of 24%.

Table 10 shows the NPLs transferred to the AMCs as well as how much has been disposed of and what value has been received in exchange. As of December 2005, the AMCs had resolved $104 billion of $156 billion of NPLs acquired, generating $22 billion in cash proceeds. To the extent that the AMCs are unable to make good on the bonds they have given the Big Four in exchange for the NPLs, the government will have to assume this obligation to prevent the banks from absorbing any losses. Still, there is the significant risk that even banks whose balance sheets have been cleaned of substantial amounts of NPLs will continue to get into difficulty if excessive credit is extended and on inappropriate terms. More generally, the NPL situation, at least in publicly available figures, for the entire banking sector in China for March 2008 is shown in Table 11. While the Big Four account for 87% of all the NPLs in the banking sector, the other domestic banks clearly have had their own loan problems.

Table 10 NPLs disposed of by asset management corporations, March 2006

	Accumulated NPLs disposed of 1999 to March 2006 (US billions)	NPLs disposed of/total NPLs (%)	Cash and non-cash received/ NPLs disposed of (%)	Cash recovered/ accumulated NPLs disposed of (%)
Huarong (BOC)	30.80	70.11	26.50	22.15
Great Wall (ABC)	33.80	80.11	12.70	10.28
Oriental (ICBC)	17.70	56.13	27.16	23.11
Cinda (CCB)	25.80	64.69	34.46	31.56
Total	108.10	68.61	24.20	20.84

Source: China Banking Regulatory Commission.

To put the NPL situation in somewhat broader perspective, Table 12 shows the equity-to-asset ratios for each of the Big Four. Comparing these ratios to the corresponding NPL ratios in Table 9 one sees the still precarious condition

system was introduced, requiring general provisions of 1% of total loans classified as pass to cover potential losses, and specific provisions of 2, 25, 50, and 100% of the amount of loans classified as "special mentioned," sub-standard, doubtful, and loss, respectively. CBRC required that the Big Four and the joint stock commercial banks adopt this classification system from 2004 and for all banks by the end of 2005. The provisioning requirements were to be implemented by the end of 2008.

Table 11 China's reported non-performing loans, March 2008

	Non-performing loans		
	Amount (US$ billions)	Percentage of total loans	Percentage of GDP
State-owned commercial banks (Big Four)	155.9	7.05	4.38
Joint stock commercial banks	12.1	2.11	0.34
City commercial banks	7.3	2.90	0.20
Rural commercial banks	1.8	3.68	0.05
Foreign banks	0.5	0.49	0.01
Total	177.6	5.78	4.99
Memo			
Asset management corporations	110.9		4.1

Source: People's Bank of China, China Banking Regulatory Commission, and Milken Institute staff estimates.

Table 12 Equity to total assets of the Big Four

Percentages, end of year	2001	2002	2003	2004	2005	2006	2007
Agricultural Bank of China	5.3	4.6	4.0	1.9	1.7	1.6	1.5
Industrial and Commercial Bank of China	4.5	3.8	3.3	2.9	3.9	6.3	6.2
Bank of China	6.6	6.7	5.8	5.5	4.9	7.9	7.9
China Construction Bank	3.9	4.7	5.3	5.0	6.3	6.1	6.2
Aggregate of the Big Four	5.0	3.0	4.6	3.8	4.4	5.5	5.6

Source: BankScope and Fortune Global 500.

of all four institutions, especially ABC, which for all practical purposes is insolvent based upon its real net equity position.[41]

To put the condition of the Big Four in better perspective, various performance measures of each of the Big Four are compared to the foreign commercial banks (FCB) operating in China, and Citibank.[42] As Chart 15 shows, each of the Big Four has substantial room for improvement based upon these measures before being in as good an overall financial condition as Citibank.[43] The Chinese banks in the best overall condition are CCB and BOC, while ABC is in the worst condition. What is particularly noticeable is that each of the Big Four has loan loss reserves that are less than 100% of its NPLs, whereas in the case of Citibank the percentage is nearly 174%. By not provisioning more for

---

[41] The Chinese government is well aware of this situation and was in the process of recapitalizing ABC in 2008.

[42] As of June 2006, 71 foreign-funded banks have opened 214 operational institutions in China; in particular, 25 cities have been opened for corporate RMB business; 26 foreign financial institutions have made equity investment in 18 domestic banks totaling US$17.9 billion; 23 joint-venture fund management companies and 8 joint-stock securities companies have been established; 42 foreign entities have become QFIIs (Governor Zhou Xiaochuan, PBOC, September 21, 2006).

[43] Of course, Citibank suffered significantly from the US subprime mortgage market meltdown and related problems that emerged in 2007.

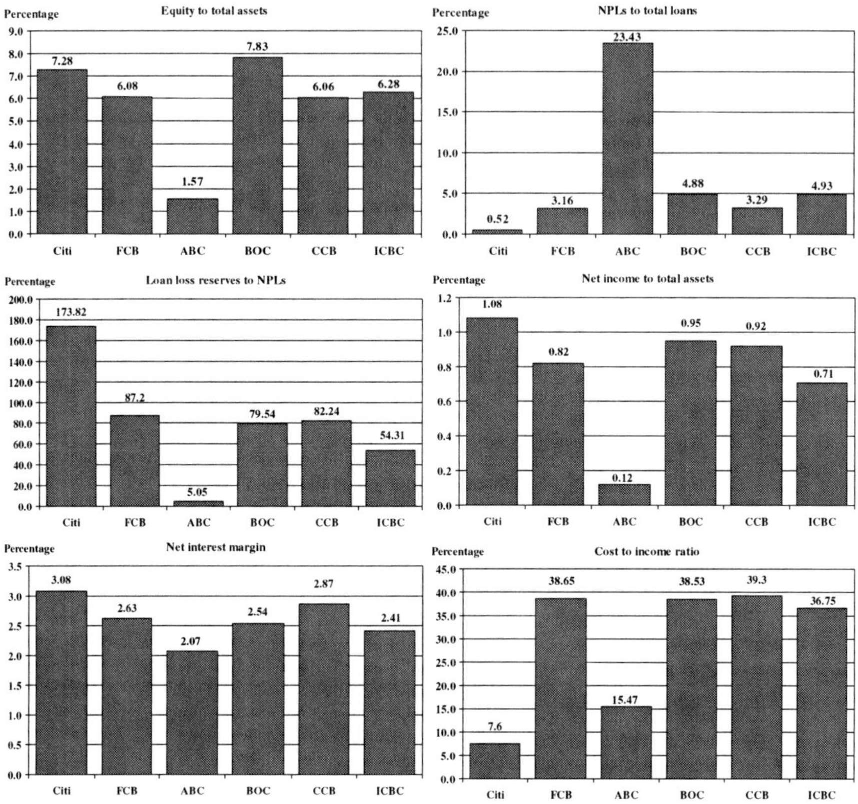

Chart 15 The Big Four's performance compared to foreign banks and Citibank, 2007
Source: BankScope.

NPLs, the net income for each the Big Four is higher than otherwise. Despite this situation, however, BOC, CCB, and ICBC were able to raise substantial amounts of new capital with initial public offerings (IPOs). Specifically, CCB went public in October 2005 and raised $8 billion, BOC went public in May 2006 and raised $11 billion, and ICBC went public in October 2006 and raised $22 billion, the latter being the biggest IPO in history at the time.[44]

The biggest concern at the moment for China's banking sector is the rapid growth in bank credit that is being used to finance various investment and real estate projects, as noted earlier. Loan growth to private sector was 20.3% in 2003, 11.2% in 2004, 9.2% in 2005, 14.3% in 2006, and 19.3% in 2007, cumulatively far faster growth than growth in nominal GDP. Chart 16 shows the improvement in the aggregate NPL ratio for the Big Four as already discussed. It is clear that there has been a dramatic reduction in that ratio to less than 10% from more

[44] In 2007, the total assets of CCB are $903,291; ICBC are $1,188,800; BOC are $820,198, ABC are $828,317, and BoCom are $288,920 all in USD million.

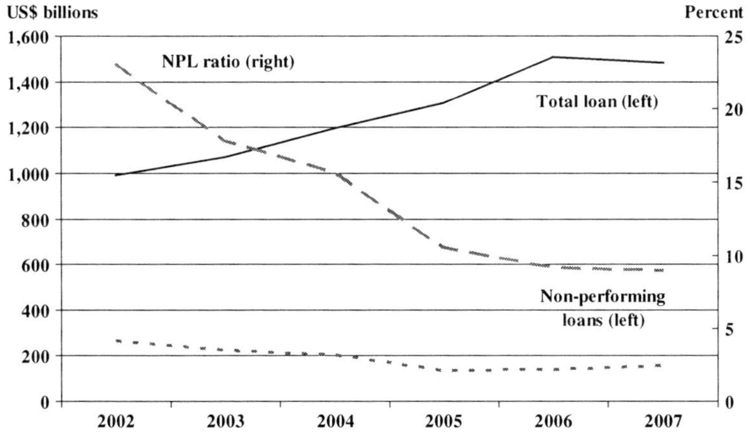

Chart 16 The Big Four's non-performing loan ratio, 2002–2007
Source: People's Bank of China, China Banking Regulatory Commission, and various press releases.

than 20%. The chart also shows, however, that at the same time the total loans of the Big Four have increased nearly 50%. The amount of NPLs has declined but not in proportion to the increase in total loans. It is, therefore, no surprise that the NPL ratio has declined quite sharply over the past several years. The issue now is what portion of all the new loans that have been made in recent years will become non-performing loans as they age. If enough of them are contributing to the "excess production" noted by Prime Minister Wen, then China's banks may need help in disposing of NPLs once again. It is worth noting that if this happens it would not be unique to China. Many transitional country governments have tried to "commercialize" state-owned banks and discovered that it is difficult to produce a lasting change in incentives within these institutions without a change in ownership. Thus, for example, Hungarian authorities recapitalized their state banks annually from 1991 to 1994, before finally selling those banks to foreign investors. The banks continued making losses for a few more years (before becoming profitable), but it was foreign shareholders who suffered. And Polish authorities, recognizing the problems with reforming state banks and yet not willing to sell them all immediately, chose to use stock options, which could only be exercised after privatization, to align managerial incentives with the goal of true commercialization.

The bottom line, as suggested earlier and also as seen in other transition countries, is that banks cannot be reformed in isolation. To the extent that state enterprises still are making losses, they will require financing, and China's banks may be pressed to comply. After all, the banking sector can perform no better than the enterprise sector and the financial sector infrastructure permit.

Apart from this potential problem, China's banking sector has another issue that merits constant attention in the transition from a centrally planned economy to a socialist market economy. This issue involves the development of a "credit culture" in which risk and return considerations are the primary determinants in the allocation of credit. This requires well-trained accountants, lawyers, and risk analysts who are capable of implementing a policy in which banks price loans on the basis of risk and credit be made available to firms of all sizes and ownership structures on equal terms. China currently has a shortage of such skilled individuals. Furthermore, as regards pricing, Chart 17 shows that before 2004, the rates charged on loans and paid on deposits at banks were tightly regulated by the government so as to lock in a predetermined net interest margin. This was done by setting benchmark rates based upon which bank rates were allowed to vary only within specified limits.[45] Available information indicates that lending and deposit rates at banks are fairly well clustered even after 2004, however, which limits competition among banks for deposits and suggests that loans are not being priced fully on the basis of risk.[46] Again, this pattern was seen in other transition countries, with loan pricing being driven more by the needs and condition of the enterprise sector than the requirements of commercial banks. Podpiera (2006) finds that lending rates do not differentiate among different credit risks, and that banks seem to lend without regard to enterprise profitability. This behavior is consistent with that in other transitional economies in which the state enterprise sector had yet to downsize as much as needed and were still absorbing a large share of bank credit.

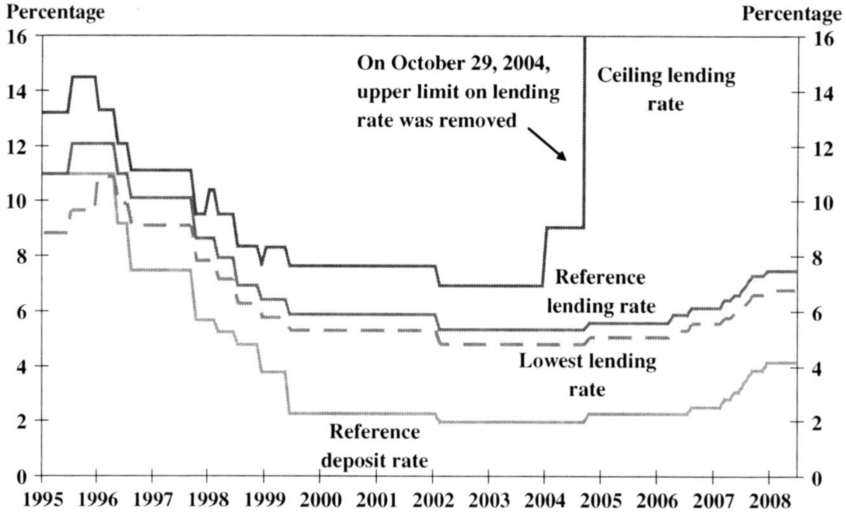

Chart 17 Bank lending and deposit rates (1 year)
Source: People's Bank of China, International Financial Statistics, and International Monetary Fund.

[45] See Ong (2004).

[46] See Dobson and Kashyap (2006).

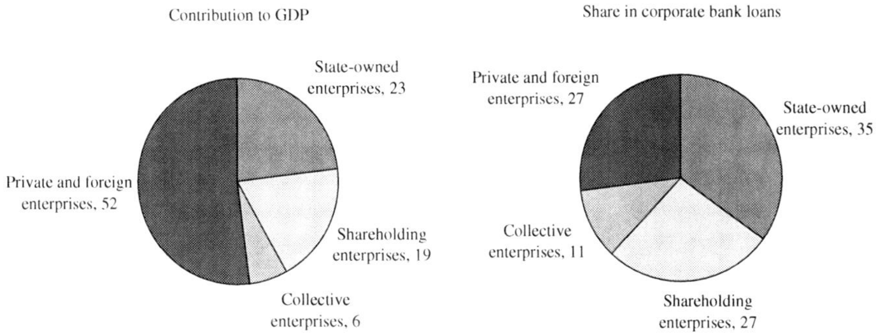

Chart 18 Private enterprises: contribution to GDP vs. share of corporate bank loans
Source: National Bureau of Statistics and the People's Bank of China.

As regards the allocation of credit, Chart 18 shows that private and foreign enterprises contribute slightly more than half of GDP but receive only about one-fourth of total corporate loans from banks. Conversely, state-owned enterprises and collective enterprises contribute only about one-fourth percent of GDP but receive nearly half of corporate loans from banks. This suggests that credit is being allocated inefficiently, perhaps due still to excessive local, if not central, government influence in bank lending decisions, and is consistent with the lack of differentiation according to credit risk, just noted above.[47] Chart 19

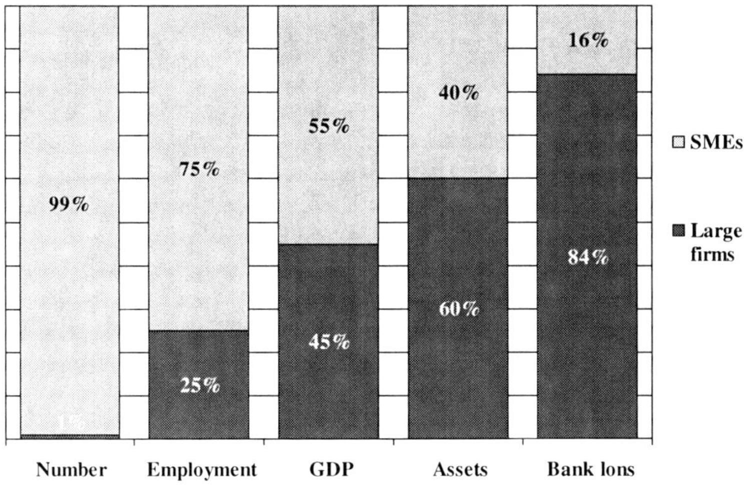

Chart 19 Most bank loans go to large firms
Source: National Bureau of Statistics and the People's Bank of China.

[47] Du and Girma (2007, p. 37) report that "[u]ntil 1998, the four state-owned commercial banks ... were instructed not to lend to private enterprises."

reinforces this view, by showing that small and medium size enterprises (SMEs) contribute a disproportionate amount to GDP but receive a small proportion of bank loans. Liang (2006, p. 22) points out that "[i]n the least developed provinces, overall 60% of financing for the small-and-medium-sized enterprises (SME) comes from informal sources (sometimes over 70%), while the corresponding share is 30% in coastal areas." Furthermore, Liang indicates that "[t]he interest rates charged by informal financial institutions are significantly above the lending rates charged by the state-owned banks."

More generally, President Hu Jintao's signature slogan is the drive for a "harmonious society" – one that would bridge the widening income gaps and ease the strains that are causing social unrest (*Wall Street Journal*, November 22, 2006, p. A4). As applied to financial development, Mr. Xiang Junbo, Deputy Governor of PBOC, stated on September 1, 2006, that:

> Financial industry is the core of modern economy. More efforts should be made to build a harmonious financial system compatible with the comprehensive, balanced and sustainable economic development. To be explicit, we will make efforts in the following aspects. First, harmonize the relationship between economic and financial development. Second, foster a harmonious system for financial institutions. Third, build a harmonious financial market. Fourth, promote the development of regional financial industry in a harmonious way. Fifth, blueprint the harmonious reform, development and opening-up of financial industry.

These are certainly commendable goals and hopefully ones that will be achieved through the recent and ongoing reforms in China's financial system.

6 Summary and Conclusions

China is undoubtedly unique and abounds both with substantial opportunities and with significant challenges. Its rapid rate of GDP growth and the boom in exports and international reserves are without precedent. The latter phenomenon of course is a joint product: not only is it unprecedented for an emerging market to be such a large creditor, but it is equally unique for a reserve currency country to be such a large debtor. Still, the reserve buildup is at least in part a testimony to China's competitiveness and of course to its massive savings rate. Moreover, by joining the WTO and welcoming capital inflows, it is signaling a desire to open its economy to international influences and, in turn, to influence international developments.

The government likewise is to be commended for taking on the challenge of reforming an immense financial system. This sector is a challenge because it is necessarily the mirror image of the real economy and accordingly cannot be reformed in isolation. To the extent that there are "zombie enterprises," that is, firms that are dead in the sense of not being able to be managed without sustaining losses and yet still alive and utilizing resources, the financial sector, and usually the banks, will be called on to provide funding. Since the state enterprise sector is still large, the government faces the daunting task of transforming the zombie enterprises into viable enterprises. The balancing act being undertaken by authorities is to keep managing the economy so that the rapid growth from the non-state sector will be able to cover the losses of the state sector.

Chinese officials are aware of this challenge. Unfortunately, the problems do not end there. The further difficulty is that just as the public sector around the world has not proved to be an efficient manager of enterprises, it has also not been an efficient manager of banks.[48] A solution that would seem to work in theory would be to grow the private sector's role in the banking system, using banks that operate on market principles as a way to continually starve inefficient enterprises of credit, while supplying credit to the productive enterprises. Finding a way to make this work in practice will require both finesse and good fortune on a scale commensurate with China's growing importance in the world economy.

Acknowledgment The authors are extremely grateful for the excellent assistance provided by Tong Li and Wenling Lu.

Appendix 1: China's International Investment Position, 2006 and 2007

US$ billion	2006	2007		2006	2007
Net position	**611**	**1,022**	**B. Liabilities**	**1,033**	**1,266**
A. Assets	**1,644**	**2,288**	**1. Foreign direct investments**	**613**	**742**
1. Direct investments abroad	**91**	**108**	**2. Portfolio investment**	**121**	**143**
2. Portfolio Investment	**229**	**240**	2.1 Equity securities	107	125
2.1 Equity securities	2	19	2.2 Debt securities	14	18
2.2 Debt securities	228	221	**3. Other investments**	**300**	**381**
3. Other investments	**252**	**406**	3.1 Trade credits	104	132
3.1 Trade credits	116	142	3.2 Loans	99	103
3.2 Loans	67	89	3.3 Currency and deposits	59	98
3.3 Currency and deposits	47	50	3.4 Other liabilities	38	47
3.4 Other assets	21	126			
4. Reserves assets	**1,073**	**1,535**			
4.1 Monetary gold	4	5			
4.2 Special Drawing Rights	1	1			
4.3 Reserves position in the fund	1	1			
4.4 Foreign exchange	1,066	1,528			

Source: State Administration of Foreign Exchange.

[48] The French banking system used to be cited as an exception to this statement, until the massive failure of Credit Lyonnais. And the German banking system, the other exception, has been beset by inefficiency and losses in their state banks.

Appendix 2: Top 10 Chinese Mergers and Acquisitions Abroad, January 1995–June 2008

Deal value US$ millions	Completion date	Acquirer	Target	Target nationality	Target industry	Cash only (Y/N)
14,316	1-Feb-08	Aluminum Corp of China; Alcoa Inc	Rio Tinto plc (12%)	United Kingdom	Mining	Y
5,490	15-Feb-08	Industrial & Commercial Bank of China – ICBC	Standard Bank Group Ltd (20%)	South Africa	Finance	Y
4,180	26-Oct-05	China National Petroleum Corp – CNPC	PetroKazakhstan Inc	Kazakhstan	Oil & gas	Y
3,652	10-Aug-06	China Petroleum & Chemical Corp – SINOPEC	Udmurtneft OAO (99.49%)	Russian Federation	Oil & gas	Y
3,425	15-Dec-06	Bank of China Ltd	Singapore Aircraft Leasing Enterprise Pte Ltd (SALE)	Singapore	Transportation	Y
3,117	24-Mar-08	China Huaneng Group	Tuas Power Ltd	Singapore	Utility & energy	Y
3,000	14-Aug-07	China Investment Corp	Blackstone Group LP (10%)	United States	Finance	Y
2,981	14-Aug-07	China Development Bank	Barclays plc (2.64%)	United Kingdom	Finance	Y
2,935	4-Apr-08	State Administration of Foreign Exchange	Total SA (1.6%)	France	Oil & gas	Y
2,692	19-Apr-06	China National Offshore Oil Corp – CNOOC	Oil & Gas Assets (Akpo Offshore Oil & Gas Field in Nigeria)	Nigeria	Oil & gas	Y

Source: Dealogic.

References

Allen, Franklin, Jun Qian and Meijun Qian. 2005. "China's Financial System: Past, Present, and Future." Wharton Center for Financial Institutions Working Paper No. 05-17.

Asian Development Bank. 2004. "People's Republic of China." In: *Asian Development Outlook 2004*. New York, USA: Oxford University Press, pp. 65–75.

Bank for International Settlements. 1999. "Strengthening the Banking System in China: Issues and Experiences." Bank for International Settlements Policy Papers No. 7.

Barth, James R., Rob Koepp and Zhu Zhongfei. 2004. "Institute View: Disciplining China's Banks." *Milken Institute Review*, Second Quarter, pp. 83–92.

Barth, James R., Douglas Arner, Berry Hsu, Wei Wang and Zhou Zhongfei (eds.). 2007. *Financial Restructuring and Reform in Post-WTO China*. Alphen ann den Rijn, Netherland: Kluwer Law International.

Barth, James, Gerard Caprio, Jr., and Ross Levine. 2006. *Rethinking Bank Regulation: Till Angels Govern*. New York, USA: Cambridge University Press.

Berdekin, Richard C. K. 2008. *China's Monetary Challenges: Past Experiences & Future Prospects*. New York, USA: Cambridge University Press.

Boyreau-Debray, Genevieve and Shang-Jin Wei. 2005. "Pitfalls of a State-Dominated Financial System: The Case of China." NBER Working Paper No. 11214.

Brandt, Loren and Xiaodong Zhu. 2002. "What Ails China? A Long-Run Perspective on Growth and Inflation (or Deflation) in China." In: *East Asia in Transition: Economic and Security Challenges*, edited by A. E. Safarian and Wendy Dobson. Toronto: University of Toronto Press.

Catin, Maurice, Xubei Luo and Christophe Van. Huffel. 2005. "Openness, Industrialization and Geographic Concentration of Activities in China." World Bank Policy Research Working Paper No. 3706.

Chen, Jianguo, Ben Marshall, Jenny Zhang, and Siva Ganesh. 2006. "Financial Distress Prediction in China." *Review of Pacific Basin Financial Markets and Policies*, 9(2), 317–36

Chen, Xiaogang, Michael Skully, and Kim Brown. 2005. "Banking Efficiency in China: Application of DEA to Pre- and Post-Deregulation Eras: 1993–2000." *China Economic Review*, 16(3), 229–45.

Chen, Zhian, Donghui Li, and Fariborz Moshirian. 2005. "China's Financial Services Industry: The Intra-industry Effects of Privatization on the Bank of China Hong Kong." *Journal of Banking and Finance*, 29, 2291–324.

China Banking Regulatory Commission. 2007. http://www.cbrc.gov.cn

China Insurance Regulatory Commission. 2007. http://www.circ.gov.cn

China Quarterly Update. August 2006.

China Securities Regulatory Commission. 2007. http://www.csrc.gov.cn

Claessens, Stijn, Asli Demirguc-Kunt, and Harry Huizinga. 1998. "How Does Foreign Entry Affect the Domestic Banking Market." World Bank Policy Research Working Paper No. 1918.

Clarke, George, Robert Cull, and Mary Shirley. 2005. "Bank Privatization in Developing Countries: A Summary of Lessons and Findings." *Journal of Banking and Finance*, 29, 1905–30.

Crystal, Jennifer, Gerard Dages, and Linda Goldberg. 2002. "Has Foreign Bank Entry Led to Sounder Banks." *Current Issues in Economics and Finance*, 8(1), 1–6.

Das, Udaibir, Marc Quintyn, and Kina Chenard. 2004. "Does Regulatory Governance Matter for Financial System Stability? An Empirical Analysis." International Monetary Fund Working Paper 04/89.

Dekle, Robert and Guillaume Vandenbroucke. 2006. "Whither Chinese Growth? A Sectoral Growth Accounting Approach." Mimeo, Department of Economics, Stanford University.

Demirguc-Kunt, Asli and Enrica Detragiache. 1997. "The Determinants of Banking Crises: Evidence from Industrial and Developing Countries." World Bank Policy Research Working Paper No. 1828.

Demirguc-Kunt, Asli and Enrica Detragiache. 1999. "Financial Liberalization and Financial Fragility." World Bank Policy Research Working Paper No. 1917.
Demirguc-Kunt, Asli and Enrica Detragiache. 2005. "Cross-Country Empirical Studies of Systemic Bank Distress: A Survey." World Bank Policy Research Working Paper No. 3719.
Dobson, Wendy and Anil K. Kashyap. 2006. "The Contradiction in China's Gradualist Banking Reforms." *Brookings Papers on Economic Activity*, 37(2), 103–162.
Dollar, David and Aart Kraay. 2005. "Neither a Borrower Nor a Lender: Does China's Zero Net Foreign Asset Position Make Economic Sense?" World Bank Policy Research Working Paper No. 3801.
Domac, Ilker and Maria Soledad Martinez-Peria. 2000. "Banking Crises and Exchange Rate Regimes: Is There a Link?" World Bank Policy Research Working Paper No. 2489.
Dooley, Michael P., David, Folkerts-Landau, and Peter M. Garber. 2003a. "An Essay on the Revived Bretton Woods System (September 2003)". NBER Working Paper No. W9971. Available at SSRN: http://ssrn.com/abstract = 447259
Dooley, Michael P., David, Folkerts-Landau, and Peter M. Garber. 2003b. "An Essay on the Revived Bretton Woods System," NBER Working Paper No. W9971.
Du, Jun and Sourafel Girma. 2007. "Finance and Firm Export in China," *Kyklos*, 60(1), 37–54.
Eichengreen, Barry and Andrew K. Rose. 1998."Staying Afloat When the Wind Shifts: External Factors and Emerging-Market Banking Crises." NBER Working Paper No. 6370.
Eichengreen, Barry and Carlos Arteta. 2000."Banking Crises in Emerging Markets: Presumptions and Evidence." Center for International and Development Economics Research (CIDER) Working Papers C00-115.
Eichengreen, Barry. 2006. "China's Exchange Rate Regime: The Long and Short of It." Columbia University's Conference on Chinese Money and Finance.
Fan, He. 2002. "How Far is China Away from a Financial Crisis." Thailand Development Research Institute, Bangkok, Thailand.
Fang, Xinghai. 2005. "Reconstructing the Micro-Foundation of China's Financial Sector." In: *Financial Sector Reform in China*, edited by Yasheng Huang, Tony Saich and Edward Steinfeld. Cambridge, Massachusetts: Harvard University Asia Center, pp. 19–28.
Frankel, Jeffrey. 2006. "Could the Twin Deficits Jeopardize U.S. Hegemony?" *Journal of Policy Modeling*, 28(6), 656–663.
Garcia-Herrero, Alicia, Sergio Gavila and Daniel Santabarbara. 2006. "China's Banking Reform: An Assessment of Its Evolution and Possible Impact." *CESifo Economic Studies*, 52(2), 304–363.
Goldstein, Morris. 2004. "Adjusting China's Exchange Rate Policies." Institute for International Economics Working Paper No. 04-1.
Goldstein, Morris and Nicholas Lardy. 2004. "What Kind of Landing for the Chinese Economy." Institute for International Economics Policy Briefs in International Economics No. PB04-7.
Goldstein, Morris. 2005. "Renminbi Controversies." Prepared for the Conference on Monetary Institutions and Economic Development, Cato Institute.
Goldstein, Morris and Nicholas Lardy. 2005. "China's Role in the Revived Bretton Woods System: A Case of Mistaken Identity." Institute for International Economics Working Paper No. 05-2.
Hu, Fred. 2001. "China's WTO Accession as a Catalyst for Capital Account Liberalization." *Cato Journal*, 21(1), 101–11.
Institute of International Finance, Inc. 2006. "Corporate Governance in China: An Investor Perspective." Task Force Report.
International Monetary Fund. 2005. "People's Republic of China: 2005 Article IV consultation—Staff Report; Staff Supplement; and Public Information Notice on the Executive Board Decisions." IMFCountry Report NO. 05/411.

Kaminsky, Graciela and Carmen Reinhart. 1999. "The Twin Crises: The Causes of Banking and Balance-of-Payment Problems." *The American Economic Review*, 89(3), 473–500.

Klingebiel, Daniela. 2000. "The Use of Asset Management Companies in the Resolution of Banking Crises: Cross-Country Experiences." World Bank Policy Research Working Paper No. 2284.

Kuijs, Louis. 2005. "Investment and Saving in China." World Bank Policy Research Working Paper No. 3633.

Lane, Philip R. and Sergio Schmukler L. 2006. "The International Financial Integration of China and India." IMF-World Bank Annual Meetings in Singapore.

Levine, Ross. 1997. "Financial Development and Economic Growth: Views and Agenda." *Journal of Economic Literature*, XXXV(June), 688–726.

Levine, Ross. 2005. "Finance and Growth: Theory and Evidence." In: *Handbook of Economic Growth*, edited by Philippe Aghion and Steven Durlauf. The Netherlands: Elsevier Science.

Liang, Hong. 2006. "China's Investment Strength is Sustainable." Goldman Sachs Global Economics Paper No. 146.

Lin, Changyuan. 2003. "Financial Conglomerates in China." Chinese Academy of Social Sciences, Center for International Law Studies Working Paper No. 2003020011.

Ma, Guonan. 2006. "Sharing China's Bank Restructuring Bill." *China & World Economy*, 14, 19–37.

Makin, John. 2004. "China: The Unplannable, Planned Economy." American Enterprise Institute for Public Policy Research Economic Outlook.

Mao, Yiwen. 2002. "Establishing China's Financial Vulnerability Indicator System after WTO Accession." *Economic Science*, 5, 11–18. 毛一文 "进入 WTO 后中国金融脆弱性监测指标体系之设计"《经济科学》2002年第5期.

McKinnon, Ronald and Gunther Schnabl. 2003. "China: A Stabilizing or Deflationary Influence in East Asia? The Problem of Conflicted Virture." Mimeo, Department of Economics, Stanford University.

McKinnon, Ronald. 2005a. "China's New Exchange Rate Policy: Will China Follow Japan into a Liquidity Trap?" Mimeo, Department of Economics, Stanford University.

McKinnon, Ronald. 2005b. "Exchange Rate or Wage Changes in International Adjustment? Japan and China versus the United States." Center for European Economic Research Discussion Paper No. 05-64.

Ministry of Finance, People's Republic of China. 2006. http://www.mof.gov.cn

Moreno, Ramon. 2002. "Reforming China's Banking System." Federal Reserve Bank of San Francisco, *Economic Letter* No. 2002.

National Bureau of Statistics, 2007. http://www.stats.gov.cn

OECD. 2005. *Economic Surveys: China*. Paris: OECD Publishing.

Ong, Lynette. 2004. "Flexible Rates Boost Bank Reform in China." *Asia Times Online*, January 8.

Pamlin, Dennis and Baijin Long. 2007. "Rethink China's Outward Investment Flows" WWF International. April. http://www.wwfchina.org/wwfpress/publication/policy/rethink.pdf

Park, Albert, and Kaja Sehrt. 2001. "Tests of Financial Intermediation and Banking Reform in China." *Journal of Comparative Economics*, 29(4), 608–44.

Pei, Guifen and Sayuri Shirai. 2004. "China's Financial Industry and Asset Management Companies: Problems and Challenges." The 21st Century Center of Excellence Program-Policy Innovation Initiative: Human Security Research in Japan and Asia.

People's Bank of China. 2005. "2005 China's Financial Stability Report." People's Bank of China. Translated by the Milken Institute staff.

People's Bank of China. 2007. http://www.pbc.gov.cn/english/

Podpiera, Richard. 2006. "Progress in China's Banking Sector Reform: Has Bank Behavior Changed?" IMF Working Paper No. WP/06/71.

Prasad, Eswar, Thomas Rumbraugh, and Qing Wang. 2005. "Putting the Cart Before the Horse? Capital Account Liberalization and Exchange Rate Flexibility in China." *China & World Economy*, 13(4), 3–20.

Sachs, Jeffery D. and Wing Thye Woo. 2003. "China's Growth after WTO Membership." *Journal of Chinese Economics and Business Studies*, 1(1), 1–31.

Schlotthauer, Nicolas. 2000. "Currency and Financial Crises: Lessons Learned From the Asian Crises for China?" University of Wurzburg Economic Papers No. 15.

Sharma, Krishnan. 2001. "The Underlying Constraints on Corporate Bond Market Development in Southeast Asia." *World Development*, 29(8), 1405–19.

Sun, Laixiang and Damian Tobin. 2005. "International Listing as a Mechanism of Commitment to More Credible Corporate Governance Practices: The Case of the Bank of China (Hong Kong)." *Corporate Governance: An International Review*, 13(1), 81–91.

Sun, Lijian. 2002. "Rethinking the Vulnerability of China's Financial System." *Finance and Trade Economics*, 3, 5–12. 孙立坚"再论中国金融体系的脆弱性",《财贸经济》2004年第3期.

Talley, Samuel, Marcelo M. Giugale, and Rossana Polastri. 1999. "Capital Inflow Reversals, Banking Stability, and Prudential Regulation in Central and Eastern Europe." World Bank Policy Research Working Paper No. 2023.

The People's Bank of China. 2006. http://www.pbc.gov.cn

US Treasury Department. 2006. "Report to Congress on International Economic and Exchange Rate Policies."

Wagner, Wolf. 2004. "The Liquidity of Bank Assets and Banking Stability." Cambridge Endowment for Research in Finance Working Paper No. 18.

Wang, Changyun. 2005. "Ownership and Operating Performance of Chinese IPOs." *Journal of Banking and Finance*, 29, 1835–56.

Whalley, John and Xian Xin. 2006. "China's FDI and Non-FDI Economies and the Sustainability of Future High Chinese Growth". NBER Working Paper No. W12249.

Wu, Zhiwen. 2003. "Financial Vulnerability: Theories and Empirical Analysis on China (1991–2000)." *Economic Review*, 2, 96–100. 伍志文"金融脆弱性:理论及基于中国的经验分析(1991–2000)"《经济评论》2003年第2期.

Xinhua News Agency. 2005. *China Money*, Vol. 11, No. 42.

Yu, Peter K., Gordon G. Chang, Jerome Cohen, Elizabeth C. Economy, Sharon Hom, and Adam Qi Li. 2003. "China and the WTO: Progress, Perils, and Prospects." *Columbia Journal of Asian Law*, 17, 1–29.

Yusuf, Shahid and Kaoru Nabeshima. 2006. "Two Decades of Reform: The Changing Organization Dynamics of Chinese Industrial Firms." World Bank Policy Research Working Paper No. 3806.

Zhao, Zibing. 2005. "An Analysis on the Reform Costs of Bank of China and China Construction Bank." *Securities Market Weekly*, September 28, 2005. 赵自兵"中行、建行改革成本分析",《证券市场周刊》2005年9月28日.

Zhu, Xingqiang. 2004. "Development of China Banking Industry and Restructuring Practices of BOC." Bankers' Association for Finance and Trade's 14th Annual Conference on International Trade.

China's Financial Sector: Contributions to Growth and Downside Risks

Albert Keidel

Abstract China has a two-part financial system with a competitive market-based component and a public, government-directed component. Both have reformed rapidly since China's reforms began in 1978. The market-based component is immature and subject to numerous systemic weaknesses, while the government-directed component, which also suffers shortcomings, performs essential funding for infrastructure and other underpinnings of China's sustained rapid growth. Critics claim that China's financial system is inefficient, with banks considered technically insolvent. But a realistic evaluation of the system's resources and accomplishments, including investment rates of return and efficiency in generating sustained growth, can only conclude that China's financial system is performing well and is likely to continue to do so. China's newly articulated strategy for financial reforms going forward clearly intends to pursue gradual commercialization of the whole system—a process that can be expected to last 20 or 30 years. In the meantime, ongoing improvements in government-directed credit will continue to ensure adequate investments in the necessary substructures for competitive for-profit economic expansion.

Keyword China's financial sector · Financial reforms

Any evaluation of China's financial system and its prospects must concentrate on its contribution to China's economic growth and to related solutions to a range of domestic economic goals. The evolution of China's financial system, in all its various dimensions, is in midstream, with its many market and non-

---

This paper was prepared for "China's Changing Financial System: Can It Catch Up With, Or Even Drive, Growth?," a conference sponsored by Networks Financial Institute at Indiana State University and held in Indianapolis on January 25, 2007.

A. Keidel (✉)
Carnegie Endowment for International Peace, Washington, D.C., USA
e-mail: akeidel@carnegieendowment.org

J.R. Barth et al. (eds.), *China's Emerging Financial Markets*,
The Milken Institute Series on Financial Innovation and Economic Growth 8,
DOI 10.1007/978-0-387-93769-4_3, © 2009 by Milken Institute

market aspects reforming simultaneously. Its hybrid nature, with aspects considered by foreign observers to be not only unconventional but inefficient, in fact appears to serve China's current needs relatively well. The requirements for continued reform include maintenance and improvement of non-market, policy-directed components at the same time that immature, market-based components struggle to overcome the considerable handicaps imposed by the human resource and institutional shortcomings of a country with a GDP per capita in 2006 below US 2,000 dollars.

China has faced and continues to face a range of domestic economic challenges directly associated with its rapid growth and market system reforms. The most important challenges are (1) job creation to restructure China's labor force away from low productivity rural interior activities, (2) accelerating construction of urban infrastructure, and (3) countering the weakness of China's tax base and other public financial resources.[1] China, starting as it has from very low levels of GDP per capita, is attempting to leap ahead into middle–income-country status in the span of only several decades. Its economic, social, and political foundations are all changing and expanding at once.

A cornerstone of Chinese economic and financial policy, therefore, is the requirement for China to continue to support rapid economic growth and job creation at the same time that it modernizes its financial system. In this setting, it is useful to emphasize the two-part nature of China's financial system—a market-based competitive component and a government-directed public component.

1 China's Changing Market-Based Financial System, 1978–2006

China's market-based financial system was essentially nonexistent in 1978, at the outset of the post-Mao reform period. Today, it has most of the institutional forms of a traditional modern financial system, even though the functionality of those institutions is immature and even though the financial role of other nontraditional institutions, especially China's planning commission, is especially strong. The system's evolution from 1978 till today has been relatively rapid, and change continues at an impressive pace. China's premier chairs a special meeting every 5 years to map out strategies for subsequent phases in China's financial sector reform, the most recent being in early 2007.

When what the Chinese call "Reforms and Opening up to the Outside World" began in late 1978, China's economy was governed little by monetary factors. Instead, plans, quotas, directives, and ration coupons allocated virtually all goods and services, including all labor, investment, material inputs,

[1] Keidel 2004. Albert Keidel, "Prospects for Continued High Economic Growth in China" (Paper presented at POSRI international Forum on China's Development, Seoul, Korea, November10, 2004); http://www.carnegieendowment.org/files/Keidel_Prospects.pdf

and distribution of final product. Nevertheless, money still mattered. Government budgets were prepared and examined, and deficits were avoided. Prices—the link between physical flows and money—were administratively set to keep real and monetary flows in balance. The banking system consisted essentially of a single mono-bank that acted as a comptroller for government budgetary activity, which included the finances of nearly all enterprises and government agencies—their investment decisions, allocation of funds from depreciation charges and distribution of all profits. Government finance and economic activity were thus merged—with a miniscule policy role for taxation or credit of any kind.

Economic reforms over almost three decades have relentlessly increased the role of independent financial activity. First, in the 1980s, socialist communes in rural areas were broken up into family farmed units. State-owned enterprises were placed under the control of individual managers, who were in principle hired to deliver profitability. Bankruptcy became a legal possibility. As reforms disbanded many ration systems, prices adjusted in the direction of scarcity and demand for higher quality products like cotton cloth and vegetables. China's mono-bank broke into a central bank and four large so-called commercial banks. Other bank-like institutions and activities appeared, including trust and investment companies, local investment banks, finance companies, rural and urban credit institutions, savings clubs, and even experimental private banks. Credit instruments included so-called bank loans, government treasury bills, a smattering of corporate bonds, and a wide variety of informal promises to pay issued by local governments and their various projects. The decade ended with financial turmoil and reform-induced social unrest at Tiananmen in 1989.

A second phase of economic and financial reforms in the 1990s greatly accelerated the pace of change. Price reforms eliminated food ration coupons but at the cost of high rates of inflation in the period 1992–1995. Stock markets, albeit heavily government manipulated, were launched early in the decade, along with indigenous brokerages and investment banks. Corporate governance initiatives advanced more modern forms, including stock share companies and boards of directors. Some government bonds became tradable on secondary markets. Internal controls for major commercial banks strengthened dramatically as part of inflation control efforts.

The process of establishing a legal framework for these reforms also gathered momentum in the 1990s with passage of a central bank law by the National People's Congress (NPC), a commercial bank law, and a company law. China in the mid-1990s created three so-called policy banks, for agriculture, foreign trade, and domestic infrastructure, as a way of relieving commercial banks of the burden of making government policy directed loans, which continued on a large scale nevertheless. Indeed, recognition that many so-called bank loans from the 1980s had been prompted by government policy rather than profitability led to a series of steps in the late 1990s to recapitalize the four main commercial banks by transferring bad loans to holding tanks called Asset

Management Companies (AMCs). Such transfers were at the same time part of an aggressive reform of corporate management that resulted in widespread closures, mergers, and layoffs—with as many as 50 million workers laid off between 1996 and 2005.

Insulated from the 1997 Asian Financial Crisis because of strictly managed short-term international capital flows, China nevertheless struggled late in the 1990s with unacceptably slower GDP growth and declines in rural household consumption—mainly because of domestic policy errors. Despite these overall difficulties, by the end of the 1990s, China's economic and financial institutions had survived 10 years of dramatic change.

The greatest pressure for market-based economic and financial reform in the new century came from China's 2001 accession to the World Trade Organization (WTO), which included a range of requirements for reform and increased competition in banking and insurance. Beginning in December of last year (2006), foreign banks must in principle receive equal national treatment in China's domestic banking markets. WTO accession did not, however, allow foreign investment banks and brokerages the controlling access to China's domestic market that they had hoped for.

Continued recapitalization of state-owned commercial banks since 2,000 ushered in a stronger role for the central bank in the process of financing such bailouts. This central bank role, including creation of a new quasi-AMC named, for short, Huijin, in part was backed by rapidly growing foreign exchange reserves. Increased reserves fed heavily by capital inflows in turn prompted introduction of exchange rate system reforms that significantly increased the potential for flexibility in the price of China's currency. The decade has also seen reforms creating or strengthening financial regulatory bodies overseeing banks, insurance, and securities markets. Expansion of the banking system to so-called second tier and stock share banks, already significant in the 1990s, continued, as did activities of relatively new urban municipal banks, converted from earlier urban credit cooperatives. In recent years, three of China's four major commercial banks have issued stock on Hong Kong and domestic stock markets and accepted minority strategic investments from some of the world's largest banks.

It is impossible to mention here all dimensions of China's market-based financial system and its reforms to date, but the pace of change has been intense and has drawn China into a wide range of multilateral and bilateral international collaboration and consultation relationships.

Nevertheless, China's market-based financial system remains immature in nearly all dimensions. At the formal national and provincial level, it is decades away from playing the full-fledged mature role financial systems play in more established market economies operating at higher standards of living—like those in Hong Kong, Japan, North America, and Europe. The markers of China's financial immaturity include the system's opaque corporate client base, whether state-controlled or private, its shaky consumer credit client base, governance weaknesses in financial institutions themselves, immature regulatory institutions, ineffective supporting legal and judicial institutions, and inadequate accounting standards and institutions. At the same time, as we have seen, early stage reforms addressing just these elements have advanced rapidly in the recent decade and can be expected to continue for several decades more.

When describing China's market-based financial system it is essential to give an important place to what Chinese financial and investment statistics call "self raised funds." These are the combination of equity contributions and retained earnings, including depreciation charges, which firms and families apply directly to capacity expansion in ways that seem potentially most profitable to them. In this sense, these funds are highly market oriented. What is more important, these private funds are reportedly much larger as a source of investment funds than bank loans. In other words, evaluation of the scale and efficiency of China's market-based financial system must necessarily include evaluation of the effectiveness of such private flows. Their scope and opportunity for profitable return is arguably greatly expanded by the large-scale public investments in education, public health, transport, and communications which have underpinned recent decades of rapid growth.

China's current and future challenge is to continue the rapid pace of market-based financial reforms while at the same time sustaining China's overall high speed economic growth. In this regard, it is important to acknowledge the effectiveness and growth contribution of the second, non-market, dimension to China's financial system.

2 China's Publicly Directed Financial System

China's evolving and so-far-successful method for meeting the public financial dimensions of its many development challenges has utilized a public finance and fiscal system that goes beyond relying on market-based finance, government taxes, direct government borrowings, and budgetary allocations. Without the successful operation and reform of government-directed finance, rapid growth of the kind China has implemented since 1978—and expects to continue for several decades—is difficult to imagine.

China's domestic fiscal and public finance system relies on a number of fundamental non-market components. First is its capture, directly and indirectly, of citizen and business deposits in financial institutions as a major source of public funds. Second is the public administrative channeling of these funds, mainly through development banks and the so-called commercial banks, to bottleneck investments vetted by public investment evaluation agencies—most importantly the planning commission (now officially known as the National Development Reform Commission (NDRC)). Third is the administrative disciplining of public investment projects for cost-effectiveness and timely repayment of related loans, as project related fees, taxes, and profits become available. Fourth is Communist Party and government pressure on large firms in bottleneck sectors to fund rapid expansion of their operations. Finally, fifth, China's central bank, far from being independent, is necessarily an integral part of this quasi-public investment funding system.

At the outset of reforms in the early 1980s, virtually all Chinese finance was government-directed at one level or another. Superficial reform of the banking system and company governance in this decade in principle converted government budgetary control to autonomous decisions on use of bank loans and retained earnings. In practice, investment and labor remuneration decisions were heavily guided through the Party affiliations of leaders and managers in most financial and corporate entities. Since before the reform period, state enterprises and collectives routinely played a public investment and management role, using internal funds for infrastructure, social services, and employment maintenance as a public good. A 1980s example of a partial formal reform in this system, which in practice changed little, was the "disbursement to loan" (*bogaidai*) policy converting government budgetary disbursements for corporate activities to state bank loans supporting those same activities. Few of these "policy" loans were ever repaid, leaving them as nonperforming assets on bank balance sheets.

Important reforms in the 1990s gradually honed the use of policy lending to restrict it more narrowly to "public goods" investment lending in two very different dimensions. The first is public infrastructure—roads and railroads, urban and rural water systems, ports, airports, government offices, educational institutions, and, in a less strictly public goods sense, telecommunications backbones, electric power generation and distribution grids and other energy supply networks, especially gas and petroleum. The scale of the need for such investments was far greater than China's weak tax base and budgetary borrowing could support.

The second "public goods" component interprets economic development leadership as a public resource. Investments in this category have encouraged expansion of productive capacity more rapidly, in the opinion of government officials, than market forces would foresee as necessary or profitable—in basic industries like steel, chemicals, and telecommunications and in services like transportation, tourism, and healthcare. In many cases, the bulk of actual investment funds in these sectors came from retained earnings and other equity-related sources, but bank lending also continued to play a role.

The 1990s also strengthened the independent financial role of banks in particular by allowing them to opt out of lending for many public projects they found financially unattractive. At the same time, management of public and quasi-public expenditures continued to improve with the introduction of competitive bidding for implementation contracts on many public projects. At the same time, the same reform of state enterprises in the later 1990s that produced so many closings, mergers, and layoffs also eliminated many corporate lending obligations for state banks.

Since 2000, reform in the public dimension of China's financial system is best represented by the growing role of China's State Development Bank, created as part of banking reforms in the middle 1990s. The State Development Bank raises funds by selling bonds to state-owned commercial banks and has become a sophisticated issuer of a wide range of instruments. In addition to supporting major infrastructure projects like dams and airports, it has evolved a strategy of making numerous modest loans to many of China's municipalities and counties for a wide range of infrastructure and other public projects. Its compliance strategy has been to insist that any county or municipality that wants to receive lending for a new project must remain up-to-date on the servicing of its existing debt to the Development Bank. As a consequence, it reportedly has the healthiest balance sheet of any Chinese bank and is one of the most profitable banks in Asia.

In sum, China's publicly directed financial mechanism is an integral part of its overall financial system. Its effectiveness in large part reflects China's administratively set low deposit rates at state commercial banks—supported by the limited alternative passive investment opportunities for citizens and companies. These low deposit rates help ensure a reliable low cost flow of funds for strategic public investments, defined broadly. It is this public and quasi-public lending which arguably enables the hardware and software underpinnings of China's largely competitive profit-oriented economic expansion. Any evaluation of China's financial system and its prospects, therefore, must recognize that both market-based and government-directed dimensions are inseparable aspects, the Siamese twins as it were, of China's financial system.

3 Evaluating the Effectiveness of China's Financial System

China's two-part financial sector is open to criticisms that it allocates investment funds inefficiently. In addition, some critics write that low interest rates and government-directed credit saddle the banking system with excessive and poor quality loans, which will eventually require government-assisted workout. China's high rate of national savings—over 40% of GDP in 2005—is presented as evidence of excessive and inefficient lending.[2]

Evaluation of these criticisms and China's financial sector performance itself, however, leads to the opposite conclusion. China's financial system appears to generate a reasonably good rate of return to investment and has succeeded in sustaining over 15 years of rapid growth, with capital investment efficiency roughly equivalent to India's.

One of the crudest measures of investment effectiveness is one of the most persuasive because it is so straightforward—the incremental capital to output ratio (ICOR). This is the ratio, for any year, of (a) how much capital is contributed

---

[2] Goldstein, Morris and Nicholas R. Lardy, "What Kind of Landing for the Chinese Economy?" Policy Brief in International Economics, PB04-7, Peter G. Peterson Institute for International Economics, November 2004, http://www.iie.com/publications/pb/pb04-7.pdf

to productive processes by the end of the previous year and (b) how much additional output is generated in the current year as a result. There are a number of ways to calculate ICORs, but in low-inflation countries with relatively stable investment rates, the variations are not large. It is also important to acknowledge that ICORs can vary significantly from one year to the next because of variations in demand-induced growth, so rather than reporting individual yearly results, it is more meaningful to consider 5-, 10-, and even 15-year averages.

For China, a major factor in calculating its ICOR is to agree on an accurate real GDP growth rate. After its 2004 economic census, China revised its official growth rates for recent years, to an average annual growth rate of 9.5% for the 5-year period 2001–2005. The GDP measurement method behind these averages is known as the production method. Using a different method, the expenditure method, which is arguably more widely used internationally, the average growth for this 5-year period is either 11.9 or 12.3%, depending on data choices for household consumption.[3]

Given China's rate of investment in fixed assets as a share of GDP supporting growth in these 5 years, roughly 39%, different growth rate statistics yield different average ICORs—an ICOR of 3.9 with official growth data and an ICOR of 3.1 with expenditure account growth data. For the 15-year period 1991–2005, China's ICORs are 3.4 and 3.3 for official and expenditure methods, respectively.

These ICOR measures of overall investment efficiency are respectable. Similar calculations by the author for India,[4] with its heavily market-based financial sector, are 4.1 and 5.3, respectively, for 2001–2006 and 1991–2006. China's ratio of investment required for new output gains is thus significantly lower than India's, even though India's economic growth is based more heavily on services sectors, which are by their nature less dependent on capital investment for growth. Even if we select favorable years for India, to avoid its poor growth year of 2002–2003, India's 3-year ICOR for 2003–2006 is 3.5, roughly in the range calculated for China over longer periods.

For rapidly growing Asian economies in earlier decades, Kwan (2004) reports that Japan's ICOR in the 1960s was 3.2, while South Korea and Taiwan in the 1980s were 3.2 and 2.7, respectively.[5] To the degree that these records are better than China's, they are only marginally so.

Some research appears to dispute these results, but on closer analysis, China's respectable measures for investment efficiency hold up to scrutiny. In the same research note cited above, Kwan calculates China's ICOR for the

---

[3] For the methodologies behind these different estimates by the author, see Albert Keidel's "China's GDP Expenditure Accounts," *China Economic Review*, 12(4), 355–67 (2001).

[4] Using GDP and fixed-asset investment data from IMF, *International Financial Statistics*, various issues. Note: India uses a non-calendar, April–March, fiscal year period to report its annual economic statistics.

[5] Chi Hong Kwan, "Why China's Investment Efficiency is Low—Financial Reforms are Lagging Behind," RIETI, *China in Transition*, June 18, 2004, http://www.rieti.go.jp/en/china/04061801.html

3-year period 2001–2003 but obtains a significantly higher figure of 5.0 by using lower, pre-revision growth rates and by using a measure of investment known to be too high because it includes purchases of land and used equipment.[6] With revised official growth data and a fixed asset investment share taken from China's national accounts (that averages 35% for the relevant 3 years), China's ICOR for 2001–2003 calculates as 3.8, significantly lower than Kwan's result.

In short, by the measure of its ability to allocate investable funds in ways optimal for sustaining high speed growth over many years, China's financial system seems to have been doing its job quite well so far. A second empirical exercise, measuring the overall rate of return to investment in China, corroborates these results.

A recent National Bureau of Economic Research working paper by Bai et al., cited already,[7] calculates annual non-labor income as a percentage of China's total net accumulated capital stock and obtains a rate of return on capital that falls from 25% in 1993 to 17.5% in 2001 before rising to 21% in 2005. The authors note that even as China's share of GDP allocated to fixed asset investment rose above the 40% level in 2005, the rate of return on capital held steady. Adjusting their methodology to allow similar calculations for China and all countries in the Penn World Tables, Bai et al. report that China's rate of return to capital was higher than that for 49 other economies, that is, higher than for all but two economies in the sample.[8]

These empirical results are useful. They qualify the common theoretical impression that China's financial system must be inefficient because of government's heavy interference directing credit to infrastructure and other "strategic" projects. China's financial system is also thought to be inefficient because of the still limited role for foreign firms in its investment banking and brokerage businesses. Finally, as mentioned above, the high level of investment as a share of GDP is considered by many to be a sign of wasteful investment. Whatever the logic of these criticisms, actual developments in China's economy as reflected in overall economic performance imply that such theories require significant adjustments for a real-world economic setting such as China's.

4 Risks to China's Financial System

Given that China's financial system appears to be performing adequately, and given the current and future needs of China's economy, what are the risks that this financial system could suffer a major crisis? The cursory review below of

[6] For a more detailed description of various statistics on fixed investment in China, see Chong En Bai, Chang-Tai Hsieh, and Yingyi Qian, "The Return to Capital in China," NBER Working Paper 12755, December 2006, www.nber.org/papers/w12755, p. 9.

[7] Bai et al. (2006), cited above.

[8] Bai et al. (2006), Fig. 10.

the various dimensions of China's financial system indicates that the only significant risks of crisis would stem from policy blunders in the direction of privatizing banks and other institutions too precipitously or opening China to short-term capital inflows and outflows prematurely. In other words, many of China's non-market government interferences in financial sector operations serve in important ways to protect the system from debilitating crises such as those encountered by Mexico in the middle 1990s, non-China East Asia in 1997, Russia in 1998 and Argentina in 2001. Sector by sector treatment shows why China's risk of such crisis is extremely low—barring overly exuberant liberalizing blunders. In all these considerations, one central underpinning of China's financial system's stability is the lack of independence for its central bank, the Peoples Bank of China.

China's three development banks, created in 1994, and its postal savings bank, reconstituted in 1986, form one of the system's stablest components. Their assets are largely national infrastructure projects and officially sanctioned activities, implicitly guaranteed by local and central governments. For the postal savings system—recently converted into a state-owned bank—a large share of assets is in central bank deposits. These institutions' liabilities, with the possibly significant exception of the Export Import Development Bank, are all in domestic currency deposits and bonds so that in the case of asset quality deterioration—such as failures of local governments to repay loans in an economic slump—central bank liquidity support presents a maximum risk of inflationary pressure—which the central bank has shown more than willing to sterilize by selling its own paper. The risk of crisis from these institutions is thus virtually nonexistent.

In the area of China's financial sector risks, commercial banks have received the most attention, with a number considered technically insolvent, given the alleged poor quality of their loan portfolios. These assessments rely on statistics for nonperforming loans (NPLs) which are of questionable quality, even though the formal reporting system has been reformed from the lenient original Chinese system to one closer to international standards. The strong likelihood is that NPLs are a more serious problem than official data indicate, although several factors argue in the other direction (e.g. that some client firms do not service loans because they can get away with not doing so, or that NPLs were especially serious during the growth recession of the later 1990s, when NPLs were underreported, whereas now that corporate financials and debt service have improved, they may not be underreported any more).

The critical insight for evaluating these institutions is the realization that China's commercial banks are not really banks. Despite their initial public offerings (IPOs) and foreign strategic investors, they are basically government controlled deposit-taking institutions. The central bank, which is forbidden by the central bank law from lending directly to the state budget, appears, however, quite free to backstop all kinds of financial institutions with little regard for what happens to its own balance sheet. The quality of its assets appears to be irrelevant to China's financial system's health, and its liabilities are essentially currency in circulation, reserve deposits, and central bank bonds issued to absorb that currency when necessary. Most of the banking system is thus in effect still an extension of the central bank, which is of course in no way independent from policy makers. The high degree of continued government ownership and control is in effect a limitless pool of contingent assets hidden in the books of these so-called banks. This is not a system at risk for financial failure.

In addition to the major state-owned commercial banks, China's banking system contains numerous "second tier" mid-sized specialized and "share holding" banks as well as relatively small urban cooperative banks. In terms of risks posed by the creation of new NPLs during the recent 2002–2004 surge in bank lending, these secondary banks, especially the relatively young urban cooperative banks, were the most irresponsible—not the large "big four" state commercial banks.

Risks associated with poor management of these other, second and third tier, banks have an interesting twist. The government might indeed allow one or more of these to fail. China's central bank governor has publicly stated that this would be a possibility. By stripping all equity stakes from "owners" of such a poorly managed bank—while compensating depositors or transferring their claims to other banks—bank regulators and the central bank could discipline the entire second tier banking community by weakening the moral hazard associated with confidence on the part of many of these firms that they would not be allowed to fail. Rather than precipitating a crisis, engineered failure of one or more such institutions would be a major step forward in market-based banking reform.

Chinese formal domestic bond markets consist largely of exchanges in the negotiable share of treasury bills outstanding, certain large corporation company bonds, sale of paper by specialized banks, including the central bank and development banks, to commercial banks, and experimental sale of renminbi (RMB) denominated paper by international institutions like the International Finance Corporation and the Asian Development Bank. With the exception of a few issuances by the Ministry of Finance (MOF) of longer term treasury bills, there is little long-term basis for determining a Chinese yield curve, and in any event, prices on what secondary markets there are find themselves subject to direct and indirect government supervision.

The main reason that China's bond markets are so underdeveloped is the bad reputation of bonds and bond issuers in China's recent decades. Failure to honor both corporate bonds and local government bonds irritated not only the purchasers but also the central bank, which in general helped make good on such losses. In general, therefore, China's bond market is immature for good reason and is likely to develop slowly as a share of financial intermediation. In the absence of crisis prone bond transaction patterns, such as the large-scale economy-wide issuance of high yielding junk bonds to support risky real estate or other investments, bond markets are unlikely to become the source of significant financial risk for a decade or more.

China's stock markets, like its bond markets, are immature and hampered by poor information about listed companies, in spite of government efforts to administratively select the candidates best qualified for listing. China's stock markets in 2006 enjoyed a recovery after a several-year slump induced by failed efforts to resolve one of the markets' most problematic aspects. For most listed firms, the shares that are openly traded on the market have generally been only a subset of shares outstanding. The overhang of "nontraded" shares, once government indicated they might become traded, dampened prices until early 2006, when a new approach promised to chip away at, if not eliminate, the overhang without undermining shareholder equity values.

Recent IPOs have indicated that a second shortcoming is still serious—underpricing of IPO issues to provide a windfall to those with access to pre-IPO purchase options. For many years Chinese stock market clients used the markets more as a gambling mechanism or get-rich-quick vehicle, since those with privileged access to underpriced initial offerings frequently saw the prices of their assets jump considerably on the first day of trading. China's stock markets thus still cannot and are not taken seriously as well-functioning financial institutions. The most fundamental reason remains that information about the listing companies is still too unreliable to support a well-functioning market. With stock markets' place in the economy still so thin, its fortunes will not be in a position to influence a countrywide crisis for at least a decade. One illustration of its essential insignificance is the abysmal performance of the market up to early 2006, while the overall economy boomed.

Finally, the array of institutional investors in China is large and growing, from insurance companies to pension funds to trust companies, finance companies, and mutual funds. Many institutions and practices are in their infancy, such as mutual funds and qualified domestic/foreign institutional investor schemes (QDIIs and QFIIs). Many larger institutions, such as insurance companies, are also state-owned or state-controlled. Others, such as certain pension funds, have had little chance to accumulate assets, remaining pay-as-you-go systems with no major role in financial activities. Finally, some, like large international trust and investment companies, are on the fringes of legality by borrowing or accepting investments from abroad while investing domestically. The quality picture for many of these institutions is mixed, but none of them is large enough or poorly enough operated to represent a major risk of financial crisis any time soon. Trust and investment companies (TICs), especially those engaged in international transactions, could threaten crisis because of obligations denominated in foreign currencies, but China's management of the Guangdong international TIC failure during the 1997–1998 Asian financial crisis showed that a nimble, if uncodified, regulatory arrangement is potentially operational.

In short, because of the heavily regulated nature of China's short-term international capital flows, the major risks posed by one or another institutional failing are virtually all denominated in local currency. The real risk of a local currency crisis would thus only become significant if government unwisely tried to privatize a major bank while its balance sheet still relied on the contingent assets represented by government control and central bank accommodation. Such privatization would be a major blunder any time in the coming decade, and such complete privatization is indeed not likely for several decades.

The second major risk to China's financial system would emerge from a too early opening up to short-term capital flows. Without adequate internal controls in corporations and financial institutions, and without effective regulatory bodies to ensure operational discipline for such internal controls, freeing up capital flows would expose the economy to the all but irresistible temptation to borrow internationally on terms denominated in foreign currencies at rates that looked attractive because they did not include foreign exchange risks. China's exchange markets and relatively small, and vulnerable capital markets would find themselves exposed to the kind of one-two punch of speculative surges in and out of both markets that Hong Kong endured during the Asian financial crisis of 1997. China's domestic enterprises have many years if not decades to go before their internal controls have matured, and regulatory agencies need both to consolidate their functions and significantly strengthen their oversight capabilities. Until these tasks are completed, opening the capital account to unmanaged short-term flows would invite a crisis. In sum, barring major policy blunders privatizing large state banks or liberalizing international capital flows, the risk of financial crisis in China is remote.

5 Current Reforms and China's Ultimate Finance Challenge

As introduced briefly at the outset of this essay, China's financial system, in two parts, has undergone rapid change in recent decades, and especially in the last 12 years. With the completion in early 2007 of China's most recent once in 5 years national financial reform work conference, the current reform emphasis has shifted clearly in several directions that point to a long-term phasing out of government-directed finance in favor of a more commercially oriented system. The communiqué from the conference outlined a number of steps which, with some exceptions, emphasized continuity with past reforms rather than a sudden or dramatic new departure.[9]

For example, emphasis on preparing the last of China's "big four" commercial banks, the Agricultural Bank of China (ABC), for stock market listing is a continuation of the process begun in 2003, when China's cabinet, the State Council, announced its intention to convert all of the big four banks to stock share governance systems. ABC has by far the worst balance sheet in the big four, so listing will require lengthy preparation.This meeting emphasized the continuation of this reform direction.

---

[9] Based on New China News Agency (Xinhua) reports on-line, January 20, 2007: http://news.xinhuanet.com/politics/2007-01/20/content_5630446.htm in Chinese.

Most interesting, perhaps, from a system reform perspective, is the work conference's decision to begin the introduction of commercial banking operations, but not deposit taking, for the State Development Bank (SDB), the largest of China's three development banks.While the adjustment will apparently start gradually, SDB will begin making commercial loans to for-profit enterprises, although the bulk of its business will continue to be infrastructure and other public projects, and it will continue to raise funds through its state-of-the-art (for China) bond issuances.But reform directions for the SDB, ABC, and related Agricultural Development Bank (ADB) indicate the very long-term goal of commercializing most of China's current two-part financial system.

In this regard, an extension of the ABC's reform is the work conference's additional emphasis on reform of all rural credit systems, especially rural credit cooperatives (RCCs), which despite the launch of major reforms in 2004 still face a severely underpatronized rural client base where the potential for micro-credit and other appropriate instruments is seen as an important vehicle for reviving the rural economy—and by so doing assist China's poverty-level households and an ambitious priority program to construct a "new rural community." RCCs were effectively bankrupt throughout the country at the end of the 1990s, and accelerated RCC reform is a natural development in pursuing a long-term goal of commercializing rural credit in ways that contribute to rural households and firms' commercial viability.

Many other aspects of the financial sector program going forward represent both continuity and long-term preparations for commercialization of the system. The 2007 work conference stressed its emphasis on building and strengthening all aspects of capital markets, but especially corporate bond markets, in part by increasing transparency and strengthening regulatory capabilities. The meeting also stressed strengthening international competition—a clear priority given the December 2006 coming into force of WTO accession requirements granting national treatment to foreign banks operating in China. But goals in this category also include stronger commercial operations in foreign exchange markets and more capital account opening—presumably through QDIIs and QFIIs.

Finally, the 2007 workshop results mentioned the need to achieve rough balance in international payments, and they encouraged further reforms in interest rates (such as for deposits, loans, and interbank activity) and improvements to monetary policy mechanisms. All these programs conform to a pattern stressing gradually increased commercialization of the whole system.

The outcome of China's 2007 financial work conference thus directs attention to what is China's ultimate financial sector challenge. At some point, China will have had to have dismantled its government-directed credit apparatus and have in place, ready to step to the fore, a mature and competitive modern financial sector. This means, in the best of all worlds, that the structure and partially mature dimensions of the eventual modern commercial system must continue to take shape and gain experience while the government-directed dimension continues to improve the way it carries out its essential functions of funding public and other strategic projects on a scale and at a pace that a private commercial system could never accomplish.

The final conversion to a fully commercial system is more than 20 years away and possibly more than 30 years, according to opinions of knowledgeable Hong Kong financial specialists. In the meantime, the question is not whether China's financial system can catch up with the rest of the economy but how it can continue to do the job of underpinning its success as it gradually grooms its replacement—a fully commercialized financial system for the middle of this century.

Part II
Monetary Policy and the Foreign Exchange Market

Monetary Policy Implementation in China: Past, Present, and Prospects

Bernard J. Laurens and Rodolfo Maino

Abstract While much has already been achieved, monetary policy implementation in China is still in transition. The effectiveness of the current framework, which still relies intensively on rules-based measures, is likely to diminish over time as the sophistication of the economy increases. The authorities are faced with the following challenges: (i) the choice of a nominal anchor; (ii) the choice of an operating target; (iii) the choice of operating instruments; and (iv) the right timing to introduce greater flexibility of the exchange rate. This chapter reviews the framework for monetary policy implementation in China by summarizing the practice of monetary policy over the past 30 years and by discussing the way forward.

Keywords Monetary policy formulation · Monetary policy implementation · Financial sector reforms

Since China embarked on a gradual but far-reaching reform of its economic system back in 1978, monetary policy implementation by the People's Bank of China (PBC), under the leadership of the CPC Central Committee and the State Council, has faced tremendous challenges. In particular, when the Communist Party formally embraced the view that the market system was not incompatible with the ideals of socialism and proclaimed the idea of establishing a "socialist market economy" the tasks at hand have involved establishing the institutional and operational frameworks that would allow the PBC to rely on market-based instruments for the conduct of monetary policy. It has involved not only building capacity at the PBC central bank but also undertaking the structural reforms that are needed for market-based allocation of financial resources to be effective and to work smoothly. For the PBC, it has also meant modernizing its strategic and

Opinions in the paper are those of the authors.

B.J. Laurens (✉)
International Monetary Fund, Washington, D.C., USA
e-mail: blaurens@imf.org

J.R. Barth et al. (eds.), *China's Emerging Financial Markets*,
The Milken Institute Series on Financial Innovation and Economic Growth 8,
DOI 10.1007/978-0-387-93769-4_4, © 2009 by Milken Institute

operating frameworks at different stages of market development (Box 1). Hence, an evaluation of the progress achieved in establishing market-based operating procedures and frameworks for monetary policy conduct, as well as scope for further modernization, needs to take into account the overall policy environment, including macroeconomic conditions, market participation limitations, and institutional constraints. In the remainder of this chapter, we review the circumstances which provide the backdrop for monetary policy implementation in China; we review the practice of monetary policy; and we discuss the way forward.

Box 1 Monetary policy implementation at different states of market development

Central bankers around the world generally agree on the benefits of using market-based monetary policy instruments. Following a trend initiated in the 1970s in industrial countries, central banks in most developing countries and emerging market economies have attempted to regulate overall liquidity conditions in the economy through financial operations in the domestic money markets. The objective of these central banks has been to influence the underlying demand and supply conditions for central bank money. The move was parallel in the monetary area of the trend toward enhancing the role of price signals in the economy in general. It aimed at improving domestic savings mobilization and strengthening their market allocation.

The process was not without difficulties in countries that did not succeed in developing their money markets. Country experiences show that the timing and speed of moving toward reliance on money market operations must be tailored to country's circumstances. A stylized sequencing can be mapped into successive stages, including (i) establishing key functions in those areas where a central bank typically has responsibilities; (ii) reliance on rules-based instruments (i.e., instruments based on the regulatory power of the central bank, such as reserve requirements, or deposit, or refinance facilities available to the banks on demand, under certain preset conditions) in view of limited market development; (iii) fostering interbank market development and introducing money market (i.e., market-based) operations, while rules-based instruments retain an important role; and (iv) full reliance on money market instruments.

Source: Laurens (2005).

1 Backdrop For Monetary Policy Implementation In China

China's macroeconomic and financial sector attributes have shaped monetary policy implementation by the PBC since it adopted the functions of a central bank back in 1984. As China moved from a centrally planned economic system to one where market forces are called to play the dominant role in financial resources, operating procedures for monetary policy implementation have been adjusted in a gradual fashion, consistent with a distinctive characteristic of China's approach to economic reforms.[1] However, some 15 years after the November 1993 milestone decision of the Third Plenum, interest rates in China are not yet fully liberalized.[2] Such a situation reflects the still unfinished agenda of the transformation of the centrally planned economy.

What are the macroeconomic and financial sector attributes which provide the backdrop for monetary policy implementation in the recent period? Regarding *macroeconomic attributes*, China is still struggling with what the economic literature has qualified as the "Inconsistency Triangle" hypothesis, which illustrates the impossibility of maintaining a fixed exchange rate regime, free capital flows, and an independent monetary policy. China's current main challenge is associated with the implementation of a tightly managed exchange rate system in the face of large foreign exchange inflows. The ensuing policy dilemma is complicating reliance on interest rates to manage aggregate demand, as policy tightening may result in larger capital inflows. Reliance on administrative controls to restrain credit and investment growth has helped deflect some of the pressure, and it has provided some monetary policy autonomy, which can be taken advantage of to keep low interest rates. However, the restrictions have opened the door for informal credit markets to flourish and for real interest rates to increase. Rules-based and administrative measures will have an impact on the SME sector and become less effective as the grip of the state on the financial sector decreases and trade-related foreign exchange flows develop. Eventually, despite extensive capital controls, de facto capital mobility may undermine the sustainability of the policy mix.[3]

Indeed, strong external sector performance and capital inflows, and the policy of keeping the nominal exchange rate stable, have resulted in sharp increases in monetary aggregates. Large-scale sterilization operations (and recourse to administrative controls and lending guidance, as elaborated below) have allowed the PBC to control the growth of banks' excess reserves and avoid high inflation. The PBC was also able to contain the cost of

---

1 See in particular Mehran, Quintyn, Nordman and Laurens (1996).

2 The Third Plenary Session of the 14th Central Committee of the Communist Party of China laid down the goals of establishing a socialist market economy, hence allowing the market to play a decisive role in resource allocation (see Mehran et al., 1996). In December 1993, the State Council indicated that the goal of the monetary policy is to maintain the stability of the value of the currency and thereby promote economic growth, ending a period during which it pursued the dual goals of currency stability and economic development.

3 The growing openness of the Chinese economy and the liberalized current account will make it increasingly difficult to insulate the economy from international financial markets. In particular, leads and lags in trade payments and remittances can be a channel for circumventing capital controls. Ma and McCauley (2005) suggest that capital controls in China have been rather leaky, leading to nonforeign direct investment capital flows in response to relative yields as well as currency expectations.

sterilization operations thanks to capital controls as well as moral suasion in the placement of its sterilization instruments and, until the most recent period, the PBC was able to issue its securities (hence mop up liquidity from the system) at interest rates that have been lower than the average return on its international reserves. However, rapid credit growth and sharp increases in real estate prices have been areas of concern. The combination of these events is making it increasingly difficult to simultaneously maintain a closely managed exchange rate regime, cope with capital inflows, and pursue an independent monetary policy.

The policy steps followed for the transformation of China's financial sector (Box 2) aimed at strengthening the efficient allocation of resources in the economy. While considerable progress was achieved, the *financial sector attributes* are those of a sector in transition, First, commercial banks dominate the financial sector, and equity and bond markets are relatively underdeveloped.[4] Second, banks are growing at a fast pace due to the high saving rate, depositor confidence, and the lack of other investment vehicles and instruments. Third, while the banks underwent a gradual transition toward market principles and measures have been taken to modernize and restructure the large state-owned banks, the stability of the sector is yet to be firmly ensured, and it will take time before fundamental changes of behavior can take root.[5] Several issues deserve to be underlined in that regard. Overall, financial resources allocation appears to be suboptimal. Wholly and partially state-owned companies continue to absorb most of the funding from the financial system, while private enterprises which account for 52% of GDP, receive only 27% of the total credit. Furthermore, a low equity market capitalization and a small number of corporate bond issues inhibit funding to large private companies and productive infrastructure projects, thus resulting in a misallocation of capital.[6] Regarding commercial banks' financial position, although China has raised the minimum capital requirement for banks since 2004, it remains below that of other countries in the region (Fig. 1). Banks' earnings, before extraordinary items and taxes, are also below some other Asian economies as a percentage of total assets (Fig. 1). Nonperforming loans (NPLs) in the banking sector have declined markedly since 2005 to current estimates of 6% of total loans, although some financial analysts place the NPLs ratio at a much higher level.

[4] Commercial banks intermediate about $^3/_4$ of the capital in the economy (McKinsey Global Institute 2006). For the first three quarters of 2007, bank loans represented more than 80% of the volume of financing, equities 8% and corporate bonds 3% (PBC, Q3 2007 Monetary Policy Report).

[5] Evidence that the state-owned banks have substantially changed their behavior and become market oriented is unclear; see Karacadag (2003), Barnett (2004) and Podpiera (2006).

[6] McKinsey Global Institute (2006) suggests that China's investment efficiency has declined: investment needed to produce US$1.00 of GDP increased from US$3.30 in the first half of the 1990s to US$4.90 since 2001 (40% more than required by other Asian emerging market economies).

Box 2 Key Policy Steps in the Transformation of China's Financial Sector

Inflationary pressures that emerged in 1985 led to a stabilization program in early 1988 (the "rectification program"), in which stabilization was given priority, and the so-called theory of "harmless inflation" that had been influential fell out of favor among Chinese policy makers. During that time, the two-tier banking system that had been established at the end of the 1970s was strengthened.

Following the next round of inflation, starting in 1993, the third plenary session of the 14th CPC Central Committee outlined and approved a comprehensive reform strategy in which financial reforms are mentioned as a key element to strengthen the capability for market-oriented macroeconomic management. In December 1993, the State Council indicated that the goal of monetary policy is to maintain the stability of the value of the currency and thereby promote economic growth, ending a period during which it pursued the dual goals of currency stability and economic development.

Through the 1990s, China's banking sector's main challenge was to strengthen its "credit culture," which suffered from policy lending (i.e., lending on the basis of administrative interventions) and the so-called "relationship-based lending" (i.e., lending based on the personal relationships between enterprises managers and banks). Enhancing China's credit culture was long and difficult. A key step on this path was the nation's first National Financial Work Conference held in November 1997, which set out a "vertical management" system for the commercial banks, whereby central and local governments were prohibited from interfering with loan decisions.

At the end of the 1990s, nonperforming loans (NPLs) in the banking system stood at 25%, although international accounting standards would have put them at above 40%, and a number of banks were technically insolvent. Such poor performance contributed to buttressing China's resolve to restructure the sector. In February 2002, at the second National Financial Work Conference, plans were made to strengthen financial supervision, and in 2003 the China Banking Regulatory Commission (CBRC) was established. It was also decided to kick off a new round of reforms on the commercial banks, clean up bank balance sheets, and proceed with financial restructuring, with a view to make the major commercial banks financially sound. Consequently, significant progress has been made in reforming China's banking sector. While it may be too early to evaluate the impact of these reforms on banks' behavior, some of the large state-owned banks seem to have developed internal controls able to slow the creation of new NPLs (Podpiera, 2006).

Sources: Mehran et al. (1996), Podpiera (2006), and Zhou (2008).

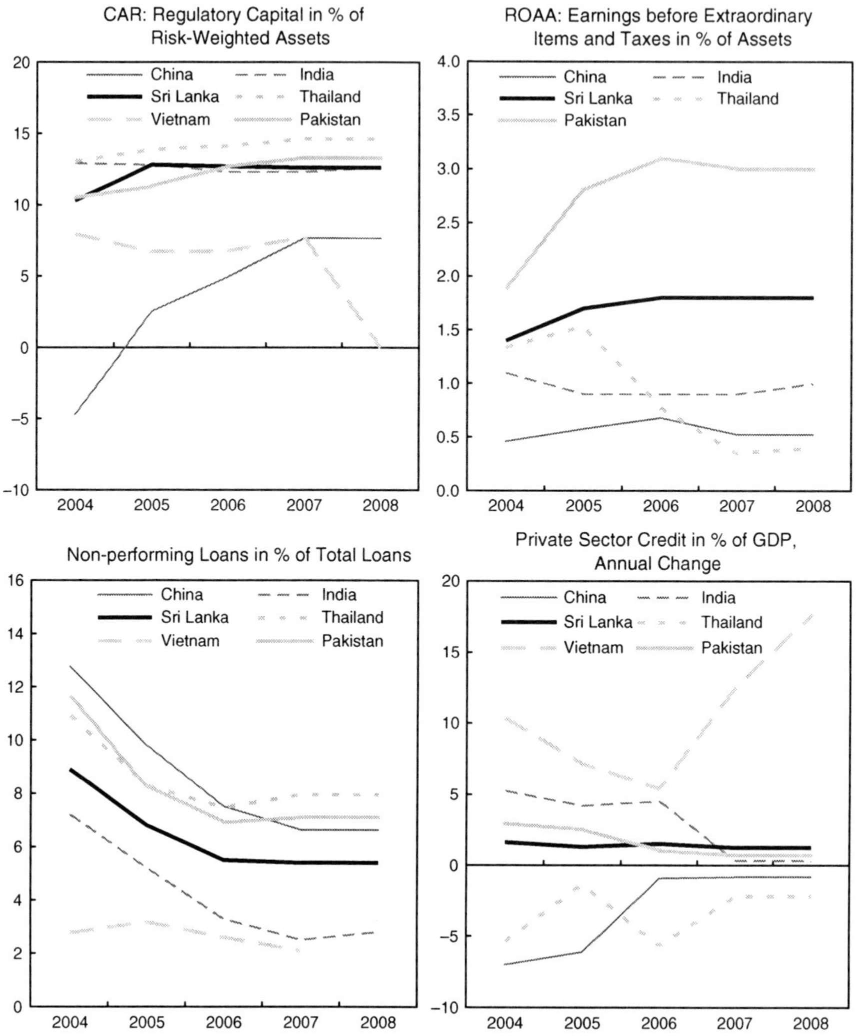

Fig. 1. Vulnerability indicators amongst selected Asian economies

Table 1 China: development of capital market and direct financing, 2005–2007

	Volume of financing (RMB billions)			As a percentage of total financing (%)		
	2005	2006	2007	2005	2006	2007
Bank loans	2462	3269	3921	76.0	78.1	71.7
Commercial papers	473	250	229	14.6	6.0	4.2
A Shares	34	151	591	1.0	3.6	10.8
Trust & designed loans	69	289	512	2.1	6.9	9.4
Corporate bonds	201	227	218	6.2	5.4	4.0
Total	3239	4186	5470	100.0	100.0	100.0

Source: PBC.

Recently, against the backdrop provided by low interest rates and increased stock prices, households and firms have tended to invest in stock and mutual fund markets, thereby relatively decreasing the amounts allocated to deposits and bonds (Table 1).

The still unfinished agenda of economic transformation from the formerly centrally planned to the market-based economy, as illustrated by China's macroeconomic and financial sectors attributes, has important implications for monetary policy implementation. Following the staged approach discussed above in Box 1, China cannot yet rely fully on market-based instruments, and rules-based instruments have retained an important role. On the other hand, greater reliance on market forces in the allocation of financial resources would be highly desirable, even necessary, to speed up the restructuring of the remnants of the "old" economic system. Therefore, the monetary authorities have to strike a balance, which means applying judgment and taking measured risks.

2 China's Practice of Monetary Policy: Past and Present

China's monetary policy in the last three decades has involved reliance on monetary targeting which has been implemented with increasing flexibility, and the PBC has introduced market-based monetary policy instruments, but it has continued to rely a great deal on rules-based and administrative measures for systemic liquidity management.

2.1 The Practice of Monetary Targeting in China

Until the late 1980s, China relied on a centrally planned economic system. In 1986, it moved to a monetary strategy anchored on intermediate monetary targets. During the period 1986–1993, targets on currency and on banks' loan portfolios were adopted as intermediate targets.[7] A second phase began in September 1994 when the PBC announced money supply indicators for M0, M1, and M2. In 1996, it formally treated money supply as an intermediary target. A third phase started in 1998 when the credit ceilings were eliminated, leaving M2 as the single intermediate target. At the beginning of the year the PBC typically announces the expected growth for M2 which would be in line with its inflation objective (Table 2). During the year, the growth of monetary and credit aggregates is closely monitored and deviations from the expected outcome for money and inflation may prompt a change in the monetary policy stance. However, the PBC does not attempt to meet the announced expected objective for M2. Under that framework, inflation and growth are the final targets, and monetary aggregates are used as information variables, together with other economic indicators, such as growth of credit and investment.

---

[7] During that period, monetary policy was aimed at achieving the dual goals of currency stability and promoting economic development. In December 1993, the State Council established that the goals of monetary policy were to maintain the stability of the value of the currency and thereby promote economic growth.

Table 2 China: targeted and actual values for monetary aggregates, 1994–2004

	M1 growth (in percent y/y)		M2 growth (in percent y/y)	
Year	Target	Actual	Target	Actual
1994	21	26.2	24	34.5
1995	21–23	16.8	23–25	29.5
1996	18	18.9	25	25.3
1997	18	16.5	23	17.3
1998	17	11.9	16–18	15.3
1999	14	17.7	14–15	14.7
2000	15–17	16.0	14–15	12.3
2001	13–14	12.7	15–16	14.4
2002	13	16.8	13	16.8
2003	16	18.7	16	19.6
2004	17	13.6	17	14.6
2005	15	11.8	15	17.6
2006	14	17.5	14	16.9
2007		21.0	16	16.7

Source: Geiger (2006) and PBC.

Inflation in China has been remarkably low and stable but has recently picked up significantly since 2005. A quantitative analysis of inflation helps highlight the following features:

- Higher growth rates for M1 and M2 during the period 2004–2008 correspond to higher inflation, suggesting that money remains a valid indicator of inflationary pressures (Fig. 2).
- The volatility of inflation has generally been low (Fig. 2). Furthermore, recent shocks to inflation have been relatively short-lived.[8]

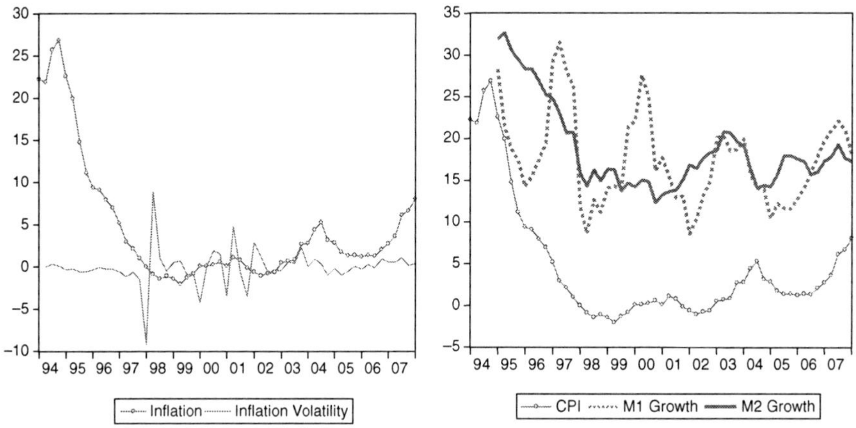

Fig. 2. China: inflation and money growth, 1994–2008 (in percent)

[8] Autoregressive models show that the sum of the coefficients for AR(1) and AR(2) is about 1, suggesting that the half-life of inflation shocks is about 2–3 quarters.

- Inflation in China is correlated with both the nominal effective exchange rate and output. The contemporaneous correlation between quarterly inflation and the nominal exchange rate, in recent times, is relatively high (–0.8), thus suggesting that nominal appreciations of the exchange rate materialize concomitantly with lower inflation.
- Based on Granger causality tests, we cannot reject the hypothesis that the nominal exchange rate does not Granger cause inflation, but we do reject the hypothesis that inflation does not Granger cause the exchange rate. Hence, it seems that that Granger causality runs one-way from inflation to the exchange rate and not the other way, thereby suggesting that the pass-through from the exchange rate to inflation is low and operates with a long lag. Appendix 1 advances a more accurate analysis of the degree of exchange rate pass-through to consumer prices.

Quantitative effects of monetary policy in China are studied using a structural vector autoregresion (SVAR) presented in Appendix 2. Some of the findings include the following:

- Output shocks have a strong positive impact on the consumer price index (CPI).
- An increase in M1 has a statistically significant effect on prices for almost a year, thereby underscoring the rationale for a greater focus on monetary aggregates as intermediate targets.
- An interest rate increase has the expected (negative) result on output, although the response is statistically insignificant at the 5% level.
- Changes in oil prices are statistically significant at the 5% level and persistent.

Changes in monetary aggregates have not behaved in a similar pattern with the inflation rate (Fig. 2). Moreover, as inflation pressures are diminishing, the informative role of monetary aggregates like M1 and M2 has fallen. Estrella and Mishkin (1997) argue that it is because of the noise caused by velocity shocks and the instability of money demand that arises from structural changes in financial systems. However, plotting both monetary aggregates by using a Kernel graph against the inflation rate (Fig. 3) shows that the association between inflation and M1 and M2 is high when the inflation rate is also high. In particular, at lower inflation rates the relation between money and inflation loses its strength (i.e., in the short run the relationship may not be stable).

While closely monitored by the PBC, so far, concerns about asset price changes have not been referred to for rationalizing a change in the monetary policy stance. The PBC seem to have taken the view, shared by most central banks, that asset prices should not be a target for monetary policy. Nevertheless, asset prices should be monitored with a view to assess whether such movements bring about inflationary or deflationary pressures to the overall economy. Contrary to most central banks, the PBC has at its disposal tools to respond to what it may consider disorderly movements in asset prices, such as

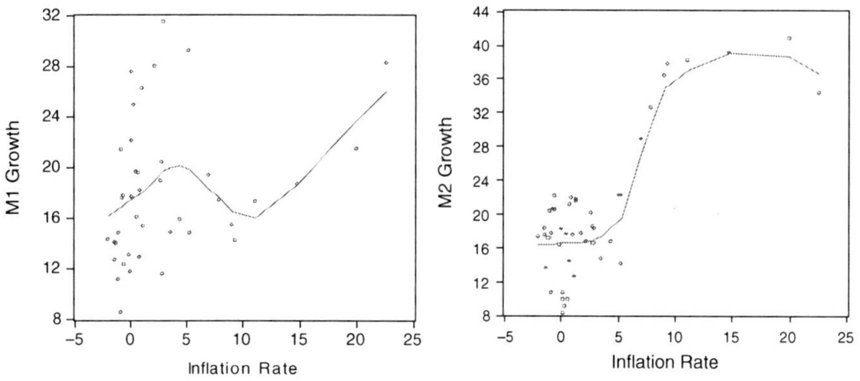

Fig. 3. China: inflation and money growth—Kernel graph, 1994–2008 (in percent)
Source: International Financial Statistics and authors' calculations.

regulations on the minimum share of down payments on mortgages, or limitations on the ability of securities houses to get funding on the interbank market.[9]

2.2 *Systemic Liquidity Management in China*

Monetary and exchange system reforms in China have emphasized institution building at the PBC, as well as financial markets development, so that the PBC can rely on interest rates as the operating target of monetary policy. Although the PBC has developed a full range of monetary instruments, and nationwide money and foreign exchange markets have been established, interest rates have not yet fully liberalized, and monetary policy still relies primarily on rules-based instruments and administrative measures.

2.2.1 Monetary Policy Instruments

The PBC has developed a set of monetary instruments broadly consistent with international practice (Box 3). These instruments have been used to prevent a build up of excess reserves in the system (which in turn could have led to inflationary pressures) that could have resulted from the massive injection of liquidity in the system as a consequence of the massive purchases of foreign exchange by the PBC. The large-scale sterilization operations took the form of

[9] In March 2005, the PBC eliminated the preferential interest rate on housing loans and it raised the down payment on consumer housing loans from 20 to 30% in cities and areas where real estate prices are considered to be rising too fast. In June 2006, banks were allowed to lend only 70% of house value, down from 80%. Regarding stock market prices, the ability of securities houses to get interbank funding is more restrictive than for other financial institutions (see below, section on China's interbank market).

open market operations (issuance of PBC bills and of repurchase operations) and extensive and growing reliance on reserve requirements.[10] The cost of sterilization was contained because of the large share of sterilization through reserve requirements which are remunerated at below market prices (currently 1.89%, compared to 4% on PBC bills), and a positive differential between foreign and domestic money market rates, although in the aftermath of the sub-prime crisis in the United States, domestic rates have started to trend above US rates. In addition to the opportunity cost of reserve requirements, the cost of this policy for China's banks has been particular high when banks' deposit rates have been kept above money market or PBC bills rates (Fig. 4). Lending and deposit rates seem to be disconnected from short-term interbank rates during the period under consideration.

Box 3 Main monetary policy instruments in some globalized economies

China	**Standing facilities (SFs):** The PBC operates two SFs whereby banks can obtain automatic collateralized lending (ACL) from the PBC at the rediscount rate minus 27 bps, and an excess reserves facility (ERR) whereby banks' excess reserves are remunerated at a below market rate. **Open market operations (OMO)** were introduced in 1993, discontinued in 1997, and re-introduced in May 1998 in the form of outright transactions on bonds, later replaced by repurchase transactions. In June 2002, the PBC started using reverse t-bonds repos to cope with forex inflows. In September 2002, when it ran out of t-bonds, the PBC started to auction its own bills. OMOs are conducted several times a week through a primary dealer system. In December 2005, the PBC made an experimental use of foreign exchange swaps; however it emphasized the anecdotal nature of these transactions. **Reserve requirements (RRs):** The ratio was reduced from a peak of 13–8% in March 1998, and to 6% in November 1999. In 2003 and 2004, the PBC raised the ratio to 7 and 7.5%. In April 2004, the PBC adopted a differentiated system: banks with capital adequacy ratios or asset quality below certain standards have to hold higher required reserves. The RRs ratio was raised three times in 2006 (in June, August and

[10] The supply of liquidity resulting from foreign exchange purchases was sterilized in the range of 80–90% over the period 2003–2007. At end 2007, central bank bills amounted to 3.5 trillion yuan, to which is to be added 0.6 trillion of repo operations, compared to a sterilization of liquidity through reserve requirements of about 4.3 trillion yuan (see, PBC, *Financial Work of the PBC Since 2003*, March 2008).

	November), 10 times in 2007 (January, February, twice in April, May, July, September, October, November and December), and 6 during the first semester of 2008 (January, March, April, May and twice in June) to the current levels of 17.5% (a lower ratio applies to rural credit cooperatives to encourage finance to the rural economy). RRs are remunerated at an unchanged rate of 1.89% since 1998.
	Interest rates controls have been dismantled except for a mechanism whereby banks are subject to a ceiling on their deposit rates and a floor on their lending rates. In 2006, the PBC has increased twice (in April and August) the benchmark loan rates and once the benchmark deposit rates (in August). In 2007, it raised the benchmark loan and deposit rates 6 times (March, May, July, August, September and December).
	Administrative measures: *Window guidance* on credit growth and sectoral allocation is used, which appears to involve lending volume guidelines. Some have argued that it has been a fairly successful instrument because the governor of the PBC, in charge of implementing it, is a higher-ranking official than those at commercial banks. The PBC has also at times issued *special central bank bills* (i.e., not voluntary or market-based) to banks with relatively rapid credit growth and ample liquidity.
HK SAR	**Sales and purchases of Hong Kong dollars** for US dollars when the HK$/US$ exchange rate reaches the weak (strong) side convertibility undertaking, respectively, under the Linked Exchange Rate System to prevent the HK$ from moving outside the trading band. The weak (strong) side convertibility undertaking is 7.85 (7.75) HK$/US$.
	Discount Window: Banks can borrow Hong Kong dollar funds overnight through repurchase agreements using Exchange Fund paper as collateral. The discount rate on the first half of the bank's holdings of the Exchange Fund paper is the maximum of 150 bps over the US Federal Funds rate target and the average five-day moving average of the overnight and 1-month HIBOR rates. The rate on the remaining Exchange Fund paper is the maximum of 500 bps above this rate, and the daily overnight HIBOR rate.
Singapore	**Open market operations:** daily using short-term money market instruments with fixed tenors: SGS repos/reverse repos; FX swaps/reverse swaps; and direct borrowing/lending.
	Standing facilities: end of day liquidity facility (2% over 1-month SIBOR); intra-day liquidity facility; borrowing and

	lending rates (+/– 50 basis points of reference rate, equal to weighted average of dealer bids for overnight deposits).
	Other: 3% Minimum Cash Balance, unremunerated, with 2-week averaging provisions between 2 and 4%. Foreign exchange interventions (aimed at maintaining the currency within an unannounced trade-weighted band).
India	**Open market operations:** Market stabilization bonds (91-day to 1 year); overnight liquidity adjustment facility.
	Liquidity adjustment facility: repo and reverse repo operations (overnight).
	Other: 7.5% Cash Reserve Ratio, to be fully met on a weekly basis; at least 70% of the requirement also has be met on a daily basis; foreign exchange intervention (aimed at smoothing volatility).
	Sources: PBC (2008) and Kramer et al. (2008).

Overall, the PBC was able to achieve its immediate objectives, as evidenced by gradual reduction of banks' excess reserves (Fig. 5), although this result was achieved at the price of higher reserve requirements, particularly in the most recent period. It is noteworthy in particular that the trend toward a reduction of the combined required and excess reserves in the early 2000s was discontinued starting in 2003. In any case, while the sterilization policy cannot tackle

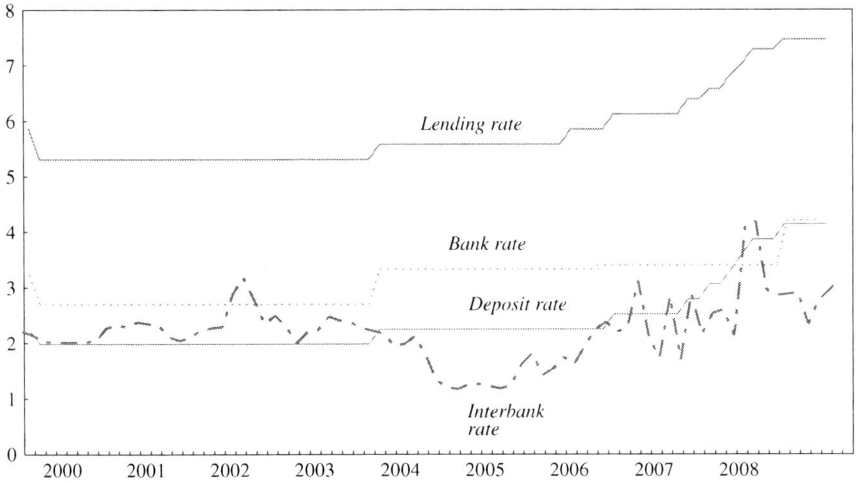

Fig. 4. China: structure of interest rates, 2000–2007
Source: IMF, International Financial Statistics, and PBC.

Fig. 5 China: required and excess reserves (December 2000–March 2008)
Source: PBC, Quarterly Monetary Policy Reports.

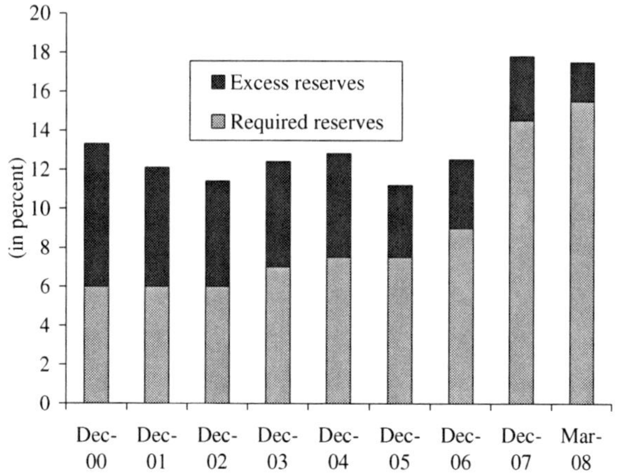

the root cause of the excess liquidity, it has helped create a relatively stable monetary and financial environment for economic growth and structural adjustments.[11]

Yet, increased reliance on reserves requirements (during the period January 2007–June 2008, the reserve ratio has been raised 16 times) suggests that the PBC is finding it harder to reconcile all its objectives, and the cost of maintaining a managed exchange rate and an independent monetary policy are mounting. During the period 2000–2006, commercial banks were able to satisfy increasing levels of required reserves by lowering their excess reserves. In the subsequent periods, higher required reserves became binding as excess reserves had reached lower levels and could probably not be reduced further.[12] The greater role assigned to window and credit policy guidance that was introduced in 1998, at the time when the PBC eliminated bank-by-bank credit ceilings, is another indication of the increasing policy dilemma faced by the PBC. This instrument became "institutionalized" starting in June 2003, when the PBC published a notice aimed at curbing the expansion of real estate lending, and its usage is reported in the PBC Quarterly Reports. Enhancing the role of price signals in the economy calls for reduced reliance on rules-based measures and greater reliance on market-based operations, as has been the case in other globalized economies in Asia (Box 3).

[11] See *Monetary Policy Report*, People's Bank of China, 2008 Q1.

[12] If reserve requirements are changed frequently and without warning, banks will have s greater incentive to hold excess reserves to use as a buffer and to invent substitutes for deposits that are not subject to this uncertain imposition. Hence, the money multiplier may become less sensitive to variations in reserve requirements, and the link to ultimate targets will be weakened.

2.2.2 Money and Foreign Exchange Markets Development

In the mid-1990s, the development of nationwide money market became a priority in order to enhance monetary policy effectiveness and strengthen the foreign exchange market. Currently, China's money market is made of three main sub-markets. The first component is the *interbank market*, where banks lend funds among themselves from overnight to 4 months. Trading is concentrated in the one- to seven-day range; the seven-day loan rate is the CHIBOR market's benchmark. The *interbank bond market*, now the largest bond market, is the second component of the money market where the PBC bills are traded. This is a liquid market, supported by the constant supply of PBC bills (3- to 12-month maturities, and a small number of 3-year bills). The MOF as well as policy and commercial banks issue debt into this market. Finally, the *bond repo market*, the third component of the money market, is for short-term borrowing. It tends to be less volatile and more liquid than the CHIBOR market. Since 1997, the repo rate has been set by the market, and the most active contracts have terms of 1–7 days. The 7-day repo is used as a benchmark rate.

Regulatory limitations have been a source of money market segmentation. In particular, disorders in the financial industry in the early 1990s motivated establishing a separation between securities and banking business, including, at the beginning of 1997, the decision that commercial banks should withdraw from repo trading on the stock exchange and carry out repo trading on the interbank market only. The fear was that short-term borrowing by securities companies in the interbank market could lead to contagion, as changing conditions in the capital market would be directly reflected in changes in the interbank market. While restrictions on the behavior of the various market participants have been relaxed, there remain sources of market segmentations such as restrictions on the maturity of transactions, which are differentiated according to three categories of participants, or trading limits, which are differentiated according to five categories of participants.[13]

Following the July 21, 2005 announcement of the adoption of new exchange rate arrangement whereby the renminbi value is set with reference to a basket of currencies, the PBC implemented a number of policy measures to enhance the operations of the foreign exchange market. In particular, a market-maker system and over-the-counter (OTC) transactions in the spot foreign exchange market was introduced, while maintaining the matching system in the Shanghai Foreign Trading System (CFETS). The OTC market is now the backbone of the spot market.[14] The PBC also launched RMB and foreign exchange swaps and

---

[13] For instance, the PBC regulation for interbank lending that came into effect as of August 6, 2007 limits to one year the maximum maturity of interbank transactions for commercial banks; 3 months for insurance companies, and seven days for securities companies. Commercial banks can trade up to 8% of their liabilities; and foreign funded banks and securities companies respectively up to twice and 80% of their capital.

[14] At the end of March 2006 trading in the OTC market stood around 30 times trading in CFETS.

RMB interest rate swaps on a pilot basis to improve the pricing mechanism of financial derivatives. The PBC also allowed access of more market participants to the foreign exchange market, with 64 member banks dealing in the inter-bank RMB forward market. Although turnover in the foreign exchange market has risen over time, reaching US$9 billion in 2007 on a daily average, the market lacks depth.[15] Finally, a primary dealer system for PBC foreign exchange transactions was established with a view to allow, in due time, a gradual exit strategy of the PBC from the foreign exchange market.[16]

These reforms should enhance the capacity of the PBC to manage the exchange rate with greater flexibility. Greater uncertainty about the exchange rate (although so far the exchange rate has been tightly managed), together with OTC trading should provide incentives to financial institutions to develop risk management tools (settlement arrangements, credit limits, etc.) while alleviating the credit risk that is borne by the CFETS. Furthermore, the setting up of market makers for the foreign exchange market is also a constructive development. By providing the market with two-way prices, market makers play an important role in price discovery mechanism and market development. Market makers can also act as the primary counterparts of the PBC in its official intervention, and the PBC can rely on them to collect market intelligence that is not currently available via the CFETS. Therefore, PBC communication and signaling should be facilitated.

2.2.3 Interest Rate Liberalization

An emphasis on the risks of financial sector reform has led to placing interest rates liberalization relatively late in the sequence of economic reform in China, and to favoring a gradual approach (i.e., waiting to see the outcome of the previous reforms before embarking on the next steps). Gradualism has been possible because, given a high savings ratio, avoiding distortions may have not been critical to savings mobilization and high growth rates were achieved with relatively low efficiency in resource allocation. In any event, real interest rates have tended to be positive, which is atypical of a financially repressed system.

The plan for liberalizing interest rates was laid out in November 1993 at the Third Plenary Session of the Fourteenth Communist Party Central Committee. In 2002, the Sixteenth National Congress reiterated the need to advance interest rate market reforms and optimize financial resource allocation. In 2003, the Third Plenary Session of the Sixteenth Central Committee pointed to the need to establish a robust mechanism for market interest rates, and monetary policy actions to steer them in a direction consistent with economic objectives.

---

[15] See BIS Triennial Survey on Foreign Exchange Markets, 2007.

[16] The primary dealer system is expected to help strengthen the transmission of the central bank's policy intentions in its foreign exchange operations as well as the effectiveness of those operations.

The sequencing of interest rates liberalization was carefully crafted. It involved first lifting restrictions on wholesale transactions then gradually liberalizing retail transactions. Deposit and lending interest rate on foreign currencies were liberalized before those on local currency, starting with loans followed by deposits, and with long term and large amounts first, followed by short term and small amounts. Beginning in 1996, restrictions started to be lifted on wholesale transactions, including bond and interbank market operations. The measures included liberalizing interbank market rates; liberalizing the primary market for government securities; adjusting the PBC refinancing rate and make it a reference rate for the money market. Wholesale transactions are now fully liberalized, as well as interest rates on foreign currency denominated instruments.

Regarding retail banking operations, the sequence involved first allowing banks to price counterparty risks on customers within a floating margin, then fully liberalize lending and deposit rates (see Mehran et al. 1996). The authorities first reduced the number of administered interest rates; adjusted bank lending rates to industrial and commercial enterprises more frequently to reflect changes in the PBC reference rate; and allowed financial institutions to price their lending operations within a floating margin.[17] In 2004, important steps were made with respect to retail operations, leading eventually, in October 2004, to the removal of ceilings on lending rates and of a floor on deposit rates. However, a floor was retained for lending rates, and a ceiling for deposit rates, differentiated by maturity (3, 6, and 12 months, and 2, 3, and 5 years). The rationale of such a rather uncommon mechanism of interest rates controls is to protect banks' intermediation margins.[18]

3 The Way Forward

Several issues need to be investigated before one can attempt to outline propositions for moving forward. First, one has to determine what should be the role of money in the strategy of the PBC: is there still a role for monetary analysis in the strategy of the PBC? We attempt to answer that question by looking at the already large body of empirical research that as attempted to ascertain the reliability of money as an intermediate target for China or, more broadly as an information variable for monetary policy conduct. Thereafter, we discuss the obstacles to reliance on interest rates as

[17] The liberalization of lending rates was not always smooth. In 1987 banks were allowed to charge higher rates on working capital loans up to 20% above the respective ceilings. In May 1996 the margin was reduced to 10% to alleviate financial costs to enterprises. In April 1999, the margin was expanded to 30% for loans to SMEs but remained at 10% for large enterprises (see People's Bank of China, 2005).

[18] Zhou (2005) argues that removing the limits may result in improper market competition.

the operating target of monetary policy. Finally, we advance some propositions for moving forward toward full reliance on market-based frameworks for monetary policy implementation.

3.1 Money as an Intermediate Target: Empirical Evidence for China

3.1.1 Xie (2004)

Xie (2004) analyzes China's monetary policy for the period 1998–2002. Using correlation analysis and Granger-causality tests he finds a strong relationship between base money and broader monetary aggregates (M1 and M2) and that, to some extent, money supply is endogenously determined. Using a cointegrated vector autoregression and a vector error-correction model, Xie investigates the relationship between money supply, inflation, and economic growth. He concludes that within a long-term horizon, monetary aggregates do not affect economic growth but do determine the inflation rate in both the short and long term. In its 2005 Q1 Monetary Policy Report, the PBC reports on the stability of the relationship between money supply, economic growth, and price stability for the period 1980–2003, during which China experienced four episodes of inflation and one of deflation. During these episodes money supply and output moved in parallel. China experienced financial deepening and a decline in money velocity despite periodic fluctuations: velocity rose as economic growth accelerated, and moderated as economic growth slowed.

3.1.2 Geiger (2006)

In a 2006 paper covering the period 1994–2002, Geiger (2006) analyzes the effectiveness of China's monetary policy and in particular whether monetary variables have a close relationship to inflation and whether inflation can be controlled via the PBC's monetary policy instruments. Geiger first makes the point that money and credit targets were missed frequently, and he finds a weak relationship between the intermediate target and the interest rate, thus suggesting that interest rate transmission channel monetary policy is weak. He observes that the inflation objective was met even during the 1993–1994 overheating episode; price stability was maintained subsequently; and inflationary pressures during 2003–2004 were contained. Geiger assigns these achievements to a well-managed mix of price- and quantity-based measures. He argues that window guidance during the 2003–2004 expansionary economic cycle was critical for the successful outcome in the absence of a well-functioning interest rate channel of monetary transmission. He concludes that monetary indicators (as intermediate targets) remain relevant given the vague relationship between interest rates and inflation; interest rates should only be supportive rather than a leading instrument. In particular, he hints that an important reason for the use of monetary targeting is the search of a nominal anchor.

Geiger notes that distortions are preventing the interest rate channel from functioning. Rather than pointing against the adoption of a short-term interest rate as the operational target of monetary policy, this points to the need to strengthen the interest rate transmission channel. Indeed, only then a price-based monetary strategy, as was officially introduced in 1998, can be successful.

3.1.3 Green and Chang (2006)

Green and Chang (2006) ran a regression between reserve money and foreign exchange inflows for the period January 2003–March 2006 to assess the controllability of reserve money and M2. They found that changes in the adjusted inflows explained 78% of the changes in reserve money, suggesting that the PBC is able to control reserve money. They ran a regression between reserve money and M2 and found that they were not closely correlated. Therefore, even if the PBC can control reserve money, it does not have an easy way of managing M2, due to an unstable multiplier. They found that bank loans were an accurate predictor of M2 in the short-run, with the impact fading after 5 months. They found also a relationship between M2 growth and bank loan growth, with demand deposits having the largest impact on lending. However, they noted that M2 growth had accelerated in recent months, while bank loan growth had more or less stabilized. This may reflect increased disintermediation due to the development of commercial paper or informal financial sector lending, in response to PBC window guidance during 2005–2006. These findings suggest that even if bank lending is under control, M2 may not automatically follow.

3.1.4 Laurens and Maino (2007)

Laurens and Maino (2007), confirming the findings by Green and Chang (2006), find that the money multiplier has proved to be unstable and not reliable to control M2 given the abrupt changes in its behavior (Fig. 6). The Augmented

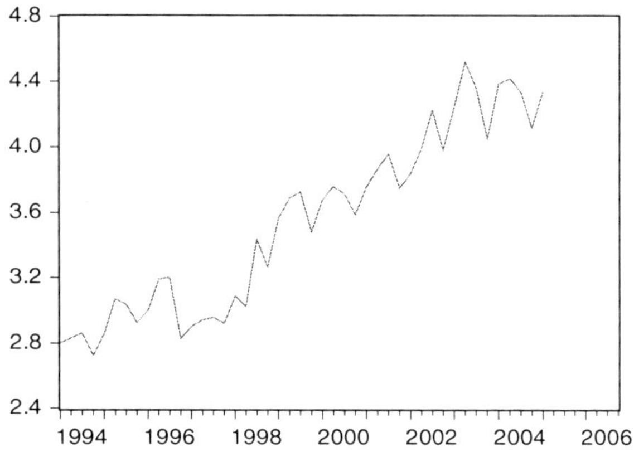

Fig. 6 China: money multiplier

Dickey-Fueller (ADF) Test provides intuition about the reliability of the multiplier for monetary policy conduct. The ADF statistic value for the series is –1.059 and the associated one-sided p-value (for a test with 40 observations) is 0.7223. Hence, we cannot reject the null hypothesis (the multiplier having a unit root) at conventional test sizes. Conceptually, we cannot reject the idea that a shock or innovation in the series is permanent.

Laurens and Maino (2007) also show that the velocity at which money rotates also poses problems for monetary policy conduct. Based on a univariate time series analysis (unit root tests) we reject the stationarity of the income velocity of M2. Being non-stationary, velocity would deviate from the trend over time. The velocity of money shows a trend of irregular deceleration since 1994 which perhaps contributed to the PBC inability to achieve its money targets. The trend might be related to the decrease in the opportunity costs of holding money (inflation and interest rates) and the (slow) technological progress related to payments instruments. However (see Appendix 3), money demand seems to be a stable function of GDP, interest rate, and inflation in the long run. Moreover, monetization is increasing: the demand for nominal money more than fully adjusts to prices in the long run so that the desired level of real balances increases.

The use of a nominal anchor in China is illustrated with a stylized model of inflation.[19] A time series model is advanced where the variability of inflation depends on long-run inflation, its persistence, and the variability of the shocks affecting it:

$$\pi_t = (1 - \phi)\pi^* + \phi\pi_{t-1} + \omega_t \tag{1}$$

where π^*represents long-run inflation rate (target rate), ϕ captures the persistence of shocks to inflation $((|\phi| < 1))$, the error term ω represents uncorrelated inflation shocks distributed with mean zero and standard deviation σ_ω.[20] The variability of inflation is given by

$$\sigma_\pi = \frac{\sigma_\omega}{(1 - \phi^2)} \tag{2}$$

The results are shown in Table 3. The standard deviation of inflation shocks is low (1.01%). The inflation process, however, is highly persistent (0.92).

Selecting a nominal anchor would involve determining restrictions on the parameters of Equation (1), $\pi^*, \phi, \sigma_\omega$. Any announcement on inflation

---

[19] A nominal anchor is a nominal variable that policymakers use to tie down the price level: it helps promote price stability, and limit the time-inconsistency problem of discretionary monetary policy. A credible nominal anchor is important to control inflationary expectations and provide confidence in monetary policy whereby agents can distinguish between movements in relative prices (necessary for consumption and investment decision making) and those associated with the price level.

[20] Data corresponds to the International Financial Statistics, various issues. A smooth estimate of the long-term trend component of inflation is obtained by means of a Hodrick-Prescott filter.

Table 3 China: persistence and variability of inflation, 1994–2004

Parameters		Memo item	
π *	ϕ	σ_{ω}	σ_{π}
2.0	0.92	1.01	6.52

Source: Authors' calculations based on quarterly data.

expectations (targets) should be credible in order to act as a nominal anchor. In China, constraints on nominal variables such as the nominal exchange rate or the nominal stock of money have been extensively used as anchors since the 1990s. A credible commitment to inflation control may advance clear constraints on ϕ and σ_{ω} by relying on a forward-looking monetary policy that reacts to future inflationary pressures.

To assess the effects of monetary policy and other policy-related variables on output, exchange rate, and prices, Laurens and Maino (2007) have estimated a five-variable Vector Autoregression (VAR) model to characterize monetary policy and study the impact of the money on inflation and output for the period 1994–2005, quarterly. A VAR methodology places minimal restrictions on how monetary shocks affect the economy, and hence, it seems suitable for monetary time series available. The model can be represented by an unrestricted form such as,

$$y_t = A(L)y_t + u_t \tag{3}$$

where y_t is a vector including endogenous variables (log of real GDP, CPI, exchange rate, short-term interest rate, monetary aggregate, M2, federal funds rates); A(L) corresponds to the matrices of coefficients to be estimated whose lag lengths are usually determined by Schwartz and AIC criteria, and u_t represents a vector of innovations that may be contemporaneously correlated and uncorrelated with their own lagged values and their right-hand side variables.

Estimates from this VAR indicates that[21]

- Prices react to a disturbance in money, although the impact tends to moderate in the medium term. In particular, the results show the persistence, long-lived, of a money shock on inflation: confirming the significant influence of money in determining inflation, as implicitly implicated by Geiger (2006).
- Money does not seem to have any long-run real effect on output.
- The impact of interest rate changes depends on the ease of propagation of the effect of monetary tightening as well as on agents' reactions. A key aspect is the extent to which a change in the central bank policy rate affects the term

[21] The limited data set used for the study might have caused significant standard errors urging us to adopt a cautionary tone in presenting the results.

structure of interest rates (the yield curve)—especially short-term money market rates, and long-term rates.

Monetary policy transmission along the yield curve heavily depends on the structure and organization of financial markets, with deeper markets allowing for more rapid and predictable transmission. As for the impact, the balance sheet positions of economic agents influence the relative importance of marginal and average interest rates effects. Clearly, an interest rate cut reduces the marginal cost of borrowing, which boosts current spending, hence aggregate demand. In addition, rising average interest rates reduce cash-flow and spending but raise savings.

3.2 Obstacles to Reliance on Interest Rates as an Operating Target in China

There are several potential obstacles to the effectiveness of interest rates as an operating target for monetary policy conduct in China. First, some of the attributes of China's economy and financial sector can potentially limit the effectiveness of the interest rate transmission channel for monetary policy in China. Second, one may argue that the PBC does not have yet in place the monetary frameworks and instruments to conduct full-fledged market-based monetary policy. In the following paragraphs, we discuss these two issues.

3.2.1 Interest Rate Transmission Channel

The effectiveness of the interest rate transmission channel could be held back due to insufficient progress in establishing a commercially driven financial sector. In particular, the banking sector exhibits several problems that complicate the transmission of monetary policy to the real sector. First, the restructuring of the banking sector has not been completed yet, and there are still some banks with high level of nonperforming loans and little capital. Second, banks' operational reforms are only starting, and it will take time before they are truly commercially oriented and will be able to price risks properly. Third, there are obstacles to the responsiveness of firms and individuals to the price of capital. Firms, in particular SOEs, may still be operating in the context of the quantitative framework whereby the credit channel is the main means of influencing aggregate demand. Financial and enterprise reforms over the last decade should, however, have meant that the interest rate has more influence, but it is difficult to measure progress in this area. Against this background, one could, however, argue that greater reliance on price signals in the conduct of monetary policy is precisely what is needed to speed up the "commercialization" of the financial sector.

Another potential obstacle to the effectiveness of the interest rate transmission channel has to do with current market segmentation. First, the 1995 Banking Law established a de facto two-tier commercial banking system. The Law created commercial banks that are subject to prudential ratios and international standards of portfolio risks, as well as policy-lending banks which are not subject to similar regulations. The Law also separates the activities of commercial banking and securities industries by not allowing the former group to engage in trust and investment and stock trading, as well as investing in real estate, NBFI, and enterprises. Second, money market segmentation, as explained above, is another obstacle to greater reliance on interest rates. Typically, central banks target a short-term interbank lending rate at which financial institutions trade their balances with the central bank among themselves. In turn, the actions of the central bank in the interbank market can spread to the other components of the financial markets because market participants are typically allowed to operate in several financial markets. As explained above, the limitations in place in China do not allow such arbitrage activities. Therefore, the monetary policy actions of the PBC in the interbank market cannot migrate to the other components of China's financial markets. Against that background, one could make the point that market segmentation is a necessary second best solution in support of a monetary policy strategy anchored on administrative measures. A shift away from administrative measures and toward market-based monetary policy implementation would imply lifting the obstacles to financial markets integration.

3.2.2 Monetary Frameworks and Instruments

High banks' excess reserves are an obstacle to full reliance on market-based monetary policy. Indeed, while they have declined significantly during the 2000s, as already elaborated (Table 2), they stand at a high level.[22] Mopping up liquidity aggressively may have involved allowing short-term interest rates to rise, which would have increased sterilization costs and could have attracted additional capital flows. The repeated increases in the reserve requirement since 2006 have helped reduce excess reserves. However, one has to be mindful of the potentially distortionary impact of high ratios, in particular, given that the remuneration of required reserves is lower than money market rates. In addition, reliance on reserve requirements does not offer the flexibility of open market operations.

[22] A level of excess reserves of more than 10% of required reserves stands particularly high compared, for instance, to the Euro area, where excess reserves amount to less than 1% of required reserves.

A last obstacle to full reliance on market-based monetary policy is the limited political and instrument autonomy (respectively autonomy with regard to objectives and instruments) of the PBC.[23] In China, all the decisions regarding the level of the interest rates or of reserve requirement ratios have to be approved by the State Council.[24] Such a framework may not provide all the flexibility that is needed to respond in a timely manner to economic developments. Moreover, the multiplicity of objectives assigned to the PBC creates "noise" in policy implementation and complicate the communication policy of the central bank.

3.3 Strengthening China's Strategic Framework

Notwithstanding China's persistently low inflation rate, the adoption of a full-fledged inflation targeting framework does not seem a viable option at this juncture. The lack of central bank operational independence, weaknesses in the production of reliable medium-term inflation forecast, and concerns about the stability of the banking sector are among a number of significant impediments to adopting inflation targeting. Furthermore, careful consideration needs to be given to the role that the PBC should play with regard to financial stability and how it could be incorporated with the central bank's mandate to ensure price stability, before a decision is made with regard to adopting an inflation-targeting regime.[25] In this regard, while increased attention has been paid to financial stability following the financial turmoil that emerged in late 2007, the relationships between central bank autonomy and financial stability is an issue which deserves further research.

China's monetary strategy is still in transition toward one that must go beyond the analysis of monetary aggregates, as it is clear that a money target would not constitute a good stand-alone nominal anchor. From a conceptual point of view, based on the level of confidence that empirical evidence provides, the role of money can range from being used to define quantitative targets to being used to supplement the short-term risks to price stability with medium-term risks. We found that money growth and inflation tend to be highly correlated in the long run, suggesting that intermediate guidelines for monetary

---

[23] Arnone et al. (2007) present indices of central bank autonomy for a broad representation of central banks around the world.

[24] Article 2 of the PBC law stipulates *The People's Bank of China shall, under the leadership of the State Council, formulate and implement monetary policy*. Additional information provided in the PBC website indicates that *the PBC needs to report to the State Council its decisions concerning the annual money supply, interest rates, exchange rates and other important issues specified by the State Council for approval before they are put into effect. The PBC is also obliged to submit work report to the Standing Committee of the National People's Congress on the conduct of monetary policy and the performance of the financial industry.*

[25] See Ferguson (2002) for a discussion on financial stability as an explicit central bank objective.

aggregates can still play a useful operational role to stabilize inflation and provide timely evidence to help assess the sustainability of an asset price boom. Although in the long run there is a recognizable link between money growth and inflation in China, the low inflation environment in China up to 2006 made it difficult for policy makers to manage inflation based on money targets given that short-run instabilities may add some noise in the decision-making progress. The current increasing inflationary process imposes new restrictions on policy makers. The monetary policy decision-making process must also include a systematic real sector analysis, as well as evaluate and cross-check the information relevant to assessing risks to price stability, in a way similar to frameworks in place in advanced economies.[26] This approach requires putting a lot of emphasis on research, modeling, internal communication, and discussion. It makes necessary regular meetings to discuss conjectural events, preparation of material to inform policy makers, and elaboration and communication of forecasts and reports. At some point, the PBC may announce a long-run inflation goal as a priority for monetary policy to help tie down inflation expectations.[27]

Such a monetary strategy needs to be supported by a high level of effective autonomy at the central bank so as to be in a position to undertake monetary policy operations that are needed to achieve its inflation objective. That involves economic analysis and developing short-term leading indicators, with a view to move progressively toward macro-econometric modeling. Finally, the policy decision-making process needs to be based on a consistent, efficient, and well-structured process for the economic analysis and the forecasting cycle which allows to fully integrate economic and monetary analyses into the decision-making process Finally, in such a policy environment characterized by increased uncertainty, the communication of the central bank is key and should be reinforced, not only with market participants but also with the public at large.

3.4 Strengthening China's Operational Framework

To be in a position to move forward and rely on a monetary strategy centered on inflation control, as elaborated above, the PBC needs to streamline its policy objectives so as to enable adoption of a short-term interest rate as the monetary policy operating target.[28] Such a policy would not be incompatible with the PBC's other objectives such as maintaining the profitability of the state-owned banks and

[26] See Appendix 5 for a short review of the ECB experience, and Mishkin (2000) for a review of the experience of selected industrialized countries with monetary targeting.

[27] See Goodfriend and Prasad (2006).

[28] See Appendix 4 for an evaluation of the relevance of an interest rate as the operating procedure.

the resulting maintenance of a mechanism to monitor banks' margins or its desire to influence the structure of banks' loan portfolio through window guidance.[29]

The current structural excess of liquidity in the banking system complicates day-to-day systemic liquidity management. Consideration should be given to conducting monetary policy from a structural liquidity deficit position. Reliance on administrative measures for monetary policy conduct, including window guidance and the forced placement of PBC bills, suggests that the PBC is not confident that liquidity-absorbing market-based monetary operations would allow achieving its overall policy objectives. In shallow markets, reliance on market-based monetary operations can be facilitated when the central bank conducts the bulk of its monetary interventions in the form of liquidity-providing operations. This reduces the scope for collusion or overshooting because the banking system has no choice but to borrow from the central bank. Hence, in the short-term, the central bank can achieve a particular liquidity objective and still control the interest rate at which it lends to the system, for instance, by using a volume tender. This is not the case when the central bank conducts the bulk of its monetary interventions in the form of liquidity-absorbing operations. In that case, banks have a choice between lending to the central bank or to their customers.[30] While a move to a structural liquidity shortage could be instigated at any time, in the case of China, it would be best implemented in combination with a gradual exit strategy of the PBC from the foreign exchange market. Indeed, since the growth of banks' reserves is attributable to international reserves accumulation, such timing would help reduce the need to expand continually the magnitude of the financial operations aimed at creating a liquidity shortage.

4 Conclusions

While much has already been achieved, monetary policy implementation in China is still in transition. China has achieved a level of financial reforms which places the monetary authorities in a strong position to enter the final stage of central bank modernization toward full reliance on market forces for monetary policy implementation. The gradual, but uninterrupted, reform process has obviated the need for radical changes along the way. However, the effectiveness

[29] The exact specification of the target should be such as to avoid strictly committing the PBC to control the short term interest rate very precisely. The PBC could announce that its short-term bills rate (for instance a maximum bid rate) would communicate the stance of monetary policy and explain that it would normally expect short-term interbank rates to remain on average close to this policy rate. Alternatively, it could declare its short-term bills rate to be its operational target, mentioning, however, that this does not mean that this rate cannot fluctuate to some extent around the pre-announced target level.

[30] See Laurens (2005) for a discussion on ways to create a structural liquidity shortage.

of the current framework, which still relies intensively on rules-based measures, is likely to diminish over time as the sophistication of the economy increases.

The first challenge has to do with the *choice of a nominal anchor*. The most suitable strategy for China appears to be an eclectic monetary policy framework, whereby the growth in money supply and bank credit extension are used as intermediate guidelines for the determination of short-term interest rates, together with a systematic real sector analysis and a cross-checking exercise for assessing risks to price stability.

The second challenge has to do with the *choice of an operating target*. Adoption of a short-term interest rate would bring about a more efficient allocation of financial resources and savings, therefore contributing to enhanced risks management. An important prerequisite for shifting to full-fledged market-based monetary policy conduct would be to grant the PBC full discretion to make interest rate changes so that it can start using its policy interest rate more actively. Such a move appears the most urgent policy measure at this juncture.

The third challenge has to do with the *choice of operating instruments*. In conjunction with a shift to a short term as the operating target for monetary policy, the PBC must place greater reliance on market-based instruments for systemic liquidity management. However, this will probably have to await the exit of the PBC from the foreign exchange market.

The fourth and last challenge has to do with the *flexibility of exchange rate*. As discussed, China is experiencing increasing difficulty to maintain a tightly managed exchange rate regime, de facto free capital flows, and an independent monetary policy. While strengthened capital controls may be expected to provide some temporary breathing space, sooner than later the benefits of such a policy will dissipate, leaving greater exchange rate flexibility as the only long-term viable option for resolving the current policy dilemma.

Appendix 1 The Degree of Exchange Rate Pass-Through to Consumer Prices

The following log-linear regression specification captures the dynamic relationship between inflation and the nominal effective exchange rate

$$\Delta cpi_t = \alpha + \sum_{j=1}^{Q} \beta_j \Delta cpi_{t-j} + \sum_{k=0}^{R} \gamma_k \Delta neer_{t-k} + AX_t + \varepsilon_t \tag{4}$$

where t refers to time, cpi is the log of the aggregate consumer price index, $neer$ is the log of the nominal effective exchange rate, X is a vector of control variables (including the log of the monetary aggregate M2), and ε is the error term. The dynamic form was estimated by Ordinary Least Squares using quarterly data (1994–2008). All variables are stationary in first differences, and the appropriate lag structures were determined by the Bayesian Information Criteria (parameters Q and R). The full pass-through from and exchange rate shock to inflation (φ) is obtained by inverting Equation (4), which is

$$\phi = \frac{-\sum_{j=0}^{R} \gamma_j}{1 - \sum_{i=1}^{Q} \beta_i} \tag{5}$$

Estimates of the long-run pass-through imply that a 10% nominal depreciation generates an increase in inflation of nearly a half-percentage point.

Exchange rate pass-through into consumer prices, 1994–2008

	Coefficient	Std. Error	t-Statistic	Prob.
C	0.032736	0.030927	1.058500	0.2954
Δ(cpi (t–1))	–0.520557	0.144906	–3.592375	0.0008
Δ (cpi (t–2))	–0.245922	0.162543	–2.512972	0.1371
Δ (CPI (t–3))	0.008756	0.014239	1.984898	0.5417
Δ NEER	0.123825	1.042025	0.118831	0.9059
Δ NEER (t–1)	–0.371184	1.041612	–0.356356	0.7232
D((M1))	–4.36E-05	8.69E-05	–0.501330	0.6185
R-squared	0.225123	Mean dependent var		0.010714
Adjusted R-squared	0.124053	S.D. dependent var		0.149620
S.E. of regression	0.140032	Akaike info criterion		–0.971391
Sum squared resid	0.902012	Schwarz criterion		–0.711164
Log likelihood	32.74186	Hannan-Quinn criter.		–0.871320
F-statistic	2.227383	Durbin-Watson stat		1.954292
Prob(F-statistic)	0.057143			

Dependent Variable: D((INFLATION))
Sample (adjusted): 1995Q1 2008Q1
Included observations: 53 after adjustments

Although the estimated pass-through is significant, it could have been even higher in the absence of administered prices.

The long-run exchange rate pass-through is complemented here with an impulse response function to depict its dynamics. The figure below suggests that the pass-through process takes about a year to complete, thereby reflecting a relative persistence of the inflation process.[31]

[31] The dotted lines represent 90% confidence intervals. The vertical axis shows the deviation from the baseline level of the target variable in response to a one standard deviation (SD) change to the shock variable, while the horizontal axis presents the number of quarters elapsed after the shock.

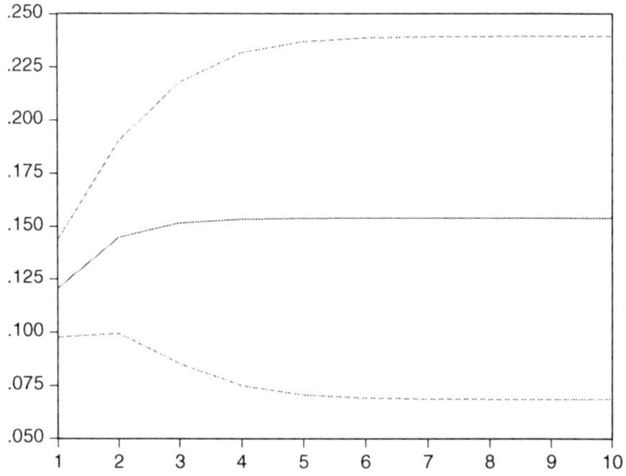

An impulse response function of a 1% depreciation in the NEER

Appendix 2 Identifying Monetary Policy Shocks: An SVAR Analysis

This section seeks to identify monetary policy shocks and simulate their impact on output and inflation by using a Structural Vector Autoregression (SVAR) methodology. A non-recursive identification scheme is presented to generate response of output to a contractionary monetary policy shock. The model assumes the economy to evolve as

$$A_0 y_t = k + A_1 y_{t-1} + ... + A_q y_{t-q} + u_t \tag{6}$$

where $y_t = \left[i_t^* x_t p_t m_t neer_t i_t oil_t\right]$ represents a $n \times 1$ data vector including the fed funds rate as a foreign interest rate (i^*), real GDP (x), domestic CPI (p), monetary aggregate (m), NEER, domestic interest rate (i); and the (world) oil price index (oil), k is a vector of constants, A_k is an $n \times n$ matrix of coefficients (with $k = 1, \ldots, K$), and u_t is a white-noise vector of structural shocks.

Some contemporaneous restrictions were imposed to identify the structural shocks. In particular:

- Domestic prices respond contemporaneously to oil price shocks and to output;
- The oil price index is exogenous with respect to all the variables in the system;
- The domestic interest rate is affected by shocks to all other variables included in the system;
- The fed funds rate and domestic output respond contemporaneously to the oil price within a period (quarter), but the latter is not affected by the former contemporaneously (zero restriction);
- Firms adjust output in response to policy shocks or financial market shocks with a lag;

- Money (M1 and M2) responds to domestic output and interest rates, consistent with standard money demand theory; and
- The NEER responds to output, prices, the oil price, and domestic interest rates.

The main results from the SVAR (impulse-response functions) are on output and prices.[32] The main results are summarized below [33]:

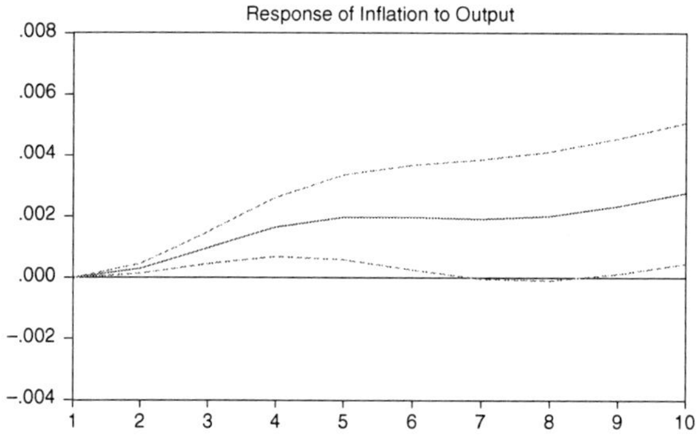

Output shocks have a strong positive impact on the CPI. The impact lasts for at 6–7 quarters and becomes statistically nonsignificant after that point.

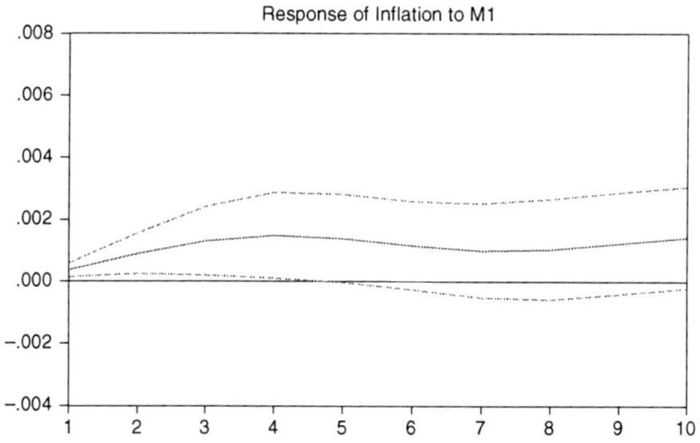

The effect of an increase in M1 has a statistically significant effect of almost a year on prices. This effect underscores the rationale for a greater focus on monetary aggregates.

[32] Reversing the ordering of the variables does not affect qualitatively the results. Hence, ordering the variables for the impulse response functions has little effect and the Cholesky responses are similar to unrestricted ones. We also note that the correlation matrix of the VAR residuals is close to diagonal.

[33] The dotted lines in the figures represent 90% confidence intervals. The vertical axis shows the deviation from the baseline level of the target variable in response to a one standard deviation (SD) change to the shock variable, while the horizontal axis presents the number of quarters elapsed after the shock.

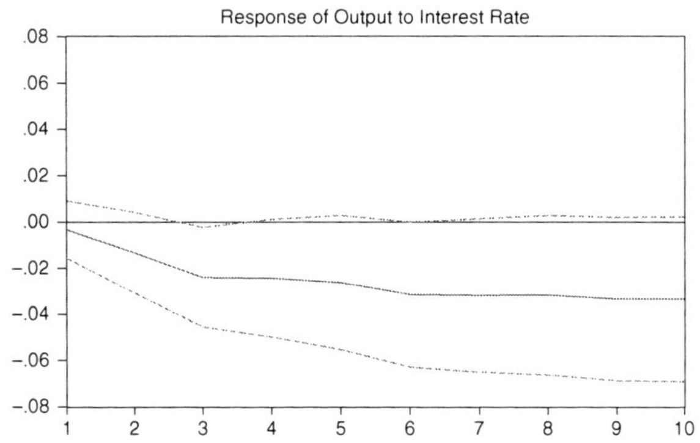

The effect of an interest rate increase on output has the expected result. However, the response is statistically insignificant at the 5% level.

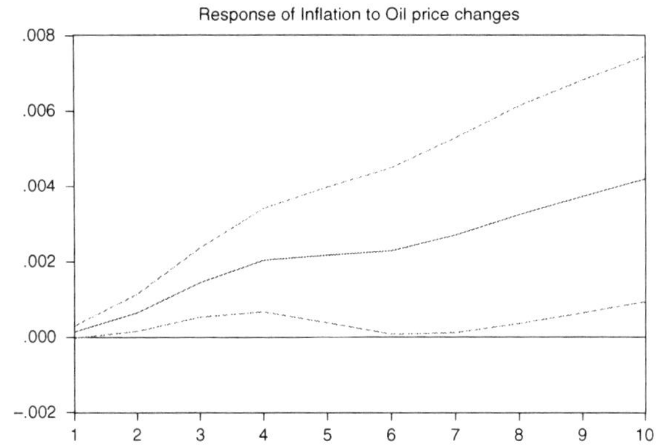

Changes in oil prices are statistically significant at the 5% level and persistent.

Appendix 3 Modeling Money Demand in China

Money demand equations are adequate instruments to examine the long-run relationship between money and prices. In particular, money demand becomes an important analytical tool, when monetary policy is not geared toward ensuring the clearing of the money market through the use of the nominal interest rate. According to our findings, the existence of a stable long-run relationship (cointegration) between monetary aggregate M2 and its determinants cannot be rejected. Consequently, M2 exhibits a stable long-run relationship with key macroeconomic variables such as inflation, real GDP, and interest rates. The demand for nominal M2 adjusts to price movements in the long run, thus leaving unchanged the desired level of real balances (there exists long-run homogeneity between money and prices).

The following long-run specification for the demand for money balances is estimated and supported by the data:

$$(m - p)_t = c + \beta_1 y_t - \beta_2 i_t - \beta_3 \pi_t \tag{7}$$

where m, p, y, and π denote, respectively, M2, the price level, real GDP, and inflation. All variables are in logarithms with the exception of interest rates, and they have been seasonally adjusted. Also, all variables were taken from the International Financial Statistics with the exception of GDP that belongs to a recent revision provided by the Chinese authorities. It is expected that real money demand is positively related to the level of real income and negatively related to the rate of interest and inflation.

The least squares regression for the period 1994 (first Quarter) to 2008 (first quarter) provides the following results:

Variable	Coefficient	Std. error	t-Statistic	Prob.
C	1.111514	0.672826	1.652010	0.1060
GDP	1.135239	0.100385	11.30887	0.0000
I	–0.059250	0.017886	–3.312695	0.0019
π	0.004890	0.006832	0.715688	0.4781
AR(1)	0.626404	0.124890	5.015651	0.0000
R-squared	0.991411	Mean dependent var		7.878369
Adjusted R-squared	0.990593	S.D. dependent var		0.544817
S.E. of regression	0.052843	F-statistic		1222.147
Sum squared resid	0.117280	Prob(F-statistic)		0.000000
Durbin-Watson stat	1.934899			

The estimated short-run demand function shows that the coefficients associated with the interest rate and inflation (the latter not statistically significant) are null while the associated impact of economic activity is large.

The empirical results support the stability of money demand.[34] The maximal eigenvalue and trace eigenvalue statistics – with a degrees of freedom adjustment ($\lambda^a_{\max}$ and λ^a_{trace}) – reject the null hypothesis of no cointegration in favor of one, and possibly two cointegrating relationships as presented in the following table:

Hypothesized No. of CE(s)	Eigenvalue	Trace statistic	0.05 Critical value	Prob.*
0	0.580080	73.67913	47.85613	0.0000
1	0.351435	36.36844	29.79707	0.0076
2	0.338191	17.74975	15.49471	0.0225
3	6.59E-06	0.000284	3.841466	0.9886

MacKinnon-Haug-Michelis (1999) p-values

[34] The ADF tests (not shown here) cannot reject the null hypothesis of the presence of a unit root in all series suggesting the existence of a stochastic trend thus implying that they are stationary in first differences.

Cointegration analysis tests for the existence of a set of coefficients, namely, the cointegrating vector that defines a linear combination of M2, income (proxied by Real GDP below?), interest rates, and inflation which is stable over time.[35] Accordingly, these findings suggest that the residuals of the money demand equation are stationary meaning that M2, income, interest rates, and inflation are cointegrated.

The next table shows the estimation results (normalized cointegration coefficients).

Dependent variable: real money balances (M2)		
Variables	Estimate	Std. error
Real GDP	1.84	0.035
Interest rate	–0.01	0.003
Inflation	0.01	0.001

Overall, the models suggest that the growth in real monetary aggregates (M2) since 1994 was primarily driven by a significant increase in real output. While the decline in inflation and interest rates have contributed to increasing money demand, their effects were relatively small.

Appendix 4 The Case for Using the Interest Rate as the Operating Procedure

In view of the weakening of the relationship between money (and credit) and inflation, following Walsh (2003) we now test the desirability of relying on interest rates as the operating procedure for monetary policy in China. The basic issue is whether the central bank should keep the interest rate constant or should it hold a monetary quantity constant, thus allowing interest rates to move, to be better positioned to achieve its inflation objective. In most cases, the goal of monetary policy is to select an instrument of monetary policy to minimize the variance of output deviations. Hence, following Walsh (2003), we state a simple variant of a basic IS-LM model in log terms:

$$Min\ E(y_t^2) \tag{8}$$

$$y_t = B_1 r_t + u_t \tag{9}$$

$$m_t = y_t + B_2 r_t + e_t \tag{10}$$

[35] If the variables involved are not cointegrated, then the differences among them could become larger as time goes by, without a tendency to return to a stable path together.

where represents output and $y = 0$ is the economy equilibrium level of the output gap when there are no shocks; r_t is the nominal rate of interest[36]; m_t represents a nominal monetary aggregate, and u_t and e_t are stationary uncorrelated stochastic process.[37] From (7) we obtain

$$r_t = \frac{m_t - y_t - e_t}{B_2} \tag{11}$$

Now plugging (6) in (8) we obtain

$$y_t = B_1 \left[\frac{m_t - y_t - e_t}{B_2} \right] + u_t \tag{12}$$

Solving for y_t,

$$y_t = \frac{B_1}{B_2 - B_1} m_t - \frac{B_1}{B_2 - B_1} e_t + \frac{B_2}{B_2 - B_1} u_t \tag{13}$$

The objective function then becomes

$$E[y_t]^2 = \frac{-B_1^2 \sigma_e^2 + B_2 \sigma_u^2}{(B_1 - B_2)^2} \tag{14}$$

When the interest rate is used as the policy instrument, the money market is in equilibrium because the money stock adjusts endogenously to be at the same level as money demand. Therefore, setting the interest rate such as $E(y) = 0$ we get

$$E_i(y_t)^2 = \sigma_u^2 \tag{15}$$

Then, the criteria to choose the interest rate as operating procedure (instead of a money-supply operating procedure) is the following:

$$E_i(y_t)^2 < \sigma_u^2 \tag{16}$$

or

$$\frac{-B_1^2 \sigma_e^2 + B_2 \sigma_u^2}{(B_1 - B_2)^2} < \sigma_u^2 \tag{17}$$

This is equivalent to the following condition:

$$\sigma_e^2 > \frac{(B_1 - 2B_2)}{B_1} \sigma_u^2 \tag{18}$$

---

36 We use the benchmark rate for RMB denominated deposit rate.

37 The level has been normalized to equal 1. Hence the log of the price level is zero ($p = 0$).

or

$$\sigma_e^2 > [1 - \frac{(2B_2)}{B_1}]\sigma_u^2 \tag{19}$$

Simply put, the interest rate might be chosen as an operating target (i) whenever the variance of the money demand disturbances is larger, (ii) the LM is steeper, and (iii) the IS curve is flatter. In other words, the interest rate would respond as a reliable operating target when money demand is perceived as unstable and difficult to predict over short-time periods, when changes in interest rates convey significant influence on output (thus inducing greater output stability), and when changes in interest rates are not significant enough to stabilize output through the money market. Applying this setup to China, we get results which imply that an interest rate would be desirable as the operating target for monetary policy conduct in China.

$$\begin{gathered} \sigma_e^2 > [1 - \frac{(2B_2)}{B_1}]\sigma_u^2 \\ 4.3830 < 37.3303 \end{gathered} \tag{20}$$

Appendix 5 The Evolving Role of Money: The ECB's Monetary Policy Strategy

The primary objective of the European Central Bank's (ECB) is price stability. Policy decisions are based on economic analysis (shorter term price movements largely influenced by interplay of supply and demand in goods, services, and factor markets) and monetary analysis (longer term price trends closely linked to underlying trends in the money stock). A framework for internal decision making aims at providing the Governing Council with all relevant information and analysis required for taking policy decisions; external communication provides the public with a clear, consistent framework to explain policy decisions and their rationale. There is no monetary target.

The ECB has decided to give importance to monetary analysis. As part of the monetary pillar, there is a focus on the analysis of the components and counterparts of M3. This decision was made in recognition of the fact that monetary growth and inflation are closely related in the medium-to-long run. This relationship provides monetary policy with a nominal anchor beyond the horizons conventionally adopted to construct inflation forecasts, underpinning the medium term orientation of monetary policy. Macro projections play an important but not an all-encompassing role. There are other variables to include, such as a broad range of price and cost indicators; aggregate demand and its components; labor and financial markets conditions; fiscal developments; and private sector expectations based on market prices and surveys. Research has shown that longer-term movements in monetary growth lead longer term movements in HICP inflation. The lead time is of relevance for policy decisions, given likely lags in transmission.[38]

In assessing the outlook for price stability, the short-to-medium-term indications coming from economic analysis are cross-checked with the medium-to-long-term perspective coming from monetary analysis. Monetary developments contain information about the state of the economy which – regardless of whether money plays an active role in the transmission mechanism of monetary policy – should be integrated into the policy-making process. Monetary and credit aggregates can also provide timely evidence to help assess the sustainability of an asset price boom. Empirical research has shown that asset price bubbles were often preceded by excessive monetary developments.

References

Arnone, Marco, Bernard J. Laurens, Jean Francois Segalotto, and Martin Sommer, 2007, *Central Bank Autonomy: Lessons from Global Trends*, IMF Working Paper 07/88.

Barnett, Steven, 2004, "Banking Sector Developments," in *China's Growth and Integration into the World Economy*, IMF Occasional Paper No. 232, edited by Esward Prasad.

Bruggeman, Annick, Gonzalo Camba-Mendez, Bjorn Fischer, and Joao Sousa, 2005, "Structural Filters for Monetary Analysis: The Inflationary Movements of Money in the Euro Area," ECB Working Paper No. 470.

Estrella, Arturo and Frederic S. Mishkin, 1997, "Is there a role for monetary aggregates in the conduct of monetary policy?" *Journal of Monetary Economics*, 40, 279–304.

Ferguson, Roger, 2002, "Should Financial Stability be an Explicit Central Bank Objective," in *Challenges to Central Banking from Globalized Financial Systems*, International Monetary Fund.

Geiger, Michael, 2006, *Monetary Policy in China (1994–2004), Targets, Instruments and their Effectiveness*, Wűrzbug Economic Papers No. 68.

Goodfriend, Marvin and Eswar Prasad, 2006, *A Framework for Independent Monetary Policy in China*, IMF Working Paper No. 06/111.

Green, Stephen, 2005, *Making Monetary Policy Work in China: A Report from the Money Market Front Line*, Working Paper No. 245, Stanford Center for International Development.

Green, Stephen and Jason Chang, 2006, *On the Ground, Asia. The PBC's Big Money Problem*, Standard Chartered, June.

Hardy, Daniel, 1993, *Reserve Requirements and Monetary Management: An Introduction*, IMF Working Paper No. 93/35, Washington: International Monetary Fund.

Karacadag, Cem, 2003, "Financial System Soundness and Reform." In: Wanda Tseng and Markus Rodlauer (eds.) *China: Competing in the Global Economy*, 149–172.

Kramer, Charles, Hélène K. Poirson and A. Pradad, 2008, *Challenges to Monetary Policy from Financial Globalization: The Case of India*, IMF Working Paper No. 08/131.

Laurens, J. Bernard, 2005, *Monetary Policy Implementation at Different Stages of Market Development*, IMF Occasional Paper No. 244.

Laurens, J. Bernard and Rodolfo Maino, 2007, *China: Strengthening Monetary Policy Implementation*, IMF Working Paper No. 07/14.

[38] See Bruggeman et al. (2005).

Ma, Guonan and Robert N. McCauley, 2005, *Are China's Capital Controls Still Binding?* Bank for International Settlements.

MacKinnon, James G., Alfred A. Haug, and Leo Michelis, 1999, "Numerical distribution functions of likelihood ratio tests for cointegration," *Journal of Applied Econometrics*, 14, 563–577.

McKinsey Global Institute, 2006, *Putting China's Capital to Work: The Value of Financial System Reform*, McKinsey Global Institute.

Mehran, Hassanali, Bernard Laurens and Marc Quintyn, 1996, *Interest Rate Liberalization and Money Market Development: Selected Country Experiences*, International Monetary Fund.

Mehran, Hassanali, Marc Quintyn, Tom Nordman and Bernard Laurens, 1996, *Monetary and Exchange Reforms in China: An Experiment in Gradualism*, IMF Occasional Paper No. 141.

Mishkin, Frederic S., 2000, "From Monetary Targeting to Inflation Targeting: Lessons from the Industrialized Countries," in *Banco de Mexico, Stabilization and Monetary Policy: The International Experience*.

People's Bank of China, *Quarterly China Monetary Policy Reports* (various editions), People's Bank of China Monetary Policy Analysis Group.

People's Bank of China, 2004, *Challenges to China's Monetary Policy*, BIS Papers No. 23, pp. 124–127.

People's Bank of China, January, 2005, *Report on Advancement of Interest Rate Market Reforms*, People's Bank of China Monetary Policy Analysis Group.

People's Bank of China, March, 2008, Financial Work at the PBC Since 2003, People's Bank of China.

Podpiera, Richard, 2006, *Progress in China's Banking Sector Reform: Has Bank Behavior Changed?* IMF Working Paper No. 06/71.

Prasad, Eswar, Thomas Rumbaugh, and Qing Wang, 2005, *Putting the Cart Before the Horse? Capital Account Liberalization and Exchange Rate Flexibility in China*, IMF Policy Discussion Paper, PDP/05/1.

Walsh, Carl, 2003, *Monetary Theory and Policy*, Second edition, The MIT Press, Cambridge, Massachusetts, London.

Xie, Ping, 2004, *China's Monetary Policy: 1998–2002*, Working Paper No. 217, Stanford Center for International Development.

Zhou, Xiaochuan, March, 2005, *Exclusive interview with the People's Daily*.

Zhou, Xiaochuan, 2008, *Instability and Evolution of the Financial System*, People's Bank of China.

The China Monetary Policy Handbook

Jonathan Anderson

Abstract The monetary policy plays a critical role in the Chinese economy. This report takes a detailed and fundamental look at each of the following questions: (i) How does policy work? (ii) Which variables does the People's Bank of China (PBC) target? (iii) Does it have market-based tools? (iv) Does it have effective control of interest rates and liquidity? (v) Can it really influence growth and inflation? Or is the economy "beyond control,"chronically lurching into overheating, asset bubbles, and eventual sharp downturn. It also summarizes in part much of the work we have done on monetary and financial markets over the past few years.

Keywords Chinese economy · Chinese monetary policy · Monetary and exchange rate policy · Chinese asset prices and monetary policy

1 Overview and Summary

If we had to choose the single most misunderstood and confusing aspect of the Chinese economy, one that generates by far the most questions from outside investors, it would be the role of monetary policy.

After all, here is a country with a virtually fixed exchange rate, a commercial banking system and a central bank that were essentially rebuilt from scratch over the past two decades, and heavy reliance on administrative controls and directives in key parts of the economy. How does policy work? Which variables does the People's Bank of China (PBC) target? Does it have market-based tools? Does it have effective control of interest rates and liquidity? Can it really influence growth and inflation? Or is the economy "beyond control," chronically lurching into overheating, asset bubbles, and eventual sharp downturn.

J. Anderson (✉)
UBS, Hong Kong, China
e-mail: jonathan.anderson@ubs.com

J.R. Barth et al. (eds.), *China's Emerging Financial Markets*,
The Milken Institute Series on Financial Innovation and Economic Growth 8,
DOI 10.1007/978-0-387-93769-4_5,

This report takes a detailed and fundamental look at each of the above questions, summarizing in part much of the work we have done on monetary and financial markets over the past few years. The key findings are as follows.

First and foremost, we believe that the PBC and other related agencies generally get a "bad rap" from outside investors and analysts, who tend to see the monetary authorities as unreconstructed relics of the socialist planning era without much grasp of market tools. In our experience, this view has more to do with the historically unprecedented and painful boom-bust cycle of the 1990s than it does with the present situation; the current reality is very different. While the Chinese policy toolkit is not complete, policy makers have quickly evolved a more useful and stable set of instruments – and instruments that are generally more market-based than many investors realize. This is a crucial conclusion, as it underlines our call for continued strong growth over the next 5 years.

On the interest rate front, China still maintains a floor on bank lending rates and effectively fixed deposit rates, but other rates in the money and bond markets are freely floating. What is more, the effects of commercial bank rate controls are often overstated, since the bank lending rate is now being set by supply and demand at the margin (although artificially depressed deposit rates do have an impact on the economy). PBC policy rates are not used much, if at all, but this is because the PBC targets the quantity of base money rather than the price, and because high FX reserve inflows mean that the short-term sterilization rate is now the de facto policy rate in China. And despite the widespread view that mainland interest rates are far too low, there is no clear evidence that this is the case for rates in general; in particular, the corporate cost of capital is reasonable or even high by Asian historical standards.

Quantitative management is the true "workhorse" of Chinese monetary policy – and there is nothing wrong with this in principle. Investors tend to forget that using the volume of base money liquidity as the intermediate policy target is every bit as "market-based" as targeting interest rates, and historically practiced by central banks around the world. In fact, with the distortions introduced by state ownership of firms and banks there are good arguments in favor of quantitative management over interest rate tools in China. There is also a separate issue of direct administrative controls on commercial bank credit in the mainland, which are clearly distortionary from an economic point of view, but even here the system has evolved from detailed line-item credit planning 20 years ago to less invasive "window guidance" ceilings on overall credit growth (which are generally only invoked in periods of rapid credit acceleration or overheating).

One of the most controversial facets of the Chinese economy today is the combination of a quasi-pegged exchange rate, record-high trade surpluses, very large foreign exchange (FX) reserve inflows and extensive domestic sterilization policies to mop up the resulting liquidity. There are two points to make here: First, despite the large external surpluses and FX reserve accumulation, there is no sign that FX inflows are "overwhelming" domestic monetary policy. The bulk of these inflows has been sterilized, the credit cycle is broadly under control, and money market interest rates are still relatively low. Indeed, China is still well behind other countries in the region in terms of the size and scope of sterilization operations.

Second, this implies that the fixed exchange rate regime has not taken away monetary independence, regardless of the level of renminbi (RMB) undervaluation. Why? In part because China is a relatively large, domestically oriented economy and in part because of binding controls on external capital inflows. On the other hand this situation cannot last forever, particularly if large surpluses persist, and the authorities would be well advised to let the currency adjust more significantly over the next few years in order to reduce trade pressures.

Another more recent development which has raised questions among investors is a shift by the PBC toward active, repeated increases in the commercial bank required reserve ratio. Contrary to the common perception, these ratio hikes are not actually a macro tightening measure; rather, they are simply another means of sterilizing FX inflows, aimed at keep domestic liquidity constant on a net basis. As a result, there is no "ceiling" on the ratio in the near future, and the central bank will likely continue to use required reserve increases for a while to come. Eventually, however, the accumulated costs to the banking system will start to matter, and we expect the PBC to shift its focus toward longer-term bonds as the next favored sterilization instrument.

Perhaps the most visible Chinese trend of all has been the dramatic recovery of the equity market, with six-fold returns in domestic A shares over the past 2 years. The common view is that mainland asset prices are being pushed up by excessively loose monetary and interest rate policies together with large external inflows, but our analysis suggests that most important factor is actually the extreme historical imbalance between China's accumulated stock of bank deposits and the small initial holdings of equity and property assets. In this situation the PBC cannot do much to prevent asset price bubbles, since raising rates and tightening liquidity at the margin is not very effective. Finally, we note that with the exception of high-end markets in selected cities, mainland property prices are nowhere near as frothy as the stock market, i.e., this is a local rather than a nationwide issue.

Where does Chinese monetary policy go from here? Based on current trends, we believe the PBC and the financial system will move much closer to their counterparts in higher-income countries over the next 5–7 years, with (i) a more privatized banking system with the state playing a passive role, (ii) a larger and better-functioning bond market, (iii) freely floating commercial bank interest rates, (iv) a shift from quantitative to interest-rate policy targeting, and (v) the removal of administrative "window guidance" constraints. On the external front, we expect a more liberalized (albeit still controlled) capital account regime with a stronger and more flexible renminbi exchange rate. A combination of currency appreciation and natural market forces should also help bring the trade surplus back toward a more balanced position.

Where could things go wrong? Our main concerns lie with the sustainability of China's present external surpluses and the strategy of large-scale intervention and sterilization over the medium-term. As discussed in the report, the mainland economy is still a good way away from the "hard choices" recently faced by countries like Thailand and India – but this will not be the case forever, and as China liberalizes its economy the authorities need to make sure it has taken the necessary steps to rebalance its trade position and make the renminbi more flexible.

2 The Backdrop

Key points in this section:

- China's financial system and its central bank are both relatively recent creations, and still a work in progress.
- The state also still plays a significant role in the mainland economy, which introduces distortions in resource allocation and commercial decision-making.
- Nonetheless, the modern market is winning out; China has made enormous strides over the past decade in gaining control over macroeconomic instruments and achieving economic stability.
- The PBC has not yet reached "state of the art" central banking, i.e., inflation targeting and price-based management in a fully flexible financial market – but it is important to remember that even the most developed countries have not been there very long.

Before we go into a discussion of monetary policy proper, we need to review the broader background against which policy takes place, including a few elements that make China relatively unique among major global economies.

2.1 The Financial System – A Work in Progress

The first point to make is that China's commercial banking system, equity and bond markets, and indeed the central bank itself as a separate policy institution are all very recent creations, at least by post-war standards. Of course China has a history of financial innovation and institution-building stretching back thousands of years, but with the establishment of the People's Republic of China in 1949 the government followed a classical Marxist pattern, closing down the preexisting financial structures and replacing them with a monobank structure that allocated resources according to central and local budgetary plans.

It was not until the 1980s that the mainland first began to separate enterprise balance sheets from the national plan, and first split off the financial system into commercial banks providing loans on the one hand and a distinct central bank managing policy on the other. At it was not really until the mid-1990s, when the government was reestablishing control over the economy following the runaway bubble of 1991–94, that the PBC consistently began to use modern monetary instruments.

A decade later, the entire financial system is still very much a work in progress, with banks widening commercial operations beyond "plain vanilla" lending and improving internal governance structures, equity and bonds markets just coming back on line in the past few years, and the PBC still working to establish a complete set of policy instruments (see the banking system discussion in *How To Think About China, Part 3, Asian Economic Perspectives, 5 September 2005* for further details).

2.2 The Role of the State

Another crucial issue in the mainland economy is the role of the state in commercial decisions and resource allocation – and here as well the current environment is very much a work-in-progress. As far back as 25 years ago, private ownership and enterprise barely existed, and in theory the state ran the economy as a planning exercise. Again, it was not until the 1980s that the government broke up collective farms and established individual farming, gave state companies independent accounting systems and relative commercial freedom, and allowed small private enterprises to come on the scene.

Even today, after two decades of gradual privatization and organic private growth, the state still directly owns roughly one-quarter of the productive economy and a slightly higher share of industry (Chart 1, see *How To Think*

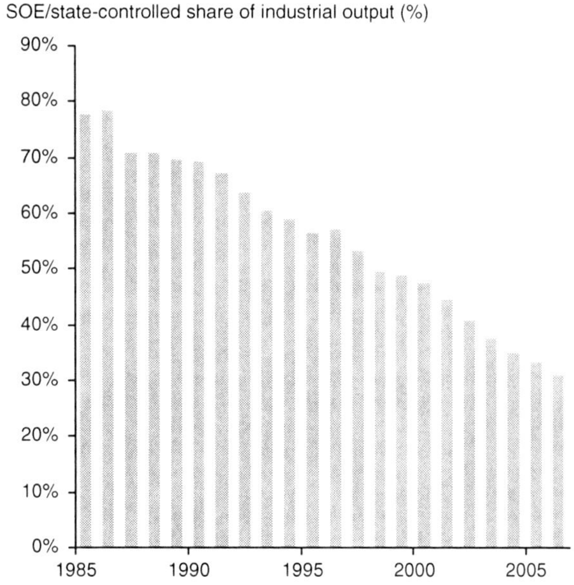

Chart 1 The state share of Chinese industry
Source: CEIC, UBS estimates

About China, Part 1, Asian Economic Perspectives, 6 January 2005 for further discussion). And more important still, the banking system remains predominantly state-owned; the government maintains an absolute majority share in the largest commercial institutions accounting for two-thirds of bank loans and assets and appoints top bank managers as civil servants. If we include indirect holdings through state agencies and enterprises, the state has a majority in most smaller commercial banks as well.

This means that the scope for formal and informal involvement in commercial decision-making is still a part of mainland economic life. For the most part, the central government is trying actively to promote an efficient banking system, but local and regional authorities have strong ties to their local banking counterparts, and the recent spate of financial corruption cases highlight the distortions in the banking system.

One of our consistent findings over the years is that both state lenders and state borrowers have an incentive to take excessive risks, with the view that capital is cheap and the state will always step in to cover losses. This puts the onus on the government to directly monitor and control state banks' balance sheets. And indeed, when central policies have been watchful, banks are generally well-behaved. However, when the government has taken an expansionary, pro-growth stance, the economy has traditionally shown a marked tendency toward overinvestment.

Another very relevant aspect of state control for the purposes of this report is the part government and party structures play in monetary management itself. Unlike developed countries, where central banks have both legal and functional independence and are free to pursue consistent policy aims, in China the PBC is subordinate to the State Council in monetary policy decisions – and everything from credit targets to interest rate movements are formally decided at a higher level, with conflicting interests from various ministries and agencies historically having a large influence on the process.

2.3 The Rise of the Market

Despite these historical handicaps and continued objective distortions, however, the mainland has also made dramatic progress over the past decade in gaining control over macroeconomic instruments and achieving economic stability. And as we will show in subsequent sections, one of the biggest mistakes investors can make is to judge Chinese policy today by the experience of the past 15 years.

You can see this in the behavior of monetary aggregates. In the 1980s, China saw fiercely overheated money and credit expansion, with growth rates jumping to 30% y/y and remaining at that pace for a number of years, before coming off sharply in the latter part of the decade (Chart 2). Exactly the same pattern occurred in the 1990s: a protracted round of very excessive money growth

Chart 2 Money and credit growth
Source: CEIC, UBS estimates

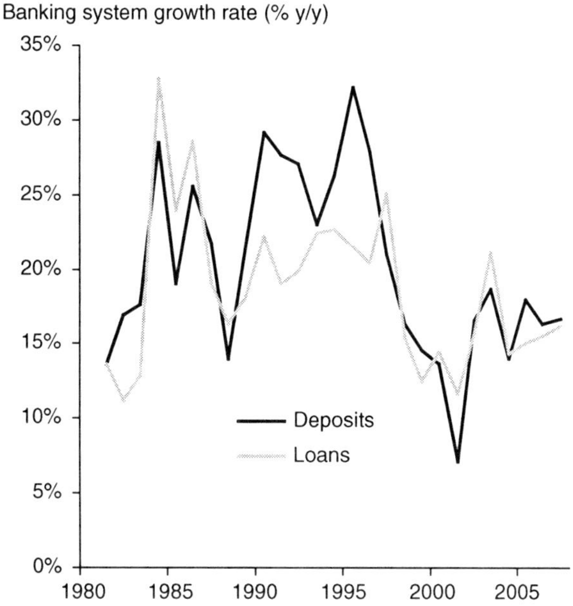

followed by a sharp contraction. By contrast, in the last 6 years loan growth barely spiked above 16% y/y on an annual basis and has quickly settled back into a more stable range.

As a result of the volatility in monetary aggregates in the 1980s and 1990s, China saw equally dramatic swings in real growth and inflation. Chart 3 below shows our estimates for real GDP and domestic demand growth rates since 1980. As you can see, the economy careened from nearly 15% y/y in 1984–85 to outright recession by the end of the decade, then back to strong double-digit growth followed by another sharp downturn in the 1990s. On the inflation front, as well, CPI growth went from 20% y/y in the mid-1980s to nearly zero, then jumped to nearly 25% y/y at the peak in 1994 before dropping into deflation only a few years later (Chart 4).

Looking at the charts, however, it is clear that the economy has visibly settled down since the beginning of the decade. Real GDP growth has averaged 10%, with very small annual deviations, and inflation rates have been slowly and steadily climbing from the late 1990s' trough. This may come as a surprise to many outside investors, who generally assume that Chinese volatility has been increasing over the past 7 years – but as the charts show, nothing could be further from the truth.

What changed? How has the economy escaped the extraordinary swings that characterized previous decades? A large part of the answer is the reversal of the contributing factors we discussed above. State ownership may still account for one-quarter of commercial activity today, but two decades ago the figure would have been 70–80%. The *role* of the state in economic activity has changed as

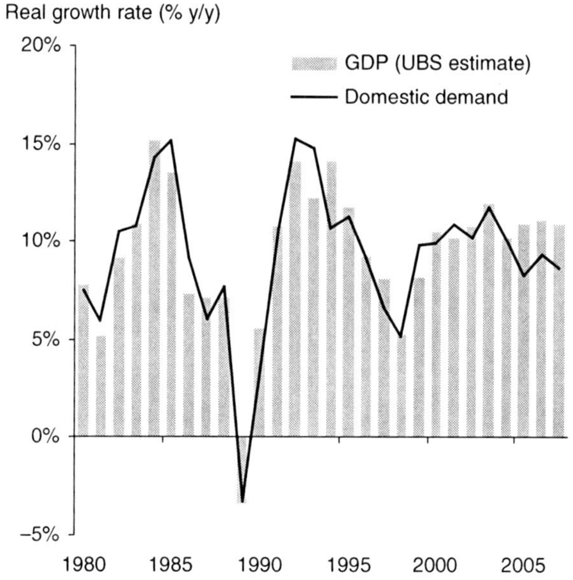

Chart 3 China's boom-bust economy
Source: CEIC, UBS estimates

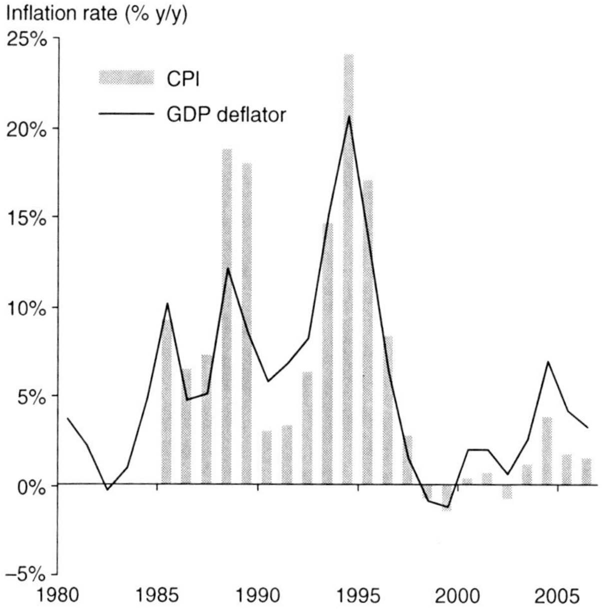

Chart 4 China's boom-bust inflation
Source: CEIC, UBS estimates

well; as we showed in *How To Think About China, Part 1*, the economy has undergone a striking evolution over the past 20 years to a more commercial, market-based system, and formal government interference is now concentrated in regulatory and investment decisions in a limited number of state-led sectors.

Finally, compared to the situation just 10 years ago the authorities now have much more experience in macroeconomic management – in part precisely because of the lessons learned from the last two boom-bust cycles. China now has a professional central bank and aggressive financial market regulators who, while not fully independent, are enjoying a higher degree of technical autonomy and internal credibility than ever before in the mainland's post-war history. Indeed, foreign visitors to Beijing are routinely surprised at the level of competence in the monetary authorities, especially for a low-income developing nation.

2.4 *Financial Market Underdevelopment*

Another important aspect of the Chinese policy environment is the historical lack of viable non-bank financial markets, i.e., domestic bonds, equities, and related financial instruments. Just look at Chart 5 and 6 below; the first shows the composition of liquid financial wealth in China, including bank deposits,

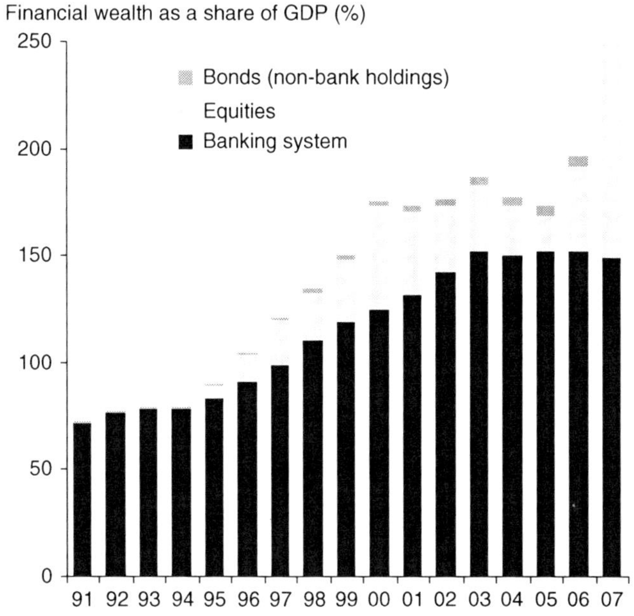

Chart 5 Liquid wealth holdings in China
Source: CEIC, UBS estimates

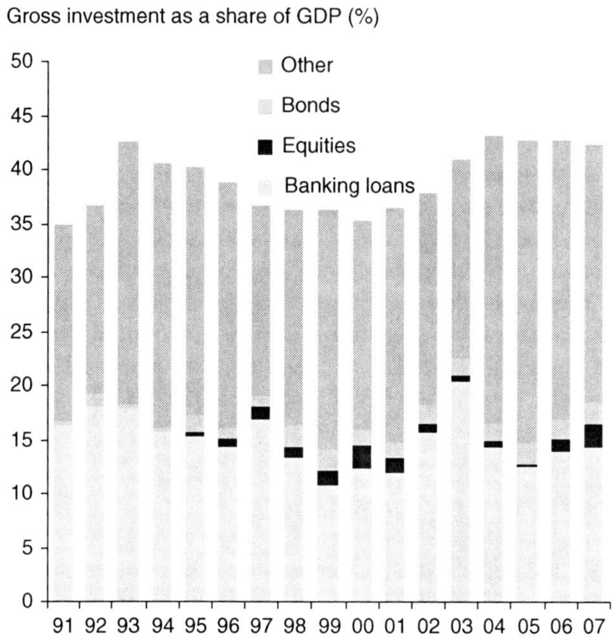

Chart 6 Investment finance in China
Source: CEIC, UBS estimates

bonds, and equities, while the second shows the breakdown of annual investment by financing category for the same instruments (the "other" category is mostly retained earnings).

As you can see, for most of the past two decades the banking system has effectively been "the only game in town" for Chinese savers, accounting for roughly 90% of total financial wealth holdings on average. It has also been the only real source of market financing for firms, accounting for roughly the same share on the investment side.

This is all the more true since China also maintains a closed external capital account regime, which makes it very difficult for households and firms to repatriate savings offshore or borrow abroad for investment needs (we will discuss capital account restrictions in greater detail below).

What does this mean for the economy? In fact, the lack of developed alternative financial markets is both negative and positive from a policy point of view. Negative, since limiting the number of saving and investment channels automatically reduces the efficiency of capital allocation, and has led to a visibly "overbanked" economy in China.

However, it is also positive in the sense that it makes the financial system more forgiving of policy mistakes and allows the authorities time to develop monetary instruments. If financial markets do not play a significant role in the economy, then even large swings in market flows or pricing do not affect the broader growth outlook, i.e., China has never really faced either a domestic or external "margin call".

The situation is changing rapidly today, as the government liberalizes equity and bond markets at home and gradually opens the capital account abroad. This also implies a change in the response function to monetary policy – holding the central bank to a higher standard, if you will – but keep in mind that these changes are occurring in large part because the PBC and the regulators are becoming more confident in their ability to carry out market-based monetary management.

2.5 Defining Our Terms: What Do We Mean by "Market-Based" Monetary Policy?

Finally, we need to take a moment to define our terms. What do we mean by monetary policy, and what do we mean by "market-based" policy? Is the global benchmark to which the PBC and other policy agencies should be held? And how relevant is developed economy experience for China?

In general, there are three distinct aspects to monetary policy in any economy. The first is the *final policy target* for central banks, which is the economic outcome the authorities are trying to influence; this could be inflation, nominal growth, the level or growth rate of the overall money supply, the exchange rate, or other variables.

The second is the *intermediate target*, or the main policy instrument used to reach the goal; here the main choice is between "price-based" policy, i.e., setting short-term interest rates and letting the base money stock adjust accordingly, and "quantity-based" policy, i.e., targeting the volume of base money and letting interest rates adjust.

The third aspect is the broader policy environment, including other administrative controls as well as the state of the overall financial system. Does the government directly control commercial bank interest rates? Are there restrictions on the operation of the money market? Do alternative financing channels operate freely? And is the capital account open or closed?

A few quick points here will prove very salient to the subsequent discussion. To begin with, there is a big difference between "money targeting" as a final policy target and "money targeting" as an intermediate policy tool. The first refers to central banks who have broad money M2 or M3 as their end goal (i.e., rather than inflation or growth). The second refers to banks that may have inflation, exchange rates, or nominal growth as their end target but use quantitative adjustments in the base money stock rather than policy interest rate adjustments to deliver the results.

Next, when we talk about "market-based" monetary policy, this has nothing to do with which targets the central bank chooses *per se*; instead, the term refers to the presence or absence of administrative controls on economic activity. To be more specific, setting policy interest rates and setting the quantity of base money as intermediate instruments are *both* "market-based" measures (again, one sets a price while letting quantities adjust; the other sets a quantity while letting prices adjust). So are inflation targeting, fixed exchange rate regimes and monetary targeting as final policy goals. From an economic theory point of view, all of these are equally market-driven.

2.6 A Review of Developed Country Experience

When investors today think about "state of the art" monetary policy, they generally think of a central bank which follows a stable (if not rigorously strict) inflation target using policy interest rates as its sole intermediate tool and operates in a free and open financial market environment. This has indeed become the de facto academic standard and is a pretty good description of how the US Federal Reserve Board and the European Central Bank function today. By comparison, the Chinese monetary authorities – who, as we will see below, follow a nominal growth target using quantitative base money tools as well as a number of direct administrative controls – look extremely unusual to most outside observers.

However, we also need to keep in mind that the current "developed country consensus" is a very recent development. As far back as two decades ago, things looked very different even in some of the most advanced global economies.

Prior to the 1970s, most European countries had fixed exchange rate regimes under the Bretton Woods system, making the international value of the currency the most important final policy target; domestic inflation and even nominal growth were decidedly secondary issues on a day-to-day basis. And in contrast to current practice, even more developed financial systems were riddled with administrative controls and restrictions, from closed capital accounts to widespread controls on interest rates, and outright credit controls and limitations on market development. Indeed, as we will see below, in many respects Chinese monetary policy today is a good deal more market-friendly and "modern" than for key European central banks in the 1960s.

In the 1970s, with the breakdown of the Bretton Woods system, central banks were forced to rethink broad policy goals and strategies – but virtually no one opted for the orthodox inflation targets that increasingly define central banking today. Instead, most banks initially focused on nominal growth targets (driven by the fashionable "Phillips curve" analysis at the time) and then turned to more rigid monetary targets in reaction to rising inflation. In fact, there was a period in the late 1970s and early 1980s when nearly every major developed central bank (United States, United Kingdom, Germany, Canada, Switzerland, to name but a few) considered itself a quantitative targeter. And throughout the decade, controls on interest rates, capital flows, and financial development remained fairly strict.

It was not really until the 1980s and beginning of the 1990s that we would call a "modern" financial and monetary policy environment came into being. Driven by academic advances, central banks began to hone their attention on inflation. Interest rate caps in the United States and Europe were dismantled. Credit controls were removed and external capital flows were liberalized. Investors everywhere began focusing on policy interest rates as the main indicator of financial conditions. And this is broadly where we find ourselves today.

But again, as a global phenomenon this modern construct has only existed for the past 20 years or so. And as we go through the detailed analysis in this report, one of our most consistent findings will be that simply because Chinese monetary policy is much closer to global practice a few decades back *does not* mean that the PBC has no monetary tools and is not using market-based instruments.

3 Interest Rates

Key points in this section:

- China still maintains a ceiling on bank deposit rates and a floor on lending rates – but the latter is no longer binding at the margin, and money market and bond rates are also market-determined.
- Official PBC policy rates are essentially meaningless for the economy at present, since with the exception of the sterilization bills rate they are rarely used.
- The main purpose of continued commercial bank interest rate controls is to prop up net interest margins in the state banking system.
- Deposit rates would clearly rise if they were liberalized, but there is no evidence that the overall level of interest rates is "too low" in China.

We begin this section with a brief introduction of the various rates used in China today.

Lending and deposit rates. First up are commercial bank interest rates. Mainland banks offer a plethora of lending and deposit rates, and a full discussion of domestic and foreign-currency rates is well beyond the scope of this report; however, end-October 2007 benchmark rates for key maturities on household and corporate deposits as well as corporate loans are shown in Chart 7.

These benchmark rates are not set by banks themselves; rather, they are determined directly by the PBC. In fact, however, the rates used in actual transactions can differ. Up until 2004 commercial banks were not allowed to deviate from the published rates by more than 10%, but since the beginning of 2004 the PBC has removed the floor on deposit rates and the ceiling on lending rates – i.e., banks are free to pay any rate for deposits as long as the rate is at or below the benchmark deposit rate and charge any rate for commercial loans as long as the rate is at least 90% of the benchmark lending rate or above.

Chart 7 Commercial bank benchmark rates, October 2007
Source: People's Bank of China

Current Deposits Rate	**0.81%**
Time Deposits Rate: 3 Months	**2.88%**
Time Deposits Rate: 6 Months	**3.42%**
Time Deposits Rate: 1 Year	**3.87%**
Time Deposits Rate: 2 Year	**4.50%**
Time Deposits Rate: 3 Year	**5.22%**
Time Deposits Rate: 5 Year	**5.76%**
Base Lending Rate: 6 Months	**6.48%**
Base Lending Rate: 1 Year	**7.29%**
Base Lending Rate: 3 Year	**7.47%**
Base Lending Rate: 5 Year	**7.65%**
Base Lending Rate: 10 Year	**7.83%**

In practice, this has yielded de facto fixed deposit rates but also more floating lending rates. As we showed in *The Sword Hanging Over Chinese Banks (Asian Focus, 15 December 2006)*, China's overly crowded banking system and the resulting intense competition for deposits effectively guarantees that banks cannot feasibly offer deposit rates below the published benchmark level. In fact, if the government were to completely liberalize interest rates tomorrow, we believe average deposit rates would rise sharply (about which more in the final section below).

By contrast, average lending rates have already begun to rise above the mandated benchmark floor, as commercial banks gradually widen the scope of lending to include more small- and medium-sized firms, and price risk accordingly. Since the 2004 lending rate liberalization, PBC data now show that roughly 50% of loans outstanding carry an interest rate above the reference floor, with an average upward margin of around 15%, or some 100 basis points. And this implies that the majority of new loans contracted over the past 2 years were at rates above the reference floor. Data from our UBS financials research team show the same trend; between 2004 and the first half of 2007, the average gross interest yield of the five large listed state banks rose by more than 120 basis points, while the average reference lending rate only rose by around 80 basis points over the same period. We are still in the early days of this "delinkage" process, of course, but the fact remains that the lending floor no longer seems to bind at the margin.

The behavior of benchmark lending and deposit rates over time is shown in Chart 8. As you can see, rates were relatively high in the inflationary period from 1990 to 1995, and then fell sharply in the latter part of the decade, with deposit rates set well below lending rates. Since 2005, the PBC has once again begun to hike benchmark rates as a response to higher growth and higher inflation. We will have more to say on all these trends further below.

Central bank rates. Like almost all central banks around the globe, the PBC also quotes a full range of policy rates on direct monetary operations. The four main categories are (i) the so-called PBC "base" or benchmark rate, which is

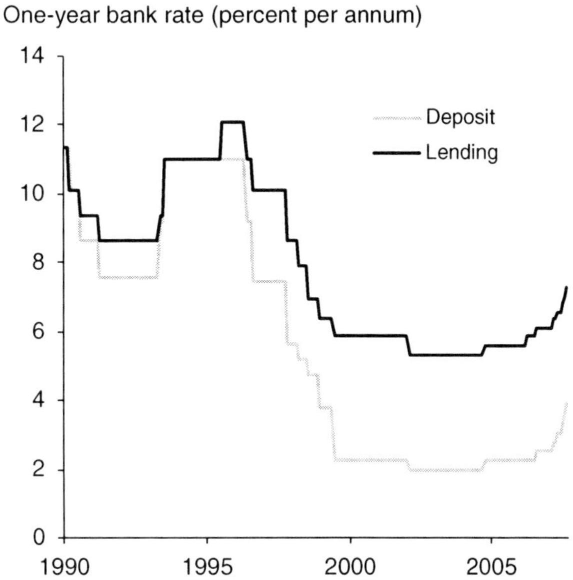

Chart 8 Commercial bank reference rates
Source: CEIC

used when the central bank provides refinance credit on a fixed-term basis to the banking system, (ii) the rediscount rate, which is applied when the PBC enters into repurchase operations involving commercial bank paper, (iii) the rate of remuneration on required and excess reserve deposits with the central bank, and (iv) the yield on PBC bills, i.e., debt paper issued at various maturities for sterilization purposes.

The level of these rates as of end-August 2007 is shown in Chart 10, and the trend in rates is shown in Chart 9 above. The first three categories are

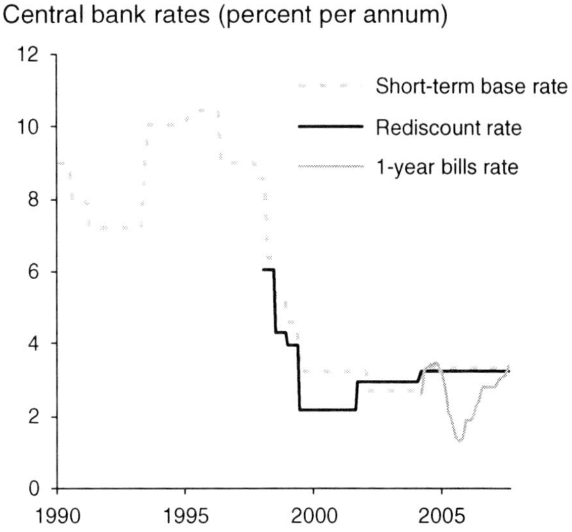

Chart 9 PBC rates
Source: CEIC

Chart 10 PBC interest rates, October 2007
Source: People's Bank of China

Base: Less Than 20 Days	3.33%
Base: 3 Months or Less	3.60%
Base: 6 Months or Less	3.78%
Base: Annual	3.87%
Rediscount Rate	3.24%
Required Reserves	1.89%
Excess Reserves	0.99%
PBC bills 3-month	2.80%
PBC bills 1-year	3.25%
PBC bills 3-year	3.74%

determined by the PBC directly (the base rate and the interest rate on reserve deposits are fixed, while the quoted rediscount rate is an effective floor; the PBC has flexibility to transact at higher rates if needed).

Meanwhile, the yield on PBC bills is set in weekly auctions with commercial banks in a "semi-floating" manner. We say semi-floating since the PBC has experimented with different auction structures over the past 3 years, including fixed-volume auctions where the yield is set competitively as well as fixed-yield auctions where volumes can vary widely. In addition, the PBC has sometimes canceled auctions when it appeared that the yield demanded by commercial banks was "too" high.

Money market rates and bond yields. Finally, we have short-term money market interest rates and longer-term yields on corporate and government bonds. These are essentially free market rates, set independently according to underlying supply and demand conditions in the banking system and the economy.

On the short end of the curve, the bulk of the market is driven by interbank trading, including traditional commercial banks as well as brokers, insurance companies and other non-bank financial institutions. The National Interbank Funding Center records daily trading results as so-called CHIBOR (China interbank offered rate) rates, including straight lending and repo transactions across a range of maturities extending from overnight lending to 120 days; by far the most liquid are the overnight and 7-day maturities. There is also a growing commercial paper market, where firms can discount short-term paper with commercial banks. Maturities run from one month to one year and rates tend to hover above comparable CHIBOR repo rates.

In view of the volatility of CHIBOR rates (see below), over the past 12 months the government has also attempted to introduce a Shanghai-based market maker system, or SHIBOR, where a dozen or so major institutions undertake to provide liquidity in order to achieve a more stable market. In practice, to date SHIBOR rates have simply followed CHIBOR rates without any noticeable decrease in volatility.

The behavior of money market interest rates is shown in Chart 11 on the next page. As you can see, short-term rates fell sharply after China's hard landing in

Chart 11 Money-market rates and bond yields
Source: CEIC, UBS estimates

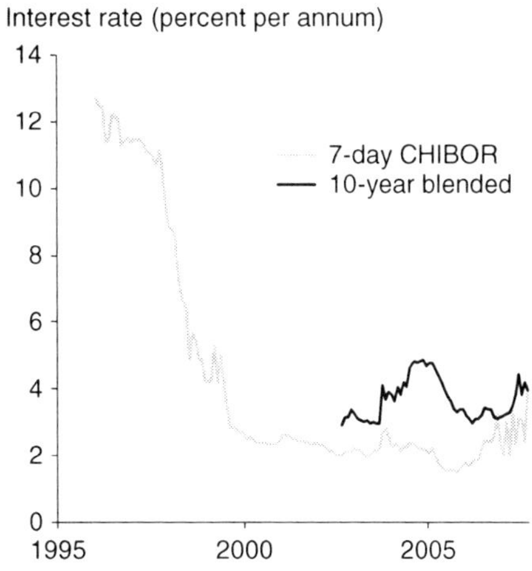

the late 1990s and remained low (at or below 2% per annum) for most of the following decade. It has only been in the last 12 months that short-term rates began to spike up and trade in a more volatile manner; we will have more to say about this in the next section.

On the long end of the curve, almost all of the action is driven by government bonds – a reflection of the extremely restrictive administrative controls on corporate bond issuance to date. National treasury bonds, together with related policy financial bonds, account for roughly 90% of total outstanding long-term securities and an even greater share of market trading and turnover.

Chart 11 shows the behavior of long-term bond yields as well (in this case, the constant-maturity 10-year yield as quoted by the National Interbank Funding Center; data-listed bonds on the Shanghai and Shenzhen exchanges show very similar trends). Long yields have been rising on trend for the past 2 years and are currently between 4.0% and 4.5% per annum.

3.1 Why Does China Have Interest Rate Controls?

At this point we should pause to address the question of why China maintains floors and ceilings on commercial bank interest rates in the first place. Historically, of course, lending and deposit rates were simply mandated as part of the overall economic and credit plans. But as we discuss further below, the days of dictated credit allocation are long gone, at least as a macroeconomic phenomenon, and both the central government and the financial regulators are actively pushing banks toward more market-oriented behavior, including commercial lending decisions, internal governance controls, risk management systems, rigorous audits, and the like. So why bother with continued interest rate controls?

Clearly the answer is not to ensure low cost of capital for state firms. As we show below, Chinese real lending rates are actually on the high side by east Asian standards – and remember that the authorities keep a *floor* on bank lending rates, not a ceiling.

On the deposit side, many analysts have focused on the need to keep the return on domestic liquid asset holdings low to avoid foreign capital inflows and ensure that intervention and sterilization operations remain profitable. We agree that this has been a source of general concern for the PBC over the past few years, but keep in mind that deposit ceilings outdate China's balance of payments surplus by many years (and keep in mind also that the evidence shows that external capital controls are still binding, see further below).

Rather, in our view the main reason for interest controls is to protect state bank margins. If you look back to Chart 8 above, you will see that commercial bank deposit and lending rates were virtually identical at the beginning of the 1990s – but by the end of the decade, the government had inserted a large "wedge" between deposit and lending rates, effectively ensuring that commercial banks had some of the widest net interest margins in the Asian region and in emerging markets more generally.

What happened during the 1990s? For the banking system, by far the biggest event was the explosion of credit growth in the 1991–95 bubble, followed by the macroeconomic hard landing and a sharp drop in corporate profitability in the second half of the decade. As a result of this boom-bust cycle, most independent analysts estimate that anywhere from 50 to 60% of the loans given prior to 1996 went bad (see *How To Think About China, Part 3* for further discussion on this point).

In this environment, the government was forced to artificially increase net interest margins by a considerable amount in order to ensure that state banks continued to see positive cash flow. This explains the floor on lending rates and the ceiling on deposit rates – and why the authorities are perfectly happy to see lending rates above the floor and deposit rates below the ceiling.

The government did initiate an aggressive program of NPL writedowns and state-led recapitalization beginning in 2003, which has taken away much of the historical bad debt problem, but this is still a work-in-progress (the last remaining major state bank to undergo restructuring is the Agricultural Bank of China, which should be completed in 2008). As late as 2005, we calculated in earlier research that even a 100 basis-point increase in deposit rates would have been enough to eliminate the entire pre-tax profit of China's "big four" state commercial banks; the ratio improved slightly in 2006 but not significantly.

3.2 How the System Works – And Which Rates to Watch

Now, having introduced the various interest rates in China we can now turn to the more important question: Which rates "matter"? That is, which rates do the policy authorities effectively target? And which rates have a real impact on the economy?

Our answer is simple – and perhaps surprising for many investors: The most important interest rates to watch are (i) short-term money market rates and (ii) commercial bank deposit rates. The reason we single out these two is that they are the only rates that are both effectively determined by policy actions at the margin (whether directly or indirectly) *and* have a substantial impact on economic trends.

Why central bank policy rates do not matter. Let us explain what we mean by process of elimination, starting with central bank interest rates. In an average developed economy, the policy lending or discount rate usually serves as an "anchor" for money market rates; in other words, since the central bank stands ready to buy or sell liquidity freely at the policy rate, other short-term rates do not deviate very far from central parity. Take the US economy as an example: as you can see in Chart 12 below, 1-month CD rates are virtually indistinguishable from the Fed Funds rate, and the same is true for 3-month Treasury bill rates as well.

Chart 12 These rates are close
Source: CEIC

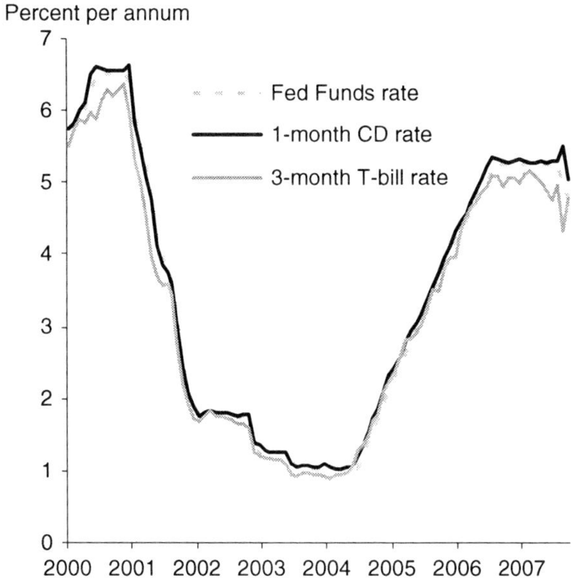

Now look at the relationship between Chinese money-market and policy rates in Chart 13. For the past 7 years there has hardly been any correlation at all; 7-day CHIBOR rates and 3-month sterilization bill rates are generally well below the PBC base and rediscount rates – and the two categories often move in opposite directions.

Why do not policy rates "work" in China? The first answer is that unlike the Fed, the PBC does not actually stand ready to buy and sell at these rates. In fact,

Chart 13 These rates are not close
Source: CEIC, UBS estimates

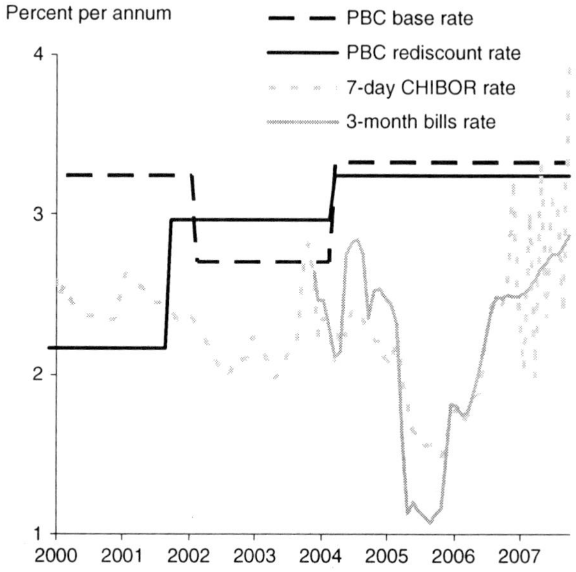

the PBC does relatively few transactions in the short-term market at all, and this is particularly true on the net emission side.

Consider Charts 14 and 15, which show the volume of PBC repo and reverse repo transactions respectively. When the central bank engages in repo

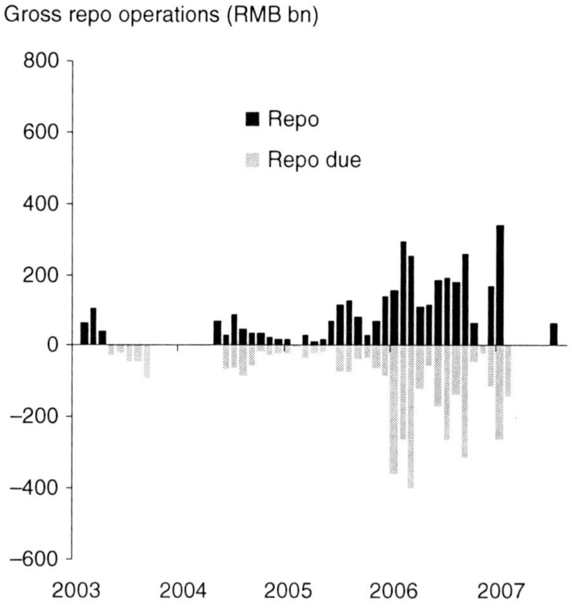

Chart 14 PBC repo transactions
Source: PBC, UBS Rates strategy

Chart 15 PBC reverse repo transactions
Source: PBC UBS Rates strategy

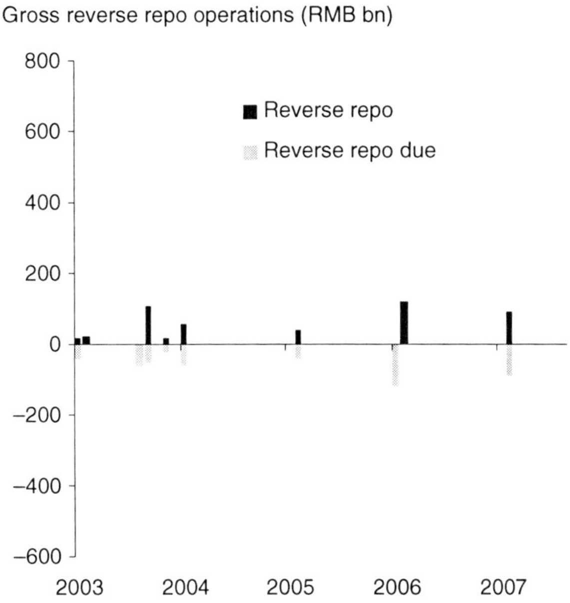

operations, it is taking liquidity out of the market (the dark grey bars in Chart 14 show the monthly gross repo volume, and the light grey bars show the subsequent gross unwinding of the repos); as you can see, the PBC was fairly inactive in the repo market from 2003 to 2005, then had a more aggressive bout of operations during 2006 – and for the past nine months has done virtually nothing.

Turning to reverse repo operations in Chart 15 – i.e., transactions aimed at putting net liquidity *into* the market – it is very clear that this window has effectively remained closed. With the exception of a small, quickly reversed liquidity injection in January and February every year (tied to the Chinese New Year holidays), the PBC has not undertaken any operations at all since 2004.

The same is true for refinance lending under the PBC base rate. The central bank has provided directed credit on a one-off basis to rural credit institutions and state-owned commercial banks in order to fund NPL write-downs, but other than that we have not seen any general net liquidity injection through the base lending window for the past 4 years. If anything, the PBC has steadily let outstanding refinance credit retire over the period (about which more below in the section on sterilization). Once again, the policy window has effectively been closed.

Why have not we seen more active two-way operations on the part of the central bank? This brings us to the second answer to our question above: As we will see below, for most of the past decade the Chinese financial system has been loaded with strong excess liquidity – and for the last 5 years has seen additional inflows to the tune of US $15–20bn a month (and closer to US $40bn a month in

2007). In this environment, since 2003 PBC monetary policy has consisted of one overriding goal: to drain liquidity from the system. And that drainage has not been carried out through short-term lending windows, but rather through sterilization operations further out along the curve, and more recently through increases in the required reserve ratio; see the discussion in later sections.

This helps explain why the PBC has been absent from overnight lending markets. And thus why money market rates have deviated so visibly from policy rates in the mainland – and why they have been so consistently *below* official policy rates. And, finally, why the PBC has not made more than a small token adjustment to either the base rate or the refinance rate in the past few years. Simply put, these rates do not matter very much in China today.

Why bond yields do not matter. The same is true for longer-maturity bond yields. In developed countries, bond yields play an important role in determining the overall cost of capital and in passing inflation expectations through to the rest of the economy; this is because most developed bond markets are both large and liquid. In the United States and EU, for example, corporate and government bonds make up around half of liquid financial wealth, and a similar share of external corporate fundraising.

Not so in China, however. As of end-2006, the total stock of mainland bank deposits was roughly US $4.5 trillion . . . compared to only US $800 billion of outstanding corporate and government bonds. And if we exclude bonds held in the banking system itself, that number falls to only US $130 billion, i.e., a tiny fraction of overall wealth.

You can see this from Charts 5 and 6 in the previous section above, which shows the breakdown of liquid financial wealth holdings as a share of GDP and the breakdown of annual gross investment flows by financing category respectively. In every respect, the role of bonds is very small relative to that the banking system. In fact, if we strip out government spending, commercial bank lending accounts for nearly all "external" investment financing in China, i.e., investment expenditure not covered by internal corporate funds.

Why do not bonds play a bigger role in the Chinese economy? To begin with, since the early 1990s the government has actively suppressed the development of the corporate bond market. Strict controls were adopted during the 1991–94 bubble to prevent excessive investment in the economy, and in the ensuing years the authorities have been very slow to liberalize new issuance policies.

Second, China has always maintained a relatively conservative fiscal policy. The national budget deficit reached a peak of around 4% of GDP in the late 1990s – a time when the government did issue new bonds in sizeable quantities – but the economic upturn since the beginning of this decade brought sharp increases in tax revenue, which in turn has meant a drop in new government issuance.

The result is as seen in Chart 11 above: Because of the relative shortage of long-dated paper, restrictions on corporate access to the market and the high levels of liquidity in the banking system, for the past decade bond yields have been significantly below corresponding long-term bank lending rates. This will change over time as the authorities liberalize the corporate bond market and increase quasi-government issuance (see the final section of this report), but in our view it will be a long time indeed before Chinese bond yields "matter" to the same degree as in more developed economies.

Why official bank lending rates do not matter. This point may be a bit confusing for most investors; after all, we just showed that commercial bank lending is virtually the sole source of outside financing for investment, and this means that bank lending rates effectively determine the marginal cost of capital for the entire economy. Among the factors impacting real growth and inflation in China, lending rates would have to be near the top of the list.

All of this is true, of course – but what we mean to say is that *official* reference lending rates do not matter, for the simple reason that they are no longer binding at the margin. As discussed in the previous section, since the PBC removed the loan rate ceiling nearly 4 years ago the average rate for loan transactions has gradually risen above the published reference rate. Although a sizeable portion of outstanding loans are still at the reference rate, the majority of new loans are not, which significantly reduces the impact of formal rate hikes (or cuts, for that matter) by the policy authorities. This is not to say that very large official rate increases (hundreds of basis points, for example) would not have a significant impact on the economy, but it does help explain why changing reference rates at the margin has not had any real effect on growth over the past few years.

Why money market rates matter. And now to the rates that do matter, in terms of the ability of policy actions to translate into actual economic results. First up are short-term CHIBOR and SHIBOR money market rates. We already argued that these rates are determined by market conditions rather than the central bank – but as we will show below, in an environment where the PBC targets quantitative monetary aggregates rather than the price of money, short-term money market rates are the only interest rates that react immediately to changes in the supply of liquidity in the system. In other words, they are the single best real-time "barometer" of the monetary policy stance in China.

You can see this in the day-to-day behavior of rates; since the middle of 2006, overnight and seven-day rates have spiked up sharply every time the PBC hiked reserve requirements in the past year, and for that matter every time another large company issued a domestic IPO, indicating a relative shortage of funds in the market (Chart 16). And then rates have inevitably come back down as new daily FX reserve inflows have replaced the lost liquidity. As we will show below, the average movement of money-market rates is an extremely accurate reflection of excess liquidity balances in the banking system.

These short-term rates also matter because they increasingly represent the marginal cost of funding to smaller banks and non-bank financial institutions in the system. Larger state-owned commercial banks account for the lion's share of deposits in the system, and in the past year or two we have seen a shift in net borrowing pattern, which many smaller institutions becoming chronic net users of short-term money market funds in order to finance new growth.

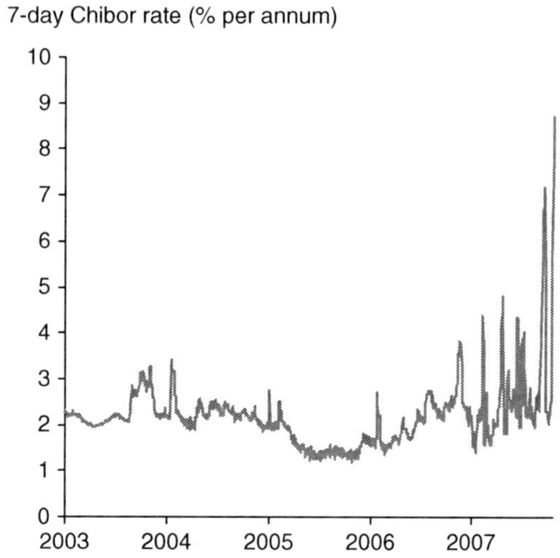

Chart 16 Money-market rates on a daily basis
Source: CEIC, UBS estimates

Why deposit rates matter. In contrast to the official reference lending rates we discussed a few paragraphs above, the published PBC deposit rate ceilings continue to play a much more important role in the Chinese economy. To begin with, the latter are binding; nearly every commercial bank in the country quotes deposit rates that are exactly at the reference ceiling. And this means when the PBC changes official rates the actual rates change immediately as well, one for one.

It also implies that market-clearing "equilibrium" deposit interest rates are above the official ceiling, i.e., deposit rates in China are held artificially low. As we will show below, this has potentially significant repercussions in asset markets, especially when nearly all financial savings is held in the banking system. So while changing deposit rates at the margin does not affect the corporate cost of capital, it directly affects the return earned by households and firms on deposit asset holdings and thus affects relative asset prices.

Finally, changes in official deposit rates affect banks earnings and margins, precisely because the deposit ceiling is binding while the lending floor is not: if the PBC raises deposit and lending reference rates in equal amounts, the effective deposit rate still goes up by more than the effective lending rate, potentially lowering profits in the banking system. And as we showed above, the authorities have traditionally been extremely sensitive about the state of commercial bank balance sheets.

3.3 Does the PBC Use Policy Rates?

Now let us turn to one of the most important findings of the report: Whether we compare with other countries in the region or with global counterparts, the PBC is one of the least active central banks in using its policy interest rates.

Chart 17 Not very active in moving rates
Source: CEIC, UBS estimates

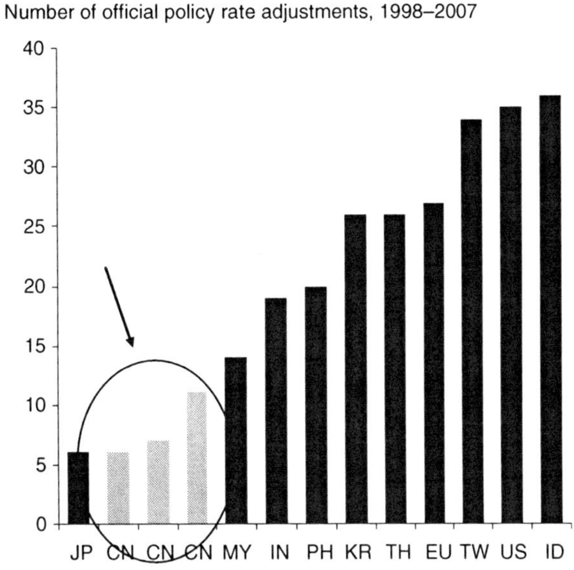

Consider Chart 17, which shows the number of official policy rate adjustments in selected countries from 1998 to 2007. Over that ten-year period, the ECB made more than 25 rate adjustments; the US Federal Reserve moved the Fed Funds rate around 35 times, or nearly four per year. The average for Asia ex-Japan (excluding China) was easily more than 20 adjustments.

By contrast, the PBC only changed its base lending rate five times and the repo rate six times over the same period; the PBC was a bit more aggressive on commercial bank reference lending rates, with 11 adjustments, but this was still far below the regional average (see the light green bars in the chart). Of all the countries we reviewed, only Japan was less active in moving rates – and this is primarily because the BoJ was following its "zero interest rate" policy for most of the period in question; in earlier decades, the BoJ was actually much closer to the United States and EU in terms of rate changes.

The PBC has also been far less aggressive than other central banks in terms of the magnitude of rate changes. Chart 18 shows the peak-to-trough swing in real policy interest rates (calculated using "core" CPI inflation for each country in the sample) across Asian and global economies since 1999. Real policy rates in high-inflation Asian countries such as India, Indonesia and the Philippines varied by more than 10 percentage points over the period; for the United States, EU and more moderate-inflation Asian countries, the average was around six percentage points. In China, however, the figure is closer to three percentage points regardless of which policy rate we use. Once again, only Japan was less active in changing rates over the period.

The bottom line is that China does not use policy interest rates as an active cyclical management tool. You can see this very clearly in Chart 19, which plots

Chart 18 Not very aggressive in rate swings
Source: CEIC, UBS estimates

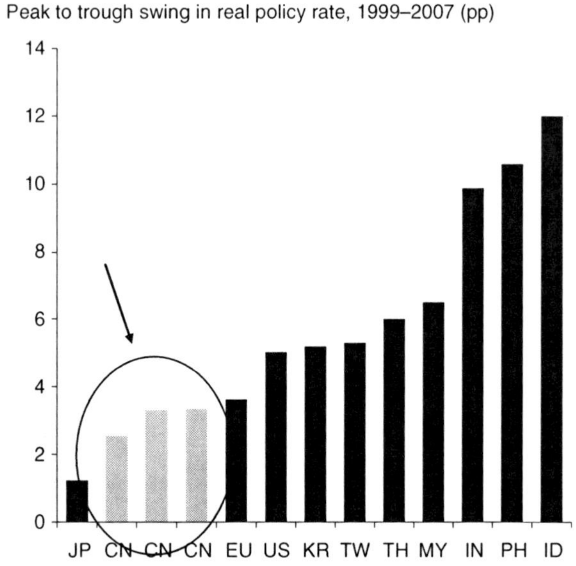

Chart 19 Real policy rates in China and the United States
Source: CEIC, UBS estimates

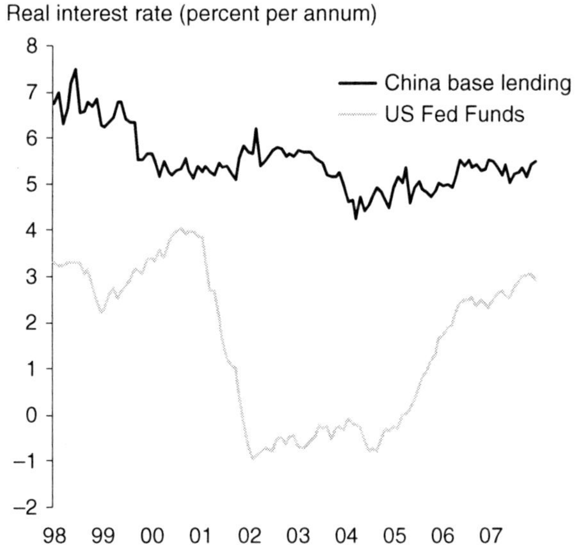

the path of the real commercial bank reference lending rate against the real US Fed Funds rate during the past decade.

When the US economy went into recession in 2001, the Fed cut nominal short-term interest rates by more than 500 basis points, which corresponded to a 500 basis-point change in *real* short term rates as well. In the ensuing recovery, the Fed also brought rates back up sharply in both nominal and real terms. In China, by contrast, the PBC has effectively kept real reference rates constant for the past 10 years – even as the economy went from hard landing in 1997–99 to recovery in 1999–2001 to outright boom in 2001–03, then to slowdown in 2004–05 and back again in the past 2 years.

In other words, even when the PBC does adjust interest rates, it does not behave like other central banks, who tend to move rates in a proactive, counter-cyclical manner. According to Chart 19, the PBC generally changes rates to *follow* inflation, not to lead it.

3.4 *Why Does Not China Use Interest Rate Tools More Aggressively?*

So why does not the PBC target policy rates more aggressively? Part of the answer is that in China the central bank does not have autonomy to make interest rate adjustments on its own. Rate decisions are formally made by the State Council Monetary Policy Commission – a body chaired by the PBC but representing other ministries and agencies as well – and in practice this means obtaining approval from the senior Chinese government leadership before significant changes are made. In our view, this is one of the key reasons why the monetary authorities have been so inactive on this front over the past decade.

However, this is not the only reason. As we will see below, the PBC has traditionally focused on other intermediate policy instruments, targeting the *quantity* of base money instead of the price and relying on administrative credit controls as well to rein in bank lending during periods of overheating.

Does this make sense? In our view, it does. To begin with, remember our earlier finding that targeting monetary aggregates rather than interest rates is an equally valid method of carrying out policy. And this has been particularly relevant for China over the past half-decade; as we discuss in the following sections, since 2003 the economy has faced unprecedented foreign exchange inflows under the fixed renminbi exchange rate regime – which means that the PBC has been forced to undertake continuous, sizeable sterilization operations in order to keep those inflows from flooding into domestic liquidity markets. These operations have been carried out at relatively flexible interest rates, of course, but the rates themselves naturally play a secondary role to the sheer volume of cash that needs to be "mopped up" on a monthly basis. In other words, whether it wanted to or not the central bank has effectively been pushed into a quantitative money management role.

Next, even in the absence of sterilization there are still good arguments for the PBC to use a combination of quantitative and administrative tools rather than relying on interest rates. As we discussed earlier on, the structure of the Chinese economy is still quite different from developed counterparts, or for that matter from most of its emerging neighbors; the fact that one quarter of GDP still accrues to state-owned firms, and in particular that the bulk of the banking sector is still in state hands, introduces very specific distortions in economic incentives.

Over the past few years, for example, the authorities faced what was essentially a state-led, sectoral overheating problem, as local governments and state enterprises poured excessive amounts of money into a handful of industrial sectors; on top of this, public and private developers were taking on far too much speculative leverage to build residential and commercial property. By contrast, the rest of the economy was broadly in balance, with strong demand growth, more reasonable capacity expansion and no real signs of inflationary pressures.

In this environment, the government had a choice: either rely solely on market-based measures and hike rates sharply, or levy sector-specific restrictions on lending and investment. Significantly raising interest rates would surely have slowed the economy, but mostly at the expense of the "good" part of the economy, which would see their funding costs increase and margins decline. Meanwhile, a rate hike might not have any effect on demand for inefficient, redundant industrial projects, since state-led and speculative borrowers are far less focused on the return to capital (or, for that matter, repaying loan principal).

As a result, the authorities chose to impose controls on an industry-by-industry basis. In our view, this was probably the correct choice: it clearly worked, as we will see in the following section, while still allowing dynamic growth in the rest of the economy. And these controls are not necessarily inconsistent with sound economic practice; the theory of the "second-best" openly states that non-market distortions are best met with similar non-market tools.

So while most economists would agree that the PBC should use all policy tools at its disposal in a more flexible manner, in the current economic environment there is also sound logic in focusing on other instruments rather than interest rates alone.

Finally, and once again, a couple of reminders before we leave this topic: First, just because the PBC keeps *policy* rates relatively stable does not mean that *overall* interest rates in the economy are inflexible. As we showed above, official short-term policy rates do not act as an "anchor" for other interest rates in the economy for the simple reason that they are not used, and both commercial lending rates and interbank money market rates are already set in a more or less market-determined fashion. The key remaining rigidity in the economy is the structure of deposit interest rates – but these have less impact on real growth and inflation and more on asset prices (see further below for details).

Second, as we discussed above, Chinese monetary policy today is simply not that much different from policy, say, in European central banks or even in the United States in the earlier post-war era, neither in terms of the lack of focus on policy rate instruments nor in terms of deposit interest rate controls.

3.5 Are Interest Rates "Too Low"?

Let us now turn to a related issue, and perhaps one of the most common questions raised by investors around the world: Are Chinese interest rates "too low"?

After all, bank lending rates, bond yields and money market rates may be flexible and set increasingly according to market conditions – but in an environment where the bulk of national savings is effectively trapped in commercial deposit accounts earning an artificially low return, is it not true that the entire rate structure is biased downward by this distortion? With nominal GDP growing at 12% on average since the beginning of the decade, should not average lending rates be of a similar magnitude, instead of the 8% we see now?

Now, we have no problem with the argument that deposit interest rates are set too low in China; we already saw above that average commercial bank deposit rates are almost exactly at the reference rate set by the PBC, which implies that nationwide rates would rise if the central bank removed the ceiling. But this does not necessarily mean that the entire rate structure would need to rise – and indeed, if we look at overall rates in the economy, they do not look particularly low by Asian historical standards.

Let us explain what we mean. The common "rule of thumb" that nominal interest rates should be equal to the nominal growth rate in the economy (or, equivalently, that the marginal product of capital should be equal to real GDP growth) holds up fairly well over time in developed economies, and this helps explain its popularity among global investors.

But this rule of thumb has never remotely applied to high-growth Asian economies. Chart 20 shows the behavior of real interest rates (using the average

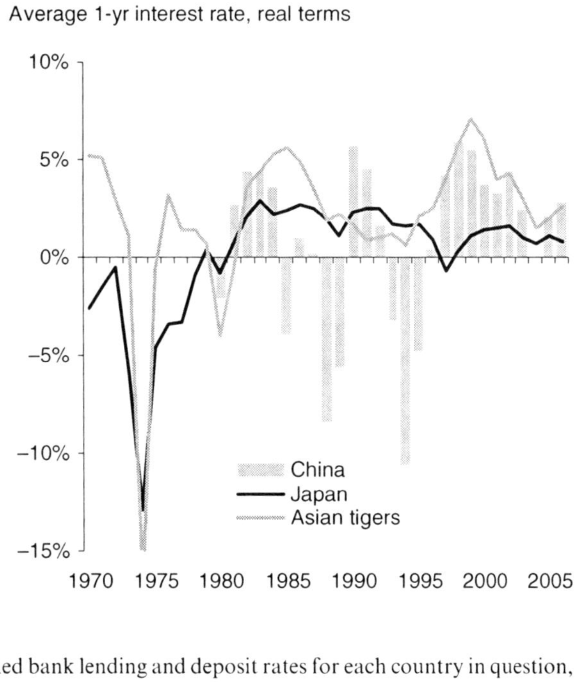

Chart 20 Real interest rates in Asia since 1970
Source: CEIC, Datastream, UBS estimates[1]

[1] We use the average of published bank lending and deposit rates for each country in question, and have attempted to come as close to a standard one-year rate as possible within the constraints of the data.

of lending and deposit rates) in Japan and the four Asian "tigers" over the past four decades, and Chart 21 shows the average level during the peak growth period; as you can see, average real rates were barely above zero in Japan and around 1.5% in the Asian tigers, far below the real rate of economic growth in every case.

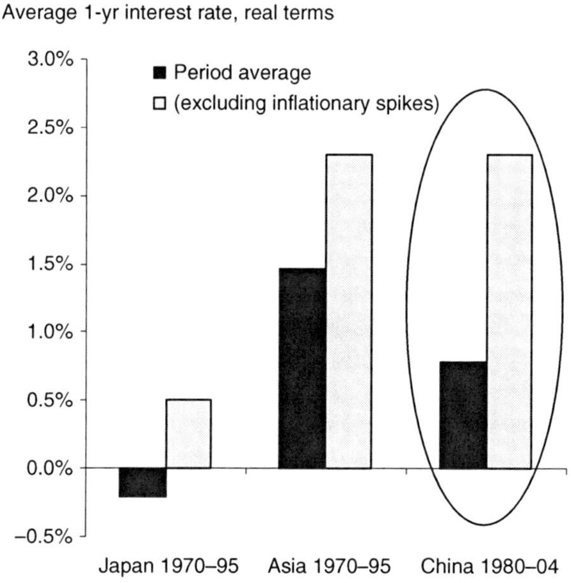

Chart 21 Average real interest rates in Asia
Source: CEIC, Datastream, UBS estimates

Why were interest rates so low compared to growth rates? As we showed in *How To Think About China, Part 5 (Asian Economic Perspectives, 15 November 2005)*, the single biggest determinant of real interest rates in the region has been the domestic savings rate. And with average savings ratios of 35–40% of GDP during their high-growth periods, more than twice as high as those in the United States or the EU, these Asian economies were able to sustain much higher investment ratios and thus much higher growth rates than their developed counterparts but also with lower average returns to capital and lower interest rates.

It should come as no surprise that China, with domestic saving rates now approaching 50% of GDP, shows a similar result; defined using the average of lending and deposit rates, real interest rates have fluctuated between 1 and 2% per annum since 1980, very much in line with regional experience. And as we saw earlier, if we just focus on lending rates deflated by core inflation, China's current real cost of capital is around 6% – well above the historical level in Japan and the tigers.

To restate our finding from the previous subsection, we would argue that a large part of China's tendency toward investment booms stems from the lack of credit discipline on the part of state banks and state-oriented borrowers, and not from mispricing of credit *per se*.

4 Quantitative Measures

Key points in this section:

- The PBC uses quantitative base money targets as its main intermediate policy tool, combined with direct administrative controls on overall credit growth.
- Base money targeting is just as "market-based" as policy interest rate targeting and has generally been effective in China. Moreover, this effectiveness is rising over time as banking system excess liquidity declines.
- Administrative "window guidance" controls are much weaker than former sector-by-sector credit allocation practices and can also be seen as a natural response to remaining state distortions in other parts of the economy.
- Focusing on loan-deposit ratios and broad money growth is misleading in the current economic environment.

The main point of this section is simple: Just because the PBC does not use interest rates as its intermediate target to adjust monetary policy, this *does not* mean that the central bank has no policy tools.

Begin with the following two charts, showing the path of bank lending and real construction activity since the beginning of the decade. In 2002–03 China saw a sharp upturn in credit growth, reaching 25% y/y at the peak of the boom cycle – and then an equally sharp drop when the authorities tightened in 2004, down to nearly 10% y/y (Chart 22). And if we turn to the construction sector the 2004 contraction was even more pronounced, with real construction growth falling to low single-digit levels by the second half of the year (Chart 23). Clearly, the PBC achieved a very significant policy tightening, even if policy interest rates were virtually untouched.

The same is true when we turn to the longer-term behavior of money and credit (Chart 24 below, which is a repeat of the Chart in the first section of this report). In the 1980s money and credit growth jumped to 30% y/y and remained at that pace for a number of years before the subsequent downturn. This pattern repeated itself in the 1990s: A large, protracted credit boom with unprecedented levels of liquidity growth followed by a sharp contraction.

By contrast, in the latest cycle loan growth barely spiked on a full-year basis and has quickly settled back into a more stable range. Again, the implication is that the economy is managed more effectively now than at any time in the past few decades.

How does this management work? The answer is quantitative monetary measures. In China, these come in two forms: (1) "standard" quantitative

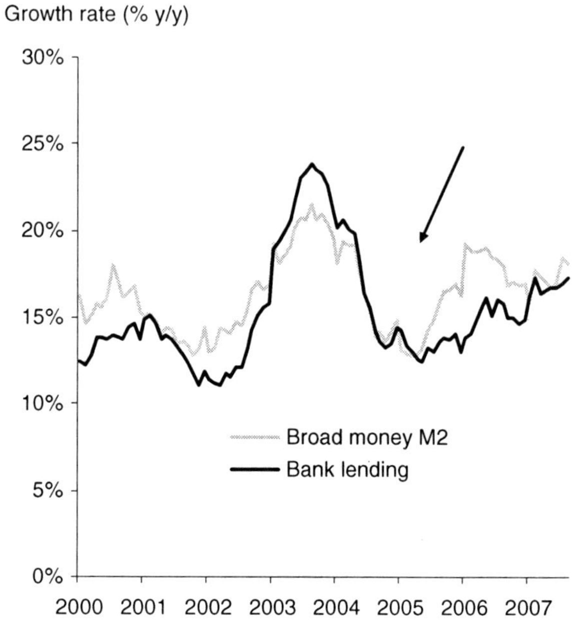

Chart 22 Bank credit growth
Source: CEIC, UBS estimates

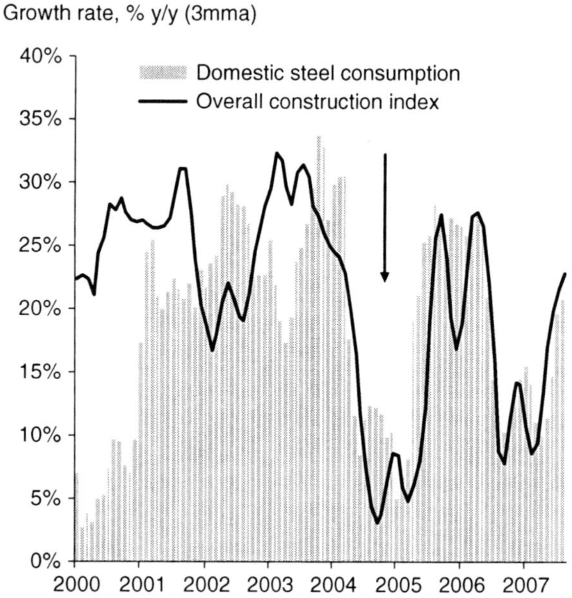

Chart 23 Real construction growth
Source: CEIC, UBS estimates

intermediate policy tools, i.e., directly targeting the level of base money in the economy, as practiced at various times by many central banks around the world, and (2) non-market administrative controls on the banking system that restrict their ability to lend out.

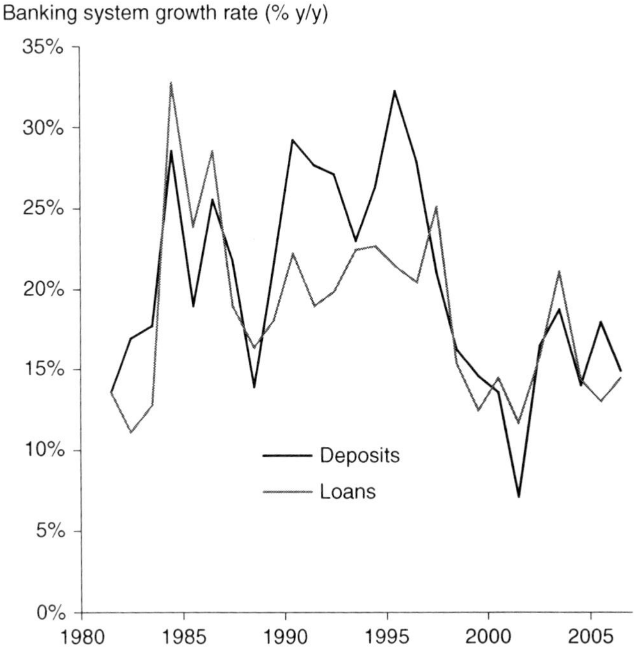

Chart 24 Long-term money and credit growth
Source: CEIC, UBS estimates

4.1 Money Base Targeting

Let us begin with a review of economic theory. In a fractional-reserve banking system (which is what you have in China as well as in virtually every developed economy) central banks operate by providing "high-powered" liquidity, or so-called base money, to commercial banks, who in turn use these funds to create new loans and deposits via the money multiplier. And as discussed above, there are essentially two ways for central banks to carry out a market-based monetary policy.

The first is to determine the price of high-powered funds in the economy by setting policy interest rates, such as the Fed Funds rate in the United States or similar discount rates in Europe and Japan, and let the market determine the quantity of liquidity injected into the economy based on those rates. Broadly speaking, this is the way the US Fed, the ECB, and the majority of other central banks currently carry out monetary policy.

The alternative is to set the quantity of high-powered liquidity in the system and let the market determine the price. Again, this may sound unusual to modern investors used to thinking about short-term interest rates as the sole indicator of the policy stance, but as we showed earlier this is the way many developed central banks operated in the 1970s and 1980s, and a number of institutions still focus on the volume of base money as a primary or secondary monetary tool. In particular, with extremely large intervention and sterilization operations a good number of Asian central banks are effectively quantitative base money targeters as well (see the next section below for further details). And we would stress again that this quantitative approach is no less "market-based" in principle than setting policy interest rates.

Here is how it works in China. To start with, take a look at the long-term relationship between "high-powered" base money growth and broad money M2 growth, as shown in Chart 25 below.[2] As it turns out, the correlation is very strong; the reason broad money and credit could grow at 30% y/y or more in the

Chart 25 Base money growth (long view) Source: CEIC, UBS estimates

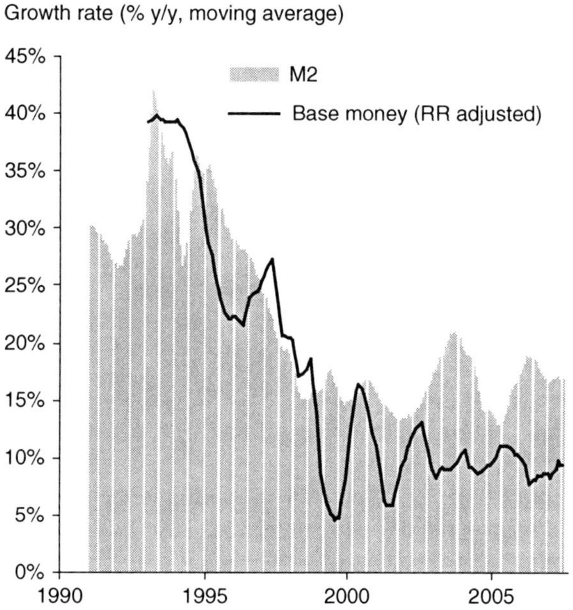

first half of the 1990s was that the PBC was emitting base liquidity into the economy at the same rate. And once the PBC tightened up on base money growth, the pace of overall M2 and credit expansion dropped as well. In other words, the credit multiplier is broadly stable – at least in a long-term sense – and intermediate base money targeting can be effective.

And in vivid contrast to our earlier finding that the PBC has not been very active in adjusting policy interest rates, we see much more evidence of policy activity when we look at quantitative liquidity. The green bars in Chart 26 show

[2] The base money growth figures in these two charts are adjusted for changes in the required reserve ratio.

Chart 26 Base money growth (short view)
Source: CEIC, UBS estimates

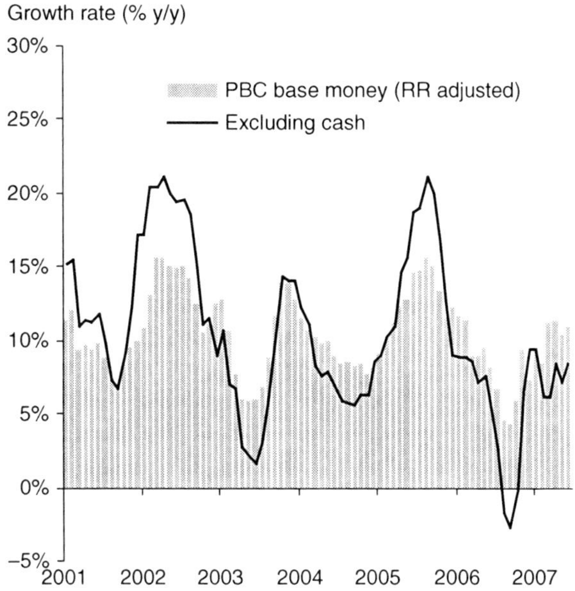

overall base money growth, and the dark line shows the growth rate excluding cash, i.e., how much liquidity is going to the commercial banking system, and both the line and the bars move a lot. In 2003 and 2004, the PBC undertook successive waves of tightening, restricting the amount of funds going to the banking system; by 2005 the PBC began to loosen, injecting greater amounts of liquidity in order to stabilize the credit cycle. By 2006 the authorities were clearly back in tightening mode, with very weak base money growth, and policy has remained relatively cautious through 2007.

4.2 Administrative Controls

This is far from the entire story, however. If you go back to Charts 22 and 23 at the beginning of this section and review the sharp contraction in credit growth and real construction growth in 2004, you will notice that the correction was much more pronounced than the underlying slowdown in base money growth in Chart 26. Market interest rates did rise in 2004, but also not very aggressively. In short, looking at the standard monetary policy indicators alone, we would not have expected such a strong reaction in economic performance. How exactly did the authorities achieve the real slowdown that year?

The answer is direct administrative controls on the banking system. In addition to base money management, the Chinese government also adopts formal targets for aggregate money and credit growth as part of its annual planning exercise. Normally these are indicative only and banks have deviated significantly according to market conditions, but when lending activity gets too strong (or, for that matter, too weak) the PBC and the bank regulator make active use of "window guidance" measures, which essentially means administrative pressure on banks to rein in growth or face sanctions in the form of liquidity penalties or even personnel changes.

In an average year PBC window guidance might be used in a preventative sense, i.e., warning banks when overall credit growth is approaching a worrisome level or when lending to certain sectors starts to look too frothy – but in late 2003, when aggregate bank lending reached 25% y/y, construction activity growth exceeded 30% y/y and short-term lending to real estate developers was running at 80% y/y or more, the authorities took more aggressive action. The PBC and the regulators actually went to each individual bank, forcing institutions to recall speculative loans to the property and construction sectors, canceling infrastructure projects and re-imposing capitalization requirements at the micro level. And this, in our view, is how the actual 2004 tightening was achieved.

Now, why do the authorities rely on administrative controls if the PBC already has market-based tools in the form of quantitative base money management? Because although over the longer term base money policy seems to work, in 2004 the government faced two specific issues.

First, the banking system had an unusually high level of excess reserves. Tightening up on high-powered liquidity works well if commercial banks are running "lean" – i.e., if they have already fully lent out against the existing stock of base money – but if banks have significant amounts of unused liquidity quantitative tightening policies may take a long time to have an effect.

Chart 27 below shows the excess reserve ratio for the Chinese financial system since the beginning of the decade, defined as total base money less required

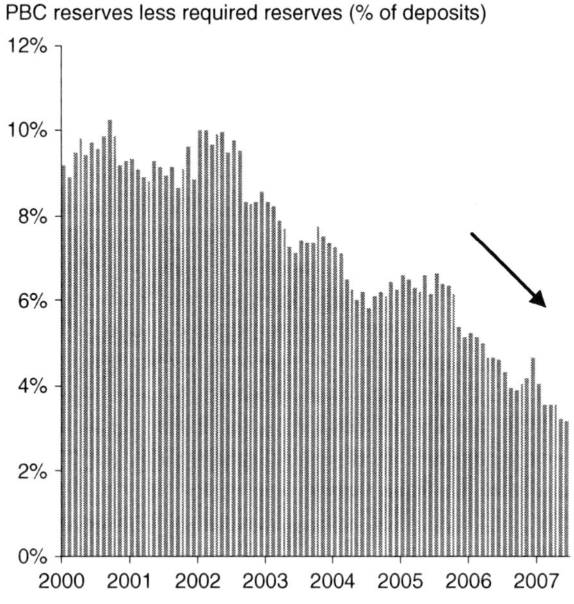

Chart 27 Banking system excess liquidity
Source: CEIC, UBS estimates

reserves as a share of overall deposits. As you can see, in 2000–02 the ratio was around 10%, an extremely high level by historical standards (and an extremely high level by regional and global standards as well). This helps explain how banks were able to increase credit growth so rapidly in 2002–03 and also explains why the PBC was so quick to turn to direct credit controls: With this overhang of excess liquidity, it would have taken a very long time indeed to reduce balances to the point where base money tightening began to "bite."

The second issue, as discussed above, was the very skewed sectoral nature of the overheating problem. Local governments and state enterprises were pouring excessive amounts of money into a handful of industrial sectors; on top of this, public and private developers were taking on far too much speculative leverage to build residential and commercial property. By contrast, other sectors such as light manufacturing and services were broadly in balance, with strong demand growth, more reasonable capacity expansion, and no real signs of overheating pressures.

Once again, in this environment economy-wide tightening would have had a disproportionate impact on the "good" part of the economy, which would see their funding costs increase and margins decline. Meanwhile, tighter overall credit conditions might not have had an effect on demand for inefficient, redundant industrial projects, since state-led and speculative borrowers are far less focused on the return to capital.

4.3 Are Not Administrative Controls Distortionary?

Does not economic theory teach us that relying on direct controls is distortive and inefficient? For the most part yes, but keep in mind that in China's case there are substantial mitigating factors as well.

First of all, there is a very large and crucial difference between detailed state interference to allocate capital and credit on a sector-by-sector or project-by-project basis on the one hand, and general controls on the overall pace of credit growth on the other. The former is distortionary and runs counter to the fundamental operation of a market economy, while the latter has been utilized to some extent by most developed countries at one time or another.

The point here, of course, is that China has long since abandoned detailed credit controls at the sectoral or project level as a matter of policy. As we discussed in the first section above, there is still a regular practice of preferential credit treatment at the local level, with local governments intervening in lending decisions to allocate resources to favored projects, but even here we showed that local intervention and overinvestment by state-owned enterprises has waned visibly over the past decade.

Second, while the PBC does use "window guidance" moral suasion techniques as a regular policy practice, full-on administrative tightening measures at the aggregate level like those in 2004 are actually a relatively rare occurrence in this decade – in contrast, say, to the 1980s and 1990s, when overall credit ceilings were still an important part of financial decisions.

Next, to repeat the point made earlier, economic theory also teaches us that non-market distortions may be best dealt with through similar non-market actions (this is the theory of "second-best"). And given the remaining distortive role of the state in the mainland economy, overall credit controls are not necessarily inconsistent with sound economic practice.

And finally, even the softer central bank "window guidance" is gradually losing ground in favor of a purer market-based quantitative management regime. Why? Because banks no longer have large excess reserve balances, and this makes base money targeting much more effective today than it was even a few years ago.

You can see this in Chart 27 above; from 10% at the beginning of the decade, the financial system excess reserve ratio has now fallen to under 3% of deposits, a number much closer to the "normal" bank reserve buffer held in other fractional reserve economies. As a result, as we showed in the previous section, liquidity movements have started to have a very visible impact on short-term rates (shown once again in Chart 28). And this is just how things are supposed to work in a market economy: Quantitative liquidity tightening both slows credit growth and pushes up interest rates in the system.

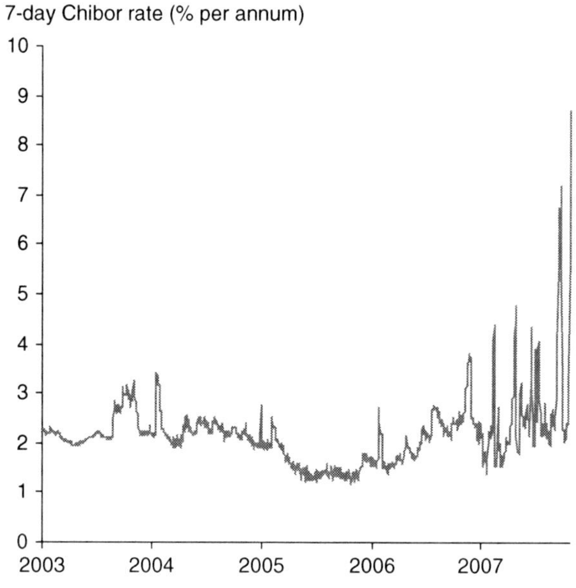

Chart 28 Money market interest rates
Source: CEIC, UBS estimates

4.4 *Can China Really Control Credit at All?*

Over the past few years some analysts have argued that China has no effective control over credit growth at all, due to the prevalent role of the informal "curbside" financial market (or the "shadow banking system").

As a reminder, in addition to regular banks, China has always had an active informal lending market. This reflects state banks' historical mandate to finance state-owned enterprises (SOEs); smaller and private companies were left to their own devices to fund growth, which meant either retained earnings, borrowing from family and friends, or turning to local moneylenders. And controls on deposit and lending interest rates in the commercial banking system meant that even as banks changed their focus to more market-based lending, smaller firms remained almost completely outside the system.

In the curbside market, interest rates are set according to separate supply and demand trends, usually at a multiple of official rates. Such markets exist in virtually every economic center and have been the focus of numerous domestic studies over the years, most of which have tended to put the volume of activity anywhere from 10 to 20% of official financing. And during the 2004 official credit tightening, curbside interest rates rose sharply – a sure sign that firms who were cut off from commercial bank lending were attempting to turn to the shadow market for financing.

However, we do not believe the curbside market has played a significant role in financial cycles; i.e., in our view official credit policy tightening is effective after all. We say this for the following reasons:

It is one thing to have an unofficial financing market that accounts for as much as 20% of commercial bank credit activity. However, in order for that market to significantly offset the effects of, say, the 2004 macro policy tightening, it must have ballooned to nearly 100% of the formal banking system virtually overnight. This is challenging for any emerging market – and a virtual impossibility in the case of China, where the banking system already accounts for nearly 200% of GDP, four times the global average and one of the highest ratios in the world. Curbside markets are (i) regionally and locally fragmented, usually limited to a very small group of mutual acquaintances, and (ii) do not benefit from credit multiplier effects, as would the formal banking system.

Also, if the curbside market were really able to offset the effects of official credit policy, then in theory we should not see formal or informal interest rates going up at all during periods of tightening; as a rule of thumb, the more liquid the shadow market, the less rates should rise when new demand comes on line. But in 2004, for example, the best available reports suggested that curbside market rates doubled during the tightening period, from 12–15% per annum to more than 25% per annum.

Most anecdotal stories about the curbside market involve drainage of deposits out of the formal banking system. However, in the past few years we have never seen anything unusual or suspicious in the deposit figures at the macro level, and no evidence that depositors are exiting banks during periods of tightening.

Lastly – and in our view most important – consider the behavior of construction activity growth in Chart 23 above. The lion's share of the 2002–03 credit upturn was due to property and real estate lending, and as a result, the lion's share of the 2003–04 credit slowdown came from the property and construction sector as well. Sure enough, when we compare official bank lending growth with real construction activity growth we get a very close fit. No sooner had the authorities tightened property lending than we saw a sharp downturn in construction growth.

The bottom line, as we see it, is that (i) the informal lending market continues to play an important role in financing growth for the small and medium enterprise sector, but (ii) there is no evidence that firms in China can avoid the effects of official macro policy by shifting credit demand back and forth between commercial banks and "outside" lenders. For further discussion, please see *Tall Tales of the Curbside Market (Asian Focus, 18 November 2004).*

4.5 What About M2 and M3?

One final note before we end this section concerns the behavior of broader money aggregates such as M2 and M3 in China. It is true that the PBC has been able to maintain general control over the credit cycle since 2003, with annual growth rates more or less stable in the mid-teens. However, it is also true that M2 has been expanding at a consistently faster pace over the past 4 years – and estimates of M3, which increase other liabilities on banks' balance sheets, are increasing faster still. As a result, the overall banking system loan-deposit ratio has fallen considerably; is not this a sign that the banking system actually has a large excess liquidity overhang that is in constant danger of rushing into the real economy, i.e., that the PBC may not have control of monetary policy after all?

Our general answer is no, and the reason is sterilization. In an environment where the central bank is locking up large amounts of liquidity on the asset side of banks' balance sheets in sterilization instruments such as bills or higher reserve requirements, we would expect both a falling loan-deposit ratio and a significant gap between M2/M3 growth and credit growth. The key here is that in a high sterilization economy the loan-deposit ratio essentially becomes a meaningless statistic – which is why we look directly at the excess liquidity ratio in Chart 27 above – and broad money growth becomes "delinked" from its ability to drive real growth or inflation through the credit multiplier (although, as we will see further below, it still has the potential to influence asset markets).

This brings us to the issues of the external balance of payments, FX inflows, and sterilization, which are the topics of the next section of the report.

5 The Open Economy – Capital Controls, Exchange Rates, and Sterilization

Key points in this section:

- China's fixed exchange rate and large trade surpluses have led to historically unprecedented FX inflows, forcing the PBC to undertake sizeable domestic sterilization operations.
- However, despite common fears that the situation is heading for a breakdown, we conclude that sterilization is sustainable for the time being – and thus that the central bank has monetary policy independence.
- This is in part due to China's closed capital account, with controls still binding at the margin.
- Many more open economies in the Asian region have much larger sterilization operations than China does and have yet to run into trouble.

We now turn to one of the most interesting, debated, and outright confusing aspects of monetary policy: the role of the exchange rate, FX reserve flows, and sterilization.

The key questions are well-known and recognized in the investment community: Can China maintain an independent monetary policy and a peg at the same time? Are large-scale foreign exchange inflows and large-scale sterilization imposing costs on the economy? And does renminbi exchange rate undervaluation effectively doom China to overheated growth, high inflation and asset bubbles?

Our answers run as follows. To begin with, as China liberalizes its financial and external capital markets it will not be able to run an independent monetary policy forever – but for the time being we do not yet see a serious threat to PBC independence in policy tools. As discussed above, the central bank has been broadly successful in controlling growth and inflation.

Second, while the current strategy of sterilizing FX inflows does have costs, those costs are still relatively small (and, of course, on a net basis sterilization is still a profitable trade for the central bank). And third, while China does currently have a problem with buoyant asset markets, there is no evidence that this is being driven by an undervalued currency.

5.1 *Fixed Exchange Rates and Domestic Monetary Policy*

All fixed or quasi-fixed exchange rate regimes run according to the same principle: The central bank stands ready to buy or sell its national currency in exchange for other currencies at a given rate. Regardless of whether that rate is fixed outright or crawling over time, the salient point is that at any given moment of time, the central bank is a fixed-price "market maker", i.e., both the buyer and seller of last resort.

Chinese practice has been no exception. The PBC is by far the largest participant in the mainland foreign exchange market, intervening to buy and sell forex to keep the price of the renminbi stable. When mainland exporters earn US dollars and want to sell them in order to pay domestic costs, more often than not the Chinese counterpart bank will sell the dollars on to the PBC in exchange for renminbi, and vice versa for importers looking to buy forex.

Now, if private supply and demand for foreign exchange is relatively balanced, then the central bank has an easy task; it simply buys FX balances from one set of players and sells them to another. However, if there is a large gap between private supply and demand at the going exchange rate, then the situation is very different. For an excess supply of foreign exchange on the market, the central bank ends up buying much more forex than it sells – and selling much more domestic currency than it buys. In case of excess demand, the opposite is true: the central bank becomes a net seller of forex and a net buyer of domestic currency.

For China, this is not just an academic side note; net central bank FX sales and purchases have recently become one of the most crucial concerns in the mainland macro policy environment. The bars in Chart 29 below show official FX reserve accumulation (which is very close to but not exactly the same as PBC intervention) in nominal US dollar terms, and the line shows accumulation as a share of GDP. For most of the past 20 years, the official forex market was relatively balanced; the PBC was normally a net buyer of foreign currency, but the quantities involved were very small: only US $1.3bn per month on average between 1986 and 2002, or less than 2% of GDP.

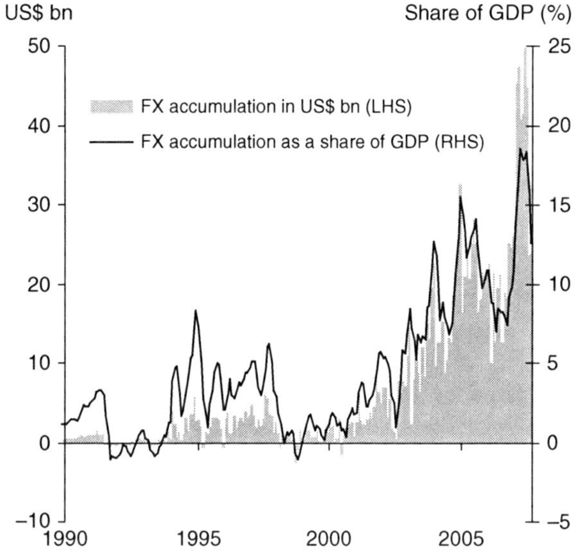

Chart 29 Net official FX accumulation in China
Source: CEIC, UBS estimates

However, since the beginning of 2003 the situation changed radically. In the past 4 years monthly net accumulation has jumped to nearly US $25bn on average, or around 13% of GDP – and closer to US $40bn per month since the beginning of 2007. And as we will discuss further below, most of the shift is due to a sharp increase in the mainland trade surplus, but for the moment the salient point is that the PBC has been buying up an enormous amount of foreign exchange by historical standards, to the point where many observers are concerned about the impact of chronic exchange rate undervaluation and large-scale FX intervention on the domestic economy.

What do foreign exchange operations have to do with domestic monetary economy? A great deal; when central banks are buying excess FX balances from the market, they are selling domestic currency, and when central banks are selling forex in the market they are buying domestic currency.

When the PBC buys US $1bn from domestic commercial banks, it credits those banks' correspondent accounts with roughly RMB7.5bn at current exchange rates, i.e., it effectively "prints" new liquidity that did not exist before and hands it over to the banking system. Conversely, when the PBC sells dollars to commercial banks, it deducts an offsetting amount of renminbi from banks' correspondent accounts – i.e., it takes liquidity out of the banking system.

So if the PBC is now buying US $40bn worth of foreign exchange per month from other banks, it is automatically also injecting roughly RMB300bn worth of base money into the domestic economy on a monthly basis.

And this highlights one the key macroeconomic problems with a fixed exchange rate: If the economy has a high external surplus, this can mean a very large, even uncontrollable increase in domestic liquidity through FX intervention, which would in turn fuel high growth and inflation. Or, by the same token, if the external balance is in deficit, the result could be a sharp domestic liquidity crunch.

5.2 A Short Primer on Sterilization

However, to date neither of these has occurred in China. If you look at the green bars in Chart 30, you will see that the rush of FX liquidity into the mainland economy should have pushed up domestic base money by 40% y/y or more over the past few years – but as we saw above, actual base money has only grown by around 10% per year (the dark line in the chart).

Why? Because the PBC "sterilized" anywhere from two-thirds to three-quarters of the gross liquidity inflows through offsetting domestic operations (see Chart 31). Exactly as the name implies, sterilization operations are aimed at neutralizing the monetary impact of foreign exchange inflows. If forex intervention is pushing too much base money liquidity into the economy, the central bank can effectively "take the money back" in one of the following ways:

Chart 30 Base money growth by component
Source: CEIC, UBS estimates

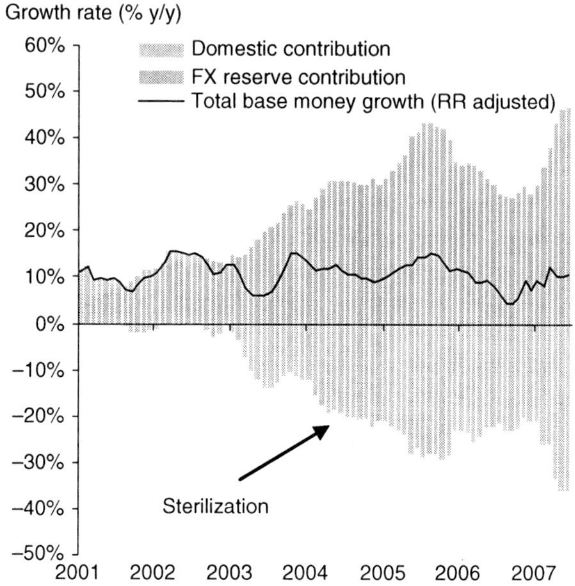

Chart 31 Sterilization operations
Source: CEIC, UBS estimates

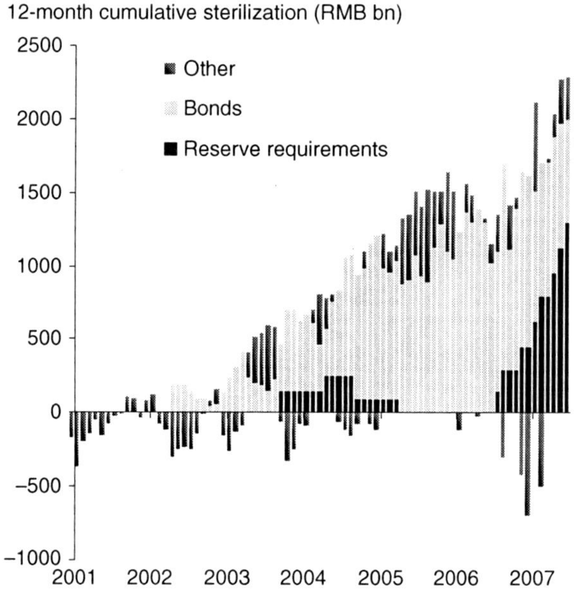

- sell central bank holdings of government bonds to commercial banks in exchange for base money;
- borrow back base money from commercial banks by issuing short-term central bank debt;

- offset the liquidity injection through other measures such as recalling outstanding central bank loans to commercial banks; or
- simply "freeze" the funds by hiking the required reserve ratio; this prevents banks from lending out excess liquidity in the rest of the economy.

In practice, the PBC uses most of these tools to ensure that the extremely high volume of FX intervention does not result in a domestic liquidity "blowout." The grey bars in Chart 30 above show the implied sterilization effort, which again suggests that the central bank has been effectively mopping up the lion's share of FX funds coming into the economy.

How does it work? Charts 32 and 33 below walk through the detailed mechanics of how standard debt-based sterilization operations affect central bank and commercial bank balance sheets. The key points are that (i) the central bank offer commercial banks an interest-bearing instrument, and (ii) in return, commercial banks agree to take funds out of their free reserve accounts and "lock them up" in term-dated assets elsewhere on their balance sheet (the alternative is for the central bank to administratively raise the required reserve ratio, and we discuss this separately in the next section below).

Chart 32 Sterilization, part 1
Source: CEIC, UBS estimates

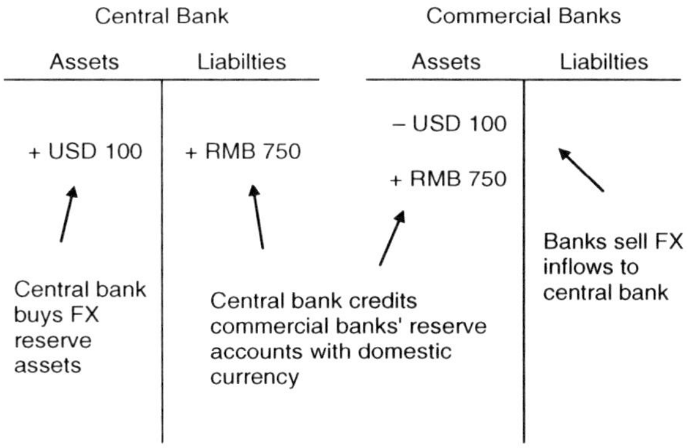

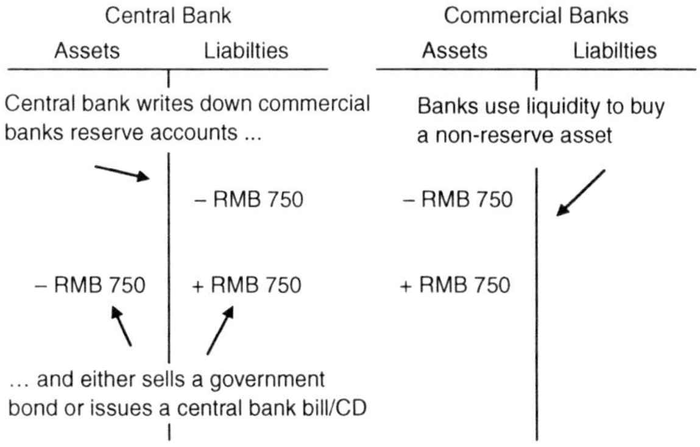

Chart 33 Sterilization, part 2
Source: CEIC, UBS estimates

Putting the story in total value terms, in the 12 months from mid-2006 to mid-2007 the PBC bought an estimated US $360bn worth of foreign currency in direct intervention in the marketplace, emitting some RMB2.8tn of domestic base money to commercial banks in the process. However, the PBC withdrew RMB2.2tn through sterilization operations over the same period, so that the total net increase in base money was only RMB600bn.

Of the total sterilization effort, roughly two-thirds came from administrative increases in the commercial bank required reserve ratio and one-third was due to short-term bill issuance (Chart 31 above) – a sharp change from 2004 and 2005, when virtually all of the sterilization came from short-term PBC bills. We will discuss the issue of reserve requirements in detail in the next section further below.

5.3 How Long Can It Last?

In other words, so far the PBC really *has* been successful in its chosen role of managing the domestic money supply even in the face of large foreign inflows, thanks in large part to extensive sterilization operations.

But does not this fly in the face of the standard wisdom that a country cannot run an independent monetary policy under a fixed exchange rate? Is China somehow exempt from this logic, or are there hidden pressures in the system?

Our answer is that China cannot play the "sterilization game" forever, simply issuing domestic debt or hiking reserve requirements *ad infinitum* without running into problems. In the long run, a combination of rising interest rates and capital account liberalization should make sterilization unsustainable.

This also means that the recent trade and current surpluses cannot go on forever without causing trouble in the domestic economy, i.e., the Chinese authorities would be well-advised to take measures to bring the imbalance down over the medium term. As we discussed in *The Real Case for Revaluation (Asian Focus, 13 July 2007)*, there are good arguments that the trade surplus will eventually peak and fall under its own weight – but we also concluded that the pace of renminbi exchange rate appreciation needs to pick up visibly in order to speed the process and ensure that the authorities can maintain domestic independence.

On the other hand, however, we do not see any serious pressures building yet – and there is no reason to suspect the situation will reach a breaking point any time soon. This is because of (i) China's closed capital account, (ii) structurally low (and artificially administered, in the case of deposits) interest rates, and (iii) the relatively low external exposure of the economy. Let us go through each of these in turn.

5.4 Interest Rates

To understand the role of interest rates in monetary sterilization, consider how sterilization operations affect central banks' balance sheets: When the central bank buys foreign exchange through printing domestic currency, it gains an interest-bearing asset on one side of the balance sheet and a non-interest (or very low interest) liability on the other. Subsequently, when the central bank sterilizes the domestic liquidity impact, it generally replaces non-interest liabilities (i.e., base money) with higher-interest liabilities (i.e., bonds or sterilization bills).

In this case, the stability of the overall exchange rate and monetary strategy depends crucially on whether the interest income the central bank receives on FX reserves is higher or lower than the interest it pays on sterilization debt. If domestic short-term rates rise above average overseas rates, then a central bank engaging in sizable sterilization operations can run significant net losses at the margin – and in the worst-case scenario, the authorities might be forced to give up FX intervention altogether and let the exchange rate jump upward in order to protect domestic monetary integrity.

This is what happened, for example, in Thailand in late 2006; the Bank of Thailand (BoT) had raised short-term interest rates repeatedly in order to rein in inflationary pressures at home, but a combination of trade surpluses and portfolio capital inflows also led the BoT to intervene heavily in foreign exchange markets and sterilize the resulting liquidity inflows at home. With onshore interest rates at or above US levels and significant appreciation pressures on the baht, global investors took advantage of the positive carry to speculate on the exchange rate in increasing amounts; this, in turn, meant that the BoT faced the prospect of ever-increasing losses on its balance sheet. At the end of the day, the central bank was left with little choice but to either let the baht soar upward, which would impose losses on Thai exporters, or administratively restrict capital inflows, essentially placing the losses on portfolio investors. In the event, the BoT chose the latter (see *The Strange Case of Thai Capital Controls, Asian Focus, 19 December 2006*, for full details).

However, the PBC has never had to worry about worsening onshore/offshore spreads. The light green line in Chart 34 below shows the yield on one-year PBC sterilization bills (the most common maturity issued), while the darker line shows our estimate for the average interest yield on official FX reserves.[3] As you can see from the chart, for most of the past 3 years domestic sterilization rates have always been well below the offshore reserve yield, and the spread is still around 100 basis points today. In other words, the PBC

---

[3] The currency weights are 65% USD, 35% EUR and 10% JPY, and the maturity weights are 67% 10-year yields and 33% 3-month rates.

Chart 34 Chinese vs. offshore interest rates
Source: CEIC, UBS estimates

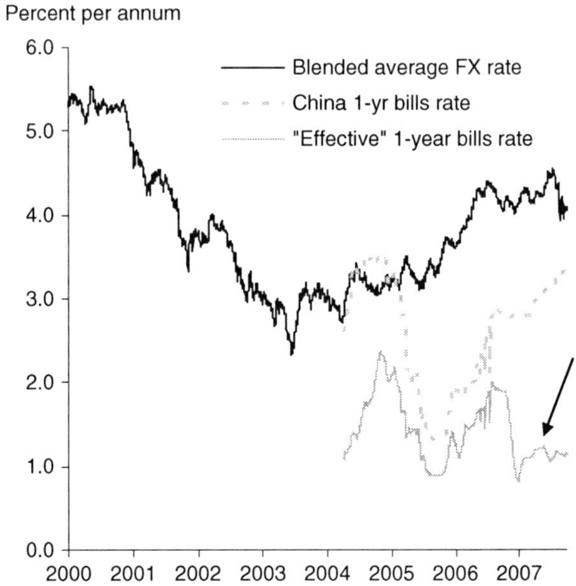

continues to make a healthy marginal profit when it intervenes to buy FX reserves and then sterilizes the inflows at home.

Now, it is true that the onshore one-year rate has been rising consistently over the past few quarters, in line with the drop in commercial banks' excess liquidity balances and the trend rise in overnight interest rates in Charts 27 and 28 above. But this is far from reaching a critical stage at present, for the following reasons:

First, remember that the PBC does not issue a full dollar of domestic debt for every US $1 of FX reserves it buys. As discussed earlier, the actual sterilization ratio runs between 60 and 75% on average, which means that the central bank can avoid flow losses even if domestic interest rates are, say, one-third higher than global rates.

Second, as we saw in Chart 31, over the past year the PBC has been moving away from short-term bill issuance in favor of administrative increases in the required reserve ratio. One of the reasons for this shift, of course, is that reserve requirement hikes are costless for the central bank, spreading the costs around the commercial banking system instead (this still leaves the question of sustainability at the commercial bank level, but we will argue in the next section below that the costs to the banking system so far have been very small indeed).

As a result of these two factors, the "effective" interest cost of sterilizing when calculated against a full dollar of inflows is well below the nominal one-year yield on PBC debt. The grey line in Chart 34 above shows our best estimate of this effective yield, calculated as the nominal one-year rate multiplied by the ratio of actual interest-bearing domestic bill issuance per dollar of FX inflows. As you can see, the effective interest cost to the PBC of sterilization is only 1–1.5% per annum – and has actually been falling over the past year.

As a final note, keep in mind that even if domestic rates were to rise considerably above world levels, with roughly US $1.4tn in FX reserves compared to only US $600bn in outstanding sterilization debt the PBC could afford to absorb marginal net interest losses and still make money on its overall balance sheet for a substantial period of time. Again, the bottom line here is that we still have a long way to go before we worry about the price of sterilization operations from a macroeconomic point of view.

5.5 The Capital Account

The other main macroeconomic buffer that keeps monetary policy independent is China's relatively closed capital account. This is also crucially important; in the Thailand case above, for example, it was not the prospect of positive onshore interest differentials *per se* that alarmed the central bank so much as the prospect of an ever-increasing flood of speculative funds.

Indeed, most countries that have run into trouble sustaining large-scale sterilization operations do so not only because of rising interest rates but also because of capital inflow pressures that can lead to relentless volume growth over time. If the central bank is an active borrower in liquidity markets at home, this causes interest rates to rise; as interest rates go up, so do external portfolio inflows – and with it the need for ever-greater sterilization. In the worst case, a "vicious circle" of intervention and inflows can overwhelm the central bank's capacity to control the situation, leading either to high inflation and real overheating at home or a forced exchange rate adjustment.

This is a prime example of the "impossible trinity" of international economic theory, which states that a small open economy can choose to fix its exchange rate, domestic interest rates, or the domestic money supply, but not all three at the same time. If the exchange rate is fixed, then interest rate differentials will naturally lead to large inflows or outflows of capital; these flows will either cause significant fluctuations in the domestic money stock, or else move domestic interest rates (or both). And if the monetary authorities attempt to skirt the inevitable by sterilizing capital inflows, they will end up exacerbating the reaction in another area (in this case, by causing interest rates to rise).

So how has the PBC managed to control the exchange rate, domestic liquidity, *and* interest rates so well over the past few years? In part, because China is not a small open economy but rather a vast continental country with relatively small real exposure to the outside world. Even annual FX reserve inflows in excess of US $400bn – an enormous sum, more than 13% of Chinese GDP – imply base money growth of only 30%, an amount that the PBC has readily offset through domestic liquidity operations.

And in part, because China does not have free and open portfolio capital flows. The mainland foreign exchange market is open for current account transactions involving trade in goods and services, but the official capital account is still relatively closed, limited to foreign direct investment and a small range of borrowing, lending and asset transactions. On paper, in fact, China has by far the most closed capital regime of all major economies in the region (see the latest *Complete RMB Handbook, Asian Economic Perspectives, 18 September 2006* for further details).

5.6 A Closer Look at Capital Account Restrictions

Now, in fairness, we should note that there is a sizable, ongoing debate over whether the Chinese capital account is indeed closed in practice or whether speculative inflows and outflows are already becoming a serious concern for the central bank. And given the importance of this topic for monetary policy independence, we thought we would walk through the arguments in detail here.

The first part of the debate concerns the volume of mainland portfolio flows. Despite the formal restrictions, it is also a widely recognized fact that China has significant informal portfolio flows, including so-called "hot" money that regularly flows in and out of the economy.

How do we define portfolio capital flows? If we take overall FX reserve growth and subtract the current account and net foreign direct investment, we get a broad series for "other" capital flows; conceptually, this is equal to recorded portfolio flows in the balance of payments plus so-called "errors and omissions". This is by no means a perfect measure of portfolio capital movements; there could be unrecorded trade transactions captured in errors and omissions, or capital flows disguised as trade transactions in the current account, valuation changes, and other accounting issues that bias the numbers. The measure is also much broader than just speculative "hot" money, since it includes legal longer-term portfolio transactions as well. But it has the strong advantage of being internally consistent and, much more important, consistent across countries.

The Chinese data for the past 20 years are given in Chart 35. As you can see, the mainland has seen periods of sizable portfolio capital outflows, reaching 8% of GDP at the trough in late 1998. And for the past few years there have been bouts of equally large capital inflows.

How does this compare with other Asian countries? Chart 36 below shows two sets of data: first, the peak capital inflow or outflow for each country as a share of GDP over the past two decades (using the same definition as for China

Chart 35 Chinese portfolio flows
Source: CEIC, UBS estimates

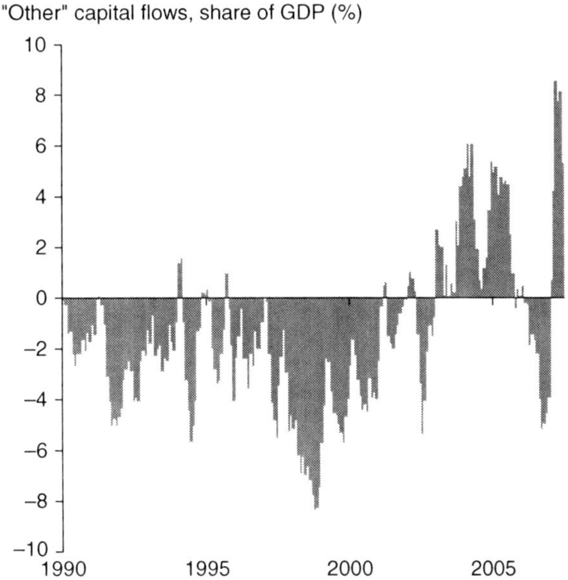

Chart 36 Portfolio flows in regional perspective
Source: CEIC, UBS estimates

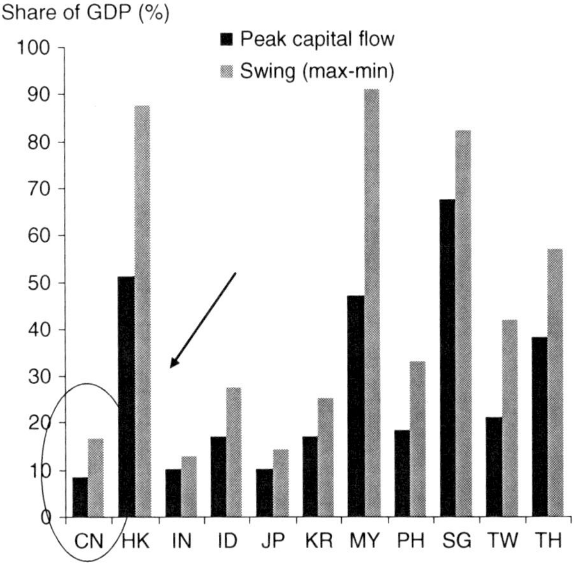

above), and second, the maximum peak-to-trough swing as a share of GDP for the same period.

The magnitude of mainland capital flows has clearly never been anywhere near as large as for small economies such as Singapore, Malaysia, or Hong

Kong. But when you compare with other larger countries like India, Indonesia, Japan or Korea, China does not look very different at all. In fact, as a share of GDP peak capital flows were nearly identical – despite the fact that most of these countries have much more open capital regimes on a formal basis.

Now look at Charts 37 and 38, which show the historical path of "other" capital flows for Japan and India. Comparing with Chart 1 above, with the

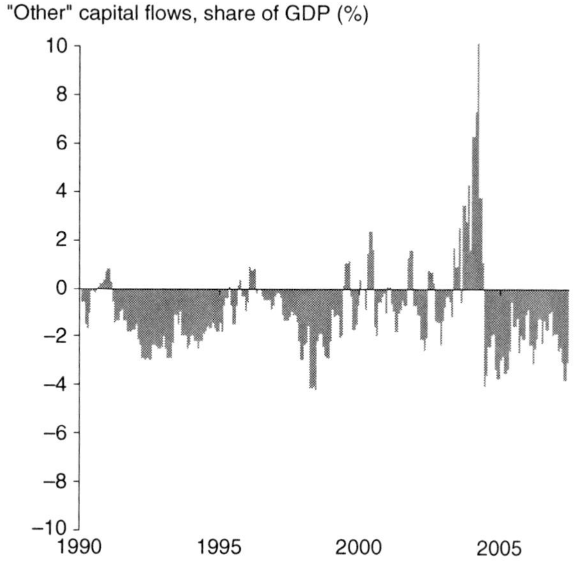

Chart 37 Capital flows – Japan
Source: CEIC, UBS estimates

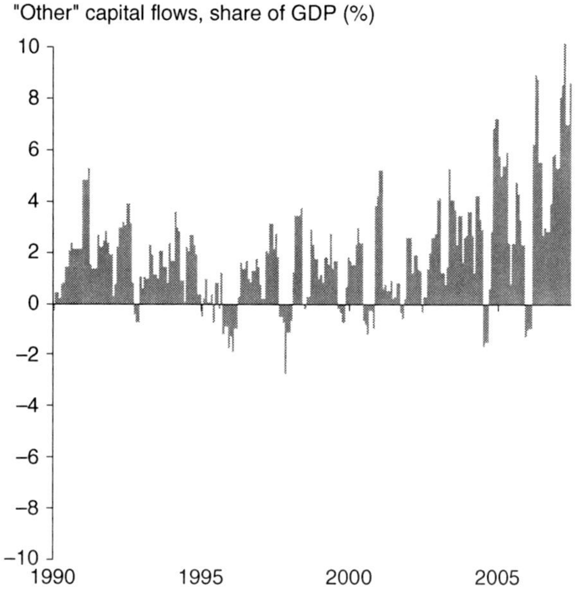

Chart 38 Capital flows – India
Source: CEIC, UBS estimates

exception of a brief spike in 2003, Japan never saw inflows or outflows even half the size of China's recent swings. And although India's gross flows have been larger, they have been nowhere near as volatile.

Finally turn to Chart 39, showing the same series for the remaining Asian economies on a collective basis. Even though most of these countries had much larger capital volumes individually, taken together they look surprisingly similar to China in Chart 36, with peak inflows of around 8% of GDP and outflows of the same.

Chart 39 Capital flows – other Asia
Source: CEIC, UBS estimates

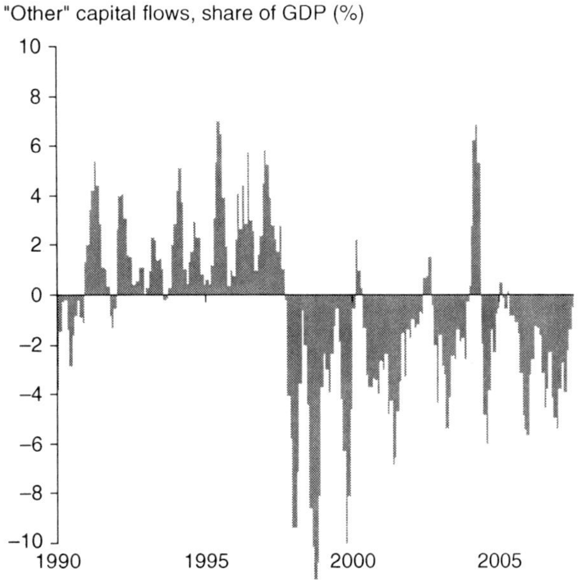

The bottom line is that on a volume basis China's capital account does not look very closed at all. Why? In part because China has a fully open current account, as well as an extremely liberal FDI regime by emerging market standards. In this environment, with banks and firms heavily involved in international trade and investment transactions, it is often difficult to separate current account flows from capital movements – and all too easy to disguise informal "hot" money flows.

However, it is not enough to point to large historical volume of flows. What we really want to know is how "binding" existing controls are *at the margin*, i.e., how responsive are portfolio flows to changes in interest rates and exchange rate expectations? It is precisely this marginal responsiveness that determines whether the PBC has functional independence in running domestic monetary policy.

So what drives Chinese capital flows? Is it marginal relative interest rate and forward exchange rate returns? Or is it because of other factors altogether? Let us begin with Charts 40 and 41, which show the relationship between net portfolio capital inflows, exchange rates, and interest rates.

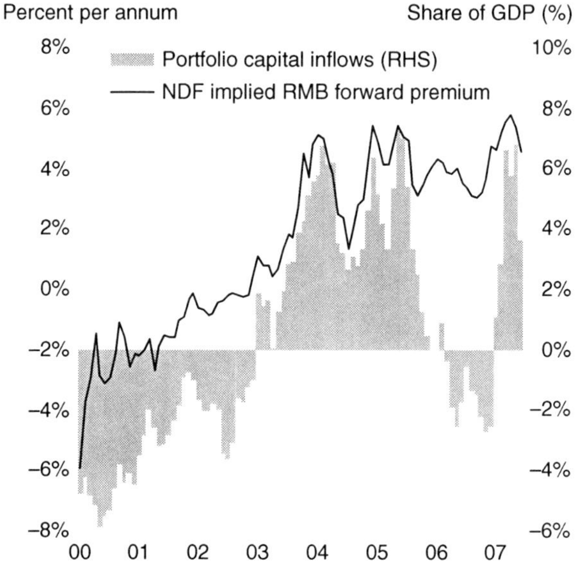

Chart 40 What drives capital flows? (1) Source: CEIC, UBS estimates

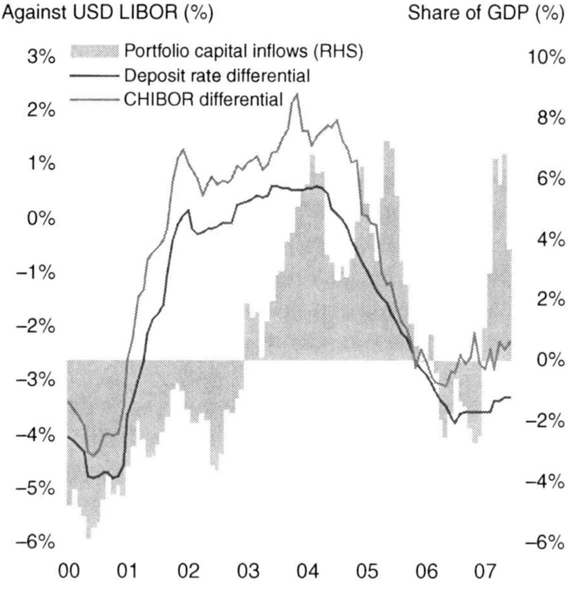

Chart 41 What drives capital flows? (2) Source: CEIC, UBS estimates

As it turns out there is a visible historical relationship between the volume and direction of capital flows and expected renminbi appreciation (as measured by the premium/discount on the renminbi against the US dollar in the offshore non-deliverable forward, or NDF market). When the NDF market expected the renminbi to depreciate against the dollar in 2000–02, portfolio funds flowed out of China – and when expectations turned to appreciation, funds flowed back in (Chart 40). The same is broadly true for the differential between local renminbi interest rates and offshore US dollar rates, as shown in Chart 41.

On the other hand, the relationship is far from clear. On the offshore forward side, we could just as easily argue the opposite: That the NDF premium rose because money was now flowing back into China, rather than the other way around. And NDF market movements cannot explain the sharp turnaround in capital flows in late 2005 and 2006. And turning to Chart 41, while the drop in the onshore/offshore interest differential due to rising Fed rates is correlated with the 2005–06 drop in flows, it does not seem to explain the resurgence in inflows in 2007, nor can differentials explain why net flows remained negative in 2001–03.

Indeed, there is an equally good case that informal capital does not respond to interest rates or currency at all but rather to asset market returns. If you look at Chart 42 below, the sharp turnaround from net portfolio outflows to net inflows in 2003–05 was exactly correlated with the Shanghai property market bubble, while the recent 2007 surge coincided with the unprecedented rally in China's A share equity market.

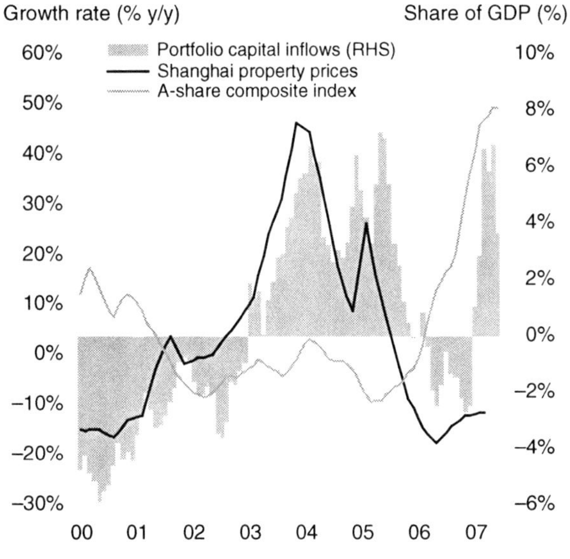

Chart 42 What drives capital flows? (3)
Source: CEIC, UBS estimates

This jibes well with anecdotal evidence from banks and firms, which clearly points to property and equities as the main investment destinations for "hot" money. Although once again, we could also argue that it was hot money flows that pushed up asset markets, rather than the other way around.

In short, simply looking at the preceding charts does not give us a definitive answer. Does it matter? Very much indeed; there is a crucial difference between a finding that portfolio capital responds aggressively to moderate changes (i.e., hundreds of annualized basis points) in relative interest rate or exchange rate returns, and one that it takes *thousands* of basis points in *monthly* asset returns to pull capital into the country. In the first case, the central bank would be significantly constrained in its ability to carry out monetary policy, and in the latter we would conclude that that domestic policy is independent.

Luckily, we have more direct measures of effective independence using the so-called arbitrage approach. The idea is straightforward: in the extreme case of a small open economy with perfectly free capital flows and a fixed peg to the US dollar, domestic interest rates should be exactly equal to US dollar rates (since any significant deviation would immediately be arbitraged away). And the further we move away from these three assumptions, the lower the correlation between domestic and overseas interest rate movements.

With this in mind, we follow Ma and McCauley (2007) in testing arbitrage conditions on two fronts. Chart 43 shows the relationship between Chinese domestic one-year interest rates and the implied one-year renminbi yield in the

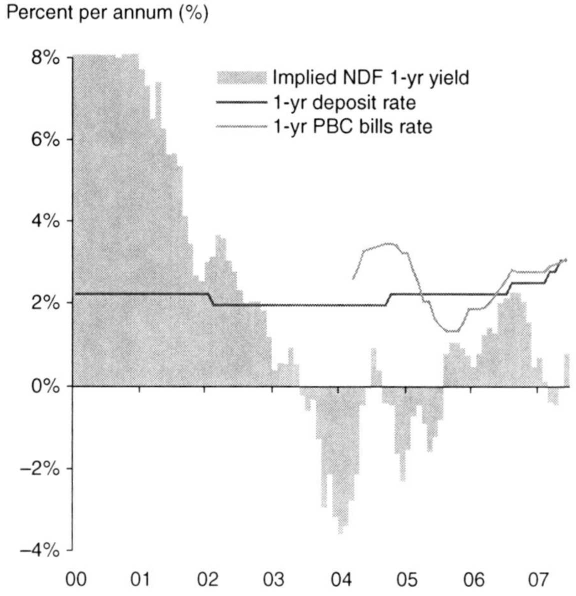

Chart 43 Implied NDF differentials
Source: CEIC, UBS estimates

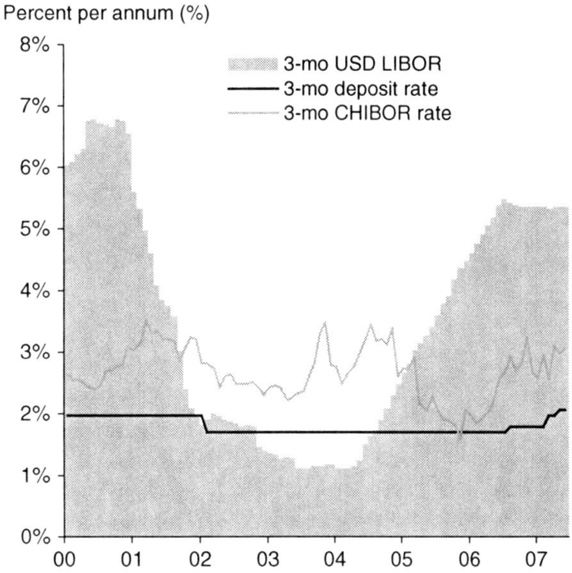

Chart 44 Uncovered differentials
Source: CEIC, UBS estimates

NDF market, and Chart 44 shows the uncovered relationship between onshore renminbi and offshore US dollar three-month rates.[4]

As you can see, there is no visible correlation whatsoever between onshore and offshore interest rates in either case. This could mean that portfolio capital flows are not responsive at all to changes in relative interest rates, or it could mean that capital flows do react to interest differentials but are too small relative to the size of the economy to have any impact on domestic liquidity conditions.

In either case, our bottom-line conclusion is that as far as money markets are concerned capital controls are effectively binding – and thus that Chinese monetary policy is still independent.

5.7 *Size Matters*

One final point on the question of sterilization concerns regional comparisons. Chart 45 below shows the current cumulative stock of outstanding sterilization instruments (defined as the cumulative difference between FX reserve flows and base money growth since the beginning of the decade) by country.

The bottom line here is that (i) sterilization is far from a unique China phenomenon, and (ii) in fact, China is a relatively minor player by Asian

[4] Remember that the NDF premium/discount on the renminbi defines the forward exchange rate against the dollar; the amount of expected renminbi appreciation is in turn is by definition equal to the difference between US dollar interest rates and an "implied" renminbi interest rate for the period in question. We use the one-year NDF forward rate and the one-year US dollar LIBOR rate to derive the implied renminbi one-year yield in the chart.

Chart 45 Cumulative sterilization in Asia
Source: CEIC, UBS estimates

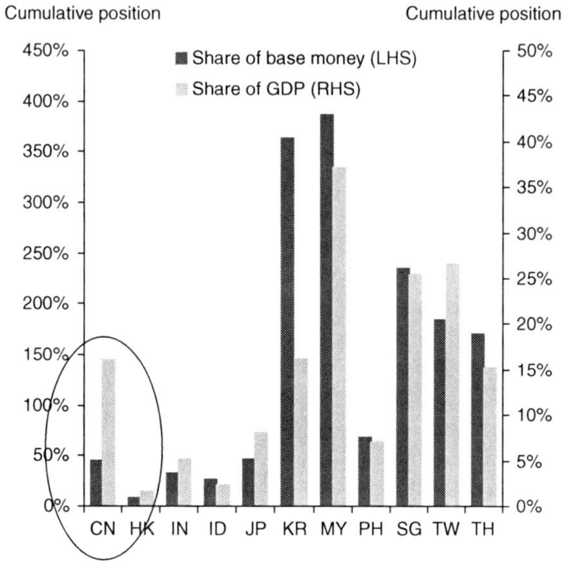

standards. The stock of mainland sterilization debt may now be 15% of GDP and around 50% of base money – but this pales in comparison to economies like Malaysia, Korea, Taiwan, and Singapore, where the exposures can be three to four times as big.

What is more, these are all smaller economies with much more open capital markets; if we want to say that sterilization is causing serious problems in a large economy like China, we first have to explain why it has not caused greater trouble in the rest of the region. We went through the numbers and analysis in detail in *The Return of Asia, Part 6 (Asian Economic Perspectives, 14 June 2007)* and concluded that even in these smaller cases we still have a good ways to go before sterilization operations become a significant issue for the economies in question, which should help put China's own situation into perspective.

5.8 China and the Fed

The above conclusions should help deflate the pervasive myths about China and the US Fed. Over the past few years hardly a month has gone by that did not see prominent statements in the financial press claiming that with an exchange rate fixed to the US dollar, the mainland economy is effectively "importing" its monetary policy from the Federal Reserve and is therefore powerless to control domestic growth.

This may be true for a very small economy like Hong Kong, but our analysis has shown that this is not true for China, where foreign inflows have had virtually no impact on domestic liquidity conditions. Once again, we find that the combination of a large domestic economy and a relatively closed capital account has given the mainland monetary authorities all the tools they need to control growth at home.

So what explains the successive credit booms of the past years? The short answer is that overheated lending has been almost completely a domestic phenomenon, fueled by large pre-existing excess liquidity holdings in the banking system, which in turn were the result of aggressive PBC monetary stimulus in earlier years.

5.9 Is There a "Negative Equity" Threat?

Before we conclude this section, we should say a few words on the topic of central bank net equity. As of end-June 2007, the net foreign asset position of the PBC stood at RMB10.5 trillion, compared to statutory capital of only RMB22 billion and another RMB900 billion in "other items", which is where the PBC records cumulative operating profits and losses.

Now, what would happen if the renminbi were to suddenly appreciate by 10% against its reserve-weighted basket of currencies (mostly the US dollar and various European units)?

Mathematically speaking, the value of net foreign assets would immediately fall by more than RMB1 trillion in domestic currency terms – i.e., enough to wipe out the entire stock of accumulated net PBC profits as well as its statutory capital. And this prospect has weighed heavily on the minds of many investors: what does it mean for the PBC, or any other central bank, to have negative net worth?

In practice, the answer is "not much", and even if the PBC were to see its net equity position turn negative we would not expect any significant implications for monetary policy.

The first reason, from a pure accounting perspective, is that the PBC does not actually adjust its statutory capital position for profits or losses. If renminbi appreciation were to result in a valuation loss, this would be recorded in the "other items" category – which has actually been negative in the past and could easily be negative again – leaving statutory capital unchanged. In other words, even if the PBC went into negative net equity in a broader sense, it would not necessarily impact the more politically sensitive capital position.

Of course, this would mean stopping profit remittances to the budget, and in cases where central banks have actually written down statutory capital they generally need to turn to fiscal authorities for a new capital injection. But this is primarily a political issue, with potential loss of independence if the government is forced to intervene. For the PBC, which does not have formal policy independence in the first place, this is hardly an issue in the current environment.

Much more important is the underlying economic point that for central banks, the existence of negative or positive net equity does not necessarily have implications for actual monetary policy, since unlike commercial entities central banks are not legally required to "repay" their liabilities. In a modern fiat banking system domestic base money (cash notes plus commercial bank reserve deposits) is simply a claim on the central bank itself, not backed by any other physical or financial asset; and other liabilities such as short-term sterilization debt are simply an eventual claim on base money. Even central banks' "net worth" is nothing more than an accounting entry denominated in domestic base money, i.e., once again, a claim on the central bank itself. Which means that from a purely macroeconomic point of view, there is no necessary reason for central banks to have positive rather than negative equity capital.

The real issue here is a question of "stocks" vs. "flows": in economic practice there is a large distinction between a revaluation impact on the *level* of equity capital and *flow* losses or profits on monetary operations. A central bank can have positive net worth today but still lose control of monetary policy if it is facing a spiralling domestic cost of sterilization in the face of large external inflows. By the same token, if a central bank has positive net interest earnings on its balance sheet then even a negative equity position today would eventually turn positive again over time, without affecting ability to set interest rates and other policy parameters in the meantime.

Sure enough, if we look back on the many dozens of historical negative equity examples, without exception the cases that required wrenching policy adjustments and statutory recapitalization arose due to flow losses on monetary operations, either because of costly net sterilization or else pressure from the government to provide quasi-fiscal subsidies to the rest of the economy. By contrast, central banks that had large one-off writedowns due to revaluation or other factors were generally happy to operate with negative equity for a period of time.[5]

6 Reserve Requirements

Key points in this section:

- The PBC has begun increasing the commercial bank required reserve ratio steadily over the past year.
- Reserve ratio hikes are just another form of sterilization, similar to bill issuance, aimed at mopping up FX inflows. Raising the required reserve ratio does not necessarily tighten liquidity on a net basis.

---

[5] For further information on central bank capital and experiences with negative net equity, see Dalton, J., and Dziobek, C. (2005): "Central Bank Losses and Experience in Selected Countries." *IMF Working Paper*, No. WP/05/72, April 2005, Stella, P. (1997): "Do Central Banks Need Capital?" *IMF Working Paper*, No. 97/83, July 1997, Stella, P. (2002): "Central Bank Financial Strength, Transparency, and Policy Credibility." *IMF Working Paper*, No. WP/02/137, August 2002.

- Reserve requirements are still not high by historical emerging market standards. Also, the cost to banks is positive, but very small at present.
- There is no theoretical "upper limit" on the reserve ratio; the PBC will likely continue to use ratio hikes as a monetary tool for a while to come.

One of the most interesting recent changes in Chinese monetary policy has been the sudden shift toward reserve requirement adjustments as a tool of monetary management. As you can see from Chart 46, after the large cut in the commercial bank required reserve ratio in 1997 the PBC kept the ratio more or less steady for the next 8 years, with marginal adjustments up and down as the liquidity situation warranted.

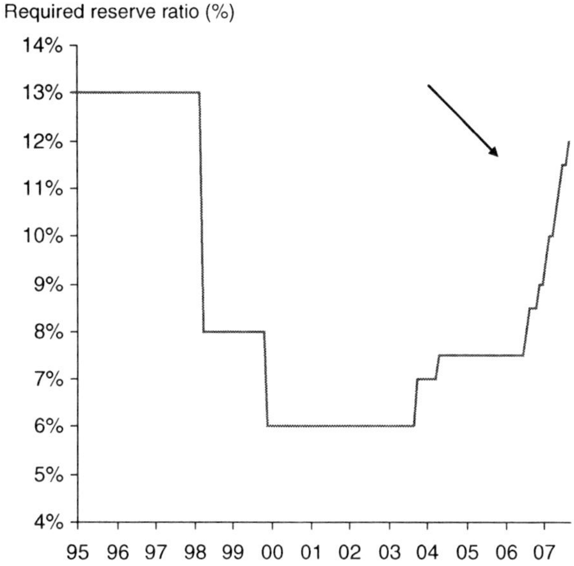

Chart 46 The big policy change
Source: UBS estimates

Since the latter part of 2006, however, the PBC has shifted to a pattern of regular, steady increases in the reserve ratio, with an unprecedented total of ten hikes in the past 15 months alone. This policy shift has caused a great deal of confusion among investors, many of whom are not used to thinking about required reserve ratios as a monetary policy instrument, and as a result we decided to devote a separate section to explaining what it means.

The first point to make is that an increase in reserve requirements is simply another form of monetary sterilization, aimed at mopping up FX inflows, and in this sense not very different from issuing short-term bills or long-term debt to the market. As a result – and contrary to the common perception in the market – hiking the reserve ratio does *not* necessarily mean tightening liquidity conditions on a net basis; this depends on whether the amount of funds withdrawn from active use by "freezing" them in required reserves is lower or higher than the gross liquidity inflow from FX reserve purchases.

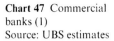

Chart 47 Commercial banks (1)
Source: UBS estimates

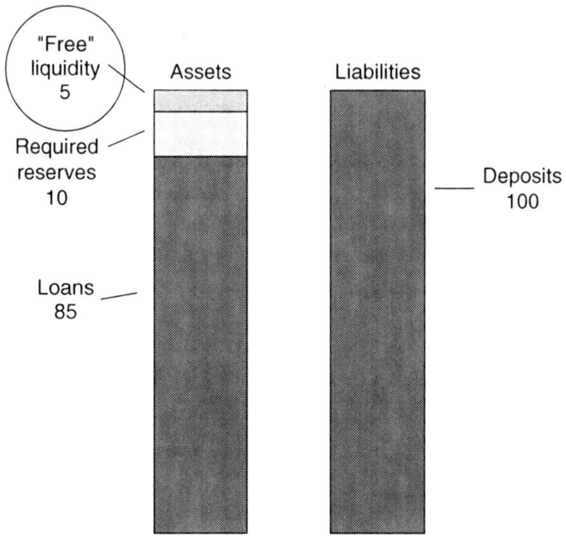

A simple example will help. Let us start with a hypothetical snapshot of the aggregate commercial banking system balance sheet in Chart 47 below. On the liability side, imagine that commercial banks have RMB100 in total deposits. On the asset side of the balance sheet, banks have two main entries: loans outstanding to the rest of the economy in the amount of RMB85, and funds on deposit with the central bank amounting to RMB15. As discussed in previous sections, this latter figure is base money, i.e., total liquidity created by the central bank.

The crucial point here is that these funds held at the central bank are broken into two separate categories: the first is "required" reserve deposits, and the second is "free" reserve liquidity. In our hypothetical example, the central bank requires all commercial banks to hold funds on deposit in the minimum amount of 10% of deposits, or RMB10; these funds are effectively frozen, as banks cannot use them to increase lending or invest in other assets.

The remaining RMB5 is "free" liquidity, i.e., funds held at the central bank that could potentially be used for other purposes. Why do banks hold excess liquidity above the required amount instead of using it to increase loans and deposits? The answer is that in every economy with a fractional reserve system, banks tend to hold more than the required minimum to cover potential liquidity swings or other prudential needs. For the purposes of our simple example, let us assume that banks generally try to hold a 5% excess reserve buffer, and that the central bank considers this to be a "neutral" level of liquidity.

Now let us imagine that the economy faces a big, sudden external windfall. Export earnings jump by a large margin, the trade surplus skyrockets upward, and instead of netting out their foreign exchange positions with each other, companies are now coming to the banking system with a big excess supply of foreign exchange to convert to domestic currency – equal to RMB10, or a full 10% of all domestic deposits in the economy.

In this case, commercial banks take RMB10 worth of foreign exchange from exporting firms and create new domestic currency deposits for them in the amount of RMB10. At this point, total bank liabilities have gone up by RMB10, offset by RMB10 in new FX assets. Assuming (as in the Chinese economy) that banks are not allowed to hold significant net foreign exchange positions, the next thing to happen is that commercial banks go to the central bank to exchange the foreign exchange for domestic currency. As a result, the central bank buys the RMB10 worth of foreign exchange (which causes official FX reserves to rise by the same amount), and in return credits commercial banks with RMB10 in new deposits on their central bank reserve accounts.

At the end of the day, the commercial bank balance sheet now looks like this (Chart 48):

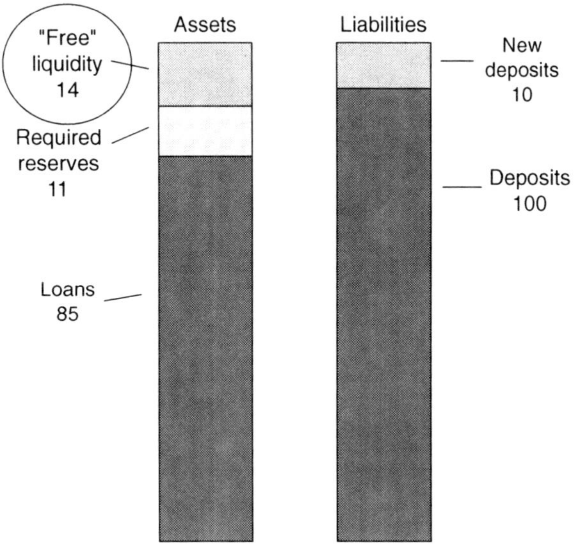

Chart 48 Commercial banks (2)
Source: UBS estimates

On the liability side, as explained above, deposits have risen by RMB10. On the asset side, total holdings at the central bank (i.e., base money) have also increased by RMB10. Because of the higher deposit base, banks now have to hold RMB11 in required reserves – but "free" liquidity has jumped from RMB5 to RMB14.

The problem now, of course, is that commercial banks now have far more excess liquidity than they usually hold, which means that if the central bank does not take measures to bring those excess balances back to more normal levels, banks are likely to start lending aggressively into the real economy.

In practice, the central bank has two choices of action if it wants to sterilize that liquidity. The first is to do what China has been doing aggressively since

2003: Borrow the money back by issuing short-term central bank bills. In exchanging reserve deposits for bills, the aggregate stock of base money goes down, since sterilization debt is not counted as free reserve deposits and cannot be used as required reserves if banks increase their loan and deposit base.

If the central bank issues RMB9 worth of sterilization bills, the new commercial bank balance sheet would look like Chart 49 below. Banks now hold RMB9 in short-term debt on the asset side of their balance sheet . . . and the stock of free liquidity has fallen back to RMB5. The risk of a credit boom has receded, and monetary policy is back to a neutral stance.

Chart 49 Commercial banks (3)
Source: UBS estimates

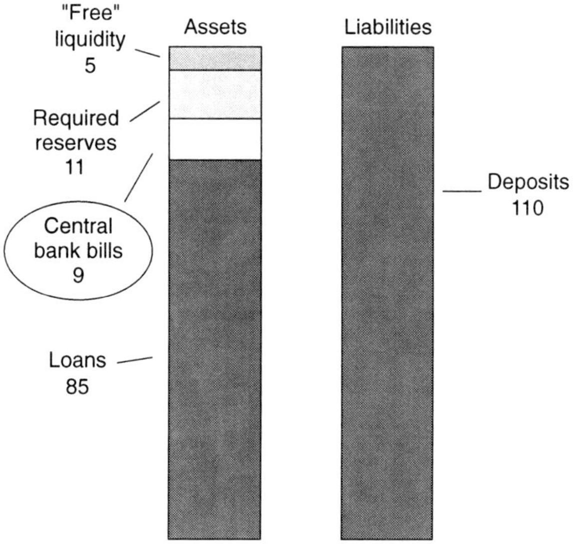

The other option is simply to "freeze" the funds by raising the required reserve ratio, i.e., force banks to apply more reserve funds to their existing deposit base, leaving less excess liquidity for future expansion. In our example, if the central bank were to increase the reserve ratio from 10 to 18%, commercial banks would be left with the situation shown in Chart 50 above.

In this case, *all* of the new liquidity inflows arising from FX purchases are now parked in the required reserve account. And as you can see from the light grey bar in the above chart, banks' free liquidity is right back at the original RMB5 level. Once again, policy is back to a neutral stance.

Why choose the second option? From a central bank perspective, reserve requirements have some very real advantages over debt-based sterilization. When the PBC increases the required reserve ratio the funds are effectively frozen forever, or at least until the central bank decides to lower the ratio again. Moreover, central banks do not have to pay a market interest rate on required reserve deposits; in fact, many are not legally required to pay an interest rate at

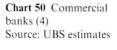

Chart 50 Commercial banks (4)
Source: UBS estimates

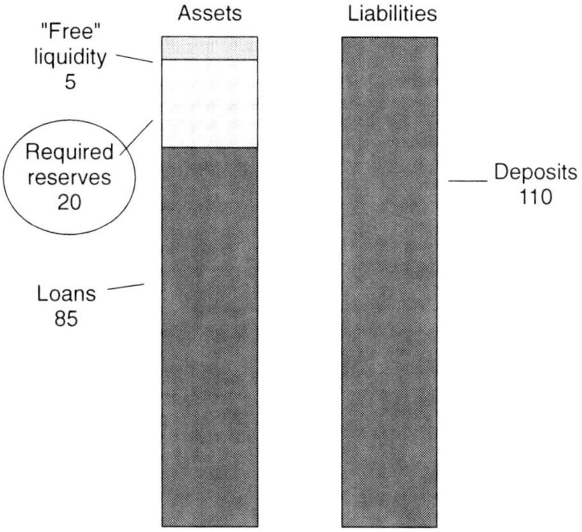

all. In practice, most central banks in a fractional reserve system choose an intermediate remuneration level (the PBC pays just under 2% per annum, less than the current market short-term interest rate).

These considerations become more important when faced (as China is) with large, chronic balance of payments surpluses; as the amount of short-term bills outstanding rises, central banks naturally begin to focus on the large sums that have to be rolled over on a regular basis. If the authorities were to be caught by surprise with a sudden jump in interest rates, the sterilization "game" could potentially break down very quickly.

Needless to say, the cumulative amount of sterilization debt outstanding is still much lower in China than in other Asian economies, as shown in Chart 45 above. However, China is the only one among the high-sterilization economies with a sharply rising balance of payments surplus over time – and in our view, this explains why the PBC was the first to move to reserve requirement hikes as an insurance policy against future volatility.

6.1 The Cost to Banks

This strategy is not completely "win-win", however. It has clear advantages for the central bank, but also shifts the costs onto the commercial banking system. Think back to the hypothetical situation in Chart 50 above. Banks originally had deposits of RMB100 and loans of RMB85. Then new deposits of RMB10 came into the system, and banks were forced to put another RMB10 into their required reserve account. How does this affect bank profits? Well, they still have the original RMB100 of deposits and RMB85 of loans, and their earnings on this part of the balance sheet have not changed. And the formal remuneration on the RMB10 of required reserves (around 2% in China's case) does at least go some way toward balancing out the interest costs of the new RMB10 of deposits (which earn around 3%).

So banks do not necessarily lose money because of the hike (although their gross margins have fallen when measured as a share of total assets). The main impact is on the opportunity cost; in an ideal world (from banks' point of view) they would have been able to lend out against those new deposit funds. To stress the point again, higher reserve requirements lower bank margins somewhat, but not the nominal level of bank profits.

There is also a separate issue of the distributional effects of the reserve requirement "tax". We just showed that the banking system as a whole does not really lose money if reserve ratio hikes are used to offset new liquidity inflows. However, the impact on *individual* banks can be quite different, and institutions that have not taken part in new inflows would clearly record losses as a result of the hikes.

The reason is that reserve requirements are an extremely blunt instrument, affecting all banks in the economy equally even if individual circumstances are very different. Think about the inflows example above: what if only one bank were involved in foreign exchange transactions, so that all the new excess liquidity inflows were concentrated in a single financial institution? If the central bank issues sterilization debt, it can be fairly confident that most of the paper will end up in that bank, since it has the most excess liquidity, i.e., sterilization through debt issuance is a "targeted" liquidity management tool.

By contrast, reserve ratio hikes force every bank in the system to top up their reserve accounts, regardless of who actually holds excess liquidity. In our single FX bank example from the previous paragraph, the central bank would be effectively taxing every other commercial bank in the economy, forcing them to turn to the one liquid bank to borrow funds in order to meet the new requirement.

In practice, we do not see this as a big concern for the banking system at present. As we showed further above, short-term money market interest rates do spike up dramatically once every four to six weeks in line with the timing of reserve ratio increases, but this is a very temporary phenomenon; on average, the cost of interbank funds is still very moderate and rising only gradually. Meanwhile, the combined effects of strong growth, government recapitalization and low deposit rates have led to sharp increases in commercial bank profits form 2005–07.

6.2 China's Misleading Loan-Deposit Ratios

At this point, we are in a position to comment on what we see as very misleading loan/deposit ratios in China. Many clients have noted that the ratio of aggregate loans to deposits in the financial system has fallen from around 85% 10 years ago to less than 65% today – and have concluded as a result that banks have an ever-growing stock of excess liquidity.

In fact, nothing could be further from the truth. To see why, take a close look at Charts 47 through 50 in our simple example above. In Chart 47, commercial banks began with a loan/deposit ratio of 85%. As new deposit funds flowed into the system, however, our hypothetical authorities took action to neutralize the liquidity effects, either through central bank debt issuance or through reserve requirements. In both cases, the end result was that banks were prevented from lending out those new deposits, which meant a fall in the aggregate loan/deposit ratio to 77%.

But this does not mean that banks have more excess liquidity; quite the opposite, excess liquidity levels actually fell as a share of deposits. The L/D ratio misses the point that the rising "gap" between loans and deposits is due to money that is essentially frozen, either in sterilization instruments or higher reserve deposits.[6]

And this is the case for the mainland economy as well. As we mentioned, China's headline loan-deposit ratio has fallen steadily over the past decade, but once we add back in the cumulative impact of sterilization operations (including reserve requirement hikes), it turns out that the "adjusted" ratio has not fallen at all – and has in fact risen visibly over the last 5 years, exactly in line with the drop in banks' excess liquidity we showed in Chart 27 above.

6.3 *How High Is Too High?*

The next question concerns the level of the required reserve ratio. The prevailing view is that every hike means less liquidity in the banking system. Is there an optimal ratio level? And how do we know if the ratio is "too high"?

International comparisons are not very useful here. In developed economies, where central banks depend more or less exclusively on interest rates as their money management tool, reserve requirements are used for prudential reasons only and tend to be set at very low levels. In general, sudden and sharp increases would be seen as restrictive and an unwarranted interference in banks' livelihoods.

In emerging markets, however, the situation is very different. During periods of high inflows in the 1980s and 1990s, countries like Malaysia took aggregate reserve ratios from less than 4% up to nearly 13%, and marginal reserve requirements in Korea rose from 5% to as high as 30% at various points.

[6] The astute reader would be tempted to reply that banks could simply sell their sterilization bills to increase liquidity, but this is not correct. In general, sterilization instruments can only be held by banks, which means that the central bank has complete control over the amounts banks hold.

When Latin American nations were fighting external inflows in the 1980s, marginal requirements ranged from 20% all the way up to 100%. And this does not include the impact of other related measures such as taxes on capital inflows or FX-related bank transactions. By these standards, China's current base ratio of 12.5% does not look particularly large.

More important still, the idea that the PBC is actually tightening liquidity balance with every ratio increase turns out to be a myth. Consider once again the earlier example; the economy experienced a large FX liquidity inflow, which the central bank sterilized by hiking reserve requirements. These two operations broadly offset each other, and at the end of the day the nominal level of excess liquidity in the system was unchanged. If those inflows persisted every month, the central bank could hike the reserve ratio every month ... and the level of excess liquidity in the system would still be unchanged. Here, increasing reserve requirements is like being on a treadmill, stepping forward continually just to remain in one place.

And this is essentially where the PBC has found itself in the past year: since the beginning of 2007 monthly FX reserve purchases have averaged nearly US $40bn, or US $120bn per quarter, which translates into or more than RMB900bn worth of domestic liquidity coming into the economy every quarter. By contrast, each 50 bp hike in the required reserve ratio takes roughly RMB180bn out of the system, and for the past year the PBC has hiked the ratio on average once every six weeks, which means RMB360bn worth of withdrawal on a quarterly basis.

This, in turn, means that there is no clear "maximum" level of reserve requirements. If China continues to run large external surpluses and FX reserves continue to flow in at the current pace, the PBC could easily end up raising the required reserve ratio to 15% and then 20% and perhaps even 30% without strong undue impact on the banking system as a whole (although this is not necessarily true for individual banks).

6.4 Where Does It End?

Once again, let us stress the conclusions that (i) hikes in the required reserve ratio are not really tightening liquidity on a net basis, and (ii) as a result, we could see continued reliance on this policy tool for a good while to come.

However, it is also clear that the PBC cannot rely on reserve requirements forever. The current impact on commercial bank profitability may be very small – and vastly outweighed by strong trend banking system profit growth over the past 2 years from other sources – but the costs are real nonetheless, and a policy of *ad infinitum* ratio increases would eventually threaten banks' income and their ability to operate. This is all the more true given our view that commercial banks will begin to see growth and profits squeezed over the medium-term through other factors (see *The Sword Hanging Over Chinese Banks, Asian Focus, 15 December 2006* for further details).

So how does it end in the medium term? In all likelihood, the PBC's "exit strategy" from reliance on required reserve hikes will involve a combination of two factors: First, a gradual decline in the magnitude of China's external balance of payments surplus, which in turn will depend on the authorities' willingness to push up the pace of RMB appreciation (see *The Real Case for Revaluation* for more details).

And second, a switch to yet other sterilization instruments. With the creation of the China Investment Corporation (or CIC, i.e., the new mainland sovereign wealth fund), the Ministry of Finance has issued US $200bn worth of long-term domestic currency bonds to fund its operations, most of which have ended up in the hands of the PBC and can be used for sterilization purposes (see the previous section for further details). As the CIC widens its scope going forward, we expect further long-term bond issuance from the Ministry of Finance as well.

Essentially, this means that the gross costs of sterilization would be shifted from the banking system to the budget. This is not a permanent solution – but remember that like the PBC, the Ministry of Finance is expected to make net profits on sterilization operations in the near term, and the current fiscal position should allow China to absorb eventual net sterilization losses for a good while to come.

7 Asset Prices and Monetary Policy

Key points in this section:

- Low real deposit rates have generally contributed to strong equity and other asset price growth in China.
- However, in our view the real driver of the stock market has been the extraordinary historical underweight position in equities as a share of financial wealth.
- This means that central bank monetary policy has almost no impact on equity prices at the margin – leaving regulatory intervention as the main tool to influence the market.
- Despite the pervasive investor view, nationwide property prices are not even keeping up with urban incomes; property "bubbles" are limited to a few liquid and transactable markets.

The logical starting point for this section is a discussion of China's domestic "A share" equity market, which to many investors looks like a very sizable bubble indeed. From a peak of 2200 earlier in the decade, the Shanghai composite index reached its lowest point at 1060 in mid-2005 before jumping to 2700 by end-2006 and a high of over 6000 in the fourth quarter of this year (Chart 51). This makes China by far the best

Chart 51 The Chinese stock market takes off
Source: CEIC, UBS estimates

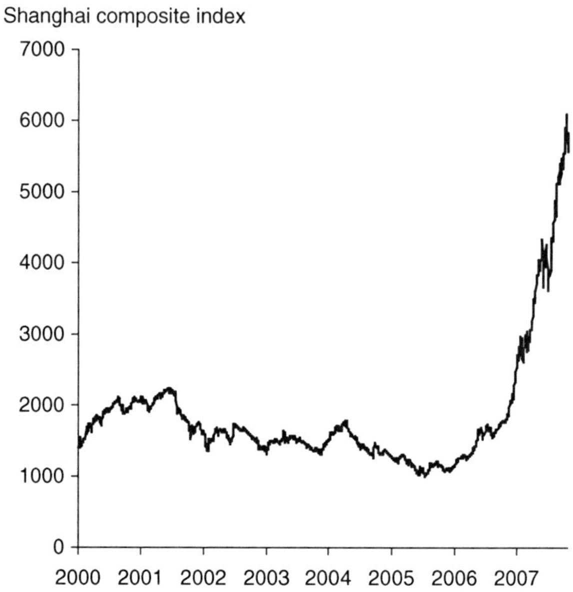

performing stock market of any major developed or emerging country over the past 12 months, and it has also brought continued flood of questions and confusion about the relationship between asset prices, domestic liquidity and official monetary policy.

7.1 What Drives the Market?

The most common view in the financial markets is that mainland stock prices are driven by excessively loose monetary policy, in the form of massive FX liquidity inflows and low or negative real deposit rates.

However, we do not find either of these last two points compelling. On the liquidity side, whether we look at new base money growth or the pace of aggregate bank credit expansion in the economy, momentum has been quite stable in the past few years; indeed, the average growth rate since 2004 has been well below that of the first part of the decade (Chart 52). The same is true for commercial bank free reserve liquidity; as we saw above, in the past 2 years excess liquidity balances have fallen to their lowest level since the PBC began compiling bank statistics (Chart 53).

Others point to FX flows as the main factor behind the A share boom, but as discussed above, PBC sterilization policies have actually been very successful to date in preventing external funds from swamping the domestic market. And

Chart 52 Credit growth
Source: CEIC,
UBS estimates

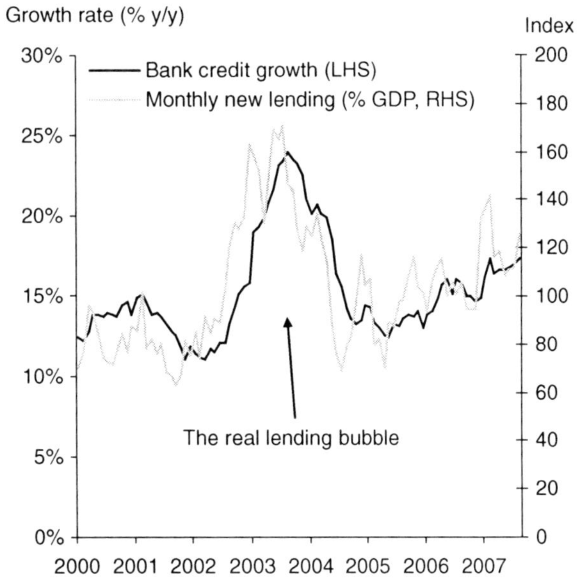

Chart 53 Bank liquidity
Source: CEIC,
UBS estimates

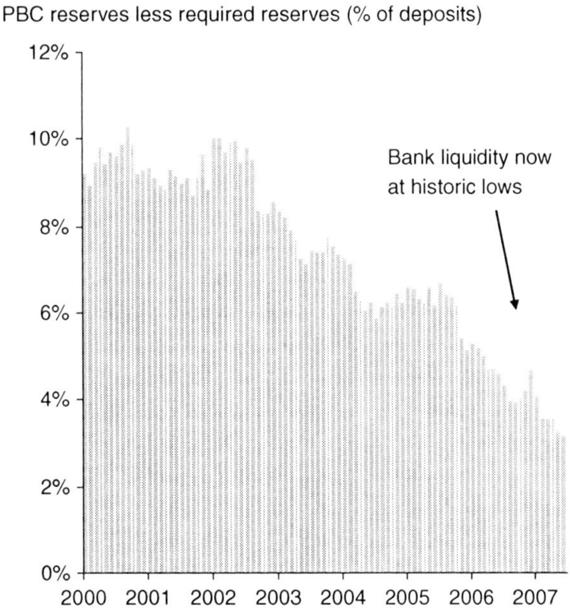

even if we take the entire gross amount of FX reserve inflows, the monthly figure accounts for only a tiny portion of the overall pickup in transaction volumes in the equity market, or for that matter estimated domestic retail inflows (Chart 54).

Chart 54 Not exactly a big influence
Source: CEIC, UBS estimates

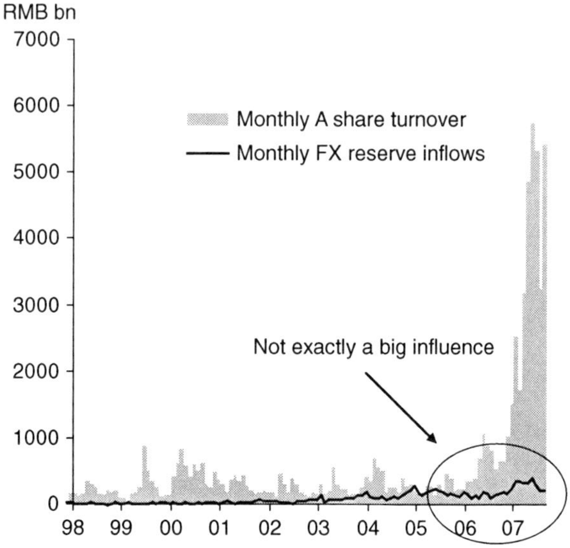

What is more, looking at the external accounts, our best estimate of portfolio capital flows in Chart 35 above shows that the peak of hot money inflows was in 2003 and 2004; by contrast, money actually been flowed *out* of China on a net basis all through 2006, and it was not until long after the domestic equity boom got underway that speculative funds finally began to return to the market in 2007.

In short, if we just focus on indicators of domestic liquidity growth and monetary policy, 2006 was probably the least attractive year for the beginning stock market rally in a long, long time. If anything, the A share market should have run in 2000–01, when excess reserves in the banking system were at their peak . . . or 2002, when both base and broad money were expanding rapidly . . . or in 2003–04 when external capital inflows were at their peak . . . or at the beginning of 2005, when short-term interest rates were at historic lows and the PBC was again pumping base money into the system . . . but by 2006 none of these indicators were supportive of an asset market boom.

Nor do low or even negative deposit returns necessarily tell the whole story. Mind you, there is little doubt that real deposit rates have been trending downward since the late 1990s as underlying inflation has increased, and that the real return went into negative territory in 2003–04 and again this year when measured against headline CPI inflation (although real rates are still significantly positive against core CPI, and roughly zero against upstream price measures, see Chart 55). And this environment almost certainly contributed to the buoyancy of stock prices in recent years.

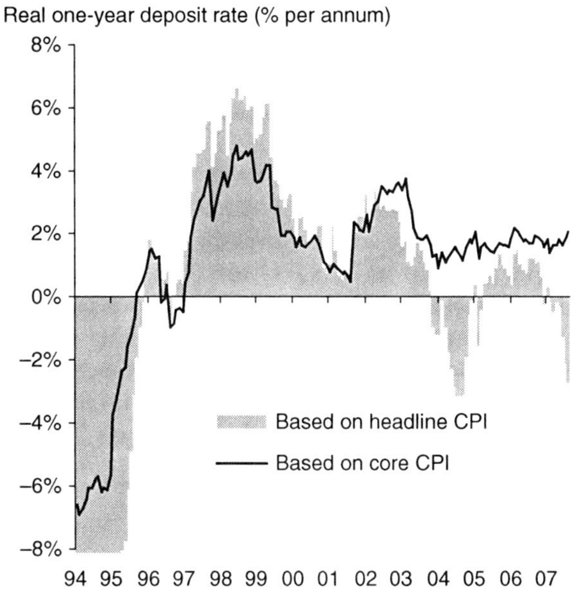

Chart 55 What about deposit rates?
Source: CEIC, UBS estimates

However, remember from the interest rate section above that low interest rates are very much the norm in high-growth Asian markets. In fact, even taking the region as a whole China's real deposit return was not particularly low during the 2005–07 boom; Chart 56 shows average real deposit rates using headline CPI inflation across Asia over the past 3 years. As you can see, Indonesia,

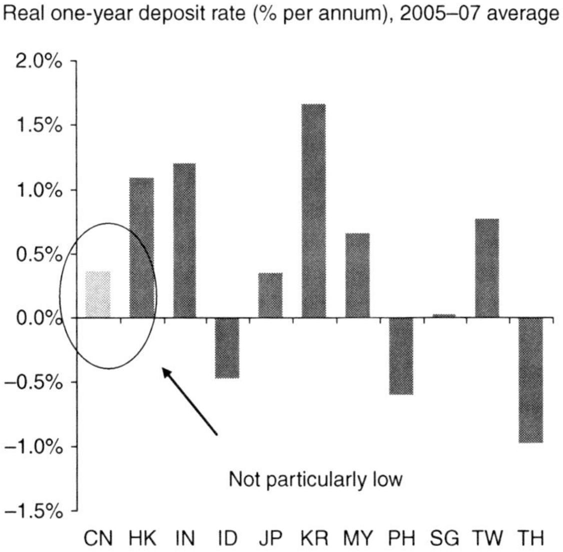

Chart 56 Not particularly low
Source: CEIC, UBS estimates

Japan, the Philippines, Singapore, and Thailand all had real interest rates lower than China – and none of them had anything approaching a six-fold stock market increase. Nor, for that matter, is there any identifiable correlation at all between real deposit returns and equity market performance on a cross-country basis.

Perhaps our point is best made in the following way: With core CPI inflation at 1.5% y/y and estimated "structural" CPI inflation including medium-term food and energy trends currently running at around 3% y/y, we could easily argue that the mainland 1-year deposit rate should be at or above 5% per annum rather than the current 3.6%; this would already put the real deposit return above that in any other Asian country in recent years. However, we have a hard time believing that a 150–200 bp increase in nominal deposit rates would have made a significant difference in countering expected gains of 15% or more *per month* in the stock market over the past 2 years.

7.2 *The Real Story*

What, then, do we see as the real underlying driver of the Chinese equity boom? In our view, the most important factor has been the extraordinary historical underweight position on the part of mainland firms and households.

Just look at Chart 57, which shows the breakdown of liquid financial wealth across global economies as of end-2005. For regions like the United States, EU and Japan, which have mature bond markets, total equity market capitalization usually accounts for 25–30% of total liquid financial assets; in non-Japan Asia, where bond markets are relatively underdeveloped, equities tend to play a stronger role at nearly 40% of financial wealth (and this is true even in the poorest economies we cover).[7]

Then turn to the bars for China. The sixth bar from the right shows the comparable breakdown for the mainland economy as of end-2005, at the beginning of the A share recovery. As of 2005, the entire domestic equity market accounted for only 9% of financial wealth, far below the regional average and far below the norm even for developed countries as well. Instead, most of China's accumulated savings was simply locked up in the banking system, to a much greater degree than anywhere else in Asia.

The magnitude of that relative underweight position was so vast that even in September 2007, after an eight-fold gain in total stock market capitalization from the 2005 trough, domestic equity holdings still only account for 35% of financial wealth in the mainland economy (the far right bar in the Chart) – i.e.,

---

[7] Chart 57 differs from Chart 5 above in that the earlier Chart only includes bonds held outside the banking system; this proved difficult to calculate on a cross-regional basis and so Chart 57 includes the total stock of government and corporate bonds outstanding. See *The Return of Asia, Part 4* (*Asian Economic Perspectives, 20 November 2006*) for further details.

Chart 57 The real story
Source: CEIC, UBS estimates

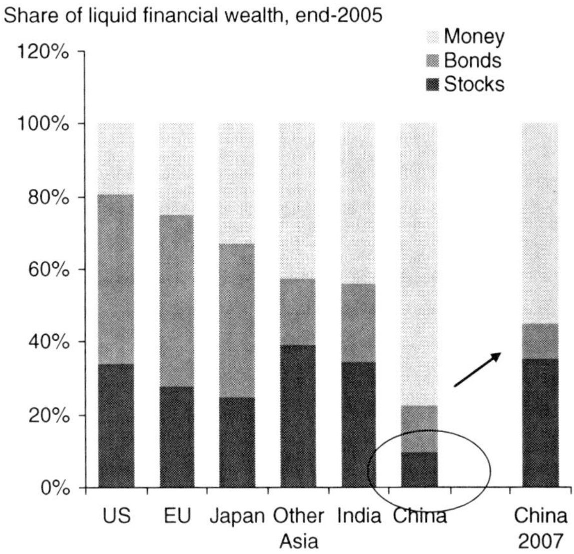

China is *only now* coming into line with the regional average for stock market weighting in overall financial portfolios.

These historical conditions helps explain how the A share market could rise when it did, even when new flow liquidity conditions were relatively unfavorable. In our view, the story runs as follows:

At the beginning of the decade, the average price/earnings ratio for the Shanghai and Shenzhen indices stood at 60 times, far higher than in any other regional market and higher than Chinese historical levels, indicating an overvalued market by almost any standard. By 2003 the ratio had fallen to 40, but was still very much on the high side for domestic investors. It was not until late 2005, when the average P/E ratio stood at around 15, that the market started to price in expectations of future upside.

Another factor was structural reform. From 1999 through 2004 the government tabled a number of plans to sell down non-tradable state shares into the market... and every time they did the domestic equity market fell sharply, which in turn forced the government to retract. Effectively, the spectre of future state share reform was a constant source of downward pressure on prices. However, by 2005 the authorities had adopted a "market-friendly" solution, reimbursing minority shareholders for the estimated losses involved in selling down state shares.

In other words, by late 2005 the two biggest sources of negative market sentiment (overvaluation and the unresolved overhang of non-tradable state shares) had disappeared. And despite some of the most unfavorable flow liquidity trends in a decade, the A share market was able to double and double again over the next 24 months. Why? Because Chinese savers had nearly US $5 trillion in cash and deposits to throw at the equity market once they became convinced that it was a profitable prospect.

7.3 What This Means for the PBC

The story above presents a clear problem for the monetary authorities, since it means their ability to control the market is extremely limited. Consider the following question: if the PBC wanted to cool off the equity market, what could it do?

We already saw above that the PBC has a comparably easy time controlling credit growth. All it has to do is tighten up on new base money liquidity going into the banking system through sterilization operations; when commercial banks' excess reserves holdings fall, they cannot lend out as much into the economy. And if worse comes to worst, the central bank can still make active use of administrative "window guidance" controls on bank credit operations.

Indeed, as we saw above, this is precisely what happened over the past few years: the PBC tightened up on base money policy and tightened controls on bank lending, and as a result liquidity levels dropped and credit growth slowed visibly on a trend basis. However, the A share market did not slow at all; instead, it began to rise – and then began to spiral upward at a record-breaking pace.

The reason, as we see it, is that equity inflows are not really financed by *new* credit growth but rather by portfolio reallocation from the existing stock of financial assets, and one of the most surprising and salient facets of the Chinese equity market is the lack of leverage or gearing in the system.

Of course the financial press is full of anecdotes about homeowners hocking their flat to a pawn shop to play the market and companies diverting loans for stock speculation, but the fact remains that such loan diversion (and indeed all brokerage margin lending) is technically illegal in China. And there is very little hard evidence to show that new credit creation has played a significant role in the A share rally. In fact, every time the regulatory authorities have stepped in over the past 18 months to try to cool off overheated investor sentiment, the market has traded sideways rather than down – just the opposite of what we would expect to see if there were a sizeable "margin call" at play (Chart 51).

As we saw in Chart 57 above, with US $5 trillion still sitting in the banking system households and firms have not really needed to leverage up to buy shares; to date, all they had to do was collectively attempt to shift their current portfolio composition. And in this environment, the question of whether that US $5 trillion sum has been increasing or decreasing by a few hundred billion dollars a year as a result of monetary policy decisions has been decidedly second-order.

What about interest rates? Why has not the PBC been hiking rates much more aggressively in order to rein in the overheated equity market? In our view, there are three reasons behind the central banks' reticence:

First, as we argued above the current level of nominal and real lending rates is arguably about right for the real economy. And this puts the PBC in the same boat as other central banks with a balanced real growth outlook but a booming asset market: if you react too aggressively to the latter, you risk causing a sharp slowdown in the former, and in this situation banks have nearly always come down on the side of real growth and inflation, with are their formal policy targets. Of course there is presently a very heated debate in academic and policy circles over the proper role of asset prices in monetary management – but for the time being, we have very few examples of rate hikes or quantitative tightening actually stopping an asset bubble in "mid-stride".

Second, the case for interest rate actions in China is especially weak given our argument that there is not much leverage in the market today, i.e., that equity prices are driven by the very sizeable pool of accumulated savings in the banking system. If portfolio reallocation is indeed the main factor behind the market rally, then raising the price of new credit or slowing credit growth is not likely to have a big impact on the process, and it should come as no surprise that the PBC has been very vocal in its view that managing the equity market is a job for the regulators and not for the central bank.

The PBC could of course raise deposit rates in order to increase the return on monetary assets and slow the flow of funds into the equity market, but this brings us back to the discussion in previous sections above: deposit rate increases of 100–200 bp are not likely to have any significant effect on stock prices, but could have a very considerable negative impact indeed on commercial banks' net income position given the ongoing restructuring of bank balance sheets.

7.4 China's Two Liquidities

On a more theoretical note, what we are really saying is that there are two very different concepts of liquidity in China: one that drives the "real" economy, i.e., macro growth and inflation, and another that drives asset markets. Under present circumstances, the two have almost nothing to do with each other – and most important, the PBC only controls the first with virtually no influence whatsoever on the second.

You can see the point in Chart 58, which we published in other research earlier this year. The dark green bar in the Chart is the total size of excess reserve liquidity in the commercial banking system today, corresponding to the figures in Chart 27 above. This is the total amount of funds available for banks to put new loans out into the economy, which in a heavily bank-dependent economy like China's represents the ability to drive overall effective real demand and spending at the margin. More important, this is the liquidity pool that is directly controlled by the PBC through its monetary policy. And as you can see, the numbers here are quite small, around RMB1.2 trillion in excess reserves as of this writing, which now represents less than 3% of bank deposits.

By contrast, the light green bar shows the total accumulated stock of bank deposits and cash held in the economy today, around RMB37 trillion, which as we argued is the pool of liquidity currently driving asset markets. The point, of course, is that the central bank has virtually no control over the size of (or, for

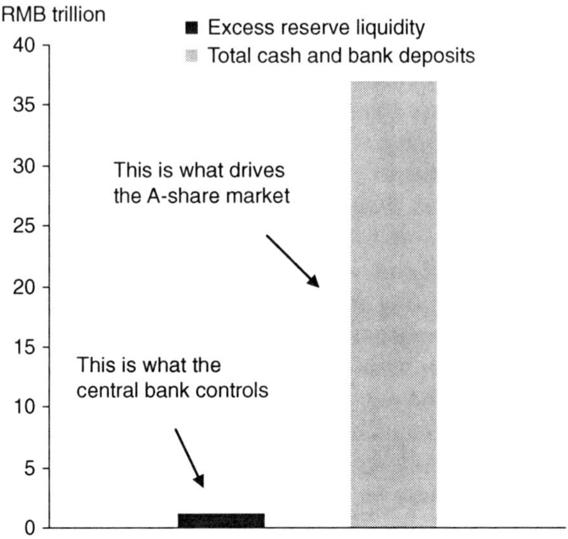

Chart 58 China's two liquidities
Source: CEIC, UBS estimates

that matter, the relative return on) these funds, and as a result the equity market has enjoyed very abundant liquidity support indeed.

This will not be the case forever. As the portfolio reallocation process reaches a mature stage – which, according to Chart 57 above, may be happening already – the market should become increasingly constrained by the ability to create new lending and leverage in order to drive prices further, which is uniformly the case in more developed countries. As this happens, the center of gravity will shift from the large bar to the smaller bar in Chart 58, giving the PBC more effective control over the process at the margin.

7.5 The M1 Myth

At this point in the discussion, many investors would be tempted to point out that there is in fact one monetary aggregate that shows a consistent, strong positive correlation with the equity market on a flow basis: "narrow" money M1. As shown in Charts 59 and 60, the relationship between M1 growth and equity price growth is almost one-to-one in the Asian region as a whole, and very strong in China as well. Indeed, for many investors fluctuations in M1 are the most important barometer of financial market liquidity; surely this is an indication that loose monetary policy and excess liquidity growth are fundamentally responsible for the A share rally?

Our answer is no, and there are two fundamental reasons why the above statement is wrong.

First, M1 may be a measure of monetary liquidity, but it is not a measure of liquidity *creation*. The only way for new money to be created in any economy is

Chart 59 The Asian M1 myth
Source: CEIC, UBS estimates

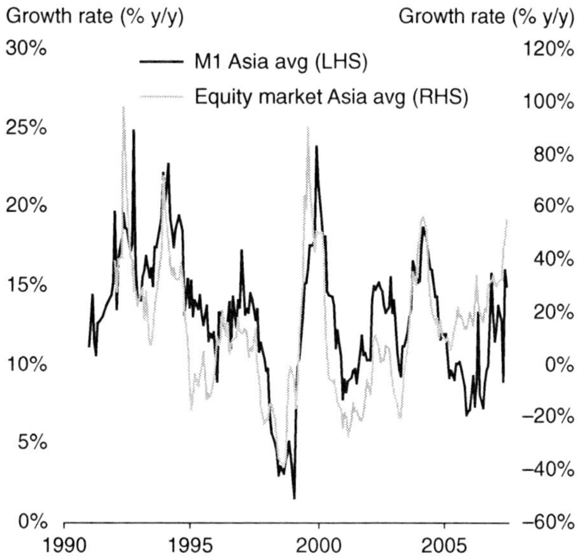

Chart 60 The China M1 myth
Source: CEIC, UBS estimates

for the central bank to issue new base money, or for banks to lend out more against a given level of base money, thus increasing broad money M2. By contrast, narrow money simply measures one sub-category of overall monetary holdings by maturity – a sub-category that households and firms can move in and out of at will by adjusting portfolio allocation, without any necessary tie to broad monetary conditions. In theory, M1 can double overnight even when the central bank is in the middle of a draconian monetary tightening; it can also fall by half even when central bank is printing new money at full throttle.

And second, as we showed in *M1 – Still a Myth (Asian Focus, 14 August 2006)*, equity prices may be highly correlated with M1 movements for every country in Asia, but as you can see from closer inspection of the two charts above, the causality actually runs in the opposite direction. In short, it is not M1 growth that drives the stock market, but rather the stock market that drives M1 growth.

Why? Think about the definition of narrow money, i.e., cash and demand deposits in the banking system. When asset returns are high relative to deposit interest rates, households and firms tend to shift out of long-term deposits and into cash or demand holdings in order to invest in the market. Analogously, when asset returns are low, investors move back into long-term deposits.

7.6 The Bank Deposit Myth

And this brings us to another common myth in the Chinese economy, one that concerns the behavior of bank deposits in the stock market boom. According to some estimates, the A share market saw more than RMB3.2 trillion of new domestic fund flows during 2006. As we saw above, the main (indeed, virtually the only) source of financing for equity purchases in China is the accumulated stock of savings in the banking system.

So if RMB3.2 trillion left the Chinese banking system to go into the domestic stock market in 2006 – a full 10% of outstanding bank deposits that year – then should we not have seen a sharp fall in the level of M2? And does not the fact that M2 actually grew by 16% over the same period mean that the PBC was pumping in massive amounts of new liquidity to prop up bank balance sheets, also fueling the stock market rally in the process?

Many investors might respond "yes" to both these questions, but the answers are actually "no" and "no". The reason is that, counterintuitive as it may same, money does not really leave the banking system when investors trade stocks. When Chinese firms and households take funds out of the bank to buy equities, the proceeds of the sale go to . . . other firms and households, who take the funds and deposit them right back in the banking system (it may take an entire chain of transactions to achieve this end result, but the end result is nonetheless the same). Indeed, from a theoretical point of view the only real leakage out of the banking system comes from *new* issuance of shares, and the total for A shares in 2006 was RMB180 billion, a far smaller amount.[8]

[8] The reason new share issuance is a "leakage" is that the issuing companies would have otherwise presumably borrowed the funds from the banking system; this implies lower credit growth and thus lower deposit growth. Even this argument is tenuous in an environment where the monetary authorities are administratively dampening credit growth (since the fact that companies are moving into equity finance doesn't necessarily lower aggregate credit creation in this case), but over the medium term we do expect disintermediation out of the Chinese banking system to have a significant effect on balance sheet growth.

How then was the portfolio reallocation in Chart 57 above achieved? Very simple: the price of existing equity holdings was bid up sharply as deposit liquidity flowed through the market (before returning to banks), and the resulting rise in market capitalization increased the relative share of equities in households' and firms' financial portfolios.

7.7 What About Property Assets?

What about the property market? In theory, the liquidity pool supporting housing prices is exactly the same at the pool pushing up equities; with no effective means of control by the monetary authorities, should we not see the same bubble-like behavior in Chinese real estate markets . . . and indeed, are we not seeing it already?

The answer is that in some regional markets we already have; think of the Shanghai high-end bubble of 2003–04 or the growing Shenzhen boom today. However, on a nationwide basis we see no real evidence whatsoever of an overall "Chinese property bubble", nor do we real prospects for one to develop in the near future. And this makes property markets very different from the mainland A share market today.

We went through the details in *Will Property Follow A Shares? (Asian Focus, 20 September 2007)*, but the basic story is as follows. Chart 61 shows the best available nationwide figures on land and property price movements over the past decade. The various series are not completely compatible, but they all show

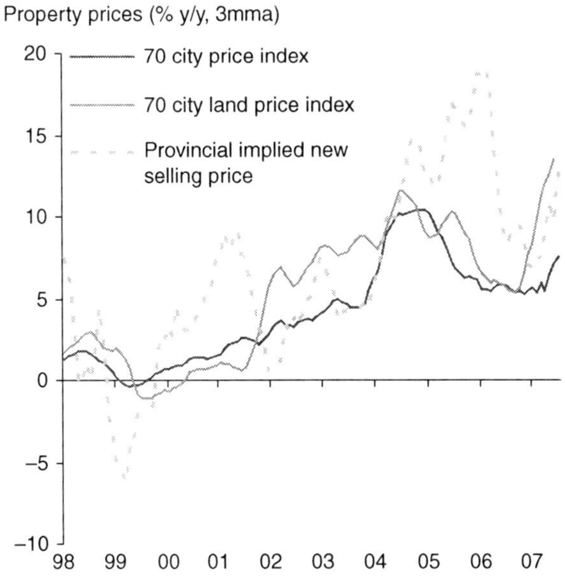

Chart 61 Property and land prices in China
Source: CEIC, UBS estimates

broadly similar trends: (i) property and land prices have been rising at an increasing pace for the last 10 years; (ii) there was a relative boom in 2004–05 followed by a slowdown in 2005–06; (iii) prices are now picking up again in 2007, and growing at an average pace of around 10% per year.

Now for the key question: Is nationwide property price growth of 10% y/y a "lot"? In a mature economy like the United States the answer might be yes, but for China we would have to say no. The reason is that nominal GDP increased by 16% y/y in the first half of 2007, and urban household income grew 17% in nominal terms over the past twelve months; in fact, when we track property and land prices relative to GDP and household income over time the ratio has been falling steadily over the past decade regardless of the price series we use. In other words, the official data uniformly show that housing and other property is becoming *more* affordable over time (Charts 62 and 63).

Chart 62 Property prices against GDP
Source: CEIC, UBS estimates

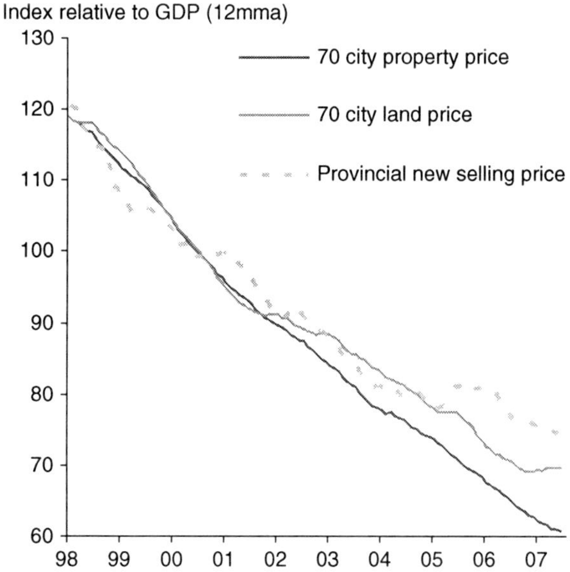

Needless to say, this is exactly the opposite of what we have seen in regional or global instances of actual housing bubbles. In larger economies like the United States and Japan, housing prices normally rose by 15–25% as a share of national income before seeing a correction; in the case of Hong Kong and the United Kingdom, relative prices jumped by 60% or even 80% (see Charts 64 and 65).

In other words, the official Chinese data show no sign whatsoever of unsustainable price increases on a nationwide basis.

Mind you, this conclusion flies in the face of many investors' own experience; since a visit to China's top-tier cities generally leaves the impression that

Chart 63 Property prices against income
Source: CEIC, UBS estimates

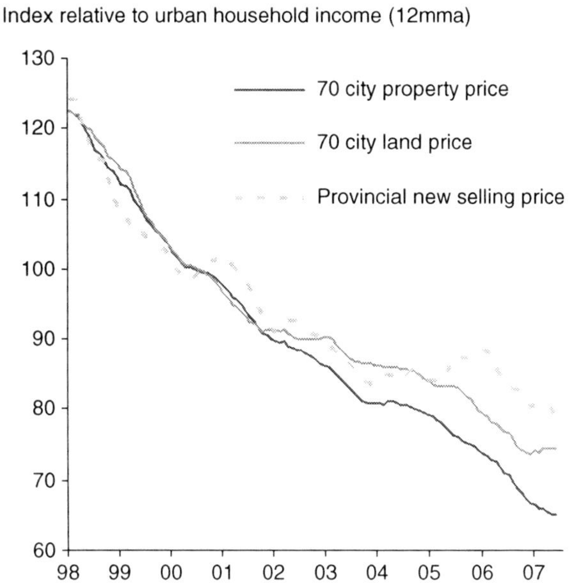

Chart 64 United States and United Kingdom
Source: CEIC, UBS estimates

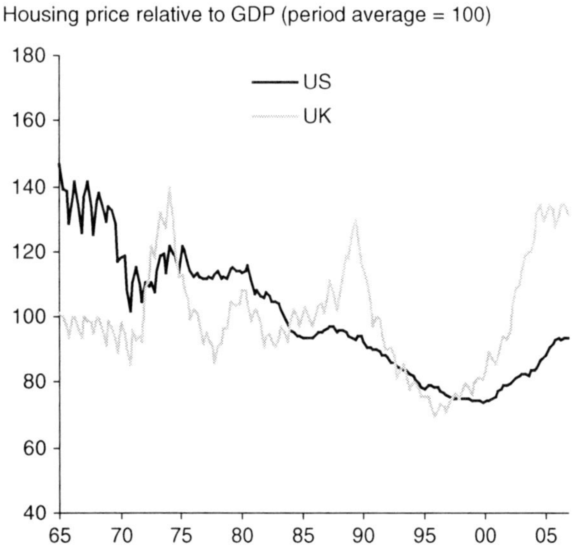

housing prices are rising much more rapidly. At the peak in 2004, Shanghai high-end flats were appreciating at 70–80% per year, and according to market reports the price for new developments in Shenzhen is now increasing at a 50% pace. How can we say that overall prices are only rising by 10% y/y or even less?

Chart 65 Japan and Hong Kong
Source: CEIC, UBS estimates

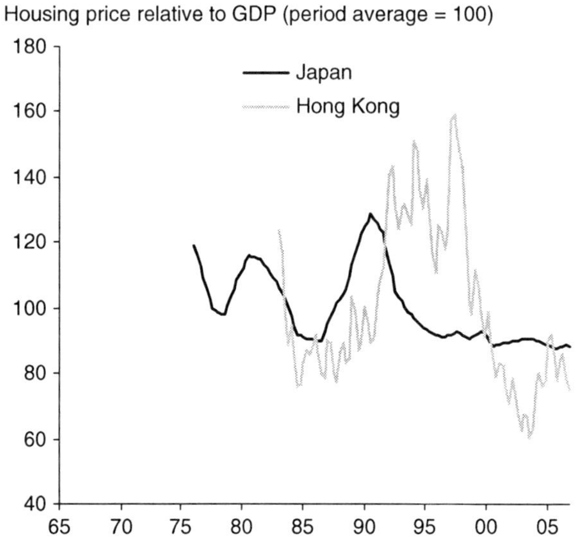

To begin with, as tempting as it is to assume that price trends in, say, Shanghai are a good proxy for the country as a whole, nothing could be further from the truth. In fact, even when we include the broadest surrounding administrative areas including all suburbs as well as associated rural counties, China's top five cities taken together still account for only 14% of the total nationwide property market, and probably only half that share if we restrict ourselves to the core urban area. And with vast differences in the level of tradability between regions (about which more below), there is no necessary reason to expect that top-tier urban markets would reflect trends in other parts of China.

Also, whenever we hear housing price figures quoted for individual markets, the numbers almost invariably refer to high-end or luxury apartments, and almost invariably to projects by established, recognized developers. This is natural, of course, since most international investors are only active in that market segment and usually get information during property visits to listed development companies; most published market research by real estate specialists is also heavily skewed toward high-end office and residential markets.

However, keep in mind that luxury development – as defined in the official Chinese statistics, which generally means anything above RMB8,000–RMB10,000 per square meter for first-tier cities – accounts for only 20% of the primary market in cities like Shanghai and Shenzhen, perhaps 15% in Beijing, and well under 10% in the broader urban market as a whole. The same is true for first-tier developers; foreign developers together with large domestic listed developers account for less than 10% of total building construction revenues.

Once we take these facts into account the official statistics no longer look particularly distorted or understated. In fact, they have done a very good job of capturing China's local property bubbles: in the 2003–04 Shanghai boom, for example, luxury segment growth of 70% y/y or more probably meant an increase of only half that magnitude in the overall market, and sure enough, the NBS data recorded a 30% y/y peak increase for Shanghai as a whole. Exactly the same math holds up for Shenzhen, where the most recent data show overall prices shooting past 20% y/y (if 20–30% y/y city-wide growth does not sound impressive, remember that even at the very peak of the 1990s Hong Kong property bubble *aggregate* city-wide housing was going up at a 40% per year in at most in nominal terms – and this was driven by much faster increases in leveraged credit than in China, see below).

7.8 Why No Property Bubble?

So far, so good, but this still leaves us with a large pool of financial assets in the banking earning a very low real return. We have already seen how portfolio reallocation out of bank deposits can affect the domestic equity market; even if property markets are not showing bubble-like traits today, is it not just a matter of time before they start to skyrocket? And in particular, if the A share market rally ends, would this not push a very large amount of liquid funds into physical property in search of the "next big thing"?

We do not believe so – at least not to anywhere near the same degree as stock prices, and not on a nationwide basis. Of course China will continue to have local "mini-bubbles" in individual cities and regions, and we should also expect overall housing price inflation continue to pick up gradually over the medium term, but here are three very good reasons not to look for a nationwide property bubble in China:

First, there is no "national" Chinese property market. Property markets are driven by local conditions in every big country, of course, but this is particularly true in emerging markets and China is no exception. Local economic trends, regulations and liquidity differ widely, and the lack of substitutability between provinces and urban areas has led to a very weak correlation between geographical markets. Studies of the US economy, for example, show a rising positive relationship among the various states – but only in the past few decades, relatively late in the development process, and correlation between individual European markets remains very low indeed.

Second, "transactability" also varies enormously between regions. Nowhere is the above point more true than in the simple ability to buy and sell in individual markets. Among first-tier cities, for example, Shanghai and Shenzhen have by far the most liberal regulatory regime, in the sense that transactions such as property transfer and title clear in a matter of weeks and the buyer is then free to resell. In Beijing, by contrast, it can take a new buyer 2 years or more to receive title on an apartment or villa, which significantly reduces effective liquidity in the market.

It should come as no surprise, then, that Shanghai and Shenzhen prices have tended to rise a lot faster than in Beijing – and, more generally, that larger and richer cities have seen higher price inflation than in their less developed counterparts. You can see this clearly (at least for those with good eyesight) in Chart 66, which shows the peak property price growth rate over the past 7 years by a major city in China.

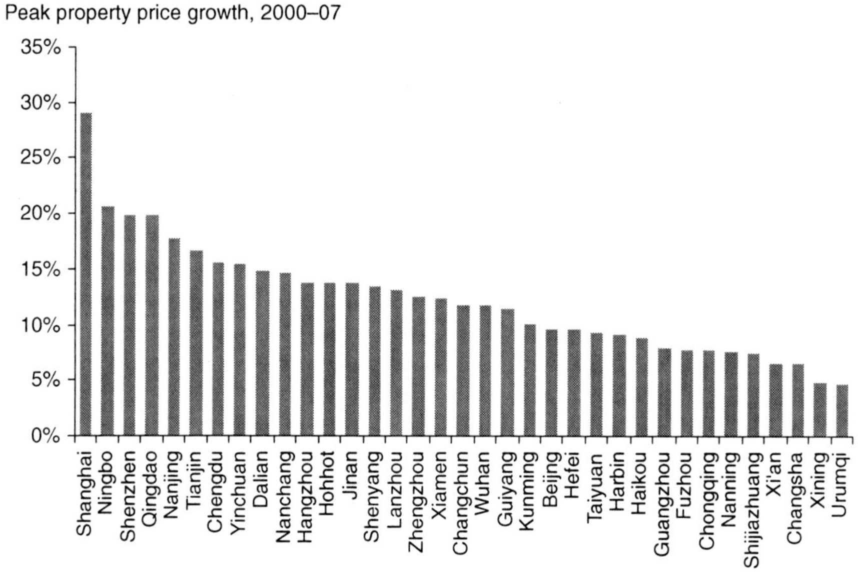

Chart 66 Price trends by city
Source: CEIC, UBS estimates

Finally, leverage opportunities are limited. Compared to equity markets, property markets require much greater access to borrowed capital in order to thrive. Of the RMB35 trillion in banking system deposits in China today, around half are household savings; this translates to around RMB13,000 per person. Any deposit holder in the country can withdraw any fraction of this amount and open an equity trading account the same day, which helps explain why A shares have boomed over the past 2 years. However, there are relatively few households with RMB200,000 (the cost of an average mid-market 70 sqm urban flat in China) of free cash in the bank – and very few indeed with the RMB750,000 or more required to enter the high end in larger cities.

In other words, effective property demand requires leverage in the form of an active mortgage market. And as we showed above, banks' ability to accelerate lending growth is already quite limited given the very low excess reserve ratio in the financial system. And this helps explain why mortgage lending is only barely

Chart 67 Consumer and mortgage lending
Source: CEIC, UBS estimates

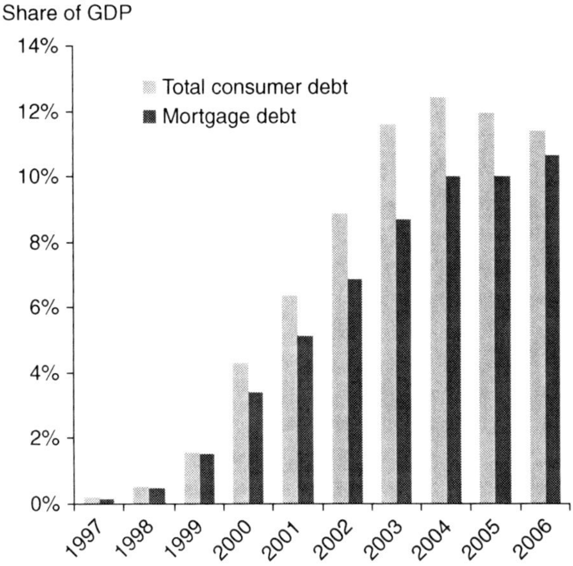

keeping up with GDP growth in recent years (Chart 67) – in sharp contrast with the mortgage credit booms that fueled almost every housing bubble in recent global history.

8 The Way Forward

Key points in this section:

- To repeat our main conclusion, the PBC is still way off from global "best practice" in monetary policy – but is also doing a very respectable job of managing the economy even by historical developed standards. And this means that the way forward will be one of gradual evolution rather than radical policy shifts.
- The next steps include continued bank privatization, interest rate liberalization, removal of administrative credit controls, financial market liberalization, continued capital account opening and a move to a flexible exchange rate. In our view, each of these could be achieved in the five-year horizon.
- We do not share market fears of an overheated domestic economy or runaway inflation, and even a sharp equity market correction should not have a significant impact on overall economic or monetary trends.
- Rather, in our view the biggest risk to the policy outlook is the prospect of an ever-increasing trade and balance of payments surplus – which could eventually destabilize the economy.

If we could sum up the findings of the above analysis, we would say that the PBC and the government have already made enormous progress in monetary management. The policy environment today is very different indeed from what it would have been 10 or 20 years ago, in terms of the tools used, the responsiveness of the economy to market-based measures and experience and quality of the policymakers themselves. As a result, while China is still far from "state of the art" central banking practice, it is already broadly consistent with historical policymaking in post-war developed economies. The mainland authorities have done a surprisingly good job of keeping the economy under control in the present cycle, and we do not see strong near-term macro risks at present.

In this final section, we look at the future prospects for Chinese monetary policy. Our discussion here falls into two categories: first, the likely trends over the next 5 years as the mainland continues to refine its policy practices, and second, the potential medium-term risks to the monetary environment. On the former side, here are our projections for the coming half-decade.

Better domestic monetary management. As we discussed earlier, the PBC is now much better placed to regulate money and credit growth than at any time in the past decade. This is in part because the level of excess liquidity in the banking system has now fallen to reasonable levels, which means that base money management practices have already begun to have a more visible impact on the cost of funding in the economy.

Another important factor is that commercial banks themselves are also undergoing a fundamental change in business practices. We already showed that the center of gravity in economic activity is moving from state enterprises to more private, commercial firms; the government is also busy privatizing large portions of the state banking sector. Moreover, banks now face proficient and aggressive regulators who were almost completely absent only15 years ago (see *How To Think About China, Part 3* for further discussion of these points). All of these changes mean that market lending risks and cost-of-capital considerations are now effective in a way they were not before.

Phasing out of administrative credit controls. We also discussed the fact that the government long since abandoned central credit allocation at the sectoral and firm level in favor of overall credit guidance – and in recent years even these aggregated controls have only been invoked when the macro situation warranted. In our view, with market-based policy now starting to "bite" it will not be long before even these softer controls are phased out as well, as the PBC has always viewed them as a practical tool rather than a fundamental philosophical necessity. We do expect the economy will continue to have problems with local government interference in banking decisions, but even here the problems are much less prevalent than they were historically.

Commercial bank interest rate liberalization. The same finding applies for the current controls on commercial bank interest rates; indeed, the PBC has long since stressed its intention to remove controls over the medium term. Again, our view is that the most important factor here is the state of commercial bank balance sheets and the ongoing recapitalization of the larger institutions. One these constraints are lifted within the next few years, we expect the authorities to lift deposit rate ceilings, remove the remaining floors on lending rates and let rates float more or less freely accounting to monetary conditions.

Rising interest rates more generally. As this happens, we expect the average level of interest rates to go up, in part because of the removal of deposit rate caps but also because of rising inflationary pressures through the end of the decade. We will have more to say about inflation in the mainland economy further below.

An eventual move to interest rate-based policy management. With standard monetary policy tools becoming more effective, banks more responsive to funding costs and broad interest rate ceilings removed, we also believe it will only be a matter of time before the PBC shifts to more active use of policy interest rates as its intermediate monetary target, in line with current global best practice.

However, we already saw that this change will depend crucially on the PBC "exiting" large-scale FX intervention and sterilization operations, and as we discuss below, it is not at all clear how fast this will happen.

Financial market liberalization and development. Over the next 5 years we expect significant changes in the structure of the mainland financial system – not just the historic opening of domestic equity and bond markets as a tool for general corporate finance, now underway, but also the establishment of new financial instruments and derivatives markets. As this process matures and financial portfolios diversify away bank deposits, we would also expect the current tendency toward asset price bubbles to fade.

Further opening of the capital account. In light of the present large trade and current account surpluses, the mainland authorities are already taking steps to remove external capital account restrictions in order to promote capital outflows, particularly in equity mutual funds and corporate outward FDI, and in our view this marks the beginning of a continuous trend toward more external opening. Of course it is highly unlikely that China will have anything close a free and unfettered portfolio capital flows regime in 5 years' time, but nonetheless we expect the capital account to gradually play a greater role in monetary policy.

Fading FX intervention and sterilization. Of all the points in this section, the question of FX intervention and sterilization is perhaps *the* crucial issue for the future of Chinese monetary policy independence. As we noted above, the PBC has managed very well to date in the face of large inflows, and we do not foresee undue problems in the near future. However, over the medium term there is a stronger policy imperative to make sure that the very large external surpluses recorded in 2006 and 2007 begin to come down, allowing the central bank to get off the intervention/sterilization "treadmill".

How will this occur? In our current forecasts, we expect the external trade and balance of payments surpluses to peak as a share of GDP during 2008 and then decline over the medium term as a result of four factors: (i) faster renminbi exchange rate appreciation going forward, (ii) a natural decline in heavy industrial capacity growth as a result of lower investment activity in the past few years, (iii) slower US demand and thus slowing Chinese exports, and (iv) stronger capital outflows due to ongoing liberalization (see *The New China – Back to the Real World, Asian Economic Perspectives, 1 March 2007*, and *The Real Case for Revaluation*, cited above, for further details).

Greater renminbi exchange rate flexibility. As long as China's external surpluses remain high, there will be strong pressure for the renminbi to appreciate in real terms – which in turn will make it difficult for the PBC to allow the currency to fluctuate purely in line with market forces. However, once the current surpluses subside, we do expect the authorities to gradually adopt a floating exchange rate regime; this is also a long-term stated goal of the current administration.

8.1 Where Could It Go Wrong?

So far the discussion above paints a fairly rosy picture of policy trends going forward, i.e., broad control over the macroeconomic environment, continued improvement in policy instruments and a steady move toward global best practice in central banking and regulation. Where could this scenario go wrong?

In general, we find that investors tend to focus on five macroeconomic risk factors: overheated growth, rising inflation, an equity or property market collapse, rising global financial exposure and the possibility of ever-increasing external surpluses. While we agree that all of these could arise as potential issues for the medium-term outlook, we do not see the first four as serious concerns for the time being. By contrast, we certainly do share medium-term concerns about the size and growth of China's external imbalances, and in our view this is the one to watch.

Real growth overheating. The first issue is the growth outlook, and with headline real GDP growth of 11.5% y/y in the first three quarters of 2007 – up considerably from the official rate in previous years – many observers conclude that China has no effective control over the economy and that the inevitable result will be a painful "hard landing".

However, we would note that even if we take the official data at face value there is no clear sign of domestic overheating. Look at Chart 68 below, which shows official real GDP growth by expenditure category.[9] If we focus on the behavior of domestic construction and investment spending, as shown by the bottom two bars in the chart, then it is clear that these demand categories have, if anything, actually *slowed* slightly over the past few years, and this is

[9] Note that the data in Chart 68 differ somewhat from the published overall GDP growth figures by industry; the reason is that we have taken the expenditure side GDP data, which are only published in nominal terms, and deflated them using the official GDP deflator. The two sets of data are not entirely consistent, but the broad picture is still very relevant.

Chart 68 What overheated demand?
Source: CEIC, UBS estimates

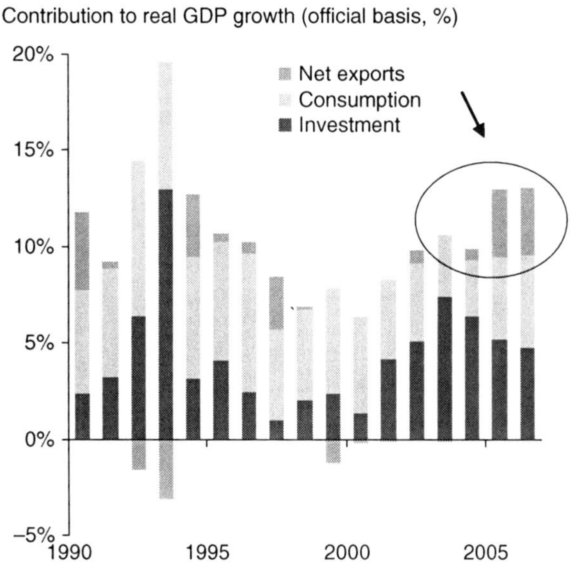

particularly true for investment expenditure. This means that all of the pickup in headline GDP growth is coming from net exports, which exploded from zero contribution to growth in 2004 to more than three percentage points on average over the past 2 years.

Put another way, the GDP numbers suggest that domestic demand is running at 9% y/y . . . while domestic production is running at nearly 12% y/y. In this case, the problem the authorities face is not excess demand at all (after all, 9% is very much in line with our estimate for medium-term sustainable growth) but rather excess supply.

This is not all, however. Keep in mind that we do not use the official GDP figures to measure historical growth trends in China; we prefer to use our own estimates derived from other data in the economy. And these figures actually show stable real GDP momentum over the past few years – i.e., it is not clear whether there has been a real growth acceleration in the first place.

Consider for example our broadest in-house measures of growth in the mainland economy: the UBS Expenditure and Physical Activity indices (explained in Footnotes 10 and 11 below). Both indicators show a sharp pickup in activity between 2000 and 2003 – but in each case, overall growth momentum either stabilized or actually slowed over the next 4 years. Significantly, neither index shows a jump to historical highs over the past four quarters (Charts 69 and 70).

This view is confirmed by virtually every other available piece of macro data in the Chinese economy. We last went through the details thoroughly in *Runaway, Runaway? (Asian Focus, 20 July 2007)*, and would refer the reader to that report for further color, but the upshot is that when looking at credit growth, fixed asset expenditure, construction demand, excess liquidity balances,

Chart 69 UBS Expenditure index[10]
Source: CEIC, UBS estimates

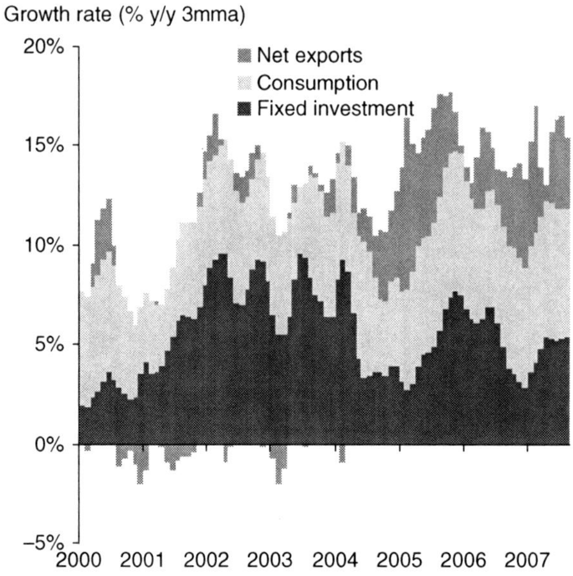

industrial profitability and inventories, real import spending and a host of physical indicators there is nothing to suggest that the authorities are far behind the curve on macro policy. And as a result we are not looking for a sharp tightening of liquidity or credit, nor do we see a looming hard landing in the economy. Instead, in our view the authorities are much more likely to focus on "supply side" policies to redude existing excess capacity and lower the trade surplus.

Inflation. The next issue is the pervasive view that China is now facing a sudden and sharp increase in economy-wide inflation – again, a sign that the PBC does not have effective monetary control and will have to make wrenching policy adjustments in order to rein in a runaway economy.

Now, we have no argument at all with the idea that mainland inflation is rising on a structural basis. As you can see from Chart 71, the CPI, the PPI and the implied GDP deflator all show exactly the same trend recovery from the 1997–2002 deflationary period. As we explained in *The New China – Back to the Real World*, the main drivers have been rising food prices, tighter labor

---

[10] The UBS Expenditure index measures the pace of real expenditure growth in three broad categories: household consumption, fixed asset investment and net exports, based on monthly trade and investment data and quarterly household expenditure surveys. These are the three main components of GDP from the expenditure side as well, so in principle there should be broad correlation between our index and overall GDP. On the other hand, keep in mind that the Expenditure index excludes other important GDP components such as government spending, inventory accumulation and services trade, which means that the index tends to overstate actual growth in practice.

Chart 70 UBS Physical activity index[11]
Source: CEIC, UBS estimates

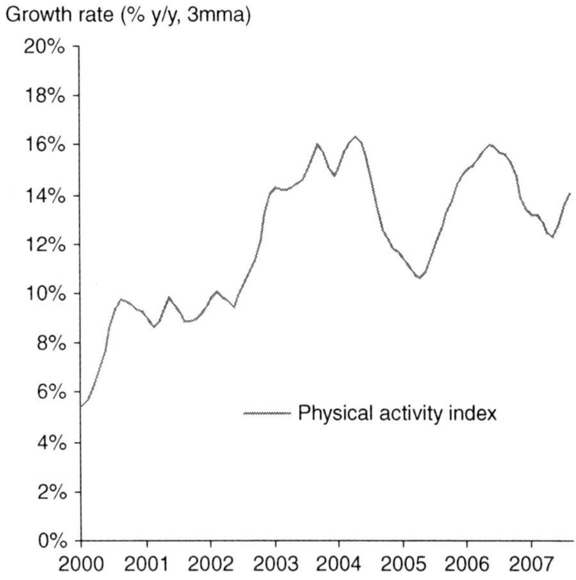

conditions in the low-end rural migrant sector, rising commodity prices and a strong trend recovery in corporate profitability – all of which we see as continued structural factors over the next few years as well.

However, keep in mind two points. The first is that according to the indicators in the chart, underlying structural inflation today is probably around 3% y/y, i.e., hardly a "blowout" by emerging market standards, and a rate that leaves plenty of room for further upside without straining the credibility of the central bank.

Second, it is safe to say that the real source of concern is not this 3% underlying trend, but rather the sudden and aggressive jump in headline CPI inflation from 2 to 6.5% y/y over the past six months. And here, the evidence suggests that this is only a temporary uptick, with supply shortages leading to very large price increases in a couple of concentrated goods categories but no sign of widespread price rises. As you can see from Chart 72, as of the latest data the entire 2007 acceleration has come from food; non-food goods and services inflation has been stable since the beginning of the year.

More important, *all* of the increase in food inflation has come from meat and eggs prices (Chart 73). In the remaining food categories (grain, dairy, fruits, vegetables, tobacco, beverages) price growth actually slowed in 2007

[11] The UBS Physical Activity index is a composite of five sub-indices, all based on physical volume growth data at the sectoral level: electricity production, passenger and freight haulage, agricultural production, construction activity (including new construction starts and completions, total floorspace under construction and land development) and industrial production (derived for bottom-up data for individual goods categories).

Chart 71 The return of inflation
Source: CEIC, UBS estimates

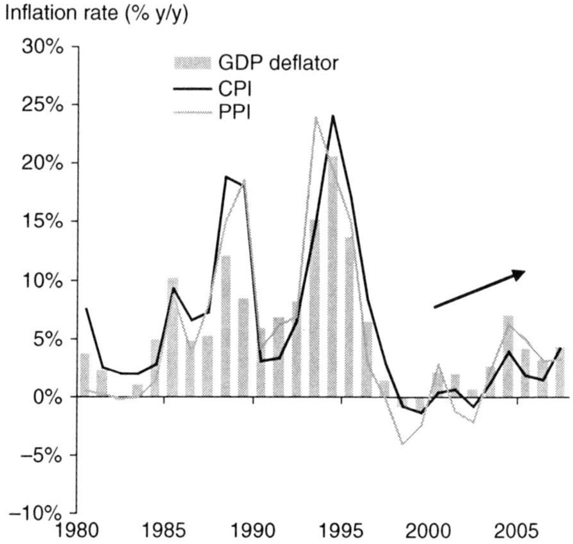

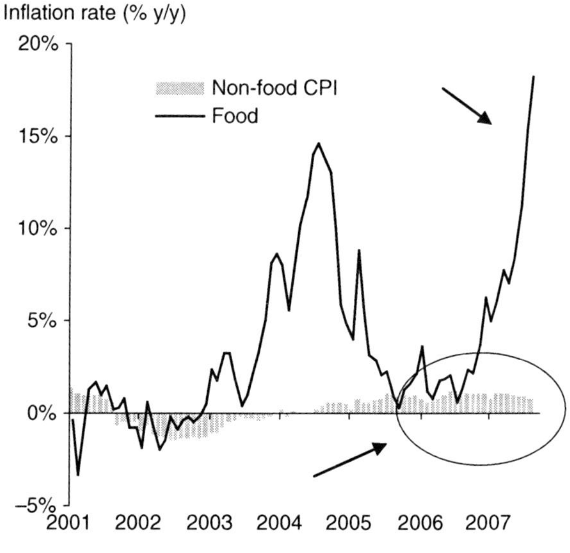

Chart 72 It is just food
Source: CEIC, UBS estimates

compared to the previous year. As a result, we expect headline CPI inflation to slow visibly in the first half of 2008 as meat and egg supply constraints are alleviated. And in the meantime we do nt expect significant policy actions by the PBC.

Asset market collapse. We discussed the main trends in mainland equity and property markets earlier on, and will not repeat the full analysis here. The key additional questions we need to raise are: What happens if China has a big asset

Chart 73 It is just meat and eggs
Source: CEIC, UBS estimates

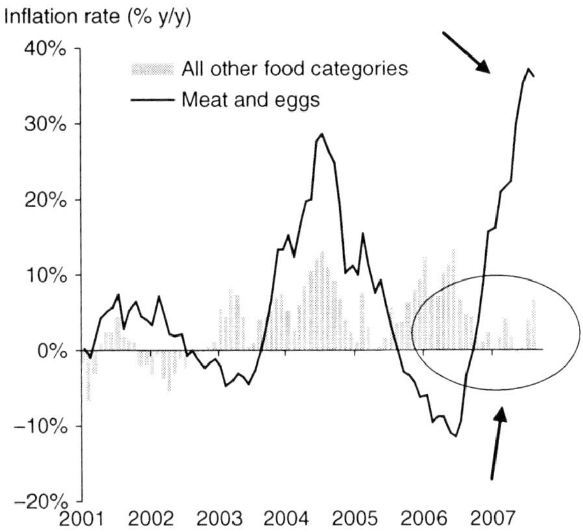

market correction? Are there implications for monetary policy or the macroeconomy in general?

We do not believe so. On the equity side, there is little doubt that the market is now extremely expensive both by global standards as well relative to China's own history (see for example Chart 74, which shows our UBS Asian Equity Strategy team's relative valuation framework for Asia ex-Japan as of end-October 2007).

However, there are three reasons why an A share downturn should not have large implications for the rest of the economy. To begin with, as we showed earlier, the A share market today is still relatively underleveraged compared to most

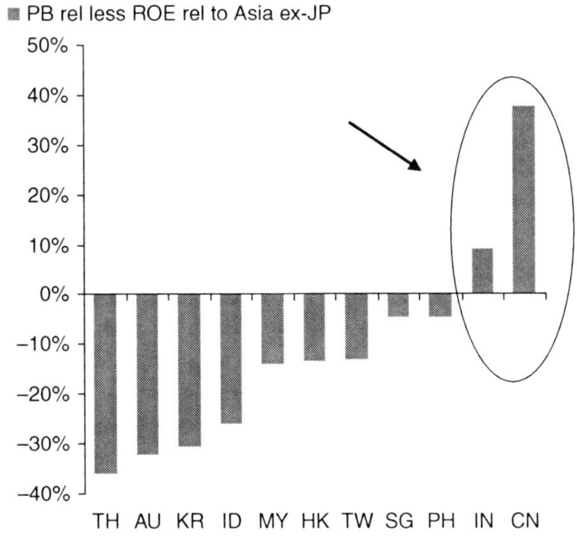

Chart 74 Asia's most expensive market (end-October 2007)
Source: CEIC, UBS estimates

neighboring and global comparators. This helps explain why the market has always traded sideways rather than down during periods of regulatory tightening; there is no real "margin call" to force a sharp correction – and no subsequent forced deleveraging of balance sheets if the market does fall.

Second, in a related point, recall from Chart 57 above that despite stock valuations that are far higher than in other economies, Chinese households and firms are still not "overweight" equities relative to their neighbors; mainland stock market holdings are only now coming into line with the global average as a share of total wealth holdings. This stands in sharp contrast to, say, the peak of the Japan or Taiwan bubbles, where the weight of the market in financial balance sheets rose to a very high proportion. As a result, any large correction from here would arguably have much less impact than the end of those earlier market rallies.

Finally, keep in mind that there is no evidence that households and firms have increased the pace of real spending in the economy over the past 2 years since the A share market rally began. In other words, stock market gains to date have essentially been treated like a one-off wealth windfall rather than a long-term increase in permanent income.

Turning to property markets, the question is even more straightforward. As discussed earlier, China does not face a property bubble on a nationwide level; in fact, the best available data show that nationwide property prices are still *falling* relative to incomes. There is a much greater risk of incipient bubbles bursting in the luxury end of a few first-tier cities, but this is far from a macroeconomic issue.

Global financial volatility. One of the key findings for the Asian region as a whole has been the lack of exposure to global credit and financial market volatility over the past few years. Of course emerging equity markets tend to rise and fall together with developed country trends – but in all of the recent periods of global market volatility, such as May–June 2006 and August 2007, the Asian region has stood out for its quiet and calm domestic interest rate and currency markets (see for example *Three Weeks Later – Bad News and Good News Revisited, Asian Focus, 20 August 2007*, for a recent review).

This was true even in small open Asian economies with very liberal capital markets, and the main factors here are strong trade and current account surpluses, conservative fiscal positions, very high international reserves and low foreign speculative exposure. All of these points are equally true for China . . . and China has an additional advantage of being large and closed. As the government liberalizes the external financial account, foreign capital flows and global market conditions will naturally play a greater role in the domestic economy, but judging by Asian experience the mainland has a long way to go indeed before financial events in New York or London begin to have a serious impact on PBC decisions at home.

Structural external surpluses. Finally, we come to the one area that in our minds presents the greatest risk to Chinese policy over the next 5 years: the prospect that ever-increasing trade and current surpluses will sooner or later take a toll on the ability to carry out independent monetary operations.

To repeat our conclusions from above, the current strategy of large-scale intervention and sterilization operations has proven both stable and sustainable for the time being, and looking forward the PBC should easily have the instruments to continue for the next couple of years without undue stress.

However, our medium-term outlook depends heavily on the premise that the overall external surplus will peak and then fall over time, allowing the authorities to reduce FX intervention and eventually wind down sterilization debt issuance altogether. What happens if instead the surpluses continue to rise over the next years, from a current account surplus of 11% in 2007 toward 15% by 2009 and even higher still by the end of the decade?

Over time, this could become a much more serious issue for the PBC and the government. Why? Because a combination of rising inflation, falling bank liquidity and expected interest rate liberalization is almost certain to push up both short- and long-term interest rates over the next few years, raising the risk of outright net losses on sterilization operations.

Again, we do not worry about such losses in the near term, since (i) the PBC has a very strong income position from its high international reserves, (ii) in the near term the central bank is already moving costs to the (currently very profitable) commercial banking system via the required reserve ratio, and (iii) if and when reserve hikes become untenable, there is still lots of room in the national budget for the government to step in through bond issuance, a policy already being implemented as we write.

On the other hand, none of these sources can hold out forever in the face of a persistent, sustained increase in the external surplus. What would happen if China reached a "breaking point"? Essentially, the PBC would be faced with the unenviable choice between letting ever-greater amounts of unsterilized liquidity rush into the banking system, or letting the renminbi exchange rate appreciate sharply in an uncontrolled manner – and either of these choices could prove destabilizing for the economy.

This is why it is crucially important for the mainland government to take more serious steps to bring the trade and current account surpluses down in the near future. And in our view, this is one area where investors should keep an eye out for changes down the road.

■Analyst Certification

Each research analyst primarily responsible for the content of this research report, in whole or in part, certifies that with respect to each security or issuer that the analyst covered in this report: (1) all of the views expressed accurately reflect his or her personal views about those securities or issuers; and (2) no part of his or her compensation was, is, or will be, directly or indirectly, related to the specific recommendations or views expressed by that research analyst in the research report.

9 Required Disclosures

This report has been prepared by UBS Securities Asia Ltd, an affiliate of UBS AG. UBS AG, its subsidiaries, branches and affiliates are referred to herein as UBS.

For information on the ways in which UBS manages conflicts and maintains independence of its research product; historical performance information; and certain additional disclosures concerning UBS research recommendations, please visit www.ubs.com/disclosures.

Further Reading

This is a long chapter, but by no means a complete report. To begin with, we have tried to approach the issue of monetary policy from the point of view of non-specialist financial investors, which necessarily means simplifying some of the debates and reaching clear and useable conclusions at the end of the day. Of course there are still a host of questions and issues that warrant further discussion – and the academic literature has sharply differing views on role of monetary policy in China, including some diametrically opposed to our own. For those interested in further reading, here's a short list of papers and reports we found useful.

References

Forssboeck, Jens, and Lars Oxelheim, 2007, "The Transition to Market-Based Monetary Policy: What Can China Learn from the European Experience?", Journal of Asian Economics, Vol. 18, No. 2

Goldstein, Morris, and Nicholas Lardy, 2007, "China's Exchange Rate Policy: An Overview of Some Key Issues", Paper Presented at the Conference on China's Exchange Rate Policy, Peterson Institute for International Economics, October 2007

Goodfriend, Marvin and Eswar Prasad, 2006a, "A Framework for Independent Monetary Policy in China," IMF Working Paper No. 06/111, March 2006

Goodfriend, Marvin and Eswar Prasad, 2006b, "Monetary Policy Implementation in China," BIS Papers No. 31

Lardy, Nicholas R., 2005, "Exchange Rate and Monetary Policy in China," CATO Journal, Vol. 25, No. 1, (Winter)

Laurens, Bernard J. and Rodolfo Maino, 2007, "China: Strengthening Monetary Policy Implementation", IMF Working Paper No. WP/07/14, January 2007

Ma, Guonan and Robert McCauley, 2007, "Do China's Capital Controls Still Bind? Implications for Monetary Autonomy and Capital Liberalization", BIS Working Papers No. 233

McKinsey Global Institute, 2006, "Putting China's Capital to Work: The Value of Financial System Reform."

Podpiera, Richard, 2006, "Progress in China's Banking Sector Reform: Has Bank Behavior Changed?" IMF Working Paper No. WP/06/71, March 2006

Prasad, Eswar, 2004, China's Growth and Integration into the World Economy: Prospect and Challenges, IMF Occasional Paper No. 232

Prasad, Eswar, Thomas Rumbaugh, and Qing Wang, 2005, "Putting the Cart Before the Horse? Capital Account Liberalization and Exchange Rate Flexibility in China," IMF Policy Discussion Paper, PDP/05/1

Xie, Ping, 2004, "China's Monetary Policy: 1998–2002", Working Paper No. 217, Stanford Center for International Development

The RMB Debate and International Influences on China's Money and Financial Markets*

Priscilla Liang, Alice Ouyang, and Thomas D. Willett

Abstract Section 2 explores a number of aspects of the debate about China's exchange rate policy. The focus is not to recommend specific policies but to expose a number of false arguments that have been made in the debate in order to separate out the serious considerations on which discussions should be based. While we argue that the adoption of a floating rate is not a panacea, we suggest that exchange rate adjustments can play a productive role as part of a coordinated policy strategy.

Section 3 deals with the effects of the large payments surpluses and international capital flows on China. We find that the People's Bank of China (PBOC) has been able to successfully sterilize most of the effects of the payments surpluses on the domestic money supply so that these have not been a major cause of inflation. Speculation on currency appreciation has not been as disruptive as some expected, and international capital flows have not been a major cause of the rise and fall of China's stock market. Thus, while China has become a major force in the global economy, it has managed to maintain considerable domestic monetary and financial autonomy.

Keywords Exchange rate policy · International reserves · Capital flows · Money supply · Stock market · Inflation

*An early version of section 2 was presented at the Conference on Global Imbalances cosponsored by the Central University of Economics and Finance and the People's Bank of China in Beijing, October 2006. Valuable comments from a number of participants are gratefully acknowledged. A revision was published in Chinese in *The Chinese Banker*, 2007. The discussion has been substantially reorganized and updated for this paper.

P. Liang (✉)
California State University, Channel Islands, Camarillo, CA, USA
e-mail: Priscilla.Liang@csuci.edu

J.R. Barth et al. (eds.), *China's Emerging Financial Markets*,
The Milken Institute Series on Financial Innovation and Economic Growth 8,
DOI 10.1007/978-0-387-93769-4_6, © 2009 by Milken Institute

1 Introduction

In Section 2, we offer a perspective on the recent debates over revaluation of the RMB. Few issues in economics have generated as much controversy and conflicting arguments as the recent debates about whether there should be a substantial appreciation of China's RMB and whether the failure of this to occur has been a major cause of worrisome global imbalances. The Chinese government's recent policy of small gradual appreciations against the dollar has done little to reduce the debate on this subject and, if anything, pressures in the US Congress to take retaliatory actions have increased.

Far too often commentators on these subjects have engaged in delivering debating points rather than balanced assessments. The forcefulness with which various points are often argued distorts the complex nature of these issues and the uncertainties about some of the key empirical parameters involved. Sadly arguments sometimes even fail to follow the rules of simple logic.

A balanced analysis suggests that both China and the United States have contributed importantly to global imbalances. China's currency remains substantially undervalued and further appreciation is in the longer-run interests of both China and the rest of the world. Short-run and special interests provide major obstacles to needed adjustments, however. Exchange rate adjustments alone will not be sufficient to restore global balance, but they are an important part of the lowest-cost policy mix for doing so.

One of the major arguments that substantial revaluation is in China's own interest is the potential disruption that continuing large surpluses generate for the domestic economy. In Section 3, we analyze key aspects of such concerns. Relevant here are both the direct effects of international capital flows on domestic financial markets and the potential indirect effects of reserve inflows on excessive expansion of the money supply and credit if these inflows are not effectively sterilized. We find that to date international capital flows have not played a major role in the fluctuations in the Chinese stock markets nor have they been a major cause of domestic money and credit expansion, i.e., the PBOC has been able to effectively sterilize the large majority of these inflows. We also find that contrary to expectations, hot money flows based on expectations of RMB appreciation have not been highly disruptive.[1] These findings help explain why the Chinese government has continued to strongly limit RMB appreciation. We caution, however, that sterilization is becoming increasingly difficult, and financial liberalization is contributing to an increase in China's financial interdependence with the global economy. Thus past success in managing the limited appreciation of the RMB is no assurance of continued success.

[1] Studies have, however, found that exchange rate expectations affect the price differentials of Chinese stocks denominated in different currencies. See, for example, Burdekin (2008).

2 Sense and Nonsense in the RMB Debate

In this section, we analyze some of the key aspects of this debate, with an eye to highlighting questionable and false statements in order to help clarify the issues. The arguments we analyze are not always stated in the recent debates as starkly as they are summarized below, but this presentation is most definitely not just attacking a group of straw men. Sometimes the non sequiturs are implied rather than explicitly stated. To illustrate the nature of these non sequiturs the general format will be to begin with a true (or at least likely true) statement, followed by a false inference often made from the first statement. Some of the latter statements may in fact turn out to be true but are not valid conclusions in the sense that they logically follow from the previous premises. Each true and false statement is then followed by explanatory comments.

1. ***True***: Much of the pressure coming from the US Congress for China to revalue or have a large tax be placed on US imports from China is based on protectionist motives and/or shaky economics.

False: Therefore, China should not revalue.

Comment: This is a classic non sequitur. Showing that a particular argument against a proposition is false does not logically imply that the proposition is therefore true. The same holds with respect to arguments that the current China-US imbalance is all the fault of the United States. The policies of both countries have clearly contributed to the problem, and just blaming each other is not helpful (except for domestic political consumption). Clearly a solution requires action by both countries (and others as well).

2. ***True***: The huge US trade deficit cannot all be blamed on China.

False: Therefore, China should not need to adjust its exchange rate.

Comment: This is another non sequitur. Adjustments by China, the US, and a number of other countries are all needed if global imbalances are to be reduced to safe levels.

3. ***True***: Exchange rate adjustments alone will not correct the imbalance.

False: Therefore there is no point in adjusting exchange rates.

Comment: This is a third common non sequitur. Just because a change in the exchange rate cannot do everything it does not mean that it cannot help. The theory of economic policy shows that in general we need as many policy instruments as we have policy objectives. Both China and the United States today have internal as well as external imbalances. China has insufficient domestic spending relative to its savings, while the United States is in just the reverse position. Combining domestic policy adjustments with changes in exchange rates will allow these multiple imbalances to be reduced at lower costs than if fewer policies were used.

4. ***True***: In monetary models, exchange rate changes will have only very temporary effects at most.

False: Therefore China should not alter its exchange rate.

Comment: The monetary model gives us many insights, but it also leaves out important considerations. The monetary model correctly shows that exchange rate changes cannot be used to create permanent disequilibrium, but the role of exchange rate adjustments is to remove disequilibrium or keep it from emerging, not create permanent disequilibrium. Economists such as McKinnon (2003, 2004), who draw heavily on the monetary model but argue that China should not undertake a major revaluation sometimes forget to point out that where a country is running a large surplus, the longer run alternative to revaluation in the monetary model is higher inflation. Contrary to the standard assumptions of the monetary model, China has been largely successful so far in keeping its surplus from substantially increasing domestic inflation. Most economists think that this has been a wise choice, but it cannot be continued indefinitely. Thus to many economists, a major argument for greater appreciation is a way to avoid high inflation.

5. ***True***: The recent large US deficits have been a major stimulant to global demand and economic growth.

Questionable: Therefore they have been good for the world.

False: And therefore there is no reason to try to reduce them.

Comment: There is no question that the US deficits have been an important engine of global growth in recent years. In many ways the short-run effects have been favorable for the US and the world. But these short-run benefits are coming at the cost of future problems. It is like someone on a spending spree using borrowed money. It is fun while it lasts, but it will eventually have to come to an end, and when it does, it will be painful.

Current account deficits of the size the US has been running are not sustainable in the judgments of the vast majority of international monetary experts. The question is how the necessary adjustments will eventually be made. The longer they are postponed, the more likely is a major crisis, and the more painful and perhaps even destructive will be the final adjustments. The US needs to start bringing its excessive spending under control and countries that have been running large current account surpluses need to begin relying more on domestic stimulants to growth.

6. ***True***: Even though it is quite large in absolute size, the US current account is not a high proportion of total world savings.

False: Therefore, we do not need to worry about continued international financing of large US deficits.

Comment: Only a proportion of global savings are effectively mobile internationally, and we cannot confidently estimate how large this proportion is. Thus we do not know how large a US current account deficit would be sustainable over the medium term. A frequently used guess is that a deficit of 2 to 3% of US GDP would be sustainable, while the current deficit is on the order of 6%.[2]

---

[2] For a more optimistic view of the sustainable size of capital inflows and hence US current account deficits see Cooper (2005).

Views vary considerably about the medium-term sustainability of capital inflows. There is strong evidence that international financial flows do not typically behave like either the farsighted fully efficient markets so popular in economic models or the wild irrationality frequently asserted by market critics. Experience does suggest that market attitudes can change swiftly, as evidenced by the frequency of sudden stops in capital flows to emerging markets. Thus it is not safe to assume that because financing for the US current account deficits has been easily forthcoming so far, we can count on their continuing for the indefinite future.[3]

7. ***True***: Economists' models do not agree on how much the RMB is undervalued.

False: Therefore it does not make sense to revalue the RMB.

Comment: Estimates of the amount of RMB undervaluation, given current policies, does vary by a huge amount – from almost zero to as much as 60%. An extremely useful illustration of our inability to precisely estimate the equilibrium value of the RMB has recently been provided by Cheung et al. (2007).

Their one standard deviation confidence bounds for their estimates are around 50% of the current value of the RMB, and the two standard deviation ranges are almost 100%, including possible undervaluation. Other types of models will give different point estimates and confidence bounds, but we clearly should not put much faith in any point estimates of the degree of RMB undervaluation.[4]

This does make official management a great deal harder, but is not a valid argument against the need for substantial further revaluation. Simple measures of equilibrium exchange rates such as calculations of purchasing power parity can be way off the mark both because of problems with price indices and changes in equilibrium real exchange rates. The strongest evidence of substantial overvaluation or undervaluation is a sustained surplus or deficit in the balance of payments. Through 2003 or so it was possible to argue that China's surplus was not a fundamental disequilibrium, since it was due largely to capital inflows that could be judged to be based only on short-term speculation that would later reverse. The continued evolution of China's balance of payments, detailed in the following section, makes this argument no longer credible.

---

[3] A number of useful papers on global imbalances were presented at the following conferences: "Revived Bretton Woods System: A New Paradigm for Asian Development?" held at the Federal Reserve Bank of San Francisco on February 4, 2005, under the joint sponsorship of the Bank's Center for Pacific Basin Studies and the University of California at Berkeley's Clausen Center for International Economics (details available at http://www.frbsf.org/economics/conferences/0502/); and "Global Imbalances and Asian Financial Markets" held at University of California, Berkeley, September 29–30, 2005. (details available at http://elsa.berkeley.edu/users/eichengr/af/agenda.html).

[4] For a valuable review of recent studies and their methodologies see Cline and Williamson (2008).

For reasons that are not clear the IMF was very slow to acknowledge the fundamental nature of China's disequilibrium, but its recent reports clearly acknowledge that this is not just a temporary disequilibrium. While the RMB has been allowed to rise considerably now against the dollar, the dollar's depreciation against other currencies has meant that the RMB's overall appreciation has been much less. There is a considerable question of whether the RMB was substantially less undervalued in 2008 than it was in 2005 when appreciation began.

8. ***Likely True*****:** If China abolished all capital controls and went to a free float, the RMB would be more likely to fall than rise.

False**:** Therefore, the RMB is not currently undervalued.

Comment: Both balance of payments disequilibria and the corresponding concepts of currency overvaluation or undervaluation of currencies are based on the failure of a number of variables to be in an equilibrium relationship to one another. Thus, there are many ways to correct a disequilibrium. Comments about currency overvaluation or undervaluation are about how the exchange rate would need to change to restore equilibrium if other policies and variables remained the same. Often the optimal policy strategy is to change both the exchange rate and other policies. Further revaluation of the RMB in current circumstances should be accompanied by an expansion of domestic demand to help offset the contractionary effect of the revaluation. Likewise on the US side, depreciation by itself is not optimal. The budget deficit also needs to be cut and arguably domestic savings needs to rise.

9. ***True*****:** A large revaluation would have a disruptive effect on China's economy.

False**:** Therefore, no revaluation should be undertaken.

Comment: The fact that sudden large adjustments are disruptive is a major reason why exchange rates for most countries should be reasonably flexible to avoid the buildup of large disequilibrium.

Because of the current large disequilibrium there is no easy way to deal with the problem. However, almost certainly a mix of policy responses should be undertaken, rather than relying only on one type. Most economists believe that revaluation should be accompanied by measures to stimulate greater domestic spending and to help the reallocation of workers who lose jobs as a result of the revaluation.

10. ***True*****:** Much of China's exports contain substantial imported inputs.

False**:** Therefore, exchange rate adjustments would not influence China's trade balance.

Comment: High import content of exports affects how much revaluation is needed, not whether exchange rate adjustments will work. High levels of imported inputs reduce the effective elasticity of demand for exports. Therefore, for a given total amount of trade, a larger exchange rate adjustment is required to bring about a given percentage change in the trade balance.

The heavy use of imported inputs in China's exports also has a large influence on the geographic distribution of China's trade. The result is to channel a larger amount of the total global imbalances onto the China-US imbalance, making it look more like just a bilateral China-US issue than is really the case.

11. ***True*:** The RMB value of China's international reserves will fall if the RMB is revalued against the dollar.

***False*:** A major cost of revaluation for China is the loss in the value of its international reserves that would be generated.

Comment: The usefulness of international reserves is based on their foreign currency, not domestic currency, value. A revaluation of the RMB would generate an accounting loss for the central bank but not a real loss for China's economy. What would cause a real opportunity cost to China is a depreciation of the dollar relative to other reserve currencies that China might hold, thus reducing the value of its dollar holdings in terms of the other reserve currencies. A note of caution is in order, however. Since China is such a large holder of dollars, if the market perceived that it is rapidly switching out of dollars, this would move the market against the dollar and generate greater losses for China.

The effects on the balance sheets of China's banks and businesses can also be relevant. The domestic currency value of both dollar assets and liabilities will be reduced.

12. ***True*:** On a per capita basis, China's international reserves are not particularly high.

***False*:** Therefore, China needs all of its huge reserve accumulations.

Comment: The purpose of accumulating international reserves is to help provide external stability and protect the economy from a shortage of foreign exchange. There is no agreement among economists about how best to calculate optional reserve levels, but there is general agreement that reserve adequacy should be related to the size of potential payments deficits, including those generated by international capital flows. This in turn is related to the degree of a country's economic and financial internationalization, not directly to the size of its population. By any reasonable estimate, China's international reserves are far larger than needed.

13. ***True*:** egged exchange rates have sometimes been useful sources of stability.

***False*:** The use of China's pegged exchange rate as a nominal anchor has been the major reason for its good recent inflation performance.

Comment*:* Pegged rates have both costs and benefits. While the use of the exchange rate as a nominal anchor has had a number of successes, it has also had a number of failures (see Willett, 1998).They can sometimes be sources of instability. In the case of China, most of the effects of international reserve flows in recent years have been sterilized. Therefore, the effects on domestic inflation have been fairly limited. If these flows had not been largely sterilized, inflation in China in the last few years would have been much higher.

Pegged rates also tend to be crisis-prone. This is more of a problem for overvalued rather than undervalued currencies and with a high rather than low degree of international financial integration. Thus, this has not been as big a problem for China as for the currencies caught in the crisis of 1997–98, but speculative inflows in anticipation of RMB appreciation have been a problem at times, and as financial liberalization proceeds this will become more of a problem over time. Thus the Chinese government wisely views greater exchange rate flexibility and financial liberalization as moving together over time. The big issue is the speed at which this process should proceed.

It should also be recognized that it is not just the RMB's value against the dollar that is important. Over the 10-year period while the RMB was fixed to the dollar, China's real effective exchange rate has varied by more than 20% and switched its direction of change several times.

14. ***True*:** To work well, free floating exchange rates and international financial flows need well-developed financial markets and a strong banking system.

***False*:** Market-oriented principles imply that China should immediately terminate all of its capital controls and allow the RMB to float freely.

Comment: Well-functioning foreign exchange and financial markets do not spring up immediately when controls are removed. A highly flexible exchange rate for China is an appropriate medium or long-term goal, not a short-term one. The rash of currency and financial crises in emerging market countries during the 1990s provide ample evidence of the need to move carefully in the process of liberalization. There is also a danger, however, that such valid concerns can be used as a smoke screen to avoid needed adjustments.

15. ***True*:** China had capital controls during the Asian crisis.

***True*:** China was not hit hard by the Asian crisis.

***False*:** Therefore, capital controls were the important factor that protected China from the Asian crisis, and hence should not be liberalized.

Comment: The assertion that capital controls saved China (and India also) from the Asian crisis is often made, but there is little serious evidence to back it. Simple correlations provide only very weak support. Econometric analysis by Willett et al. (2004) suggests that China's and India's fundamentals were sufficiently strong in 2007 that they would not have faced heavy speculative attacks even with no capital controls. This finding of course does not prove that controls did not help, but the general empirical literature on capital controls and currency crises fails to show evidence that capital controls generally provide strong protection against crises. Indeed, several studies find that controls are associated with higher probabilities of crises. There are a number of good reasons why China should not immediately abandon all of its capital controls, but protection from imported crises is likely not one of them.

16. ***True*:** There are a number of similarities between today's international monetary system and the Bretton Woods system.

***False*:** Therefore, there is no reason to worry about today's global imbalances.

Comment: There are both similarities and differences between today's system and Bretton Woods. To the extent they are similar, a key issue is whether the current situation is more like the early days of Bretton Woods as Dooley et al. (2004) suggest or more like the last days before it collapsed. The current US macroeconomic imbalances are distressingly similar to those of the United States in the last days of the Bretton Woods pegged rate regime and the large surpluses in Asia and the Middle East parallel the large surpluses of Germany and Japan. Thus seeing similarities between today's regime and Bretton Woods should not necessarily be a source of optimism. For discussions of the similarities and differences between Bretton Woods and the current situation, see Eichengreen (2004) and Rose (2006).

17. ***True*:** Financial markets have not built a substantial risk premium into US interest rates (at least until the recent subprime mortgage problems).

***False*:** This is a strong indication that the worries of economists about the US budget deficits and global imbalances are greatly exaggerated.

Comment: Financial markets have in a number of cases been short-sighted and failed to give strong early warning signals of coming crises. Examples include Europe in 1992–93, Mexico in 1994–95, Asia in 1997–98 and Argentina in 2001–02. The investment of other countries' payments surpluses in the US has been a major factor helping to hold down US interest rates, with some estimates suggesting that this effect has been as much as 100–150 basis points.

18. ***True*:** China has not undertaken the type of competitive devaluation that was a major problem during the 1930s and was a major source of concern by the creators of the Bretton Woods system.

***False*:** Therefore, China's current policy has not violated its international obligations and should not be the subject of international pressure and IMF investigation.

Comment: The Bretton Woods system was extremely successful in avoiding a repeat of the beggar-thy-neighbor devaluations that were so destructive during the Great Depression of the 1930s. It was not so successful, however, in avoiding disequilibria generated by the failure of surplus countries to adjust. The problem became one of too little rather than too much adjustment.

During the Bretton Woods era, it became recognized that the failure to appreciate one's currency in the face of strong continuing payments surpluses was also a source of problems both for other countries and the stability of the system and should be avoided. This was made explicit in the international reforms that followed the breakdown of the Bretton Woods pegged exchange rate regime in the 1970s. This is the basis for IMF pressure on China to appreciate more.

In its slowness to adjust, China is being no worse than Germany and Japan in the last years of the Bretton Woods pegged exchange rate regime, but as with Germany and Japan then, this is causing serious problems for the international monetary system. (And like them, on the deficit side the United States also shares blame for inappropriate policies.)

Of course there have been many charges by members of the US Congress that China has been guilty of manipulating its exchange rate and thus should be subject to punitive tariffs according to US law. Prohibitions on exchange rate manipulation are also contained in IMF agreements, and most economists believe that the IMF rather than individual countries should make judgments about whether international guidelines are being followed. The US Treasury has resisted finding that China has been manipulating its exchange rate on a combination of technical and political grounds, but these should not be taken as strong evidence that China is playing by the rules of the international monetary system.[5]

The use of manipulation in the language of the IMF and US legislation is unfortunate, since it carries a connotation of active efforts to promote exports, while as noted above, failure to correct imbalances can also lead to major problems. What does seem clear is that we are more likely to get needed adjustments in the context of discussion of coordinated policy responses to mutual imbalances than by pointing the finger at individual countries.

3 International Influences on China's Money and Financial Markets

3.1 Evolution of China's Balance of Payment Accounts

An examination of trends in the growth of China's reserves suggests that one can identify various subperiods since 1990 (Fig. 1).

China's reserves remained stagnant in 1990 and 1991 and actually declined in 1992, as small surpluses on the current and capital accounts were more than offset by capital flight, as witnessed by the negative balance in the errors and omissions category. However, things changed once the Chinese Yuan was officially devalued from 5.8 CNY per US dollar to 8.45 in January 1994. Between 1992 and 1996 the surplus in the capital account exceeded the current account deficit, and "illegal" capital flight (as proxied by the errors and omissions balance), such that reserves rose briskly during this period. The country's current account shifted to a surplus from 1997 onwards, though the capital account surplus diminished, while capital flight continued. In aggregate, between 1997 and 2000, China's reserves remained more or less stagnant. Since 2001, however, China has experienced large and growing surpluses on both the capital and

[5] For a detailed analysis of the US Treasury's reports on China see Frankel and Wei (2007).

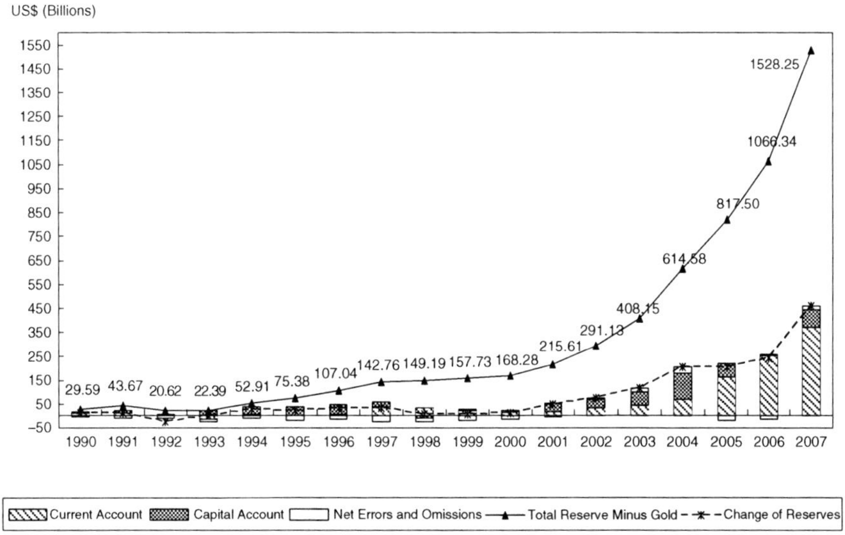

Fig. 1 Trends in China's balance of payments transactions, 1990–2007
Source: IFS Data published by IMF.

current accounts, while even the errors and omissions balance turned positive. Thus, reserves increased markedly during this period – almost eightfold.

3.1.1 The Composition of China's Current Account

China's current account has been in surplus since the devaluation in 1994 and has risen briskly after China joined WTO in 2001. Figure 2 shows that China's trade surplus is the main contributor to the huge current account surplus. The amount has increased from US \$34 billion in 2001 to US \$315 billion in 2007, reaching 11.3% of GDP. The preferential tariff policy and inexpensive labor costs have attracted many foreign-funded enterprises to transfer their processing sector into China. The consequence is that the processing trade resulting from foreign-funded enterprises has contributed 81% of the total trade surplus. To lower the trade surplus, China has made policy adjustments, such as canceling export tax rebates for 553 high-pollution and high-energy-consumption products, and lowering import tariffs for some products. In addition, current transfers have also been increasing, and reached US \$38 billion by 2007. Some of the increase has likely been short-term speculative capital flows into China through personal remittances.[6]

[6] The evidence of a large amount of short-term speculative capital inflows into China could be found from the increase in the current transfer, security investment, and the error and omissions (Zhang, 2005).

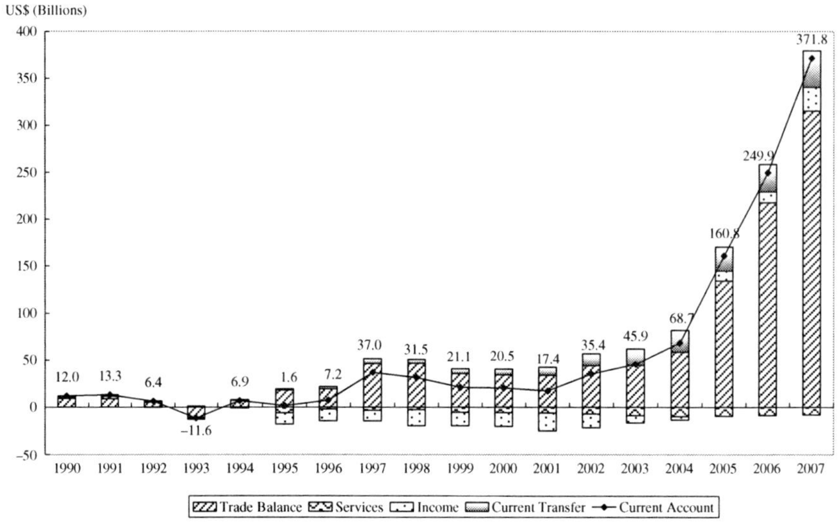

Fig. 2 Composition of China's current account, 1990–2007
Source: IFS data published by IMF.

3.1.2 The Composition of China's Capital Account

Figure 3 shows the composition of China's capital account. The capital account reached its highest point of US $110.65 billion in 2004. But since then, the capital surplus sharply decreased to US $6 billion in 2006 due to a large amount of portfolio investment outflow. A large part of capital outflow was due to

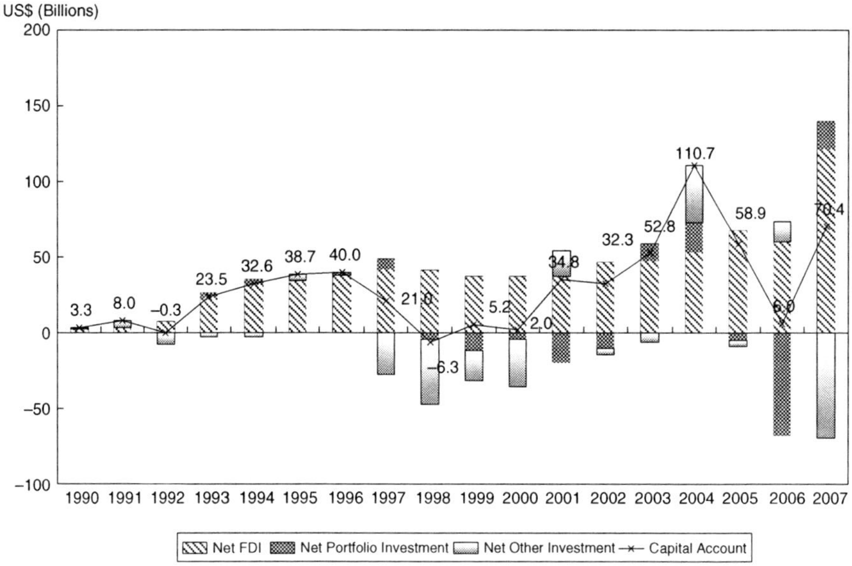

Fig. 3 Composition of China's capital account, 1990–2007
Source: IFS data published by IMF.

domestic enterprises and financial institutions engaging in IPOs overseas in 2006. Thirty-four domestic enterprises generated over US $38.7 billion through IPO or issuance of new shares in Hong Kong stock market, while three big financial institutions, Bank of China, China Merchants Bank, and Industrial and Commercial Bank of China, also generated US $11.12 billion, US $2.53 billion, and US $16.04 billion, respectively. The capital account surplus has risen sharply again to US $70 billion due to a surge of net FDI in 2007.

Since early 1990s, FDI has consistently been in surplus. Figure 4 shows the FDI inflows and outflows in China. In a single year of 2007, the net FDI grows almost double compared to the previous year. Most FDI inflows go into nonfinancial sectors, such as manufacturing and real estate sectors in China.

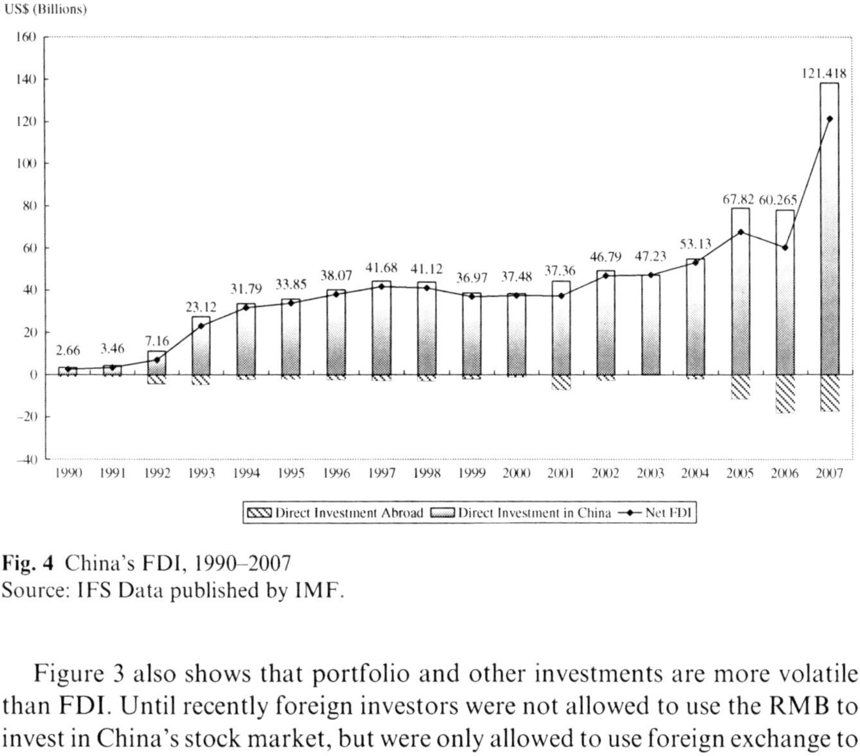

Fig. 4 China's FDI, 1990–2007
Source: IFS Data published by IMF.

Figure 3 also shows that portfolio and other investments are more volatile than FDI. Until recently foreign investors were not allowed to use the RMB to invest in China's stock market, but were only allowed to use foreign exchange to invest in certain authorized shares that are called B shares. But at the end of 2002 China launched the Qualified Foreign Investment Institutions (QFIIs) to invest in domestic securities markets (which include A-shares, treasuries, convertibles and corporate bonds); it obviously contributed part of the increase in both equity and debt securities investment.[7] In addition, China also launched the Qualified Domestic Investment Institutions (QDIIs) in May 2006 to generate domestic funds investing abroad. By the end of 2007, QDIIs has

[7] Forty six QFII investors with a total US$9.5 billion got approved from the China Securities Regulatory Commission by early 2007.

contributed US $35.3 billion capital outflows. Figure 5 shows the changes of the composition of the portfolio investment from 1990 to 2007.

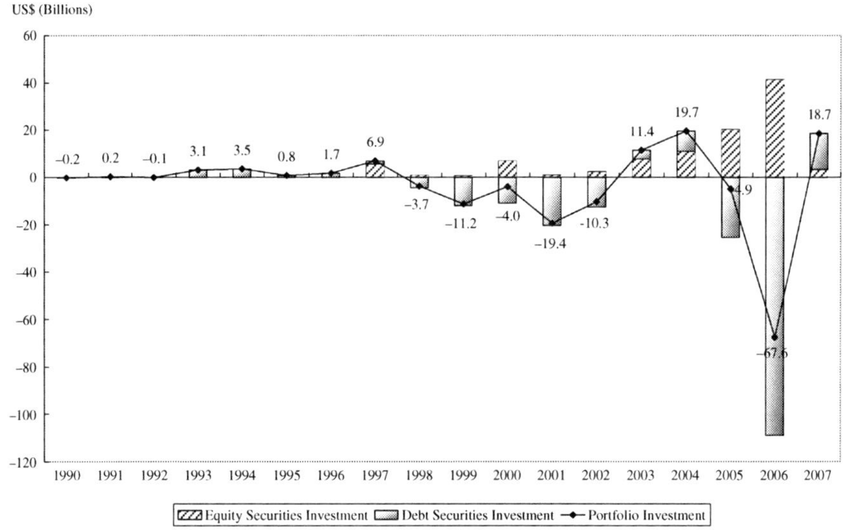

Fig. 5 Composition of China's portfolio investment, 1990–2007
Source: IFS data published by IMF.

Other investment includes short- and long-term loans, trade credits, and transactions in currency. Due to the government injection of US $45 billion into four state-owned banks to recapitalize, other investment had a US $58.82 billion deficit in 2003. There was a US $70 billion deficit in other investments in 2007, mainly contributed by the increase in trade credits.

3.2 Monetary Sterilization Policies in China

What are the monetary consequences of the huge reserve buildup in China? Figure 6 shows that, since December 2002, domestic high-powered money creation proxied by the growth in broadly defined net domestic assets (NDA)[8] has remained rather low if not negative. This helped moderate the increase in the domestic monetary base (MB) and overall money supply ($M2$) (Fig. 7), suggesting that the Peoples Bank of China (PBC) was actively neutralizing the impact of the reserves buildup using various policies and instruments. Two conventional sterilization policies frequently used by the PBC are open market

[8] Broadly defined net domestic assets (NDAs) equals monetary base (MB) minus net foreign assets (NFAs).

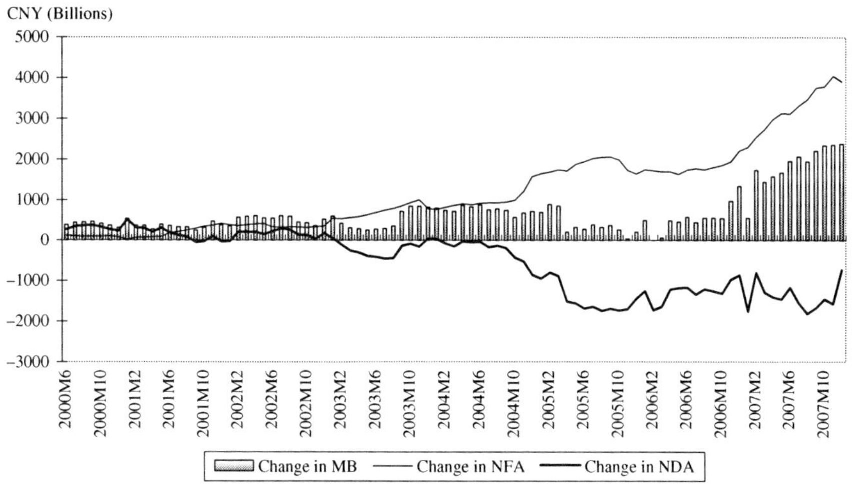

Fig. 6 Monthly annual change in NFAs, NDAs, and reserve money in China, 2000
Source: IFS data published by IMF.

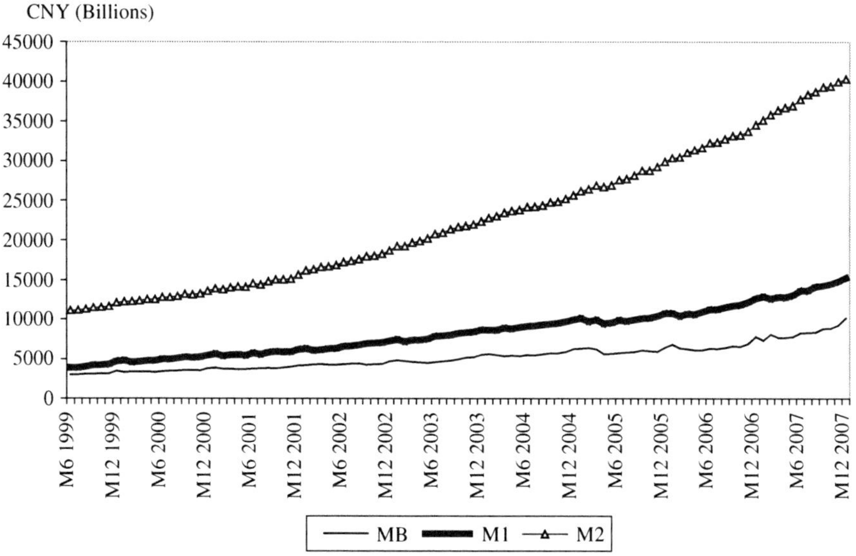

Fig. 7 Reserve money in China, 1999–2007
Source: IFS data published by IMF.

operations (OMOs) and raising reserve requirements (He et al., 2005). In early 1998, the PBC used treasury bonds or securities as the sterilization tools. But since September 2002, the PBC has replaced all outstanding securities with central bank bills (CBCs) for use in its open market operations (OMOs).

Figure 8 reveals the sharp growth in PBC issuances in the last five years. In addition, the PBC has begun to issue short-term repurchases ranging from 7 to 182 days to do sterilization in these three years.[9]

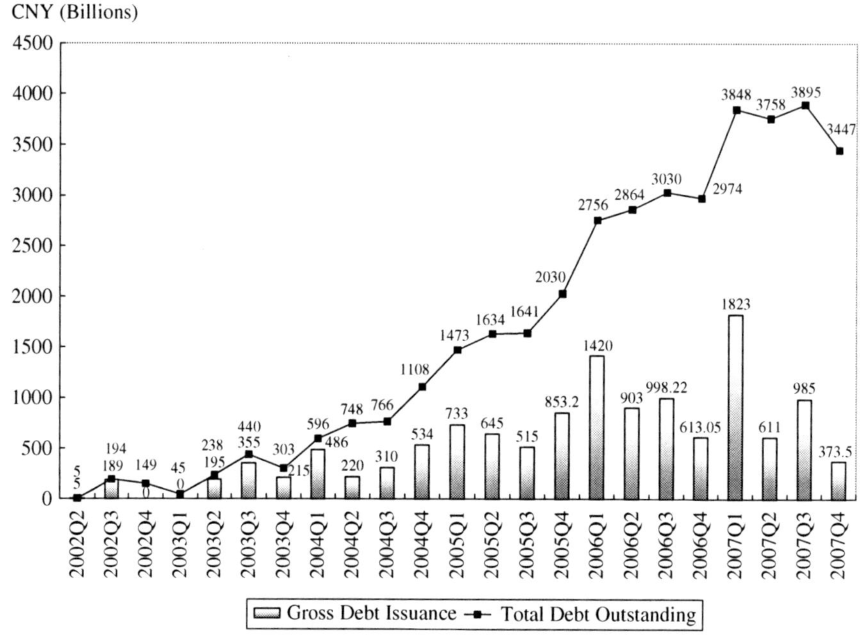

Fig. 8 Issuance of central bank bills and total PBC debt outstanding, 2002–2007
Source: IFS data published by IMF and the PBC website.

Since 1998, the PBC has required state banks to hold greater levels of bank reserves to reduce the money multiplier. The PBC has also been increasing the benchmark interest rate to curb liquidity growth and has undertaken a series of market-based interest rate reforms, such as broadening the floating band of financial institution lending rates at the beginning of 2004.[10] These monetary policy actions have been accompanied by administrative measures including window guidance to halt the nongovernment-approved construction loans and cool down specific sectors. Other measures, such as moral suasion and risk warnings, have also been conveyed to commercial banks to try to maintain "reasonable" credit growth and optimize resource allocation. The government also introduced measures to curb the rapid escalation of property prices in May

[9] He et al. (2005) outline some of the improvements/changes made by the PBC in its conduct of OMOs in 2003–2004.

[10] In addition, commercial banks have been allowed a greater degree of autonomy in deciding medium and long-term CNY loan interest rates.

2006 (Ma, 2006). China has used new monetary sterilization instruments to make its monetary policies more flexible. In the following section, we will discuss what kinds of instruments the PBC has used for sterilization.

3.2.1 Open Market Operations

The PBC has used open market operations (OMOs) to sterilize more frequently in recent years. In early 1998, the PBC used treasury bonds or securities as the sterilization tools. But since the PBC replaced all outstanding securities with central bank bills in September 2002, central bank bills have been broadly used in the open market operations. Figure 8 shows that the PBC has issued CNY 765 billion in 2003 and then has issued even more central banks bills in 2007, up to RMB 3,793 billion, to control monetary growth pressure that resulted from the huge reserve accumulations. The PBC began to carry out repurchases in May 2004 to enhance the efficiency of open market operations. Since then, the PBC has frequently used short-term obverse repurchases of open market operations to mop up the excess liquidity. The repurchase operations range from 7 to 182 days. From the updated data, CNY 280 billion central bank bills and CNY 231 billion obverse repurchases have been issued in the first five months in 2008.

In addition to issuing central bank bills and doing repurchases, the Chinese government issued CNY 1,550 billion Special Treasury Bonds to domestic commercial banks on the inter-bank bond market to purchase US $200 billion foreign exchange for the National Foreign Exchange Investment Company as operating capital. This not only contracts domestic liquidity, but also increases the PBC's holdings of treasury bonds, and provides another effective tool to do open market operations.

3.2.2 Legal Reserve Requirement Ratio

Another tool to manage the excess liquidity in the money market is to adjust legal reserve requirement ratios. This can reduce the money multiplier, and further decrease money creation. Table 1 shows that the PBC has increased the legal reserve requirement ratios considerably since 2007. The ratio has been raised 10 times in a single year of 2007, and then another 4 times to 17% in the first half of 2008.

3.2.3 Interest Rate Policy and Market-Based Interest Rate Reform

Interest rate policy is another instrument used frequently by the Chinese government to manage excess liquidity in the money market, including the adjustment of central bank base interest rates, central bank lending rates, rediscount rates, and deposit reserve rates. The PBC raised the base deposit and lending rates eight times in 2007. Tables 2, 3, and 4 list China's deposit reserve rates, central bank lending rates, and rediscount rates, base deposit, and lending rates, respectively.

Table 1 Legal reserve requirement ratio in China, 1984–2008

1984	Reserve requirement was 20% on business deposits, 40% on demand deposits, and 25% on demand deposits in rural credit cooperatives.
1985	Reserve requirements reduced to 10% for all deposits.
1987	Reserve requirement raised to 12% to control overheating and inflation.
1988	Reserve requirement raised to 13%.
March 1998	Legal reserve requirement reduced to 8%. Financial institutions can now decide the excess reserve requirement.
November 1999	Legal reserve requirement reduced to 6% to stop deflation.
September 2003	Legal reserve requirement raised to 7% to prevent inflation.
April 2004	The system of differentiated reserve requirements ratio was re-adopted. Legal reserve requirement raised to 7.5% for most financial institutions. However, in order to support the agricultural credit and reform of the rural credit cooperatives, urban and rural credit cooperatives were exempt from the new reserve requirement for the time being, while the current 6% ratio still applied to them. The reserve requirement for financial institutions with poor capital adequacy and asset quality rose to 8%.
2006 July 5	Legal reserve requirement raised to 8%.
August 15	Legal reserve requirement raised to 8.5%.
November 15	Legal reserve requirement raised to 9%.
2007 January 15	Legal reserve requirement raised to 9.5%.
February 25	Legal reserve requirement raised to 10%.
April 16	Legal reserve requirement raised to 10.5%.
May 15	Legal reserve requirement raised to 11%.
June 5	Legal reserve requirement raised to 11.5%.
August 15	Legal reserve requirement raised to 12%.
September 25	Legal reserve requirement raised to 12.5%.
October 25	Legal reserve requirement raised to 13%.
November 26	Legal reserve requirement raised to 13.5%.
December 25	Legal reserve requirement raised to 14.5%.
2008 January 25	Legal reserve requirement raised to 15%.
March 25	Legal reserve requirement raised to 15.5%.
April 25	Legal reserve requirement raised to 16%.
June 15	Legal reserve requirement raised to 17%.

Source: Adapted from China's 2003 and 2004 Annual Monetary Report and the PBC website.

In addition, the PBC has undertaken a series of market-based interest rate reforms, such as broaden the floating band of financial institution lending rates in the beginning of 2004. For commercial banks and urban credit cooperatives, the upper band was extended to 170% of the benchmark rate announced by the PBC and to 200% for rural credit cooperatives. The lower band remained at 90% of the benchmark. Meanwhile, commercial banks were allowed to have more discretion. For example, the lender and borrower can both decide the medium and long-term CNY loan interest rates. The upward floating of interest rate and higher discretion not only provide more space for commercial banks to do risk management, but may also be able to reduce lending turnovers (decreasing the money multiplier) by increasing the borrowing costs.

Table 2 Deposit reserve rates, central bank lending rates, and rediscount rates in China

Adjustment date	Legal reserve rate (%)	Excess reserve rate (%)	Central bank lending rate				Rediscount rate (%)
			One-year (%)	Within six months (%)	Within three months (%)	Within twenty days (%)	
5-1-96	8.82	8.825	10.98	10.17	10.08	9	**
8-23-96	8.28	7.92	10.62	10.17	9.72	9	**
10-23-97	7.56	7.02	9.36	9.09	8.82	8.55	**
3-21-98	5.22		7.92	7.02	6.84	6.39	6.03
7-1-98	3.51		5.67	5.58	5.49	5.22	4.32
12-7-98	3.24		5.13	5.04	4.86	4.59	3.96
6-10-99	2.07		3.78	3.69	3.51	3.24	2.16
9-11-01							2.97
2-21-02	1.89		3.24	3.15	2.97	2.70	2.97
12-21-03		1.62					
3-25-04			3.87	3.78	3.6	3.33	3.24
3-17-05		0.99					
1-1-08			4.68	4.59	4.41	4.14	4.32

Source: PBC website.

Note: 1. The legal reserves account was combined with the excess reserves account in March 1998.

2. ** represents that the rate float 5–10% below the central bank lending rate with the same maturity.

Table 3 Base deposit rates and time deposit rates in China

		Time deposit					
Adjustment date	Deposit rate (%)	Three-month (%)	Six-month (%)	One-year (%)	Two-year (%)	Three-year (%)	Five-year (%)
4-15-90	2.88	6.30	7.74	10.08	10.98	11.88	13.68
8-21-90	2.16	4.32	6.48	8.64	9.36	10.08	11.52
4-21-91	1.80	3.24	5.40	7.56	7.92	8.28	9.00
5-15-93	2.16	4.86	7.20	9.18	9.90	10.80	12.06
7-11-93	3.15	6.66	9.00	10.98	11.70	12.24	13.86
5-1-96	2.97	4.86	7.20	9.18	9.90	10.80	12.06
8-23-96	1.98	3.33	5.40	7.47	7.92	8.28	9.00
10-23-97	1.71	2.88	4.14	5.67	5.94	6.21	6.66
3-25-98	1.71	2.88	4.14	5.22	5.58	6.21	6.66
7-1-98	1.44	2.79	3.96	4.77	4.86	4.95	5.22
12-7-98	1.44	2.79	3.33	3.78	3.96	4.14	4.50
6-10-99	0.99	1.98	2.16	2.25	2.43	2.70	2.88
2-21-2002	0.72	1.71	1.89	1.98	2.25	2.52	2.79
10-29-04	0.72	1.71	2.07	2.25	2.70	3.24	3.60
8-19-06	0.72	1.80	2.25	2.52	3.06	3.69	4.14
3-18-07	0.72	1.98	2.43	2.79	3.33	3.96	4.41
5-19-07	0.72	2.07	2.61	3.06	3.69	4.41	4.95
7-21-07	0.81	2.34	2.88	3.33	3.96	4.68	5.22
8-22-07	0.81	2.61	3.15	3.60	4.23	4.95	5.49
9-15-07	0.81	2.88	3.42	3.87	4.50	5.22	5.76
12-21-07	0.72	3.33	3.78	4.14	4.68	5.40	5.85

Source: PBC Web site.

Table 4 Base lending rates in China

Adjustment date	Six-month (%)	One-year (%)	One to three years (%)	Three to five years (%)	Above five-year (%)
4-21-91	8.1	8.64	9	9.54	9.72
5-15-93	8.82	9.36	10.8	12.06	12.24
7-11-93	9	10.98	12.24	13.86	14.04
1-1-95	9	10.98	12.96	14.58	14.76
7-1-95	10.08	12.06	13.5	15.12	15.3
5-1-96	9.72	10.98	13.14	14.94	15.12
8-23-96	9.18	10.08	10.98	11.7	12.42
10-23-97	7.65	8.64	9.36	9.9	10.53
3-25-98	7.02	7.92	9	9.72	10.35
7-1-98	6.57	6.93	7.11	7.65	8.01
12-7-98	6.12	6.39	6.66	7.2	7.56
6-10-99	5.58	5.85	5.94	6.03	6.21
2-21-02	5.04	5.31	5.49	5.58	5.76
10-29-04	5.22	5.58	5.76	5.85	6.12
4-28-06	5.4	5.85	6.035	6.12	6.39

Table 4 (continued)

Adjustment date	Six-month (%)	One-year (%)	One to three years (%)	Three to five years (%)	Above five-year (%)
8-19-06	5.58	6.12	6.3	6.48	6.84
3-18-07	5.67	6.39	6.57	6.75	7.11
5-19-07	5.85	6.57	6.75	6.93	7.2
7-21-07	6.03	6.84	7.02	7.20	7.38
8-22-07	6.21	7.02	7.20	7.38	7.56
9-15-07	6.48	7.29	7.47	7.65	7.83
12-21-07	6.57	7.47	7.56	7.74	7.83

Source: PBC website.

China introduced the Shanghai Interbank Offered Rate (SHIBOR), the Chinese LIBOR, into market on January 4, 2007 as a landmark in China's interest rate system reform. Figure 9 shows the movement of SHIBOR since October 8, 2006. The SHIBOR is calculated by China's National Interbank Funding Center, based on the arithmetic average of interbank loan interest rates quoted by 16 commercial banks, which are primary dealers in the interbank market or the market makers in the foreign exchange market. The rate ranges from overnight to one year. The launch of the SHIBOR is a touchstone to further liberalize interest rates and the benchmark to form the market-based basis interest rates.

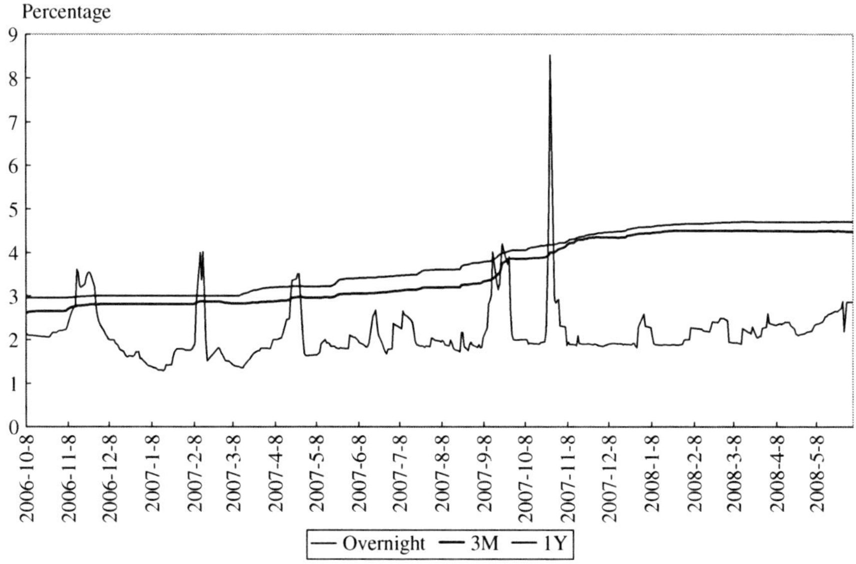

Fig. 9 Shanghai interbank offered rate (SHIBOR)
Source: SHIBOR website: http://www.shibor.org/shibor/web/html/index.html

3.2.4 Window Guidance

Since raising rediscount rates and legal reserve requirement may slow down macroeconomic activity the PBC has also used measures like window guidance to halt the nongovernment-approved construction loans to cool down specific sectors. This was used by the PBC three times in 2003 (July, August, and September) and once in March 2004.[11] To further contract hot money flowing into the real estate market, the Chinese government announced a strengthening of commercial real estate mortgages, and more frequently conducted window guidance to caution both domestic and foreign commercial banks on loan growth, especially loans for certain industries with high risks of excess capacity.

Meanwhile, financial institutions were also encouraged to increase their credit support to agriculture and small and medium-sized enterprises (SMEs). Commercial banks were required to offer quality financial services and funding for the procurement of agricultural produce. Other guidance, such as moral suasion and risk warnings, was also conveyed to commercial banks in the regular monthly meetings.

3.2.5 Capital Controls

While restricting speculative investments and short-term borrowings inflows, the PBC has loosened controls on capital outflows. China used to encourage long-term capital inflows, such as foreign domestic investment (FDI), and restrict capital outflows. But to ease appreciation pressures, a series of new policies for loosening controls on capital outflows have been issued by the PBC. For example, beginning in 2007, the cash limit of local currency that a person can carry in and out of the country was raised from the previous RMB 20,000 to RMB 50,000. Also, since December 2004, individual Chinese can transfer assets out of China, and Chinese students who study abroad can carry more money out of China. In addition, a Qualified Domestic Institutional Investors (QDII) system has been introduced. By the end of 2007, QDIIs had invested US $30.3 billion (including National Social Security Fund) overseas.

3.2.6 Estimating the Extent of Sterilization in China

Most existing literature of estimating the extent of sterilization can be classified into three groups. With the assumption that capital flows are exogenously determined, the first group simply uses OLS to estimate a central bank's monetary reaction function such as the one below:

$$\Delta NDA_t = c_0 + c_1 \Delta NFA_t + X'\beta + u_t \tag{1}$$

[11] Refer to Terada-Hagiwara (2004) and China's Annual Monetary Policy Report in 2004.

where ΔNDA_t and ΔNFA_t represent the change in net domestic assets (a proxy for domestic money creation) and net foreign assets (a proxy for international reserves), respectively, and X represents other explanatory variables that might influence a monetary authority's reaction. $c_1 = -1$ implies that an increase of international reserves is fully sterilized by monetary authorities, while $c_1 = 0$ implies no sterilization. But in some instances, ΔMB_t or $\Delta M2_t$ is used instead of ΔNDA_t. If this is the case then $c_1 = 0$ represents full sterilization since a rise of international reserves does not significantly impact the monetary base (or broad money). For example, Burdekin and Siklos (2008) use the quarter data from 1990 to 2002, and regress both the change of base money and M2 on the change of foreign reserves. They find that China's broad money had significantly increased by the reserve accumulation during the sample period, even though the base money remained quite constant. Based on their empirical results, one unit increases in the change of foreign reserves leads to decrease of 0.1–0.2 units in the change of based money, but M2 growth has significantly been raised by 0.11 units.

The second group uses a Vector Autoregression (VAR) model, to estimate the lagged effects of NDAs and NFAs. The standard form of a VAR model is as follows:

$$\Delta NDA_t = \alpha_{10} + \sum_{i=1}^{k} \alpha_{1i} \Delta NDA_{t-i} + \sum_{i=1}^{k} \beta_{1i} \Delta NFA_{t-i} + e_{1t} \tag{2a}$$

$$\Delta NFA_t = \alpha_{20} + \sum_{i=1}^{k} \alpha_{2i} \Delta NFA_{t-i} + \sum_{i=1}^{k} \beta_{2i} \Delta NDA_{t-i} + e_{2t} \tag{2b}$$

The advantage of using the VAR model is that one can trace the time path of the various shocks on the variables included in the VAR system through the derived impulse response function. For example, if an unexpected shock from foreign reserves results in an offsetting decrease in domestic money creation, i.e., β_1 will be close to -1 if monetary authorities fully sterilize, and then declined to zero if the effect gradually decrease. An important limitation that one has to be aware is that the VAR approach tends to treat all variables as symmetrically endogenous. Therefore, it cannot estimate the contemporary effect of variables without restrictions due to the issue of identification. He et al. (2005) and Cavoli and Rajan (2006) find that China has almost fully sterilized its reserve accumulation, but the extent of sterilization in China during the sample period of 2003 to 2004 is somewhat greater than the period between 1998 and 2002.

Due to the possible endogeneity issue between domestic and foreign components of the monetary base, the third group of studies estimates as set of simultaneous equations between NDAs, and NFAs. The typical model specification is:

$$\Delta NFA_t = \alpha_{10} + \alpha_{11}\Delta NDA_t + X_1'\beta_1 + u_{1t} \tag{3a}$$

$$\Delta NDA_t = \alpha_{20} + \alpha_{21}\Delta NFA_t + X_2'\beta_2 + u_{2t} \tag{3b}$$

where X_1 and X_2 are the vectors of controls in the balance of payment function and monetary reaction function, respectively. Equations (3a) and (3b) are the balance of payments and the monetary reaction functions, respectively. The value of α_{11} is referred to as so called the "offset coefficient", which can be used to measure the degree of capital mobility. $\alpha_{11} = 0$ implies no capital mobility since international capital flows are not affected by a change in domestic money creation. Follow the same logic, $\alpha_{11} = -1$ implies perfect capital mobility. The value of α_{21} is referred to as so called the "sterilization coefficient", which is used to measure the extent of sterilization. The expected value of the sterilization coefficient again is bound between 0 and –1. The former represents no sterilization, while the latter represents fully sterilization.

Ouyang et al. (2007) uses monthly data between June 1999 and September 2005, and applies two-stage least squares (2SLS) to estimate the simultaneous equations. The empirical results show that the degree of capital mobility in China is around –0.63 to –0.7, indicating a substantial degree of capital mobility despite China's capital controls. The estimated sterilization coefficients range around –0.92 to –0.97, indicating a heavy sterilization policy was conducted during the sample period.

The paper has also used recursive estimation to find the dynamic behavior of offset and sterilization coefficients. The results suggest that the *de facto* capital mobility in China remained fairly stable between early 2003 and mid 2004, but increased significantly thereafter. In the early part of the estimation period the offset coefficients were quite low, around –0.1 to –0.2, but by the end of the period had increased to around –0.7, indicating a substantial increase in effective capital mobility. However the recursive estimation does not indicate any corresponding decline in sterilization. Indeed the extent of sterilization was found to have slightly increased in 2005 compared to 2004.

To sum up, most studies find that China has heavily sterilized the international reserves to release the substantial inflationary pressure since the 1990s. The extent of sterilization is generally over 90%. This in turn explains how China has been able to maintain relatively low rates of money growth and until recently, inflation (Fig. 10) despite the continuing large balance of payments surpluses.

3.3 RMB Appreciation Expectations and Their Influence on China's International Capital Flows and Stock Markets

Conceptually we may think of a country's balance of payments as having two major components – the underlying balance reflecting economic and financial

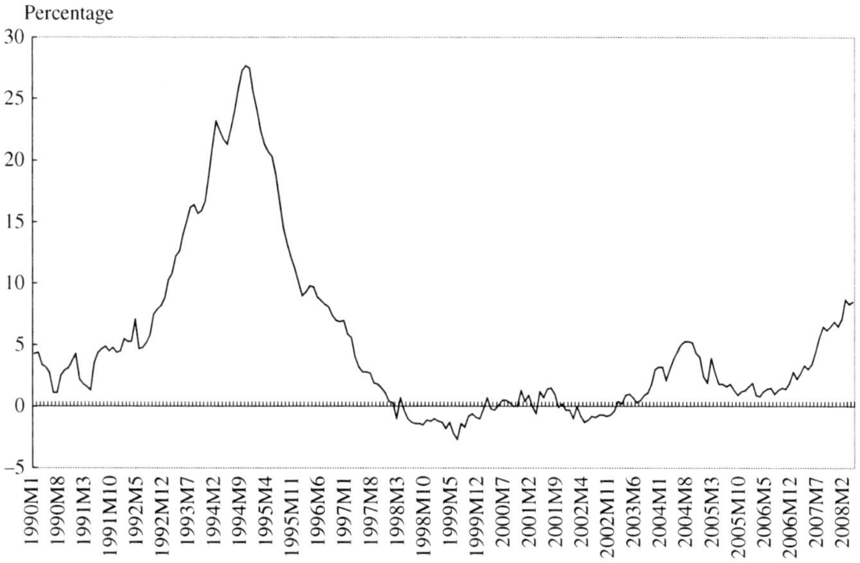

Fig. 10 Inflation in China (annual CPI percentage change), 1990–2008
Source: IFS data published by IMF and the National Bureau of Statistics of China website.

conditions and speculative capital flows reflecting expectations of changes in exchange rates and other policies. Considerable concern was expressed before the unpegging of the RMB in 2005 that while appreciation would reduce the underlying payments surplus, small appreciations from an initial position of substantial disequilibrium could generate expectations of greater future appreciation and hence generate large speculative capital inflows that could disrupt financial markets and lead to an overall increase rather than decrease in the balance of payments surplus. The continued growth in China's balance of payments surplus and the bubble in its stock market are consistent with these fears, but more detailed analysis of the data suggest that hot money flows were not the major cause of either development.

One year after China joined the WTO, China's net errors and omissions account turned into a surplus from a twelve-year continuous deficit. Such a shift generally reflects changes in unrecorded capital flows. A year later, China's net portfolio investment account followed suit and moved into surplus in 2003 (Table 5). These capital inflow trends continued in 2004. In addition, other investment account contributed US $37.9 billion more inflows. Two popular measures of hot money flows, one, the non-FDI capital account, and two, the combination of portfolio flow and net errors and omissions, both showed hot money inflows to China during 2003 and 2004. The non-FDI capital account, in particular, reached US $84.6 billion inflows in 2004. Economists suspected that widespread expectations of RMB appreciation had brought large speculative capital flows into China during these two years (Prasad and Wei, 2005).

Table 5 Balance of payments (US$ billions)

	1995	1996	1997	1998	1999	2000	2001	2002	2003	2004	2005	2006	2007
Changes in international reserve	22.48	31.6	35.7	6.43	8.51	10.5	47.3	75.5	117	206.4	207	247	462
Current account	1.618	7.24	37	31.5	21.1	20.5	17.4	35.4	45.9	68.66	161	250	372
Goods	18.05	19.5	46.2	46.6	36	34.5	34	44.2	44.7	58.98	134	218	315
Service	–6.09	–2	–3.4	–2.8	–5.3	–5.6	–5.9	–6.8	–8.6	–9.7	–9.4	–8.8	–7.9
Income	–11.8	–12	–11	–17	–14	–14.7	–19	–15	–7.8	–3.52	10.6	11.8	25.7
Transfer	1.434	2.13	5.14	4.28	4.94	6.31	8.49	13	17.6	22.9	25.4	29.2	38.7
Financial account	38.68	40	21	–6.3	5.21	1.96	34.8	32.3	52.8	110.7	58.9	6.02	70.4
FDI	33.85	38.1	41.7	41.1	37	37.5	37.4	46.8	47.2	53.13	67.8	60.3	121
Portfolio investment	0.79	1.74	6.94	–3.7	–11	–3.99	–19	–10	11.4	19.69	–4.9	–68	18.7
Other investment			–28	–44	–21	–31.5	16.9	–4.1	–5.9	37.91	–4	13.3	–70
Net error and omission	–17.8	–16	–22	–19	–18	–11.9	–4.9	7.79	18.4	27.05	–17	–13	16.4
Hot money (port + net error/omission)	–17	–14	–15	–22	–29	–15.9	–24	–2.5	29.8	46.74	–22	–80	35.1
Non-FDI capital account (including errors and omissions)	–13	–14	–43	–66	–50	–47.5	–7.4	–6.7	23.9	84.57	–22	–63	–32

Source: IFS.

On July 21, 2005, the Chinese government announced an RMB appreciation of 2.1%, a switch from pegging to the dollar to an undisclosed basket of currencies and a new policy of allowing gradual changes in parity over time. On May 18, 2007, it widened the daily floating band (for RMB against the US dollar) from 0.3 to 0.5%. On April 10, 2008, RMB traded at below seven Yuan per USD for the first time. By the end of May 2008, the RMB had gained more than 17% against the dollar since July 2005. However, because of the dollar's depreciation, the overall appreciation of the RMB was much less. Thus it was not surprising that a major turnaround in China's trade and current accounts had not occurred by mid 2008.

The RMB's 2005 adjustment was small, but it was the first sign that the value of RMB could be determined more by market forces in the future. Since the RMB was severely undervalued, market watchers expected it to appreciate further and economists were concerned that a one-way bet on RMB appreciation would cause huge speculative inflows. Figure 11 shows that appreciation of the RMB spot exchange rate has lagged behind that of the 12-month Nondeliverable Forwards (NDFs) rate (a measure of market expectations) since November 2002.

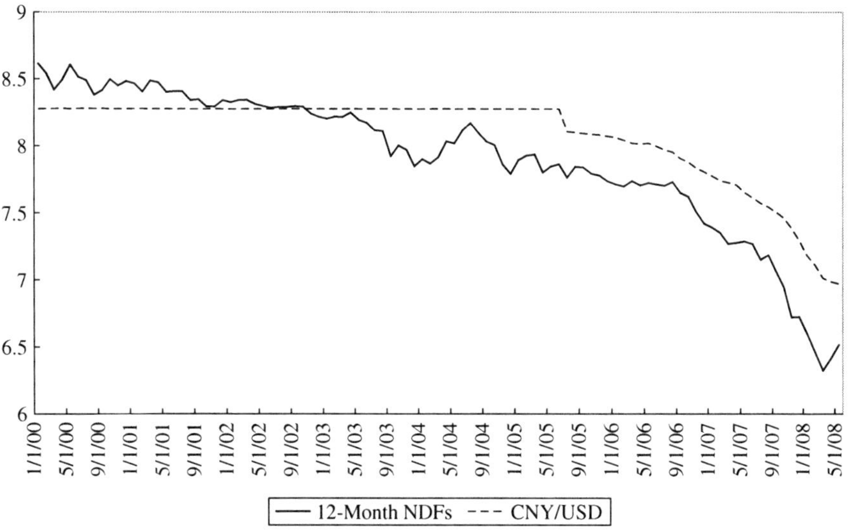

Fig. 11 RMB spot exchange rates and twelve-month non-deliverable forward rates
Source: Bloomberg.

As expected, the small appreciation in 2005 had little impact on China's trade growth. China's trade and current account surpluses grew by over 100% that year. However, its reserves that had been growing rapidly barely increased. Analyzing the balance of payments data, we find that China's decreasing rate of reserve growth was mainly due to reductions in the capital and financial accounts, which declined 46.8% to US $58.9 billion in 2005. The reduction in the financial account was largely caused by portfolio and other investment outflows. Thus instead of stimulating greater capital inflows, as many feared, there was more capital outflow.

This unusual phenomenon continued in 2006 with strong trade and current account growth of over 50%, but with lower reserve growth of a little under 20%. China's financial account decreased another 90% to only US $6 billion in 2006. Even though the account for other investments was in surplus, portfolio outflows were at a historical high of US $67.6 billion. This absence of evidence of strong speculative capital inflows after the RMB began to appreciate is consistent with the behavior of ex rate expectations as reflected in the behavior of the forward rate. Rather than generating expectations of more rapid future appreciation as many economists feared, Fig. 11 records relatively little change in the rate of expected future depreciation for the first year after the RMB was unpegged.

Beginning in 2006 China's stock markets began to boom (Fig. 12). The three major Chinese stock indices – Shanghai Component Index (SH), Shenzhen Composite Index (SZ), and Hang Seng China Enterprise Index (HSCE) gained 121, 113, and 53%, respectively, during the year. A plausible hypothesis would be that with heightened appreciation anticipation, international speculative inflows would flow into the Chinese stock markets, contributing to their boom. On the contrary, however, not only was portfolio investment in deficit

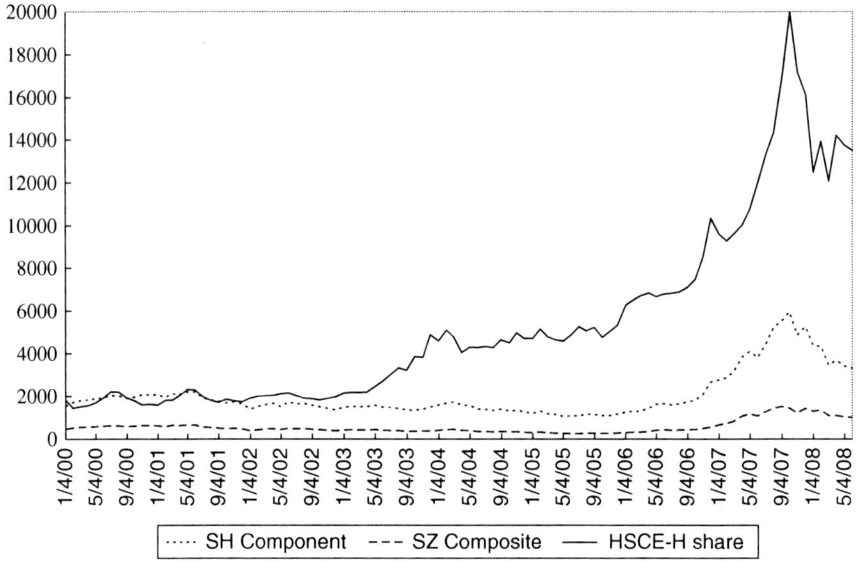

Fig. 12 Chinese stock indices
Source: Bloomberg.

but also the net errors and omissions account turned negative in 2005 and 2006. Combining portfolio investment and net errors and omissions, there were US $21.7 billion of hot money outflows in 2005. This rose to US $80.4 billion in 2006. Another hot money measure, the non-FDI capital account, showed US $21.6 and US $63.6 billion outflows in 2005 and 2006 (Fig. 13). Thus, we cannot find evidence of speculative inflows into China from the official balance of payment data. The PBOC also confirmed that there were little speculative inflows from expectations of RMB appreciation.

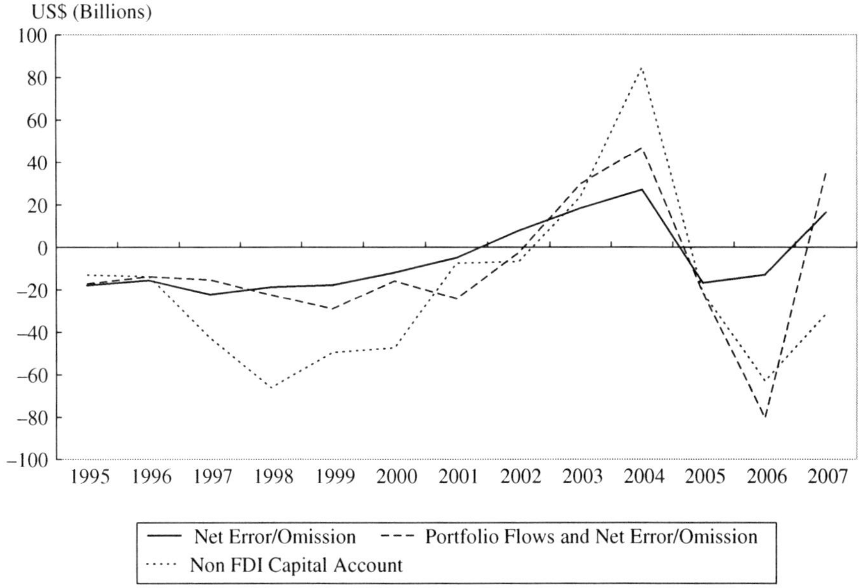

Fig. 13 Hot money flows
Source: IFS and authors' calculations.

By 2004, interest rates had begun rising in China. The upward movement of interest rates accelerated in 2007 as inflationary concerns began to mount. In the United States, the fallout from the subprime crisis led the Federal Reserve to drive down the federal funds rate from 5.25% in September 2007 to 2.25% in March 2008 (Fig. 14). The interest rate differential between China and the United States reversed direction within a short period. Interestingly, as the interest differential shifted in favor of China, the expected rate of future appreciation of the RMB also increased. These developments combined to yield a substantial increase in the expected returns from holding short-term interest-bearing assets in China relative to the United States.

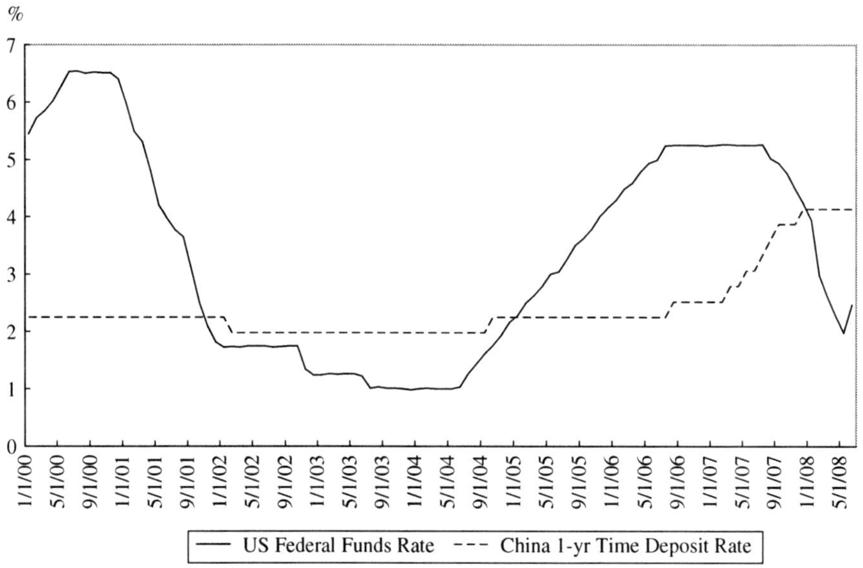

Fig. 14 US and China interest rates
Source: CEIC database.

The year 2007 also saw the Chinese stock bubbles peak and burst. The Shanghai Component Index (SH), the Shenzhen Composite Index (SZ), and the Hang Seng China Enterprise Index (HSCE) gained 114, 134, and 109%, respectively, within nine months, reaching peaks at the end of September 2007. The drops in the markets were as dramatic as their rises. By mid-2008, the two Mainland China indices had fallen by over 50%. The Hong Kong H-share Index lost 40% within 5 months.

China's financial account increased more than 11-fold to US $70.4 billion in 2007. Portfolio inflows and the surplus on net errors and omissions add up to US $35.1 billion, indicating hot money inflows. But the other hot money measurement, the non-FDI capital account, showed outflows of US $31.5 billion for the year. Thus we do not get a clear picture of speculative flows in 2007 from the annual balance of payments data.

The greatest part of China's stock market boom occurred during the first 9 months of 2007. If international flows were a major reason for the Chinese stock markets overheating, we should have observed large inflows during the first half of the year. But portfolio investment showed a deficit of US $4.8 billion for the first 6 months of the year. Hot money calculated from portfolio inflow and the errors and omissions surplus was only US $8.3 billion. Thus, we can conclude that international capital flows were not a major cause of the Chinese stock market bubble during early 2007. Likewise, we cannot explain the bursting of the bubble by any major shift in exchange rate expectations. The bubble appears to have been largely home grown.

4 Concluding Comments

Most international monetary experts believe that the current global imbalances present a serious danger to the world economy over the medium-to-longer term. The current situation is unlikely to be sustainable and if needed, adjustments continued to be postponed, then the eventual adjustment will be much more painful, likely involving a major international financial crisis that will pose major challenges to international cooperation.

What is the outlook for bringing about substantial reductions in global imbalances before a major crisis erupts? There are some encouraging signs. The quality of the dialogue between the American and Chinese governments has improved greatly. The US government has backed off of its initial ill-founded advice that China should swiftly abolish all of its capital controls and move promptly to a free float. The Chinese government has acknowledged in turn China's self-interest in moving toward a more flexible exchange rate regime and rebalancing China's economy to increase domestic consumption and to become less reliant on exports as a primary source of growth. However, while the IMF has belatedly begun to play a role in attempting to promote coordinated actions to promote adjustments, its success so far has been meager at best.[12] Nor has the United States taken substantial steps to put its fiscal house in order. Thus the overall progress to date has been quite limited.

A major reason that China has continued to resist more rapid appreciation is that, as we have discussed, China has so far been quite successful in limiting the effects of capital inflows and the huge surpluses on its domestic money and financial markets. Its stock market boom and bust has not been correlated with changes in international capital flows or exchange rate expectations, and the PBC has been able to sterilize a high proportion of reserve inflows so that while there has been an overheating of the economy this has been caused primarily by domestic factors rather than monetary expansion generated by reserve increases. Furthermore, and contrary to the expectations of many economists, the slow appreciation of the RMB was initially accompanied by reduced rather than increased speculative capital inflows. Apparently the instability of heavily managed exchange rates applies much more strongly to overvalued than to undervalued exchange rates.

There are signs, however, that sterilization is becoming increasingly difficult for the PBC and is imposing substantial costs on the banking sector. With the rising concerns about inflation generated by the huge increases in food and raw material prices there should be stronger incentives for more rapid appreciation as an anti-inflationary measure.

On the other hand, the recent slowing of Chinese export growth will stimulate domestic pressures to reduce the rate of appreciation. The report of slower

[12] See Bird and Willett (2007). For a strong critique of the IMF's performance, see Mussa (2008).

growth in June 2008 was quickly followed by a call from a senior official from the communist part's policy research office calling for slowing appreciation.[13]

Still, the biggest problem is that most of the actions needed to promote longer run rebalancing of the world economy involve short-run costs that governments are reluctant to impose on themselves and their citizens. The major source of short-run political pressure is a perverse one – the forces that have pressured the US Congress into seriously considering imposing harsh trade sanctions on China unless substantially greater RMB appreciation is undertaken. Such measures would hardly be in the overall interests of the United States, much less the world economy, but it would benefit particular influential import competing economic interests in the United States, just as postponing major adjustments is in the short-run interests of Chinese exporters. Let us hope that both America and China will find a way to act based on their longer run interests that are harmonious, rather than on the conflicting short-run interests of particular groups.

References

Bird, G. and T. D. Willett. (Oct.–Dec. 2007). "Multilateral Surveillance: Is the IMF Shooting for the Stars?" *World Economy*, 8(4), 167–89.

Burdekin, R. C. K. (2008). *China's Monetary Challenges: Past Experiences and Future Prospects*. New York: Cambridge University Press.

Burdekin R. C. K. and P. L. Siklos. (2008). "What has Driven Chinese Monetary Policy Since 1990? Investigating the People's Bank of China Policy Rule," *Journal of International Money and Finance*, 27(5), 847–59.

Cavoli, T. and R. S. Rajan. (2006). "The Capital Inflows Problem in Selected Asian Economies in the 1990s Revisited: The Role of Monetary Sterilization," *Asian Economic Journal*, 20(4), 409–23.

Cheung, Y., C. Menzie, and F. Eiji. (Sept. 2007). "The Overvaluation of the Renminbi's Undervaluation," *Journal of International Money and Finance* 26(5), 762–785. Also NBER Working Paper No. 12850.

Cline, W. R. and J. Williamson. (2008). "Estimates of the Equilibrium Exchange Rate of the Renminbi". In M. Goldstein and N. Lardy (eds.), *Debating China's Exchange Rate Policy*, pp. 131–154. Washington, DC: Peterson Institute for International Economics.

Cooper, R. N. (2005). "Living with Global Imbalances: A Contrarian View". *Policy Briefs in International Economics*. Institute for International Economics.

Dooley, M. P., D. Folkerts-Landau, and P. Garber. (2004). "The Revised Bretton Woods System," *International Journal of Finance and Economics*, 9(4), 307–313.

Eichengreen, B. (2004). "Global Imbalances and the Lessons of Bretton Woods," NBER Working Paper No. 10497.

Frankel, J. A. and S. Wei. (2007). "Assessing China's Exchange Rate Regime," NBER Working Paper No. 13100.

Goldstein M. and N. Lardy (eds.). (2008). *Debating China's Exchange Rate Policy*. Washington, DC: Peterson Institute for International Economics.

[13] See "China's trade surplus shrinks by 20%" *Financial Times*, July 11, 2008, p. 4.

He, D., C. Chu, C. Shu, and A. Wong. (2005). "Monetary Management in Mainland China in the Face of Large Capital Inflows," *Research Memorandum* 07/2005, Hong Kong Monetary Authority (HKMA), April.
Holland, T. and D. Lague (2004). "Wasteful Transfusion", *Far Eastern Economic Review*, January 22, pp. 26–29.
Hu, F. (2004). "Capital Flows, Overheating, and Nominal Exchange Rate Regime in China," *mimeo*, Goldman Sachs.
Kim, S., S. H. Kim, and Y. Wang (Nov. 2004). "Macroeconomic Effects of Capital Account Liberalization: The Case of Korea," *Review of Development Economics*, 8(4), 624–39.
Ma, G. (2006). "Who Pays China's Restructuring Bill?" Working Paper No.2006-04, CEPII.
McKinnon, R. and G. Schnabl (2003). "China: A Stabilizing or Deflationary Inflation in East Asia? The Problem of Conflicted Virtue," Working Paper No. 23, Hong Kong Institute for Monetary Research.
McKinnon, R. and G. Schnabl (2004). "The Return to Soft Dollar Pegging in East Asia: Mitigating Conflicted Virtue," *International Finance*, 7, 169–201.
Moreno, R. (2001). "Pegging and Macroeconomic Performance in East Asia", *ASEAN Economic Bulletin*, April.
Mussa, M. (2008). "IMF Surveillance over China's Exchange Rate Policy". In M. Goldstein and N. Lardy (eds.), *Debating China's Exchange Rate Policy*, pp. 279–335. Washington, DC: Peterson Institute for International Economics.
Ouyang, Y. A., R. S. Rajan, and T. D. Willett. (2007). "China as a Reserve Sink: The Evidence from Offset and Sterilization Coefficients" *mimeo*.
Prasad, E. and S. Wei. (2005). "The Chinese Approach to International Capital Flows: Patterns and Possible Explanations," NBER Working Paper No. 11306.
Rose, A. (2006). "A Stable International Monetary System Emerges: Bretton Woods, Reversed," Paper presented at a conference on Financial and Commercial Integration, UC Santa Cruz, September 29–30. (http://sccie.ucsc.edu/webpages/JIMF-agenda.html)
Terada-Hagiwara, A. (2004). "Reserve Accumulation, Sterilization, and Policy Dilemma," *ERD Policy Brief Series* No. 31, Asian Development Bank.
Tornell, A. and A. Velasco (2000), "Fixed Versus Flexible Exchange Rate Regimes: Which Provides More Fiscal Discipline," *Journal of Monetary Economics*, 45, 399–436.
Willett, T. (1998). "The Credibility and Discipline Effects of Exchange Rates as Nominal Anchors", *The World Economy*, 21, 303–26.
Willett, T. D., Ekniti Nitithanprapas, Isiriya Nitithanprapas, and Sunil Rongala. (2004). "The Asian Crises Reexamined". *Asian Economic Papers*, 3(3), 32–87
Xin, Z. (2007). "Inflows of Hot Money to be Curbed," China Daily, June 27. http://www.chinadaily.com.cn/china/2007-06/27/content_903359.htm
Zhang, L. (2005). "China's External Imbalance: Diagnosis and Prescription", *mimeo* (May).

The United States–China Currency Dispute: Is a Rise in the Yuan Necessary, Inevitable, or Desirable?

John A. Tatom

Abstract China-bashing has become a popular media and political sport. This is largely due to the US trade imbalance and the belief, by some, that China is responsible for it because it manipulates its currency to hold down the dollar prices of its goods, unfairly creating a trade advantage that has contributed to the loss of US businesses and jobs. This chapter reviews the problem of the large trade imbalance that the United States has with China and its relationship to Chinese exchange rate policy. It examines the link between a Chinese renminbi appreciation and the trade balance and also whether a generalized dollar decline could solve the global or Chinese–US trade imbalance. The consensus view explained here is that a renminbi appreciation is not likely to fix either the trade imbalance with China or overall. If these perceived benefits of a managed float are small or nonexistent, then perhaps they should be pursued anyway because of small costs or even benefits for China. Section 4 looks at the costs of a managed float in terms of the benefits of the earlier peg. Opponents of a fixed dollar/yuan exchange rate ignore the costs of a managed float for China, especially with limits on currency convertibility. These costs are outlined here in order to provide an economic basis for the earlier fixed rate and China's reluctance to appreciate. Finally it is suggested that the necessary convertibility on capital account, toward which China is moving, could easily result in yuan depreciation under a floating rate regime. This is hardly the end that China critics have in mind, and it is not one that would improve US or other trade imbalances with China.

Keywords Exchange rate policy · Currency manipulation · Current account imbalance

---

An earlier version of this chapter appeared in the *Global Economy*, Volume 17, issue 3, article 2, pp. 1–13. Article reprinted with permission from the publisher, The Berkeley Electronic Press, ©2007. Originally published in Global Economy Journal, available at http://www.bepress.com/gej/vol7/iss3/2/.

J.A. Tatom (✉)
Networks Financial Institute at Indiana State University, Indianapolis, IN, USA
e-mail: john.tatom@isunetworks.org

J.R. Barth et al. (eds.), *China's Emerging Financial Markets*,
The Milken Institute Series on Financial Innovation and Economic Growth 8,
DOI 10.1007/978-0-387-93769-4_7, © 2009 by Milken Institute

China-bashing has become a popular media and political sport. This is largely due to the US trade imbalance and the belief, by some, that China is responsible for it because China manipulates its currency to hold down the dollar prices of its goods, unfairly creating a trade advantage that has contributed to the loss of US businesses and jobs. The attacks reached a new plateau in February 2005 with a congressional proposal to impose a 27.5% tariff on Chinese goods entering the United States unless China immediately "revalues," or raises the value, of its currency, the renminbi, whose basic unit is the yuan, by 27.5%, the midpoint of a range of estimates that China undervalues the yuan relative to the US dollar by 15–40%. While this proposal became the centerpiece of federal policy efforts to address the Chinese trade imbalance, the proposed legislation died with the end of the last Congress. In the meantime, China began to push up the value of the yuan in July 2005, but very slowly so that tariff proponents and other protectionists have not been satisfied that China has removed their unfair competitive advantage.[1]

This chapter reviews the problem of the large trade imbalance that the United States has with China and its relationship to Chinese exchange rate policy (Section 1). In Section 2, it examines the link between a Chinese renminbi appreciation and the trade balance. In Section 3, it looks at whether a generalized dollar decline could solve the global or Chinese–US trade imbalance. The consensus view explained here is that a renminbi appreciation is not likely to fix either the trade imbalance with China or overall. If these perceived benefits of a managed float are small or nonexistent, then perhaps they should be pursued anyway because of small costs or even benefits for China. Section 4 looks at the costs of a managed float in terms of the benefits of the earlier peg. Opponents of a fixed dollar/yuan exchange rate ignore the costs of a managed float for China, especially with limits on currency convertibility. These costs are outlined here in order to provide an economic basis for the earlier fixed rate and China's reluctance to appreciate. Finally it is suggested that the necessary convertibility on capital account, toward which China is moving, could easily result in yuan depreciation under a floating rate regime. This is hardly the end that China critics have in mind, and it is not one that would improve US or other trade imbalances with China.

---

[1] In 2007, the Hunter-Ryan proposal was reintroduced in the US House of Representatives as "The China Currency Act of 2007." This bill would add currency manipulation to the list of actionable export subsidies under World Trade Organization rules. However, the Congressional Research Service in Sanford (2007) argues that it is not clear that this is consistent with WTO rules. Senators Christopher Dodd and Richard Shelby have introduced another approach in the US Senate that would at least define currency manipulation. It would occur whenever a country has both a bilateral and overall current account surplus. No action of any sort is required and no evidence on the real or nominal exchange rate would be required. Another bill that passed the Senate Finance Committee revives the approach of Senators Charles Schumer, Max Baucus, Chuck Grassley, and Lindsey Graham. It explicitly specifies anti-dumping duties for a failure of China to appreciate its currency by a specified amount. The International Monetary Fund also toughened its rules of surveillance for currency manipulation in June 2007, at least partially at the urging of the United States to do so.

1 The US Trade Deficit and China

The US current account deficit, the excess of imports of goods and services or unilateral transfers abroad, has climbed steadily and inexorably to record territory since 1991, except for slight improvements in 1995 and 2001. In 1991, the current account balance was a small surplus of US $2.9 billion, the first surplus since 1981 and the last. Since then the deficit has climbed to a preliminary US $856.7 billion, or 6.5% of GDP, in 2006. This is the largest deficit in US history, measured both in billions of dollars and as a percentage of GDP. Such a large deficit is also unusual in comparison with the experience in other countries, but when measured as a percentage of GDP, it is not uncommon elsewhere, sometimes remaining very large for many years. More often than not, however, such a high level of the deficit, especially if unsupported by rapid growth, ends in a financial crisis.

The risk of a financial crisis arises because current account deficits must be financed, that is, the excess of imports over exports must be paid for. When foreign credit is extended to a country year in and year out in such large amounts relative to GDP, there is eventually concern about the ability of the country to repay its foreign credit or even to service its debt to foreigners through interest or dividends. If creditworthiness comes into question, creditors become less inclined to continue lending and may even begin to reduce it, putting upward pressure on interest rates and downward pressure on the currency in the borrowing country. There are other reasons for concern about deficits that are more transitory and political but more popular and pressing as well. In particular, many politicians and workers fear that goods and services have been moved abroad and raised unemployment. Businesses that produce exportable goods and services and those that compete with imports view weak exports relative to imports as damaging competition and sometimes lead efforts to protect the domestic economy. Thus, opposition to current account deficits is easily mobilized, despite the positive benefits associated with them.

The connection to China comes from the fact that the US trade imbalance with China is its largest bilateral imbalance. In 2006, the current account deficit with China was US $261.7 billion or 30.5% of the total. To some analysts, this suggests large shifts of business and employment to China and makes China the bull's eye for US protectionists, especially for calls to push China to raise the foreign prices of its goods by dramatically boosting the value of its currency. This movement has been reinforced by support of advocates of letting markets determine the nominal exchange rate through a flexible exchange rate system.

Chinese authorities did begin to push up the value of its currency, the renminbi, whose basic unit is the yuan, against the dollar in July 2005, after being essentially fixed since 1994. But recall that the pressure in Congress was to raise the prices of Chinese goods by 27.5% through a tariff, if it did not occur through a rise in the dollar price of the yuan, or a currency appreciation. This is an indication of how much some people think that Chinese goods and services are underpriced when sold in the United States. Yet the rise in the dollar price of the yuan has been only 6.8% from July 2005 until February 2007. It rose 3.4% in the first year and has risen slightly faster in the past year, up 3.9% in the year ending in February 2007. This is hardly a breakneck response to US pressures. Moreover, while the appreciation has quickened recently, so has US inflation so that the dollar prices of Chinese goods are not rising much faster than dollar prices of US goods. Thus, there has been little gain in the pricing competitiveness of US goods. This lack of competitiveness gains highlights the importance of what is called the *real exchange rate*, the observed nominal exchange rate adjusted for prices in the two countries.

It is the real exchange rate that affects the price competitiveness of two countries' goods, not the nominal exchange rate. China's currency could rise in value relative to the US dollar, but if China's yuan prices are rising more slowly than the dollar prices of US goods, China's goods could end up selling at lower prices in the United States than US goods do. The real exchange rate is the nominal yuan price of the dollar times the relative price level in the United States relative to China. Chart 1 shows the nominal exchange rate for the dollar in terms of yuan as well as the real exchange value of the dollar constructed using the US consumer price index (CPI) divided by the CPI in China, where each is set equal to 100 in 2005. The nominal and real exchange rates are the same in 2005.

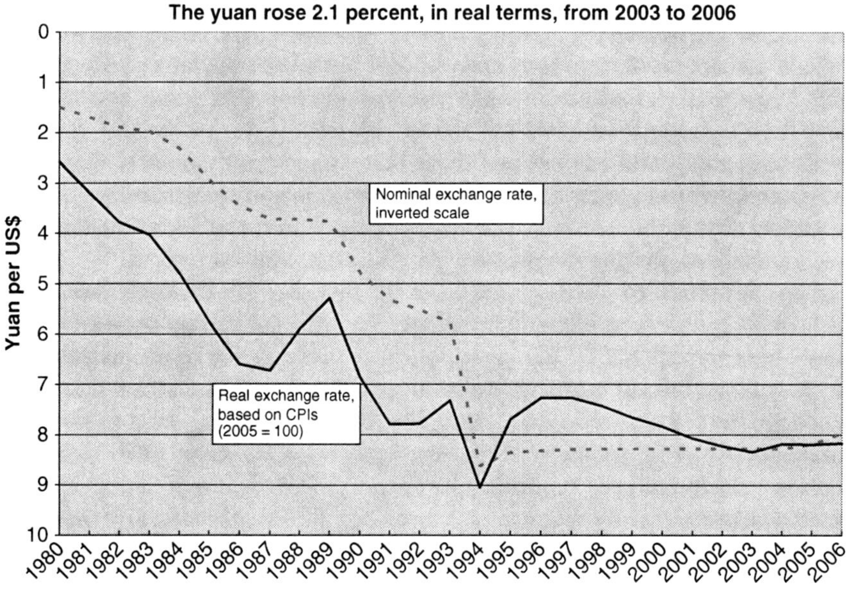

Chart 1 The Chinese currency has begun to slowly rise

Note that an inverted scale is used to measure the exchange rates so that increases in either line reflect an improvement in the respective value of the yuan. Since the exchange rate is the yuan price of the dollar, an increase in the value of the yuan (in dollars) means a fall in the value of the dollar (in yuan). Increases in the exchange rate, as shown, are increases in the value of the yuan and reductions in the value of the dollar, as desired, but it is the use of the inverted scale that accomplishes this. Like nearly all explanations of exchange rates and their movements, the conventional effort to make the discussion as simple as possible is unusually complicated.

If the yuan were undervalued and fixed, as critics claim that it has been, it would be expected to appreciate in real terms through faster inflation in China than in the United States. This would occur because an undervalued yuan would accelerate China's export growth and restrict its imports, putting upward pressure on prices, wages, and rates of return for its exports and its import-competing industries, until the cost advantage is eliminated. This would be fostered by the general inflow of dollars, which would accumulate at the central bank as reserves and support more inflationary growth of the Chinese money supply. The responses to an undervalued yuan would lead to a rise in Chinese prices relative to US prices pushing up the real exchange rate for the yuan, given the nominal exchange rate.

This has not occurred to any large degree over the past 13 years. Such a long period of adjustment to a peg makes claims of currency manipulation sound oxymoronic. How can a country be said to manipulate its currency when its nominal value has not changed for more than 10 years? And how can an unfair trading advantage persist for over a decade when prices in the United States and/or in China have been free to respond to the demands created by any undervaluation, eliminating it in the process? [2]

2 Could Yuan Appreciation Solve the US Current Account Imbalance?

In order to reduce US demand for Chinese goods and promote Chinese demand for US exports, it is the real exchange rate for the yuan that must rise, not the nominal rate. Note that in Chart 1 the real exchange rate began rising in 2003, 2 years before China relaxed the peg of the yuan to the dollar and began to raise the nominal value of the yuan. The real exchange rate for the yuan can rise independently of the nominal rate. The real exchange rate has not risen any

[2] Two strong proponents of the view that China has manipulated its currency and some of their initial commentary supporting institutional responses are Bergsten (2004) and Goldstein (2005). Absent moves in nominal exchange rates, neither notes in their numerous criticisms that the long decline in China's real exchange rate followed double-digit inflation and a partially offsetting currency depreciation that created a 24.5% appreciation of the currency in 1994–1996 (see Chart 1). About 60% of this renminbi overvaluation was eroded away by subsequent US inflation that was faster, on average, than Chinese inflation.

faster since the peg was relaxed than it did over the two years before that action. On an annual average basis, the real exchange value of the yuan rose 1.9% in 2004, and only rose 0.2% from 2004 to 2006.

Thus it is not surprising that there has been no improvement in the bilateral trade balance with China; the price change that would bring improvement about has been weaker since the yuan began to rise from what it was before the relaxation of the peg. China has implemented an appreciation of its currency, but it has not "floated" the yuan, or allowed the marketplace to determine its price. International finance specialists refer to the current exchange rate policy regime as a "managed float," because the central bank, the People's Bank of China (PBOC), has intervened daily to insure that movements in the nominal exchange rate do not deviate from the bank's desired path, dictated by the government.

Forcing up the value of the renminbi could presumably improve the US trade balance with China, but there are other forces that could forestall improvement. For example, a rapid nominal appreciation could be offset by Chinese producers offsetting the upward pressure on the dollar prices of their goods by reducing their yuan export prices. In effect, they could take reduced profit margins. Similarly, US importers could lower their margins, absorbing part of the rise in the dollar cost of the goods they purchase from China in order to maintain prices and sales. Of course neither course is sustainable in the long run because reduced margins affect the long-term viability of the enterprises. But it can be a potent offset, neutralizing the effects of a foreign currency appreciation. The same forces could frustrate adjustment for US exports to China. Chinese importers of US goods could refuse to pass along the price cuts that yuan appreciation would allow, taking the lower yuan prices of US goods as increased profit rather than passing along those savings to their customers and selling more US exports in China. US exporters could also attempt to capture some of the price cut that a higher valued yuan would allow by raising dollar prices of their exports without disrupting sales. Again, these are not sustainable actions in the long run, but the short run could, in these cases, be measured in years instead of months. Ignoring these adjustments, a large enough rise in the nominal and real value of the yuan could reduce the bilateral trade balance with China.

Larger yuan appreciation might improve the balance of trade with China, but it would not fix the overall US imbalance. US buyers would switch away from the more expensive Chinese goods, but they would switch to the next cheapest source of goods that benefit from low-wage production, which is not likely to be a US supplier. In fact, this shifting has been occurring without yuan appreciation, as increases in wages or other costs in China have fostered shifting of sourcing of imports to Vietnam, Indonesia, or other countries with lower wages relative to productivity. Similarly if US exports to China rise, there will be upward pressure on US prices of those goods so that there will be reduced exports elsewhere. More importantly, the Chinese policy actions that would support a higher valued yuan, essentially deflationary monetary growth, would frustrate the effort to raise the real exchange rate by forcing down yuan prices relative to US prices, leaving US prices of Chinese goods in line with those in the United States, despite the higher yuan.[3]

3 What About a Generalized Dollar Depreciation?

Even a more generalized fall in the value of the dollar against our trading partners would not be likely to eliminate the US current account deficit or even to reduce it much, at least for very large declines ranging up to say 30–40% or so. A recent study by Bailey and Lawrence (2007) finds that a 20% fall in a broad measure of the value of the dollar would be sufficient, with other steps, to restore balance in trade, although not in the current account balance. The conventional wisdom based on most studies is that a much larger and historically unprecedented decline would be necessary to eliminate the current account deficit. The largest sustained decline in the index Bailey and Lawrence refer to was in 1985–1988 when it fell by 35.7%. While the current account balance improved, it was not eliminated until some years later. The same measure of the real exchange rate has fallen almost as much as suggested by Bailey and Lawrence and others in recent years; from February 2002 until February 2007 the Fed's broad measure of the real exchange rate for the US dollar fell 16.1%. Nonetheless the current account deficit has worsened from 3.8% in the year ending in the first quarter of 2002 to 6.5%, according to preliminary data, in 2006. Of course there are many other factors influencing the current account balance and there are lags in the impact of exchange rates on trade, but the recent experience is not encouraging.

The more important limitation on the ability of a dollar depreciation to affect the US current account balance is the source of the imbalance. Current account imbalances for a country are reflected in imbalances in the financial account. Thus, if a country imports more goods and services than it exports, it has a matching financing flow from the rest of the world to pay for its excess imports. The central issue is which causes which? Does a country run a deficit in its current account because it is able to borrow excessively abroad to pay for the excess imports, or does it run a current account imbalance because the rest of the world is trying to acquire more of its assets than it seeks to acquire abroad? The conventional US imbalance story emphasizes the former, the United States borrows abroad to finance its excessive imports. But the other possibility is that foreigners want to acquire US assets, flooding the country with foreign currency that is used to buy imports of goods and services that are more attractive than foreign assets. The difference in these two extreme conceptual scenarios is that the dollar falls in the former case when foreigners must be induced to hold dollar assets and rises in the second case when the foreigners are trying to induce

[3] McKinnon (2005) makes this point in a broader review of problems with yuan appreciation.

US residents to acquire their assets, goods, or services in return for US assets. The strength of the dollar over the period of the climbing current account deficit, despite a decline since 2002, suggests that it is not excessive US consumption that is driving the current account deficit, but the excessive demand of foreigners for US assets that has powered the current account deficit to historic levels.

The principal solution to current account imbalances will come from market adjustments unless policy makers here or abroad intervene to force an adjustment. Capital inflows to the United States will eventually slow or decline as rates of return abroad become more attractive relative to the United States. The corresponding excess of imports of goods and services will adjust in tandem. Policies that make the United States a less attractive market for investment or make foreign countries more attractive can reinforce that adjustment. Whether this will involve movements in the exchange rate for the dollar will depend on its current overvaluation or undervaluation and on the effects of policy actions on the value of the dollar in the short-to-medium term.

4 The Costs of the Managed Float

Yuan appreciation in nominal terms is not necessary to achieve US policy interests, and it could damage Chinese development, which is not in the geopolitical or economic interest of the United States. If the yuan were undervalued and fixed, it would be expected to appreciate in real terms through faster inflation in China than in the United States. This would occur because an undervalued yuan would accelerate China's export growth and restrict its imports, putting upward pressure on prices, wages, and rates of return for its export sector and its import competing industries, until the cost advantage is eliminated. This would be fostered by the general inflow of dollars, which would accumulate at the central bank of reserves and support more inflationary growth of the Chinese money supply. China has resisted, to some extent, this inflationary money growth by administrative restrictions on interest rates and credit, and through reserve requirement increases. Nevertheless, the response to an undervalued yuan would lead to a rise in Chinese prices relative to US prices pushing up the real exchange rate, given the nominal exchange rate.

The cost of an appreciation of the yuan is best understood by looking at the benefit of a peg. China had a history of bouts of very rapid inflation during the early years of reform and rapid growth (Chart 2). Until 1994, occasional mismanagement of monetary policy led to periods of rapid inflation and currency depreciation. Inflation and currency depreciation threatened foreign investors and the domestic public alike, reducing investment and growth. In order to restore price stability by providing an anchor for prices and expectations, China pegged the yuan's value to the dollar in 1994. This had the intended effect of restoring monetary stability and essentially eliminating inflation for

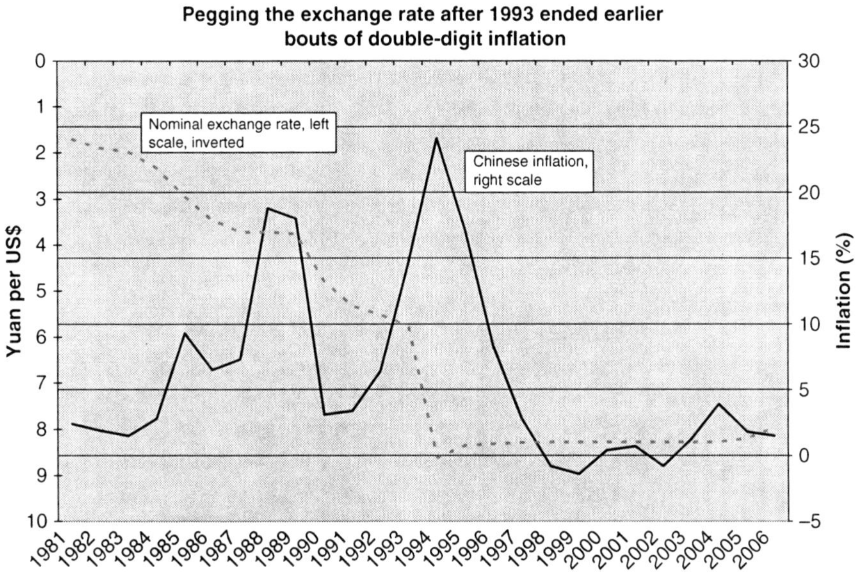

Chart 2 Exchange rate stability reduced inflation

more than a decade. This, in turn, created a very favorable investment climate. Relaxing the discipline of a sustainable fixed exchange rate regime risks freeing the central bank to unintentionally bring back excessive money creation and inflation. This would not only endanger strong investment and growth, it would also create the tensions that earlier led to popular unrest, including the Tiananmen Square crisis in 1989.

Eventually China's recent efforts to strengthen its financial markets will begin to pay off allowing for liberalization of its international financial arrangements and a freely functioning foreign exchange market. Until then, the discipline of a currency peg and its demonstration effects for foreign and domestic investors alike would be valuable and a key safeguard for policy. The risk of a policy error is heightened by abandoning the peg too early. Relaxing the peg too much, or forcing a managed appreciation too rapidly, will lead to unsustainable capital inflows as speculators bet on the appreciation of the currency, creating unsustainable growth of money, real output and employment, and inflation. This would be a replay of the appreciation pressures that led to the eventual breakdown of other Asian pegs and crisis in 1997. China has kept itself isolated from many of the extreme possibilities seen during that earlier era in Asia, but it would not be immune if investors believed that continuing appreciation is possible.

The irony of the managed appreciation of the yuan is not just the risk to China's rapid and stable growth, but it also arises from the fact that a competitive and accessible capital market would mean allowing larger and free outflows from China. Capital outflows are currently highly restricted and small. Despite China's rapid growth and scarce capital, private investors in China have limited access to high-yield financial assets. Bank deposits are the principal asset available, and they have very low, regulated yields. Individuals push an unusually large flow of saving through these low-yield accounts, largely because they do not have competitive local markets or access to foreign capital markets where they can find higher and yet safer rates of return. As China relaxes access to external assets, such as foreign bank accounts, mutual funds, foreign stocks or bonds, it will force higher banking standards on domestic firms and find that citizens are able to diversify their assets and increase both the returns and safety of their asset holdings. A large capital outflow would put strong downward pressure on the yuan, however. Thus, opening the capital market to substantially boost the welfare of domestic households and the competitiveness of the domestic financial services industry has now become hostage to US political pressures to manipulate the currency in the opposite direction.[4]

5 What Is the "Right" Yuan-Dollar Exchange Rate?

Proponents of the view that the yuan is undervalued point to the large and persistent bilateral trade deficit that the United States has with China. There is no reason why any one country's trade with another has to balance, however. Economic theory and accounting only dictate that in the long run a country's overall current account balance with all countries will tend to balance. And even then, the "long run" for this purpose is often counted in decades. A bilateral trade balance is not evidence of an imbalance, at least in the sense that there are economic forces that would eventually eliminate it, or in the sense that it will ever have to go away or that its persistence implies excess costs or risks to either country.

International financial theory predicts that the real exchange rate of a currency is "stationary," which means that it fluctuates around its mean, with no tendency to drift off and a systematic tendency to move back to the mean if for some reason it is moved away from it. This occurs because of "purchasing power parity" (PPP), which holds that the same bundle of goods and services will tend to sell for the same price (in a given currency). As a result, the exchange rates must adjust to reflect price differences in the domestic price levels in the

[4] China surprised markets when it announced in late-August 2007 a large opening of its capital market by allowing private citizens open access to investment in the Hong Kong equity market. This produced a sharp surge of 2.9%, similar to the 2.5% rise after mid-May 2007 announcement of the intention to relax rules for individual investors. Some analysts expect a cumulative outflow with full liberalization that would exceed current reserve holdings, if China's freed investors diversified their portfolios as much as typical OECD or other Asian countries.

two countries, or, given a fixed nominal exchange rate, price levels adjust to make PPP hold. PPP rests on the ability to profitably arbitrage price differences when it does not hold.

An example of how PPP works might clarify the point. Suppose, for the sake of argument, that PPP holds but China appreciates the nominal value of the yuan by 27.5%. PPP implies that such an appreciation would cause the price level in China to fall eventually by 27.5% relative to prices in the United States. The reason is that the nominal, and initially real, appreciation of the yuan by 27.5% would lead Chinese goods to rise by 27.5% in dollar terms and US goods to fall by 27.5% in yuan terms. Thus the Chinese and Americans would buy more US goods and fewer Chinese goods, putting upward pressure on US prices and downward pressure on Chinese prices. Since the Chinese market is so small relative to the United States, most of the pressure would fall on the Chinese market. The temporary incentive to switch purchases from Chinese to US goods would continue until prices in China fell by 27.5% relative to US prices and then PPP would be restored.

Some price differences across countries could arise from taxes, transport cost, or natural endowments of specialized resources. These differences in prices cannot be easily eliminated by arbitrage, so PPP may not as readily hold in these cases. Even when there are such factors, however, the real exchange rate is expected to be stationary in the long run so long as these distorting factors remain unchanged or change in a nonsystematic way. But again, the long run can be very long.

The real value of the yuan shown in Chart 1 appears to have a downward drift in the value of the yuan, or upward drift in the value of the dollar until 1991. This should not be surprising, however. The chart begins soon after reform and the opening of the Chinese market began. Highly centralized socialist economies attempt to control prices and hold the prices of essential consumer goods and services at artificially low levels and to control access in order to ration them. They also control exchange rates and access to foreign exchange. In China's case, it appears that the real exchange rate may have been set artificially high so that foreign demand was relatively low and domestic demand for foreign goods and foreign exchange (dollars) were rationed. As the economy opened, the real exchange rate fell. It might seem that it could take a long time for the real exchange rate to become stationary. Some simple statistical tests of the absence of stationarity strongly reject this, however. These so-called augmented Dickey-Fuller tests show that there is no significant trend, and a "unit root," the absence of stationarity, can be strongly rejected at conventional significance levels. Depending on the period used (from 1980 or from 1991), it would appear that the real exchange rate has been slightly overvalued, but by no more than 1% in 2006. Of course, it is not possible to have much confidence in such a conclusion based on only 25 years data for an economy in such dramatic transition, but the results are surprising, powerful, and suggestive. A more detailed analysis by Cheung et al. (2007) provides stronger support for this conclusion, however.

6 Conclusion

US policy toward China has been to exert strong pressure to get the Chinese to appreciate the yuan as part of its opening up of its foreign exchange and other financial markets to international competition. The focus is on the latter opening, but the expectation is that the currency would appreciate as many other policy makers and industry leaders hope. With a flexible, market-driven exchange rate, market participants determine the right price for a currency in real time, minute by minute, so that it is difficult to argue that the exchange rate is "wrong." Under a fixed exchange rate, such as that maintained for over 10 years by the Chinese, market pressures arising from underpriced or overpriced currencies do not move the exchange rate but instead move prices in each country to eliminate any undervaluation or overvaluation. Price rigidities suggest that this process could be much slower than exchange rate changes. In any event, theory and evidence today favor the notion that PPP and real exchange rate stationarity are the long-run determinates of the exchange rate and of international pricing relationships. The evidence suggests that, either way, the yuan may be very close to correctly valued for the long term. Opening the capital markets further could put strong downward pressure on the renminbi, creating further turmoil among trading partners. Any effort to force more nominal exchange rate appreciation could be deflationary for China, damage US exports and bilateral trade balance, and it would fail to have any effect on the overall US balance. The value of a symbolic appeasement of short-term protectionist interests unfortunately could have greater value than avoiding such risks.

References

Bailey Martin Neil, and Robert Z. Lawrence, "Can America Still Compete or Does it Need a New Paradigm?" Peter G. Peterson Institute for International Economics *Policy Brief* No. 4–9, December 2006.

Bergsten C. Fred, "The IMF and Exchange Rates," Testimony before the Committee on Banking, Housing and Urban Affairs, United States Senate, May 19, 2004.

Cheung Yin-Wong, Menzie D. Chinn, and Eiji Fujil, "The Overvaluation of Renminbi Undervaluation," National Bureau of Economic Research Working Paper 12850, June 2007.

Goldstein Morris, "Currency Manipulation and Enforcing the Rules of the International Monetary System," Paper Prepared for the Institute for International Economics, September 23, 2005.

Sanford Jonathan E, "Currency Manipulation: The IMF and WTO," Congressional Research Service Report for Congress, May 7, 2007.

McKinnon Roland I., "Currency Wars," *Wall Street Journal*, July 29, 2005.

New Estimation of the Renminbi Regime

Jeffrey A. Frankel

Abstract The chapter addresses the question: what precisely is the exchange rate regime that China has put into place since it announced a move away from the dollar peg in 2005? Is it a basket anchor with the possibility of cumulatable daily appreciations, as was announced at the time? We apply to this question a new approach to estimating countries' de facto exchange rate regimes, a synthesis of two techniques. One technique estimates implicit de facto currency weights when the hypothesis is a basket peg with little flexibility. The second technique is used to estimate the de facto degree of exchange rate flexibility when the hypothesis is an anchor to the dollar or some other single major currency. It is important to have available a technique that can cover both dimensions, inferring weights *and* inferring flexibility. The synthesis adds a variable representing "exchange market pressure" to the currency basket equation, whereby the degree of flexibility is estimated at the same time as the currency weights. This approach reveals that by mid-2007, the RMB basket had switched a substantial part of the dollar's weight onto the euro. The implication is that the appreciation of the RMB against the dollar during this period was due to the appreciation of the euro against the dollar, not to any upward trend in the RMB relative to its basket.

Keywords Band · Basket weights · China · De facto · Exchange market pressure · Exchange rates · Foreign currency · Foreign exchange · Intervention · Managed float · Peg · Regime · Renminbi · Reserves · Target zone · Yuan

Chinese authorities announced in 2005 a switch to a new exchange rate regime. The exchange rate would henceforth be set with reference to a basket of other currencies, with numerical weights unannounced, allowing a movement of up to ±0.3% within any given day. Although this step was originally accepted at face

J.A. Frankel (✉)
Kennedy School of Government, Harvard University, Cambridge, MA, USA
e-mail: jeffrey_frankel@harvard.edu

J.R. Barth et al. (eds.), *China's Emerging Financial Markets*,
The Milken Institute Series on Financial Innovation and Economic Growth 8,
DOI 10.1007/978-0-387-93769-4_8, © 2009 by Milken Institute

value in public policy circles, early statistical tests confirmed that skepticism was in order. The tests found that the basket assigned overwhelming weight to the dollar and that the degree of flexibility had hardly increased at all. This chapter conducts an updated evaluation of what exchange rate regime China has actually been following. The update consists of more than merely adding another year or two of data, as important as that is to the result.

The earlier RMB studies used a technique originally introduced by Frankel and Wei (1994) to estimate the weights in a currency basket. This technique regresses changes in the value of the local currency, in this case the RMB, against changes in the values of the dollar, euro, yen, and other currencies that may be in the basket. The equation is correctly specified to infer the weights in the case of a perfect basket peg, with an R^2 of 1, but is on less firm ground if the authorities allow even a relatively small band of flexibility around the central parity. This approach neglects to include anything to help make sense out of the error term under the alternative hypothesis that the country is not perfectly pegged to a major currency or to a basket but rather has adopted a degree of flexibility around the anchor.

Meanwhile another branch of the regime classification literature is designed to uncover the true degree of flexibility of an exchange rate regime. It has the drawback that it is unable to infer what is the relevant anchor; typically the anchor currency is chosen a priori. This chapter applies a new synthesis technique, which brings these two branches of the literature together to produce a complete equation suitable for use in inferring the de facto regime for the RMB across the spectrum of flexibility *and* across the array of possible anchors.

1 The New Regime

The Chinese currency had been effectively pegged to the US dollar at the rate of 8.28 RMB/dollar from 1997 until July 21, 2005. On that date, the People's Bank of China (PBOC) proclaimed – after a minor initial revaluation of 2.1% – a switch to a managing float regime "with reference to a basket of currencies." The announcement was billed as a major regime change.

As is often the case with currency baskets, the Chinese weights were not made public. Speculation ensued after the announcement about which currencies were in the new reference basket and what their weights were. Jen (2005), for example, guessed that the weight on the dollar was 85%. On August 9, 2005, PBOC Governor Zhou Xiaochuan (2005) disclosed a list of 11 currencies as constituents of the reference basket, in a speech in Shanghai marking the opening of the central bank's second headquarters. He revealed that the basket emphasizes four major currencies: the US dollar, the euro, the yen, and the Korean won. In addition, Governor Zhou stated that the other seven currencies in the basket are the Singapore dollar, the British pound, the Malaysian ringgit, the Russian ruble, the Australian dollar, the Thai baht, and the Canadian dollar.[1] The governor said that these currencies were chosen because of their economies' importance for China's current account. Still not announced were the weights on these currencies, or the frequency and the criteria with which these weights might be altered. In this chapter, we test for all 11 currencies in an Appendix table. In light of Governor Zhou's statement and the earlier results in Frankel and Wei (2007), we will concentrate on the four major currencies. We are very short of data points when using the new synthesis technique, because it requires the use of data on reserves and the monetary base which for China, as for most countries, are only available on a monthly basis.

The newly announced regime would allow a movement of up to ±0.3% in bilateral exchange rates within any given day. (This band was later widened to ±0.5%). In theory, the daily band could cumulate, at the maximum, to a strong trend of 6.4% per month; this would require, however, both that movement among the major currencies is low and that the Chinese authorities make maximum use of the 0.3% band. In practice, the cumulative trend has been only a small fraction of the hypothetical maximum. The trend has been dwarfed by movements in the dollar against the euro, yen, and other currencies.

Although the announced change in official policy was originally taken at face value in public policy circles, it soon became clear that, at least for the remainder of 2005, the currency remained closely linked to the dollar. Subsequently, in 2006, the RMB indeed started to give a little weight to some non-dollar currencies, but the process was very slow. In 2007, the RMB appreciated more against the dollar. This much is known, but public commentary usually fails to distinguish whether the appreciation was attributable to a shift in basket weights away from the dollar toward non-dollar currencies, or to a greater degree of exchange rate flexibility, or to a trend appreciation. In our econometric analysis of precisely what exchange rate regime China has followed since July 2005, we take account of the likelihood that the regime has evolved over the 3 years.

2 The Old Technique

If a country announces the adoption of a basket peg, and reveals a list of currencies that may be included in the basket, but does not reveal the exact weighting of the component currencies, how would one ascertain what is the true exchange rate regime? Previous studies of this question for other currencies have used a particular technique to estimate the implicit weights: Frankel (1993), Frankel and Wei (1994, 1995), Bénassy-Quéré (1999), Ohno (1999), Frankel et al. (2000), and Bénassy-Quéré et al. (2004).

---

[1] Frankel and Wei (2007) found no significant role for these currencies, during most of the subsequent two years, with the partial exception of the ringgit.

The weight-inference technique is very simple: One regresses changes in the value of the local currency, in this case the RMB, against changes in the values of the dollar, euro, yen, and other currencies that are candidate constituents of the basket. In the special case where China in fact follows a perfect basket peg, the technique is an exceptionally apt application of OLS regression. It should be easy to recover precise estimates of the weights. The fit should be perfect, an extreme rarity in econometrics: The standard error of the regression should be zero, and $R^2 = 100\%$.

The reason to work in terms of changes rather than levels is the likelihood of non-stationarity. Concern for non-stationarity goes beyond the common refrain of modern time series econometrics, the inability to reject statistically a unit root, which in many cases can be attributed to insufficient power. One of the most important hypotheses we are testing is that the authorities have allowed the yuan to drift away from a basket, perhaps via an upward trend. Thus it is important to allow for nonstationarity. Working in terms of first differences is the cleanest way to do so. We should include a constant term to allow for the likelihood of a trend appreciation in the RMB, whether against the dollar alone or a broader basket. Algebraically, if the RMB is pegged to currencies $X1$, $X2$, ... and Xn, with weights equal to $w1$, $w2$, ... and wn, then

$$logRMB(t+s) - logRMB(t) = c + \sum w(j)\,[logX(j,t+s) - logX(j,t)] \quad (1)$$

This is as good a place as any to address a nagging methodological question. How do we define the "value" of each of the currencies? This is the question of the numeraire.[2] If the exchange rate is truly a basket peg, the choice of numeraire currency is immaterial; we estimate the weights accurately regardless.[3] If the true regime is more variable than a rigid basket peg, then the choice of numeraire does make some difference to the estimation. Some authors in the past have used a remote currency, such as the Swiss franc.

A weighted index such as a trade-weighted measure or the SDR (Special Drawing Right, an IMF unit composed of a basket of most important major currencies) is probably more appropriate. Here is why. Assume the true regime is a target zone or a managed float centered around a reference basket, where the authorities intervene to an extent that depends on the magnitude of the

[2] Frankel (1993) used purchasing power over a consumer basket of domestic goods as numeraire; Frankel and Wei (1995) used the SDR; Frankel and Wei (1994, 2006), Ohno (1999), and Eichengreen (2006) used the Swiss franc; Bénassy-Quéré (1999), the dollar; Frankel et al. (2000), a GDP-weighted basket of five major currencies; and Yamazaki (2006), the Canadian dollar. Bénassy-Quéré et al. (2004) propose a modification of the methodology, with a method of moments approach; the claim is that the results then do not depend on the choice of a numeraire currency.

[3] If the linear equation holds precisely in terms of any one "correct" numeraire, then add the log exchange rate between that numeraire and any arbitrary unit to see that the equation also holds precisely in terms of the arbitrary numeraire. This assumes the weights add to 1, and there is no error term, constant term, or other non-currency variable.

deviation; this seems the logical alternative hypothesis in which a strict basket peg is nested. The error term in the equation represents shocks in demand for the currency that the authorities allow to be partially reflected in the exchange rate (but only partially, because they intervene if the shocks are large). Then one should use a numeraire that is similar to the yardstick used by the authorities in measuring what constitutes a large deviation. The authorities are unlikely to use the Swiss franc or Canadian dollar in thinking about the size of deviations from their reference point. They are more likely to use a weighted average of major currencies. If we use a similar measure in the equation, it should help minimize the possibility of correlation between the error term and the numeraire. Similarly, if there is a trend in the exchange rate equation (a constant term in the changes equation) representing deliberate gradual appreciation of the currency, then the value of the RMB should be defined in terms of whatever weighted exchange rate index the authorities are likely to use in thinking about the trend. These considerations suggest a numeraire that is itself composed of a basket of currencies. Here, as in Frankel and Wei (2007), we choose the SDR.[4]

There is a good argument for constraining the weights on the currencies to add up to 1. However weak one thinks the link to the reference basket might be, or however large or small the weight on the dollar, the authorities must view movements in the RMB through the metric of distance from some reference rate or effective exchange rate. The easiest way to implement the adding up constraint is to run the regressions with the changes in the log RMB value on the left-hand side of the equation transformed by subtracting off the changes in the log value of one of the currencies, say the won, and the changes in the values of the non-won currencies on the right-hand side transformed in the same way.

To see this, we repeat equation (1):

$$\begin{aligned}\Delta \, log\, RMB_t &= c + \sum w(j)\, [\Delta \, log X(j)_t] \\ &= c + \beta(1)\, \Delta \, log\, \$_t + \beta(2)\, \Delta \, log\, €_t + \beta(3)\, \Delta \, log\, €_t + \alpha\, \Delta \, log\, won_t\end{aligned}$$

We want to impose the adding up constraint $\alpha = 1 - (1) - (2) - (3) \ldots$
We implement it by running the regression equation (2):

$$\begin{aligned}[\Delta \, log\, RMB_t - \Delta \, log\, won_t] &= c + \beta(1)\, [\Delta \, log\, \$_t - \Delta \, log\, won_t] \\ &+ \beta(2) [\Delta \, log\, ¥_t - \Delta \, log\, won_t] + \beta(3))[\Delta \, log\ _t - \Delta \, log\, won_t]\end{aligned} \quad (2)$$

One can recover the implicit weight on the value of the won by adding the estimated weights on the non-dollar currencies and subtracting the sum from 1.

[4] Among the extensions and robustness checks in that paper was a check whether the results were sensitive to the numeraire, as between the SDR and gold.

(This coefficient estimate is reported in the last row of the tables.) Imposing the constraint sharpens the estimates a bit.[5]

3 The Old Results

Shah et al. (2005) adopted the weight-inference methodology to study the Chinese currency basket after July 2005 and found that the RMB was still tightly pegged to the dollar and no other currencies. However, the only candidate currencies that they considered in the RMB basket were the dollar, the yen, the euro, and the pound, probably unaware of the 11-currency disclosure made by the Chinese central bank (with the won on the list of four prime suspects, rather than the pound). In addition, their sample covered only the initial few months after July 21, 2005. Frankel and Wei (2006) extended to 11 the components of the basket, but found that the RMB regime in the second half of 2005 was still a tight dollar peg – as tight as that of the Hong Kong SAR regime. Ogawa (2006) found the same. Eichengreen (2006, pp. 22–25) had daily observations of data that ran from July 22, 2005, to March 21, 2006, and found a dollar weight around 0.9, but with no evidence of a downward trend in the weight, and no significance on non-dollar currencies.

Each of these four papers was too early to catch the evolution in 2006. Yamazaki (2006, p. 8) updated the estimation and found some weight had shifted to the euro, yen, and won; but he estimated the equation in terms of levels rather than changes (risking non-stationarity), did not allow for a trend, did not allow for the other currencies on the list, and had a relatively small number of (bimonthly) observations.

Frankel and Wei (2007) found continued evolution of the Chinese exchange rate regime over the 2-year period from July 2005 to August 2007. In the first 6 months following the announced shift by the Chinese central bank to a managed floating regime with reference to a basket of 11 currencies, China gave such heavy weight to the US dollar that it was indistinguishable from a dollar pegger. However, after February 2006, there were signs of increased flexibility. First, in the spring of 2006, some weight in the basket was temporarily shifted to other currencies: the Malaysian ringgit, the Korean won, the Russian ruble, and the Thai baht. Surprisingly, throughout the sample, there was not an iota of evidence of any positive weight assigned to the yen or the euro. Second, beginning in the fall of 2006, in addition to the lesser weight on the dollar (an estimated weight of 0.9 rather than 1.0 as in the earlier periods), the association between the RMB and the reference currency basket became slightly looser. There was a non-negligible trend of appreciation against the basket.

[5] The choice of which currency to drop from the right-hand side in order to impose the adding up constraint, in this case the won, is completely immaterial to the estimates. The choice of which currency to use as numeraire, by contrast, *is* material to the estimates (to the extent that the true regime differs substantially from a perfect basket peg).

4 Updated Results with Daily Data, Using the Traditional Technique

Estimation of the RMB basket *using the traditional approach*, on daily exchange rate data, is updated through October 2008 in Table 1. We take advantage of the abundance of daily data to estimate the parameters in a rolling regression by 3-month subperiods, thereby allowing the regime to evolve rapidly over time. (Table 3 in Appendix estimates the parameters

Table 1 Updated estimation of weights in RMB basket with daily exchange rate data

	Evolution of RMB Basket Weights from 6-22-2005,3-month windows, ending on the month shown							
	(1)	(2)	(3)	(4)	(5)	(6)	(7)	(8)
Coefficient	8/2005	9/2005	10/2005	11/2005	12/2005	1/2006	2/2006	3/2006
usd	0.805***	0.968***	0.957***	0.980***	0.972***	0.996***	0.979***	0.965***
	(0.123)	(0.017)	(0.034)	(0.030)	(0.028)	(0.015)	(0.018)	(0.019)
eur	–0.146	–0.013	–0.019	–0.004	–0.001	–0.023**	–0.018	–0.015
	(0.100)	(0.019)	(0.028)	(0.025)	(0.025)	(0.011)	(0.016)	(0.015)
jpy	0.315	0.027	0.048	0.019	0.007	0.017	0.026**	0.031**
	(0.200)	(0.016)	(0.029)	(0.028)	(0.022)	(0.014)	(0.012)	(0.013)
Constant	0.001	0.000	0.000	0.000	0.000	0.000	0.000	0.000
	(0.000)	(0.000)	(0.000)	(0.000)	(0.000)	(0.000)	(0.000)	(0.000)
Observations	63	63	63	63	61	63	61	64
R-squared	0.84	0.98	0.95	0.96	0.98	0.99	0.99	0.99
krw	0.027	0.019	0.015	0.004	0.022	0.010	0.013	0.019

	Evolution of RMB Basket Weights from 2-22-2006, 3-month windows, ending on the month shown							
	(1)	(2)	(3)	(4)	(5)	(6)	(7)	(8)
Coefficient	4/2006	5/2006	6/2006	7/2006	8/2006	9/2006	10/2006	11/2006
usd	0.947***	0.932***	0.929***	0.895***	0.905***	0.895***	0.939***	0.965***
	(0.020)	(0.021)	(0.022)	(0.031)	(0.033)	(0.045)	(0.033)	(0.028)
eur	0.003	0.005	0.007	–0.020	–0.031	–0.007	–0.033	0.047
	(0.015)	(0.018)	(0.023)	(0.032)	(0.029)	(0.034)	(0.031)	(0.035)
jpy	0.008	0.009	0.020	0.051*	0.078***	0.037	0.041	–0.060
	(0.014)	(0.017)	(0.020)	(0.028)	(0.023)	(0.031)	(0.030)	(0.036)
Constant	0.000	0.000	0.000	0.000	0.000*	0.000	0.000**	0.000*
	(0.000)	(0.000)	(0.000)	(0.000)	(0.000)	(0.000)	(0.000)	(0.000)
Observations	62	63	62	62	62	61	62	63
R-squared	0.99	0.98	0.98	0.95	0.95	0.91	0.94	0.96
krw	0.042	0.054	0.044	0.074	0.048	0.075	0.053	0.048

	Evolution of RMB Basket Weights from 10-22-2006, 3-month windows, ending on the month shown							
	(1)	(2)	(3)	(4)	(5)	(6)	(7)	(8)
Coefficient	12/2006	1/2007	2/2007	3/2007	4/2007	5/2007	6/2007	7/2007
usd	1.005***	0.973***	0.930***	0.814***	0.924***	0.947***	0.925***	0.796***
	(0.038)	(0.048)	(0.060)	(0.035)	(0.050)	(0.064)	(0.074)	(0.076)
eur	0.006	0.010	0.018	0.068**	0.071*	0.003	0.024	0.009
	(0.038)	(0.030)	(0.034)	(0.027)	(0.040)	(0.041)	(0.049)	(0.040)
jpy	–0.023	–0.019	0.007	0.020*	0.019	0.043	0.052	0.028
	(0.035)	(0.027)	(0.019)	(0.011)	(0.015)	(0.028)	(0.045)	(0.028)
Constant	0.000**	0.000**	0.000*	0.000	0.000	0.000**	0.000**	0.000
	(0.000)	(0.000)	(0.000)	(0.000)	(0.000)	(0.000)	(0.000)	(0.000)
Observations	61	63	61	64	61	64	63	64
R-squared	0.95	0.94	0.91	0.94	0.93	0.87	0.85	0.89
krw	0.011	0.036	0.045	0.098	–0.014	0.007	–0.001	0.167

Table 1 (continued)

	Evolution of RMB Basket Weights from 6-22-2007, 3-month windows, ending on the month shown							
Coefficient	(1) 8/2007	(2) 9/2007	(3) 10/2007	(4) 11/2007	(5) 12/2007	(6) 1/2008	(7) 2/2008	(8) 3/2008
usd	0.869***	0.895***	0.886***	0.843***	0.824***	0.862***	0.878***	0.972***
	(0.060)	(0.042)	(0.078)	(0.061)	(0.065)	(0.055)	(0.041)	(0.034)
eur	0.032	0.004	0.034	0.044	0.054	0.045	0.019	0.003
	(0.042)	(0.037)	(0.035)	(0.031)	(0.040)	(0.030)	(0.026)	(0.023)
jpy	−0.012	−0.013	−0.002	0.037**	0.035**	0.040**	0.044***	0.026
	(0.021)	(0.016)	(0.019)	(0.017)	(0.015)	(0.015)	(0.017)	(0.018)
Constant	0.000*	0.000	0.000**	0.000**	0.001***	0.001***	0.001***	0.001***
	(0.000)	(0.000)	(0.000)	(0.000)	(0.000)	(0.000)	(0.000)	(0.000)
Observations	63	62	63	63	62	63	61	64
R-squared	0.89	0.89	0.87	0.90	0.88	0.85	0.96	0.97
krw	0.111	0.114	0.082	0.076	0.087	0.054	0.059	−0.001

	Evolution of RMB Basket Weights from 2-22-2008, 3-month windows, ending on the month shown*							
Coefficient	(1) 4/2008	(2) 5/2008	(3) 6/2008	(4) 7/2008	(5) 8/2008	(6) 9/2008	(7) 10/2008	(8) 11/2008
usd	0.959***	0.991***	0.949***	0.973***	0.958***	0.992***	0.989***	0.971***
	(0.027)	(0.027)	(0.026)	(0.029)	(0.034)	(0.027)	(0.026)	(0.039)
Eur	0.015	0.029	−0.012	−0.027	0.035	0.049**	0.052***	0.070**
	(0.034)	(0.032)	(0.031)	(0.032)	(0.024)	(0.020)	(0.019)	(0.028)
Jpy	0.026	0.009	0.063*	0.064*	−0.005	−0.030	−0.031	−0.022
	(0.022)	(0.030)	(0.035)	(0.033)	(0.028)	(0.019)	(0.021)	(0.027)
Constant	0.000**	0.000**	0.000**	0.000	0.000	0.000	0.000	0.000
	(0.000)	(0.000)	(0.000)	(0.000)	(0.000)	(0.000)	(0.000)	(0.000)
Observations	62	64	63	64	62	60	38	18
R-squared	0.97	0.96	0.97	0.96	0.99	1.00	1.00	1.00
Krw	0.001	−0.028	−0.000	−0.010	0.012	−0.011	−0.010	−0.019

***$p<0.01$, **$p<0.05$, *$p<0.1$
Robust standard errors in parentheses

month by month, allowing for even more rapid evolution.) As in earlier studies, the weight on the dollar remains close to 1.0 throughout 2005 and 2006.[6] In some periods thereafter the dollar weight falls significantly below 1.0, in the range 0.8–0.9 from mid 2007 through early 2008. In some of these months, the R^2 does fall as low as 0.85 showing a – rather limited – degree of flexibility around the anchor. Flexibility also shows up in the form of a positive trend in the value of the RMB which, though very slight, is statistically significant in many months. In many of the estimation intervals, the Korean won or Japanese yen seem to be the currencies that make up the non-dollar share (particularly January–May 2006, and September 2007–February 2008, respectively).

During the months July–October 2008, which are covered by the last three rolling regressions of the sample, the yen and won drop out, and the statistically significant weight instead shifts to the euro. Though the euro's estimated weight never rises above 0.07, the R2 returns to 1.0, suggestive of a basket peg.

[6] Excluding June 2005, the month of the discrete revaluations.

When we estimate month-by-month, in Appendix Table 3, the weight on the dollar more often drops statistically below 1.0. The yen, the won, and the euro are each occasionally significant, though none consistently so. When we include the full array of 10 currencies in the basket, in Appendix Table 4, the Malaysian ringgit joins the list of those that are occasionally significant.

5 The New Technique

Although the weight-inference technique is well specified if the true regime is a tight basket peg, as noted, it may be less well specified if the true regime allows flexibility. For any currency, it is very likely that in practice the basket peg is not perfect. If the basket peg is relatively tight, one can still expect to estimate the weights with fairly tight standard errors. One can also estimate a trend appreciation term with no problem. But one is also interested in estimating whether the authorities allow increased flexibility relative to the weighted basket, for example, how wide the band is. It stands to reason that the looser the link, the lower the R^2. But in the event of substantial flexibility, there is no theorem that says that the equation is correctly specified, the weights accurately estimated, or the R^2 an appropriate calibration of the degree of flexibility. Indeed, one can imagine a fall in the R^2, resulting from an increase in external shocks to economic fundamentals instead of from any further loosening of the exchange rate regime.[7]

There are by now many attempts to discern the true "de facto" exchange rate regimes that countries actually follow, along the spectrum from fixed to floating, with a continuum of flexibility in between. Among the most prominent are Calvo and Reinhart (2002) and Levy-Yeyati and Sturzenegger (2003, 2005). Their classification schemes count as a de facto floater a country that has high variability of the exchange rate, relative to variability of reserves, and count as fixed a country that has low variability of the exchange rate relative to reserves.

It is important when inferring the de facto flexibility of an exchange rate regime to look beyond the variability of the exchange rate in itself. One currency could show a higher degree of variability than another, and yet this might be because the former has been subject to larger shocks than the latter, rather than because the authorities intervene less and allow a given shock to show up more in the form of price movement. It is for just such reasons that the classification schemes of Calvo and Reinhart (2002) and Levy-Yeyati and Sturzenegger (2003, 2005) do not look at exchange rate variability alone

[7] One can see from graphs in Frankel and Wei (2008) how commodity producers tend to have higher variability in exchange market pressure, regardless whether they are peggers, floaters, or in between.

(prices of currencies) but rather compare it to variability in reserves or money supplies (quantities of currencies). The question is: When there is a shock that increases international demand for the RMB, to what extent do the authorities allow it to show up as an appreciation and to what extent as an increase in reserves. In this chapter, we frame the issue in terms of the Exchange Market Pressure variable, which is defined as the percentage increase in the value of the currency plus the increase in reserves (expressed as a fraction of the monetary base).[8] When this variable appears on the right-hand side of an equation and the percentage increase in the value of the currency appears on the left, a coefficient of 0 signifies a completely fixed exchange rate (no changes in the value of the currency), and a high coefficient signifies a floating rate (few changes in reserves).

One possible limitation of these and other papers that estimate flexibility versus stability of exchange rate regimes is that they sometimes have to make arbitrary judgments regarding what is the major currency in terms of which flexibility and stability are to be defined. The dollar is the most common choice. This may be fine for most western hemisphere countries. But for many others, particularly in Asia and the Pacific, the relevant foreign currency is neither the dollar nor the euro but some (possibly trade-weighted) basket. It would be better to let the data tell us what is the relevant anchor for a given country, especially for those that are not clearly in either the dollar or euro camp, rather than making the judgment subjectively or a priori.[9]

The new equation that we now apply is a synthesis of the inferred-weights technique (Frankel and Wei, 1994, etc.) and the flexibility criterion (Levy-Yeyati and Sturzenegger, 2003, 2005, etc.). Since the RMB and many other currencies today purportedly follow variants of Band-Basket-Crawl, it is important to have available a technique that can cover both dimensions, inferring weights *and* inferring flexibility.[10]

6 New Estimation

Our equation is:

$$\Delta\ logRMB_t = c + \sum w(j)\ \Delta\ logX(j)_t + \delta\Delta emp_t\} + u_t \tag{3}$$

where $\Delta\ emp_t$ denotes the percentage change in exchange market pressure, that is, the increase in international demand for the RMB, which may show up either

[8] The progenitor of the Exchange Market Pressure variable, in a rather different context, was Girton and Roper (1977).

[9] Clearly many of the authors of these papers are fully aware of the issue.

[10] Frankel and Wei (2008).

in the price of the RMB or the quantity of the RMB depending on the policies of the Chinese monetary authorities (floating vs. fixed). Here we define the percentage change in total exchange market pressure by

$$\Delta\ emp_t \equiv \Delta\ logRMB_t + \Delta\ Res_t / MB_t$$

The $w(j)$ coefficients capture the de facto weights on the constituent currencies. The coefficient δ captures the de facto degree of exchange rate flexibility: a high δ means the currency floats purely, because there is no foreign exchange market intervention (no changes in reserves); $\delta = 0$ means the exchange rate is purely fixed, because it never changes in value; most currencies probably lie somewhere in between.

We repeat equation (3), with the major basket currencies made explicit:

$$\Delta\ logRMB_t = c + \sum w(j)\ [\Delta\ logX_t] + \delta\ \{\Delta\ emp_t\} + u_t \qquad (3')$$

$$= c + w(1)\Delta\ log\ \$_t + w(2)\ \Delta\ log\ €_t + w(3)\ \Delta\ log\ ¥_t + w(4)\ \Delta\ log\ won_t + \\ + \delta\ \{\Delta\ emp_t\} + u_t\ .$$

We want to impose the adding up constraint $w(4) = 1 - w(1) - w(2) - w(3) - \ldots$ We implement it by running the regression equation (3):

$$[\Delta logRMB_t - \Delta log\ won_t] = c + w(1)\ [\Delta log\ \$_t - \Delta log\ won_t] \\ + w(2)\ [\Delta log\ €_t - \Delta log\ won_t] + w(3)\ [\Delta log\ ¥_t - \Delta log\ won_t] + \delta\{\Delta logEMP_t\} + u_t \qquad (4)$$

The results reported in Table 2 come from the estimation of this equation. Here the weight on the dollar falls more dramatically in 2007, to 0.6, and the weight on the euro rises more dramatically to a highly significant 0.4. The significance is impressive in that there are so few data points in each of these regressions (only 12 per year). The coefficient on exchange market pressure is statistically significant and in excess of 0.2, in 2005 and again in 2007. This indicates a surprising degree of exchange rate flexibility.[11] But the upward trend is gone. In fact the constant term, though not usually significant, is always negative.

---

[11] For comparison, the coefficient exchange market pressure in the case of the Australian and Canadian dollars – two floaters – only ever gets as high as 0.3 or 0.4 – Frankel and Wei (2008). In theory, if changes in reserves precisely captured foreign exchange intervention and nothing else, the estimated δ should approach 1.0 in the case of pure floaters. In practice, reserves often change for reasons other than intervention.

Table 2 Rolling 12-month regressions of value of RMB against values of other currencies and Δ EMP

Δ (EMP) defined as [res(t)–res(t–1)]/mb(t–1) + [exr(t)–exr(t–1)]/exr(t–1)12-month windows, ending on the month shown

	(1)	(2)	(3)	(4)	(5)	(6)	(7)	(8)
Coefficient	06M7	06M8	06M9	06M10	06M11	06M12	07M1	07M2
usd	0.710***	0.776***	0.749***	0.737***	0.909***	0.870***	0.786***	0.756***
	(0.105)	(0.132)	(0.154)	(0.150)	(0.147)	(0.213)	(0.175)	(0.105)
jpy	0.149*	0.090	0.107	0.122	–0.015	0.025	0.014	–0.095
	(0.069)	(0.096)	(0.103)	(0.109)	(0.098)	(0.140)	(0.124)	(0.085)
eur	0.109	0.124	0.120	0.118	0.029	0.034	0.056	0.116
	(0.086)	(0.125)	(0.127)	(0.116)	(0.117)	(0.131)	(0.094)	(0.096)
Δ emp	0.269**	0.215*	0.250*	0.254*	0.137	0.139	0.176	0.179***
	(0.095)	(0.108)	(0.114)	(0.113)	(0.100)	(0.157)	(0.104)	(0.047)
Constant	–0.005*	–0.003	–0.004	–0.004	–0.001	–0.001	–0.002	–0.003*
	(0.002)	(0.003)	(0.003)	(0.003)	(0.003)	(0.004)	(0.003)	(0.002)
Observations	12	12	12	12	12	12	12	12
R-squared	0.985	0.975	0.973	0.975	0.984	0.979	0.964	0.967
krw	0.031	0.010	0.024	0.023	0.077	0.070	0.144	0.222
	(1)	(2)	(3)	(4)	(5)	(6)	(7)	(8)
Coefficient	07M3	07M4	07M5	07M6	07M7	07M8	07M9	07M10
usd	0.756***	0.866***	0.860***	0.757***	0.788***	0.820***	0.746***	0.745***
	(0.067)	(0.167)	(0.151)	(0.159)	(0.192)	(0.130)	(0.146)	(0.148)
jpy	–0.140	–0.019	–0.007	–0.013	–0.037	0.013	0.028	0.033
	(0.089)	(0.092)	(0.097)	(0.103)	(0.079)	(0.074)	(0.101)	(0.102)
eur	0.169**	0.006	0.016	0.049	0.041	0.006	–0.063	–0.058
	(0.068)	(0.120)	(0.111)	(0.105)	(0.121)	(0.084)	(0.174)	(0.181)
Δ emp	0.187***	0.100	0.109	0.133**	0.118	0.116	0.067	0.078
	(0.029)	(0.073)	(0.058)	(0.056)	(0.078)	(0.064)	(0.080)	(0.073)
Constant	–0.004***	–0.000	–0.000	–0.001	–0.001	–0.000	0.002	0.002
	(0.001)	(0.003)	(0.003)	(0.003)	(0.004)	(0.003)	(0.004)	(0.004)
Observations	12	12	12	12	12	12	12	12
R-squared	0.975	0.913	0.917	0.877	0.875	0.925	0.924	0.930
krw	0.215	0.147	0.131	0.207	0.208	0.162	0.289	0.280
	(1)	(2)	(3)	(4)	(5)	(6)	(7)	
Coefficient	07M11	07M12	08M1	08M2	08M3	08M4	08M5	
usd	0.774***	0.944***	0.747**	0.633**	0.613***	0.515***	0.597***	
	(0.165)	(0.176)	(0.242)	(0.182)	(0.171)	(0.111)	(0.130)	
jpy	0.026	–0.086	0.054	0.053	0.059	0.042	0.030	
	(0.126)	(0.113)	(0.109)	(0.094)	(0.081)	(0.082)	(0.083)	
eur	0.153	0.228	0.212	0.375	0.357**	0.445***	0.397***	
	(0.259)	(0.233)	(0.253)	(0.205)	(0.143)	(0.073)	(0.105)	
Δ emp	0.123	0.108	0.198	0.280**	0.290***	0.281***	0.249**	
	(0.088)	(0.087)	(0.117)	(0.087)	(0.076)	(0.063)	(0.097)	
Constant	–0.001	0.000	–0.002	–0.006	–0.006	–0.006**	–0.004	
	(0.004)	(0.004)	(0.005)	(0.004)	(0.003)	(0.002)	(0.003)	
Observations	12	12	12	12	12	12	12	
R-squared	0.922	0.930	0.895	0.926	0.967	0.970	0.966	
krw	0.047	–0.086	–0.014	–0.061	–0.030	–0.002	–0.024	

***$p<0.01$, **$p<0.05$, *$p<0.1$

Robust standard errors in parentheses

7 Conclusions Regarding the Recent Chinese Exchange Rate Regime

Reporting in the financial press has focused on the 2005–2008 appreciation of the RMB against the dollar. The focus is understandable, both because this is the question of political interest, and because looking at a 2005–2008 graph of the dollar/yuan exchange rate seems to tell a clean story of an appreciation trend that, though starting out very small, gradually escalated in an exponential way. If this accelerating trend were in fact deemed part of the current regime, one could extrapolate it and predict more serious appreciation in the future.

Our results – with the benefit of more recent data and a technique that allows for changes in currency weights as well as changes in the rigidity of the peg – suggest that the regime probably is not best described as a dollar peg with a trend appreciation. Rather, the regime that has recently been in effect is better described as a basket peg with some weight on a non-dollar currency, the euro in particular. By mid-2007, the weight on the dollar had fallen to 0.6, and the weight on the euro had risen correspondingly to 0.4. The euro now apparently plays almost as important a role as the dollar. It follows that the appreciation of the RMB against the dollar in 2007 was attributable to the appreciation of the euro against the dollar, not to a trend effective appreciation of the RMB. The distinction in characterizations of the regime could make a big difference for the future. Our results suggest that if the euro in the future reverses its 2005–07 appreciation against the dollar, the Chinese currency may automatically do the same thing unless the regime evolves again (necessitating further estimation).

Acknowledgment The author would like to thank Danxia Xie for excellent research assistance and the Mossavar-Rahmani Center for Business and Government for support. Part of this chapter draws on "New Estimation of China's Exchange Rate Regime," *Pacific Economic Review* (Wiley), special issue, "China's Impact on the Global Economy," edited by Menzie Chinn, 2009.

Appendix: Estimation of Weights with Daily Exchange Rate Data, but Without EMP Variable

Table 3 Five-currency basket month by month, June 2006–September 2008

Evolution of RMB Basket Weights from 6-22-2005,window size: 1 month

Coefficient	(1) 6/2005	(2) 7/2005	(3) 8/2005	(4) 9/2005	(5) 10/2005	(6) 11/2005	(7) 12/2005	(8) 1/2006
Usd	0.666***	0.980***	0.985***	0.952***	0.929***	0.973***	0.980***	1.000***
	(0.141)	(0.018)	(0.032)	(0.056)	(0.101)	(0.020)	(0.026)	(0.017)
Eur	-0.120	0.063	-0.103	-0.033	-0.012	-0.087***	0.018	-0.022
	(0.183)	(0.054)	(0.061)	(0.048)	(0.111)	(0.028)	(0.033)	(0.027)
Jpy	0.605***	0.035*	0.010	0.056	0.051	0.014	0.005	0.065***
	(0.191)	(0.019)	(0.022)	(0.052)	(0.087)	(0.015)	(0.015)	(0.012)
Krw	-0.121	-0.000	0.019	0.016	-0.005	0.008	0.037	-0.022
	(0.148)	(0.009)	(0.035)	(0.047)	(0.089)	(0.022)	(0.023)	(0.017)
Constant	0.001*	0.000	0.000	0.000	0.000	-0.000	0.000	0.000
	(0.001)	(0.000)	(0.000)	(0.000)	(0.000)	(0.000)	(0.000)	(0.000)
Observations	21	20	22	21	20	22	19	22
R-squared	0.88	0.99	0.99	0.99	0.96	1.00	0.99	0.99
Gbp	-0.031	-0.078	0.089	0.008	0.037	0.092	-0.040	-0.023

Coefficient	(1) 2/2006	(2) 3/2006	(3) 4/2006	(4) 5/2006	(5) 6/2006	(6) 7/2006	(7) 8/2006	(8) 9/2006
Usd	0.945***	0.921***	0.929***	0.861***	0.940***	0.863***	0.861***	0.984***
	(0.044)	(0.039)	(0.027)	(0.045)	(0.032)	(0.077)	(0.059)	(0.045)
Eur	0.062	-0.026	-0.035	-0.003	-0.018	0.056	-0.056	0.108
	(0.052)	(0.034)	(0.023)	(0.042)	(0.039)	(0.160)	(0.039)	(0.080)

Table 3 (continued)

Coefficient	(1) 2/2006	(2) 3/2006	(3) 4/2006	(4) 5/2006	(5) 6/2006	(6) 7/2006	(7) 8/2006	(8) 9/2006
Jpy	0.027	0.024	0.008	0.078	0.086**	0.032	0.132***	-0.181**
	(0.024)	(0.031)	(0.015)	(0.050)	(0.034)	(0.061)	(0.023)	(0.081)
Krw	0.056*	0.079**	0.025**	0.120**	0.016	0.087	0.019	0.044
	(0.030)	(0.031)	(0.011)	(0.044)	(0.031)	(0.081)	(0.056)	(0.050)
Constant	0.000	0.000	-0.000	0.000	0.000	0.000	0.000**	0.000
	(0.000)	(0.000)	(0.000)	(0.000)	(0.000)	(0.000)	(0.000)	(0.000)
Observations	20	22	20	21	21	20	21	20
R-squared	0.99	0.99	0.99	0.98	1.00	0.97	0.99	0.97
Gbp	-0.090	0.002	0.073	-0.057	-0.024	-0.038	0.045	0.046

Coefficient	(1) 10/2006	(2) 11/2006	(3) 12/2006	(4) 1/2007	(5) 2/2007	(6) 3/2007	(7) 4/2007	(8) 5/2007
Usd	0.958***	0.975***	1.238***	0.804***	0.828***	0.754***	0.996***	0.867***
	(0.074)	(0.053)	(0.117)	(0.062)	(0.053)	(0.074)	(0.078)	(0.201)
Eur	-0.070	0.018	0.007	0.037	0.102*	0.115**	-0.077	-0.246**
	(0.121)	(0.121)	(0.146)	(0.054)	(0.057)	(0.049)	(0.069)	(0.089)
Jpy	0.048	-0.047	-0.113*	-0.025	0.026	-0.004	0.185	-0.005
	(0.049)	(0.062)	(0.058)	(0.031)	(0.016)	(0.021)	(0.140)	(0.121)
Krw	0.045	0.032	-0.160	0.184**	0.008	0.146**	-0.109**	0.160
	(0.070)	(0.040)	(0.135)	(0.069)	(0.075)	(0.069)	(0.041)	(0.102)
Constant	0.000	0.000	0.000	0.000	0.000	-0.000	0.000	0.000
	(0.000)	(0.000)	(0.000)	(0.000)	(0.000)	(0.000)	(0.000)	(0.000)
Observations	21	22	18	23	20	21	20	23
R-squared	0.98	0.98	0.97	0.98	0.98	0.98	0.92	0.90
Gbp	0.019	0.022	0.028	0.001	0.036	-0.011	0.006	0.224

Coefficient	(1) 6/2007	(2) 7/2007	(3) 8/2007	(4) 9/2007	(5) 10/2007	(6) 11/2007	(7) 12/2007	(8) 1/2008
Usd	0.855***	0.723***	1.012***	0.863***	0.711***	0.911***	0.855***	0.858***
	(0.100)	(0.112)	(0.124)	(0.085)	(0.138)	(0.084)	(0.115)	(0.101)
Eur	0.353*	0.035	-0.020	-0.016	0.034	0.088	0.050	0.042
	(0.172)	(0.075)	(0.095)	(0.056)	(0.085)	(0.085)	(0.075)	(0.065)
Jpy	0.028	0.050	-0.034	0.010	0.066*	0.049	-0.018	0.044
	(0.054)	(0.035)	(0.028)	(0.033)	(0.037)	(0.036)	(0.042)	(0.035)
Krw	-0.138	0.198***	-0.022	0.204	0.130	0.016	0.104	0.065
	(0.159)	(0.044)	(0.131)	(0.155)	(0.090)	(0.093)	(0.155)	(0.080)
Constant	-0.000	0.000	0.001	-0.000	0.000	0.000	0.001*	0.001**
	(0.000)	(0.000)	(0.000)	(0.000)	(0.000)	(0.000)	(0.001)	(0.000)
Observations	20	21	22	19	22	22	18	23
R-squared	0.87	0.97	0.94	0.94	0.97	0.96	0.90	0.98
Gbp	-0.099	-0.007	0.065	-0.061	0.060	-0.063	0.009	-0.009

Coefficient	(1) 2/2008	(2) 3/2008	(3) 4/2008	(4) 5/2008	(5) 6/2008	(6) 7/2008	(7) 8/2008	(8) 9/2008
Usd	0.897***	1.014***	0.970***	0.983***	0.971***	1.147***	0.945***	0.925***
	(0.043)	(0.060)	(0.053)	(0.079)	(0.058)	(0.122)	(0.049)	(0.058)
Eur	0.005	0.064	0.166*	-0.081	-0.070	0.094	0.187***	0.023
	(0.032)	(0.087)	(0.079)	(0.059)	(0.102)	(0.086)	(0.056)	(0.030)
Jpy	0.081***	-0.026	0.001	0.066	0.173***	-0.072	-0.049	0.001
	(0.026)	(0.057)	(0.055)	(0.039)	(0.050)	(0.094)	(0.032)	(0.028)
Krw	0.115**	-0.070	-0.012	-0.039	0.014	-0.124	0.029**	-0.022*
	(0.044)	(0.047)	(0.067)	(0.049)	(0.024)	(0.075)	(0.013)	(0.012)
Constant	0.001**	0.000	0.000	0.001**	0.000	-0.000	0.000	0.000
	(0.000)	(0.000)	(0.000)	(0.000)	(0.000)	(0.000)	(0.000)	(0.000)
Observations	20	21	21	22	20	22	20	18
R-squared	0.99	0.95	0.95	0.96	0.93	0.95	0.99	0.98
Gbp	-0.098	0.018	-0.126	0.071	-0.089	-0.045	-0.112	0.074

***$p<0.01$, **$p<0.05$, *$p<0.1$
Robust standard errors in parentheses

Table 4 Ten-currency basket by 3-month periods, June 2006–September 08

	Evolution of RMB Basket Weights from 6-22-2005, 3-month windows, ending on the month shown							
	(1)	(2)	(3)	(4)	(5)	(6)	(7)	(8)
Coefficient	8/2005	9/2005	10/2005	11/2005	12/2005	1/2006	2/2006	3/2006
usd	0.560**	1.066***	1.317***	0.649***	0.926***	0.865***	0.826***	0.726***
	(0.247)	(0.045)	(0.219)	(0.139)	(0.116)	(0.068)	(0.075)	(0.072)
eur	−0.091	−0.029	0.008	0.010	0.032	−0.040	−0.028	−0.015
	(0.068)	(0.034)	(0.042)	(0.033)	(0.042)	(0.024)	(0.017)	(0.019)
jpy	0.015	0.020	0.032	−0.001	−0.009	0.021	0.032**	0.029**
	(0.069)	(0.018)	(0.031)	(0.022)	(0.022)	(0.016)	(0.013)	(0.013)
sgd	0.653**	−0.023	−0.056	−0.010	−0.028	−0.057	−0.097***	−0.074
	(0.280)	(0.047)	(0.086)	(0.057)	(0.058)	(0.038)	(0.035)	(0.049)
myr	−0.043	−0.120**	−0.324	0.314**	0.094	0.132**	0.152**	0.264***
	(0.132)	(0.058)	(0.221)	(0.135)	(0.128)	(0.064)	(0.068)	(0.074)
rub	−0.058	0.050	−0.002	−0.018	0.009	0.059**	0.080***	0.070**
	(0.148)	(0.057)	(0.080)	(0.055)	(0.054)	(0.027)	(0.029)	(0.034)
aud	−0.091	0.019	0.018	0.039	0.007	0.010	−0.010	−0.019
	(0.068)	(0.017)	(0.030)	(0.025)	(0.025)	(0.015)	(0.016)	(0.015)
thb	0.021	−0.003	0.053	0.130*	0.025	0.003	0.020	0.017
	(0.082)	(0.028)	(0.051)	(0.071)	(0.067)	(0.023)	(0.018)	(0.017)
cad	−0.002	−0.015	−0.066**	−0.099***	−0.069*	−0.003	0.013	−0.003
	(0.041)	(0.015)	(0.027)	(0.026)	(0.036)	(0.022)	(0.016)	(0.016)
Constant	0.000*	0.000	0.000	0.000	0.000	0.000	0.000	−0.000
	(0.000)	(0.000)	(0.000)	(0.000)	(0.000)	(0.000)	(0.000)	(0.000)
Observations	63	63	63	63	61	63	61	64
R-squared	0.91	0.98	0.96	0.98	0.98	0.99	0.99	0.99
krw	0.035	0.036	0.020	−0.013	0.013	0.009	0.013	0.005

	Evolution of RMB Basket Weights from 2-22-2006, 3-month windows, ending on the month shown							
	(1)	(2)	(3)	(4)	(5)	(6)	(7)	(8)
Coefficient	4/2006	5/2006	6/2006	7/2006	8/2006	9/2006	10/2006	11/2006
usd	0.864***	0.912***	0.926***	0.899***	0.791***	0.748***	0.825***	0.921***
	(0.038)	(0.038)	(0.032)	(0.047)	(0.069)	(0.086)	(0.088)	(0.160)
eur	−0.012	0.033	0.013	0.011	−0.092**	−0.051	−0.056	0.043
	(0.028)	(0.026)	(0.027)	(0.041)	(0.038)	(0.060)	(0.053)	(0.163)
jpy	0.005	0.001	0.016	0.052	0.060**	0.009	0.028	−0.047
	(0.014)	(0.020)	(0.021)	(0.035)	(0.029)	(0.037)	(0.036)	(0.041)
sgd	0.002	0.010	0.057	0.007	0.059	−0.060	−0.135**	−0.075
	(0.042)	(0.044)	(0.050)	(0.067)	(0.054)	(0.073)	(0.062)	(0.063)
myr	0.062	0.087**	0.063**	0.062*	0.056*	0.180**	0.203***	0.092**
	(0.055)	(0.039)	(0.028)	(0.035)	(0.031)	(0.077)	(0.071)	(0.036)
rub	0.051	−0.071*	−0.057*	−0.078*	0.110	0.135	0.137	0.049
	(0.060)	(0.039)	(0.033)	(0.046)	(0.085)	(0.123)	(0.114)	(0.285)
aud	−0.009	−0.015	−0.006	−0.018	0.014	0.024	0.031	−0.021
	(0.014)	(0.013)	(0.018)	(0.022)	(0.023)	(0.028)	(0.026)	(0.025)
thb	0.005	0.010	−0.016	0.021	−0.027	−0.014	−0.050	0.003
	(0.023)	(0.034)	(0.034)	(0.050)	(0.036)	(0.045)	(0.038)	(0.022)
cad	0.016	0.007	−0.007	0.001	0.006	−0.007	−0.007	0.016
	(0.021)	(0.019)	(0.016)	(0.019)	(0.019)	(0.030)	(0.021)	(0.021)
Constant	−0.000	0.000	0.000	0.000	0.000	0.000	0.000**	0.000
	(0.000)	(0.000)	(0.000)	(0.000)	(0.000)	(0.000)	(0.000)	(0.000)
Observations	62	63	62	62	62	61	62	63
R-squared	0.99	0.98	0.98	0.96	0.96	0.92	0.95	0.96
krw	0.014	0.026	0.009	0.042	0.023	0.036	0.025	0.020

Table 4 (continued)

	Evolution of RMB Basket Weights from 10-22-2006,3-month windows, ending on the month shown							
	(1)	(2)	(3)	(4)	(5)	(6)	(7)	(8)
Coefficient	12/2006	1/2007	2/2007	3/2007	4/2007	5/2007	6/2007	7/2007
usd	0.983***	0.953***	0.918***	0.814***	0.962***	1.080***	1.006***	0.802***
	(0.089)	(0.098)	(0.115)	(0.067)	(0.108)	(0.139)	(0.133)	(0.093)
eur	0.010	0.002	-0.030	0.075	0.024	0.083	0.080	0.014
	(0.062)	(0.053)	(0.059)	(0.053)	(0.089)	(0.101)	(0.093)	(0.062)
jpy	-0.030	-0.028	-0.008	0.008	0.013	0.050	0.055	0.033
	(0.037)	(0.029)	(0.023)	(0.015)	(0.022)	(0.033)	(0.047)	(0.037)
sgd	-0.016	0.037	0.068	0.063	0.021	-0.046	0.005	0.022
	(0.076)	(0.084)	(0.096)	(0.059)	(0.063)	(0.061)	(0.084)	(0.082)
myr	0.050	-0.007	-0.060	-0.059	-0.071	-0.019	-0.042	-0.058
	(0.036)	(0.040)	(0.079)	(0.054)	(0.105)	(0.064)	(0.061)	(0.051)
rub	0.055	0.047	0.106	0.032	0.027	-0.212	-0.124	0.008
	(0.094)	(0.079)	(0.100)	(0.056)	(0.154)	(0.170)	(0.129)	(0.088)
aud	-0.000	-0.023	-0.013	-0.031*	0.044	0.017	0.020	0.010
	(0.048)	(0.046)	(0.046)	(0.018)	(0.030)	(0.031)	(0.035)	(0.028)
thb	-0.034*	-0.026**	-0.023*	-0.002	0.006	-0.010	-0.008	-0.002
	(0.018)	(0.013)	(0.013)	(0.007)	(0.012)	(0.008)	(0.009)	(0.010)
cad	-0.020	0.004	-0.018	-0.018	-0.005	0.031	-0.003	-0.006
	(0.025)	(0.025)	(0.026)	(0.023)	(0.030)	(0.042)	(0.047)	(0.031)
Constant	0.000*	0.000**	0.000**	0.000	0.000	0.000	0.000**	0.000
	(0.000)	(0.000)	(0.000)	(0.000)	(0.000)	(0.000)	(0.000)	(0.000)
Observations	61	63	61	64	61	64	63	64
R-squared	0.96	0.94	0.92	0.94	0.93	0.87	0.85	0.89
krw	0.003	0.040	0.061	0.117	-0.021	0.026	0.011	0.178

	Evolution of RMB Basket Weights from 6-22-2007, 3-month windows, ending on the month shown							
	(1)	(2)	(3)	(4)	(5)	(6)	(7)	(8)
Coefficient	8/2007	9/2007	10/2007	11/2007	12/2007	1/2008	2/2008	3/2008
usd	0.900***	0.908***	0.971***	0.827***	0.893***	0.871***	0.909***	0.903***
	(0.074)	(0.070)	(0.098)	(0.134)	(0.113)	(0.100)	(0.105)	(0.094)
eur	0.043	0.035	0.136	0.034	0.219	0.133	0.102	-0.056
	(0.069)	(0.080)	(0.094)	(0.121)	(0.145)	(0.103)	(0.121)	(0.112)
jpy	-0.022	-0.019	-0.032	0.050	0.040	0.037	0.039	0.015
	(0.025)	(0.025)	(0.028)	(0.034)	(0.029)	(0.026)	(0.024)	(0.026)
sgd	0.107	0.061	0.042	-0.016	0.011	-0.028	-0.009	0.025
	(0.071)	(0.069)	(0.071)	(0.074)	(0.080)	(0.075)	(0.080)	(0.042)
myr	-0.129**	-0.092	-0.001	0.069	0.147*	0.198**	0.064	0.020
	(0.051)	(0.058)	(0.054)	(0.067)	(0.077)	(0.089)	(0.060)	(0.040)
rub	-0.005	-0.035	-0.150	-0.032	-0.360	-0.204	-0.141	0.117
	(0.100)	(0.127)	(0.142)	(0.207)	(0.225)	(0.158)	(0.184)	(0.182)
aud	0.006	-0.005	-0.046	0.001	-0.031	0.000	-0.014	0.024
	(0.027)	(0.029)	(0.033)	(0.033)	(0.032)	(0.029)	(0.027)	(0.025)
thb	0.008	0.003	-0.050	0.006	-0.005	-0.004	0.003	0.008
	(0.013)	(0.018)	(0.035)	(0.037)	(0.027)	(0.023)	(0.016)	(0.015)
cad	-0.039	-0.006	0.014	0.016	0.042	0.019	0.003	-0.046
	(0.032)	(0.027)	(0.028)	(0.026)	(0.026)	(0.029)	(0.029)	(0.028)
Constant	0.000*	0.000	0.000**	0.000	0.001***	0.000**	0.001***	0.000**
	(0.000)	(0.000)	(0.000)	(0.000)	(0.000)	(0.000)	(0.000)	(0.000)
Observations	63	62	63	63	62	63	61	64
R-squared	0.91	0.90	0.88	0.90	0.90	0.88	0.96	0.97
krw	0.131	0.150	0.115	0.046	0.043	-0.022	0.045	-0.012

Table 4 (continued)

	Evolution of RMB Basket Weights from 2-22-2008 3-month windows, ending on the month shown							
	(1)	(2)	(3)	(4)	(5)	(6)	(7)	(8)
Coefficient	4/2008	5/2008	6/2008	7/2008	8/2008	9/2008	10/2008	11/2008
usd	0.837***	0.831***	0.868***	0.883***	0.852***	0.953***	0.921***	0.579
	(0.102)	(0.069)	(0.075)	(0.073)	(0.074)	(0.059)	(0.076)	(0.680)
eur	−0.043	−0.021	0.053	0.007	0.025	0.064	0.014	−0.236
	(0.144)	(0.076)	(0.097)	(0.063)	(0.058)	(0.046)	(0.057)	(0.517)
jpy	0.008	−0.008	0.036	0.027	−0.012	−0.050*	−0.052*	0.025
	(0.032)	(0.029)	(0.024)	(0.034)	(0.031)	(0.025)	(0.029)	(0.098)
	Evolution of RMB Basket Weights from 2-22-2008 3-month windows, ending on the month shown							
	(1)	(2)	(3)	(4)	(5)	(6)	(7)	(8)
Coefficient	4/2008	5/2008	6/2008	7/2008	8/2008	9/2008	10/2008	11/2008
sgd	0.118*	0.082	0.192	0.190*	0.179**	0.171***	0.196**	0.480
	(0.060)	(0.065)	(0.133)	(0.101)	(0.080)	(0.058)	(0.080)	(0.451)
myr	0.050	0.098*	0.077	0.069	0.006	0.063	0.021	0.004
	(0.045)	(0.051)	(0.054)	(0.073)	(0.070)	(0.057)	(0.051)	(0.132)
rub	0.069	0.048	−0.234	−0.166**	−0.096	−0.059	0.047	0.359
	(0.235)	(0.127)	(0.153)	(0.076)	(0.079)	(0.066)	(0.077)	(0.730)
aud	−0.007	−0.011	−0.020	0.005	0.004	−0.024**	−0.027**	0.001
	(0.031)	(0.033)	(0.039)	(0.036)	(0.028)	(0.011)	(0.011)	(0.025)
thb	0.006	0.015	0.045	−0.003	0.063	−0.096*	−0.096	−0.151
	(0.017)	(0.053)	(0.048)	(0.068)	(0.078)	(0.055)	(0.062)	(0.154)
cad	−0.008	0.029	0.020	0.019	−0.016	−0.001	−0.005	−0.036
	(0.030)	(0.026)	(0.029)	(0.038)	(0.036)	(0.026)	(0.031)	(0.067)
Constant	0.000	0.000**	0.001***	0.000**	0.000	0.000	0.000	0.000
	(0.000)	(0.000)	(0.000)	(0.000)	(0.000)	(0.000)	(0.000)	(0.001)
Observations	62	64	63	64	62	60	38	18
R-squared	0.97	0.97	0.97	0.97	0.99	1.00	1.00	1.00
krw	−0.030	−0.062	−0.036	−0.031	−0.006	−0.021	−0.019	−0.026

***$p<0.01$, **$p<0.05$, *$p<0.1$
Robust standard errors in parentheses

References

Bénassy-Quéré, Agnès, 1999, "Exchange Rate Regimes and Policies: An Empirical Analysis," in *Exchange Rate Policies in Emerging Asian Countries*, edited by Stefan Collignon, Jean Pisani-Ferry, and Yung Chul Park, Routledge, London, pp. 40–64.

Bénassy-Quéré, Agnès, Benoit Coeuré, and Valérie Mignon, 2004, "On the Identification of de facto Currency Pegs," *Journal of Japanese and International Economies* 20(1), 112–127, March.

Calvo, Guillermo and Carmen Reinhart, 2002, "Fear of Floating," *Quarterly Journal of Economics* 117(2), 379–408.

Eichengreen, Barry, 2006, "China's Exchange Rate Regime: The Long and Short of It," revision of paper for Columbia University's conference on Chinese money and finance held in New York on February 2–3.

Frankel, Jeffrey, 1993, "Is Japan Creating a Yen Bloc in East Asia and the Pacific?" in *Regionalism and Rivalry: Japan and the US in Pacific Asia*, edited by Jeffrey Frankel and Miles Kahler, University of Chicago Press, Chicago, pp. 53–85.

Frankel, Jeffrey, 2006, "On the Yuan: The Choice Between Adjustment Under a Fixed Exchange Rate and Adjustment under a Flexible Rate," in *Understanding the Chinese Economy*, edited by Gerhard Illing, CESifo Economic Studies, Munich.

Frankel, Jeffrey, 2009, "New Estimation of China's Exchange Rate Regime," in *Pacific Economic Review*, special issue, "China's Impact on the Global Economy," edited by Menzie Chinn, Wiley.

Frankel, Jeffrey, Sergio Schmukler and Luis Servén, 2000, "Verifiability and the Vanishing Intermediate Exchange Rate Regime," in *Brookings Trade Forum 2000*, edited by Susan Collins and Dani Rodrik, Brookings Institution, Washington DC.

Frankel, Jeffrey and Shang-Jin Wei, 1994, "Yen Bloc or Dollar Bloc? Exchange Rate Policies of the East Asian Economies," in *Macroeconomic Linkages: Savings, Exchange Rates and Capital Flows*, edited by Takatoshi Ito and Anne Krueger, University of Chicago Press, Chicago, pp. 295–329.

Frankel, Jeffrey and Shang-Jin Wei, 1995, "Emerging Currency Blocs," in *The International Monetary System: Its Institutions and its Future*, edited by Hans Genberg, Springer, Berlin, pp. 111–143.

Frankel, Jeffrey and Shang-Jin Wei, 2006, "Currency Mysteries," May 28.

Frankel, Jeffrey and Shang-Jin Wei, 2007, "Assessing China's Exchange Rate Regime," *Economic Policy* 51, 575–614, July.

Frankel, Jeffrey and Shang-Jin Wei, 2008,"Estimation of De Facto Exchange Rate Regimes: Synthesis of The Techniques for Inferring Flexibility and Basket Weights," *IMF Staff Papers*, 55, 384–416.

Girton, Lance and Don Roper, 1977, "A Monetary Model of Exchange Market Pressure Applied to the Postwar Canadian Experience," *American Economic Review* 67(4), 537–548, September.

Jen, Stephen, 2005, "Chinese RMB Basket Still a Mystery," *Global Economics Forum*, Morgan Stanley, August 19.

Levy-Yeyati, Eduardo and Federico Sturzenegger, 2003, "To Float or to Trail: Evidence on the Impact of Exchange Rate Regimes on Growth," *American Economic Review*, 93(4), 1173–1193, September.

Levy-Yeyati, Eduardo and Federico Sturzenegger, 2005, "Classifying Exchange Rate Regimes: Deeds vs. Words," *European Economic Review*, 49(6), 1603–1635, August.

Ogawa, Eiji, 2006, "The Chinese Yuan after the Chinese Exchange Rate System Reform", *China & World Economy*, 14(6), 39–57, November–December.

Ohno, Kenichi, 1999, "Exchange Rate Management in Developing Asia," Working Paper No. 1, January, Asian Development Bank Institute.

Shah, Ajay, Achim Zeileis, and Ila Patnaik, 2005, "What is the New Chinese Currency Regime?" Unpublished, November.

Yamazaki, Kazuo, 2006, "Inside the Currency Basket," Columbia University and Mitsubishi UFJ Trust and Banking Corp., December.

Zhou, Xiaochuan, 2005, "Governor's Speech at the Opening of the Shanghai Headquarters of the People's Bank of China (in Chinese)," www.hexun.com, August 10. Speech (in English) on PBoC website: http://www.pbc.gov.cn/english//detail.asp?col = 6500&ID = 82

The Chinese Imbalance in Capital Flows

John A. Tatom

Abstract China has three major imbalances: a trade surplus, a capital account surplus and a large annual build up, and a very high level of international reserves. Capital flows, especially flows of US government securities, are also important in assessing the bilateral and overall imbalances in transactions. China has a capital account surplus reinforcing its current account surplus and the accumulation of foreign exchange reserves, mainly US dollar denominated assets. This is unusual because a sustainable fixed or floating requires that countries with large current account surpluses run capital account deficits.

The worst consequences of imbalances have been the build-up of large, low-return foreign exchange. These reserves have led to rapid growth in money and credit and, in turn, to a sharp acceleration in inflation, something that China had assiduously avoided since 1994 and that has raised serious doubts about the credibility of the monetary authorities and damaged its inflation-fighting reputation. Moreover, efforts to offset money growth and inflation have deepened existing inefficiencies in the financial system, which China had hoped to begin remedying by its efforts to recapitalize and list its banks' equities on stock exchanges. China could eliminate these imbalances by policies that would reduce growth. An alternative solution is to lift restrictions on capital outflows, allowing households and business to diversify their wealth holdings and realize higher returns and/or less volatility in their own income and wealth. This would transform future asset growth from massive central bank holdings of US securities to holdings of higher return and lower risk assets abroad. Such a step also would eliminate pressures on the People's Bank of China (PBOC), allowing for more rapid deregulation of banks, slower money, and credit growth and lower inflation.

Keywords Capital account imbalance · Capital controls and banking inefficiencies · Capital outflows and financial development · Exchange rate management · Banking regulation

---

J.A. Tatom (✉)
Networks Financial Institute at Indiana State University, Indianapolis, IN, USA
e-mail: john.tatom@isunetworks.org

J.R. Barth et al. (eds.), *China's Emerging Financial Markets*,
The Milken Institute Series on Financial Innovation and Economic Growth 8,
DOI 10.1007/978-0-387-93769-4_9, © 2009 by Milken Institute

Chinese international capital transactions are critically important components of their economic relations with the rest of the world. But these transactions are not balanced and could have important effects on its economic performance and growth possibilities and could create significant geopolitical issues. International trade in goods and services attracts the most attention, with China running a large surplus.[1] But international trade is not simply about goods and services. Capital flows are a large and significant aspect of China's international transactions. Typically such flows provide the mirror image of a country's balance on trading goods and services. More importantly, capital flows can have a more important effect on economic activity and on economic growth. Capital inflows are an important source of financing for domestic investment activities, and the "direct" component of capital inflows often bring with them not only the investments in productivity that are financed but also productive entrepreneurial, organizational, and management skills. Capital outflows provide a source of profitable business expansion for domestic firms, accessing new markets, technologies, and resources, and for investors (consumers, business, and government) who gain access to new financial products, better rates of return or lower risk on financial assets.

Chinese capital inflows are open and are large relative to gross domestic product (GDP). In the past few years, capital outflows from China have been sizable, but have fallen short of the capital inflow, so that China has persistently had a net capital inflow to go along with its current account surplus. To maintain the exchange rate, which would otherwise appreciate the value of domestic currency, the yuan, the People's Bank of China (POBC) has had to acquire the excess funds flowing into the currency and hold it as official reserve assets, principally in US treasury securities, or other foreign currency assets. Because of the large surpluses, China has been under international pressure, especially from the United States, to appreciate the value of its currency, in order to change trade and investor behavior to eliminate the surpluses in its international accounts.

Generally China's so-called imbalances—a large current account surplus, a capital account surplus, and a large annual accumulation of foreign exchange or official reserve assets generally—have been viewed as problems for its trading partners and for its consumers. This article provides some perspective on these problems, how they are related, and some potential remedies. The focus here is on the capital account imbalance and how it might be used to restore some balance to international payments accounts. But first, in Section 1 the trade situation is reviewed to set the stage for the discussion. Section 2 discusses the capital account, and Section 3 provides a discussion of some potential remedies. Section 4 provides a summary and some concluding remarks.

---

[1] The current account refers to Balance of Payments accounting where the current account measures the exports (credit, +) and imports (debit, –) of goods, services, income payments for resource services, and unilateral international transfers.

1 The Chinese Trade Imbalance

China has a relatively large current account surplus. Table 1 shows the current account balance for 2007, measured in US dollars and as a percentage of GDP.

Table 1 Chinese international capital and financial transactions: 2007 (millions of dollars)

(Credits +; debits –)	
Capital account	
Capital account transactions, net	**3,099**
Financial account	–
Chinese-owned assets abroad (increase/financial outflow (–))	**1,206,332**
Chinese official reserve assets	–461.9
Gold/7/	0
Special drawing rights	–78.9
Reserve position in the International Monetary Fund	239.7
Foreign exchange	–461.9
Unofficial assets	–170,805
Direct investment	–16,995
Foreign securities	–2,324
Other assets	–151,486
Foreign-owned assets in China, (increase/financial inflow (+))	**241,215**
Direct investment	138,413
Chinese securities	20,996
Other liabilities	81,806
Statistical discrepancy (sum of above items with sign reversed)	**16,402**

Source: State Administration of Foreign Exchange (2008)

The Chinese current account surplus is one of the largest in the world relative to GDP. It reflects exports of goods and services that amounted to 41.4% of GDP in 2007, while imports of goods and services were a huge, but smaller, 31.9% of GDP. Both figures reflect the high degree of openness of Chinese trade. The current account surplus attracts considerable attention, especially in the United States, which has a large current account deficit. This can be seen in Chart 1, where the current account as a percentage of GDP for 1982–2007 is shown. The current account deficit in the United States is a reverse image of the surplus in China, though this largely reflects the persistence and growth of each balance over the period.

It is this similarity that attracts so much popular interest in both countries, with US critics pointing out that there is a strong link between these two balances and that the US deficit may even be caused by the trade and exchange rate policies that, in their view, hold down the prices of Chinese goods, largely by fixing the yuan–dollar exchange rate, so that US firms and consumers buy a relatively large amount of Chinese exports and export little of their relatively high-priced goods and services to China. As evidence, critics point to a

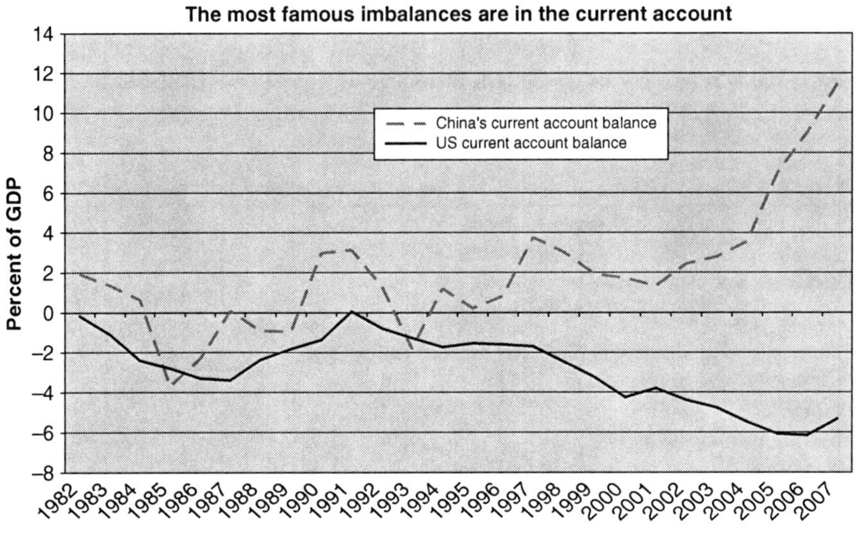

Chart 1 China's and US current account imbalances
Source: US Bureau of Economic Analysis

relatively large build-up of foreign exchange or official reserve assets in China, which they believe indicates the imbalance because the Chinese are willing to allow their central bank, the PBOC, to acquire this excess flow of dollars to China and hold it in very low interest US government securities instead of allowing the yuan to appreciate, which would reduce China's exports/US imports and boost China's imports/US exports to restore balance, or at least move toward balance in each country's current account balance.

There are many errors in this analysis, which render it false. The most basic problems are that trade is only one aspect of international transactions so that attempts to intervene in trade can have undesirable effects on capital flows and on the exchange rate, and, second, trade with one country is not the source of a nation's overall trade imbalance. The latter is influenced by the capital account and by other macroeconomic features of an economy.[2] It is not the purpose here to explore these fallacies, but the data do suggest that US and Chinese international trade in goods and services is dominated by the other. The United States is China's largest trading partner, the number one customer for its exports and the third largest supplier of China's imports, behind Japan and South Korea,

[2] See Tatom (2007) for a discussion of some of the arguments over the US–China trade imbalance and the likely lack of justification and the ineffectiveness of bilateral exchange rate or trade policy actions in eliminating a multilateral imbalance. Cheung et al. (2008) provide supporting evidence that the Renminbi is not misaligned so that efforts to force a currency appreciation are doomed to failure, as they did earlier (2007). See also Bailey and Lawrence (2006).

respectively. China trade is a significant share of the US current account deficit.[3] The United States does not play as large a role in China's capital flows except for the purchases of the PBOC purchases of US government securities which are a large share of the overall capital outflows.

2 The Capital Account Imbalance

Table 1 shows the Chinese capital account in 2007. It is included to provide the more detailed components of the capital flows discussed here. First note that it is officially called the "financial" account and that there is, in fact, another account called the "capital" account. The real capital account in the official balance of payments statistics of countries is for movements of real capital items, particularly (gifts), of used equipment across borders. It is typically very small. The capital transactions of interest here are the acquisition or sales of financial assets, especially for direct investment abroad or for foreign direct investment, or portfolio investment in bonds and stocks, or in bank deposits or loans. These financial transactions are lumped together as capital inflows or outflows here, and their net balance is referred to as the capital balance here.

Some countries, including China, do not include official reserve balances in the financial account, and, instead, account for these "below the line" as the financing item for any remaining balance of payments. The Chinese account is rearranged here to include them in the financial account. Central banks typically hold most of their foreign exchange in US Treasury securities.

2.1 China's Capital and Foreign Exchange Transactions

The simplified table for China in 2007 is given in Table 2 based on this more detailed information. The table also shows the current account balance in order to show the relationship to the capital account, and it shows the change in reserves, which are a large component of the overall capital inflow into the United States. In 2007, US capital inflows were US $1.9 trillion, or 13.4% of GDP, with almost one-quarter of that coming from Chinese purchases of US government securities for their foreign exchange reserves. One problem with the growing US capital inflows is that an increasing share of inflows is due to foreign central banks acquiring US government securities as an instrument for holding their growing foreign exchange holdings. This is especially true

---

[3] In 2007, the US current account deficit with China was US $289.7 billion, 39.2% of the overall US current account deficit. China's leading trade partner, the United States, accounts for 32.5% of China's trade in goods and services, while the United States' top trade partner, Canada, accounts for 16.8% of US trade; China, accounts for 10.3%.

Table 2 China has relatively large capital inflows

China balance of payments 2007		
(Billions of US dollars)	China	% GDP
Capital inflows	$241.2	7.4%
Capital outflows	170.8	5.3
Capital balance	70.4	2.1
Current account balance	371.8	11.5
Change in reserve assets	461.7	14.2

Source: State Administration for Foreign Exchange

for China, for example, which added US $461.7 billion to its reserve assets in 2007 alone and has accumulated about US $1.8 trillion in reserve assets.

If the US capital inflow and surplus is due to foreigners financing the US trade deficit, then the United States remains exposed to the potentially growing unwillingness of foreign monetary authorities, especially the Chinese, to holding larger and larger amounts of relatively low-interest rate US government securities.[4] The large size of these additions to reserves each year is a risk to the US economy, because these securities yield relatively low returns to foreign central banks, and there is currency risk, especially in recent years that makes holding these dollar-denominated securities a poor return asset for many foreign central banks. The addition of these assets to foreign central bank balance sheets also has other adverse consequences abroad. Expanding central bank reserves also expands the monetary base and the domestic money stock, and this in turn creates higher inflation in the country. Because of these consequences, foreign central banks, especially the PBOC, could reduce their holdings of dollar-denominated assets by refusing to acquire them or by substituting other foreign exchange assets for dollars. This could have a substantial effect on the value of the dollar and the level of US interest rates, in the view of some analysts. However, simply switching the currency in which to hold reserves would have little or no effect on the currency markets, according to most analyses. Suppose China did this, then the supply of currencies it acquires would fall relative to dollars in the rest of the world, and this would put upward pressure on the value of the dollar elsewhere so that there would be little or no effect on the value of the dollar or US interest rates overall.

The other reaction of central banks acquiring what is viewed as excessive and perhaps increasingly risky dollar-denominated assets, ending the reserve accumulation in dollars or any other currency, would lead to an appreciation of the

[4] Phillips (2008) suggests that the overall US capital inflow is at risk because of concerns over future policy or simply the large indebtedness of the United States to the rest of the world. The diversification, liquidity, return, and safety benefits to foreign investors in the United States are not written in stone, and policy discussions and decisions over the past year raise doubts about the extent of those benefits in the future. The concentration of foreign exchange holding in a single increasingly risky name is more likely to be the tripwire for adverse global capital market developments.

local currency vis-à-vis the dollar, with all the macroeconomic effects that this would have on the domestic country as well as on the United States.

In China, capital inflows and outflows are a larger share of GDP than in many countries. The capital inflows are especially large as foreign investors are attracted by the openness of trade and the attractive cost of resources relative to productivity in China. Foreign direct investment in China in 2007 was US $138.4 billion, more than half the total capital inflows. This flow compares favorably with the US total foreign direct investment of US $204.4 billion, which is only about 11% of the total US capital inflow that year. China's attractiveness for foreign direct investment leads that of emerging markets and most of the world.

In most countries, especially those with floating exchange rates, the capital account balance typically mirrors the current account and is often the driving force determining the current account balance. It is the overall balancing item in such a country, where there is little government or central bank intervention in the foreign exchange market and little or no attempt for any other reason to manage international reserves. Exchange rates are allowed to adjust so that the balance of payments balances without any required intervention by the central bank. The capital account balance is not the balancing item in a country like China, however. Indeed, the Chinese capital account balance usually shows a surplus, as seen in Chart 2. Thus the dollars that flow into China to pay for exports are not fully used to purchase imports, and those dollars are not used to buy foreign assets, on net, either. Instead, the net dollar flow from trading goods and services is supplemented by the net dollar flow arising from the net flow of dollars to acquire China's assets. The key balancing item in the Chinese

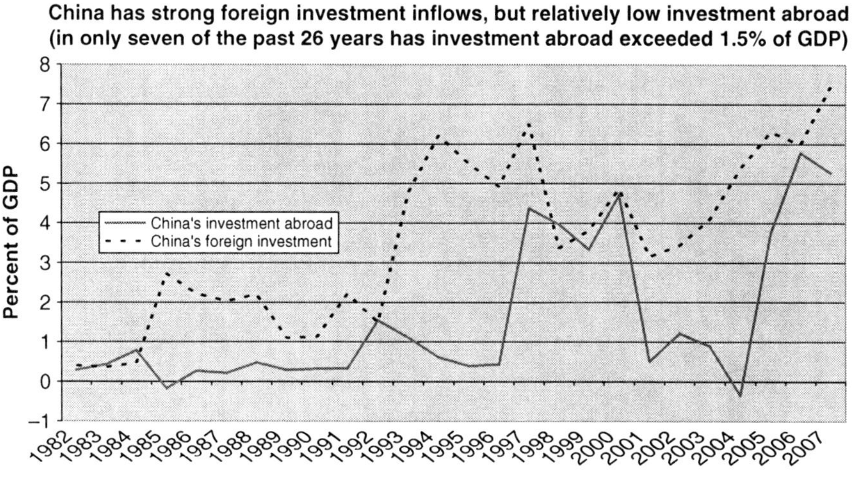

Chart 2 China has strong capital flows, but outflows are relatively weak
Source: International Monetary Fund and State Administration for Foreign Exchange

balance of payments is the official reserve assets, which reflect the rate of addition to official reserve assets. This is part of the fixed exchange rate system that China followed from 1994 to 2005 and a continuing component of exchange rate and monetary policy under the managed float policy followed since then.

Rather than a capital account deficit, which would represent China's net purchases of assets abroad, including acquisition of foreign currency balances in foreign bank accounts, China has a persistent capital account surplus. This is the major "imbalance" in the capital account that can be identified in this paper, and it feeds or enlarges the third Chinese imbalance, the large and growing accumulation of reserve assets. China's balance of payments has the classic appearance of a "mercantilist" nation aiming to enrich itself by accumulating official reserve assets by exporting its goods, services, and capital to accumulate gold or other foreign exchange reserves. The welfare losses associated with such policies date back at least to Adam Smith's classic work (1776).

The official reserve asset imbalance is shown in Chart 3, along with its principal sources, the current account and capital account balances; the other source of the change in foreign exchange reserves is "errors and omissions," which is not shown. China persistently accumulates foreign exchange, indeed it is an accelerating annual share of GDP despite rapid GDP growth. So much so, that by the end of 2007 the PBOC held US $1.5 trillion of foreign exchange, almost one half year's GDP, and growing rapidly. While the chart indicates that it is the accelerating current account balance that accounts for most of the explosive growth of reserves since 2004, the capital account also played a significant role over most of the past 25 years.

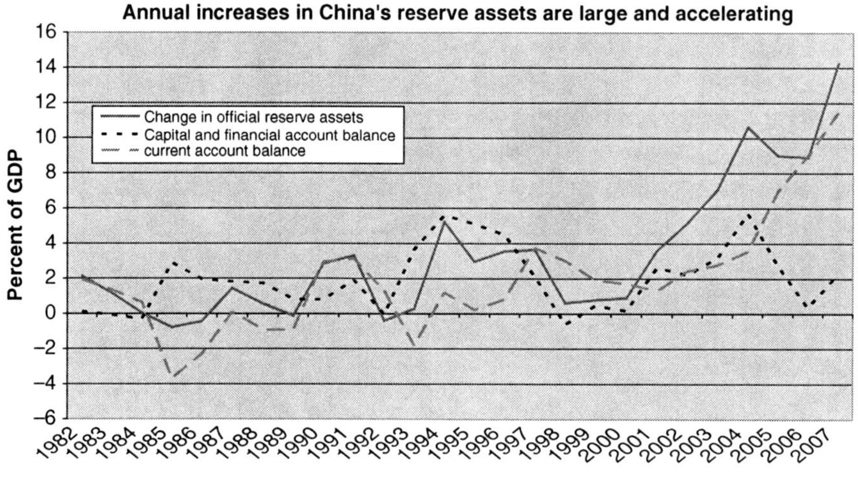

Chart 3 Chinese official reserve assets are accumulating at an accelerating rate

One perspective on the excessive level and growth of reserves is provided by a comparison of foreign exchange assets to the external spending of a nation. Credit analysts often evaluate a country's foreign exchange assets by comparing them to imports of goods and services; the standard criteria that a country has adequate reserves if they exceed 3 months or one quarter of a year's imports. The indicator suggests that the country could pay for its imports for 3 months in a crisis in which it could not obtain credit or earn foreign exchange by exporting. In China's case, the nation could meet such a crisis and cover its imports of goods, services, and assets for over a year. Chart 4 shows that China's foreign exchange (the most liquid component of official reserves, so not including gold or other international reserve assets) have grown to exceed not only its annual imports of goods and services, so four times an adequate level, but more than its purchases of goods, services, and assets abroad. At nearly 50% of GDP, China's foreign exchange is the highest in the world measured relative to GDP.

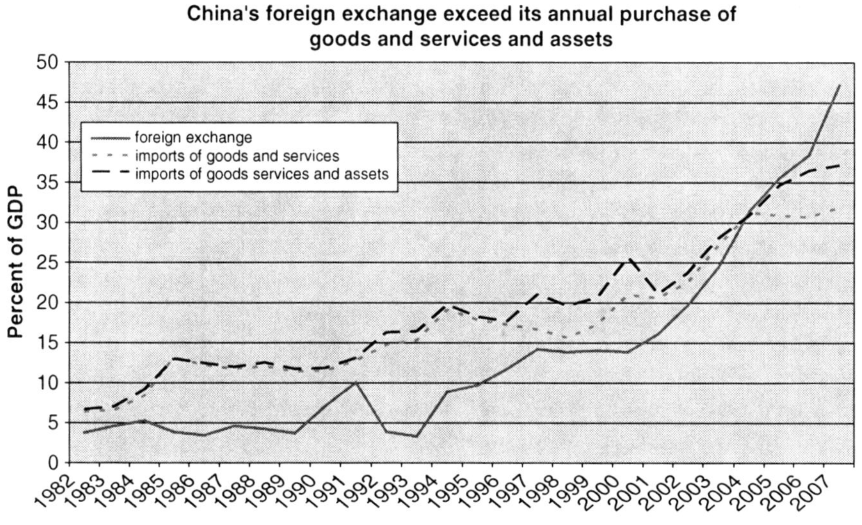

Chart 4 China's foreign exchange reserves are large relative to its annual foreign expenditures

3 Potential Remedies

The potential remedies for international transaction imbalances depend upon identifying the imbalances that are of concern. Commonly identified imbalances that have been examined here are the Chinese trade imbalances, the excessive Chinese capital account balance, and the foreign exchange level and growth in China. The second issue concerns the possibility of either country to unilaterally change these imbalances by actions directed at the other. A country's transactions with the rest of the world are in part determined by its macroeconomic performance relative to the rest of the world so that taking action to alter the economic relationship with one country simply results in substitutions of transactions with other nations. An example of this is the proposal of many US critics of the outsized imports from China who believe that actions to push up the value of the yuan will reduce those imports, improve the US trade balance, and also reduce the pace of Chinese accumulation of US government securities, thereby slowing growth of the Chinese money supply and reducing inflation. It is the case that a government can intervene in the market for its currency and bring about a change in its value, at least within limits. But such change would simply make it likely that the now more expensive Chinese goods would be replaced by cheaper imports from China's competitors, especially other Asian producers in Indonesia, Vietnam, the Philippines, and elsewhere. An appreciation of the yuan is not likely to have much effect on the US trade imbalance; it would simply move it from China to other nations.

An appreciation of the yuan against all currencies would reduce China's trade surplus and could reduce pressures on foreign exchange reserve growth, money growth, and inflation, but it would also disrupt production and employment at many domestic firms, and, more importantly, it could produce a speculative surge in capital inflows and make the capital account, monetary policy, and inflation problems worse and create a potential for a future reversal of the capital flow and currency collapse reminiscent of the patterns associated with the 1997–1998 Asian crisis.[5] Concern for the avoidance of a surge in portfolio investment and subsequent outflow is probably the second main reason for China's fixed exchange rate regime from 1994 until 2005.[6] The principal reason was to provide a monetary anchor for monetary policy and inflation. Thus, a policy of appreciation of the yuan would have little effect on the US trade imbalance, and it could have serious adverse risks on the Chinese economy within a few years.

There are several remedies that ultimately rely for their effectiveness on slowing the US and rest of the world (ROW) growth (slower import growth, improved relative prices for exports relative to imports, reduced rates of return to capital, and foreign investment) or faster growth in China. Countries do not consciously choose slower economic growth, and countries growing at their

---

[5] Goldstein and Lardy (2008) argue that the Chinese have not appreciated their currency enough since the amount allowed so far has been accompanied by a growing current account surplus and an acceleration on foreign exchange growth.

[6] Capital controls typically apply to inflows, but putting restrictions on inflows or outflows reduce incentives for foreigners to invest in a country. Chilean restrictions on capital inflows outflows from 1991-98 were expected to insulate the country from the sudden stops of capital inflows associated with the financial crises in Asia. Instead, the restrictions acted as a disincentive to invest in the country and the undesired fall in the capital account balance was accomplished by a surge in outflows instead of a decline in inflows. See Forbes (2007) for evidence of how these restrictions also raised the cost of capital for smaller traded domestic firms and Gallego et al. (2000) and Cowan and De Gregorio (2005) for overviews and lessons from the Chilean experience.

capacity rates are not easily encouraged to pursue inflationary policies or policies that waste resources in order to gain some short-term output gain. Countries sometimes do take up protectionist policies that indirectly slow growth and reduce current account deficits and capital account balances, but such actions damage domestic business and citizens and so have little to recommend them.

The most obvious step that the Chinese could take is to open up the capital account.[7] Beginning in February 2007, current account transactions were liberalized so that Chinese businesses, both domestic and non-domestic, could freely move foreign exchange across the border for import or export purposes. The same is not true for capital account transactions, especially capital outflows.[8] Capital outflows are quite limited for Chinese households and investors. That is a primary reason for the small capital outflows, even in recent years. Removing restrictions would reduce the net capital inflow and foreign exchange build-up in China dollar for dollar with each dollar increase in capital outflow, probably turning net inflows into net outflows. Such a reduction in the foreign exchange build-up would reduce asset growth at the PBOC and the associated pressure on the money supply and inflation.

Under current Chinese monetary and financial policy, the PBOC has attempted to insulate monetary growth from the increase in foreign exchange by raising reserve requirements at banks. In effect, the People's Bank increased bank reserves by buying up the dollars coming into the country and then raised reserve requirements so that banks would have to hold these reserves instead of

[7] Cappiello and Ferrucci (2008) focus on the importance of opening the capital account and moving toward a flexible exchange rate as sequenced steps to reduce the opportunity cost of a fixed exchange rate system. They do not single out the benefits of lifting capital outflow restrictions, however, which are emphasized here. People's Bank of China Deputy Governor Xiang (2006) provides an excellent review of China's financial sector and economic development and outlines the next steps to be taken. He notes the importance of a harmonious relation between economic development and development of the financial sector. He also points to the importance of developing internal financial markets and opening the sector to global competition.

[8] Chinese authorities have made recent changes in tax incentives for capital inflows that will reduce such investments, but these changes are strongly in the interest of promoting economic efficiency and equality and may actually boost the attractiveness of investing in China. Earlier, in order to promote direct investment, tax incentives were given that lowered the income tax rate paid by foreign firms. These may have been successful in priming the pump for foreign investment, but they misallocated capital and other resources within the economy. Ending those subsides will improve the integrity of the tax system and of economic policy, even if they have a slight negative effect on capital inflows. Unfortunately, regulators have offset the benefits of these steps by tightening restrictions on majority or even minority ownership of foreign acquisitions in the financial services industry and by regulatory delays in approving such acquisitions. Regulators have also cracked down on capital inflows that have come from inflated invoicing of exports, forcing more rapid and exact documentation to convert dollar receipts into Renminbi. Making foreign investment subject to changing and arbitrary rules, as well as limiting the potential for control of domestic financial firms severely diminishes the attraction of investing in China.

being able to lend them out, expanding credit and deposits. Of course, the reserve requirement increases were not fully offsetting so that money, credit, and inflation have accelerated in the past several years despite these efforts. Reserve requirements at large Chinese banks have been raised steadily since July 2006 when the reserve ratio was 8%, to more than double that burden, 17.5% in June 2007. Such increases substantially affect the cost, efficiency, competitiveness, and profitability of domestic banks. For every yuan of deposits, banks now must hold 0.175 yuan in non-interest-bearing reserves and are able to cover the interest and other costs of these deposits by lending out the remaining 0.825 yuan. These increases in reserve requirements have left Chinese banks with reserve requirement costs that are among the highest in the world, despite a global trend toward reducing or eliminating reserve requirements in order to boost international competitiveness among banks.

Associated with the restrictions on financial markets, Chinese monetary authorities also limit the interest rates that banks can pay depositors and that they can charge on loans. In April 2006, before the central bank began to attempt to restrain the growth of money and credit, banks could pay 2.25% on deposits and could not charge more than 5.31% on loans. Both of these rates were higher than the 1.2% inflation rate over the previous year. As reserve requirements rose, reducing banks' spreads or margins on loans, and as inflation rose, monetary authorities raised both rates but raised deposit rates by less and both rates by less than inflation rose. By December 2007, the lending rate had been raised to 7.47%, while the rate paid to depositors had risen to 4.14%, with the latter substantially below the inflation rate of 6.5%. Inflation accelerated in 2008, further reducing the negative real rate earned by depositors and reducing the real lending rate to negative territory. Banks lost profitability due to these changes, and depositors lost as well. If borrowers can obtain credit, they face negative real interest rates, but in a regulated environment such as this one, interest rates cannot be used to allocate credit, and so scarce credit does not go to its highest valued social use.

In this environment, harmonious workings of financial markets become less likely. Savers are exploited by a financial system that offers negative returns and no access to higher yield opportunities domestically or abroad, so firms face credit rationed by criteria other than interest rates or profitability of the use of scarce credit, and banks are caught in the middle, earning lower returns and higher costs than their competitors abroad or other domestic business. The inefficiencies and waste of resources that are created by all of these regulations and inflation have been characterized as repressed financial markets, and such markets are a major obstacle to growth.[9] Lifting restrictions on capital outflows would end the circumstances (growth of foreign exchange reserves, money, credit, and inflation) that have given rise to the more extensive repression of financial markets in China.

---

[9] See Beim and Calomiris (2001) for an extended discussion of the conditions and effects of repressed financial markets.

Allowing greater freedom for domestic investors to diversify wealth portfolios by investing abroad would reduce the problems that Chinese imbalances create for China. It would push the capital account balance toward deficit. It would also reduce the size and growth of China's huge holding of foreign exchange in low-return US government securities. It would also raise returns on Chinese wealth, reduce risk, improve the financial system, and ease the pressures on the exchange rate, monetary policy, and inflation. Increasing Chinese private capital outflows would also switch the accumulation of foreign exchange assets in the United States to private financial assets. In one sense this is simply switching the composition of assets from US government securities to stocks, bonds, and bank deposits in the United States. However, this diversification benefits the United States by reducing the concentration of exposures to China. It also would put upward pressure on the US dollar because the asset demands of China would be desired portfolio or direct investments instead of residual purchases arising from excessive dollar flows into China.

Capital outflows from a country are aimed at improving the rate of return on domestic wealth and/or reducing risk of these returns, sometimes simply through diversification, or from relatively attractive profit opportunities. Domestic business can expand markets and access to foreign resources through direct investment abroad. Exposure to foreign markets increases productivity of domestic firms because of exposure to more demanding and more diverse markets abroad and because of new knowledge and capabilities of foreign technology and resources. In the case of the domestic financial market, international capital outflows provide significant competition, providing opportunities for upgrading productivity, rates of return and risk reduction through better products, or better processes for management of domestic resources. Outflows of capital for foreign portfolio investment are imports of capital and act in much the same way as imports of goods and services in terms of influencing competitive pressures, offering new products and technologies and new ideas of how to better serve domestic financial customers.

One of the biggest development problems facing China is the upgrading of its financial system and making it globally competitive.[10] China's outstanding growth record stands in marked contrast to its largely state-owned, failed financial institutions. While most analysts argue that China is the exception, it is not. The same arguments have been made in other more open Asian economies (see Rohwer 1995); the evidence suggests that Asian growth success has come despite the backward financial markets, which held back even greater

[10] Demirguc-Kunt and Levine (2008b) provide a detailed review of the literature on the finance-growth linkage and they provide new evidence that government policies have significant effects on the operations of the financial system and on access to financial services by large segments of the population. Their review shows that "The services provided by the financial system exert a first-order impact on long-run economic growth." (p. 2).

growth.[11] Chinese government recapitalization of large banks in recent years yielded well-capitalized state-majority owned banking firms, but without directly addressing the incentive problems of state-owned companies and the institutional framework that led to the predominance of policy lending by domestic banks and the pattern of insolvent banks. China has entered a brief window of opportunity in which to make the banking system efficient and competitive before the earlier problems of insolvency and inefficiency return. Increased competition from internationally competitive banks is the most direct route to achieving the desired high quality, sustainably profitable financial institutions.[12]

China has a captive financial market because of restrictions on capital outflows. Investors have essentially three options for unusually high saving: saving at highly regulated banks at extremely low rates of interest or investing in their own proprietary firms, or investing in asset accumulation at home, especially in housing, but again restrictions on financing put this option out of the reach of typical households. Investing in entrepreneurial activity is the most risky option, but given the incredibly low rate of interest payable at banks this is an attractive option. Even before the explosion of foreign exchange, money, credit, and inflation, and the consequent steps to offset some of these problems by reserve requirement changes detailed above, onerous restrictions on bank pricing created political and business incentives that restrained the growth of vibrant and competitive financial markets. Opening capital outflows would create new wealth creation opportunities for investors, banks, business, and government, and it would create strong pressures from all of these groups, especially banks initially damaged by enhanced competition, to reduce excessive regulation of banks and to develop a profitable and competitive sector. By enhancing the performance of the financial system, such a policy would reduce inequality and reduce poverty.[13]

There has been some progress on this front, especially for direct investment. But the few notable steps prove that these are exceptional. In 2008, the most prominent direct outflows from China to the United States have been the approval of New York branches for China Construction Bank and, on

---

[11] Some analysts argue that Asia, or at least China, is the exception to the rule that the quality of financial institutions is a critical determinant of economic growth and development. Maksimovic et al. (2008) find evidence that formal financial institution finance is associated with faster firm growth, but funds raised from alternative channels is not. Moreover, they find that this result is not due to the selection process for firms that have access to formal financial institutions.

[12] Porter (1998) emphasized the role of competition in open goods markets for upgrading the competitiveness of domestic enterprise and boosting economic growth. In the case of financial services firms, such improved competitiveness will arise through the import of capital from abroad.

[13] Demirguc-Kunt and Levine (2008a) provide evidence that the more developed the financial system is the lower is income inequality and poverty and the greater is access by low income households to financial services.

August 5, 2008, for the Industrial and Commercial Bank of China. The latter is the biggest bank in China and it is 74.8% owned by the People's Republic of China. China Aluminum Company (Chinalco) acquired almost 15% of Rio Tinto, the Australian mining firm, in February 2008 for almost US $15 billion and proposed to acquire 11% more in August 2008. Haier was rumored in the financial press to be acquiring GE's small appliance division, and Lenovo is rumored to be acquiring the remainder of IBM's consumer products division.

Earlier notable Chinese investments in the United States include Lenovo's acquisition of IBM's laptop business, Haier's opening of a US headquarters and sales operation for small consumer appliances, and, until its July 2008 sale to its partner Cleveland Clifts, United Mining Company's, a subsidiary of Chinese steelmaker Laiwu, 30% ownership of United Taconite. Of course there are other Chinese companies in the United States, but the list is not long. In one sense, it is very impressive that there is direct investment from China in the United States; other emerging markets are more focused on developing their own business sector and do not expect to have profitable opportunities from expanding abroad.

The greater opportunity for deregulation of the capital account would come from allowing investors to access financial assets abroad, either directly or through lifting of restrictions on Chinese financial firms offerings of foreign financial assets. In August 2007, China surprised markets by allowing private citizens open access to investment in the Hong Kong equity market. This had a large impact on outflows from the mainland to the Special Administrative Region. This action, referred to as the "through train" policy, was halted in November 2007 but not before Hong Kong's Hang Seng Index rose 55%. It is unclear when this outlet will resume. But full liberalization would likely make a huge dent in China's stock of international reserves over time, and it would ease pressures on the yuan, the US dollar, China's inflation, and risks to the international financial system. Moreover, allowing full access to foreign assets through mainland firms would greatly boost the banking system's competition and lead more directly to improvement in the competitiveness of China's financial industry.

4 Summary and Conclusions

China has been at the heart of global discussions of international imbalances in economic relations. China has three major imbalances: a trade surplus, a capital account surplus and a large annual build-up, and very high level of international reserves. Moreover, foreign central banks, with the PBOC being the leader, have a large annual growth in holdings of US government securities, which they hold as foreign exchange reserves. In large part, the attention to the bilateral relations of the United States and China is due to the central role that the dollar has played in China's exchange rate system; the Renminbi was pegged to the US dollar as the anchor for Chinese monetary policy from 1994 to 2005 and has remained the key currency in its managed float since then. But the other reason for attention to this bilateral relation is political and business concern that China's exports are responsible for US imports and for the trade imbalances in both countries.

Capital flows, especially flows of US government securities, are also important in assessing the bilateral and overall imbalances in transactions for China and the United States. What stands out here is that China has a capital account surplus to go along with its current account surplus, reinforcing its accumulation of foreign exchange reserves, mainly US dollar denominated assets. This is unusual for several reasons. Most important is that countries with large current account surpluses usually run deficits in their capital accounts, as excess foreign exchange that is not used to buy imports are used to purchase, on net, assets abroad. For example, Switzerland, which exports more relative to GDP and has a larger current account balance on this basis, runs a corresponding deficit in its capital account, as relatively large domestic saving, capital inflows, and large foreign exchange inflows on its current account are used to acquire assets abroad for its domestic and international investors. The reverse offsetting balance—a current account deficit and capital account surplus—is observed in the United States.

It should be noted that this is a more "normal" pattern for a rapidly growing merging market economy—a current account deficit and a capital surplus, because such countries demand superior quality foreign resources, materials, and capital goods to expand capacity, and hence they have current account deficits, and they also offer global investors relatively high rates of return so that the country will have net foreign investment in their countries. Some of China's major competitors had such a pattern before the Asian crisis in 1997–1998, but its increased sensitivity to a reversal of capital inflows has led them to pursue slower growth and to run surpluses in trade and continuing outflows of capital, on net. China's special circumstances have allowed the authorities to indulge an even stronger sense of security by building reserves that even some of its Asian competitors could not afford.

The worst consequences of imbalances have been the build-up of large, low-return foreign exchange that has actually had negative returns since the managed float began in 2005. These reserves have led to rapid growth in money and credit and, in turn, to a sharp acceleration in inflation, something that China had assiduously avoided since 1994 and that has raised serious doubts about the credibility of the monetary authorities and damaged its inflation-fighting reputation. Moreover, efforts to offset money growth and inflation have exposed and deepened existing inefficiencies in the financial system, which China had hoped to begin remedying by its efforts to recapitalize and list its banks' equities on stock exchanges.

China could attempt to eliminate these imbalances by restricting its openness or subsidizing imports, but such policies would reduce growth. Ironically, Chinese policy makers could boost growth and aim to increase consumer and business demand for imports, but this too would lead to costly resource misallocations and would be challenged by greater foreign investment inflows. China could also try to limit capital inflows, but this would restrict the ability to import technology, organizational, and other human capital that accompanies foreign investment. Limiting portfolio inflows would reduce the efficiency and liquidity of financial markets, raising the cost of scarce capital resources.

The most obvious solution proposed here is to lift restrictions on capital outflows, allowing households and business to diversify their wealth holdings to realize higher returns and/or less volatility in their own income and wealth. This would soak up excess foreign exchange and transform future asset growth from massive central bank holdings of US government securities to holdings of more attractive assets in the United States or elsewhere. Such a step would eliminate the pressures on the PBOC, allowing for more rapid deregulation of banks, slower money, and credit growth and slower inflation.

References

Bailey Martin N. and Robert Z. Lawrence, "Can America Still Compete or Does It Need a New Paradigm?" Peter G. Peterson Institute for International Economics *Policy Brief*, No. 4–9, December 2006.

Beim David O. and Charles W. Calomiris, *Emerging Financial Markets*, New York: McGraw Hill/Irwin, 2001.

Cappiello Lorenzo and Gianluigi Ferrucci, "The Sustainability of China's Exchange Rate Policy and Capital Account Liberalization," European Central Bank Occasional Paper No. 82, March 2008.

Cheung Yin-Wong, Menzie David Chinn and Eiji Fujii, "Pitfalls in Measuring Exchange Rate Misalignment: The Yuan and Other Currencies," National Bureau of Economic Research Working Paper No. 14168, July, 2008.

Cheung Yin-Wong, Menzie David Chinn and Eiji Fujii, "The Overvaluation of Renminbi Undervaluation," National Bureau of Economic Research Working Paper 12850, June 2007.

Cowan, Kevin and Jose De Gregorio, "International Borrowing, Capital Controls and the Exchange Rate: Lessons from Chile," National Bureau of Economic Research Working Paper No. 11382, May, 2005.

Demirguc-Kunt Asli and Ross Levine, "Finance and Economic Opportunity," World Bank Policy Research Working Paper No. 4468, January 2008a.

Demirguc-Kunt Asli and Ross Levine, "Finance, Financial Sector Policies, and Long-Run Growth," World Bank Policy research Working Paper No. 4469, January 2008b.

Forbes Kristin J., "One Cost of the Chilean Capital Controls: Increased Financial Constraints for Smaller traded Firms," *Journal of International Economics* 71, April 2007.

Gallego Francisco A., Leonardo Hernandez, and Klaus Schmidt-Hebbel, "Capital Controls in Chile: Effective? Efficient?" Econometric Society World Congress 2000 contributed paper No. 0330, 2000.

Goldstein Morris and Nicholas Lardy, "China's Currency Needs to Rise Further," Financial Times, July 23, 2008.

International Monetary Fund, International Financial Statistics, July 2008 and Various Earlier Issues.

Maksimovic Vojislav, Asli Demirguc-Kunt, and Meghana Ayyagari, "Formal vs. Informal Finance: Evidence form China," World Bank Policy Research Working Paper No. 4465, January 2008.

Phillips Michael M., "Capital Flow From Emerging Nations to U.S. Poses Some Risks," *The Wall Street Journal*, June 23, 2008.

Porter Michael E., *The Competitive Advantage of Nations*, New York: Simon and Schuster Adult Publishing Group, June 1998.

Rohwer Jim, *Asia Rising*, London: Nicholas Brealey Publishing, 1995.

Smith Adam and Andrew Skinner, *An Inquiry into the Nature and Causes of the Wealth of Nations*, Penguin Classics edition, 1982, original 1776.

State Administration for Foreign Exchange, "China's Balance of Payments Maintains a Twin Surplus in 2007," *SAFE News*, June 5. 2008.

Tatom John A. "The US-China Currency Dispute: Is a Rise in the Yuan Inevitable, Necessary or Desirable?" *Global Economy Journal*, 17(3), article 2, pp. 1–13, 2007.

Xiang Junbo, "Harmonious Financial Development: The Expectations of the World's Economy and Financial Industry," Speech at the Opening Ceremony of the Lujiazui Financial Culture Week and Lujiazui International Financial Forum, reprinted by *Risk News*, December 11, 2006.

Some Issues Regarding China's Foreign Reserves

Jie Li, Jing Chen, and Liqing Zhang

Abstract This chapter answers some interesting questions on China's foreign reserve holdings: Are they excessive? Why so much? How to invest them? We first use the popular reserve adequacy measures to examine if China's foreign reserve holdings are excessive. All the exercises suggest that China is holding too much reserves. We then analyze the motive of reserve holdings from a new aspect: foreign reserve holdings could be self-augmented. We also investigate the problem of how to set up a better portfolio for foreign reserve investment. The simulation in our model suggests that if foreign reserves are used to hedge against potential macroeconomic risks, it may raise the social utility by 56%.

Keywords Foreign reserves · Adequacy · Self-augmented · Investment strategy

1 Introduction

The financial turmoil in international financial markets in the 1990s and the early years of the twenty-first century has motivated academia, central bankers, and practitioners to rethink about international financial architecture. In the 1990s, with the significant reduction of the restrictions on international capital movements, capital mobility has been greatly increased worldwide, among emerging markets in particular. Meanwhile, maintaining stable exchange rates to gain competitiveness in exports had been emerging markets' top priority. Pegging-greenback exchange rate regime was quite popular before the Asian financial crises. However, the "impossible trinity" tells us that pegging is not sustainable with high capital mobility and independent monetary policies. Therefore, when those Asian emerging markets' current accounts deteriorated

J. Li (✉)
Central University of Finance and Economics, Beijing, China
e-mail: jieli.cn@gmail.com

J.R. Barth et al. (eds.), *China's Emerging Financial Markets*,
The Milken Institute Series on Financial Innovation and Economic Growth 8,
DOI 10.1007/978-0-387-93769-4_10, © 2009 by Milken Institute

with the appreciation of U.S. greenback, their pegging rates were under serious currency attacks, which in turn led to currency crises.

Rebuilding international financial architecture after the crises has called for flexibility of exchange rate regimes and foreign reserve holding. One of the most important lessons we learnt from the crises is that sufficient foreign reserve holdings can serve as a buffer stock when currency is under attack. Protecting domestic currencies from future attacks boosts the precautionary demand for foreign reserves (Aizenman, 2007). However, reserve holdings in Asian countries, among other emerging markets (Fig. 1), are so significant that even precautionary demand motive may not be sufficient to explain.

(US$ billions)

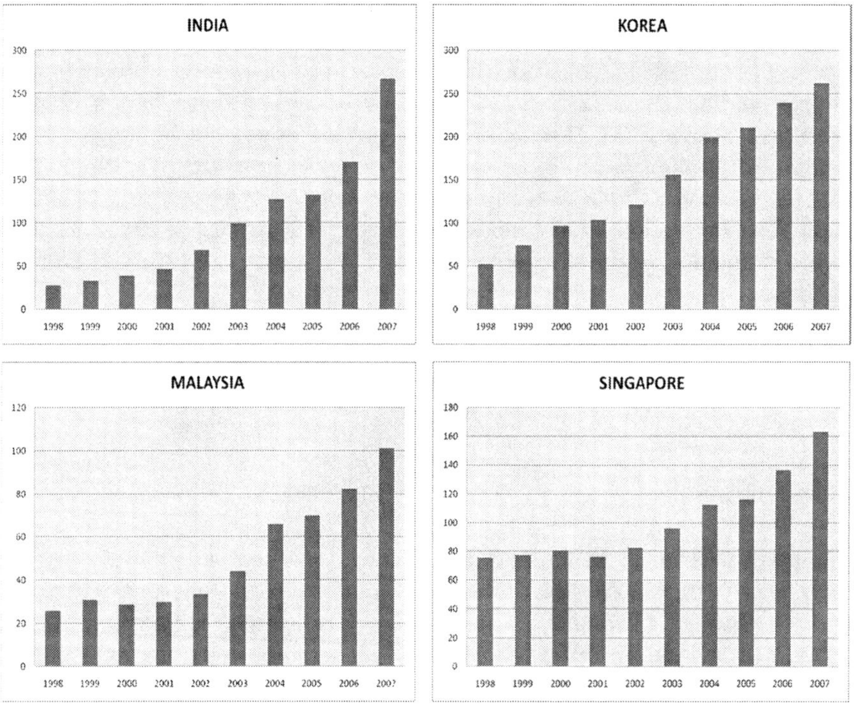

Fig. 1 Trends of reserve holding among Asian countries.
Source: BIU Country Data

Among those reserve holding countries, China is the most striking one in terms of her massive scale of reserves in relation to imports, short-term external debt, and M2 (Figs. 2, 3, 4, and 7). This chapter tries to address the following questions about China's foreign reserves: Are China's reserve holdings excessive? If yes, why? How to deal with it?

Section 2 presents some popular reserve adequacy ratios to measure if China's reserve holdings are excessive. Section 3 surveys the literature about

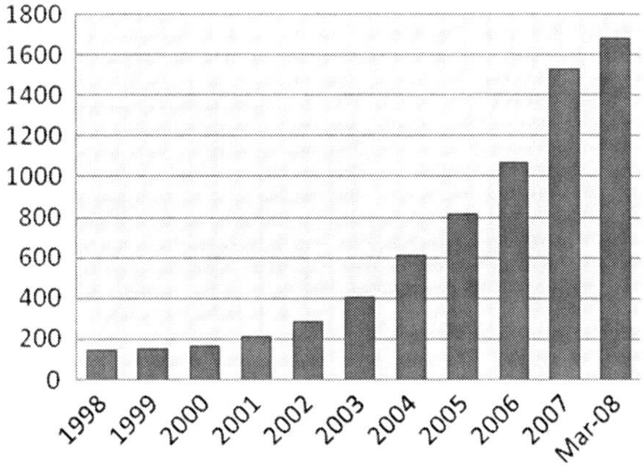

Fig. 2 China's foreign reserve holdings from 1998 to March 2008.
Source: Macrochina Database

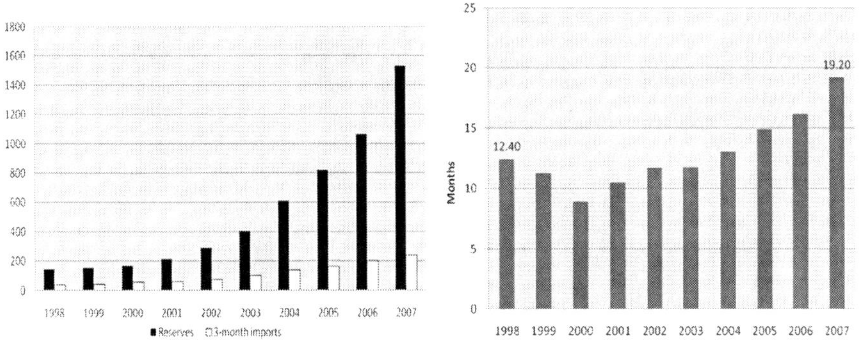

(a) (b)

Fig. 3 China's foreign reserves holdings vs. 3 months of imports.
Source: Macrochina Database

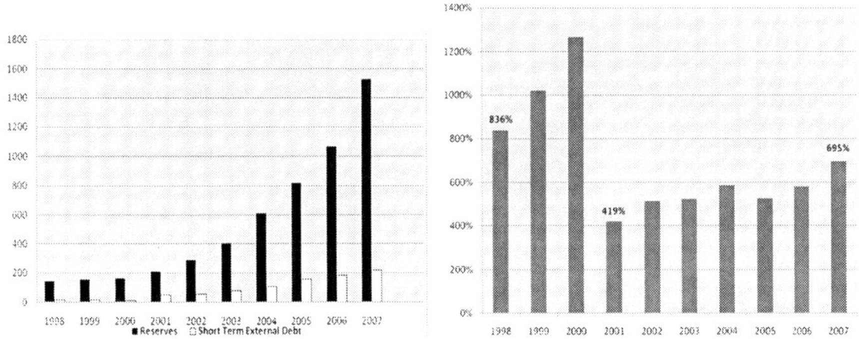

(a) (b)

Fig. 4 China's foreign reserve holdings and short-term external debt.
Source: Macrochina Database

reserve holding motives and tries to derive China's rationale for reserve holdings, while Section 4 proposes a way for China to invest her foreign reserves. Section 5 concludes the chapter.

2 Are China's Foreign Reserves Excessive?

China's foreign reserves climbed to $1682.177 billion at the end of March 2008, the increment of $35.043 billion in a single month, March.[1] Before we can answer the question about the excessiveness of China's foreign reserves, we have to investigate the closely related issue: What is the appropriate reserve adequacy measure for China? In this section, we survey the main reserve adequacy measures in the literature and practical uses, and then we give our judgment on this issue.

There are some rule of thumb indicators to determine the adequate level of foreign reserves. They are quite simple but informative and thus in wide use. These indicators can tell the capability of the foreign reserves to cover external or internal macroeconomic vulnerability. In the following, we will calculate the indicators using the data of China from 1998 to 2007 to test whether China's foreign reserves are excessive.

2.1 Reserves-to-Import Ratio[2]

In the Bretton-Woods system when capital account financial crises were rare, foreign reserves were used to absorb shocks in external payments. Smoothing out external payments, especially current account payments, to avoid the adjustment costs became the primary function of foreign reserves (Willett 1980). The rationale for the reserve–import ratio is that official foreign reserves should be adequate to pay off at least 3 months of imports. Therefore, the amount of reserves is regarded adequate if it is over 3 months of imports.

Figure 3 illustrates the reserve adequacy of China using this measure. In Fig. 3(a), the red bar represents 3-month imports, while the blue bar represents the actual reserve holdings of China. Fig. 3(b) depicts the number of months that the official reserves can pay off its imports at the current level if all the capital flows cease. As noted in Fig. 3(b), in terms of import cover, China's foreign reserves have increased from 12.4 months of imports during 1998 to 19.2 during 2007. Both figures illustrate that China's foreign reserves exceeds the adequate level by huge amounts.

But the limitation of the measure is also obvious. It focuses on current account while ignoring the capital account. It is appropriate to indicate the adequacy level of foreign reserves in the past when there were lots of restrictions

---

[1] Foreign Reserves Statistics from State Administration of Foreign Exchange of China

[2] IMF (2001). "Guidelines for Foreign Exchange Reserve Management" (September 20).

on the movement of capital flows. Meanwhile, it is more relevant to developing countries that are exposed to current account shocks and have limited access to international capital markets. But as the Chinese government is liberalizing its capital accounts gradually, it may not be the best measure to define the reserve adequacy of China.

2.2 Reserves-to-Short-Term External Debt Ratio

Short-term external debt (STED) is a measure of all debt repayment to non-residents due within the coming year. The Reserve-to-STED indicator is known as the Greenspan-Guidotti Rule, which is the most widely used in empirical researches or central banks to measure the vulnerability to capital account crises. The rule says that a country should hold enough foreign reserves to cover its STED. In other words, whenever the ratio of foreign reserves over STED is greater, the country is considered to hold "adequate" reserves. It can be the most important indicator of reserve adequacy in countries which have significant but uncertain access to capital markets.

It should be noted that China adjusted the coverage of foreign debt data significantly in 2001. External liabilities of foreign financial institutions, external trade financing within 3 months, offshore deposits of Chinese banks and medium- and long-term external debts with remaining maturity of less than 1 year are reclassified as short-term debts[3]. Though the size of STED has been increasing from 2001, foreign reserves are still sufficient to cover all short-term liabilities.

As shown in Fig. 4(a) and (b), China's foreign reserves are more than enough to cover all its STED. In addition, the difference between China's foreign reserves and STED is steadily picking up. The ratio of reserves-to-STED shown in Fig. 4(b) was 836% in 1998. It declined to 419% due to the adjustment in coverage of foreign debt and then increased to 635% at the end of 2007.

2.3 Bank of Korea Benchmark

Figure 5 makes it apparent that even if one considers a benchmark of reserve adequacy based on the sum of the 3 months' import and all short-term external debt, China still holds too much foreign reserves.

Aizenman et al (2004) show that in estimating the demand for foreign reserves the variables of trade openness are no longer significant, while short-term foreign debt and foreign shareholdings become significant after the Asian crises. Therefore, a more prudent benchmark for reserve adequacy was set up by the Bank of Korea. It takes into account not only the 3-month import and STED but also 30% of foreigners' holdings of domestic stocks.

---

[3] www.pbc.gov.cn/english//detail.asp?col = 6400&ID = 5 - 18 k

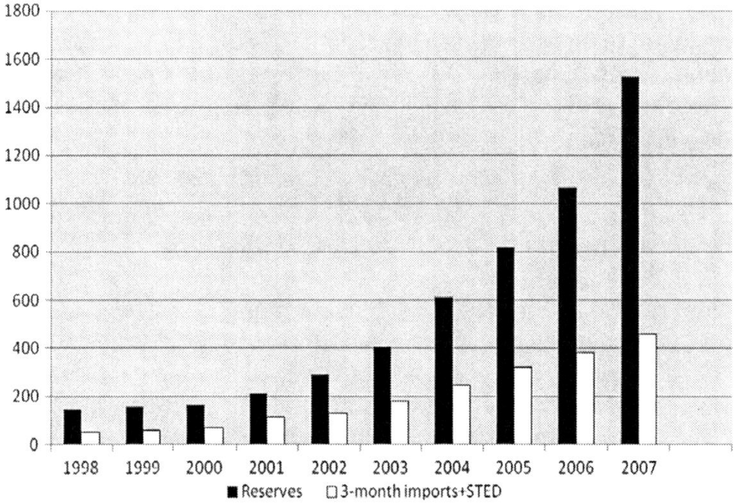

Fig. 5 China's foreign reserves and 3 months of imports plus STED.
Source: Macrochina Database

Figure 6 illustrates the implications of a coverage rule of 3 months' imports, STED, and 30% foreigners' stock holdings. The actual foreign reserve holdings in China are way above the Bank of Korea benchmark after considering the foreigners' holdings of domestic stocks.

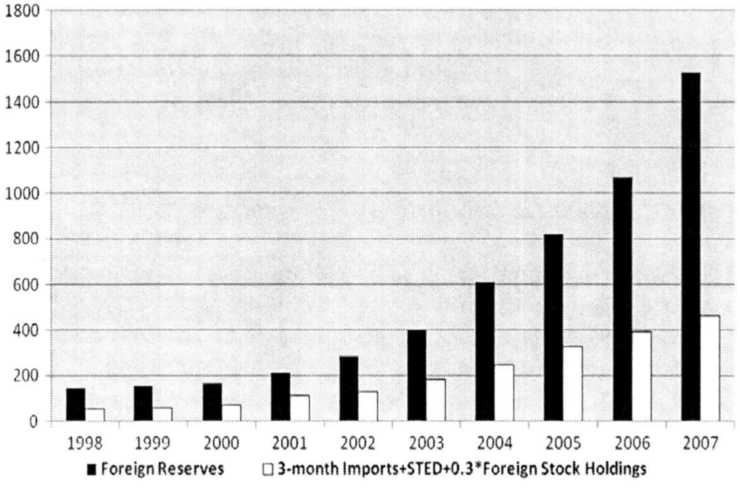

Fig. 6 China's foreign reserves and BOK benchmark
Note: (1) the data of foreign reserves, imports and short-term external debt are from "Macrochina Database," while 3-month imports equal to the annual import divided by 4.
(2) the data of foreign stock holdings from State Admistration of Foreign Exchange of China

2.4 Reserves-to-M2 Ratio

Though the reserves-to-STED ratio has been regarded as an important benchmark to assess the adequacy level of foreign reserves, it fails to take into account the potential capital flight by domestic residents during a financial crisis, the so-called internal vulnerability. Since reserves-to-M2 ratio can be used to capture the capability to cover internal vulnerability of an economy, Wijnholds et al. (2001) argues that one should take 5% of M2 as a threshold for reserve adequacy. As illustrated in Fig. 7, the reserves-to-M2 ratio of China increased from 11.5% in 1998 to 29.5% in 2007. This measure also clearly states that China's reserve holdings are beyond the adequate level.

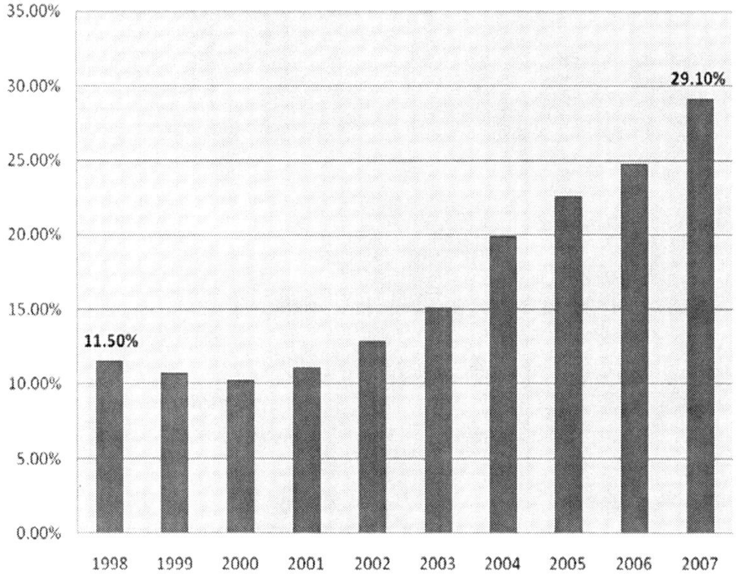

Fig. 7 China's foreign reserves/M2.
Source: Macrochina database

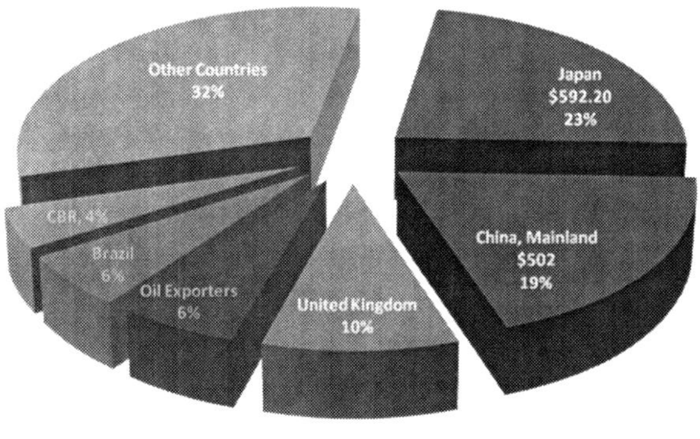

Fig. 8 Major holders of Treasury securities at the end of April 2008.
Source: http://www.treas.gov/tic/ticsec2.shtml

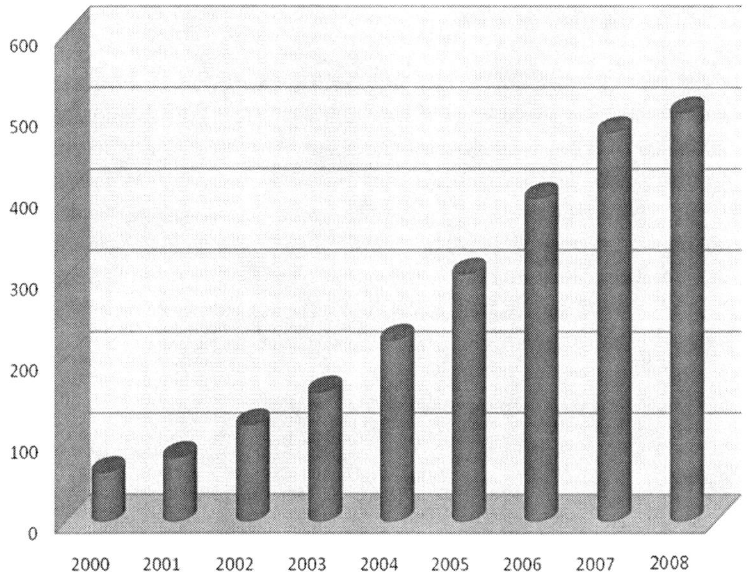

Fig. 9 Treasury securities holdings by China

2.5 Claremont Measures of Reserve Adequacy

Kim et al. (2005)[4] propose new benchmarks of reserve adequacy from replicating potential capital outflows using data during the Asian crises. Since foreign reserves are accumulated to pay off the potential capital flights by foreigners and domestic residents, the potential maximum capital flights can be used as a benchmark for reserve adequacy. During non-crisis years, there are no actual capital flights, so we can only calculate the amounts of capital flights in the past crises and scale them up as the indicators. Kim et al. calculate various capital outflows by taking into account portfolio investment, balance of financial account, and other reversible capital. Moreover, they estimate the maximum amounts of capital outflows in the most crisis-hit countries during the Asian financial crises – Indonesia, Korea, Malaysia, Philippines, and Thailand – by scaling the capital outflows with M2, GDP, and short-term external debt.

Table 1[5] shows capital outflows of the five Asian countries. In Tables 2, 3, 4, 5, and 6, we scale up the outflow figures by using the current M2, GDP, and STED data. For example, if the Indonesian-type crisis hits China in 2007, what would the capital outflows be? The estimates in Table 2 indicate that they would be $ 987.941 billion if scaled by M2, $321.927 billion by GDP, and $129.737

[4] All five authors of this paper are from Claremont Colleges. To differentiate it from others, we call the new measure as Claremont measure.

[5] Table 13 in Kim et al. (2005)

Table 1 Ratios of the greatest capital outflows to M2, GDP, and short-term foreign debt

	Ratio of capital outflow (CO) to three scales		
	Ratio of CO to M2	Ratio of CO to GDP	Ratio of CO to STD
Indonesia	−18.81%	−9.91%	−58.95%
Korea	−24.69%	−9.81%	−78.31%
Malaysia	−4.96%	−4.58%	−41.56%
Philippines	−7.44%	−4.19%	−43.42%
Thailand	−28.07%	−22.68%	−85.59%

Source: http://www.treas.gov/tic/ticsec2.shtml

Table 2 Scaled-up figures of capital outflows under Indonesian-type crisis (US $ billions)

	Scaled-up figures of capital outflows			
Year	Scaled by M2	Scaled by GDP	Scaled by STED	Actual reserve holdings
1998	−237.153	−100.916	−10.2219	144.96
1999	−272.048	−107.201	−8.94861	154.675
2000	−305.784	−118.74	−7.71066	165.574
2001	−359.752	−131.29	−29.8169	212.165
2002	−420.464	−144.082	−32.8941	286.407
2003	−502.277	−162.469	−45.4174	403.251
2004	−577.618	−191.469	−61.4902	609.932
2005	−683.404	−221.591	−92.0463	818.872
2006	−811.799	−262.261	−108.249	1066.34
2007	−987.941	−321.927	−129.737	1528.2

Table 3 Scaled-up figures of capital outflows under Korean-type crisis (US $ billions)

	Scaled-up figures of capital outflows			
Year	Scaled by M2	Scaled by GDP	Scaled by STED	Actual reserve holdings
1998	−311.288	−99.8973	−13.579	144.96
1999	−357.089	−106.119	−11.8875	154.675
2000	−401.372	−117.542	−10.2429	165.574
2001	−472.21	−129.965	−39.6092	212.165
2002	−551.901	−142.628	−43.697	286.407
2003	−659.288	−160.83	−60.3332	403.251
2004	−758.181	−189.537	−81.6844	609.932
2005	−897.035	−219.355	−122.276	818.872
2006	−1065.57	−259.615	−143.799	1066.34
2007	−1296.77	−318.678	−172.345	1528.2

billion by STED. The simulations suggest that China has built up more than adequate reserves to handle the potential capital outflows except for the period of 1998–2003 if scaled by M2.

The review of the above reserve adequacy measures applied to the case of China unanimously implies the excessiveness of China's current foreign reserve

Table 4 Scaled-up figures of capital outflows under Malaysian-type crisis (US $ billions)

Year	Scaled-up figures of capital outflows			Actual reserve holdings
	Scaled by M2	Scaled by GDP	Scaled by STED	
1998	–62.5349	–46.6391	–7.2065	144.96
1999	–71.7361	–49.5441	–6.30881	154.675
2000	–80.632	–54.8767	–5.43605	165.574
2001	–94.8628	–60.6768	–21.021	212.165
2002	–110.872	–66.5887	–23.1905	286.407
2003	–132.445	–75.0866	–32.0195	403.251
2004	–152.312	–88.4892	–43.3508	609.932
2005	–180.206	–102.41	–64.893	818.872
2006	–214.063	–121.206	–76.3158	1066.34
2007	–260.51	–148.782	–91.4652	1528.2

Table 5 Scaled-up figures of capital outflows under Philippine-type crisis (US $ billions)

Year	Scaled-up figures of capital outflows			Actual reserve holdings
	Scaled by M2	Scaled by GDP	Scaled by STED	
1998	–93.8023	–42.6676	–7.52903	144.96
1999	–107.604	–45.3252	–6.59116	154.675
2000	–120.948	–50.2038	–5.67934	165.574
2001	–142.294	–55.51	–21.9618	212.165
2002	–166.308	–60.9185	–24.2284	286.407
2003	–198.668	–68.6928	–33.4525	403.251
2004	–228.468	–80.9541	–45.291	609.932
2005	–270.31	–93.6898	–67.7973	818.872
2006	–321.094	–110.885	–79.7313	1066.34
2007	–390.764	–136.112	–95.5587	1528.2

Table 6 Scaled-up figures of capital outflows under Thailand-type crisis (US $ billions)

Year	Scaled-up figures of capital outflows			Actual reserve holdings
	Scaled by M2	Scaled by GDP	Scaled by STED	
1998	–353.902	–230.955	–14.8413	144.96
1999	–405.974	–245.34	–12.9926	154.675
2000	–456.319	–271.748	–11.1952	165.574
2001	–536.854	–300.469	–43.2914	212.165
2002	–627.454	–329.745	–47.7592	286.407
2003	–749.543	–371.826	–65.942	403.251
2004	–861.974	–438.195	–89.2781	609.932
2005	–1019.84	–507.132	–133.643	818.872
2006	–1211.44	–600.21	–157.167	1066.34
2007	–1474.3	–736.761	–188.366	1528.2

holdings. Then, the next question surfaces naturally: since it is not without cost to hold reserves[6], why does China still hold so much? We briefly review the motives of reserve holding in the literature and analyze China's case in the next section.

3 Why So Much?

There have been two competing hypotheses explaining large foreign reserve holding: active holding and passive holding. Active holding happens when a central bank recognizes the important roles by foreign reserves and thus, accumulates reserves actively. The main representative holding behavior in this category is the holding due to precautionary demand for reserves. The view of passive holding regards reserve accumulation as a by-product of other policy targets. A mercantilism view of reserve holding is a typical passive holding argument. Mercantilism interprets reserve accumulation as the consequence, not objective, of exchange rate policy. In order to gain competitiveness in exporting sectors, a government maintains relatively undervalued local currency. This leads to the booming of exports while depressing imports[7], which in turn stimulates the reserve holding through current account surplus.

There has been a large set of papers investigating active holding behavior. Aizenman and Marion (2004) attributes the reserve holding to solving the constrained optimal public finance problem facing costly tax collection, sovereign risks, and the need to finance public expenditures. Self-insurance against potential output loss from sudden stops and financial crises gives a country the precautionary motive for foreign reserves (Aizenman et al., 2005, Aizenman and Lee, 2007, Jeanne and Ranciere, 2006).

While the mercantilism view of reserve holding has long existed, the systematic analysis of passive holding is rare in the literature. Dooley et al. (2004) propose the revived Bretton-Woods within which reserve holdings are a residual of exchange rate policies. Aizenman and Lee (2007) disentangles the mercantilism from the precautionary demand for reserves. Their empirical tests show that the mercantilism is quantitatively dwarfed by precautionary motive.

We add into the discussion of passive reserve holding by introducing Li, Cun and Zhang (2008). This paper models a channel of foreign reserves being self-augmented, insofar as the existing stock of foreign reserves may lead to more inflows. Most of China's foreign reserves are taking the form of U.S. Treasury bills and bonds. This increases the supply of loanable funds in U.S. bond markets, which in turn, enables U.S. government to collect funds at a lowered interest rate. This rate encourages more investment and consumption in the United States, part of which is transferred into U.S. imports. Since China is

[6] The most popular measure of costs of holding reserves is opportunity cost which is taken as the spread of domestic interest rates and US T-bill rates.

[7] The effectiveness of this policy depends on whether it may cause devaluation of other competing countries.

United States's main importing partner, the current account of China will be improved further. This helps China to hold more foreign reserves.

The key assumption in the paper is

$$i = f(Y, r) \qquad \frac{\partial i}{\partial Y} > 0, \qquad \frac{\partial i}{\partial r} < 0$$

with *i*: U.S. interest rate; *Y*: U.S. output and *r*: part of China's reserves invested in U.S. bond markets.

In a simple two-country model, domestic (United States) and foreign (China) outputs are determined in Keynesian style:

$$Y = C(Y) + I[f(Y, r)] + \bar{G} + CA(Y, Y^*)$$
$$Y^* = C^*(Y^*) + I^*[f^*(Y^*, \bar{r}^*) + \bar{G}^*] + CA(Y, Y^*)$$
$$CA^* = -CA$$

with *C*: U.S. consumption, *I*: U.S. investment, *G*: government expenditure, and *CA*: U.S. current account. The variables in stars refer to the same economic concepts as above but in a foreign country. In a two-country setting, the sum of two countries' current accounts is zero.

The model implies:

$$\frac{\partial Y}{\partial r} = \frac{I_i f_r}{(1 - C_Y) + (1 - C^*_{Y^*})\frac{dY^*}{dY} - I_i f_Y - I^*_{i^*} f^*_{Y^*}\frac{dY^*}{dY}}$$

$$\text{with } \frac{dY}{dr} > 0$$

$$\text{In addition, } \frac{dCA^*}{dr} = \left(CA^*_Y + CA^*_{Y^*}\frac{dY^*}{dY}\right)\frac{dY}{dr} \tag{1}$$

$$\text{with } \frac{dCA^*}{dr} > 0$$

The inequality (1) implied China's foreign reserves can help boost U.S. output by lowering U.S. interest rates. The inequality (2) confirms the self-augmented process: The stock of China's foreign reserves lead to more current account surplus, which adds more into China's reserve holdings.

The simulation in Li et al. (2008) indicates that every dollar of China's foreign reserve holdings can lead to 0.07 dollar more when the self-augmented process is completed.

4 Investment of Foreign Reserves

There are three principles in foreign reserve investment: liquidity, security, and profitability (IMF 2003). Since an economy is accumulating reserves to defend its currency whenever it is under attack, the liquidity and security of foreign reserves are the most important factors in determining where to invest. In practice, most of the foreign reserves are invested in U.S. T-bills since T-bills are the perfect security to provide liquidity and security.

Therefore, the issue of profitability of foreign reserve investment has long been neglected when foreign reserve holdings are slim in scales. However, with the rapid growth of foreign reserves, their social cost cannot be ignored. Based on the estimates from Rodrik (2006), the social cost of reserve accumulation can account for 1% of GDP due to the low yields from T-bills. How to form a better portfolio to cover the social cost becomes a more crucial problem than before. Caballero and Panageas (2005) propose the investment on derivatives of VIX. Based on their simulations, the investment on VIX can increase reserve holdings by 40% when sudden stops happen.

There have been no formal models addressing the investment of foreign reserves taking into account macro business cycles. Mei and Li (2008) give a first try and argue that foreign reserves should be invested into those assets with negative correlation with domestic business cycles. This investment strategy can improve the social utility by 56% with perfect hedging. We briefly introduce the framework by Mei and Li (2008) in this section and shed light on future research.

Assume that an economy consists of two parts: the real economy[8] and foreign reserves with scales C and R, respectively. The expected return and risks of C are $E(r_c)$ and σ_c. The foreign reserves R can be invested in risk-free asset with the volume R_f at the rate of r_f. R can also be invested in risky assets with volume R_f at the expected rate of $E(R_{r_f})$. A social planner maximizes the following social utility:

$$U(r_p, \sigma_p) = E(r_p) - A\sigma_p^2 \tag{2}$$

with r_p: return of the portfolio consisting of the real economy and reserves; σ_p^2: variance of the portfolio; and A: risk aversion coefficient. The expected return and variance of the portfolio can be spelled out as

$$\begin{aligned} E(r_p) &= \frac{R}{R+C}E(r_R) + \frac{C}{R+C}E(r_c) \\ \sigma_p^2 &= \text{var}\left(\frac{R}{R+C}\sigma_R + \frac{C}{R+C}\sigma_C\right) \\ &= \left(\frac{R}{R+C}\right)^2\sigma_R^2 + \left(\frac{C}{R+C}\right)^2\sigma_C^2 + 2\rho_{R,C}\frac{RC}{(R+C)^2}\sigma_C\sigma_R \end{aligned} \tag{3}$$

What we want to track is the utility gains from investment in risky assets with negative correlation with the real economy. Case 1 describes the situation when all foreign reserves are invested in risk-free asset while Case 2 lays out the case when all or partial reserves are invested in risky assets.

---

[8] We present the model with a one-sectional real economy. The model of a multi-sectional economy follows the same spirit and can be fully tracked in Mei and Li (2008).

Case 1: All Reserves Are Invested in Risk-Free Assets

With investment in risk-free asset, we have $r_R = r_f$, $\rho_{R,C} = 0$. Then

$$E(r_p) = \frac{R}{R+C} r_f + \frac{C}{R+C} E(r_C)$$

$$\sigma_p^2 = \left(\frac{C}{R+C}\right)^2 \sigma_C^2 \tag{4}$$

$$U_0(r_p, \sigma_p) = \frac{R}{R+C} r_f + \frac{C}{R+C} E(r_c) - A\left(\frac{C}{R+C}\right)^2 \sigma_C^2$$

Case 2: All or Partial Reserves Are Invested in Risky Assets

Assume that there exists a risky asset so that its return has a correlation coefficient with the real economy: $\rho_{R_r,C}$. Thus, the social utility is

$$\begin{aligned} U(r_p, \sigma_p) =& \frac{R - R_r}{R+C} r_f + \frac{R_r}{R+C} E(R_r) + \frac{C}{R+C} E(r_C) \\ & - A\left[\left(\frac{R_r}{R+C}\right)^2 \sigma_{R_r}^2 + \left(\frac{C}{R+C}\right)^2 \sigma_C^2 + 2\rho_{R_{r,c}} \frac{R_r C}{(R+C)^2} \sigma_{R_r} \sigma_C\right] \end{aligned} \tag{5}$$

Equation (5) can be further simplified with risk-neutral social planner: $E(r_{R_r}) = r_f$.

$$\begin{aligned} U(r_p, \sigma_p) =& \frac{R}{R+C} r_f + \frac{C}{R+C} E(r_C) \\ & - A\left[\left(\frac{R_r}{R+C}\right)^2 \sigma_{R_r}^2 + \left(\frac{C}{R+C}\right)^2 \sigma_C^2 + 2\rho_{Rr,C} \frac{R_r C}{(R+C)^2} \sigma_{R_r} \sigma_C\right] \end{aligned} \tag{6}$$

Maximization of the above gives the optimal reserve holding:

$$R_r^* = -\rho_{R_r,C} C \frac{\sigma_C}{\sigma_{R_r}} \tag{7}$$

When the actual reserve holding $R_r^* \geq -\rho_{R_r C} C \frac{\sigma_C}{\sigma_{R_r}}$, R_r^* is attainable.[9] Plugging (7) into (6) gives the maximized social utility:

$$U(r_p, \sigma_p) = \frac{R}{R+C} r_f + \frac{C}{R+C} E(r_C) - A(1 - \rho_{R_r,C}^2) \frac{C^2}{(R+C)^2} \sigma_C^2 \tag{8}$$

The comparison of the utilities under the two cases is

[9] If $R_r^* < -\rho_{R_r,C} C \frac{\sigma_C}{\sigma_{R_r}}$, similar results can be obtained in Mei and Li (2008).

$$U_{max} - U_0 = A \frac{\rho_{R_r,C}^2 C^2}{(R+C)^2} \sigma_C^2 > 0 \tag{9}$$

In addition,

$$\frac{\partial(U_{max} - U_0)}{\partial A} = \frac{\rho_{R_r,C}^2 C^2}{(R+C)^2} \sigma_C^2 > 0, \frac{\partial(U_{max} - U_0)}{\partial \rho_{R_r,C}} = 2A \frac{\rho_{R_r,C} C^2}{(R+C)^2} \sigma_C^2 < 0$$
$$\frac{\partial(U_{max} - U_0)}{\partial \sigma_C} = 2A \frac{\rho_{R_r,C}^2 C^2}{(R+C)^2} \sigma_C > 0, \frac{\partial(U_{max} - U_0)}{\partial \frac{R}{C}} = -2 \frac{\rho_{R_r,C^{\sigma}}^2 C^2}{1 + \frac{R}{C}^2} < 0 \tag{10}$$

Some useful results can be derived from (9) and (10): With adequate reserve holdings, allocating partial of total reserves on risky assets can increase the social utility. Its effectiveness positively depends on risk aversion coefficient, the correlation coefficient of returns of the risky asset and the real economy, and risks of the real economy. It also negatively depends on the relative scale of the reserve holdings.

Dividing both right- and left-hand sides of (7) yields

$$\tau^* \equiv \frac{R_r^*}{R} - \rho_{R_r,C} \frac{C}{R} \frac{\sigma_C}{\sigma_{R_r}} \tag{11}$$

Therefore, the share of the optimal risky asset is determined by three factors: the correlation coefficient between the risky asset and the real economy, the relative size of the real economy, and the relative risk of the real economy.

Given a set of parameter values

$$\left(A, \frac{R}{C}, r_f, E(r_c), \rho_{R_r,C}, \sigma_C, \sigma_{R_r}\right) = (3, 0.5, 5\%, 10\%, -0.5, 15\%, 30\%)$$

A simple simulation (Table 7) suggests that the maximum of the utility gains from Case 2 is 56%.

Even though the above model is suggestive in hedging macroeconomic risks in the real economy, it does not consider the role of foreign reserves in lowering the probability of currency crisis. If we can take into account the risk from currency attacks, the model can be easily extended.

Furthermore, the current model attempts to include the profitability of foreign reserves, leaving the objectives of liquidity and security intact. The future models should endogenize the three principles of foreign reserve investment. Inclusion of liquidity and security in the objective function may lead to a measure of the necessary holding of reserves, while the excess can be used in hedging macroeconomic risks.

Table 7 Simulation

$\rho_{R_r,C}$	U_0	U_{max}	$U_{max} - U_0$	$(U_{max} - U_0)/U_0$	R_0/R	R_r/R
–0.1	5.333	5.363	0.030	0.56%	0.900	0.100
–0.2	5.333	5.453	0.120	2.25%	0.800	0.200
–0.3	5.333	5.603	0.270	5.06%	0.700	0.300
–0.4	5.333	5.813	0.480	9.00%	0.600	0.400
–0.5	5.333	6.083	0.750	14.06%	0.500	0.500
–0.6	5.333	6.413	1.080	20.25%	0.400	0.600
–0.7	5.333	6.803	1.470	27.56%	0.300	0.700
–0.8	5.333	7.253	1.920	36.00%	0.200	0.800
–0.9	5.333	7.763	2.430	45.56%	0.100	0.900
–1	5.333	8.333	3.000	56.25%	0.000	1.000

5 Conclusions

Foreign reserve hoarding has been one of the most intriguing phenomena in recent years. As the leading country in foreign reserve holding, China poses a series of interesting questions for academia: Are China's reserves excessive? What are the motives for the massive reserve holding in China? How to invest them?

This chapter surveys the rule of thumb thresholds for reserve adequacy measures and applies them to China's case. These measures unanimously point to one conclusion: China's reserves are excessive.

We conduct a brief review of researches in the motives of China's foreign holding. Distinguishing passive holding from active holding, we add into the literature by introducing a possible channel: China's reserves can be self-augmented. China's reserves provide cheap funding for U.S. treasury securities, helping U.S. maintain low interest rates. The low rates boost China's exports by increasing investment and consumption in the United States. The improved current account in China adds more to the existing stock of foreign reserves. The simulation suggests that China's reserves can be raised 7% through this channel.

We then introduce a model describing the uniqueness of foreign reserve investment: the sovereign characteristic. Different from private investment, the investment of foreign reserves should consider the effects on macro economy. Using the foreign reserves to hedge against potential macroeconomic risks helps raise the social utility by 56% (Mei and Li, 2008).

References

Aizenman, J. (2007). "Large hoarding of international reserves and the emerging global economic architecture", forthcoming, *The Manchester School.*

Aizenman, J. and J. Lee (2007). "International reserves: precautionary versus mercantilist views, theory, and evidence", *Open Economy Review*, Vol. 11, pp. 191–214.

Aizenman, J. and J. Lee, (2006). "Financial versus monetary mercantilism – long-run view of large international reserves hoarding", *NBER* WP # 12718.

Aizenman, J., Y. Lee and Y Rhee (2005). "International Reserves Management and Capital Mobility in a Volatile World: Policy Considerations and a Case Study of Korea", Forthcoming, *Journal of the Japanese and International Economies.*

Aizenman, J. and N. Marion (2004). "International reserves holdings with sovereign risk and costly tax collection", *Economic Journal* Vol. 114, pp. 569–591.

Caballero, J.R. and S. Panageas (2005). "Contingent reserves management: an applied framework", *Journal Economía Chilena (The Chilean Economy)*, Central Bank of Chile, Vol. 8(2), pp. 45–56.

Dooley, M.P., D. Folkerts-Landau and P. Garber. (2004). "The revived bretton woods system: The effects of periphery intervention and reserve management on interest rates and exchange rates in center countries", *NBER Working Paper* # 10332.

IMF (2003). "Guidelines for foreign exchange reserve management", *IMF Working Paper*.

Jeanne, O. and R. Rancière (2006). "The optimal level of international reserves for emerging market countries: Formulas and applications", *IMF Working Paper* 06/229

Kim, J.S., J. Li, O. Sula, R. Rajan and T. Willett (2004). "Reserve adequacy in Asia revisited: New benchmarks based on the size and composition of capital flows", Conference Proceedings, "*Monetary and Exchange Rate Arrangement in East Asia*", Seoul: Korea Institute for Economic Policy.

Li, J., W. Cun and L. Zhang (2008). "China's self-augmented foreign reserves", *RCFR Working Paper,* CUFE Research Center for Foreign Reserves.

Mei, S. and J. Li (2008). "Hedging mechanism against macroeconomic risks for excessive foreign reserves", *The Journal of World Economy*, Vol. 6, 2008 (Chinese).

Rodrik, D. (2006). "The social cost of foreign exchange reserves", *NBER WP* # 11952

Wijnholds, J., O. de Beaufort and A. Kapteyn (2001). "Reserve adequacy in emerging market economics", *Working Paper*, IMF, WP/01/143.

Willett, T.D. (1980). "International liquidity issues", *American Enterprise Institute for Public Policy Research*, Washington, DC.

Zhang, L. (2008). China's External Imbalance: Diagnosis and Prescriptions, *CUFE Working Paper*.

Part III
The Banking System

Institutional Development, Ownership Structure, and Business Strategies: A New Era in the Chinese Banking Industry

Allen N. Berger, Iftekhar Hasan, and Mingming Zhou

Abstract This chapter traces the structural changes in the Chinese banking industry since the 1990s and explores the role of governance in influencing the banking strategies and performance of local financial institutions. Specifically, the chapter focuses on the increasing openness to foreign ownership in local banks, the asset–liability and geographical diversification strategies undertaken by the financial institutions during these deregulatory and changing environments, and the institutional developments in the economy. Finally, the chapter links these changes with bank performance. The evidence suggests that banks with minority foreign ownership are associated with better performance, all types of diversification – captured in four dimensions: loans, deposits, assets, and geography – are associated with reduced profits and higher costs, while banks with minority foreign ownership are associated with fewer diseconomies of diversification, suggesting that foreign ownership plays an important mitigating role. We also observe a significant impact from institutional developments; gradual dominance of the market economy, growth of the private sector, and establishment of secure property rights and rule of law are important factors associated with higher bank performance.

Keywords Minority foreign ownership · Diversification · Institutional development · Chinese banking

1 Introduction

The average 10% annual real economic growth over the last decade has made China one of the most successful transitional economies so far. However, despite this performance, China's banking sector still remains relatively

A.N. Berger (✉)
Moore School of Business, University of South Carolina, Columbia, SC, USA; Wharton Financial Institutions Center, Philadelphia, PA, USA
e-mail: aberger@moore.sc.edu

J.R. Barth et al. (eds.), *China's Emerging Financial Markets*,
The Milken Institute Series on Financial Innovation and Economic Growth 8,
DOI 10.1007/978-0-387-93769-4_11, © 2009 by Milken Institute

undercapitalized, unprofitable, and saddled with nonperforming loans. In recent years, the Chinese banking sector overall has been growing rapidly and has been playing a significant role in channeling the financial resources between the depositors and borrowers, primarily the Chinese enterprises, especially the ones that are less politically connected and are left out from the exclusive privilege of financing through the capital markets.

One of the most notable features of the Chinese banking sector is that it is dominated by the so-called Big Four state-owned banks which hold almost three-fourths of the industry assets. The remaining one-fourth of the industry assets is made up of 13 national banks, a large number of much smaller local banks, and numerous foreign banks' subsidiaries and/or branches from developed as well as developing countries. Since the mid-1990s, Chinese regulators have attempted several major reforms in the banking industry to recapitalize the largest state-owned banks and take over their nonperforming loans, which, however, were not as successful as anticipated in general. One of the factors that account for the ineffectiveness of these initiatives lies in the fact that the Chinese state-owned banks, large or small, have been tightly interlocked with complicated networks of central and local government, state-owned enterprises, and other influential interest groups. Therefore, the reforms are unlikely to be successful without dealing with corporate governance, increasing business freedom, and setting up the legal and institutional foundations and environment which serve as critical external monitoring mechanisms for the Chinese banks.

First, we argue that foreign ownership plays an important role as it brings forward a more effective corporate governance mechanism. Since China gained access to World Trade Organization (WTO) in 2001, there has been significant reform of the banking system, and one of the recent approaches is to open up the Chinese banking system to foreign strategic investors, i.e., foreign investors who can only purchase minority shares in the domestic Chinese banks. For example, since 2005, three of the Big Four banks – China Construction Bank (CCB), Bank of China (BOC), and Industrial & Commercial Bank of China (ICBC) – have taken on minority foreign ownership from some global banks and international corporate giants, such as Citigroup, HSBC, Deutsche Bank, Royal Bank of Scotland, and IBM. As foreign investors take over some seats on the corporate boards and get actively involved with bank management, a new monitoring discipline emerges among the banks. Nevertheless, this change in the regulation with regard to minority foreign ownership is rather a recent trend, and there are very few studies in the literature that analyze its impact.[1] That is, although studies on majority foreign-owned banks are abundant, research on the experience of minority foreign ownership of banks is very limited.[2]

---

[1] See Berger et al. (2008a) and Garcia-Herrero and Santabarbara (2008) for some empirical studies of the role minority foreign ownership in effecting bank performance in China.

[2] See Stulz (2005) and Kho et al. (2006) for discussion on how agency problems of domestic firms allow insiders to own large equity stakes of firms in developing nations, which limits the role of foreign investors or institutions.

The deregulation of asset and geographical restrictions also create opportunities for Chinese banks to improve their performance. Before China's entry to the WTO agreement, the Chinese banks – especially the majority state-owned banks that dominated the market – had been heavily influenced by policy makers, and throughout the last few decades, they had had a very limited degree of freedom in terms of product offerings and regions in which they could operate their businesses. In fact, after 2001, the newly powered banks moved into new areas and products very rapidly, in many cases without proper expertise or knowledge of the products or even markets. This chapter also aims to report the experiences of banks' diversification strategy during their early years of autonomy and freedom.

A broader and important perspective in analyzing the Chinese banking industry is the institutional environment in which it operates. Recent analysis (e.g., Cull and Xu, 2005) claims that the inefficient banking sector and poor legal/financial infrastructure in China probably restrained the true growth and development potentials in China. While we recognize that China's legal and financial systems are not well developed – even by the standards of most developing nations – the Chinese institutional environment has been steadily improving, though these improvements are different across regions and time periods. While recent literature emphasizes the role of institutions in explaining economic transitions and growth (see, e.g., Henisz, 2000), institutional factors as potential sources of determinants of banking performance have largely been ignored (Berger and Mester, 1997). This chapter attempts to void this gap by explicitly testing this line of discussions by linking the Chinese banks' performance and the institutional environment in which they operate.

In sum, this chapter examines the roles of minority foreign ownership, focus-diversification strategy, and institutional development in the performance of the Chinese banks. We find that banks, on average, perform better in terms of both profit efficiency and cost efficiency when they are associated with minority foreign ownership, more focused business strategy, and in environments in which there are better institutions in terms of awareness of property rights and presence of private sector. Further, minority foreign ownership mitigates the diversification discount in terms of profit and cost efficiency of the Chinese banks. In addition, we find that minority foreign ownership, in general, reinforces the positive effect of institutional variables on the performance of the Chinese banks.

The rest of this chapter is organized as follows. Section 2 discusses the structural changes in the Chinese banking industry since the 1990s. Section 3 briefly reviews the literature. Section 4 describes the sample, methodology, and various measures we employ for the empirical study. Section 5 presents the empirical results, and Section 6 summarizes and concludes.

2 Structural Change in Chinese Banking: Post 1990s

2.1 *Historical Background*

The old Chinese banking system was designed in a socialist model, where the central bank, People's Bank of China (PBOC), was primarily involved in currency transaction and monetary control. A mono-bank model was in place where both the central and commercial banking activities were undertaken by the PBOC. Under the PBOC umbrella, a few large state-owned banks were given the responsibility of the lending function in some designated areas. These banks were Bank of China (BOC), China Construction Bank (CCB), Agricultural Bank of China (ABC), and Industrial and Commercial Bank of China (ICBC), now referred to as the "Big Four." It was after the mid-1980s that these "Big Four" were allowed to compete in sectors beyond their primary areas and started to get more competitive pressure from other banks. Earlier, they simply served as agents of the government, supporting their policy-lending initiatives. During the 1990s, these banks suffered from accumulated large nonperforming loans, which prompted the government to recapitalize the Big Four banks around 1998, float long-term bonds worth over US $32.6 billion, and hand over some explicit responsibilities of policy lending to some newly created policy banks or state-owned asset management companies.

The government started to take steps toward market discipline in the mid-1990s. A new set of reforms distinguished PBOC as the central bank and allowed state-owned banks to operate based on market principles. The banking market since then has witnessed the entrance of a large number of new banks in the markets competing with the state-owned banks. In 1997, for the first time, the central government refused to bail out a failing institution, the Guangdong International Trust and Investment Corporation, leaving debt holders to receive less than 13% of their initial investment.

It was two years after the Chinese membership in WTO in 2001 that the China Banking Regulatory Commission (CBRC) was set up to supervise the reforms and create regulations for the banking market. The CBRC started to provide incentives and encourage foreign investors to purchase shares in local banks up to a maximum limit of 25% of total ownership, with a limitation of a single foreign owner up to a maximum of 20%. This prompted US and European banks as well as banks from other Asian countries to enter the Chinese market. At the same time, the banks started to finance via both domestic and overseas capital markets, issuing record dollar amount of stocks in the IPO markets.

2.2 *Product and Geographical Diversification Restrictions*

As mentioned earlier, banks did not have autonomy or freedom to create their asset–liability management or geographical diversification, as they followed guidelines from the government about possible directions of their activities to lend in certain sectors and to certain customers. Also, investment banks and asset management were prohibited from entering commercial banking or insurance activities and vice versa.[3] Additionally, banks started to rely increasingly on non-traditional banking activities, earning higher fee income, cash and wealth management, and acquisitions of other banks.

In general, geographical diversification is less restricted for the Chinese national banks, i.e., they are permitted to establish branches and take deposits and lend across various regions in China, though a large number of local banks, e.g., the city commercial banks, are still limited to operate only in local regions. For example, one of the Big Four, Bank of China, boasts an extensive network across the nation and abroad with over 2,000 branches. In summary, the Chinese banks started to become more like regular banks since the 1990s, and in the post 2001 era, they have become more active in making independent banking strategies on products and locations.

2.3 Institutional Development

China is a huge country with 31 provinces and territories (including 4 municipalities). These regions varied in many ways, including market development, execution of laws and regulations, and economic growth (Aziz and Duenwald, 2001; Demurger et al., 2002). Being a country in transition, China also faced an entirely new set of institutional set-up and distribution across regions. We argue that such differences in the regional institutional development may well be associated with the efficiency of the local banking system.

The development of a new legal system in the post-socialist era of the 1990s has helped in enacting numerous new laws, regulations, and administrative rules on capital markets, property rights, and intellectual property laws on properties and products. New laws were introduced in the mid-1980s in order to protect foreign patents and after a few years, regulations went into effect that allowed firms to define property rights and separate collective and private enterprise shares. The 1994 Company Law improved property rights by establishing the firm as a legal entity. However, the adoption and implementation of these standards were uneven across regions, and according to Krug and Hendrischke (2003), they differed substantially. This was also true in the banking sector and other business sectors.

One of the most important institutional transitions that China experienced in recent history is the switch from a centrally planned economy to a market economy and the deep-rooted privatization since the 1990s. Since then, the privatization initiatives have encouraged and helped in expanding a flourishing private sector producing over one-third of the country's GDP. In 1999, China

[3] Source: Aims to diversify revenue sources, Shanghai Daily, July 18, 2008.

made a constitutional amendment and formally recognized the private sector. The private sector is still small, has limited political connections, less access to bank credit and capital markets, and relies primarily on informal financial channels and self-financing.

Overall, China experienced major changes in the economic environment and institutional developments in all areas of the economy: political, social, and economic institutions. These reforms and changes varied substantially across provinces and regions, and the chapter highlights these regional differences over time and explores how these differences matter affecting bank performance.

3 Related Literature

The finance–growth nexus was introduced by King and Levine in a series of papers in the early 1990s (King and Levine, 1993a,b,c). These papers revealed that financial deepening through banking institutions play a key role in channeling scarce financial capital to different sectors and areas of the economy. What is clear in this literature is that a good banking system can match investors and entrepreneurs effectively and can infuse capital in the right direction, eventually creating an environment for new innovations, productivity, and economic growth.

Many studies examine the performance effects of bank ownership type, especially foreign ownership. The stylized findings for developing nations are that on average, foreign banks are more efficient than or approximately equally efficient to private domestic banks, though there are variations in the findings. For example, Bonin et al. (2005a, b) use data from the transition nations of Eastern Europe and find foreign banks to be the most efficient on average, followed by private domestic banks and then state-owned banks. On the other hand, Yildirim and Philippatos (2007) also study transition nations and find the mixed result that foreign banks are more cost efficient but less profit efficient than both private domestic and state-owned banks. A more comprehensive study by Berger et al. (2004) using 28 developing nations from various regions finds that the foreign banks have the highest profit efficiency, followed by private domestic banks, and then state-owned banks. However, most of the studies in this line of research only examine the performance effects of majority foreign ownership, leaving the effects of minority foreign ownership on banks' performance largely unknown, although there are studies of minority foreign ownership of nonbanking firms in developing nations (see, e.g., Stulz, 2005; Kho et al., 2006). To our best knowledge, there are only two empirical studies so far documenting the role of minority foreign investors in the banking industry, and both are based on the evidence from China. The first study, by Berger et al. (2008a), focuses on the ownership structure finding positive and significant association between foreign ownership – both majority and minority ownership – and higher efficiency among Chinese banks. The second study, by

Garcia-Herrero and Santabarbara (2008), finds that foreign participation which consists of a minority stake in a Chinese bank appears to be most effective when the foreign bank acts as a strategic investor. Given the recent regulatory changes that allow entry of minority foreign ownership in the Chinese domestic banks, it is interesting to examine the performance effects of partial privatization and minority foreign ownership of the Big Four and other large Chinese banks.

At the same time, given the new deregulation of asset allocation and expansion in different provinces in recent years, banks in China have grown at a record pace and, in some cases such rapid expansion may have been associated with increased deterioration of asset quality. Banks traditionally want to be diversified, as banks are highly levered and diversification across sectors and regions may reduce risk. Several models of intermediation suggest that diversification makes it cheaper for institutions to achieve credibility in their role as screeners or monitors of borrowers (Diamond, 1984; Boyd and Prescott, 1986). On the other hand, some studies stand on the general consensus in corporate literature (Berger and Ofek, 1996; Servaes, 1997; Denis et al., 1997) and argue that focused institutions are likely to be better performers. The empirical evidence on this debate in the banking industry is rather mixed. The managers of diversified institutions can apply their skills and abilities to other products, or can transfer knowledge to other locations to improve performance across the organization (Iskandar-Datta and McLaughlin, 2005), or can gain economies of scope (Drucker and Puri, 2005). Diversification in financial services also enables banks to sell services to customers who demand multiple products (financial supermarkets). On the other hand, some studies believe that the cost of diversification outweighs benefits (Stiroh, 2004; Acharya et al., 2006). Laeven and Levine (2007) reported that financial conglomerates engaging in multiple lending activities have lower market values than they would if they were broken into separate financial institutions.

With respect to the benefits of geographical diversification, Deng and Elyasiani (2007) argue that geographical diversification globally could cause increased exchange rate and political risk, and difficulties of dealing with different languages, laws, and customs can also destroy shareholders' wealth. DeLong (2001) examines U.S. bank mergers with respect to both activity and geographic location and finds that banks focusing on both activity and geography were value increasing. Finally, some studies also find that geography diversification can also lead to organizational inefficiency (e.g., Klein and Saidenberg, 1998).

Most of these studies on focus-diversification issue are based on U.S. and European experience, leaving focus-diversification issue in emerging/transitional economies largely unexamined. In addition, most of the existing banking literature on China does not discuss the asset-liability management as well as geographical strategies and its impact on performance. The only exception is the study by Berger et al. (2008b), which investigates the diversification discount in the Chinese banking industry. Our study, different from Berger et al.'s (2008b), attempts to study the performance effect of the diversification strategy in the Chinese banking sector within the framework of disparate institutional development across the country.

During the late 1990s, some important work focused on the role of institutions in promoting the economy (e.g., La Porta et al., 1997, 1998). They conclude that, among others, stronger investor protection and more efficient banking institutions are correlated with better financial and economic outcomes. However, some later studies debated the extent of their influence (e.g., Rajan and Zingales, 2003). Demirguc-Kunt and Huizinga (1999) document that institutional environment can also affect commercial banks' performance. Qian and Strahan (2007) report strong creditor rights being associated with higher availability of credit.

Moreover, well-defined property rights are cornerstones for private sector development and growth. The protection of property rights facilitates the development of financial markets. Well-functioning and flexible financial markets allow entrepreneurs to embrace economic opportunities and promote growth by protecting entrepreneurs from appropriation by large market participants. Aron (2000) and Johnson et al. (2002) argue that it is the lack of property rights and availability of external finance that are the two key variables common across developing nations. In a firm-level study using Chinese data, Cull and Xu (2005) report that access to finance, ownership structure, contract enforcement, and expropriation risk are significantly associated with reinvestment decisions. Similarly, Djankov et al. (2006) observe significant influence of legal and economic institutions in fostering entrepreneurship in China. Hasan et al. (2008) explored the role of institutional development and economic growth reporting significant impact of legal and political institutions in determining the variability of economic growth in Chinese provinces.

To the best of our knowledge, there are very few studies that aim at linking institutional development and bank performance. Given the recent regulatory changes and variations of the implementations and developments of institutions across regions in China, one of our objectives in this study is to investigate whether and how the variation of regional institutional settings may affect the performance of the banking sector in China.

4 Sample and Methodology

4.1 Sample

Our sample is an unbalanced panel which includes financial data of 79 Chinese banks during the 11-year period of 1996–2006, totaling 411 observations. To focus on the role of minority foreign ownership on domestic Chinese banks' performance, we explicitly exclude any majority foreign banks, which are defined as those banks whose foreign ownership equals or exceeds 50% of total shares. In other words, our sample only includes the majority domestic Chinese banks, with or without minority foreign ownership. The basic data source is Bankscope – Fitch's International Bank Database. The major data source for branch data to construct geography diversification measures are the annual issues of Almanac of China's Finance and Banking (ACFB), 1996–2006. We also collect or double-check the data from other official sources, such as annual issues of ACFB and the China Statistical Yearbook, when Bankscope does not provide enough information or has questionable values.[4] The data source and construction of institutional variables will be discussed later in this section. All financial variables are inflation-adjusted to the base year 1996.

Among the 79 sample Chinese banks, there are the Big Four, which take up more than 66% of total commercial banking assets, and the 12 national share-holding commercial banks – known as the "second-tier" domestic banks which own about 21% of commercial banking assets in 2006. Our sample also includes 50 city commercial banks and 13 joint venture banks which take up about 4% of the total commercial banking assets in China in 2006.[5] Our sample covers over 90% of the assets of commercial banks in China.

4.2 Ownership Dummies

Table 1 summarizes the distribution of our sample observations across year, by ownership groups, and by bank size. We define majority state-owned banks as those banks whose state and state-owned enterprises ownership is greater than 50% of total ownership, and majority private domestic banks are defined as those banks whose private domestic ownership is greater than 50% of total ownership. Within the category of majority state-owned banks, we have the so-called Big Four, the four big Chinese banks which were 100% state-owned until near the end of the sample period, i.e., Bank of China, Industrial and Commercial Bank of China, Agricultural Bank of China, and China Construction Bank. Minority foreign ownership is defined as the foreign ownership in the majority domestic Chinese banks which is more than 0 but smaller than or equal to 50%. Bank size is defined based on total assets (prices are inflation-adjusted to the base year 1996) of the bank at year t, and the bank is a small bank if its assets are less than or equal to US $1 billion, a medium bank if the bank's assets are

[4] While we recognize that there may be some inconsistencies in financial data using different accounting standards, given that most of the sample banks follow Chinese Accounting Standards (CAS) while a few also prepared annual reports based on International Accounting Standards (IAS), we do not find a material difference between the financial statements of the same bank while reporting under both CAS and IAS respectively.

[5] All the city commercial banks in China, along with the joint venture and foreign banks and other banking institutions, make up the "third-tier" banks in the industry, and they take up about 30% of the total banking assets in China in 2006.

Table 1 Total observations

This table shows the distributions of our sample across years, by ownership groups and by bank size. Our overall sample is an unbalanced panel which consists of 411 observations (79 Chinese banks), covering a 11-year period from 1996 to 2006. In this table and throughout this chapter, majority state-owned banks refer to those banks whose state ownership (including stake held by state-owned enterprises, i.e., both directly or indirectly owned by the state) is greater than 50% of total ownership. Majority state-owned banks are divided into four groups: Big Four banks *without* foreign minority ownership, Big Four banks *with* minority foreign ownership, non-Big Four majority state-owned banks *without* minority foreign ownership, and non-Big Four majority state-owned banks *with* minority foreign ownership. By the same token, majority private domestic banks refer to those banks whose private domestic ownership is greater than 50% of total ownership, in the same fashion, we further divide majority private domestic banks into two groups: majority private banks *without* foreign minority ownership and majority private banks *with* foreign minority ownership. Majority foreign banks, i.e., those banks whose foreign ownership is greater than 50% of total ownership, are excluded from our sample. The bank size is defined based on total assets (inflation-adjusted, at constant price level of 1996) of the bank at year t, and the bank is a small bank if its assets are less than or equal to US $1 billion, medium bank if the bank's assets are greater than US $1 billion but less than or equal to US $20 billion, and large bank if the bank's assets are greater than US $20 billion. Sources of Data: Bankscope, annual issues of Almanac of China's Finance and Banking, 1996–2006; individual bank's financial statement, etc

	Total	1996	1997	1998	1999	2000	2001	2002	2003	2004	2005	2006
Total bank observations	411	6	9	12	31	36	35	45	52	60	68	57
Observations according to ownership												
1. Majority state-owned banks	282	5	6	8	19	24	25	31	38	41	47	38
a. Big Four banks	34	0	0	2	4	4	4	4	4	4	4	4
a.1. Big Four banks *without* foreign minority	32	0	0	2	4	4	4	4	4	4	4	2
a.2. Big Four banks *with* foreign minority	2	0	0	0	0	0	0	0	0	0	0	2
b. Non-Big Four majority state-owned domestic banks	248	5	6	6	15	20	21	27	34	37	43	34
b.1. Non-Big Four majority state-owned banks *without* foreign minority	187	5	5	5	13	18	19	24	30	31	35	2
b.2. Non-Big Four majority state-owned banks *with* foreign minority	61	0	1	1	2	2	2	3	4	6	8	32
2. Majority Private domestic banks	129	1	3	4	12	12	10	14	14	19	21	19
a. Majority private banks *without* foreign minority	96	1	2	3	10	11	9	13	12	17	16	2
b. Majority Private domestic banks *with* foreign minority	33	0	1	1	2	1	1	1	2	2	5	17
Observations according to bank size												
Small Banks: assets < US $1 billion	63	0	2	3	4	4	4	9	6	10	13	8
Medium Banks: US $1 billion<assets< US $20 billion	245	6	6	6	21	24	21	22	30	35	40	34
Large Banks: assets > US $20 billion	103	0	1	3	6	8	10	14	16	15	15	15

greater than US $1 billion but less than or equal to US $20 billion; and a large bank if the bank's assets are greater than US $20 billion.

4.3 Focus Indices

For each bank in our sample, data are available to calculate the following portfolio decompositions:

1. A disaggregated loan decomposition based on each bank's industry loans, commercial loans, real estate loans, agriculture loans, and consumer loans.
2. A disaggregated deposit decomposition based on each bank's customer demand deposits, customer savings deposits, non-bank corporate deposits, deposits by other banks, and other deposits.
3. A disaggregated asset decomposition based on each bank's total loans, deposits in other banks, financial investments (including investments in government securities, trading securities, and other financial assets), total fixed assets, and other assets.
4. A disaggregated geographical decomposition based on each bank's loans on various regions in China, including northern, eastern, central, southern, western regions.

Table 2 presents the summary statistics of the above decomposition of loan, deposit, asset, and geographic portfolios. All financial items are in billions of $US, and inflation-adjusted to the price level of year 1996.

Table 2 Summary statistics of decomposition of portfolios
Table 2 presents summary statistics of decomposition of loan, deposit, asset, and geographical portfolios. The disaggregated loan decomposition is based on each bank's loans to industry loans, commercial loans, real estate loans, agriculture loans, and consumer loans. The disaggregated deposit decomposition is based on each bank's customer demand deposits, customer savings deposits, non-bank corporate deposits, deposits by other banks, and other deposits. The disaggregated asset decomposition is based on each bank's total loans, deposits in other banks, financial investments (including investment in government securities, trading securities, and other financial assets), total fixed assets, and other assets. The disaggregated geographical decomposition is based on each bank's loans on various regions in China, including northern, central, eastern, southern, and western regions. All the financial items are in billions of US dollars, and inflation-adjusted to the price level of year 1996

Variable	Obs	Mean	Median	Std Dev.	Minimum	Maximum
Loan decomposition						
Industry loans	411	20.300	1.127	58.000	0.002	416.000
Commercial loans	411	4.487	0.294	14.700	0.000	141.000
Real estate loans	411	1.774	0.038	7.304	0.000	78.200
Agriculture loans	411	1.328	0.102	6.178	0.000	89.500
Consumer loans	411	2.326	0.309	6.981	0.000	70.700

Table 2 (continued)

Variable	Obs	Mean	Median	Std Dev.	Minimum	Maximum
Deposit decomposition						
Customer demand deposits	411	25.100	1.879	71.000	0.000	423.000
Customer savings deposits	411	15.200	0.810	44.900	0.000	384.000
Corporate deposits	411	0.123	0.004	0.418	0.000	3.849
Banking deposits	411	3.640	0.142	10.300	0.000	81.100
Other deposits	411	0.131	0.010	0.422	0.000	3.826
Asset decomposition						
Loans	411	30.600	1.931	86.600	0.000	725.000
Deposits in other banks	411	2.615	0.192	8.392	0.000	96.700
Financial investments	411	11.900	0.807	37.400	0.000	341.000
Total fixed assets	411	0.825	0.057	2.302	0.000	12.900
Other assets	411	5.566	0.379	15.400	0.000	98.900
Geographical decomposition (loans)						
Northern	411	3.070	0.000	40.100	0.000	648.000
Central	411	12.100	0.026	160.000	0.000	2410.000
Eastern	411	6.970	0.000	94.800	0.000	1760.000
Southern	411	4.040	0.000	50.700	0.000	861.000
Western	411	2.380	0.000	28.500	0.000	447.000

We then construct a measure of focus versus diversification, i.e., the Focus Index, by employing a Herfindahl-Hirschman Index (HHI) measure following Acharya et al. (2006). The Focus Index is the sum of squares of the proportions of portfolios in each classification. In our case, we construct four different Focus Indices, which are loan, deposit, asset, and geographic Focus Indices. For example, in the case of loan Focus Index, if we denote the loans in each of the five loan categories as L_i, where i = 1, 2, ..., 5, we then have:

$$\text{Loan Focus Index } = \sum\nolimits_{i=1}^{5} (L_i/Q)^2, \text{ where, } Q = \sum\nolimits_{j=1}^{5} L_j. \qquad (1)$$

Note that the Focus Index, by definition, ranges from 1/n, or 1/5 in this case, to 1, with a higher value of the index indicating a higher degree of focus (less diversification).

Table 3 presents the summary statistics of the above Focus Indices, based on the decomposition of loan, deposit, asset, and geographic portfolios. Summary statistics of subsamples of Chinese banks are also presented.

Table 3 Summary statistics of Focus Indices of loan, deposit, asset, and geographic portfolios
Table 3 presents the summary statistics of Focus Indices, and decompositions of loan, deposit, asset, and geographical portfolios follow the same definitions as in Table 2. Summary statistics of subsamples of Chinese banks by size are also presented

	Obs.	Mean	Median	Std. dev	Minimum	Maximum
Summary statistics for all observations						
Loan Focus Index	411	0.430	0.416	0.087	0.282	0.700
Deposit Focus Index	411	0.412	0.393	0.085	0.281	0.979
Asset Focus Index	411	0.524	0.517	0.111	0.273	1.000
Geographic Focus Index	411	0.804	1.000	0.358	0.046	1.000
Summary statistics for small banks: assets <US $1 billion						
Loan Focus Index	63	0.433	0.416	0.085	0.298	0.602
Deposit Focus Index	63	0.471	0.425	0.149	0.307	0.979
Asset Focus Index	63	0.601	0.577	0.165	0.383	1.000
Geographic Focus Index	63	1.000	1.000	0.000	1.000	1.000
Summary statistics for medium banks: US $1 billion < assets < US $20 billion						
Loan Focus Index	245	0.410	0.393	0.076	0.282	0.610
Deposit Focus Index	245	0.390	0.380	0.054	0.281	0.548
Asset Focus Index	245	0.527	0.528	0.098	0.273	0.941
Geographic Focus Index	245	0.953	1.000	0.182	0.079	1.000
Summary statistics for large banks: assets > US $20 billion						
Loan Focus Index	103	0.474	0.471	0.098	0.299	0.700
Deposit Focus Index	103	0.428	0.428	0.070	0.299	0.644
Asset Focus Index	103	0.470	0.466	0.061	0.336	0.593
Geographic Focus Index	103	0.328	0.097	0.361	0.046	1.000

4.4 Institutional Variables

We use three variables to capture the disparate regional institutional environments in which the Chinese banks operate. Our first institutional variable is the awareness of and respect for property rights, particularly intellectual property, and it is proxied by the number of domestic trademark applications per firm. Our hypothesis for using this variable to capture both awareness of property rights and the degree of development of secure property rights-associated institutions in each province is that more trademark applications reflect confidence in the preservation of property rights and a desire to defend them. Data on domestic trademark applications are collected from the annual issues of the Almanac of China's Property Rights, the Yearbook of China's Industrial and Commercial Administrative Statistics (which provide data starting in 1998), annual provincial yearbooks, government-sponsored trademark web site, and the online China Trademark database. Missing data are back cast using the national data and the proportions of applications in the province in 1998.

Our second institutional variable is the rule of law, and it is proxied by the number of lawyers per 10,000 people. Our motivation for the use of this variable is that an increased presence of legal professionals in a province is an indicator of the both the development of legal institutions and of the mechanisms for law enforcement. If more lawyers are at work, then there are greater efforts to promote public accountability and limit corruption. The data are collected from the Statistics Yearbook of China's Legislation and the annual issues of the Statistics Yearbooks of each province, which provide data for 1990, 1995 and 2000–2002). Additional information was collected from other web based resources, such as the China Law of Lawyering (china-lawyering.com), China Lawyers Investigation web site (www.007cn.cn), and China Lawyers web site (www.chineselawyer.com.cn). These web sites provided additional data on the number of lawyers per province or city since the 1990s. Missing data are interpolated based on nationwide growth in the number of lawyers. The population data are obtained from the National Bureau of Statistics of China.

Our third institutional variable is the presence of the private sector. We are interested in the link between private sector and banking performance because our sample period from 1996 to 2006 represents an important privatization phase for China, and the influence of privatization on the economic growth and banking sector in transitional economies is not always obvious. We follow Cull and Xu (2005) and interpret the relative size of private sector in the Chinese regional economy as a proxy for the market economy and to some extent, it also links to the extent of property rights protection. The presence of the private sector is measured by the ratio of regional private sector total fixed investment to regional total fixed investment. The data of China's private sector are from the China Economic Information Network Database and the China National Statistics Bureau.

Table 4 presents the mean and standard deviation of the above three institutional variables, namely, awareness of property rights, rule of law, and presence of private sector.

Table 4 Descriptive statistics of institutional variables by province

Table 4 presents the mean and standard deviation of our three institutional variables, namely, awareness of property rights, rule of law, and presence of private sector. Awareness of property rights is proxied by the number of trademark applications per firm. Rule of law is proxied by the number of lawyers per 10,000 people.Presence of private sector presence is proxied by the ratio of private sector total fixed investment to overall total fixed investment

		Awareness of property rights		Rule of law		Presence of private sector	
Province	Obs	Mean	Std. dev	Mean	Std. dev	Mean	Std. dev
Anhui	11	0.832	0.501	0.554	0.039	0.519	0.030
Beijing	11	3.443	1.824	5.639	1.893	0.482	0.097
Chongqing	11	1.151	0.754	1.087	0.378	0.546	0.037
Fujian	11	1.717	0.984	0.816	0.063	0.621	0.024
Gansu	11	0.266	0.099	0.172	0.030	0.323	0.026

Table 4 (continued)

Province	Obs	Awareness of property rights		Rule of law		Presence of private sector	
		Mean	Std. dev	Mean	Std. dev	Mean	Std. dev
Guangdong	11	1.991	0.860	0.943	0.065	0.633	0.069
Guangxi	11	0.622	0.332	0.507	0.077	0.487	0.021
Guizhou	11	0.652	0.332	0.558	0.077	0.349	0.015
Hainan	11	2.073	0.877	0.816	0.063	0.569	0.023
Hebei	11	0.883	0.443	0.683	0.092	0.596	0.046
Heilongjiang	11	1.277	0.721	0.783	0.088	0.386	0.127
Henan	11	0.434	0.238	0.502	0.023	0.514	0.029
Hubei	11	0.763	0.423	0.729	0.081	0.450	0.021
Hunan	11	0.834	0.508	0.730	0.072	0.507	0.022
Jiangsu	11	0.710	0.331	0.983	0.199	0.593	0.028
Jiangxi	11	0.690	0.483	0.507	0.077	0.471	0.048
Jilin	11	0.917	0.559	0.805	0.074	0.484	0.103
Liaoning	11	1.112	0.572	0.989	0.058	0.507	0.094
Inner Mongolia	11	1.358	0.810	0.172	0.030	0.412	0.087
Ningxia	11	0.894	0.467	1.207	0.147	0.367	0.079
Qinghai	11	0.560	0.282	0.834	0.044	0.328	0.109
Shaanxi	11	1.092	0.594	0.835	0.134	0.386	0.040
Shandong	11	0.860	0.384	0.632	0.085	0.594	0.058
Shanghai	11	1.104	0.483	3.333	0.711	0.578	0.106
Shanxi	11	0.526	0.281	0.887	0.072	0.393	0.101
Sichuan	11	1.535	0.826	0.558	0.077	0.528	0.064
Tianjin	11	0.579	0.242	2.007	0.190	0.546	0.087
Xinjiang	11	1.746	1.064	1.326	0.164	0.387	0.160
Tibet	11	0.316	0.151	0.217	0.034	0.089	0.040
Yunnan	11	0.923	0.517	0.558	0.077	0.381	0.028
Zhejiang	11	1.440	0.637	1.275	0.243	0.661	0.026
Total	341	1.074	0.889	1.021	1.087	0.473	0.136

The province-year institutional variables are then aggregated at the bank-year level, with the weights equaling to the proportion of each bank-year's loans in the respective province to that bank-year loans in all provinces. More explicitly, we have

$$\text{Institutional variable}_{\text{i, t}} = \sum_{j=1}^{31} w_{i,j,t} IV_{j,t} \tag{2}$$

$$\text{and } w_{i,j,t} = \frac{L_{i,j,t}}{\sum_{j=1}^{31} L_{i,j,t}} \tag{3}$$

In equations (2) and (3), j indexes the jth province in our sample, and ranges over 1, 2, . . ., 31. i indexes the ith bank in our sample, and ranges over 1, 2, . . ., 79. t indexes year, and ranges over 1996, 1997, . . ., 2006. $w_{i,j,t}$ indexes the weight of ith bank's loan in j^{th} province to total loans of ith bank in year t. $L_{i,j,t}$ indexes the total loans provided by i^{th} bank to j^{th} province in year t. $IV_{i,t}$ is the institutional variable of the jth province in year t.

These bank-year aggregated institutional variables are used independent variables in the OLS regressions that we present later.

4.5 Efficiency Measures

Cost and profit efficiency measure how close to the minimum cost or maximum profit a bank is, where the minimum and maximum are determined by best performers in the sample. We estimate efficiency levels by specifying the commonly-used translog functional form for the cost and profit functions. For convenience, we show only the cost function:

$$\begin{aligned}\ln(C/w_3z)_{it} = {} & \alpha_0 + \sum_{j=1}^{4} \delta_j \ln(y_j/z)_{it} + \frac{1}{2}\sum_{j=1}^{4}\sum_{k=1}^{4} \delta_{jk} \ln(y_j/z)_{it} \ln(y_k/z)_{it} \\ & + \sum_{l=1}^{2} \beta_l \ln(w_l/w_3)_{it} + \frac{1}{2}\sum_{l=1}^{2}\sum_{m=1}^{2} \beta_{lm} \ln(w_l/w_3)_{it} \ln(w_m/w_3)_{it} \\ & + \sum_{j=1}^{4}\sum_{l=1}^{2} \theta_{jl} \ln(y_j/z)_{it} \ln(w_l/w_3)_{it} \\ & + \textit{year dummies} + \ln\mu_{it} + \ln v_{it}\end{aligned} \tag{4}$$

where i, t index the bank and year, respectively, $j, k = 1,\ldots 4$ index the four output variables, and $\delta_{jk} \equiv \delta_{kj}$. C represents the bank's total costs. There are four outputs (y): total loans, total deposits, liquid assets, other earning assets; three input prices (w): w_1 (price of funds, proxied by the ratio of interest expenses to total deposits), w_2 (price of fixed capital, proxied by the ratio of other operating expenses to fixed assets), w_3 (price of labor, proxied by the ratio of personnel expenses to total number of employees); and one fixed netput (z): total assets. The $\ln\mu_{it}$ term represents a bank's efficiency level and $\ln v_{it}$ is a random error that incorporates both measurement error and luck. The cost function is estimated using $\ln\mu_{it} + \ln v_{it}$ as a composite error term. The normalization by bank's total assets (z) reduces heteroskedasticity, and allows banks of any size to have comparable residual terms from which the efficiencies are calculated. The normalization by the last input price (w_3) ensures price homogeneity.

A bank's cost efficiency score is determined by comparing its actual costs to best-practice minimum costs to produce the same output under the same conditions using estimates of the efficiency factor $\ln \mu_{it}$, which is disentangled from the estimated cost function residual using half-normal distributional assumptions, whereas $\ln v_{it}$ follows the normal distribution. Profit efficiency scores are estimated similarly. Total profits replace total costs and we add a constant before taking the log to avoid taking a log of negative number.

Table 5 presents the summary statistics of basic variables that are used in the profit and cost efficiency estimations, based on the approach outlined here.

Table 5 Summary statistics of variables used in efficiency estimations

Table 5 presents the summary statistics of basic variables used in the profit and cost efficiency estimations. In the translog based estimations of profit (cost) efficiency, output variables considered are total loans, total deposits, liquid assets, and other earning assets, and the input variables are w_1 (price of funds, proxied by the ratio of interest expenses to total deposits), w_2 (price of fixed capital, proxied by the ratio of other operating expenses to fixed assets), w_3 (price of labor, proxied by the ratio of personnel expenses to total number of employees). The outputs are normalized by total assets. All financial values are inflation-adjusted to the base year 1996

	Obs	Mean	Median	Std. dev.	Minimum	Maximum
Profit and cost (in billion US$)						
Total profits	411	0.212	0.017	0.772	–0.080	5.784
Total costs	411	1.088	0.098	2.821	0.000	21.200
Output quantities (in billion US$)						
Total loans (y_1)	411	26.800	1.770	71.300	0.000	426.000
Total deposits (y_2)	411	44.200	3.036	120.000	0.000	791.000
Liquid assets (y_3)	411	5.952	0.411	17.000	0.012	112.000
Other earning assets (y_4)	411	19.000	1.628	53.600	0.005	444.000
Input prices						
Price of funds (w_1)	411	0.026	0.020	0.015	0.003	0.067
Price of fixed capital (w_2)	411	0.913	0.760	0.562	0.174	2.500
Price of labor (w_3)	411	14.400	14.528	3.055	0.720	21.105
Total assets *(in billon US$)*	411	49.500	3.768	132.000	0.033	880.000

5 Empirical Results

In this section, we report our empirical evidence by modeling the Chinese banks' performance and efficiency as a function of ownership, diversification strategy, and institutional factors. More specifically, we intend to test whether the banks' performance and efficiency differ across different ownership categories, whether the banks' performance and efficiency are affected by their product diversification strategy, and whether the institutional environment in which these banks operate influences their performance and efficiency. More interestingly, we also attempt to examine whether minority foreign ownership plays an important role in explaining the improvement of banks' performance and efficiency when it interacts with the diversification strategy and institutional environment, and the possible mechanism behind.

Table 6 presents the OLS regressions of return-on-assets (ROA) on ownership, Focus Indices, and institutional variables. The Focus Index used in the regressions presented by the first two columns is the loan Focus Index, which is defined based on the loan portfolio decomposition and Focus Index in Section 4.3. In the similar fashion, the Focus Index used in the regressions presented by the third and fourth columns is deposit Focus Index, followed by asset Focus Index in the fifth and sixth columns and geographic Focus Index in the seventh and eighth columns. Besides, within each pair of columns which use the same Focus Indices, the general difference between the odd numbered column and even numbered column is that the regressions in the even numbered columns include interaction terms between minority foreign ownership and Focus Indices, and interaction terms between minority foreign ownership and institutional variables, besides the independent variables already included in the regressions presented in the odd numbered columns. In all cases, small, majority private domestic banks are suppressed in the constant.

Across all columns in Table 6 minority foreign ownership dummy is associated with positive and (most of the time) significant coefficient, which implies that the Chinese domestic banks that are associated with minority foreign ownership tend to be better performers in terms of ROA.[6] The coefficients of Focus Index are positive and significant most of the time, indicating that banks with more focused product diversification strategy tends to perform better, or equivalently, the banks who diversify more in their products are, on average, associated with lower ROA. The negative and significant coefficients of the interaction term between Focus Index and minority foreign implies imply that the minority foreign ownership plays an mitigating role when banks diversify: the banks who are associated with minority foreign ownership will suffer less from decreased ROA when they diversify in their loans, deposits, assets, or geographic portfolios.

The three institutional variables present different properties of roles in affecting ROA of the banks as shown in Table 6. The positive and significant coefficients of awareness of property rights variable indicate that banks tend to perform better when they operate in an environment in which there is more awareness and respect for property rights, and/or a higher degree of development of secure property rights-associated institutions in the environment. There is a significant literature that confirms that well-defined property rights induce agents to exert their efforts (see, e.g., Wilson, 1989; Schmidt, 1991; Shapiro and

---

[6] We are less concerned with the insignificance of the minority foreign ownership dummy coefficients in the even numbered columns because those columns include the interaction terms between minority foreign and other variables, and when higher order terms are present in the regression, significance of the lower order terms becomes less relevant. The same rule also applies to the coefficients of Focus Index and the institutional variables in the even numbered columns.

Table 6 OLS regressions of ROA on ownership, Focus Indices, and institutional variables

Table 6 presents the ordinary least square (OLS) regressions of return-on-assets (ROA) on a number of independent variables including ownership dummies, Focus Indices of portfolios, institutional variables and size dummies. Interaction terms between Focus Indices and minority foreign ownership dummy variable and between institutional variables and minority foreign ownership dummy variable are also included in some of the regressions. Small, majority private banks are suppressed in the constant. The definitions of ownership dummies follow the same as in Table 1. The definitions of decomposition of loan, deposit, asset, and geographical portfolios are the same as described in Table 2. The definitions of institutional variables follow the same as in Table 4, except that they are aggregated at the bank-year level when used in the regressions. Absolute value of t statistics in brackets, and *, **, and *** represent significance level of 10%, 5%, and 1%, respectively

	Dependent variable: ROA							
	Loan Focus Index		Deposit Focus Index		Asset Focus Index		Geographic Focus Index	
Constant	0.018***	0.018***	0.016***	0.016***	0.015***	0.015***	0.018***	0.018***
	[12.40]	[11.90]	[10.83]	[10.43]	[10.22]	[10.09]	[14.45]	[13.36]
Big Four	−0.001	−0.001	−0.001	−0.001	−0.001	−0.001	−0.001	−0.001
	[0.68]	[1.10]	[0.77]	[1.24]	[0.76]	[1.21]	[0.84]	[1.37]
Majority state-owned	−0.001*	−0.001**	−0.001*	−0.001**	−0.001	−0.001**	−0.001*	−0.001**
	[1.73]	[2.59]	[1.68]	[2.55]	[1.54]	[2.38]	[1.66]	[2.51]
Minority foreign ownership	0.001**	0.002	0.001**	0.004**	0.001**	0.002	0.001**	0.003*
	[2.51]	[0.91]	[2.54]	[2.10]	[2.34]	[1.11]	[2.57]	[1.82]
Focus Index	0.001**	0.001	0.003**	0.002	0.007**	0.005**	0.001***	0.001
	[2.18]	[0.23]	[2.45]	[1.16]	[2.58]	[2.00]	[2.67]	[0.63]
Focus Index * Minority foreign		−0.004**		−0.001**		−0.004*		−0.002**
		[2.55]		[2.38]		[1.79]		[2.23]
Awareness of property rights	0.001***	0.002***	0.001***	0.002***	0.001***	0.001***	0.001***	0.002***
	[3.34]	[4.76]	[3.21]	[4.65]	[2.85]	[4.30]	[3.35]	[4.80]
Rule of law	−0.001***	−0.001***	−0.001***	−0.001***	−0.001***	−0.001***	−0.001***	−0.001***
	[4.82]	[6.28]	[4.44]	[5.87]	[4.25]	[5.62]	[4.86]	[6.34]
Presence of private sector	0.002*	0.001	0.003*	0.001	0.003**	0.001	0.002**	0.001
	[1.68]	[0.29]	[1.77]	[0.32]	[2.14]	[0.64]	[2.21]	[0.01]
Awareness of property rights * Minority foreign		0.002***		0.002***		0.002***		0.002***
		[3.10]		[3.15]		[3.15]		[3.20]

Table 6 (continued)

	Dependent variable: ROA							
	Loan Focus Index		Deposit Focus Index		Asset Focus Index		Geographic Focus Index	
Rule of law * Minority foreign		0.001***		0.001***		0.001***		0.001***
		[3.83]		[3.65]		[3.37]		[3.76]
Presence of private sector * Minority foreign		0.006*		0.006*		0.007**		0.008**
		[1.82]		[1.95]		[2.16]		[2.22]
Medium banks	–0.001	–0.001	–0.001	–0.001	0.001	0.001	–0.001	–0.001
	[1.35]	[1.26]	[1.01]	[0.92]	[0.55]	[0.55]	[1.39]	[1.27]
Large banks	–0.002***	–0.002***	–0.002**	–0.002**	–0.002***	–0.002**	–0.003***	–0.002**
	[3.22]	[2.75]	[2.50]	[2.12]	[2.88]	[2.46]	[3.02]	[2.45]
Observations	411	411	411	411	411	411	411	411
F-statistics	6.43	6.22	6.69	6.13	7.27	6.56	6.48	6.15
R-square	0.13	0.17	0.13	0.17	0.14	0.18	0.13	0.17
Adj R-square	0.11	0.14	0.11	0.14	0.12	0.15	0.11	0.14

Willig, 1991; Laffont and Tirole, 1993; Tirole, 1994). Consequently, creditors are better off in an environment where property rights are strictly enforced.

The negative and significant coefficients of rule of law indicate that banks tend to perform better when the environment is associated with *poorer* rule of law, i.e., less development of legal institutions and less law enforcement. Such direction of the link between banks' performance and institutional environment in terms of rule of law seems contradictory to the evidence that some studies found in other countries, such as La Porta et al. (1997, 1998). But if we take the special banking environment and capital market in China into account, such a relationship is not totally surprising. First, most of the lending contracts between the banks (especially the state-owned banks) and state-owned enterprises (SOEs) are not really legally binding or strictly enforced, in the sense that in time of default, the banks do not have a lot of power to force repayment from the borrowers, or to force the borrower to file bankruptcy. On the other hand, lending to the private sector is more legally binding, and therefore, we predict that an environment with stricter rule of law exerts stronger effect on performance of lending to private sector than that to the state sector. However, most private firms in China are relatively small and rely heavily on internal finance and relationship lending, while suffering from less access to bank loans and capital markets (see, e.g., Cull and Xu, 2005). While relationship banks need to invest a great amount of resource to collect proprietary information and exert tight monitoring on their customers, it is plausible that strict enforcement of legal institutions weakens such incentives and results in sub-optimal lending decisions with a higher default rate.

With regard to the institutional aspect captured by the presence of the private sector in Table 6, we find that banks tend to perform better in an environment where there is a prosperous private sector. This is generally consistent with existing banking and growth literature, such as King and Levine (1993a,b,c). In contrast to the SOEs which tend to have a soft budget constraint in a centrally planned or transitional economy, private enterprises have more incentive to keep up good relations with banks by not defaulting. In addition, it is well documented that small private firms are more flexible in choosing profitable projects, more capable of capturing the entrepreneurial opportunities, and have more potential to achieve large improvements in performance (e.g., Frydman et al., 1999; La Porta and Lopez De-Silanes, 1999).

The interactions between each institutional variable and minority foreign ownership are all associated with positive and significant coefficients in Table 6. The positive coefficients of the interaction terms indicate that on average, with the same amount of improvement in institutional environment in terms of awareness of property rights or presence of private sector, or with the same amount of deterioration in institutional environment in terms of rule of law, Chinese banks with minority foreign ownership tend to perform better than those without minority foreign ownership.

Table 7 follows the same format as Table 6, with the only difference being that the dependent variable in Table 7 is profit efficiency instead of ROA.

Table 7 OLS regressions of profit efficiency on ownership, Focus Indices, and institutional variables

Table 7 presents the ordinary least square (OLS) regressions of profit efficiency on a number of independent variables including ownership dummies, Focus Indices of portfolios, institutional variables, and size dummies. Interaction terms between Focus Indices and minority foreign ownership dummy variable, and between institutional variables and minority foreign ownership dummy variable are also included in some of the regressions. Small, majority private banks are suppressed in the constant. Profit efficiency is calculated based on the production function specified in Table 5. The definitions of ownership dummies follow the same as in Table 1. The definitions of decomposition of loan, deposit, asset, and geographical portfolios are the same as described in Table 2. The definitions of institutional variables follow the same as in Table 4, except that they are aggregated at the bank-year level when used in the regressions. Absolute value of t statistics in brackets, and *, **, and *** represent significance level of 10%, 5%, and 1%, respectively

	Dependent variable: profit efficiency							
	Loan Focus Index		Deposit Focus Index		Asset Focus Index		Geographic Focus Index	
Constant	0.814***	0.821***	0.890***	0.886***	0.861***	0.858***	0.880***	0.878***
	[40.79]	[39.15]	[42.14]	[40.63]	[41.02]	[39.77]	[49.19]	[46.39]
Big Four	0.031**	0.031**	0.043***	0.041***	0.041***	0.039***	0.030**	0.028**
	[2.32]	[2.31]	[3.33]	[3.18]	[3.15]	[3.01]	[2.20]	[2.03]
Majority state-owned	–0.004	–0.006	–0.003	–0.005	–0.003	–0.005	–0.002	–0.003
	[0.68]	[0.87]	[0.52]	[0.79]	[0.47]	[0.71]	[0.26]	[0.46]
Minority foreign ownership	0.001**	0.004	0.002**	0.025	0.002**	0.014	0.003**	0.009
	[2.15]	[0.14]	[2.23]	[0.93]	[2.29]	[0.52]	[2.47]	[0.38]
Focus Index	0.099***	0.078**	0.063**	0.059**	0.016**	0.015	0.041**	0.041**
	[2.85]	[2.15]	[2.27]	[2.13]	[2.42]	[0.40]	[2.27]	[2.26]
Focus Index * Minority foreign		–0.045*		–0.025*		–0.011**		–0.017*
		[1.77]		[1.72]		[2.25]		[1.92]
Awareness of property rights	0.008*	0.002	0.007*	0.001	0.007*	0.002	0.008*	0.002
	[1.89]	[0.47]	[1.72]	[0.23]	[1.80]	[0.32]	[1.87]	[0.40]
Rule of law	–0.003**	–0.002*	–0.002*	–0.001**	–0.003**	–0.002*	–0.002*	–0.001
	[2.23]	[1.79]	[1.80]	[2.37]	[2.17]	[1.74]	[1.83]	[1.55]

Table 7 (continued)

	Dependent variable: profit efficiency							
	Loan Focus Index		Deposit Focus Index		Asset Focus Index		Geographic Focus Index	
Presence of private sector	0.046**	0.026	0.041**	0.020	0.042**	0.020	0.021*	0.001
	[2.26]	[1.14]	[2.00]	[0.88]	[2.01]	[0.87]	[1.92]	[0.05]
Awareness of property rights * Minority foreign		0.020**		0.022**		0.022**		0.021**
		[2.25]		[2.45]		[2.46]		[2.38]
Rule of law * Minority foreign		0.002**		0.002**		0.001**		0.001**
		[2.35]		[2.46]		[2.23]		[2.11]
Presence of private sector * Minority foreign		0.078*		0.082*		0.093**		0.098**
		[1.70]		[1.76]		[2.01]		[1.98]
Medium banks	–0.009	–0.009	–0.016*	–0.015*	–0.012	–0.012	–0.012	–0.011
	[1.12]	[1.11]	[1.88]	[1.75]	[1.45]	[1.36]	[1.45]	[1.40]
Large banks	–0.025**	–0.024**	–0.033***	–0.031***	–0.024**	–0.023**	–0.040***	–0.038***
	[2.42]	[2.31]	[2.95]	[2.77]	[2.32]	[2.17]	[3.18]	[3.00]
Observations	411	411	411	411	411	411	411	411
F-statistics	3.18	2.86	2.83	2.61	2.25	2.21	2.83	2.64
R-square	0.07	0.09	0.06	0.08	0.05	0.07	0.06	0.08
Adj R-square	0.05	0.06	0.04	0.05	0.03	0.04	0.04	0.05

Although our study includes both accounting measures and efficiency measures, in general, we consider efficiency measures superior to accounting performance measures because efficiency measures are more comprehensive in the sense that the efficiency measures take into account both inputs and outputs, and they gauge how the banks are efficiently utilizing the available resources to maximizing their profits in the case of profit efficiency (or minimizing costs in the case of cost efficiency). As mentioned earlier, we measure efficiency from pooled observations incorporating year dummies in order to avoid any estimation biases that may arise due to potential changes in bank performance due to technological progress or changes in the economic and regulatory environments. We therefore avoid time fixed effects in the secondary regressions, given the efficiency scores are adjusted for sample years, avoiding time adjustment twice.

Despite the measurement differences between ROA and profit efficiency, Table 7 presents very similar evidence as Table 6 in terms of the direction of the links between banks' performance and ownership, diversification, and institutions. Therefore, the evidence presented in Table 7 confirms our findings in Table 6.

We then turn our attention to the cost perspective of the banks. Table 8 presents the OLS regressions of the cost ratio (total expenses/total assets) on the same sets of independent variables as in Tables 6 and 7. The negative and significant coefficients associated with minority foreign ownership indicate that banks with minority foreign ownership, on average, tend to be more cost saving (i.e., lower costs/assets ratio). The negative and significant coefficients of Focus Indices imply that on average, banks with more focused strategy (less diversified) tend to be more cost saving. The positive and significant coefficients of the interaction term between Focus Indices and minority foreign ownership indicate that minority foreign ownership plays a mitigating role: Banks with minority foreign ownership, on average, tend to have lower costs/assets when they diversify compared with banks without minority foreign ownership.

Turning to our measures of institutional variables, we find that all our three institutional variables are negatively and significantly associated with the cost ratio, indicating that banks operate in environment with more awareness of property rights, and/or more enforcing rule of law, and/or higher presence of private sector, on average, tend to have lower cost ratios. We omit the discussions of the interaction terms between awareness of property rights (and presence of private sector) and minority foreign ownership because they do not have significant coefficients. On the other hand, the coefficients of the interaction term between rule of law and minority foreign ownership is significantly negative, indicating that minority foreign ownership, on average, tends to reinforce the cost-reducing effects of institutional variables in terms of better legal institutions and rule of law.

Table 9 presents the OLS regressions of cost efficiency on the same set of independent variables as in Tables 6, 7, and 8. As we mentioned earlier, we regard the efficiency measures to be superior to the accounting measures.

Table 8 OLS regressions of cost ratio on ownership, Focus Indices, and institutional variables

Table 8 presents the ordinary least square (OLS) regressions of cost ratio (total expenses/total assets) on a number of independent variables including ownership dummies, Focus Indices of portfolios, institutional variables, and size dummies. Interaction terms between Focus Indices and minority foreign ownership dummy variable, and between institutional variables and minority foreign ownership dummy variable are also included in some of the regressions. Small, majority private banks are suppressed in the constant. The definitions of ownership dummies follow the same as in Table 1. The definitions of decomposition of loan, deposit, asset, and geographical portfolios are the same as described in Table 2. The definitions of institutional variables follow the same as in Table 4, except that they are aggregated at the bank-year level when used in the regressions. Absolute value of t statistics in brackets, and *, **, and *** represent significance level of 10%, 5%, and 1%, respectively

	Dependent variable: total expenses/total assets							
	Loan Focus Index		Deposit Focus Index		Asset Focus Index		Geographic Focus Index	
Constant	0.040***	0.039***	0.028***	0.029***	0.024***	0.026***	0.024***	0.023***
	[9.78]	[9.15]	[6.31]	[6.49]	[5.57]	[5.85]	[6.45]	[6.02]
Big Four	0.006**	0.004	0.003	0.002	0.003	0.002	0.006**	0.005*
	[2.08]	[1.61]	[1.13]	[0.77]	[1.12]	[0.74]	[1.99]	[1.66]
Majority state-owned	0.004***	0.004***	0.004***	0.003**	0.004***	0.003**	0.004***	0.003**
	[3.38]	[2.70]	[3.07]	[2.40]	[3.18]	[2.51]	[2.86]	[2.15]
Minority foreign ownership	–0.002*	–0.003	–0.003*	–0.004	–0.003**	–0.004	–0.003**	–0.003
	[1.73]	[0.54]	[1.84]	[0.66]	[1.98]	[0.79]	[2.10]	[0.57]
Focus Index	–0.025***	–0.023***	–0.003***	–0.001	–0.013*	–0.009	0.009**	0.010***
	[3.58]	[3.16]	[2.59]	[0.15]	[1.74]	[1.20]	[2.57]	[2.67]
Focus Index * Minority foreign		0.001**		0.002**		0.001**		0.003*
		[2.18]		[2.31]		[2.09]		[1.74]
Awareness of property rights	–0.003***	–0.004***	–0.003***	–0.004***	–0.003***	–0.004***	–0.003***	–0.004***
	[3.86]	[4.30]	[3.77]	[4.15]	[3.47]	[3.87]	[3.81]	[4.22]
Rule of law	–0.002***	–0.003***	–0.002***	–0.003***	–0.002***	–0.003***	–0.002***	–0.003***
	[5.21]	[6.05]	[4.98]	[5.93]	[4.77]	[5.63]	[4.67]	[5.74]
Presence of private sector	–0.013***	–0.013***	–0.014***	–0.014***	–0.015***	–0.015***	–0.019***	–0.019***
	[3.17]	[2.70]	[3.28]	[2.89]	[3.53]	[3.07]	[4.08]	[3.70]
Awareness of property rights * Minority foreign		0.003		0.003		0.002		0.003
		[1.61]		[1.39]		[1.32]		[1.50]

Table 8 (continued)

	Dependent variable: total expenses/total assets							
	Loan Focus Index		Deposit Focus Index		Asset Focus Index		Geographic Focus Index	
Rule of law * Minority foreign		–0.003***		–0.003***		–0.003***		–0.004***
		[3.16]		[3.29]		[3.08]		[3.42]
Presence of private sector * Minority foreign		0.003		0.006		0.006		0.006
		[0.32]		[0.65]		[0.62]		[0.59]
Medium banks	0.003**	0.004**	0.004**	0.004**	0.005***	0.005***	0.004**	0.004**
	[2.06]	[2.17]	[2.45]	[2.44]	[2.80]	[2.71]	[2.46]	[2.58]
Large banks	–0.004*	–0.003	–0.004*	–0.003	–0.004*	–0.003	–0.001	0.001
	[1.93]	[1.51]	[1.71]	[1.48]	[1.82]	[1.49]	[0.23]	[0.15]
Observations	411	411	411	411	411	411	411	411
F-statistics	14.51	10.99	12.73	9.85	13.12	9.99	13.63	10.58
R-square	0.25	0.26	0.22	0.24	0.23	0.25	0.23	0.26
Adj R-square	0.23	0.24	0.20	0.22	0.21	0.22	0.22	0.23

Table 9 OLS regressions of cost efficiency on ownership, Focus Indices, and institutional variables

Table 9 presents the ordinary least square (OLS) regressions of cost efficiency on a number of independent variables including ownership dummies, Focus Indices of portfolios, institutional variables, and size dummies. Interaction terms between Focus Indices and minority foreign ownership dummy variable and between institutional variables and minority foreign ownership dummy variable are also included in some of the regressions. Small, majority private banks are suppressed in the constant. Cost efficiency is calculated based on the production function specified in Table 5. The definitions of ownership dummies follow the same as in Table 1. The definitions of decomposition of loan, deposit, asset, and geographical portfolios are the same as described in Table 2. The definitions of institutional variables follow the same as in Table 4, except that they are aggregated at the bank-year level when used in the regressions. Absolute value of t statistics in brackets, and *, **, and *** represent significance level of 10%, 5%, and 1%, respectively

	Dependent variable: cost efficiency							
	Loan Focus Index		Deposit Focus Index		Asset Focus Index		Geographic Focus Index	
Constant	0.456***	0.437***	0.508***	0.515***	0.491***	0.494***	0.457***	0.462***
	[12.09]	[11.11]	[12.78]	[12.61]	[12.49]	[12.23]	[13.58]	[12.97]
Big Four	–0.040	–0.040	–0.033	–0.026	–0.034	–0.029	–0.026	–0.019
	[1.59]	[1.60]	[1.34]	[1.05]	[1.40]	[1.20]	[0.99]	[0.73]
Majority state-owned	–0.023*	–0.019	–0.022*	–0.018	–0.022*	–0.018	–0.023*	–0.019
	[1.91]	[1.58]	[1.88]	[1.50]	[1.87]	[1.47]	[1.93]	[1.56]
Minority foreign ownership	0.042***	0.073	0.042***	0.056	0.043***	0.019	0.041***	0.025
	[3.31]	[1.37]	[3.33]	[1.12]	[3.36]	[0.37]	[3.23]	[0.55]
Focus Index	0.055*	0.112*	0.052**	0.054	0.030**	0.023	0.035**	0.036
	[1.84]	[1.65]	[2.01]	[1.04]	[2.43]	[0.33]	[2.03]	[1.06]
Focus Index * Minority foreign		–0.155**		–0.122*		–0.023**		–0.041*
		[2.16]		[1.91]		[2.28]		[2.17]
Awareness of property rights	0.016**	0.028***	0.015**	0.027***	0.015*	0.027***	0.016**	0.028***
	[2.05]	[3.11]	[1.97]	[3.02]	[1.95]	[2.97]	[2.08]	[3.13]
Rule of law	0.004	0.001	0.005	0.002	0.004	0.001	0.003	0.001
	[0.92]	[0.25]	[1.09]	[0.39]	[0.97]	[0.24]	[0.69]	[0.01]
Presence of private sector	0.016**	0.026	0.020**	0.021	0.021**	0.020	0.002**	0.042
	[2.43]	[0.61]	[2.52]	[0.50]	[2.53]	[0.46]	[2.04]	[0.91]

Table 9 (continued)

	Dependent variable: cost efficiency							
	Loan Focus Index		Deposit Focus Index		Asset Focus Index		Geographic Focus Index	
Awareness of property rights * Minority foreign		-0.043^{**}		-0.045^{***}		-0.044^{**}		-0.043^{**}
		[2.52]		[2.65]		[2.55]		[2.56]
Rule of law * Minority foreign		0.008^{*}		0.007^{*}		0.008^{*}		0.008^{*}
		[1.88]		[1.72]		[1.84]		[1.87]
Presence of private sector * Minority foreign		0.155^{*}		0.189^{**}		0.164^{*}		0.193^{**}
		[1.81]		[2.18]		[1.89]		[2.07]
Medium banks	–0.013	–0.013	–0.018	–0.019	–0.016	–0.018	–0.014	–0.015
	[0.84]	[0.84]	[1.13]	[1.21]	[1.02]	[1.09]	[0.90]	[0.98]
Large banks	–0.011	–0.013	–0.017	–0.023	–0.011	–0.015	0.004	–0.002
	[0.54]	[0.66]	[0.83]	[1.10]	[0.56]	[0.76]	[0.17]	[0.08]
Observations	411	411	411	411	411	411	411	411
F-statistics	4.29	4.00	4.32	3.92	4.22	3.52	4.33	3.69
R-square	0.09	0.12	0.09	0.11	0.09	0.10	0.09	0.11
Adj R-square	0.07	0.09	0.07	0.08	0.07	0.07	0.07	0.08

Therefore, the evidence presented in Table 9, in our view, is more important than what is presented in Table 8. However, in general, profit efficiency measure is regarded superior to cost efficiency as an indicator of the quality of bank management, because profit efficiency takes account of both cost and revenue performance, and thus is a more inclusive concept, given that managers have some control over both revenues and costs.

Regarding the links between minority foreign ownership, diversification strategy, and the interaction term between these two variables, Table 9 presents evidence that is consistent with Table 8.[7] Turning to our measures of institutional variables, we find that both awareness of property rights and presence of private sector are positively and significantly associated with cost efficiency, while the effect of rule of law on cost efficiency is insignificant. These findings indicate that banks are better off in terms of cost efficiency when they operate in an environment with better defined and awarded property rights, and/or a more thriving private sector.

What is more interesting is the signs of the coefficients of the interaction terms between institutional variables and minority foreign ownership. The negative and significant coefficients of the interaction term between awareness of property rights and minority foreign ownership indicate the substitute effects between property rights environment and inside monitoring from minority foreign investors, or in other words, it implies that the positive effect of minority foreign ownership on cost efficiency of the Chinese banks, on average, tends to be less observable when the banks are already operating in an environment where there is sound property rights awareness and protection. On the other hand, both the interaction terms between the rule of law and minority foreign ownership and between presence of the private sector and minority foreign ownership are positively and significantly associated with cost efficiency of the banks, indicating that minority foreign ownership, on average, reinforces the positive effect of institutional variables in terms of property rights and private sector on cost efficiency. Combining such evidence with findings in previous tables, it appears that rule of law tends to have different effects on profit efficiency and cost efficiency for the Chinese banks. As we have argued, banks operating in an environment with strict rule of law may have less incentive to spend resources in collecting proprietary information, which results in less profit efficiency (e.g., Hauswald and Marquez, 2006). However, by reducing the investment in information collection, banks may record better cost efficiency.

---

[7] When comparing Tables 8 and 9, please note that the lower costs/assets ratio in Table 8 corresponds roughly to the higher cost efficiency in Table 9, therefore, in general, the signs of the coefficients of the independent variables in these two tables are expected to be opposite to each other.

6 Conclusions

This chapter examines the role of ownership, diversification strategy, and institutional environment in affecting the performance of Chinese banks. We begin our discussion by first introducing the historical background of these banks, their major structural reforms and important transitions from servicing the centrally planned economy to servicing the current dynamic market economy, coupled with the entry of foreign investors and the qualitative changes in the institutional environment across different regions in China. We then empirically investigate the role of ownership (especially minority foreign ownership), diversification strategy, and institutions on the banks' performance by employing a sample of 79 Chinese banks over 11 years from 1996 to 2006 (totaling 411 bank-year observations).

Our evidence indicates that banks tend to perform better in terms of profits (ROA) and profit efficiency when they are associated with minority foreign ownership, more focused business strategy, and in environment where there are better institutions in terms of awareness of property rights and presence of private sector. In addition, minority foreign ownership exhibits an important mitigating effect when it interacts with diversification strategy, that is, meaning banks, on average, suffer less from diversification discount when there is minority foreign ownership. Minority foreign ownership also shows a strong reinforcing effect when it interacts with the institutional variables in terms of awareness of property rights, rule of law, and presence of private sector, that is, banks with minority foreign ownership, on average, perform better compared to banks without minority foreign ownership when they operate in the same improved institutional environment.

In terms of the cost ratio (expenses to assets) and cost efficiency, we find that minority foreign ownership, a more focused business strategy, and better institutional environment (in terms of awareness of property rights, rule of law, and presence of private sector) tend to contribute to more cost savings and better cost efficiency of the Chinese banks. Furthermore, our study also shows that minority foreign ownership mitigates the diversification discount in terms of expenses to total assets or cost efficiency. Also, our evidence shows that there is a substitute effect between property rights environment and inside monitoring from minority foreign investors, while minority foreign ownership, on average, reinforces the positive effect of institutional variables in terms of property rights and private sector on cost efficiency. One of the institutional variables, rule of law, tends to have different effects on profits and profit efficiency as opposed to costs and cost efficiency for the Chinese banks. We argue that it is because in China, banks operating in an environment with a stricter rule of law may have less incentive to spend resources in collecting proprietary information and do relationship lending to private sector, which results in less profits and profit efficiency, while such reduced investment in information collection may result in better costs and cost efficiency for the Chinese banks.

An important note is that there might be a pitfall before we can draw any strong conclusions regarding the performance of state-owned banks, as these banks have been facing pressures and directions from central and local governments to grant policy loans for political purposes, rather than for profit maximization, consistent with findings for state-owned banks in other nations (e.g., Sapienza, 2004). However, with the recent reforms and increasing pressure from the market discipline as some state-owned banks go public and acquire minority foreign ownership shares, Chinese state-owned banks have become more profit-driven in recent years, and this trend increases the relevance of studies like ours.

References

Acharya, V.V., Hasan, I., Saunders, A., 2006. Should banks be diversified? evidence from individual bank loan portfolios. *Journal of Business* 79, 1355–1412.

Aron, J., 2000. Growth and institutions: A review of the evidence. *The World Bank Research Observer* 15, 99–135.

Aziz, J., Duenwald, C., 2002. Growth-financial intermediation nexus in China. IMF Working Paper, 01/3.

Berger, A.N., Hasan, I., Klapper, L.F., 2004. Further evidence on the link between finance and growth: An international analysis of community banking and economic performance, *Journal of Financial Services Research* 25: 169–202.

Berger, A.N., Hasan, I., Zhou, M., 2008a. Bank ownership and efficiency in China: What will happen in the world's largest nation? *Journal of Banking and Finance*, forthcoming.

Berger, A.N., Hasan, I., Zhou, M., 2008b. The effects of focus versus diversification on bank performance: Evidence from Chinese banks. Working paper.

Berger, A.N., Mester, L.J. 1997. Inside the black box: What explains differences in the efficiency of financial institutions? *Journal of Banking and Finance* 21, 895–947.

Berger, P.G., Ofek, E., 1995. Diversification's effect on firm value. *Journal of Financial Economics* 37, 39–65.

Bonin, J.P., Hasan, I., Wachtel, P., 2005a. Bank performance, efficiency and ownership in transition countries. *Journal of Banking and Finance* 29, 31–53.

Bonin, J.P., Hasan, I., Wachtel, P., 2005b. Privatization matters: Bank efficiency in transition countries. *Journal of Banking and Finance* 29, 2155–2178.

Boyd, J., Prescott, E., 1986. Financial intermediary coalitions. *Journal of Economic Theory* 38, 211–32.

Cull, R. Xu, L.C., 2005. Institutions, ownership, and finance: The determinants of profit reinvestment among Chinese firms. *Journal of Financial Economics* 77, 117–146.

DeLong, G., 2001. Stockholder gains from focusing versus diversifying bank mergers. *Journal of Financial Economics* 59, 221–252.

Demirguc-Kunt, A., Huizinga, H., 1999. Determinants of commercial bank interest margins and profitability: Some international evidence, *World Bank Economic Review* 13, 379–408.

Demurger, S., Sachs, J.D., Woo, W.T., Bao, S., Chang, G., Mellinger, A., 2002. Geography, economic policy and regional development in China. Harvard Institute of Economic Research Discussion Paper Number 1950. Available at SSRN: http://ssrn.com/abstract=286672.

Deng, S., Elyasiani, E., 2007. Geographic diversification and BHC return and risk performance. Working paper.

Denis, D., Denis, D., Sarin, A., 1997. Agency problems, equity ownership, and corporate diversification. *Journal of Finance* 52, 135–160.

Diamond, D., 1984. Financial intermediation and delegated monitoring. *Review of Economic Studies* 59, 393–414.

Djankov, S., Qian, Y., Roland, G., Zhuravskaya, E., 2006. Who Are China's Entrepreneurs? *American Economic Review* 96, 348–352.

Drucker, S., Puri, M., 2008. On loan sales, loan contracting, and lending relationships, *Review of Financial Studies*, forthcoming.

Frydman, R., Gray, C., Hessel, M., Rapaczynski, A., 1999. When does privatization work? The impact of private ownership on corporate performance in the transition economies. *Quarterly Journal of Economics* 114, 1153–1191.

Garcia-Herrero, A., Santabarbara, D., 2008. Does the Chinese banking system benefit from foreign investors? BOFIT Discussion Papers 11/2008.

Hasan, I., Wachtel, P., Zhou, M., 2008. Institutional development, financial deepening and economic growth: Evidence from China. *Journal of Banking and Finance*, forthcoming.

Hasan, I., Wang, H., Zhou, M., 2009. Do better institutions improve bank efficiency? Evidence from a transitional economy. *Managerial Finance*, forthcoming.

Hauswald, R., Marquez, R., 2006. Competition and Strategic Information Acquisition in Credit Markets, *Review of Financial Studies* 19, 967–1000.

Henisz, W.J., 2000. The institutional environment for economic growth. *Economics and Politics* 12, 1–30.

Iskandar-Datta, M., McLaughlin, R., 2005. Global diversification: new evidence from corporate operating performance, Working Paper, retrieved from www.fma.org/chicago/papers/fmadiversity.pdf.

Johnson, S., McMillan, J., Woodruff, C., 2002. Property Rights and Finance. *American Economic Review* 92, 1335–1356.

Kho, B., Stulz, R.M., Warnock, F.E., 2006, Financial globalization, governance, and the evolution of the home bias, Working paper, 1–51.

King, R., Levine, R., 1993a. Finance and growth: Schumpeter might be right. *Quarterly Journal of Economics* 108, 717–737.

King, R., Levine, R., 1993b. Finance, entrepreneurship, and growth: theory and evidence, *Journal of Monetary Economics* 32, 513–542.

King, R., Levine, R., 1993c. Financial intermediation and economic development. In C. Mayer and X. Vives (eds.), Capital Markets and Financial Intermediation, pp. 156–189. Cambridge University Press, Cambridge.

Klein, P., Saidenberg, M., 1998. Diversification, organization, and efficiency: evidence from bank holding companies. Federal Reserve Bank of New York Working paper.

Krug, B., Hendrischke, H., 2001. China incorporated: Property right, privatisation, and the emergence of a private business sector in China. ERIM Report Series ERS-2001-81-ORG.

Laeven, L., Levine, R., 2007. Is there a diversification discount in financial conglomerates? *Journal of Financial Economics* 85, 331–367.

La Porta, R., Lopez-De-Silanes, F., Shleifer, A., Vishny, R.W., 1997. Legal determinants of external finance, *The Journal of Finance* 52, 1131–1150.

La Porta, R., Lopez-De-Silanes, F., Shleifer, A., Vishny, R.W., 1998, Law and finance, *The Journal of Political Economy* 106, 1113–1155.

La Porta, R., López-De-Silanes, F., 1999. The benefits of privatization: Evidence from Mexico, *Quarterly Journal of Economics* 114, 1193–1242.

Laffont, J.-J., Tirole, J., 1993. A Theory of Incentives in Regulation and Procurement, MIT Press, Cambrighe, MA.

Qian, J., Strahan, P.E., 2007. How laws and institutions shape financial contracts: The case of bank loans, *The Journal of Finance* 62, 2803–2834.

Rajan, R.G., Zingales, L., 2003. The great reversals: the politics of financial development in the twentieth century, *Journal of Financial Economics* 69, 5–50.

Sapienza, P., 2004. The effects of government ownership on bank lending. *Journal of Financial Economics* 74, 357–384.

Servaes, H., 1997. The value of diversification during the conglomerate merger wave. *Journal of Finance* 51, 1201–1225.
Schmidt, K., 1991. The Costs of Benefits of Privatization, Mimeo, University of Bonn, Germany.
Shapiro, C., Willig, R., 1991. Economic Rationales for the Scope of Privatization, Mimeo, Princeton University, Princeton.
Stiroh, K.J., 2004. Diversification in banking: Is noninterest income the answer? *Journal of Money, Credit and Banking* 36, 853–882.
Stulz, R.M., 2005. The limits of financial globalization, *The Journal of Finance* 60, 1595–1638.
Tirole, J., 1994. The internal organization of government, *Oxford Economic Papers* 46, 1–29.
Wilson, J.Q., 1989. Bureaucracy: What Government Agencies Do and Why They Do It, Basic Books, New york.
Yildirim, H.S., Philippatos, G.C., 2007. Efficiency of banks: Recent evidence from the transition economies of Europe 1993–2000. *European Journal of Finance* 13, 123–143.

China's Nonperforming Loans: A $540 Billion Problem Unsolved

Tong Li

Abstract China's banking industry has grown rapidly over the past three decades. As the major source of funding for Chinese enterprises (especially state-owned enterprises), the banking sector has helped finance the nation's transformation from a centrally planned economy to a market-oriented economy. In the meantime, large amounts of nonperforming loans have accumulated on the balance sheets of Chinese banks, partly due to the cost of reform, partly due to poor management and inadequate regulation. In 1999, four asset management corporations were established to resolve the nonperforming loan problem. As stated by the State Council, these asset management corporations would cease operation by the end of 2009. It is therefore of interest to examine the progress they have made in disposing of nonperforming loans. In this paper, the author attempts to draw a picture of how the nonperforming loan problem has developed since the mid-1990s, provide an estimate of the total nonperforming loans held by Chinese financial institutions, and assess to what extent these bad assets might pose a threat to the country's financial stability.

Keywords Chinese economy · Bank regulation · Asset management corporations · Nonperforming loans

1 Introduction

China's banking sector has grown rapidly over the past three decades. As the major source of funding for Chinese enterprises (especially state-owned enterprises), Chinese banks have helped finance the nation's transition from a centrally planned economy to a market-oriented economy. In the meantime, large amounts of nonperforming loans (NPLs) have accumulated on their balance sheets, partly due to costs inevitably incurred by the reform and partly due to poor management, lack of risk management, and inadequate governmental regulation.

T. Li (✉)
Milken Institute, Santa Monica, CA, USA
e-mail: cli@milkeninstitute.org

J.R. Barth et al. (eds.), *China's Emerging Financial Markets*,
The Milken Institute Series on Financial Innovation and Economic Growth 8,
DOI 10.1007/978-0-387-93769-4_12,

In 1999, four asset management corporations were established to resolve the nonperforming loan problem. As stated by the State Council, these asset management corporations would cease operation by the end of 2009. It is therefore of interest to examine the progress they have made in disposing of nonperforming loans. In this paper, the author attempts to draw a picture of how the nonperforming loan problem has developed since the mid-1990s, provide an estimate of the total amount of nonperforming loans held by China's financial institutions, and assess to what extent these bad assets might present a hazard to the country's financial stability.

This chapter proceeds as follows: Section 2 starts with a discussion of the changing landscape of China's banking industry in the past three decades, followed by an analysis of the composition of nonperforming loans held by commercial banks. Section 3 serves as an overview of the history and operation of asset management corporations. An estimate of the total amount of outstanding nonperforming loans will be provided in Section 4. Section 5 assesses to what extent nonperforming loans may pose threats to the stability of China's financial system.

2 How Nonperforming Loans Became a Threat to China's Financial System

2.1 A Short History of China's Banking Sector, 1978–2003

The large amount of nonperforming loans is caused by many factors. A part of these nonperforming loans are the necessary cost incurred during the country's transition from a planned economy to a market economy.

Xianglong Dai, Governor of the People's Bank of China
International Forum on Nonperforming Loan
Beijing, China
November 11, 2001

China's banking industry has grown rapidly over the past three decades. Just 10 years ago, many foreigners were not familiar with such names as the Industrial and Commercial Bank of China or China Construction Bank. Despite their large assets and wide customer base, these banks acted as the Chinese government's lending arms before 2003 and thus were considered to be entirely different animals from commercial banks, such as Bank of America and Citigroup. However, some of China's largest banks have recently been restructured and publicly listed. In September 2008, Chinese banks took three of the top ten places in a global ranking of banks by their market capitalization, with the Industrial and Commercial Bank of China being the largest commercial bank worldwide in terms of market value. China's bank assets have grown roughly 58-fold from 1985 to 2008.

Unlike the U.S. financial system, in which the debt and equity markets play roles as important as those of banks, China's financial system has, until very recently, been dominated by the banking sector. Assets of banking institutions accounted for 49% of China's total financial assets in 2007—a year in which, for the first time ever, this share dropped below 50%.[1] In contrast, the development of the equity market did not take off until 2007, while the corporate bond market remains underdeveloped. For many years, banks have served as the major funding source of Chinese firms, especially state-owned enterprises. In a sense, they helped fuel China's rapid growth over the past three decades by directing funds to investment projects initiated by the government or state-owned enterprises. Indeed, in the absence of mature and efficient equity and bond markets, the banking sector dominated the allocation of available capital for the Chinese economy.

Since China's banking sector plays such an important role in the nation's economy and allocation of resources, when nonperforming loans began to accumulate in the 1990s, concern grew that this situation might cause severe disruptions in the financial sector. It is generally believed that Chinese banks' NPL level reached a peak, relative to total loans, in the mid-1990s. Official statistics, however, were not made available. Some estimated that the nonperforming loans were as much as 35% of banks' total loan portfolios. In 1998, this translated to RMB 2.5 trillion, or approximately 31% of China's GDP.

To understand how the nonperforming loans problem emerged, it may be advantageous to take a long-term view and examine the changing landscape of China's banking industry. The People's Bank of China (PBC) remained the only state-owned bank in China until 1979, when the Agricultural Bank of China (ABC) and the Bank of China (BOC) were established. Two more state-owned commercial banks—the China Construction Bank (CCB) and the Industrial and Commercial Bank of China (ICBC)—were established in 1983 (the ABC, the BOC, the CCB, and the ICBC are commonly referred to as the "Big Four"). In the same year, the People's Bank of China formally attained legal status as China's monetary authority. Its other responsibilities, such as providing credit to state-owned enterprises, were shifted to the Big Four.

In the following decade, the Chinese government used the Big Four as its "lending arm" to allocate credit to state-owned enterprises and municipal governments. Although referred to as commercial banks, the Big Four functioned like government agencies, unlike their free-market foreign peers. Investment decisions were not based upon appropriate assessment of risks and returns but upon government instructions. Not surprisingly, nonperforming loans rapidly accumulated on their balance sheets as funds were channeled to businesses and projects, regardless of whether the loans would be repaid.

In 1993, three policy development banks—the Agricultural Development Bank of China, the China Development Bank, and the Export-Import Bank of China—were established, resuming the Big Four's role as the government's policy lending arm. This was the first step in a series of efforts to reform the

[1] The share of bank assets in all financial assets should have increased significantly in the first nine months of 2008, since bank assets have been growing steadily, while the equity market lost more than 50% of its value as compared to the end of 2007.

entire banking industry, to transform the Big Four into real commercial banks, and to fundamentally improve the efficiency of capital allocation. The legal basis for China's banking industry, the Law of the People's Bank of China and the Commercial Banking Law, were enacted in 1995. These two laws were amended in 2003. The Law of Banking Supervision was enacted in the same year. The three legal documents formally set the legal framework for the current Chinese banking sector (see Appendix for a list of key legislations for China's banking industry).

2.2 Sources of NPLs Prior to 2000

Huge amounts of NPLs accumulated in China's financial system in the 1980s and 1990s. A couple of factors contributed to this disturbing situation. First, China experienced rapid economic growth from 1992 to 1996, which was largely fueled by a wave of excessive investments in infrastructure. As growth slowed down from 1996 to 1998 (due in part to government intervention and the Asian Financial Crisis), many of the loans extended to these projects became nonperforming. Second, the lack of appropriate risk-control procedures and poor management skills at the commercial banks usually led to a lower quality of loans being originated. Third, the lack of a credit-rating system made it difficult for banks to evaluate a loan's riskiness when making lending decisions. Last and most important, the nonperforming loans were considered by many to be part of a cost paid for China's state-owned enterprise (SOE) reform.

In the 1990s, nationwide SOEs were reformed and privatized. Numerous near-insolvent SOEs were closed, merged, or restructured. State-owned commercial banks provided critical funding for these reforms, and a large portion of these loans eventually became nonperforming. To an extent, the nonperforming loan problem represents the cost of economic reform as China moved from a centrally planned to a market-oriented economy. It is only reasonable that the government would bail out the nearly insolvent commercial banks so that they could dispose of the nonperforming assets that were generated as a result of the aforementioned historic reasons. In 1999, four asset management corporations (AMCs) were established. With initial capital injected by the Ministry of Finance and additional funding support from the PBC, the AMCs served as special-purpose entities that would specialize in acquiring and disposing of NPLs from commercial banks.

3 Asset Management Corporations: Who Are They, Why Were They Established, and What Is the Progress They Have Made in NPL Disposal?

3.1 AMCs and Their Mandate

China adopted the practices of other countries when setting up the AMCs. It was decided that Chinese AMCs would hold nonperforming assets as equity (like the Resolution Trust Corporation in the United States), and there would be multiple AMCs, one for each problem commercial bank (following Sweden's decentralized NPL management model).

The first AMC, Cinda, was established in April 1999. Three other AMCs (Huarong, China Orient, and Great Wall) were established in October of the same year, each corresponding to one of the Big Four. With RMB 10 billion initial capital injected into each AMC by the Ministry of Finance, the four AMCs were established with a mandate to clean up the Big Four's nonperforming loans over a 10-year period. The plan was to remove bad assets from commercial banks' balance sheet, repackage them, then either restructure or dispose of them on a wholesale basis. Commercial banks would then be able to improve capital adequacy and improve their corporate governance so that they could be restructured from the government's policy arms into publicly listed modern financial institutions.

During the initial NPL transfer in 1999, the four AMCs purchased the Big Four's NPL portfolios at face value. Ma (2002) estimates that aside from the RMB 1.4 trillion NPLs transferred to the four AMCs, the Big Four still held RMB 2 trillion NPLs in their portfolios. In addition, the AMCs supposedly would only take care of NPLs formed due to "historic reasons"; hence any loans generated after 1999 or not from government-initiated lending were to be excluded from the transfer. As a result, the NPLs transferred from the Big Four to AMCs only accounted for part of the banks' bad assets.

AMCs, by definition, are "solely state-owned non-bank financial institutions."[2] Who regulates them? The answer: just about everyone. When AMCs were established, the PBC, the Ministry of Finance, and the China Securities Regulatory Commission (CSRC) were appointed as regulators. The China Banking Regulatory Commission (CBRC) took over part of the regulatory responsibilities when it was established in 2003.[3] Currently, the CBRC is in charge of the AMCs' daily operations, while the Ministry of Finance determines whether an NPL deal should be approved. A board of supervisors, appointed by the State Council, oversees AMCs' asset quality and evaluates the performance of its senior executives. The CSRC, State-Owned Assets Supervision and Administration Commission, the National Audit Bureau, the PBC, and the Ministry of Commerce all oversee some of AMCs' activities in their respective capacities. As shown in Fig. 1, some of these regulation functions overlap. On the other hand, some of these agencies lack the specific legal authority to be effective regulators.

---

[2] PRC State Council. Regulation on Financial Asset Management Corporations. November 1, 2000.

[3] Although the CBRC is currently the major supervisor for AMCs, the Regulation on Financial Asset Management Corporations was never amended to formally appoint CBRC as AMCs' regulator.

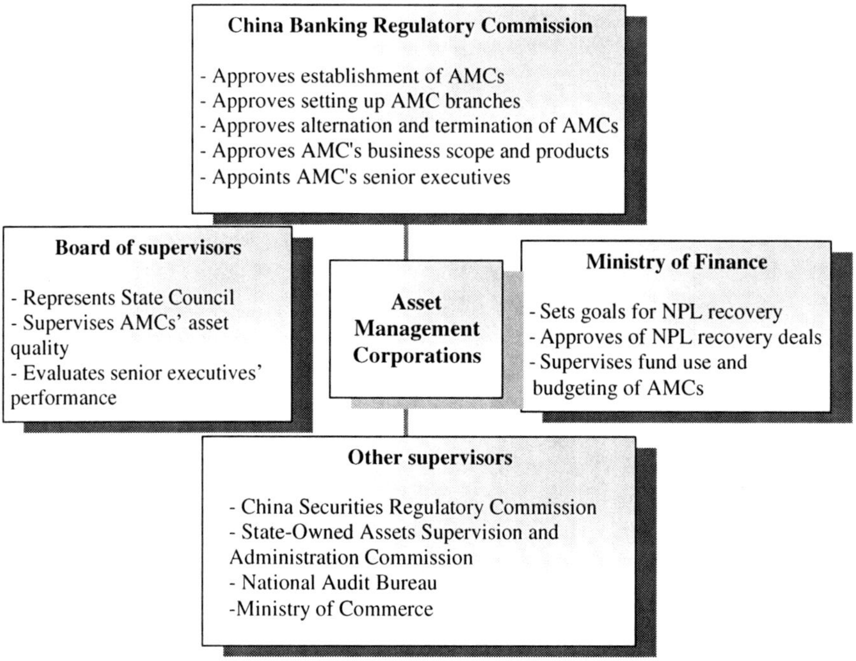

Fig. 1 Who regulates AMCs?: Multiple regulators with overlapping capacity

3.2 Funding Sources for NPL Purchases

The AMCs' funding sources include the PBC, the Ministry of Finance, funds borrowed from other financial institutions, and bonds issuance (PRC State Council, 2000). As discussed earlier, when AMCs were first established in 1999, their initial capital was provided by the Ministry of Finance. The Ministry of Finance then issued special government debts to finance the capital injection. These transactions are summarized in Table 1.

Table 1 Ministry of Finance provides initial capital to AMCs

Ministry of Finance:
• Issues debts to fund the capital transfer
• Gains sole ownership of the four AMCs
AMCs:
• Gains initial capital of RMB 40 billion(RMB 10 billion each)

The AMCs bought RMB 1.4 trillion of nonperforming loans at face value by borrowing from the PBC and issuing AMC bonds. The AMCs would pay an annual interest rate of 2.25% on both their borrowings from the PBC and AMC bonds. Also, the nontransferable bonds issued by AMCs (fully guaranteed by the Treasury) were sold to their corresponding commercial banks. As a result, bad assets on the Big Four's financial books were swapped with risk-free bonds guaranteed by the government. Their total assets and debts remained unchanged.

These funding activities increased the AMCs' leverage ratio (loan-to-equity ratio) to a fairly high 34x. Considering that these assets would lose a significant part of their value once marked to market, the AMCs have been technically bankrupt since the day they were established.

Table 2 provides a summary of the impact of the funding activities discussed above on the PBC, commercial banks, and AMCs. The net effect would be an immediate improvement in the commercial banks' asset quality. AMCs, on the other hand, would work on recovering some of these nonperforming assets by packaging and selling them to third-party investors, swapping debts for equity stakes for some companies, restructuring some others, or simply writing part of these bad assets down.

Table 2 Impacts of initial NPL transfer in 1999

The People's Bank of China
• Lends to AMCs
• Receives 2.25% annual interest rate on its lending to AMCs
Four AMCs
• Borrow from the People's Bank of China, and pay 2.25% annual interest rate on its borrowing
• Issue 10-year non-transferrable bonds to their corresponding commercial banks, and pay 2.25% annual interest rate on these bonds.[4]
• Purchase nonperforming assets from the commercial banks at face value
Commercial Banks
• Sell nonperforming loans to AMCs at full face value
• Receive AMC bonds and cash as payment

As will be discussed later, once these toxic assets are marked to market when they are sold or written down, current hidden losses will be recognized. The AMCs may fail to repay their borrowings from the PBC, in which case these borrowings will become nonperforming loans on the PBC's balance sheet. As for the AMC bonds guaranteed by the government, once AMCs fold, special government bonds will probably be issued to repay the principal on them. Also, these losses may again be transferred to another special purpose vehicle and digested over a longer time period.

During the initial NPL transfer, the four AMCs borrowed RMB 604 billion from the People's Bank of China, and issued RMB 811 billion in bonds. Table 3 provides a detailed breakdown of the funding source for each of the four AMCs.[5]

[4] It is not clear that whether the AMC bonds are explicitly or implicitly guaranteed by the Ministry of Finance.

[5] After 2003, the AMCs purchased more nonperforming loans from commercial banks at a discount. These purchases are also funded by PBC loans or AMC bonds. The difference between book value and purchase price was written down by commercial banks.

Table 3 Funding source (in RMB billions) for the four AMCs' initial NPL purchase in 1999

	PBC credit	AMC bonds	Total purchase of NPLs financed by PBC credit and AMC bonds
Huarong	95	313	408
Great Wall	346	-	346
China Orient	116	151	267
Cinda	48*	347	395**
All four AMCs	604	811	1,415**

Sources: Ma (2002), Yu (2005), author's estimates.
Note: *The number includes borrowings completed in 2000 and 2001.
**The numbers include NPLs from the China Development Bank and the People's Bank of China. A tiny portion of NPL purchases might have been paid in cash.

3.3 NPL Sales to Foreign Investors

A research report released by China Orient Asset Management Corp. (2008) indicated that foreign investors accounted for 30% of all NPL deals completed by AMCs. In contrast, state-owned investors accounted for 46%, while domestic private investors accounted for another 24%. Nevertheless, NPL sales to foreign investors attracted far more attention from the media and general public. This is partly due to the fact that any NPL deals completed with foreign investors would have been approved by State-Owned Assets Supervision and Administration Commission and the Ministry of Finance; hence more details regarding these deals would have been disclosed. In addition, these deals are generally under closer scrutiny from the public with respect to fair pricing.

Many have questioned whether the NPL sales to foreign investors would cause undue losses in state-owned assets. A large majority of these distressed assets belong to state-owned enterprises. The Big Four and AMCs are considered state-owned, as well. Disposal of underlying SOE assets at a discount price raised the question whether the regulatory agencies had performed due diligence examinations on the terms of these sales. Indeed, some of these sales with the better-quality nonperforming loans were priced at below 20%, lower than the average cash recovery ratio of the four AMCs (Jiang 2007). This is an indication that the AMCs, burdened with huge amounts of nonperforming loans and faced with the 10-year timeline, were under pressure to dispose of nonperforming assets quickly.

Auctions seem to be the fastest way to make substantial progress, even if that means lower returns compared to more time-consuming methods, such as restructuring the problematic firms. On the other hand, foreign investors with better access to funds see profitable opportunities in these distressed assets; sometimes merely by selling tangible assets in the portfolio, they were able to recover what was paid since the assets were priced at deep discounts.

As mentioned above, many government agencies oversee the AMCs in one capacity or another. Somewhat ironically, however, the supervision of AMC operations is by no means effective and consistent. There is much criticism on how the AMCs are regulated. In June 2005, the National Audit Bureau issued a report on

AMC operations from 2000 to 2003. The auditing results showed numerous problems, including fraud, violation of regulations, and inappropriate operations that involved RMB 71.5 billion worth of nonperforming assets (Liu 2005). The auditing results, to an extent, revealed the inadequacy in AMC regulations.

3.4 Current Status of China's NPLs

After great efforts to reform and recapitalize commercial banks, both the NPLs and the NPL ratios for Chinese banks have decreased over the past several years. The ratio of loan-loss reserves to nonperforming loans at major commercial banks more than doubled, from 19.1% in 2003 to 39.2% in 2007, before increasing further to 44.8% in June 2008 (see Fig. 2).

According to statistics from the CBRC, the nonperforming loan ratios at Chinese commercial banks have dropped to 5.58% in the second quarter of 2008, from 13.6% at the end of 2004. These numbers are somewhat misleading, however, since they do not include NPLs held by development banks, credit unions, and asset management corporations. Some of these institutions still hold huge amounts of nonperforming loans in the portfolio and are in urgent need of reform.

Compared to the composition of NPLs transferred to the AMCs in 1999, the composition of NPLs by industry has not changed much. Industrial loans account for 36%, followed by wholesale and retail loans at 18%. Personal loans account for 9%, while agricultural loans constitute another 8%. These

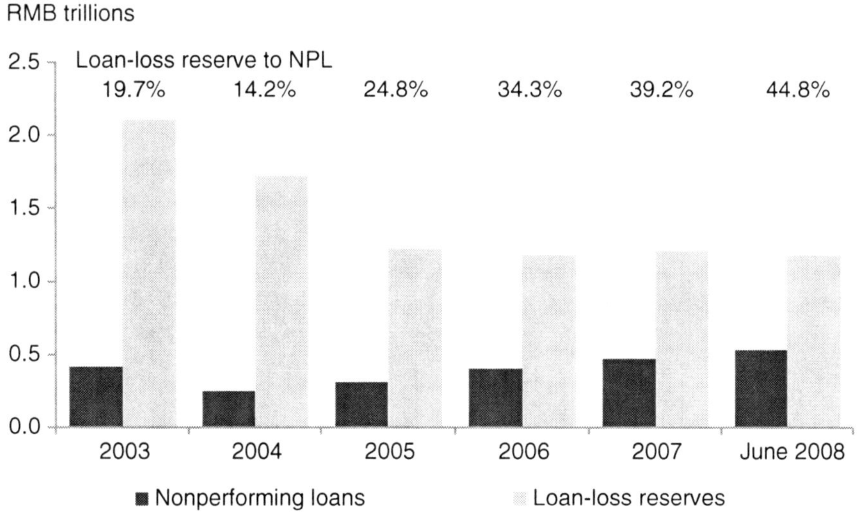

Fig. 2 Loan-loss reserves account for an ever-larger percent of nonperforming loans at Chinese commercial banks
Sources: CBRC, the author

numbers do not include nonperforming loans held by rural credit unions and the Agricultural Development Bank of China. As will be discussed later, these institutions still hold significant amounts of agricultural-related NPLs in their portfolios.

It is also worth mentioning that although personal loans are relatively new products in China, they account for 8% of all NPLs outstanding. The quality of personal loans, including credit card debt and personal mortgage debt, merits special attention, especially in the context of today's credit crisis, which originated in the United States.

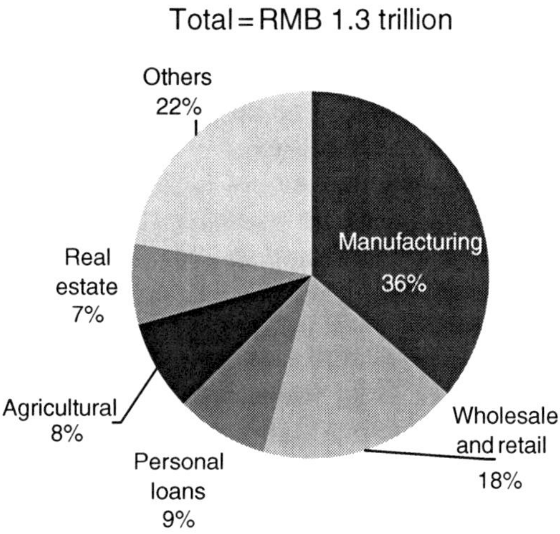

Fig. 3 Composition of outstanding nonperforming loans in Chinese commercial banks' portfolios (December 2007).
Sources: CBRC, Author's estimate

4 Estimating Total Outstanding NPLs in China's Financial System

How big exactly is China's NPL problem? The once-dire situation seemed to have improved tremendously once Chinese banks underwent major reforms and recapitalization. After a vast amount of NPLs was carved out from their balance sheets, the banks experienced immediate improvement in their asset quality. Three out of the Big Four went public after being recapitalized. However, one should always bear in mind that these NPLs did not disappear from China's financial system. The economy as a whole will eventually have to bear the cost of banking restructuring.

The Regulation on Financial Asset Management Companies (2000) states that

31. *When the AMCs are terminated, the Ministry of Finance will organize an auditing committee to audit AMCs' asset value*
32. *The Ministry of Finance will submit to the State Council a resolution for dealing with the final loss in AMC*

At the end of 2009, when the four AMCs fold, the huge losses on their balance sheets will be recognized (AMCs do not yet make their balance sheets available to the public on a regular basis). The cash recovered from NPL disposal merely covers the interest and coupon payments on borrowing from the PBC and AMC bonds. The AMC bonds issued to the Big Four will be delinquent and either be paid by the Treasury or rearranged and rolled over into new debts. The PBC loans to AMCs will also become NPLs on PBC's balance sheet. In other words, a large portion of the costs incurred in restructuring banking sector and disposing of NPLs has yet to be written down from the economy's balance sheet. NPLs transferred to AMCs are still staying in the system and pose significant risks to China's financial stability.

There are many estimates about the current amount of NPLs outstanding in China. Unfortunately, some of these estimates are flawed or no longer accurate. Some were made before the banking sector was restructured and reformed in 2003. Some carried over figures from the past, not taking into account the fact that some of these NPLs have already been written off from commercial banks' loan-loss reserves. Some have the issue of double counting in their estimates. The 2006 Ernst and Young figure, for example, included NPLs held by AMCs at face value. Ernst and Young's calculation also counted the PBC's loans to AMCs to finance NPL purchases. Their estimates hence exaggerated the outstanding NPLs in China's financial system due to double counting. Also, when NPLs are sold at a significant discount to the AMCs, it usually implies that the difference between book value and negotiated price is written down by commercial banks from their loan-loss reserves. Therefore one should not use the book value of all NPLs in an AMC portfolio when estimating NPL stock remaining in the system.

As discussed earlier, the official number is not an appropriate estimate for the size of China's NPLs either, since it does not include NPLs held by some of the most troublesome financial institutions, such as AMCs and rural credit unions. In this paper, the author attempts to give a more comprehensive estimate of the current outstanding NPLs held by China's financial institutions.

4.1 Commercial Banks

The transfer of NPLs to the AMCs partly took care of the banks' nonperforming loan stocks accumulated before 1999. More capital injections after 2003 also helped recapitalize commercial banks. However, NPLs still accounted for 6.17% of commercial banks' loan portfolios at the end of 2007. This figure further declined to 5.58% in June 2008. The NPL ratio at state-owned commercial banks was 7.43% in June 2008, higher than those of other types of banks. At the end of 2007, the outstanding NPLs held by commercial banks totaled RMB 1.27 trillion.

It should be noted, however, that some commercial banks still hold nontransferable AMC bonds in their portfolio. It is not likely that the AMCs will be able to repay any principal on AMC bonds when they fold. Nonetheless, as discussed earlier, it is generally believed that these bonds are guaranteed by the Ministry of Finance.

Table 4 Total outstanding nonperforming loans at Chinese commercial banks (2005–June 2008)

RMB billions

	2005	2006	2007	June 2008
All commercial banks	1,313.4	1,254.9	1,268.4	1,242.5
State-owned commercial banks	1,072.5	1,053.5	1,115.0	1,103.2
Other commercial banks	147.2	116.8	86.0	73.1
Joint-stock banks	84.2	65.5	51.2	50.2
City banks	5.7	15.4	13.1	12.2
Foreign banks	3.8	3.8	3.2	3.8

Source: CBRC.

4.2 Other Financial Institutions

The CBRC's annual reports define "other financial institutions" to include policy development banks and city and rural credit unions. The annual reports of policy development banks show that their NPLs totaled was RMB 90.7 billion at the end of 2007, of which RMB 64.3 billion belonged to the Agricultural Development Bank.

Little information has been made available regarding the balance sheets of rural credit unions and cooperatives. But while it is difficult to get a clear picture of the asset quality at city and rural credit unions, the NPL ratios at rural credit unions and cooperatives are recognized as among the highest of all Chinese financial institutions. According to Du (2008), NPLs held by rural credit unions and cooperatives totaled RMB 659.6 billion at the end of 2007. This is after the PBC issued RMB 247.5 billion in special government bills in order to swap part of the NPLs held by these institutions.[6]

Table 5 Nonperforming loans at other financial institutions, 2007

Institution	Nonperforming loans RMB billions, December 2007
Development banks	
China Development Bank	18.5
Export-Import Development Bank	7.9
Agricultural Development Bank	64.3
Rural credit unions	659.6
Total	750.3

Sources: China Development Bank, Export-Import Development Bank, Agricultural Development Bank, author's estimates

[6] According to Zhang (2008) and Du (2008), the PBC has issued RMB 165.6 billion special bills in exchange for nonperforming loans at rural credit unions and cooperatives. According to PBC (2007), an additional RMB 81.9 billion was issued in 2007.

4.3 Asset Management Corporations

Table 6 provides a list of NPLs transferred to or purchased by the AMCs since 1999. NPL transfers and sales to AMCs after 2004 were usually priced at a significant discount. Here we assume that the commercial banks took the losses in these transactions and have already written them down from their loan-loss reserves. Hence the AMCs have paid approximately RMB 1,812 billion in exchange for these NPLs. As the AMCs make progress in disposing of these assets, the total amount of NPLs held by the four AMCs will drop, while losses from disposing of these NPLs will be revealed in their financial books.

Table 6 AMCs purchases of nonperforming loans from commercial banks, 1999–2008

RMB billions	Face value	Actual amount paid*
Policy-oriented transfers		
1999: Initial transfer from the Big Four	1,393.9	1,393.9
1999: Initial transfer from China Development Bank	100.0	100.0
May 2004: Bank of China and China Construction Bank	196.9	59.1
Auctions		
June 2004: Bank of China and China Construction Bank	278.7	86.4
2005: Bank of Communication	64.1	32.1
June 2005: Industrial and Commercial Bank of China	459.0	137.7
2007: Bank of Shanghai	3.0	1.5
2007: Shenzhen Commercial Bank	3.5	1.8
Total	2,499.1	1,812.4

Sources: AMCs press releases, Xinhua.net, Bloomberg, author's estimate.
Note: In 2008, the AMCs purchased RMB 140 billion in face value of NPLs from China Everbright Bank. It is also reported that the Agricultural Bank of China plans to transfer RMB 800 billion of NPLs to the AMCs.
*Estimated according to various press releases by the AMCs.

According to information provided by China Orient Asset Management Corporation, it has disposed of 52.4% of all NPLs transferred and acquired as of the end of 2007, with 25.7% cash recovery ratio. It is hence reasonable to assume that all four AMCs have approximately disposed of 50% of all NPLs and have recovered 25% in cash.[7] This indicates that the AMCs still held RMB 906.2 billion NPLs on their balance sheets at the end of 2007.

[7] Statistics on NPL disposal progress made by the AMCs after the first quarter of 2006 are no longer released on a quarterly basis by the CBRC. According to AMCs press releases on January 15, 2007, their cumulative cash recovery ratio is 17.6% at the end of 2006. The 25% assumption hence should be deemed relatively high estimate for AMCs' cash recovery ratio. This assumption, however, has no impact on the author's estimate of NPLs still held by AMCs.

Table 7 Estimates of outstanding NPLs, cash recovered and losses at AMCs (2007)

	RMB billions
Face value of all NPLs before they were transferred to AMCs	2,499.1
Book value of all NPLs at AMCs	1,812.4
Of which that are still outstanding: assume 50% have been disposed	906.2
Cash recovered (assume 25% cash recovery ratio)	226.5
Losses posted by AMCs (assume 25% cash recovery ratio)	679.6

Source: Author's estimates.

4.4 People's Bank of China

Interestingly, some nonperforming loans are held by the monetary authority—the PBC. Zhang (2008) points out that among the credit provided by the PBC to municipal governments and financial institutions, a vast amount was used to swap for the bad assets on their balance sheets. In other words, the PBC provides credit so that these entities are able to repay their debts or write down bad assets, without expecting these loans to be paid back in full. These loans thus become NPLs on the central bank's balance sheet.

In addition, the PBC used to function as a commercial bank and policy development bank. It still holds historic NPLs carried over from the 1980s and 1990s, a majority of which are real estate loans in Guangdong and Hainan. Zhang (2005) estimates the total amount of the aforementioned historic NPLs to be above RMB 33 billion, while Shen (2006) states this number could be as high as RMB 100 billion. Indeed, very limited details have been made available regarding the total amount and composition of these NPLs. It is also unclear if some of them have been recovered after recent efforts made by the PBC. Therefore, these numbers will not be included in the author's estimate of NPLs to be conservative.

Moreover, it is also common practice for the PBC to provide funding to bail out financial institutions. The AMCs borrowed RMB 604.2 billion from the PBC to finance the initial NPL transfers in 1999 and 2000. In addition, the AMCs borrowed RMB 619.5 billion after 2003 to finance more purchases of NPLs from commercial banks. Also, the PBC issued RMB 30 billion credit in order to bail out bankrupt securities brokerage firms in 2004 (Zhang 2008).

The credit provided to municipal governments, banks, and non-bank financial institutions, nonetheless, should not all be counted toward the total amount of NPL outstanding. Take AMCs as example. If NPLs outstanding on their balance sheets are counted, then the central bank credit extended to AMCs for the purpose of NPL disposal should be excluded to avoid double counting. For an estimate for the nonperforming assets held by the PBC, see Table 8.

Table 8 Nonperforming loans held by the People's Bank of China

	RMB billions
Claims on AMCs	1,223.7
of which: nonperforming (assume 50% disposal progress at AMCs)	611.8
Nonperforming loans: claims on rural credit unions and cooperatives	247.5
Nonperforming loans: claims on municipal governments	141.1
Nonperforming loans: claims on brokerage firms	30.0
Total nonperforming loans	1,033.4

Source: Author's estimates.
Note: These estimates do not include historic nonperforming real estate loans formed in 1980s and 1990s.

5 Summary

Table 9 is a summary of total outstanding NPLs held by China's financial institutions. Adding up the NPLs held by commercial banks, rural credit unions, PBC, and AMCs, one can conclude that China's financial institutions held a total of RMB 3.94 trillion (or US $540 billion) of NPLs at the end of 2007.

Table 9 Total nonperforming loans in China's financial system (2007)

Institution	RMB billions
Commercial banks	
State-owned commercial banks	1,115.0
Joint-stock commercial banks	86.0
City commercial banks	51.2
Rural commercial banks	13.1
Foreign banks	3.2
Development banks	
China Development Bank	18.5
Export-Import Bank of China	7.9
Agricultural Development Bank	64.3
Rural credit unions	644.5
People's Bank of China	1,033.4
Asset management corporations	906.2
Total nonperforming loans	**3,943.2**

Source: Author's estimates.

It should be noted that this exercise of estimating the total NPLs has some limitation due to the lack of information. For example, some NPLs held by such institutions as city credit unions and postal banks are not included in this estimate because their financial status is not disclosed to the general public. The nonperforming part of PBC credit is also estimated based upon limited information.

It is also notable that a large portion of the outstanding NPLs were "historic" loans formed in the pre-reform era. Up to date, reformed Chinese commercial banks, especially those publicly listed, have done a good job of maintaining NPLs on their balance sheets at a reasonable level. Bad loans should be interpreted as the commercial banks' normal cost of business. Although a low NPL ratio undoubtedly reflects prudency of a bank's lending practice and good judgment, it is not clear whether the desired level for NPL ratio should be zero. This is because banks, like other businesses, usually are willing to take a certain degree of risk in exchange for higher returns and faster growth. A reasonable amount of NPLs held by commercial banks, therefore, should not be deemed problematic. It would be an alarming signal, however, if the outstanding amount of NPLs trends upward again from the current level. Also, special attention should be given to the NPLs on the Central Bank's balance sheets, NPLs held by rural credit unions and cooperatives, and NPLs still held by the AMCs. These bad assets, if not disposed of in a timely and efficient manner, will remain potential threats to the health of China's financial sector.

In addition, as Fig. 4 shows, although the outstanding NPL level has dropped sharply compared to 2002 and before, this amount has remained relatively flat since 2005. Indeed, the outstanding NPL level only decreased by 3.5% from 2005 to June 2008. In contrast, outstanding loans increased by more than 40% over the same period. NPL ratio has dropped by 2.8% points since 2005, of which roughly 0.3% points were contributed by the decline in NPLs and 2.5% points by the increase in total loans outstanding. Apparently, in recent years, the increase in outstanding loans has played a much larger role than the decrease in NPLs.

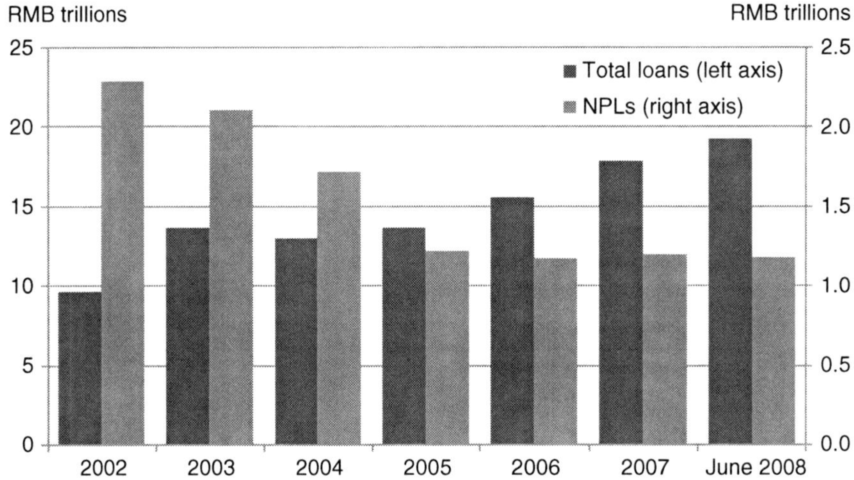

Fig. 4 Growth in outstanding loans is the major contributor to the drop in NPL ratio. Sources: CBRC, author's estimate

A potential risk with this situation is that once bank lending slows down, the NPL ratio may increase again. Such a slow down is not unlikely, if the Chinese economy cools down from a 15-year-long boom. Furthermore, since economic cycles are usually correlated with credit cycles, a slow down of the economy often implies less liquidity. Deterioration of asset quality may exacerbate the existing NPL problem during an economic downturn. Lacking a mature credit rating system for businesses and individuals, China is more vulnerable to this kind of risk, since it would be extremely difficult to find out assets and securities' market value without appropriate credit assessment.

Moreover, the ongoing credit crisis may cause some securities held by banks to be marked down to market or further written down. As of September 2008, Chinese financial institutions have written down more than US $3 billion as a result of the credit crisis. This should also raise some red flags about Chinese financial institutions' risk management practices. The ever-changing market condition can lead some good-quality assets to become illiquid in a short period, or eventually become NPLs. The magnitude of such changes can be huge. In the first six months of 2008, Chinese commercial banks have increased their loan loss reserve to total NPL ratio by 5.6% points to a historic high of 44.8%, which is a good sign that they are becoming better capitalized in response to the increased volatility in global financial markets.

6 The NPL Problem in Perspective

As discussed in Section 4, outstanding NPLs held by Chinese financial institutions were RMB 3.9 trillion or US $540 billion at the end of 2007. This is comparable to global write-downs by financial institutions during the current credit crisis since 2007, which is US $588 billion through September 2008. The savings-and-loan crisis that caused nearly 4,000 U.S. banks to fail, in contrast, only caused losses of US $150 billion, or roughly US $400 billion in today's dollar. Is the Chinese economy robust and resilient enough to digest such a large amount of NPLs without causing financial instability? Figure 5 below puts the amount of NPLs into the context of today's Chinese economy.

At the end of 2007, assets held by the banking institutions totaled RMB 53 trillion. The NPL-to-asset ratio calculated for the whole banking industry amounted to less than 9%. According to various estimates, NPLs exceeded one-third of China's GDP in 1999. Today this number has dropped to 16%. The Chinese economy has undoubtedly become more robust and resilient than it was 10 years ago. Rapid economic growth over the past decade has led to accumulation of real wealth, which should reduce the possibility of any potential financial disruption. In addition, the US $1.6 trillion foreign exchange reserve also serves as a cushion for such disruptions.

However, instability is still a concern if the government should ever opt to dispose of these NPLs in a relatively short time period. As shown above in Fig. 5, total NPLs held by financial institutions are equivalent to 16% of China's GDP, 35.3% of its foreign exchange reserve, and 79.7% of government

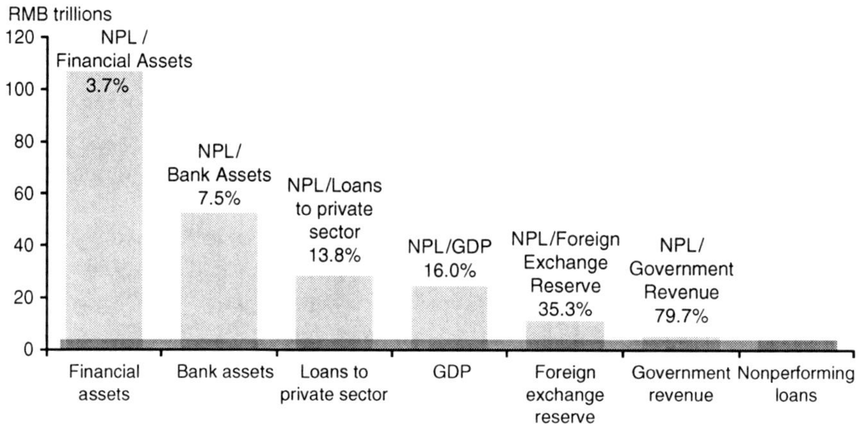

Fig. 5 Size of outstanding NPLs in perspective (2007).
Sources: CBRC, PBC, BIS, S&P, IFS, SAFE, China Bureau of Statistics, author's estimate

revenue in 2007. Apparently, the resolution cost for the NPLs will be high, and the Chinese economy will undoubtedly suffer some pain from the process one way or the other.

As the deadline for AMCs approaches, it becomes imperative for the regulators to review the NPL resolution agenda. As discussed in previous sections, when NPLs are transferred from one institution to another, the underlying risks posed to the system are by no means reduced. Some financial institutions such as the Big Four may seem much healthier after the NPLs are carved out. Nonetheless, these NPLs (thus the risks) still remain in the system and will have to be digested over a long time period. It took the four AMCs more than 8 years to dispose of roughly RMB 1 trillion of NPLs. Therefore it is not unreasonable to conclude that it may be another decade, if not longer, before China can finally claim this US $540 billion problem "solved."

Acknowledgments Tong Li is a senior research analyst at the Milken Institute. The author thanks James R. Barth, Triphon Phumiwasana and Perry Wong for helpful comments, and Dinah McNichols for insightful suggestions.

Appendix

Selected Chinese laws and regulations relevant to the establishment and operation of asset management corporations

Year	Laws and regulations
1993	Decision of the State Council on Reform of the Financial System
1995	Law on the People's Bank of China, Commercial Bank Law, Negotiable Instruments Law, Guarantee Law, Insurance Law
1996	Measures for the Administration of Foreign Exchange

(continued)

Year	Laws and regulations
1998	Securities Law
2000	Interim Regulation on the Board of Supervisors of Major State-Owned Financial Institutions
2000	Regulation on Financial Asset Management Companies
2001	Trust Law
2003	Law on Securities Investment Fund
2003	Banking Supervision Law, Law on the People's Bank of China (amendment), Commercial Bank Law (amendment)
2004	Negotiable Instruments Law (amendment)
2005	Securities Law (amendment)
2007	Property Right Law

Sources: People's Bank of China, the author.

References

Barth James R. and Gerard Caprio."China's Financial System: The Perils of Riding the Wave." *The Milken Institute Review: A Journal of Economic Policy*, Third Quarter 2007.

China Banking Regulatory Commission. Annual Report 2006.

China Banking Regulatory Commission. Annual Report 2007.

China Orient Asset Management Corporation Research Center.China Financial NPL Market Survey Report. May 2008.

Du, Yan. "Nonperforming Loan Ratio Rebounds: Rural Credit Union Reforms Imperative." 21st Century Business Herald, May 23, 2008.

Ernst and Young.Global Nonperforming Loan Report 2006. May 2006.

Fung Ben, Jason George, Stefan Hohl, and Guonan Ma. "Public Asset Management Companies in East Asia: A Comparative Study." In BIS Financial Stability Institute Occasional Paper, no.3. 2004.

Gao Cailin. "The Influence of Nonperforming Assets on Inflation and Monetary Policy." China Finance, no. 5. 2001.

Jiang Yunxiang. "AMC Transformation Proposal Halted As the Ministry of Finance and the People's Bank of China Differ in Opinions." 21st Century Business Herald, May 26, 2007.

Lardy Nicholas. "The Challenges of Bank Restructuring in China." BIS Policy Papers, no. 7, 17–39, 1998a.

Lardy Nicholas. China's Unfinished Economic Revolution. Washington D.C.: Brookings Institution Press, 1998b.

Lardy Nicholas. "China's Worsening Debts." Financial Times, June 22, 2001.

Liu Dan."A Discussion on the Auditing Results of Asset Management Corporations." *China Audit*, no. 19 (2005).

Ma Guonan. "Who Pays China's Bank Restructuring Bill?" In CEPII Working Paper, no. 2006–2004. 2006.

Ma Guonan and Ben S C Fung. "China's Asset Management Corporations." BIS Working Papers, no. 115 (2002).

PricewaterhouseCoopers. Industry Watch: PRC Non-Performing Loans (NPLs) & Asset Management Companies (AMCs). April 2002.

PricewaterhouseCoopers. NPL Asia Issue 1. October 2002.

PricewaterhouseCoopers. NPL Asia Issue 2. April 2003.

PricewaterhouseCoopers. NPL Asia Issue 3. December 2003.

PricewaterhouseCoopers. NPL Asia Issue 4. September 2004.

PricewaterhouseCoopers. NPL Asia Issue 5. April 2005.
PricewaterhouseCoopers.NPL Asia Issue 6. December 2005.
PricewaterhouseCoopers. NPL Asia Issue 7. May 2006.
PricewaterhouseCoopers.NPL Asia Issue 8. March 2007.
PricewaterhouseCoopers. NPL Asia Issue 9. May 2008.
Shen Aihua. "Huida Established to Take Care of the PBC's Nonperforming Loans." Business Watch, March 31, 2006.
Yu Ning. "A Detailed Analysis of the People's Bank of China Credits." Caijing, July 25, 2005.
Zhang, Yuzhe, and Xiu Wen. "The Cross Road for AMC Transformation." Caijing, March 3, 2008.
Zhang Min. "The Launch of Huida Leads to an Important Stage for NPLs Disposal." Caijing, July 25, 2005.
Zhao Liang. "NPLs Disposal: A Feast for Foreign Investment Banks?" China Economic Weekly, 2004.

The Evolution of Bank Lending Patterns in China: A Post-1994 Province-By-Province Analysis

Richard C. K. Burdekin and Ran Tao

Abstract Disaggregated province-by-province analysis appears to confirm the importance of ongoing redistributive lending by the big four Chinese banks together with lending to state-owned enterprises that is especially pronounced amongst the poorer provinces. Agricultural Bank of China's own allocation of loans to the weaker provinces surges after 2000. This may well reflect its greater presence in the poorer areas of the country and the potential damage exerted if its lending there were cut back. On the other hand, such lending patterns also make it unsurprising that Agricultural Bank of China has not yet followed the other big banks into public ownership.

Keywords Commercial banks · China · Lending patterns · State-owned enterprises · Provincial data · Agricultural Bank of China

1 Introduction

China's five state-owned commercial banks (SOCBs) accounted for over RMB 28 trillion in assets at the end of 2007, representing approximately 53% of the total assets in China's banking system (http://www.cbrc.gov.cn). Although occupying a less dominant market position than in the past (Lu et al., 2007), the SOCBs have benefited from substantial equity investment from both the central government and foreign investors.[1] This chapter focuses on the provincial lending patterns of the four largest SOCBs, which are the Agricultural Bank of China (ABC), the Bank of China (BOC), China Construction Bank (CCB),

[1] The potential efficiency gains associated with foreign ownership stakes in Chinese banks (Berger et al., 2008) may be limited insofar as foreign investors limit their involvement to non-core areas of SOCB operations (Leigh and Podpiera, 2006).

R.C.K. Burdekin (✉)
Claremont McKenna College, Claremont, CA, USA
e-mail: richard.burdekin@claremontmckenna.edu

J.R. Barth et al. (eds.), *China's Emerging Financial Markets*,
The Milken Institute Series on Financial Innovation and Economic Growth 8,
DOI 10.1007/978-0-387-93769-4_13, © 2009 by Milken Institute

and the Industrial and Commercial Bank of China (ICBC). These four banks formed part of the government's credit plan until 1998 and played a key role in government policy throughout our post-1994 sample period. We exclude the fifth SOCB, the Bank of Communications, which is much smaller than the others and was not classified as a large SOCB until 2007. Following new injections of public funds to reduce their non-performing loan (NPL) levels, BOC, CCB, and ICBC enjoyed successful initial public offerings (IPOs) on the Hong Kong market in 2005–2006. BOC, CCB, and ICBC have since ranked amongst the world's top ten commercial banks in terms of market value, with ICBC's rising share price actually made it the biggest lender in the world by market capitalization as of July 23, 2007 (Ren, 2007). ABC lagged far behind, however, with an NPL ratio of 23.5% at the end of 2007 and in need of substantial restructuring before it could become a viable IPO candidate.

2 State-Owned Commercial Bank Lending Practices

ABC, BOC, CCB, and ICBC first became accountable for their own profits and losses when three new policy banks were created in 1994 – the State Development Bank of China, the Import-Export Bank of China, and the Agricultural Development Bank of China.[2] The old state-directed policy loans were to be transferred to these new institutions. On the other hand, most of their bond issues aimed at supporting lending remained, in practice, heavily supported by the big four SOCBs (Barth et al., 2004). The central government continued to incorporate the SOCBs into its credit plan to finance its state-owned enterprises (SOEs), and formal funding requirements were not lifted until 1998. Even after 1998, the historical burden of prior bad loans plus ongoing protection of many SOEs continued to hamper full commercialization of the SOCBs. State-owned banks were still allocating 75% of their short-term loans to SOEs in 2003 (Chiu and Lewis, 2006, p. 208), and an ongoing concentration of bank lending in favor of provinces where SOEs are dominant is identified by Dobson and Kashyap (2006, pp. 125–126). Meanwhile, Barth and Caprio (2007, p. 26) point to SOEs and collective enterprises receiving nearly half of total corporate loans despite contributing little more than a quarter of GDP.

Under the pre-1998 credit plan, the big four banks were typically forced to make loans to the SOEs, while having no way to hold SOE managers accountable for the non-repayment of old loans. This meant that, even if an SOE had previously defaulted on loans to the same SOCB, the bank still lacked the authority to independently cut off new lending. Not surprisingly this led to rampant NPL growth. The practice of assigning loan quotas to every region under each year's credit plan further boosted the allocation of funds toward

[2] For more details on the past banking reforms, and ongoing developments under World Trade Organization membership, see Burdekin and Kochanowicz (2008). On the legal setting and regulatory challenges, see the comprehensive treatment in Barth et al. (2007).

SOEs because regions with low growth potential also tended to be the most dependent on SOEs. Philips and Kunrong (2005) show that provinces with greater SOE shares in industrial production, on average, experienced lower growth rates. The slower growth provinces with higher SOE concentrations tend to be located in China's interior, well away from the Special Economic Zones located in such coastal provinces as Shanghai and Shenzhen.

The 1998 lifting of the credit plan, and the formal elimination of minimum loan quotas for each region, was intended to increase the independence of the loan portfolios of the SOCBs. The Ministry of Finance issued RMB 270 billion (US $32.5 billion) in special bonds to recapitalize the SOCBs in 1998, followed by further substantial recapitalizations in 2003 and 2005 to get BOC, CCB, and ICBC ready for their Hong Kong IPOs. NPL ratios were drastically reduced for these three banks from the 19.9–34.4% range in 2000 to 4.7% or less by 2005 (see Burdekin and Kochanowicz, 2008). On the other hand, ABC's NPL ratio remained at inflated levels and actually registered a slight increase in the latest year, rising marginally from 23.4% in 2006 to 23.5% in 2007. Making a bad situation worse, ABC announced that the tragic May 2008 earthquake in Sichuan would likely add a further RMB 6 billion (US $860.7 million) in NPLs (*People's Daily Online*, May 20, 2008).

With the government's increased loan quotas favoring weaker economic regions and SOEs under the pre-1998 situation, the limitations on the funds left for the private sector also reduced bank profit potential, *ceteris paribus* (Burdekin and Tao, 2008). Private companies, especially those of small-to-medium size, certainly do seem to have often been completely shut out of the formal lending market (Zhu, 2002). This helps explain the observed disproportionate reliance on trade credits by Chinese firms (Ge and Qiu, 2007) along with a wide range of informal financing practices (Tsai, 2002). It is doubtful that such informal lending channels offer an effective substitute for bank loans, and curb market rates triple those of standard bank rates have been observed (Huang, 2006). Ayyagari et al. (2008) find that, whereas the majority of the 2400 Chinese firms in their 2003 sample relied on informal finance, only financing from the formal financial system was associated with more rapid enterprise growth. This suggests that limits on lending to the private sector may well have hurt not only SOCB profitability but also the performance of the firms themselves.

The theoretical framework set out in Burdekin and Tao (2008) suggests that, to the extent the SOCBs have been taking advantage of increased freedom to pursue profit maximization since 1998, this should be evidenced in reduced emphasis on lending to SOEs (as the counterpart to increased lending to the private sector) and less emphasis on the weaker economic regions. This chapter uses provincial level data to examine whether there is any support for such a change in lending patterns over time. Table 1 shows how the overall loan distributions of the big four SOCBs across China's 31 provinces, municipalities, and administrative regions evolved after 1994, based on a grouping that divides these entities into top, middle, and bottom tiers according to each year's annual per capita GDP of each region. Although some change in the loan allocation

Table 1 Loan allocation of the big four state-owned banks

ABC	2005	2004	2003	2002	2001	2000	1999	1998	1997	1996	1995	1994
High tier	52.3%	52.4%	52.2%	52.8%	50.9%	50.2%	48.2%	47.2%	53.4%	49.1%	47.5%	47.3%
Mid tier	24.1%	24.7%	24.0%	21.0%	25.1%	27.0%	29.1%	29.7%	26.3%	31.1%	26.6%	28.7%
Low tier	23.6%	22.9%	23.8%	26.2%	24.0%	22.8%	22.7%	23.1%	20.3%	19.8%	25.9%	24.0%
BOC	**2005**	**2004**	**2003**	**2002**	**2001**	**2000**	**1999**	**1998**	**1997**	**1996**	**1995**	**1994**
High tier	–	66.5%	64.3%	64.2%	64.8%	67.4%	62.8%	63.0%	63.0%	63.0%	63.8%	62.2%
Mid tier	–	19.5%	21.2%	20.8%	18.8%	20.6%	23.3%	23.3%	23.2%	23.3%	20.2%	22.2%
Low tier	–	14.0%	14.5%	15.0%	16.4%	12.1%	13.9%	13.7%	13.8%	13.7%	16.0%	15.6%
CCB	**2005**	**2004**	**2003**	**2002**	**2001**	**2000**	**1999**	**1998**	**1997**	**1996**	**1995**	**1994**
High tier	57.9%	61.4%	57.8%	58.4%	59.6%	58.8%	56.5%	54.0%	53.1%	50.9%	49.3%	45.9%
Mid tier	23.0%	21.0%	21.4%	21.8%	20.4%	22.5%	23.9%	26.3%	26.8%	29.7%	25.9%	29.2%
Low tier	19.1%	17.5%	20.8%	19.8%	20.0%	18.7%	19.6%	19.8%	20.0%	19.4%	24.8%	24.9%
ICBC	**2005**	**2004**	**2003**	**2002**	**2001**	**2000**	**1999**	**1998**	**1997**	**1996**	**1995**	**1994**
High tier	–	57.8%	58.1%	56.3%	57.9%	57.6%	54.9%	54.0%	53.8%	51.9%	51.9%	47.7%
Mid tier	–	23.3%	22.6%	23.2%	22.5%	24.6%	26.0%	26.8%	27.0%	28.3%	25.1%	29.4%
Low tier	–	18.9%	19.3%	20.5%	19.6%	17.8%	19.1%	19.1%	19.2%	19.8%	23.0%	22.9%

Source: *Almanac of China's Finance and Banking*, Beijing, 1995–2006.

Notes: China's 31 provinces, municipalities, and administrative regions are divided into three tiers according to their relative rankings based on each year's provincial nominal per capita GDP.

Foreign currency loans and deposits are included from 2000, with the US$ amounts converted into RMB using the 8.28 fixed exchange rate that applied through 2004. The annual average exchange rate value was applied for 2005.

Table 2 Regression of each province's loan-to-deposit ratio on SOE share and per capita GDP, 1994–2005

		ABC		BOC		CCB		ICBC		Four-bank aggregate		BOC + CCB + ICBC	
Ranking	Provinces	SOE	GDP	SOE	GDP	SOE	GDP	SOE	GDP	SOE	GDP	SOE	GDP
1	Shanghai	0.661***	–0.08	–2.02	–4.574***	0.525*	0.14	1.250**	–0.487**	0.826*	–0.503***	0.73	–0.608***
2	Beijing	0.27	–0.386*	0.04	–2.102***	0.20	0.07	–0.22	–0.431***	–0.27	0.01	–0.14	–0.374***
3	Tianjin	0.18	–0.542**	3.31	–7.056***	4.124**	–0.63	1.68	–2.393***	1.16	–2.139***	1.75	–3.860***
4	Zhejiang	0.62	–0.29	5.179***	–2.734**	–2.998***	1.930***	0.85	–0.114	0.33	0.23	0.52	0.14
5	Guangdong	1.63	–2.051***	1.37	–2.938***	0.33	–0.942***	0.708*	–0.711**	1.36	–1.654***	0.67	–1.336***
6	Jiangsu	0.63	–0.27	2.792*	–2.496*	–0.22	0.11	2.633**	–2.535***	1.273***	–0.931***	1.763**	–1.685***
7	Fujian	1.643**	–1.155**	5.121**	–5.600***	0.04	–0.11	1.398***	–1.160***	1.612***	–1.397***	1.827**	–1.813***
8	Liaoning	0.930**	–1.490**	3.871***	–6.538***	2.340***	–3.241***	2.510***	–4.632***	2.752***	–4.220***	2.947***	–5.353***
9	Shandong	–0.10	0.20	4.945*	–5.281***	–0.06	–0.22	2.29	–2.535**	1.103**	–1.174***	1.78	–2.212**
10	Heilongjiang	2.497**	–6.622***	4.879***	–9.421***	3.458***	–6.223***	2.419***	–4.883***	3.113***	–6.152***	3.110***	–6.369***
11	Hebei	0.37	–1.26	2.324***	–4.938***	0.809**	–2.054***	1.852***	–4.098***	1.376***	–2.778***	1.634***	–3.723***
12	Xinjiang	2.231**	–1.87	1.47	–3.856**	0.88	–3.603***	1.71	–4.456***	1.892**	–3.157***	1.13	–4.199***
13	Hubei	0.55	–5.543**	1.473**	–4.237**	0.70	–4.242**	1.99	–11.07***	1.513*	–7.207***	1.45	–7.743***
14	Hainan	2.363**	–7.41	–0.01	–5.17	–0.64	–8.232**	–0.26	–10.46***	0.50	–7.305***	–0.35	–9.051***
15	Jilin	8.250***	–13.13***	10.36***	–15.08***	5.399***	–8.404***	6.307***	–8.608***	6.480***	–9.891***	7.468***	–10.45***
16	Inner Mongolia	1.207**	–4.891***	1.466***	–5.462**	2.323***	–4.921**	1.223***	–5.565***	1.377***	–3.665***	1.543***	–6.404***
17	Hunan	1.477*	–9.331***	1.358***	–7.294***	0.43	–1.60	1.917***	–9.506***	1.509***	–7.064***	1.458***	–7.311***
18	Henan	1.35	–2.53	2.099**	–3.089**	1.43	–2.83	2.984***	–4.593***	1.832*	–3.028**	2.534**	–4.332**
19	Chongqing	2.886***	–5.224**	4.175**	–11.73**	0.55	–1.34	3.789**	–10.97**	2.792***	–5.614**	2.958**	–8.568**
20	Shanxi	0.88	–3.591**	1.357***	–4.983***	4.197***	–8.723***	1.381***	–5.101***	1.911***	–4.819***	2.033***	–7.024***
21	Qinghai	–0.45	–3.22	7.133***	–21.46***	7.257***	–18.42***	2.306***	–9.107***	3.831***	–11.43***	4.774***	–16.66***
22	Anhui	1.65	–6.679**	3.049***	–8.784***	2.353**	–8.168***	3.767***	–14.09***	2.914***	–9.056***	3.111***	–11.53***
23	Jiangxi	1.456***	–4.688***	3.369**	–16.33***	0.35	–2.361*	1.730**	–8.244***	1.612***	–6.322***	1.661**	–8.473***
24	Ningxia	0.55	–2.13	–2.64	23.46	0.642**	–2.126*	1.395***	–6.162**	0.73	–2.38	0.61	–1.00

Table 2 (continued)

		ABC		BOC		CCB		ICBC		Four-bank aggregate		BOC + CCB + ICBC	
Ranking	Provinces	SOE	GDP	SOE	GDP	SOE	GDP	SOE	GDP	SOE	GDP	SOE	GDP
25	Sichuan	2.347***	−6.260***	3.160***	−10.17***	2.924***	−8.026***	4.079***	−13.06***	2.981***	−8.358***	3.734***	−11.68***
26	Yunnan	0.63	−5.313*	2.240***	−17.33***	0.23	−1.22	0.803***	−5.316***	0.694***	−4.208***	0.918***	−6.608***
27	Tibet	−0.60	−8.643***	11.10**	28.82	−0.59	−18.58			1.54	−5.34	3.94	−3.94
28	Shaanxi	3.360**	−5.562***	4.35	−16.01***	3.377**	−6.527***	0.60	−8.013***	3.172*	−7.433***	2.07	−10.32***
29	Guangxi	0.60	−5.156**	0.20	−13.34***	−0.49	−0.76	0.03	−4.584**	0.25	−3.884**	−0.08	−5.419*
30	Gansu	0.13	−4.434**	3.323***	−25.25***	2.569***	−12.21***	1.022***	−6.684***	1.379***	−7.457***	1.694***	−12.19***
31	Guizhou	1.973**	−22.98***	−0.35	16.21	1.462***	−10.11**	1.621***	−14.68***	1.444***	−11.60***	1.429***	−11.95**

Note: ***, **, and * denote significance at the 99%, 95%, and 90% confidence levels, respectively

Table 3 Correlation coefficients for ABC before and after 2000

		SOE share			Per capita GDP		
Ranking (2000)	Provinces	Before 2000	After 2000	Difference	Before 2000	After 2000	Difference
1	Shanghai	0.92	0.94	0.01	0.46	–0.86	–1.32
2	Beijing	0.54	–0.54	–1.09	0.44	0.32	–0.13
3	Tianjin	0.29	–0.47	–0.76	0.35	–0.21	–0.57
4	Zhejiang	–0.09	–0.87	–0.78	0.06	0.60	0.54
5	Guangdong	–0.54	0.55	1.09	0.30	–0.95	–1.25
6	Jiangsu	0.16	–0.48	–0.64	0.65	0.55	–0.10
7	Fujian	0.21	0.91	0.71	0.64	–0.85	–1.49
8	Liaoning	0.14	0.13	–0.01	0.20	–0.08	–0.27
9	Shandong	–0.31	0.85	1.16	0.78	–0.88	–1.66
10	Heilongjiang	–0.04	0.93	0.96	0.15	–0.92	–1.07
11	Hebei	–0.44	0.73	1.17	0.78	–0.91	–1.69
12	Xinjiang	0.67	0.40	–0.27	0.80	–0.95	–1.75
13	Hubei	–0.52	0.73	1.25	0.72	–0.91	–1.63
14	Hainan	0.55	0.81	0.26	0.87	–0.93	–1.80
15	Jilin	0.45	0.93	0.48	–0.56	–0.94	–0.39
16	Inner Mongolia	–0.36	0.96	1.32	0.56	–0.89	–1.45
17	Hunan	–0.69	0.98	1.68	0.78	–0.98	–1.75
18	Henan	–0.49	0.04	0.53	0.72	0.02	–0.70
19	Chongqing	0.77	0.89	0.13	0.20	–0.79	–0.99
20	Shanxi	–0.50	0.60	1.09	0.75	–0.86	–1.61
21	Qinghai	–0.69	0.63	1.32	0.86	–0.93	–1.79
22	Anhui	–0.16	0.91	1.06	0.60	–0.92	–1.52
23	Jiangxi	0.20	0.94	0.74	0.60	–0.90	–1.50
24	Ningxia	–0.08	0.98	1.06	0.71	–0.92	–1.62
25	Sichuan	0.49	0.87	0.38	0.09	–0.89	–0.98
26	Yunnan	–0.56	0.71	1.27	0.72	–0.72	–1.44

Table 3 (continued)

		SOE share			Per capita GDP		
Ranking (2000)	Provinces	Before 2000	After 2000	Difference	Before 2000	After 2000	Difference
27	Tibet	–0.13	0.07	0.20	–0.91	–0.91	0.00
28	Shaanxi	0.38	0.80	0.42	0.43	–0.96	–1.39
29	Guangxi	–0.31	0.57	0.88	0.75	–0.69	–1.44
30	Gansu	–0.55	–0.64	–0.09	0.56	–1.00	–1.56
31	Guizhou	–0.68	0.95	1.63	0.70	–0.92	–1.62
		SOE share			Per capita GDP		
Average coefficients		Before 2000	After 2000	Difference	Before 2000	After 2000	Difference
Tier 1		0.13	0.19	0.06	0.40	–0.33	–0.73
Tier 2		–0.06	0.71	0.76	0.56	–0.81	–1.38
Tier 3		–0.19	0.62	0.81	0.46	–0.89	–1.35
Overall average		–0.04	0.51	0.55	0.48	–0.68	–1.16

pattern is apparent for CCB and ICBC, there is no obvious shift in the lending allocations for ABC and BOC. ABC's lending allocation to the richer provinces remained close to 50% over the 1994–2005 period, while BOC's share hovered around 65%.[3] As expected, ABC's rural base is reflected in an allocation of more than 22% of total lending to the poorest provinces. Meanwhile, BOC provided the lowest loan allocation to this group. Although CCB and ICBC both appear to lend more to the richest provinces, and less to the poorest provinces, over the sample period, CCB's shift in loan allocation is the more pronounced. The CCB loan allocation to the wealthiest regions rose from 45.9% in 1994 to 57.9% in 2005, whereas the allocation to the poorest regions dropped from 24.9% in 1994 (higher even than ABC in that year) to 19.1% in 2005.

Another way to look at the allocation of funds is to consider the average ratio of loans to nominal provincial GDP. By comparing the three tiers, we can see if proportionately more lending is going to the poorer or to the richer provinces. In this respect, ABC stands out with a far greater issuance of loans relative to GDP for the poorest provinces (Tier 3) than for the richer provinces (Fig. 1). No

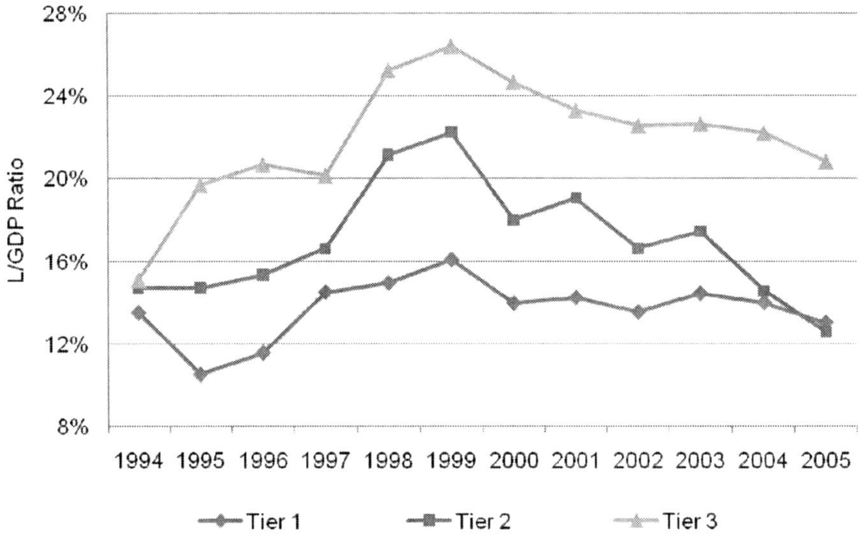

Fig. 1 ABC's average loan-to-GDP ratio for each provincial income tier
Note: The income tiers are derived from each region's per capita GDP ranking in every year, with Tier 1 being the richest group and Tier 3 the poorest. The ratios are calculated as the averages across the provinces in each tier. For details on sources and computation, see notes to Table 1

[3] ABC and CCB data extends through 2005 whereas data on the other two banks is limited to 2004. This reflects the fact that BOC and ICBC provincial lending data were no longer reported in the *Almanac of China's Finance and Banking* after 2004 (and also could not be obtained from the individual bank websites). Provincial GDP data, meanwhile, are drawn from the *China Statistical Yearbook*.

such striking pattern is evident for the other three SOCBs (see Appendix).[4] What is interesting about the pattern evident in Fig. 1 is not so much the relatively heavy loan allocation toward the poorer, typically more rural, areas where ABC's branches are concentrated, but the fact the size of the over-allocation to the poorest provinces rises sharply after the 1998 reforms. That is, although the absolute level of the ratio declines across all three income tiers, it falls by much less for the Tier 3 provinces than for the other two tiers so that the gap widens over time. This seems to imply that ABC did not take advantage of the greater freedom to exploit potentially more profitable lending opportunities in the richer areas of the country. Indeed, its loan allocation appears to have moved in the exact opposite direction. Podpiera (2006) suggests that the other SOCBs could also have done more to take advantage of the opportunities available in the richer regions, with all the SOCBs losing market share to other financial institutions in those provinces featuring more profitable SOEs.[5]

The tendency for the SOCBs to lend more to poorer provinces in the pre-1998 period (cf, Park and Sehrt, 2001) was an almost inevitable product of the old credit plan. The question is whether the abolition of the credit plan really brought about any broad-based shift in SOCB lending patterns. Based on the summary evidence reviewed so far, the support for this proposition actually seems quite limited and the lending pattern for ABC looks to have become more redistributive based on the trends depicted in Fig. 1. A more market-based approach surely implies lending relatively more to the stronger provinces over time, not less. As it stands, the poorer provinces remain heavily dependent upon SOCB lending, however. Cheng and Degryse (2007) find that raising the loans-to-provincial GDP ratio from the lowest level in their 1995–2003 sample to the highest observed level could boost future growth by more than four percentage points. With ABC having the greatest initial presence in the poorer parts of the country, it is possible that concern with the negative effects of cutting back lending there explains why this SOCB seemingly made no real move to shift its lending activity toward the potentially more profitable opportunities available elsewhere.

[4] The other figures do reveal sharp spikes in lending to Tier 3 provinces by BOC in 2004 and by CCB in 1995, driven primarily by large single-year expansions in the provision of funds to Tibet. BOC lending to Tibet increased 30-fold during 2003–2004 and CCB lending to Tibet rose by 20-fold over 1994–1995. BOC lending to Guizhou (the poorest of all the provinces) also increased five-fold during 2003–2004 while loans to Ningxia increased seven-fold.

[5] This is not, of course, to deny the progress made in lowering loan-to-deposit ratios for ABC, CCB, CCB and ICBC since 1994 as well as the greatly strengthened balanced sheets achieved by BOC, CCB and ICBC as they transitioned to publicly-owned joint stock companies (see, for example, Burdekin and Kochanowicz, 2008; Burdekin and Tao, 2008). Although SOCB efficiency levels and prudential levels continued to lag behind China's joint stock banks (Fu and Heffernan, 2007; Shih et al., 2007; Ariff and Can, 2008), recent data suggest at least some progress in closing the gap (Jia, 2008) and achieving higher profitability (Lu et al., 2007).

3 Disaggregated Province-by-Province Analysis

Park and Sehrt (2001) find that pre-1998 SOCB lending not only tended to be redistributive in nature but also reflected ties to the government's loss-making SOEs. Subsequent empirical analysis in Burdekin and Tao (2008) suggests ongoing SOE-based lending by ABC coupled with little consistent evidence of SOCB lending practices becoming less redistributive over time. In the disaggregated analysis below, we examine whether greater freedom to pursue profit maximization has, in practice, been associated with reduced emphasis on SOE lending – in addition to shedding further light on whether SOCB lending has really become any less redistributive at the individual province level. Figure 2 suggests that there is a generally positive relationship between SOCB loan-to-deposit ratios and provincial SOE shares over our 1994–2005 sample, both for the SOCBs aggregated together and for the four banks individually. The relationship appears to be quite pronounced for ABC, BOC, and ICBC, with ABC and BOC also being the two SOCBs that appeared to change their lending behavior least based on the summary data in Table 1. Figure 3 confirms that the positive relationship between SOCB loan-to-deposit ratios and provincial SOE shares is generally maintained when we divide the provinces into the three income tiers previously employed in Table 1 and Fig. 1. The positive relationship appears to be strongest for the poorest Tier 3 provinces, however, and is considerably more notable for CCB (and, to some extent, ICBC) than in Fig. 2 when all provinces were grouped together. This may well reflect the greater dependence of the poorer provinces on the SOEs and the potential damage to provincial prosperity, and perhaps stability, if lending were cut back.

Figure 4 plots SOCB loan-to-deposit ratios against provincial per capita GDP over our 1994–2005 sample. There is an apparent tendency toward redistributive lending in that the loan-to-deposit ratio generally falls as provincial per capita GDP rises. As with the relationship with SOE shares, the linkage appears quite clear cut for ABC, BOC, and ICBC. No such obvious trend is evident for CCB. When the provinces are again divided into three income tiers in Fig. 5, the negative relationship is generally maintained for ABC, BOC, and ICBC. While CCB's plot still shows no clear trend across the richest Tier 1 provinces, there is a negative relationship with per capita GDP levels over the two lower tiers (Tier 2 and Tier 3) in conformity with the overall pattern evident for the other three SOCBs. This implies that SOE-based lending and redistributive lending did indeed outlive the abolition of the credit plan in 1998. There is also an indication that SOE-based lending has been particularly pronounced in the poorer interior provinces, which tend to be more dependent upon SOEs to begin with – and hence more dependent upon SOCB lending to those SOES in order to maintain provincial output and employment levels.

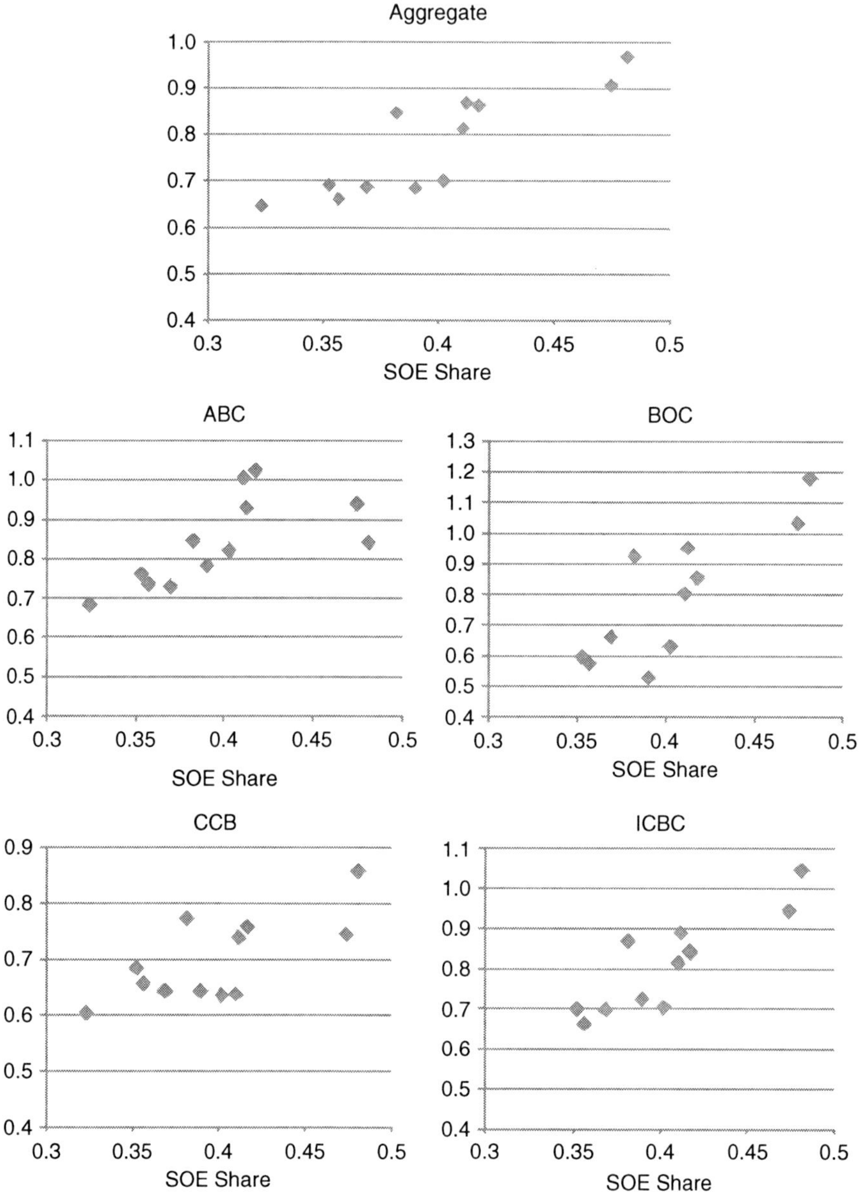

Fig. 2 Loan-to-deposit ratio vs. SOE share for the four SOCBs, aggregated and individually

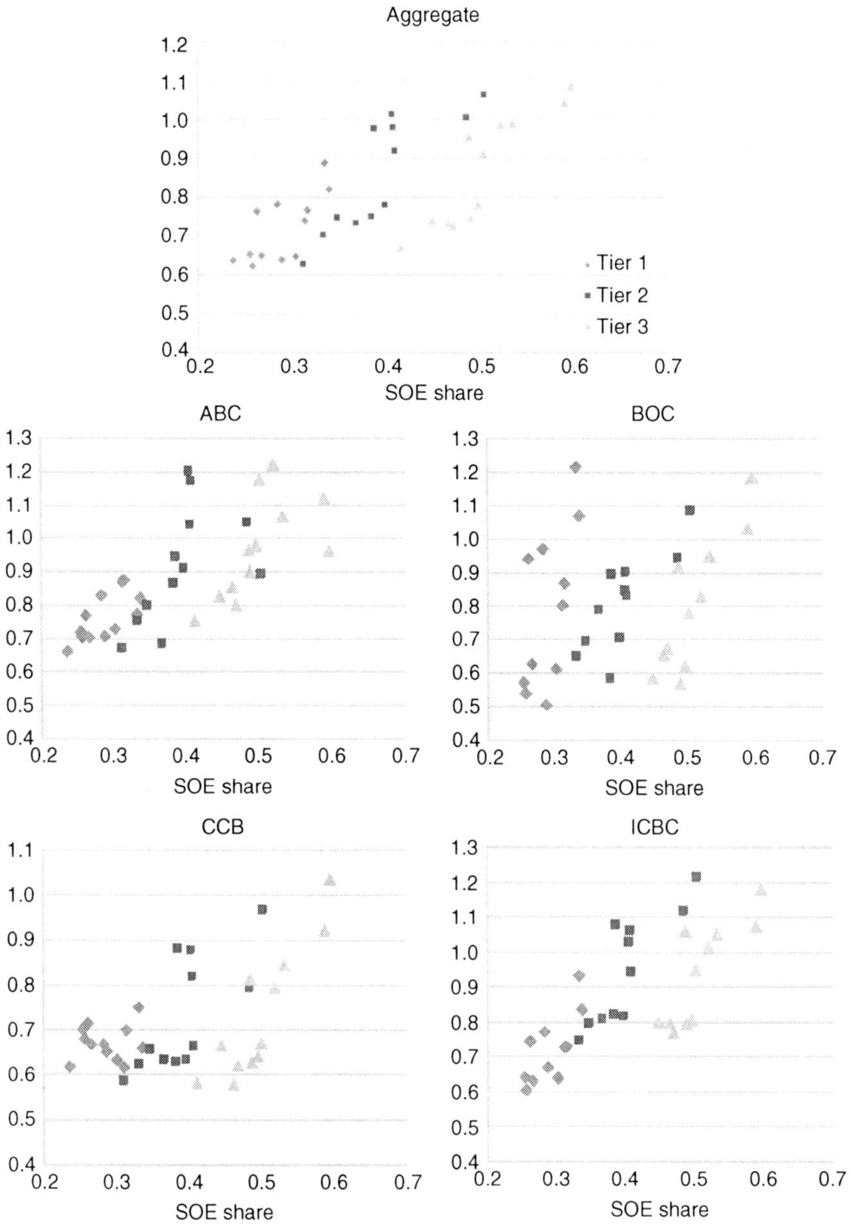

Fig. 3 Loan-to-deposit ratio vs. SOE share for the four SOCBs, aggregated and individually by provincial income tier

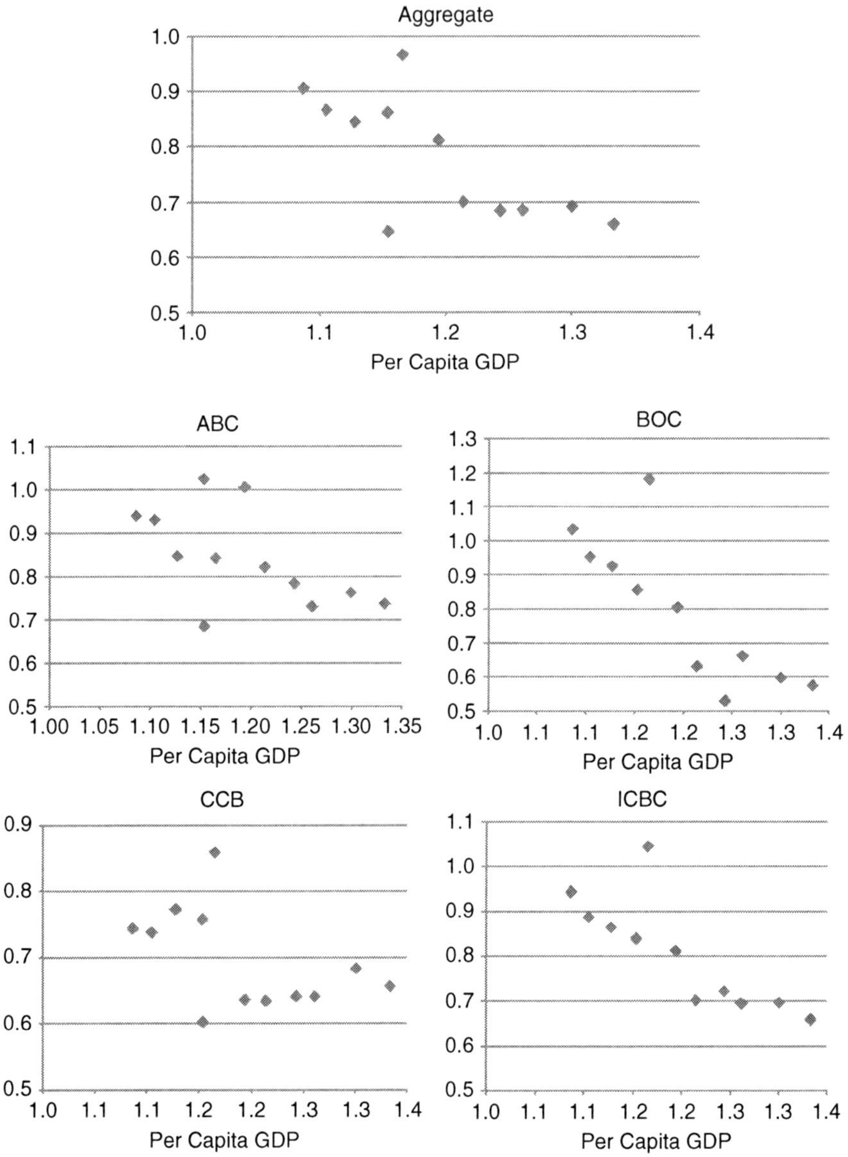

Fig. 4 Loan-to-deposit ratio vs. per capita GDP for the four SOCBs, aggregated and individually

Our final step is to examine the relationship between SOCB loan-to-deposit ratios and SOE shares and local per capita GDP at the individual province level. The SOCB loan-to-deposit ratio in each province is regressed first on the provincial SOE share and then on the per capita GDP level over our

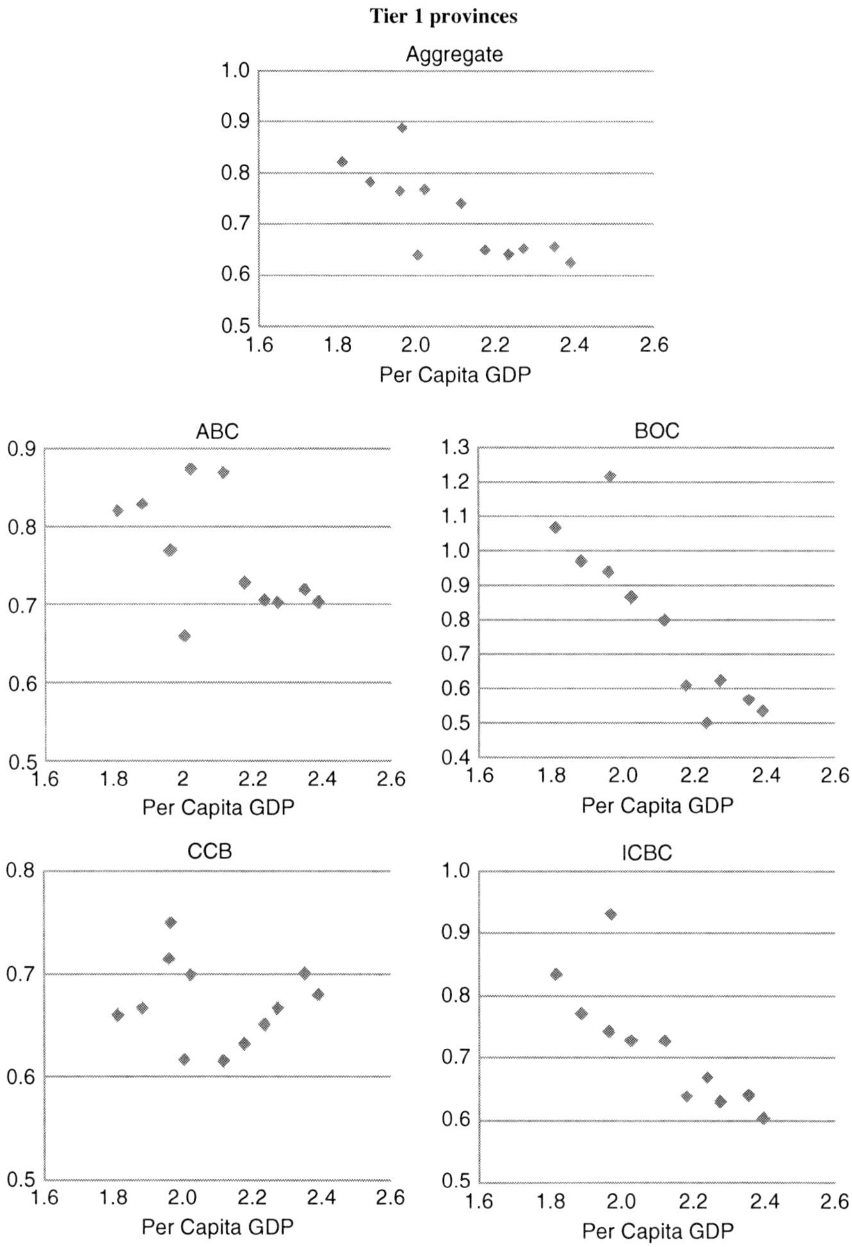

Fig. 5 Loan-to-deposit ratio vs. per capita GDP for the four SOCBs, aggregated and individually, by provincial income tier

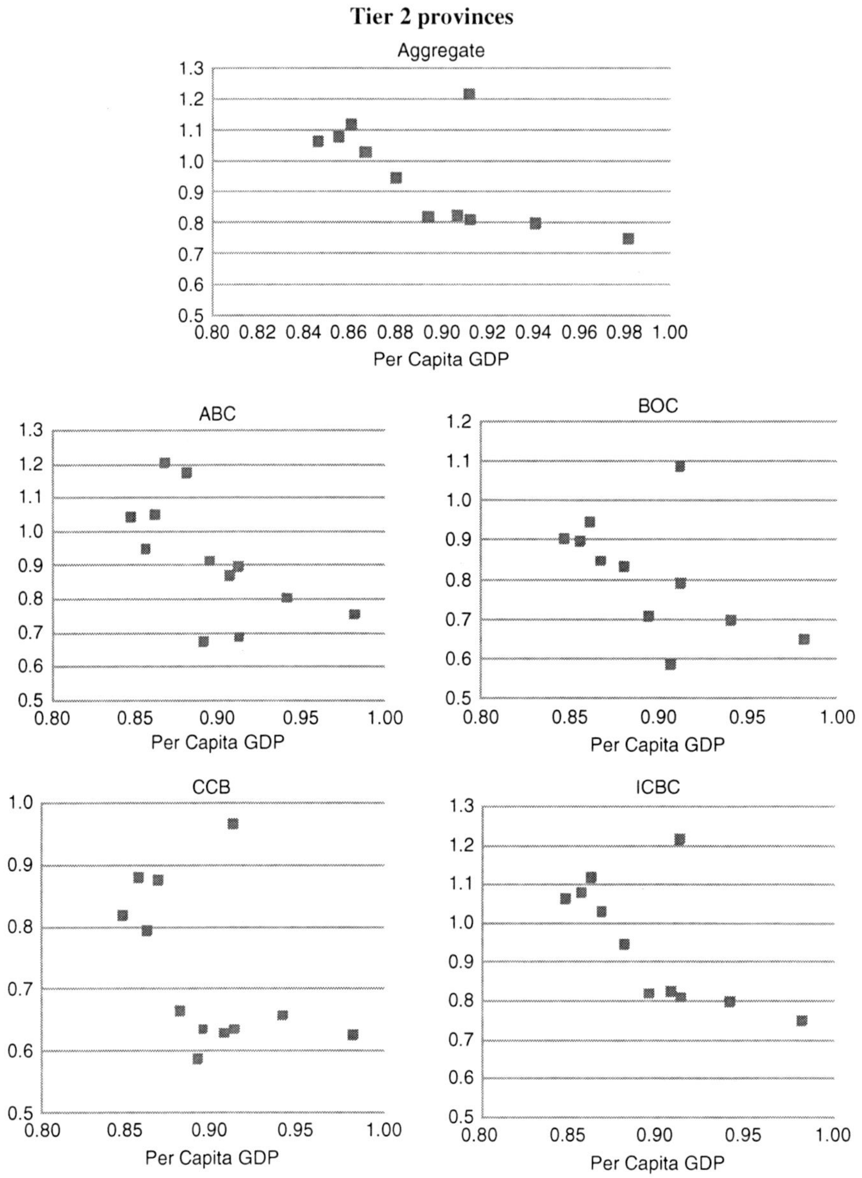

Fig. 5 (continued)

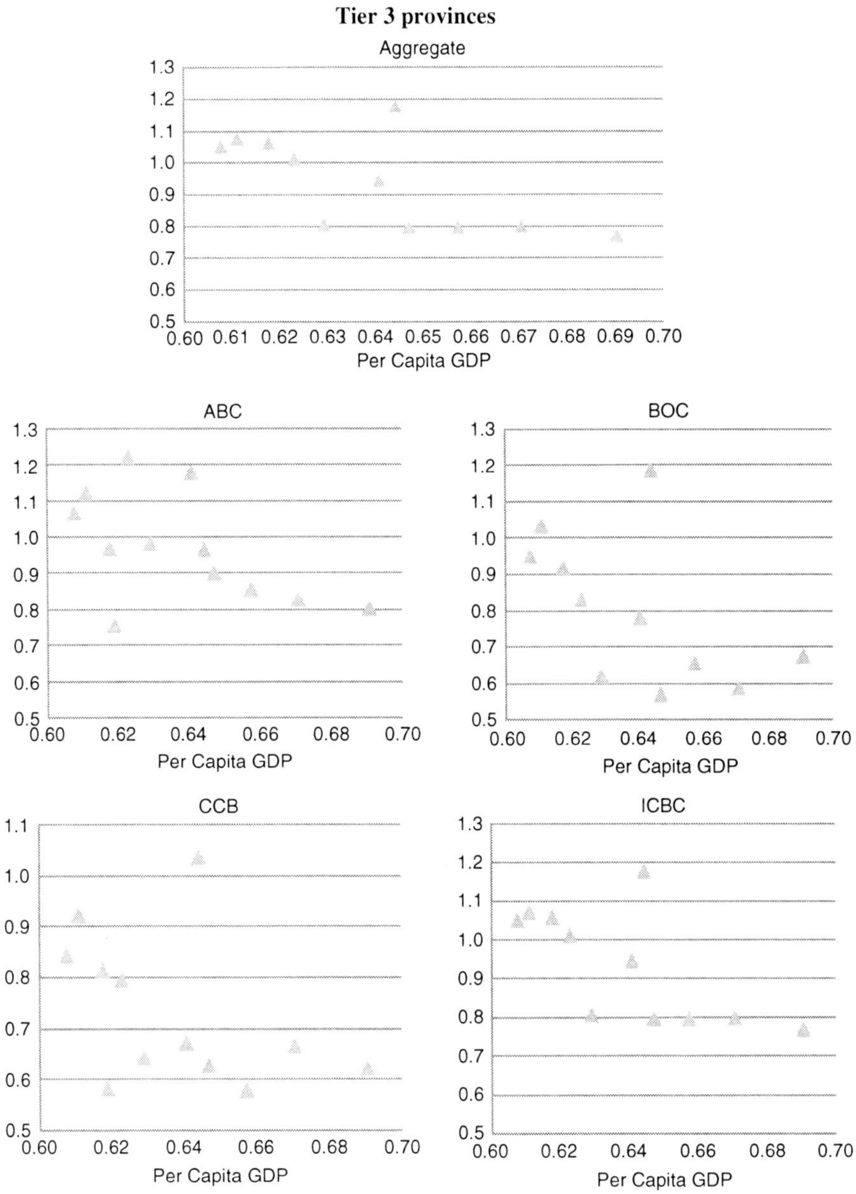

Fig. 5 (continued)

1994–2005 sample period. This analysis is done for each bank individually and for the four SOCBs aggregated together. We also consider a grouping of just BOC, CCB, and ICBC in order to allow for potentially different behavior on the part of ABC owing to its more rural lending base and lack of restructuring. Table 4 reports empirical results with the provinces listed in order of their per capita income level in 2000, going from the richest (Shanghai) to the poorest (Guizhou). Notwithstanding the relatively short time series available, most of the individual SOE coefficients are found to be positive and significant and most of the coefficients on per capita GDP are negative and significant, thereby offering support for the trends indicated in Figs. 2, 3, 4, and 5 above. More specifically, of the 31 regions, 23 show positive and significant responses to the SOE share at the 90% confidence level or better for all four SOCBS aggregated together – and 18 still show positive and significant responses when we limit it to just BOC, CCB, and ICBC. With regard to the responses to provincial per capita GDP, 27/31 show negative and significant responses when all four SOCs are aggregated together and 28/31 show negative and significant responses when ABC is excluded. In no case is any SOE coefficient significant with a negative sign or any GDP coefficient significant with a positive sign.

The results for each individual SOCB typically produce a similarly high ratio of significant coefficients and, most strikingly amongst such a large number of estimated coefficients, only Zhejiang (in the single case of CCB) has a negative and significant coefficient on the SOE share and/or a positive coefficient on per capita GDP. For SOE shares, the number of significant positive coefficients is 14/31 for ABC, 21/31 for BOC, 15/31 for CCB, and 21/30 for ICBC.[6] For per capita GDP, the number of negative and significant coefficients is 21/31 for ABC, 27/31 for BOC, 18/31 for CCB, and 29/30 for ICBC. Although these results are based on simple regressions that do not control for other variables (owing to the short available time series), the consistency in the findings of is quite remarkable. An overall pattern of SOE-based lending and redistributive lending appears to hold at the individual province level across all four big SOCBs.

We cannot sensibly use this same regression analysis to test for a possible change in SOCB behavior over our sample period owing to the already small number of total observations. We do, however, examine correlation coefficients between the SOCB loan-to-deposit ratio and the SOE and provincial income variables before and after 2000. We select the year 2000 as the dividing point, because it both gives us two equal-sized sub-samples (1994–1999 and 2000–2005) and also allows a couple of years for the SOCBs to adjust to the ending of the national credit plan in 1998.[7] There is a striking difference

[6] The total number of provinces for ICBC is only 30 because, unlike the other three SOCBs, it has no lending activities in Tibet.

[7] Experimentation with breaking the sample in 1999 produced almost identical results.

Table 4 Combined Correlation Coefficients for BOC, CCB, and ICBC before and after 2000

		SOE share			Per capita GDP		
Ranking (2000)	Provinces	Before 2000	After 2000	Difference	Before 2000	After 2000	Difference
1	Shanghai	0.72	0.87	0.15	−0.52	−0.79	−0.26
2	Beijing	−0.62	−0.48	0.14	−0.77	0.74	1.51
3	Tianjin	0.75	−0.35	−1.10	−0.99	−0.14	0.84
4	Zhejiang	0.87	−0.56	−1.43	−0.98	0.98	1.96
5	Guangdong	−0.04	0.39	0.44	−0.67	−0.80	−0.12
6	Jiangsu	0.29	−0.33	−0.62	−0.95	0.01	0.96
7	Fujian	0.52	−0.02	−0.54	−0.86	0.20	1.07
8	Liaoning	0.86	0.82	−0.03	−0.95	−0.90	0.06
9	Shandong	0.03	0.33	0.30	−0.94	−0.15	0.79
10	Heilongjiang	0.96	0.66	−0.30	−0.99	−0.61	0.38
11	Hebei	0.68	0.73	0.05	−0.91	−0.86	0.05
12	Xinjiang	−0.77	−0.01	0.76	−0.95	−0.69	0.26
13	Hubei	0.34	0.76	0.42	−0.52	−0.93	−0.41
14	Hainan	−0.67	0.60	1.27	−0.12	−0.61	−0.49
15	Jilin	0.75	0.97	0.22	−0.98	−0.94	0.04
16	Inner Mongolia	0.83	−0.71	−1.54	−0.96	0.94	1.90
17	Hunan	0.77	0.52	−0.25	−0.82	−0.55	0.27
18	Henan	0.41	0.61	0.20	−0.62	−0.40	0.22
19	Chongqing	−0.41	0.78	1.18	−0.89	−0.83	0.06
20	Shanxi	0.80	0.85	0.05	−0.93	−0.99	−0.06
21	Qinghai	0.88	0.64	−0.25	−1.00	−0.89	0.11
22	Anhui	0.74	0.74	0.00	−0.95	−0.85	0.10
23	Jiangxi	0.15	0.68	0.53	−0.95	−0.71	0.24
24	Ningxia	0.83	−0.10	−0.93	−0.95	0.06	1.01
25	Sichuan	0.77	0.69	−0.08	−0.97	−0.72	0.24
26	Yunnan	0.78	0.37	−0.41	−0.83	−0.42	0.41

Table 4 (continued)

Ranking (2000)	Provinces	SOE share			Per capita GDP		
		Before 2000	After 2000	Difference	Before 2000	After 2000	Difference
27	Tibet	–0.02	0.89	0.91	–0.39	0.34	0.73
28	Shaanxi	0.34	0.71	0.37	–0.92	–0.97	–0.06
29	Guangxi	–0.17	–0.54	–0.37	–0.29	0.27	0.56
30	Gansu	0.92	–0.63	–1.55	–0.94	–0.67	0.26
31	Guizhou	0.88	–0.21	–1.09	–0.94	–0.10	0.83
Average coefficients		SOE share			Per capita GDP		
		Before 2000	After 2000	Difference	Before 2000	After 2000	Difference
Tier 1		0.43	0.13	–0.30	–0.86	–0.15	0.72
Tier 2		0.27	0.51	0.24	–0.77	–0.59	0.18
Tier 3		0.55	0.29	–0.26	–0.83	–0.42	0.40
Overall Average		0.43	0.31	–0.11	–0.82	–0.39	0.43

between the shift in lending behavior evidenced by ABC and the pattern evident across the other three SOCBs. Consistent with the move toward more redistributive lending suggested in Fig. 1 above, we actually find that ABC lending after 2000 generally became more responsive to SOE shares, and more negatively related to provincial per capita GDP, than over the 1994–1999 period. These patterns hold for the vast majority of the individual provinces (24/31 in the case of SOE shares and 29/31 in the case of per capita GDP). With regard to the response to the SOE share, the correlation with the bank's loan-to-deposit ratio moves from positive to negative for three of the six richest provinces as well as becoming more negative for a fourth. This suggests that ABC did at least cut back on its SOE-based lending in leading areas like Beijing and Tianjin. Its overall SOE-based lending rose, however, and the correlation between its loan-to-deposit ratio and provincial SOE shares increased even for the Tier 1 group – albeit by considerably less than for Tier 2 and Tier 3 groupings.

Amongst the other three big SOCBs, the trend is more toward smaller correlations with SOE shares and more positive correlations with provincial GDP levels.[8] The combined correlation coefficients for BOC, CCB, and ICBC are presented in Table 4. The correlation with SOE shares remains positive across all three provincial tiers, and for 20/31 individual provinces, after 2000. The correlations tend to decline from the 1994–1999 levels, however, and this is particularly evident among the top provinces where even ABC showed some indications of reducing its SOE-based lending. The overall reduction nevertheless remains relatively mild overall, and there is actually a higher correlation with Tier 2 provincial SOE shares offset by declines amongst the Tier 1 and Tier 3 groupings. There is a more consistent reduction in redistributive lending after 2000 applying across all three provincial income tiers and 25/31 of the individual provinces. This offers some evidence that BOC, CCB, and ICBC lending became somewhat less redistributive and less SOE-based in more recent years. Strikingly, though, all the available evidence points toward ABC moving, seemingly quite strongly, in the other direction. Although its very high NPL ratio could be brought down via an injection of public funds of the type previously granted to the other three SOCBs, it is not obvious how future NPL growth could be contained in the face of the trends evident through 2005.

4 Conclusions

Disaggregated province-by-province analysis appears to confirm the importance of ongoing SOE-based and redistributive lending by the big four SOCBs. This pattern is quite consistent but the importance of SOE-based

[8] The strongest move n this direction is actually evidenced by BOC.

lending appears to be most pronounced amongst the poorer provinces. BOC, CCB, and ICBC do show some limited signs of reduced SOE-based lending after 2000 along with a more consistent move toward a less redistributive lending pattern. ABC, however, appears to have moved in the other direction. ABC's allocation of loans to the poorer provinces shows a sharp rise after 2000 as reflected both in its loan-to-deposit ratios and in terms of loan issuance as a share of provincial GDP. SOE-based lending by ABC also appears to have been on the rise other than for cutbacks in a handful of the very richest parts of the country. These trends may well reflect ABC's greater presence in the poorer areas of the country and the potential damage exerted on such provinces if ABC cut back on its lending and support for local SOEs. On the other hand, the lending patterns reviewed in this chapter make it unsurprising that ABC has yet to be prepared for joint stock ownership and a public listing. Could the government take the risk of cutting back on ABC's support for the poorer interior provinces in order to achieve the profitability that would likely be demanded by outside shareholders? Finally, with regard to the other big SOCBs, we should add the qualification that our sample period largely predates their transition to joint-stock companies – leaving us unable to take into account any more marked shifts in their behavior that potentially occurred after 2005.

Appendix

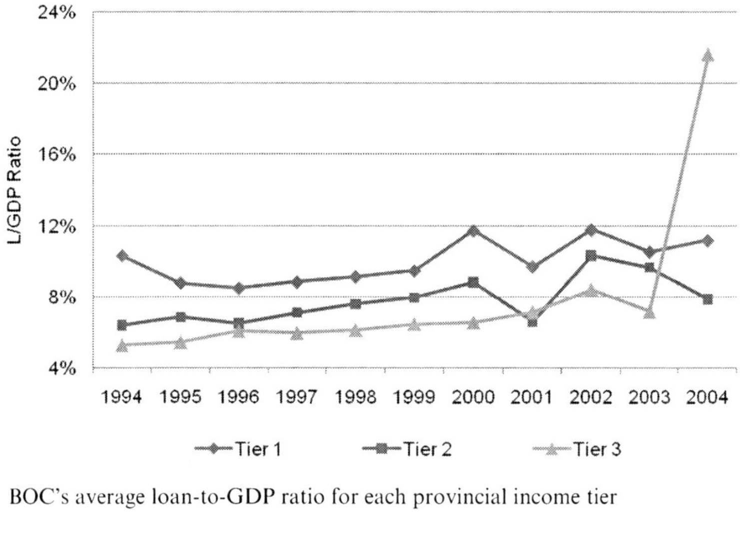

Fig. 6 BOC's average loan-to-GDP ratio for each provincial income tier

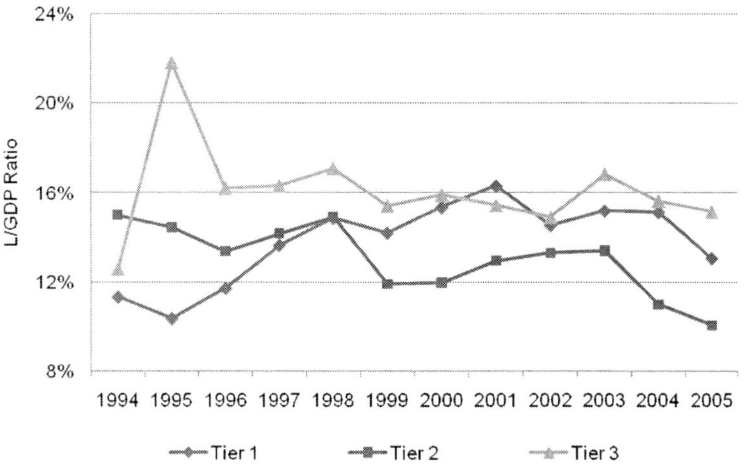

Fig. 7 CCB's average loan-to-GDP ratio for each provincial income tier

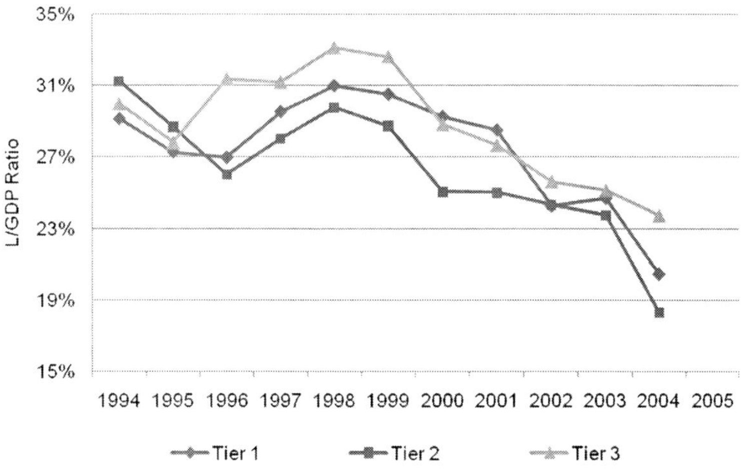

Fig. 8 ICBC's average loan-to-GDP ratio for each provincial income tier

References

Almanac of China's Finance and Banking, Beijing, various issues.

Ariff Mohamed and Luc Can. "Cost and Profit Efficiency of Chinese Banks: A Non-Parametric Analysis." *China Economic Review* **19** (June 2008): 260–273.

Ayyagari Meghana, Asli Demirgüç-Kunt and Vojislav Maksimovic. "Formal versus Informal Finance: Evidence from China." Policy Research Working Paper 4465, World Bank, Washington, DC, (January 2008).

Barth James R. and Gerard Caprio, Jr. "China's Changing Financial System: Can It Catch Up With, or Even Drive Growth." Networks Financial Institute at Indiana State

University, Policy Brief 2007-PB-05, (March 2007) [http://www.networksfinancialinstitute.org/pdfs/profiles/2007-PB-05_Barth-Caprio.pdf].

Barth James R., Rob Koepp and Zhongfei Zhou. "Institute View: Disciplining China's Banks." *Milken Institute Review*, Second Quarter (2004): 83–92.

Barth James R., Zhongfei Zhou, Douglas W. Arner, Berry F.C. Hsu and Wei Wang. *Financial Restructuring and Reform in Post-WTO China*. Alphen aan den Rijn, Netherlands: Kluwer Law International (2007).

Berger Allen N., Iftekhar Hasan and Mingming Zhou. "Bank Ownership and Efficiency in China: What Will Happen in the World's Largest Nation?" *Journal of Banking and Finance* **32** (2008, forthcoming).

Burdekin Richard C. K. and Emily Kochanowicz. "WTO Challenges and China's Banking System Today," in Richard C. K. Burdekin, *China's Monetary Challenges: Past Experiences and Future Prospects*. New York: Cambridge University Press (2008).

Burdekin Richard C. K. and Ran Tao. "China's State-Owned Banks' Lending Practices, 1994–2005: Empirical Tests and Policy Implications." *Open Economics Journal* **1** (2008): 14–24.

Cheng Xiaoqiang and Hans Degryse. "The Impact of Banks and Non-Bank Financial Institutions on Local Economic Growth in China." Discussion Paper 22/2007, Institute for Economies in Transition, Bank of Finland, Helsinki, (December 2007) [http://www.bof.fi/bofit].

China Statistical Yearbook, Beijing, various issues.

Chiu Becky and Mervyn K. Lewis. *Reforming China's State-owned Enterprises and Banks*. Northampton, MA: Edward Elgar (2006).

Dobson Wendy and Anil K. Kashyap. "The Contradictions in China's Gradualist Banking Reforms." *Brookings Papers on Economic Activity*, **2** (2006): 103–162.

Fu Xiaoqing (Maggie) and Shelagh Heffernan. "Cost X-Efficiency in China's Banking Sector." *China Economic Review* **18** (2007): 35–53.

Ge Ying and Jiaping Qiu. "Financial Development, Bank Discrimination and Trade Credit." *Journal of Banking and Finance* **31** (February 2007): 513–530

Huang Yasheng. "Do Financing Biases Matter for the Chinese Economy?" *Cato Journal* **26** (Spring/Summer 2006): 287–306.

Jia Chunxin. "The Effects of Ownership on the Prudential Behavior of Banks—The Case of China." *Journal of Banking and Finance* **32** (2008, forthcoming).

Leigh Lamin and Richard Podpiera. "The Rise of Foreign Investment in China's Banks—Taking Stock." Working Paper 06/292, International Monetary Fund, Washington, DC. (December 2006).

Lu Yan, Hung-Gay Fung and Xianfeng Jiang. "Market Structure and Profitability of Chinese Commercial Banks." *The Chinese Economy* **40** (September-October 2007): 100–113.

Park Albert and Kaja Sehrt. "Tests of Financial Intermediation and Banking Reform in China." *Journal of Comparative Economics* **29** (December 2001): 608–644.

People's Daily Online. "Quake Adds $860 mln to Agricultural Bank of China NPLs." (May 20, 2008) [http://english.people.com.cn/90001/90776/90884/6414091.html].

Philips Kerk L. and Shen Kunrong. "What Effect Does the Size of the State-Owned Sector Have on Regional Growth in China?" *Journal of Asian Economics* **15** (January 2005): 1079–1102.

Podpiera Richard, "Progress in China's Banking Sector Reform: Has Bank Behavior Changed?" Working Paper 06/71, International Monetary Fund, Washington, DC, March 2006.

Ren Daniel. "Rally Puts ICBC on Top of the World." *South China Morning Post*, (July 24, 2007), p. B1.

Shih Victor, Qi Zhang and Mingxing Liu. "Comparing the Performance of Chinese Banks: A Principal Component Approach." *China Economic Review* **18** (2007): 15–34.

Tsai Kellee S. *Back-Alley Banking: Private Entrepreneurs in China*. Ithaca, NY: Cornell University Press, (2002).

Zhu Youping. "Irrational Expectations Lead to Failure of the Transmission Mechanism – A Structural Explanation for Sustained Low Price Levels" (in Chinese), (October 9, 2002) (http://www.forumcn.com).

Determinants of Location Choice of Foreign Banks Within China: Evidence from Cities

Chung-Hua Shen, Qi Liang, and Xiang-Chao Hao

Abstract This chapter investigates location choice of foreign banks within China based on a panel data of 40 cities. Our empirical results show that the market opportunity is the most crucial factor to affect foreign bank decision to enter China cities. The labor cost is also important and the high labor cost of a city attracts more foreign banks. But the restriction on the locations of Renminbi business operation is very limited. Furthermore, we find that the city infrastructures like hardware and software environments strongly enhance the relation between market opportunity and foreign bank penetration.

Keywords Foreign banks · Location choice · Following customers, Regulation

1 Introduction

International banking activity has increased considerably in recent years. This development has motivated an increased interest in identifying the factors responsible for the growth and distribution of banking activity. Recently, China has gradually opened its domestic banking market according to the commitment of joining WTO. This gradual opening immediately attracts foreign banks to accelerate their investments in China, hoping to occupy favorable positions in the future competition. Thus, what factors affecting foreign banks set up overseas offices in China becomes an interesting question.

Previous works propose four models to investigate the determinants of international bank behaviors. The following client model, the first one, suggests that foreign banks set up the overseas offices passively in order to maintain strategic relations with the former domestic customers (Nigh et al., 1986; Goldberg and Grosse, 1994; Brealey and Kaplanis, 1996). Next, market opportunity

C.-H. Shen (✉)
National Taiwan University, Taipei, Taiwan, China
e-mail: chshen01@ntu.edu.tw

J.R. Barth et al. (eds.), *China's Emerging Financial Markets*,
The Milken Institute Series on Financial Innovation and Economic Growth 8,
DOI 10.1007/978-0-387-93769-4_14, © 2009 by Milken Institute

indicates that foreign banks are attracted by the market opportunity of the host country (Hultman and McGee, 1989; Yamori, 1998; Forecarelli and Pozzolo, 2005; Outreville, 2007). The fast rising GDP per capita, the mass population, and the development of financial markets are all market opportunity. The third one is the gravity model, which suggests that the mass (usually proxied by GDP) and distance are crucial to affect the decision of multinational banks. Both the physical and spiritual distance are considered in the literature. Finally, a less regulated environment appears an attracting factor for foreign bank entry. Focarelli and Pozzolo (2005) argued that heavily regulated banking systems are typically less accessible to foreign banks, thus reducing the probability of entry. Nigh et al. (1986), Hultman and McGee (1989), and Forecarelli and Pozzolo (2005) also point out that deregulation of the host country exerts a very positive impact on foreign banks.

The first aim of this study is to investigate the decisions of foreign banks to locate in Chinese cities. We collect information on foreign bank activities in 40 medium and large cities in China, including setting up of subsidiaries, branches or representative offices. Using the cities as the host, the conventional four models serve as our first basic test.

Next, we propose an extended test by examining whether the infrastructure of each city enhances or mitigates the above models, such as will the cities with strong infrastructure enhance the market opportunity? We consider two types of infrastructions – traffic and communication, and human capital. The former type can also be referred to as hardware environment and the latter type the software environment. Studies regarding China's non-financial foreign direct investment (FDI) have found that regional factors like the special economic zones, level of infrastructure, and labor quality have positive effects on the entry of FDI (Zhou et al., 2002; Wakasugi, 2005; Wei and Wang, 2005; Hong and Anthony, 2006; Kang and Lee, 2007), whereas the impact of labor cost is uncertain (Wei, 2000; Wu and Strange, 2000). However, previous studies typically use FDI as the proxy for testing the customers hypothesis without considering that these regional factors may also affect the decision, though possibly indirectly. Our second aim tries to fulfill this void.

This study contributes to the literature in three aspects. First, previous studies mainly examine location choice of foreign banks from or to developed countries (Nigh et al., 1986; Goldberg and Grosse, 1994; Yamori, 1998) at the national level. Few studies focus on the location choice of foreign banks in China, an emerging and transition country, and at the sub-national level. Although Leung et al. (2003) investigate why foreign banks come to China with a survival analysis and find that foreign banks has been attracted by the growing business opportunities and improved political environment, yet they do not examine why and how the foreign banks make location choice at the sun-national level. In other word, their research focuses on country characters but not city characters within China. Up to now, there are no systematic studies regarding the determinants of foreign banks' location choice within China, and thus there are no answers for the queries.

Next, studies of the determinants that affect foreign banks can be divided into three types based on the number of home countries from and to the host countries. The first type is referred to as one-to-many, denoting banks from one home country to set up overseas offices in many host countries. For example, Miller and Parkhe (1998) examined the determinants that affected US banks when establishing overseas offices in 32 countries. The second type is referred to as many-to-one, denoting banks from many home countries to one host country. Grosse and Goldberg (1991) investigated the factors that affect 35 foreign countries, banks setting up in the United States. Esperanca and Gulamhussen (2001) studied the same issue but with banks from 53 countries locating in Greece. The last type is about many-to-many, denoting banks from many home countries to many host countries. Brealey and Kaplanis (1996) investigated factors affecting the top 1,000 banks in the world from 37 countries setting up overseas offices in 82 countries and found that the trade and foreign direct investment between home and host countries are effective; see also Focarelli and Pozzolo (2005).

This study appears to be the second case, i.e., many-to-one, where many foreign banks come to China. However, though this study considers only one host country, there are many host cities. Thus, our paper has similarity and dissimilarity with the conventional many-to-one studies. Also, because it is consideration of cities, we use city infrastructure as the conditional variables to examine the indirect way.

Third, the use of non-financial FDI commonly find that labor cost plays an important role in affecting the entry of foreign manufacturing firms to China, such as the study by Wakasugi (2005) using Japanese case and Kang and Lee (2007) using Korean cases. Our finding indicates that the labor cost is not an important factor in influencing foreign banks' entry.

Fourth, we divide factors into basic factors (which is the conversional four models) and regional factors (which is our city infrastructure). Thus, we extend the literature in a slight way which helps us understand the importance of software and hardware environments.

The remaining part of this chapter is organized as follows. Section 2 introduces the development and major events of foreign banks in the last 30 years; Section 3 is literature review; Section 4 presents our empirical model. Section 5 describes data and sample construction and basic statistics; Section 6 reports the regression results; and Section 7 is our conclusions.

2 History of Foreign Banks in China

The history of foreign banks in China dates back to over 100 years. However, when the People's Republic of China was founded in 1949, the central government allowed only four foreign banks, Hong Kong and Shanghai Banking Corporation (HSBC), Bank of East Asia, Oversea-Chinese Banking Corporation (OCBC), and Standard Chartered Bank, to stay in Shanghai. After that, the development of foreign banks in China stagnated because of complex international political relation until 1978. At that time, the central government decided to open itself up to the world and launch the great reform practice. From 1978 to 2005, the development of foreign banks in China can be divided into three stages.

The first stage is the initial phase of opening-up, which started from mainly in the late 1970. In 1979, Chinese government permitted the Industrial Bank of Japan to establish the representative office of non-business. In 1981, foreign banks were further permitted to set up operational agents in five special economic zones, which are Shenzhen, Zhuhai, Xiamen, Shantou and Island Hainan. The most important impact for foreign bank entries is the pass of the stipulations of establishing foreign branches in 1983 and foreign banks and Chinese-foreign joint venture banks in 1985.[1] Xiamen international bank was set up based on the later law. However, the restrictions in setting up foreign bank offices are not deregulated.

The second phase further deregulated the location restrictions mostly. Since 1990, China government expanded the number of cities where foreign banks are permitted to set up representative offices or branches in cities outside the special economic zones for the first time. By the end of 1997, foreign banks have set up totally 175 branches in China. The fast growth of foreign banks number, however, slowed down and some of them are even closed after Asian crisis erupted in 1997. In the end of 2001, the total number of foreign banks' branches in China was only 159, and the net increase of 4 years is only 17.

The last phase is deregulation of business restriction, which is partially due to the officially returning to World Trade Organization in 2001. Before this stage, while the location restrictions are largely removed, business operation is prohibited. In 1996, authority first allows Renminbi (RMB) business by Citigroup, HSBC, Societe Generale of Tokyo-Mitsubishi in Shanghai Pudong New Zone for foreign firms only. In 2001, the restrictions are lifted for local firms within 2 years and remove all geographical restrictions. In 2005, 25 cities are allowed for foreign banks to engage in RMB business. Other deregulation continues. All of these changes suggest that foreign banks can largely free to choose the locations they want to invest.

3 Literature Review

Previous studies have considered foreign banks' location choice at the national and sub-national levels. First, a great deal of studies at the national level focus on country characteristics affecting foreign banks'

[1] The exact name of two laws are "Measures of the People's Bank of China for Regulations Relating to Establishing Resident Representative Office in China by Overseas Chinese and Foreign Banking Institutions" and "Regulations of People's Republic of China special economic zones on management of foreign banks and Chinese-foreign joint venture banks"

location choice. These studies can be divided into three types based on the number of countries from and to. The first type is referred to as one-to-many, denoting banks from one home country to set up overseas offices in many host countries. For example, Miller and Parkhe (1998) examined the determinants that affect U.S. banks to establish overseas offices in 32 countries. The second type is referred to as many-to-one, denoting banks from many home countries to one host country. Grosse and Goldberg (1991) investigated the factors that affected the decisions of 35 foreign countries' banks to set up in the United States, while Esperanca and Gulamhussen (2001) studied whether multinational banks, which come from 53 countries to the United States, follow their non-corporate customers. The last type is about many-to-many, denoting banks from many home countries to many host countries. Brealey and Kaplanis (1996) investigated factors that influenced the top 1,000 world banks from 37 countries to set up overseas offices in 82 countries. They found that the trade and foreign direct investment between home and host countries are effective; see also Focarelli and Pozzolo (2005).

Second, only a few studies have considered foreign banks' location choice at the subnational level. At the subnational level, country characters are the same for all foreign banks, so studies consider state characters within a country, such as the United States. Hultman and McGee (1990) find that Japanese presence in the US banking market is of particular significance and represents slightly over one-half of the total foreign banking presence. Simultaneously they also find most of foreign banking presences are concentrated in two states, which are New York and California. Goldberg and Grosse (1994) also find the amount and type of foreign bank activity varies greatly in states, with New York and California being by far the most important, so they examine the determinants of foreign banking activity by state and find that foreign bank presence is drawn to the states with large bank market size and fewer restrictions to entry.

4 Empirical Models

Three different measures for foreign bank penetration (*FBP*) are used in the literature. They are the percentage of foreign bank's assets over total bank assets (Nigh et al., 1986; Hultman and McGee, 1989; Goldberg and Grosse, 1994; Focarelli and Pozzalo, 2005), the financial foreign direct investment (Yamori, 1998), and the number of foreign banks' branches in the local market (Goldberg and Grosse, 1994; Shen and Chou, 2007). This chapter uses the third measure to proxy FBP because of the availability of data. In particular, FBP includes the number of foreign banks' branches and representative offices in China.

Following Goldberg and Grosse (1994) and Shen and Chou (2007), our empirical model is as follows:

$$FBP_{it} = \beta_0 + \beta_1 OPPORTUNITY_{it} + \beta_2 CUSTOM_{it} + \beta_3 REG_{it} + \beta_4 LABORCOST_{it} + \varepsilon_{ij} \quad (1)$$

$$\beta_1 = \beta_{11} + \beta_{12} INFRASTRU \quad (2)$$

$$i = 1, \ldots, N; t = 1, \ldots, T$$

where subscripts i and t denote the ith city at time t, where N is equal to 40, t ranges from 2000 to 2005, *FBP* is defined above, *OPPORTUNITY* measures the market opportunity of each Chinese city, *CUSTOMER* measures the following customer effect, *REGULATION* examines the effect of regulations on foreign banks, and *LABORCOST* is the vector of the variable of labor cost in banking industry, and *INFRASTRU* measures the infrastructure of each city.

Detailed explanatory variables are accounted for as follows.

OPPORTUNITY This study considers three proxies for market opportunity of host country, namely, *GDP* of each city (*CityGDP*) (Brealey and Kaplanis, 1996; Wezel, 2004; Margi, Mori and Rossi, 2005; Von Der Ruhr and Ryan, 2005), the value of total banking assets (*BankASSET*) (Goldberg and Grosse, 1994; Outreville, 2007), and the last is the ratio of the banking assets to city *GDP* (*BankASSET*/*CityGDP*).

CUSTOMER The following customer hypothesis is important in attracting foreign banks. Previous studies tend to use bilateral trade between two countries to measure the hypothesis (Goldberg and Grosse, 1994; Brealey and Kaplanis, 1996). Because this data is not available at a city level, we use the foreign direct investment to each city (*CityFDI*) as the proxy.

REGULATION *The regulation* is the important factor to affect the decision of foreign banks. In China, the administrator, China Banking Regulatory Commission (CBRC), gradually opens up Renminbi (RMB) business operation like saving and credit in appointed cities, such as Shanghai, Shenzhen, and Beijing. Foreign banks cannot operate the RMB business until they get the permission of CBRC. Therefore, we consider the regulation on RMB business operation (*REG_RMB*), It is a dummy variable, which is equal to unity if RMB business operation of the city is permitted by CBRC and zero otherwise. *REG_RMB* of Beijing, for example, is 1 after 2004 when it is opened up, and 0 before 2004.

LABORCOST Following Wu and Strange (2000), we use the average wage in the finance and insurance sectors, which include banking, insurance, security and trust, as city labor cost.

INFRASTRU Infrastructure is not discussed in the literature but is our conditional variables. Pervious studies have rarely considered the influence of city (country) infrastructure on foreign banks' decision in setting up overseas offices. This chapter is the first attempt to the best of our knowledge. Three proxies are considered. *CITY_ROAD* is the transportation infrastructure, *CITY_COM* is the communication infrastructure, and *CITY_HR* is the sufficiency of human capital of each city, where the transportation infrastructure is proxied by the road-paves area per capita, the communication infrastructure is proxied by fixed telephone, mobile phone and Internet user per capita, and the human capital infrastructure is proxied by the proportion of the employees that are serving in finance and insurance sectors against local total population. As suggested by Wakasugi (2005), the former two could be referred to as the hardware infrastructure and the last one the software infrastructure. See Table 2 for detailed definition of each variable and its data sources.

Equations (1) and (2) are similar to those of Shen and Lee (2006). When only Equation (1) is considered, we refer to it as "the benchmark model," but when Equations (1) and (2) are simultaneously considered, we refer to them as "the conditional models." For the conditional model, we have the following hypotheses:

1 If $\beta_{11} > 0$, and $\beta_{12} > 0$, the impact of market opportunity on foreign banks is positive, and the condition variable Z will strengthen that positive impact.
2 If $\beta_{11} > 0$, and $\beta_{12} < 0$, the impact of market opportunity on foreign banks is positive, but the condition variable Z will adversely affect that positive impact.

We will explore these two hypotheses individually in the following sections.

5 Data and Sample

5.1 Data Sources

Our panel data comprises 40 cities in China from 2000 to 2005. First, the dependent variable FBP is collected from *Almanac of China's Finance and Banking* in 2006. Next, city gross domestic product (*CityGDP*), the total size of banking assets (*BankASSET*), the ratio of to the total size of banking assets against gross domestic product (*BankASSET*/*CityGDP*), foreign direct investment(*CITYFDI*), the ratio of the industrial product of foreign firms against the industrial product of host firms by city (*INDUST*), the road-paves area per capita, (*CITY_ROAD*), fixed telephone, mobile phone and Internet user per capita (*CITY_COM*), the proportion of the employees that are serving in finance and insurance sector against local total population (*CITY_HR*) are taken from *China City Statistical Yearbook*. Last, the average wage of employees in the finance and insurance sectors (*LABORCOST*) is obtained from the *Statistical Yearbook or Economic Yearbook* of 40 cities from 2000 to 2005. See Table 2 for details.

Table 1 History of opening-up of foreign banks in China from 1980 to 2005

Phase	Year	Policy and big incident	Memo
Initial Opening-up	**1979**	Sanction non-profit agent	Bank of Tokyo set up a representative office in Beijing, which is the first subsidiary of a foreign bank since the founding of the PRC.
	1981	Sancion setting up operational agents in five special economic zones, including Shenzhen, Zhuhai, Shantou, Xiamen and island of Hainan.	The first branch of a foreign bank, Shenzhen branch of Singaporean Nanyang bank is established.
	1983	promulgate *Measures of the People's Bank of China for Regulations Relating to Establishing Resident Representative Office in China by Overseas Chinese and Foreign Banking Institutions,* sanctioning representive office set ups in Beijing and five special economic zones.	
	1984	Sanction, specially HSBC, Standard Charted Bank, OCBC and Bank of East Asia operating Renminbi business.	
	1985	Promulgate *Regulations of People's Republic of China special economic zones on management of foreign banks and Chinese-foreign joint venture banks.*	Xiamen International Bank is set up
Deregulation of Region Restrictions	**1990**	Open up Shanghai and sanction setting up operational agents.	
	1992	Open up new additional seven coastal cities	Including Dalian, Tianjin, Qingdao, Nanjing, Ningbo, Fuzhou, and Guangzhou.
	1994	Promulgate *Regulations of the Peoples Republic of China Governing Financial Institutions with Foreign Capital*, sanctioning foreign banks to set up operational agents in 11 cities.	
	1995	Open up backland cities	Including Wuhan, Xi'an, Hangzhou, Suzhou, Hefei,Chendu, Chongqi, and Shenyang; Qingdao International Bank is set up.

Table 1 (continued)

Phase	Year	Policy and big incident	Memo
	1996	Promulgate *Rules for Implementation of Regulations of the Peoples Republic of China Governing Financial Institutions with Foreign Capital, Provisional Measures for Foreign-funded Banks Setting Up Subsidiary Agents, and Shanghai Pudong New Zone, Administration of Pilot Operation of Renminbi Business by Foreign Investment Financial Institutions Tentative Procedures*	TM International Bank, the first solely foreign-funded bank, is estabished in Pudong of Shanghai; Bank of Asia invests share of China Everbright Bank
	1997	Pilot Renminbi business	City Bank, HSBC, Bank of Tokyo-Mitsubishi and Societe Generale Bank pilot to operate RMB business in Pudong of Shanghai, but the scope is limited in three types of foreign-funded enterprises and foreign residents.
	1998	Expand Renminbi pilot scope, sanctioning branches of eight foreign banks, including Societe Generale Bank, City Bank, HSBC, and other five banks to join intercompany offered market.	Shenzhen is sanctioned be the second city of piloting Renminbi business.
	1999	Promulgate *Provisional Measures of Investing to Financial Institution, Closure by Foreign Banks of Their Business Branches in China Operational Guidelines*, and *Measures for the Administration of Bank Card Business*, expanding the scope of region of customers, relaxing the limitation on size of Renminbi business, and canceling regional limitation on setting up subsidiary agents.	Restrict solely foreign-funded and sino-foreign joint venture financial institutions to invest in state-owned commercial bank; cities sanctioned to set up operational agents expand to 23 central cities; IFC invests in the shares of Shanghai Bank.

Table 1 (continued)

Phase	Year	Policy and big incident	Memo
Deregulation of Business Restrictions	**2001**	China returns WTO officially, promising that sanction foreign banks to operate RMB business for Chinese firms within 2 years, remove all geographical restrictions, sanction providing all Chinese customers with services, and the establishment of city business outlets within 5 years	Sanction to establish solely foreign-funded or sino-foreign joint venture financial leasing company; HSBC invest the share of Shanghai Bank.
	2002	Emend *Regulations of the Peoples Republic of China Governing Financial Institutions with Foreign Capita* and its implementing rules; promulgate *Provisional Measures of Qualified Foreign Institutional Investors and Qualified Domestic Institutional Investors;* Expand the city scope operating Renminbi business.	Sanction Bank of East Asia's Internet bank business; Open Renminbi business in Guangzhou, Zhuhai, Qingdao, Nanjing and Wuhan; Sanction Deutsche Bank's acquisition of Huize China Holding; Sanction City Bank to operate foreign exchange service to domestic residents; HSBC invest Pin'an Insurance Company.
	2003	Sanction Qualified Foreign Institutional Investors	Sanciton City Bank, HSBC and Standard Charted Bank to operate security trust business of Sanction Qualified Foreign Institutional Investors; and open up Renminbi business of Jinan, Fuzhou, Chendu, and Chongqing.
	2004	Sanction foreign banks to develop banking card business	Shanghai Pudong Development Bank and City Bank cooperate to issue a double-currency credit card; sanction HSBC, Mizuho Bank, City Bank, and Bank of East Asia to serve Renminbi business to sino-funded enterprises; open up Renminbi business of Kuning, Beijing, Xiamen, Xi'an and Shenyang.
	2005	Keep opening up the region of Renminbi business	Open up the Renminbi business of Shantou, Ningbo,Haerbin, Changchun, Lanzhou, Yinchuan and Nanning, which increases the number of cities operating Renminbi business to 25.

Table 2 Definitions of explanatory variables and data source

Type		Variable Name	Definition	Expected Sign	Data Source
Opportunity		*CiryGDP*	Log of the city total industrial product	+	*China City Statistical Yearbook*
		BankASSET	Log of the amount of all local financial institutions' loan of a city	+	*China City Statistical Yearbook*
		BankASSET/ CityGDP	A ratio of the amount of all local financial institutions' loan of a city versus its GDP	+	*China City Statistical Yearbook*
Customer		*CITYFDI*	Log of FDI absorbed by a city	+	*China City Statistical Yearbook*
Regulation		*REG*	If Renminbi business operation is opened up, REG is 1, else 0.	+	*News conference of CRC on the Internet*
Labor Cost		*LABORCOST*	Log of the average salary of the employee that are serving in financial and insurance industry	?	*Statistical Yearbook or Economic Yearbook of each city*
Infrastructure	**Transportation**	*CITY_ROAD*	Log of road-paves area per capita	?	*China City Statistical Yearbook*
	Communication	*CITY_COM*	Log of fixed telephone, mobile phone, and Internet user per capita	?	*China City Statistical Yearbook*
	Human Capital	*CITY_HR**	the proportion of the employees that are serving in financial and insurance industry versus local total population	+	*China City Statistical Yearbook*

Notes: Because the proportion of the employees that are serving in financial and insurance industry versus local total population is too small to exhibit the results well, so we multiple it with 100.

5.2 Descriptive Statistics

Figure 1 presents the total number of branches set up by foreign banks in China from 1980 to 2005. The starting period of 1980 is chosen because foreign banks start to set branches in China that year. There are roughly three peaks during the past three decades. The first peak appears in 1986–1987, when the authority decides to open the market and gradually phase out the restriction on foreign entrances. The second peak falls in the period of 1993–1996 when central government decides a further opening policy to allow local cities to accept more foreign banks branches. The number drops slightly during 1997–1999 due to the Asian crisis that erupted in 1997. The last peak occurred in 2004–2005 because China joined WTO, committing to open the financial market.

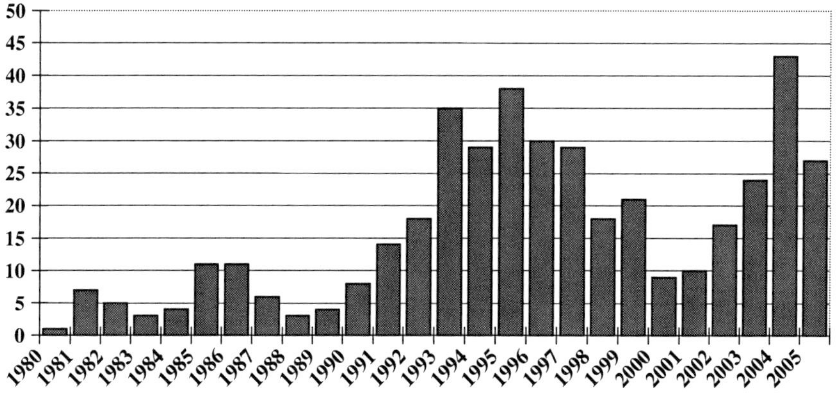

Fig. 1 Describes the change of branches set up by foreign banks in China from 1980 to 2005

Table 3 presents the historical number of FBP from home countries to China during period 1980–2005. Four interesting results are highlighted as follows. First, foreign banks from Hong Kong (91), Japan (75), the United States. (34), Germany (23), and South Korea (23) established more branches than other countries (area), where the number in parenthesis is the total number of overseas offices in China. In particular, the foreign branches set up by the United States and German banks are clustered around 1995–1996, of which the numbers are 17 and 15 and then slowly the decline after 2001. Next, the total numbers of branches from Hong Kong, Japan, and South Korea are 189, accounting for 44.47% of total branches. The percentage by the United States, Germany, France, and Britain is around 30%. Third, Hong Kong in 1981 and Japan in 1980 are the first area and country, respectively, which set up branches in China. Furthermore, their presences grow stably even during the Asian financial crisis and gain momentum after 2001. Finally, while South Korea

Table 3 The distribution of original countries (areas) and years of foreign banks' branches[1]

Country/Area	Year(1980–2005)																										
	80	81	82	83	84	85	86	87	88	89	90	91	92	93	94	95	96	97	98	99	00	01	02	03	04	05	Total
Total	1	7	5	3	4	11	11	6	3	4	8	14	18	11	29	38	30	29	18	21	9	10	17	24	43	27	425
Hong Kong		1	1			3	2	1	2		3	2	6	10	4	6	4	5	2	5	4		1	5	14	10	91
Japan	1			1	3	2	3	2				4	3	3	8	13	6	4	2	1			2	3	7	7	75
U.S.							2		1		1	2	2	4		2	3	3		4		2	2	3	3		34
Germany		1				1	1							1	3	2	2	2	4	1	2	1			2		23
South Korea													2	1	2	2	2	1			1		1	4	2	5	23
France		1				1				2		1	2	2	2	1	3	2	2					2			21
U. K.		1	1			1	2	1		1		1	2	2	1		1	2	1	2				1			20
Singapore						1						2		3	2		3	2	1			2			2		18
Italy			1				1	2			3				1	1		1	1					1	2		14
Netherlands											1			1	2	3	1		2					1	1		12
Canada		2	1												2		1	1				1			2		10
Thailand													1	2		3	2	1									9
Switzerland														1	1			1		1		1	1		1		7
Taiwan																							7				7
India																		1					1	1	2	2	7
Australia						1						1		1	1	1		1									6
Belgium				1													1		2	1		1					6
Sweden			1	1	1																1		1				5
Russia										1							1			1					1		4
Spain						1								1		1									1		4
Austria												1								1						1	3
Philippines														1		1						1					3
Portugal														1				2									3
Pakistan		1																								1	2
Kazakhstan																				1					1		2
Malaysia														1							1						2

Table 3 (continued)

Country/Area	Year(1980–2005)																										
	80	81	82	83	84	85	86	87	88	89	90	91	92	93	94	95	96	97	98	99	00	01	02	03	04	05	Total
Egypt																				1							1
Brazil																									1		1
Korea																						1					1
Cuba																				1							1
Cameroon																								1			1
Kuwait																										1	1
Mongolia																									1		1
Morocco																				1							1
South Africa																1											1
Norway																								1			1
Turkey																			1								1
Iran																							1				1
Indonesia																								1			1
Jordan																1											1

Table 3 (continued)

	City[2]																										
Country/Area	SH	BJ	GZ	SZ	TJ	DL	XM	CD	QD	WH	FZ	HZ	NJ	SY	CQ	ZH	DG	ST	SC	KM	HK	KS	NT	NB	WX	XA	Total
Total	148	102	35	32	19	13	12	8	8	7	4	4	4	4	4	4	3	3	3	2	1	1	1	1	1	1	425
Hong Kong	19	7	11	17	3	3	4	2	3	2	4	2	1	1	2	1	3	2	2		1					1	91
Japan	35	8	4	3	4	8	1	1	1	3		1	1	1	1				1				1		1		75
U.S.	14	11	3	1	2		2	1																			34
Germany	11	10	2																								23
South Korea	7	4	2	1	4	1			2					2													23
France	5	6	3	1	3		1	1		1																	21
U. K.	5	4	1	1	1	1	1	1	1			1	1			1								1			20
Singapore	6	3	2	1	1		2	2	1																		18
Italy	8	6																									14
Netherlands	4	3	1	2	1					1																	12
Canada	3	4	2												1												10
Thailand	2	2		1			1											1		2							9
Switzerland	3	4																									7
Taiwan	3	2		1																		1					7
India	4		2	1																							7
Australia	2	4																									6
Belgium	2	1	1	1									1														6
Sweden	2	3																									5
Russia		4																									4
Spain	1	3																									4
Austria		2														1											3
Philippines	1	1		1																							3
Portugal	1		1													1											3
Pakistan		2																									2
Kazakhstan	1	1																									2
Malaysia	1	1																									2
Egypt	1																										1

Table 3 (continued)

	City^2																										
Country/Area	SH	BJ	GZ	SZ	TJ	DL	XM	CD	QD	WH	FZ	HZ	NJ	SY	CQ	ZH	DG	ST	SC	KM	HK	KS	NT	NB	WX	XA	Total
Brazil	1																										1
Korea		1																									1
Cuba		1																									1
Cameroon		1																									1
Kuwait	1																										1
Mongolia		1																									1
Morocco		1																									1
South Africa	1																										1
Norway	1																										1
Turkey	1																										1
Iran		1																									1
Indonesia	1																										1
Jordan	1																										1

Note 1: Foreign banks' affiliates include branches, representative offices and several sub-branches.
Note 2: For the sake of typeset, we shorten the name of each city into two alphabets. Here SH-Shanghai, BJ-Beijing, GZ-Guangzhou, SZ-Shenzhen, TJ- Tianjin, DL-Dalian, XM-Xiamen, CD-Chengdu, QD-Qingdao, WH-Wuhan, FZ-Fuzhou, HZ-Hangzhou, NJ-Nanjing, SY-Shenyang, CQ-Chongqing, ZH-Zhuhai, DG-Dongguan, ST-Shantou, SC-Suzhou, KM-Kunming, HK-Haikou, KS-Kunshan, NT-Nantong, NB-Ningbo, WX-Wuxi, and XM-Xi'an.

lags behind Hong Kong and Japan to establish branches in the early 1990s, the presence of Korean banks increase considerably after 1992 because of the establishment of formal diplomatic relations in that year.

In short, both the proximity and development of economics are crucial factors in determining the entrance to China banking market. That is, foreign banks from countries with closer geography and culture as well as from the industrialized countries tend to join the Chinese banking market.

Table 3 presents the matrix of number of *FBP* from home countries to the host cities. Among the 10 most favored cities by foreign banks, seven are harbor cities, whereas the remaining three are Beijing (the capital), Chengdu (the largest city in Pearl River Delta region), and Wuhan (largest city in middle China), which are inner cities. Banks from Hong Kong are the most active ones in China. Also note that while Hong Kong is geographically close to Guangzhou, Shenzhen, and other Pearl River Delta region, banks from Hong Kong set up a considerable number of branches in cities far from its location, such as branches in Beijing (7), Shanghai (19) (the financial center in China) and Tianjin (3) (the center in the BorHai Bay), and other northern cities. This decision probably reflects the importance of market opportunity. Japan is another case to demonstrate this argument. Japanese banks have eight branches in their previous colony, Dalian city, but they also established many branches in cities far from their location, such as in Shanghai (35), Suzhou (1), Wuxi (1), and Nantong (1). Banks from Europe are most located in Beijing and Shanghai, indicating again the importance of market opportunity.

Table 4 reports the mean of each explanatory variable. We divide 40 cities into four divisions. Bohai Rim (in Northeast China), Yangtze River Delta (in Middle East China), Pearl River Delta (in South China), and Mid-West based on its location. Also, see the Annual Report on Urban Development of China in 2002 for the same classifications. The *CityGDP* for these four divisions are 7.20, 7.48, 6.87, and 5.89, respectively, and the *BankASSET* are 7.62, 7.48, 6.95, and 6.85 respectively, suggesting that the market opportunity of Yangtze River Delta is the most attractive. While *BankASSET*/*CityGDP* are 1.06, 1.00, 1.01, and 1.16, indicating the ratio of the banking assets to city *GDP* of Mid-West has its potential to attract foreign banks. With respect to FDI in city, our variable *CITYFDI* shows that Mid-West (8.46) is the least attractive for foreign banks among four divisions. At the same time, *LABORCOST* (9.89) of Mid-West is also the lowest. Note that in manufactory industry, low labor cost could attract more foreign investment; the same argument, however, may not apply to the financial industry. Low labor cost may indicate little low labor quality in terms of the knowledge of the financial operations. Thus, low labor cost in the financial industry may not attract foreign banks. Regarding the infrastructure, the greatest numbers of *CITY_ROAD, CITY_COM, and CITY_HR* are Pearl River Delta, suggesting the hardware and software of the division surpass other divisions.

Turning to the case of city, the largest numbers of *CityGDP* and *BankASSET* is Shanghai, followed by Beijing. Thus, it is not surprising to find that the largest number of *CITYFDI* is also on Shanghai (13.14). If both the market

Table 4 Mean value of explanatory variables of each division and city

Division[1]	City	*CityGDP*	*BankASSET*	*BankASSET/CityGDP*	*Cityfdi*	*Laborcost*	*City_Road*	*City_Com*	*City_HR*
Bohai Rim	Beijing	8.19	9.17	1.12	12.67	10.87	2.03	1.89	1.07
	Tianjin	7.63	7.91	1.04	12.51	10.14	1.91	1.17	0.59
	Shenyang	6.94	7.53	1.08	11.88	10.14	1.98	1.1	0.85
	Dalian	7.22	7.43	1.03	12.01	10.15	1.79	1.51	1.02
	Changchun	7.08	7.27	1.03	10.85	9.88	1.85	1.19	0.71
	Haerbin	6.32	7.12	1.13	10.12	10.02	1.59	1.05	0.79
	Jinan	6.82	7.32	1.07	10.67	10.08	2.27	1.1	0.80
	Qingdao	7.38	7.17	0.97	11.71	10.20	2.36	1.45	0.88
	Subtotal	**7.20**	**7.62**	**1.06**	**11.55**	**10.19**	**1.97**	**1.30**	**0.84**
Yangtze River Delta	Shanghai	9.13	8.87	0.97	13.14	10.59	2.47	1.81	1.02
	Nanjing	7.67	7.94	1.04	11.79	10.53	2.45	1.12	0.56
	Wuxi	7.33	7.09	0.97	11.64	10.25	2.83	1.38	0.68
	Suzhou	7.37	7.13	0.97	12.15	10.15	2.47	1.39	0.62
	Nantong	5.95	6.05	1.02	9.92	10.03	2.04	1.17	0.80
	Hangzhou	7.69	8.01	1.04	11.10	10.46	1.91	1.52	0.93
	Ningbo	7.18	7.25	1.01	11.40	10.36	2.05	1.79	0.98
	Subtotal	**7.48**	**7.48**	**1.00**	**11.59**	**10.34**	**2.32**	**1.45**	**0.80**
Pearl River	Fuzhou	6.25	7.09	1.13	10.85	10.20	2.00	1.47	1.12
	Xiamen	7.08	6.48	0.92	11.29	10.60	2.15	1.67	0.78
	Guangzhou	8.10	8.58	1.06	12.39	10.71	2.37	2.51	0.95
	Shenzhen	8.43	8.26	0.98	12.59	11.05	3.44	8.7	2.59
	Zhuhai	6.80	5.90	0.87	11.19	10.34	3.31	2.61	1.20

Table 4 (continued)

Division[1]	City	*CityGDP*	*BankASSET*	*BankASSET/ CityGDP*	*Cityfdi*	*Laborcost*	*City_Road*	*City_Com*	*City_HR*
	Shantou	5.85	6.04	1.03	9.31	9.80	1.66	0.82	0.44
	Dongguan	7.46	6.93	0.93	11.87	10.18	2.93	4.26	0.97
	Haikou	5.02	6.30	1.25	10.28	9.96	2.15	1.46	1.03
	Subtotal	**6.87**	**6.95**	**1.01**	**11.22**	**10.36**	**2.50**	**2.94**	**1.13**
Mid-West	Changsha	5.70	7.06	1.24	10.23	9.98	2.16	1.36	0.98
	Chengdu	6.42	7.66	1.19	10.20	10.15	2.05	1.27	0.71
	Guiyang	5.58	6.48	1.16	8.78	9.82	1.34	1.06	0.64
	Hefei	6.08	6.78	1.11	9.99	9.78	2.56	1.26	0.67
	Kunming	6.02	6.70	1.11	3.99	9.81	1.56	1.34	0.76
	Lanzhou	6.11	6.70	1.10	0.00	9.64	1.83	1.18	0.72
	Nanchang	5.81	6.44	1.11	10.05	9.89	1.84	1.31	0.84
	Nanning	5.00	6.65	1.33	9.10	9.98	2.10	1.23	0.78
	Shijiazhuang	6.40	6.86	1.07	9.49	9.95	2.10	1.18	0.88
	Taiyuan	6.06	7.03	1.16	9.23	9.65	1.98	1.06	0.80
	Urumqi	5.77	6.64	1.15	7.20	10.10	1.93	1.38	0.95
	Wuhan	7.19	7.66	1.07	11.74	9.87	1.28	0.93	0.47
	Xi'an	6.41	7.36	1.15	10.11	9.90	1.52	0.93	0.74
	Xi'ning	4.00	5.80	1.45	6.97	9.86	1.51	0.86	0.75
	Yinchuan	4.69	5.68	1.21	7.71	9.93	2.26	1.27	1.44
	Zhengzhou	5.87	7.27	1.24	8.95	9.99	1.95	1.22	1.03
	Chongqing	7.10	7.71	1.09	10.20	9.90	1.41	0.83	0.44
	Subtotal	**5.89**	**6.85**	**1.16**	**8.46**	**9.89**	**1.85**	**1.16**	**0.80**

Note 1: We divide our forty cities into four big divisions according to their location and economy relationship with each other. The four divisions are Bohai rim which includes the main big city around Bohai Bay, Yangtze River Delta which includes the most developed cities around Shanghai, Pearl River Delta which covers most big coastal cities in province of Guangdong, Fijian, and Mid-West which includes the biggest and central inland cities in China.

opportunity and following the client hypothesis are correct in China, Shanghai should be the most preferred city by foreign banks. It is interesting to note that while the largest *BankASSET/CityGDP* is Xining, the city has almost zero foreign direct investment. One reason for this is that BankAsset/CityGDP is not the appropriate proxy for market opportunity. The largest values of *LABORCOST* fall overwhelmingly on the largest cities, such as Shenzhen, Beijing, Guangzhou, Xiamen, and Shanghai. The *CITY_ROAD*, *CITY_COM*, and *CITY_HR* of Shenzhen are the greatest among our forty cities. Therefore, greater diversity is found for four divisions and our sample cities.

6 Empirical Results

6.1 Benchmark Model

Table 5 presents the correlation matrix of the explanatory variables. The correlation coefficients between each paired variables fall in the range of –0.44 to 0.6, suggesting that the multi-colinearity problem is not the concern.

Table 5 Correlation matrix of the explanatory variables

Variable	*CityGDP*	*BankASSET*	*BankASSET/ CityGDP*	*CityFDI*	*Reg*	*Laborcost*
CityGDP	1					
BankASSET	0.04	1				
BankASSET/ CityGDP	–0.42	0.88	1			
CityFDI	0.58	–0.05	–0.30	1		
Reg	0.55	–0.03	–0.25	0.33	1	
Laborcost	0.66	0.12	–0.18	0.52	0.53	1

Table 6 presents estimated results using the benchmark model. There are three specifications in the table because we consider one of three proxies for the market opportunity in turn, where the three proxies are *CITYGDP*, *Bank-ASSET*, and *BankASset/CITYGDP*, respectively. We first test the null hypothesis of no individual effects in our panel data. The *F*-statistics reported in Table 6 are equal to or above 117, rejecting the null of no individual effect. We next examine the null of random effect in our panel data using Hausman test. The bottom of Table 6 shows that two specifications reject the null and one cannot reject the null. Because the estimation results are similar regardless of random and fixed effect used, we only report the results of fixed effects models.

In Table 6, coefficients of *CityGDP* in specifications A is significantly positive, suggesting that market opportunity effect exists when the city GDP is used as the proxy. The effect of market opportunity, however, is elusive

Table 6 Basic model: Fixed effect

Variable	A	B	C	D	E	F
CityGDP	3.24*			2.95		
	(1.63)			(1.45)		
BankASSET		–0.13			–0.11	
		(–1.03)			(–0.85)	
BankASSET/CityGDP			–0.61			–0.46
			(–0.80)			(–0.60)
CityFDI	–0.30	–0.29	–0.30			
	(–0.82)	(–0.78)	(–0.80)			
Reg	–0.42	–0.28	–0.29	–0.37	–0.26	–0.24
	(–0.44)	(–0.30)	(–0.31)	(–0.39)	(–0.25)	(–0.25)
Laborcost	0.72	3.75***	3.56***	0.50	3.24***	3.07***
	(0.34)	(3.78)	(3.23)	(0.24)	(3.03)	(2.93)
Obs	240	240	240	240	240	240
R^2	0.36	0.05	0.09	0.34	0.1	0.13
F test	117***	135***	143***	118***	138***	147***
Hausman test	12.35***	–33.90	161***	12.96***	–1.71	–0.91

Notes: The F test: $F = \frac{(RSSU-RSSR)/(n-1)}{RSSU/(nT-n-k)}$, where *RSSU* is residual sum of square from the OLS model and RSSR is residual sum of square from the fixed effect model. All the six tests reject the null hypothesis, the fixed effect model is more appropriate; Hausman test: $[\beta_{re} - \beta_{fe}]'[Var(\beta_{re}) - Var(\beta_{fe})]^{-1}[\beta_{re} - \beta_{fe}]$, three groups reject the null hypothesis, while the other three accept it; t values are in parentheses; ***,**,* denote significance at 1%, 5%, and 10% level.

because the coefficients of *BankAsset* and *BankASSET* are insignificant. Thus, market opportunity once proxied by *CITYGDP* is crucial in affecting the decision of foreign banks, which is consistent with that of Goldberg and Grosse (1994) and Outreville (2007). The coefficients of *CITYFDI* are all insignificantly negative, rejecting the null of following the client hypothesis. Thus, foreign banks do not following their customers in China. This finding is interesting because the hypothesis is commonly supported by using country level data; see Nigh et al. (1986), Hultman and McGee (1989) and Yamori (1998) to show that foreign banks follow their customers to set up branches in other countries. Regarding the variable *REG*, its coefficients are all insignificantly negative, suggesting regulation on RMB business operation affects little the location choice of foreign banks.

Notably, the coefficients of *LABORCOST* are significantly positive for two of three specifications. This indicates that foreign banks go to the cities with high labor costs, which appears to be contradictory to our intuition at first glance. Unlike the manufacturing sector, where cheap labor is important–as shown in studies by Wakasugi (2005) and Kang and Lee (2007) regarding the manufacturing sectors in Japan and Korea the quality of labor—may be crucial in the financial sector. Thus, we conjecture that foreign banks prefer the cities with high labor costs reflecting their high labor quality.

6.2 Conditional Model

Table 7 presents the estimation results considering both equations (1) and (2) using panel fixed effect method. [2] Three specifications are presented, and each uses the interaction term between *CityGDP* with one of the three infrastructure variables, *CITY_ROAD*, *CITY_COM*, and *CITY_HR*, respectively. Notably, the coefficients of the three interaction terms are overwhelmingly significantly positive, suggesting that infrastructures of transportation, communication, and human resource enhance the market opportunity effect, namely, cities with better transportation, communication, and human resources together with higher GDP could attract more foreign banks. However, most of previous coefficients are insignificant except for *CITYGDP* in the third specification.

Table 7 Conditional model: Fixed effect

Variable	A	B	C
CityGDP	1.08	0.95	6.19***
	(0.54)	(0.46)	(–3.56)
CityFDI	–0.32	–0.23	–0.13
	(–0.90)	(–0.64)	(–0.39)
REG	–0.64	–0.38	–0.4
	(–0.70)	(–0.42)	(–0.45)
Laborcost	–1.30	0.68	–2.61
	(–0.62)	(0.33)	(–1.40)
CityGDP*City_Road	0.77***		
	(4.11)		
CityGDP*City_Com		0.21***	
		(3.43)	
CityGDP*City_hr			1.35***
			(5.74)
Observation	240	240	240
$\mathbf{R^2}$	0.19	0.14	0.38
Hausman test	15.18***	18.13***	10.60*

Notes: Hausman test: $[\beta_{re} - \beta_{fe}]'[Var(\beta_{re}) - Var(\beta_{fe})]^{-1}[\beta_{re} - \beta_{fe}]$. All the three tests reject the null hypothesis, so the fixed effect model is more appropriate; t values are in parentheses; ***,**,* denote significance at 1%, 5%, and 10% levels.

7 Conclusion and Discussion

This study investigates the location choice when foreign banks plan to set up overseas offices in 40 Chinese cities. We examine the effect of following customers, market opportunity, regulation, and cost of labor on the foreign bank

[2] Hausman tests in three specifications all reject the null hypothesis, so we only report the fixed effect estimation results.

decision. Also, previous studies investigate location choice of foreign banks commonly using the sample before 1980, and our investigation could be the most recent one using the sample of 2000–2005.

Our results suggest that the market opportunity is the most crucial factor to affect foreign bank decision to enter Chinese cities. Next, the labor cost is also important in affecting the foreign bank decision. However, contrary to the literatures from manufacturing industry, the high labor cost of a city attracts more foreign banks. We argue that this is because the high labor cost implies high labor quality, which is an important factor in financial industry. Despite these two positive effects, the effects of following customers and regulations are insignificant. For example, the restriction on the locations of Renminbi business operation is very limited.

Our results also show that city infrastructures strongly enhance the relation between market opportunity and foreign bank penetration. The better the infrastructure of the city, the stronger the relation is.

It is worth discussing why foreign banks do not follow their customers in our study, whereas it is widely accepted in the literature. One plausible reason is the change of the local economic environments. In the past 30 years, the economic size of many city GDPs has been double, triple, and even quadruple since 1978, implying that there are much more wealthy people now. This is particularly true in the east coast cities like Shanghai, Shenzhen, and Guangzhou. Foreign banks could expect this fast growth trend to continue; they are attracted by the opportunity to do business with wealthy locals even if customers from their home countries are not present. Furthermore, the economic policies and law become more transparent and effective, which largely release the black box concern of foreign banks in engaging in business. Outreville (2007) finds that location choice of firms is a dynamic process, and the impact caused by the rapid growth in developing countries with economic transformation in the recent decades is very significant. Our results concur with his findings.

In addition, the theory of comparative advantage suggests that the accumulation of international expansion experience of foreign banks will positively affect their location choice (Focarelli and Pozzolo, 2000). Though our study does not provide statistical analysis to test this argument, we argue that many foreign banks may have already accumulated more than 20 years' experience to understand the Chinese market before they come. This definitely affects their decision in choosing cities for their branches.

References

August Lösch, 1954. The Economics of Location, Yale University Press, New Haven.

Bagchi-Sen Sharmistha, 1991. The location of foreign direct investment in finance, insurance and real estate in the United States, Geografiska Annaler. Series B, Human Geography 73(3), 187–197.

Bagchi-Sen Sharmistha, James O. Wheeler, 1989. A spatial and temporal model of foreign direct investment in the United States, Economic Geography 65(2), 113–129.

Bartik Timothy J., 1985. Business location decisions in the United States: estimates of the effects of unionization, Taxes, and other characteristics of states, Journal of Business and Economic Statistics 3(1), 14–23.

Brealey R. A., Kaplanis E. C., 1996. The determination of foreign banking location, Journal of International Money and Finance 15(4), 577–597.

Buch Claudia M., Stefan M. Golder, 2001. Foreign against domestic banks in Germany and the US: A tale of two markets? Journal of Multinational Financial Management, 11, 341–361.

Cheng Leonard K., Yum K. Kwan, 2000. What are the determinants of the location of foreign direct investment? The Chinese Experience, Journal of International Economics 51, 379–400.

Claessens Stijn, Neeltje Van Horen, Location Decisions of Foreign Banks and Competitive Advantage, World Bank Policy Research Policy Paper, 4113.

Clarke George, Robert Cull, Maria Soledad Martinez Peria and Susana M. Sanchez, 2001. Foreign Bank Entry: Experience, Implications for Developing Countries and Agenda for Further Research, World Bank Policy Research Policy Paper, 2698.

Coughlin Cletus C., Joseph V. Terza and Vachira Arromdee, 1991. state characteristics and the location of foreign direct investment within the United States, The Review of Economics and Statistics 73(4), 675–683.

Daniels P. W., 1991. Services and Metropolitan Development, Routledge Press, London.

Esperanca J. P., Gulamhussen, M. A., 2001. (Re)Testing the 'follow the customer' hypothesis in multinational bank expansion, Journal of Multinational Financial Management 11, 281–293.

Focarelli, D. and A. Pozzolo, 2000. The determinants of cross-border bank share holdings: An analysis with bank-level data from OECD countries, Banca Italia, Paper 381.

Focarelli D., Pozzolo A. F., 2005. Where do banks expand abroad? An Empirical Analysis, Journal of Business 78(6), 2435–2463.

Gao J. T., 2007. Analysis of Regional Economics, Century Publishing Group, Shanghai.

Gao Ting, 2005. Labor quality and the location of foreign direct investment: evidence from China, China Economic Review 16(3), 274–292.

Greenhut Melvin L., 1995. Loaction Economics: Theoretical Underpinnings and Applications, Edward Elgar Publishing Company.

Gerlowski Daniel A., Hung-gay Fung, Deborah Ford, 1994. The location of foreign direct investment for U.S. real estate: an empirical analysis, Land Economics 70(3), 286–293.

Goldberg Lawrence G., Grosse Robert. 1994. Location choice of foreign banks in the United States, Journal of Economics and Business 46(5), 367–379.

Grosse Robert, Goldberg Lawrence G., 1991. Foreign bank activity in the United States: an analysis by country of origin, Journal of Banking and Finance 15, 1093–112.

Gross Dominique M., Horst Raff, Michael Ryan, 2005. Inter- and intra-sectoral linkages in foreign direct investment: evidence from Japanese investment in Europe, Journal of Japanese International Economies 19, 110–134.

He Qiang, H. Peter Gray, 2001. Multinational banking and economic development: a case study, Journal of Asian Economics 12, 233–243.

Hong Junjie, Anthony T. H. Chin, 2006. Modeling the location choices of foreign investments in Chinese logistic industry, China Economic Review, forthcoming, doi:10.1016/j.chieco.2006.07.001.

Hultman Charlies W., L. Randolph McGee, 1989. Factors affecting the foreign banking presence in U.S., Journal of banking and finance 13, 383–396.

Hultman Charlies W., L. Randolph McGee, 1990. The Japanese banking presence in the United States and its regional distribution, Growth and Change (Fall), 67–79.

Jiang Y., 2003. A study of the deepening degree of China's finance, The Theory and Practice of Finance and Economics (China) 24(3), 16–19.
Kang, J. S., Lee, H. S., 2007. The determinants of location choice of South Korean FDI in China, Japan and the World Economy 19, 441–460.
Leung M. K., Rigby D., Young T., 2003. Entry of foreign banks in the People's Republic of China: a survey analysis, Applied Economics 35, 21–31.
Liang Q., Teng Jianzhou, 2006. Financial development and economic growth: evidence from China, China Economic Review 17, 395–411.
Markusen J., Rutherford T. F., Tarr D., 2000. Foreign Direct Investment in Services and the Domestic Market for Expertise, NBER working paper.
Miller Stewart R., Parkhe Arvind, 1998. Patterns in the expansion of U.S. banks' foreign operations, Journal of International Business Studies 29(2), 359–389
Nigh Douglas, Kang Rae Cho, Suresh Krishnan, 1986. The role of location-related factors in U.S. Banking involvement abroad: an empirical examination, Journal of International Business Studies 17(3), 59–72.
Omran M., Ali Bolbol, 2003. Foreign direct investment, financial development, and economic growth: evidence from the Arab Countries, Review of Middle East Economics and Finance 1(3), 231–249.
Outreville J. Francois, 2007. Foreign affiliates of the world largest financial groups: locations and governance, Research in International Business and Finance 21(1), 19–31.
Pak Yong Suhk, Young-Ryeol Park, 2005. Characteristics of Japanese FDI in the East and the West: understanding the strategic motives of Japanese investment, Journal of World Business 40, 254–266.
Ryuhei Wakasugi, 2005. The effects of Chinese regional conditions on the location choice of Japanese affiliates, The Japanese Economic Review 56(4), 390–407.
Seth Rama, Daniel E. Nolle, Sunil K. Mohanty, 1998. Do banks follow their customers abroad?, Financial Markets, Institutions and Instruments 7(4), 1–25.
Shen Chung-hua, Chou Hsiu-Hsia, 2007. Foreign Banks in Asian Markets: The Determinants of Location Choice, working paper.
Shen, Chung-Hua, Lee Chien-Chiang, 2006. Same financial development yet different economic growth–why? Journal of Money, Credit and Banking 38(7), 1907–1944.
Tang D., 2000. The empirical test of financial deepening in China, The Study of Finance and Economics (China) 26(3), 10–14.
Tschoegl Adrian E., 2000. International banking centers, geography, and foreign banks, financial markets, Institutions and Instrument 91, 1–32.
Wakasugi Ryuhei, 2005. The effects of Chinese regional conditions on the location choice of Japanese affiliates, The Japanese Economic Review 56(4), 390–407.
Walter L., 1988. Global Competition in Financial Services: Market Structure, Protection, and Trade Liberalization, American Enterprise Institute/Ballinger, Cambridge, Mass.
Wei H. K., 2000. Location decison of investment on manufacturing industry of Europe, U.S., Japan and South Korea in China. China Industrial Economy 11, 65–73.
Wei Q. S. Wang R. F., 2005. Infrastructure and choice of FDI location, Academic Journal Graduate School Chinese Academy of Social Sciences 1, 27–34.
Wu Xiaohong, Roger Strange, 2000. The location of foreign insurance companies in China, International Business Review 9, 383–398.
Xiao H. R., Lu D., 2006. Empirical study on foreign banks' entry and its impact on banking industry of Shanghai, Journal of Financial Research(China) 1, 141–149.
Yamawaki Hideki, 1993. Location Decisions of Japanese Multinational Firms in European Manufacturing Industries, in Kirsty S. Hughes, ed., European Competitiveness, Cambridge University Press, Cambridge.
Yamori Nobuyoshi, 1997. Do Japanese banks lead or follow international business? An Empirical Investigation 7, 369–382

Yamori Nobuyoshi, 1998. A note on the location choice of multinational banks: The case of Japanese financial institutions, Journal of Banking and Finance 22, 109–120.

Ye X., Feng Z. X., 2004. Impact on foreign banks entry and banking system stability of host countries, The Journal of World Economy(China) 1, 29–36.

Zhang L., Zhang R., 2006. Foreign banks' entry and the efficiency improvement of the host countries' banking system, Nankai Economic Studies 1, 127–136.

Zhen F., Gu Ch. L., 2002. New perspectives on spatial structure research in information era, Geographical Research 2, 257–266.

Zhou Changhui, Andrew Delios, Jingyu Yang, 2002. Locational determinants of Japanese foreign direct investment in China, Asia Pacific Journal of Manament 19, 63–86.

Financial Institutions' Lending and Real Estate Property Prices in China

Perry Wong and Diehang Zheng

Abstract: The rapid increase of China's property prices in recent years, especially in major municipalities, has drawn much attention and provoked intense debates on the existence of "inflationary property values." Many believe that over-investment in the real estate sector should be blamed for the skyrocketing property prices in many municipalities. This study takes a slightly different angle by focusing on efficiency of capital allocation rather than total volume of investment. This chapter attempts to address the following question: Will efficiently allocated regional capital help hold off a potential housing price bubble? Our analysis finds a negative relationship between our proxy for loan efficiency and local property price. The finding, however, implies that when loan efficiency improves, local property price tends to be lower. Hence, effective lending policies and practices can reduce the level of "inflationary property value."

Keywords Urban · Housing · Property prices · Chinese economy · Regional · economics

1 Introduction

The rapid increase of China's property prices in recent years, especially in major municipalities, has drawn much attention and provoked intensified debates on the existence of an "inflationary property value." Many believe that over-investment in the real estate sector should be blamed for the skyrocketing property prices in many of these municipalities. This study takes a slightly different angle by focusing on the efficiency of capital allocation rather than the total volume of investment. The following questions are examined: Will efficiently allocated regional capital help hold off a potential housing price

P. Wong (✉)
Milken Institute, Santa Monica, CA, USA
e-mail: pwong@milkeninstitute.org

J.R. Barth et al. (eds.), *China's Emerging Financial Markets*,
The Milken Institute Series on Financial Innovation and Economic Growth 8,
DOI 10.1007/978-0-387-93769-4_15,

bubble? Our analysis finds a negative relationship between our proxy for loan efficiency and local property price. The finding, however, implies that when loan efficiency improves, local property price tends to be lower. Hence, effective lending policies and practices can reduce the level of "inflationary property value."

2 Background

For more than 30 years, real estate development remained stagnant in China after the socialist state was established in 1949. Housing activities mainly focused on providing living quarters for employees of emerging factories and institutions. This situation did not change until 1978, when the country's open-up policy and economic reform paved the path for substantial changes in almost every aspect of the economy. Prior to the state-owned enterprise reform that took place in the 1980s and 1990s, China promoted a "state-owned, work-units allocated and low rent" housing policy. In other words, the state, through state-owned enterprises (SOEs), owned a majority of residential housing units in urban areas. Instead of being sold to households, these housing units came as a benefit attached to employment. SOEs provided housing to employees at low rental cost. At that time, this arrangement was in line with the ongoing price control on wages and commodities as well as the "hukou" policy that discourages inter-region immigration. Not surprisingly, low housing prices have created huge demand for housing, especially in urban areas. The growth in population only exacerbated this problem.

The development of commercial real estate market came in at a much later stage in the 1990s after numerous government experiments on housing development. Several milestones have set the stage for the development of a commercial real estate market in China beginning in the early 1980s:

1. In 1982–1984, the term "commodity housing" was introduced. Commodity housing is not part of an employment benefit. Buyers or renters pay market prices based upon living areas and actual construction costs incurred plus a premium. This was the first time since 1949 that real estate became tradable.
2. In 1987, the government increased the rent for employment housing in line with the rise in income level.
3. In 1994, a milestone legal document, "The State Council Decision on Deepening the Reform of the Housing System," was enacted. This signaled that the state had changed its housing policy to promote the development of a commercial residential housing market. Households were allowed to purchase their dwelling. In addition, housing prices, especially for high-end apartments, were then partly decided by demand and supply.

The turning point for China's housing reform was 1998. The State Council issued the Administrative Law[1], which stated that housing would no longer be

[1] "The State Council Decision on Further Deepening Reform of the Housing System and Speeding Up Housing Construction", 1998.

provided as an employment benefit for employees of SOEs after December 31, 1999. In line with this document, the People's Bank of China adopted "Guidelines on Individual Housing Loans" in the same year, which allows commercial banks to extend housing loans to individuals.[2] These changes formally broke the link between employment and housing. At the same time, they also facilitated access to credit that is crucial for housing construction and household purchases. The new legislations hence accelerated the development of a residential real estate market.

Real estate development grew at an exponential speed after these changes. In less than a decade, China's real estate sector grew from virtually a scratch to an industry that contributed one-tenth of China's GDP in 2005. Total real estate assets increased from RMB 420 billion in 1996 to RMB 6.2 trillion in 2004, with the total amount invested in real estate market totaling RMB 15.8 trillion in 2005.

The rapid expansion of the real estate market also revealed many issues that persist. Chief among them is housing affordability in urban areas. Even though the central government has made housing affordability a top policy priority since day one of the housing reform, local governments and real estate developers have very different incentives and agendas. Municipal governments, for example, always choose to maximize their fiscal revenue. For them, the fee charged on land transactions is an important source of revenue; hence high land prices directly benefit local governments. In addition, high property price means high tax revenue. Furthermore, the growth of real estate industry is also an indication of government officials' achievements and one that could easily be measured and showcased. In contrast, there is no easy way to measure government officials' achievements on promoting housing affordability, especially for low- and middle-income households. As a result, local governments tend to give higher priority to the fast growth of the real estate market, rather than to affordability. For real estate developers, higher-end properties mean higher profit margins on limited lands. Without appropriate government regulations, they have no incentive to invest in affordable housing. However, on the demand side, huge pressures were mounting as rural immigration to urban areas accelerated. Growing demand and inadequate supply in affordable housing have led to the coexistence of a high vacancy rate for new units and unmet pending demand from ordinary households.

3 Commercial Banks' Role in the Real Estate Market

Bank loans are one of the major funding sources for the real estate market. Before the banking reform that took place after 2000, Chinese banks were the lending arms for the government. Bank lending to state-owned enterprises was

[2] Loans will not be extended to individuals, however, if they wish to purchase luxurious houses.

equivalent to quasi-fiscal support from the government.[3] After 2000, Chinese commercial banks became better capitalized after a series of reform efforts. Three out of the largest four commercial banks were eventually publicly listed. However, at the local level, bank branches' lending practices are still heavily influenced by municipal government.

Commercial banks play an important role in the real estate market. On the one hand, they provide critical funding for land development and infrastructure construction. On the other hand, banks loans are sometimes used to purchase properties. There are two possibilities that bank loans to real estate sector might relate to low loan efficiency. First of all, regional branches may extend loans to local investment projects because of municipal governments' interest. These projects are often "(政绩工程) (zheng ji gong cheng)[4]" which produce little economic and social returns. Many of these projects are real-estate related, in addition, so that they contribute to an increase in land price and add to the costs of local real estate properties. Secondly, some bank loans are invested on real estate properties. In some cases these investments are solely for speculative purposes. As a result, property prices are inflated. Indeed, in 2004, 76% of bank loans in Shanghai were invested in the real estate market (Le 2005). The excessive investments fueled by bank lending are blamed by many as the major factor that drove up property prices in many municipalities. The large share of bank loans that goes to the real estate market reflects fact that returns on real estate exceed returns in other sectors. This can be an indicator of relatively low productivity in other sectors, but can also be attributed to the housing price bubbles that have formed in many Chinese cities.

4 Effect of Credit Availability

Financial institutions' lending is closely correlated with property prices in both developed and developing economies, as ample research indicates. Easily available bank credit has been blamed for recent financial crises in Latin America and Asia. Credit expansion is usually observed to be associated with a property price boom in the economy. The synchronization of bank lending and property price cycles has been documented by

---

[3] The central planning system in China operated financially mainly through collecting revenue from state enterprises and allocating investment through budgetary grants. The banking system served to provide the credit needed by enterprises to implement national plans for economic output and provided and monitored cash used to cover wage costs above state-provided benefits, and credit for state purchases of agricultural products from collectives above state quotas.

[4] (政绩工程) is a Chinese term used to describe development projects that have little economic value, instead showcasing "reform and economic progress" from new policy and/or new leadership.

policy-oriented literature, such as those from the IMF (2000) and BIS (2001).[5] But the less touched upon question is whether it is the availability of credit that causes property price inflation or the efficiency of capital utilization?

Theoretically, for a region that observes significant increase in investment activities, as long as the capital has been effectively used to improve infrastructure and the quality of other resources (such as labor), the enhanced regional productivity will result in (1) higher regional income, and (2) higher demand for local assets. Both outcomes will lead to higher property prices. But when the invested capital has not been effectively used to improve regional productivity, the temporary "extra purchasing power" from the easy access to credit will inflate local asset prices, including real estate. We term the first case "property value increase" as the result of greater real demand, and the second case "property price inflation" as the consequence of extra credit.

Although the correlation between credit and property prices is widely recognized, little rigorous empirical study has been done on this relationship. Goodhart (1995) finds that property prices significantly affect credit growth in the UK. Hofmann (2001) also provides evidence of property price contributing to credit extension. Borio and Lowe (2002) show that sustained rapid credit growth combined with large increases in asset prices appears to increase the probability of an episode of financial instability. In their analysis on the Asian Financial Crisis, Collyns and Senhadji (2002) find a strong relationship between bank lending and asset price inflation, especially in the real estate market. Gerlach and Peng (2005) study the causality between bank lending and residential property prices in Hong Kong. They find that the direction of influence goes from property prices to bank credit rather than conversely. But very few authors ever addressed the impact of the regional capital investment efficiency on local property prices.

5 Methodology and Data

Following Quigley (1999), the prices in competitive markets are determined by the intersection of supply and demand:

$$P_{it} = f(Q_{it}^{d}, Q_{it}^{s}) \tag{1}$$

where P_{it} proxies housing prices in the metropolitan area, and Q_{it}^{d} and Q_{it}^{s} are quantities of housing demand and supply in city i at time t. They are characterized by

$$Q_{it}^{d} = d(P_{it}, Income_{it}, X_{it}) \tag{2}$$

and

$$Q_{it}^{s} = s(P_{it}, Vacancy_{it}, Y_{it}) \tag{3}$$

[5] The New Basel Capital Accord (2001, p. 11) has clearly recognized the nexus between property prices and credit risk. According to it, the risk weight on residential mortgage is 50%, while that on commercial mortgage is 100%.

Housing demand in city i at time t is a function of housing price level P_{it}, average income, $Income_{it}$, and a vector of exogenous variables, X_{it}. Demand is negatively correlated with price and positively correlated with income. Housing supply is a function of price level, P_{it}, vacancy rate, $Vacancy_{it}$, and a vector of exogenous variables, Y_{it}. In a competitive market, housing supply increases with price and decreases with vacancy rate. When the market follows adaptive expectation, i.e., expects a slow change in price, it is the lagged price, rather than current price, that is used to determine the demand and supply.

For an emerging economy with a strong government like China's, policy is a very significant factor that may alter or overwhelm the "competitive" market mechanism. This means that while those exogenous policies can dampen the fuction of some economic fundamentals, they can also introduce other influential elements like policy-driven regional investment. Vacancy rate does not serve as the theoretically significant guidance in many Chinese real estate markets, which is typically represented by a lengthy mismatch between higher-end housing demand and supply. Domestic investment activities and resource allocation are highly influenced by policy. Figure 2 is the scatter plot between Total RMB Loan Balance of Financial Institutions (100 million 2005 RMB Yuan) and GDP (100 million 2005 RMB Yuan) for the four municipalities (the sample in this study).

Chongqing, Tianjin and Shanghai generate higher GDP relative to the scale of total loan balance compared to Beijing. Since loan allocation is directly related to the investment allocation in China, we take this factor as investment policy proxy. Moreover, the onset of privatization in the housing market came in 1998, aiming

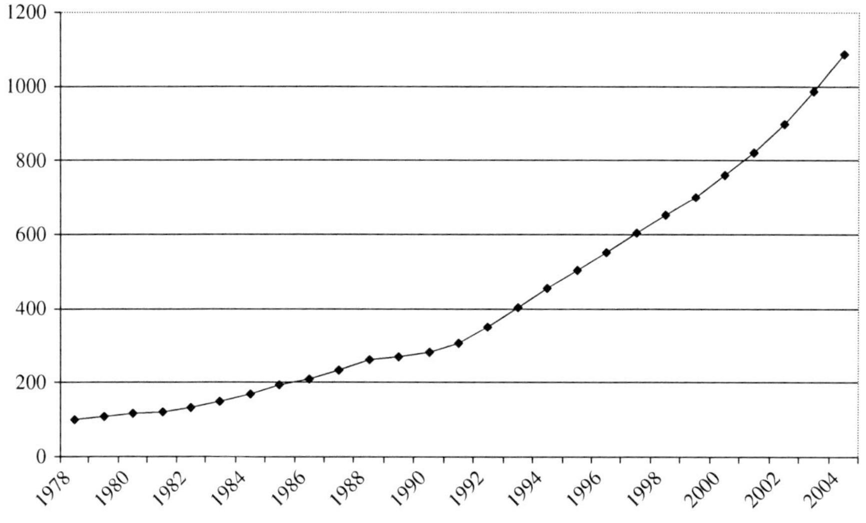

Fig. 1 China GDP Growth – Index of Constant GDP (1978–2004).
Source: World Bank 2006

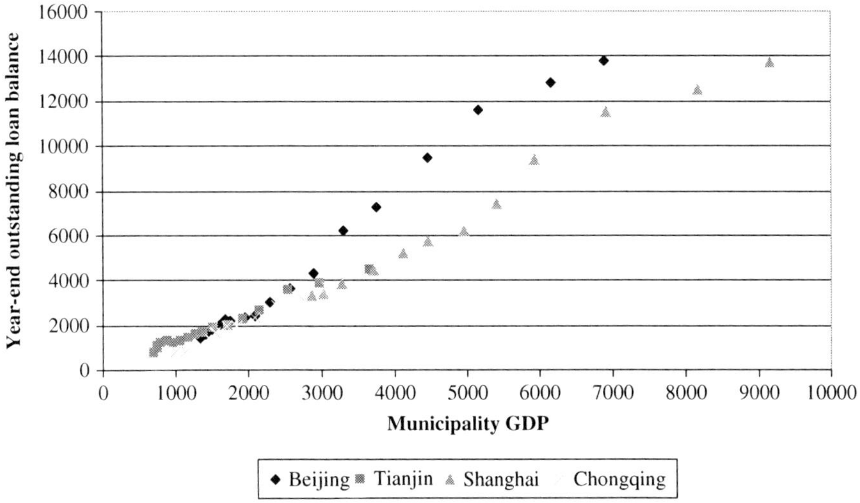

Fig. 2 Year-end outstanding loan balance and GDP in four Chinese municipalities (Constant 2005 RMB Yuan)

to end the state-controlled welfare housing system.[6] Hence, 1998 is widely taken as a structural turning point in the development of the Chinese real estate industry.

Summarizing the above factors, we can rewrite the supply and demand functions as

$$Q_{it}^{d} = d(L[P_{it}], Income_{it}, X_{it}) \tag{4}$$

And

$$Q_{it}^{s} = s(L[P_{it}], Y_{it}). \tag{5}$$

Substituting (4) and (5) into (1) and solving for P_{it} yield

$$P_{it} = f(Income_{it}, L[P_{it}], Z_{it}), \tag{6}$$

where $L[P_{it}]$ indicates lagged price in area i and Z_{it} is the vector of exogenous variables, representing the policy changes and market environment conditions.

In this study, we focus on the four Chinese municipalities directly under the central government, including Beijing, Tianjin, Shanghai, and

[6] Prior to 1998, over 90% of the urban residential housing units in China were developed and owned by state-owned enterprises (*Dan Wei*). These housing units were leased to the employees at very low rent as part of welfare for the state-run enterprises' employees and collective owned enterprises' employees. Under the PRC State Council 1998 Administrative Law, state-owned enterprises will no longer be allowed to allocate welfare housing to their employees after December 31, 1999.

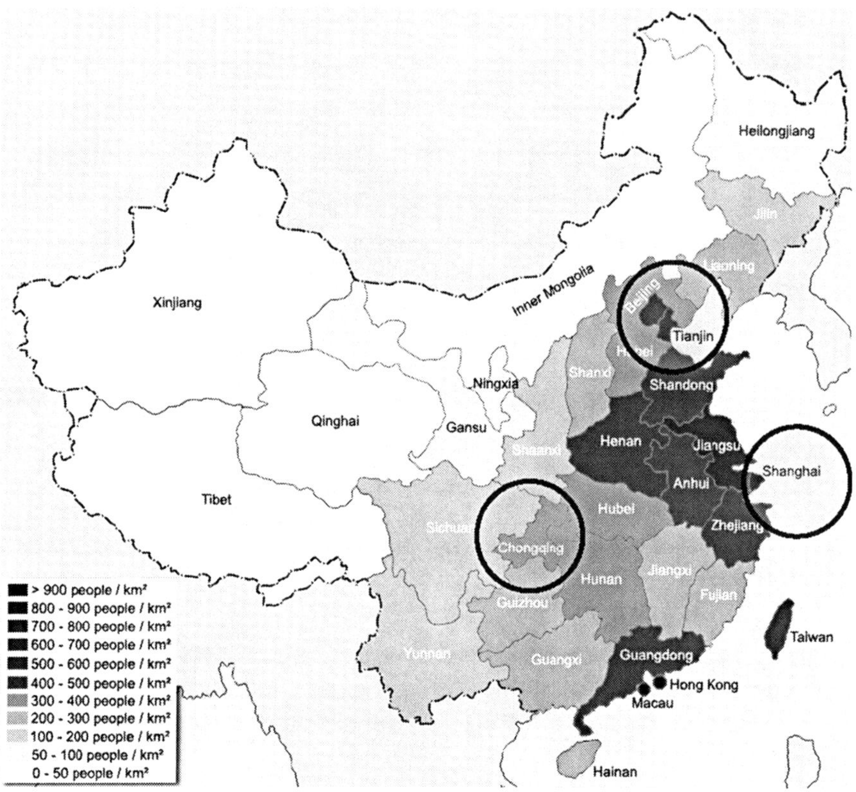

Fig. 3 China map and four municipalities

Chonqing (Fig. 3). The four municipalities have a relatively high percentage of urban population, varying between 60% (Tianjin) and 84% (Beijing, Shanghai) in 2005. Although Chonqing has the highest population (over 31 million in 2005), Shanghai, Beijing, and Tianjin have a much higher population density (2145, 937, 788 separately vs. 385 people per square kilometer in 2005). They are the centers for the corresponding regional development.[7] The data on local Chinese real estate markets, economic conditions, and population information were collected from the National Bureau of Statistics of China, local government statistical bureaus, the China Economic Information Network, and the People's Bank of China.

Table 1 presents the means and standard deviations of some key real estate market and economic variables. The annual average price per square meter of commercial real estate is calculated since related market information became

[7] Given their economic and geographic proximity, Beijing and Tianjin have had a long and complementary relationship. As Brian Hook stated in his 1998 book, Tianjin has been central to Beijing's development - just as Beijing has to Tianjin's – mainly due to its strategic coastal location.

Table 1 Mean and standard deviations for key variables Four Regional Municipalities, 1990–2005

	All Four	Beijing	Tianjin	Shanghai	Chongqing
Average Price of Commercial Real Estate (2005 RMB Yuan/sq.m)[10]	3,439 (1,600)	5,014 (842)	2,550 (519)	4,386 (1,272)	1,493 (299)
Average Price of Commercial Real Estate Index (first year = 100)	130 (28)	126 (21)	127 (26)	141 (41)	131 (26)
Population (10,000)	1,490 (829)	1,095 (45)	903 (21)	1,324 (21)	3,086 (52)
Population Density (person/sq.km)	957 (600)	778 (92)	758 (18)	2,089 (32)	374 (6)
GDP (100 million 2005 RMB Yuan)	2,863 (1,973)	3,089 (1,730)	1,600 (859)	5,370 (1,998)	1,864 (633)
GDP per Capita (2005 RMB Yuan)	21,542 (14,857)	23,409 (10,297)	17,355 (8,458)	40,446 (14,412)	6,012 (1,941)
Loan Efficiency = GDP/Loan Balance	0.787 (0.17)	0.676 (0.16)	0.781 (0.06)	0.746 (0.10)	0.997 (0.19)
No. of observations	54	16	16	11	11

[10]The time frame for each municipality regarding "average price" is as follows: Beijing and Tianjin: 1990–2005; Shanghai and Chongqing: 1995–2005.

Table 2 Models of housing price developmentDependent variable: Average Price of Commercial Real Estate (2005 RMB Yuan/sq.m)

	Model							
Variable	I-1	I-2	I-3	I-4	I-5	I-6	I-7	I-8
Price (T-1)	1.01 (21.93)	0.99 (6.42)					0.87 (14.56)	0.48 (4.09)
Price (T-2)		0.03 (0.17)						
GDP per Capita (2005 RMB Yuan)			0.07 (5.84)	0.07 (6.61)	0.08 (8.70)	0.08 (9.37)	0.02 (3.26)	0.05 (5.06)
Lagged Loan Efficiency			–3318.1 (–3.62)					
Tianjin				–2019.2 (–10.16)				
Chongqing				–2175.7 (–7.10)				
Shanghai				–1811.5 (–6.90)				
Tianjin × Lagged Loan Efficiency					–1728.2 (–2.44)	–2745.3 (–3.39)		–1775.8 (–2.35)
Chongqing × Lagged Loan Efficiency					–1413.2 (–2.53)	–2115.1 (–3.43)		–1221.2 (–2.06)

Table 2 (continued)

Variable	Model I-1	I-2	I-3	I-4	I-5	I-6	I-7	I-8
Shanghai × Lagged Loan Efficiency					−1590.0	−2726.3		−1916.2
					(−2.34)	(−3.33)		(−2.53)
Beijing × Lagged Loan Efficiency					946.7			
					(1.25)			
Beijing × Lagged Loan Efficiency, if GDP/ Lagged Loan Efficiency > 0.6						37.6 (0.05)		−306.9 (−0.40)
Beijing × Lagged Loan Efficiency, if GDP/ Lagged Loan Efficiency ≤0.6						−1411.7 (−1.12)		−1431.9 (−1.26)
After 1998			−919.6	−338.0	−426.3	−483.1	−187.2	−379.3
			(−3.13)	(−1.58)	(−2.20)	(−2.58)	(−1.24)	(−2.28)
Intercept	141.1	154.9	5116.4	3441.8	2760.9	3522.7	220.6	2019.4
	(0.84)	(0.87)	(5.52)	(14.21)	(4.34)	(5.08)	(1.31)	(2.88)
R square	0.909	0.912	0.673	0.901	0.921	0.929	0.927	0.950
No. of observations	50	47	54	54	54	54	50	50

available to the public after the local real estate market took off. It is measured in 2005 constant RMB. The average price is the lowest in Chongqing (1,439 RMB Yuan/sq.m) and highest in Beijing (5,014 RMB Yuan/sq.m) since the local market came into being. From 1995 to 2005, the average price increase in all of the four municipalities is 20%. Figure 4 shows that Beijing, an expensive market before 1995, experienced relatively low average price growth in the following ten years; while Shanghai, one of the fastest growing cities, experienced the highest growth rate among the four cities at more than 40%. Tianjing and Chongqing have much lower property prices compared to Beijing and Shanghai.

Chongqing is the city with the lowest population density. Shanghai has the highest population density at 2,089 people per square kilometer, more than double that of Beijing and Tianjin, and about six times that of in Chongqing. Within the sample period, Chongqing had the lowest GDP per capita (6,012 RMB Yuan), while Shanghai has the highest (40,446 RMB), 70% higher than Beijing's and more than double that of Tianjin.

As mentioned above, since loan allocation is directly related to the economic development and regional infrastructure investment allocation and capital inflow distribution in China, we take it as the investment policy proxy. If we

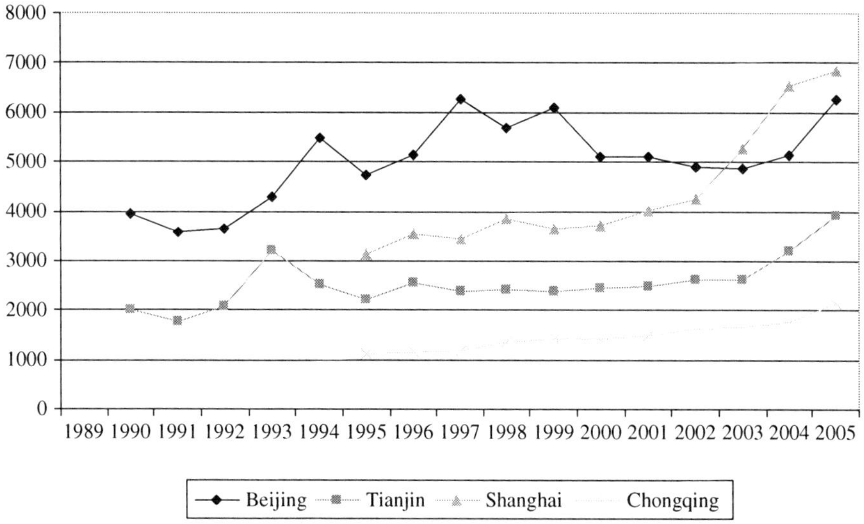

Fig. 4 Average price in four Chinese municipalities (constant 2005 RMB Yuan/sq.m.)

further assume that the outstanding loan amount of the year-end financial institutions is proportional to the regional investment intensity, the efficiency of capital utilization can be represented by the ratio between local GDP per capita and year-end outstanding loan amount. Among the four municipalities, Chongqing has the highest loan efficiency ratio, while Beijing's is the lowest. As the national capital, Beijing has very high priority in capital allocation with current government policy, whereas questions like "If the investment really used

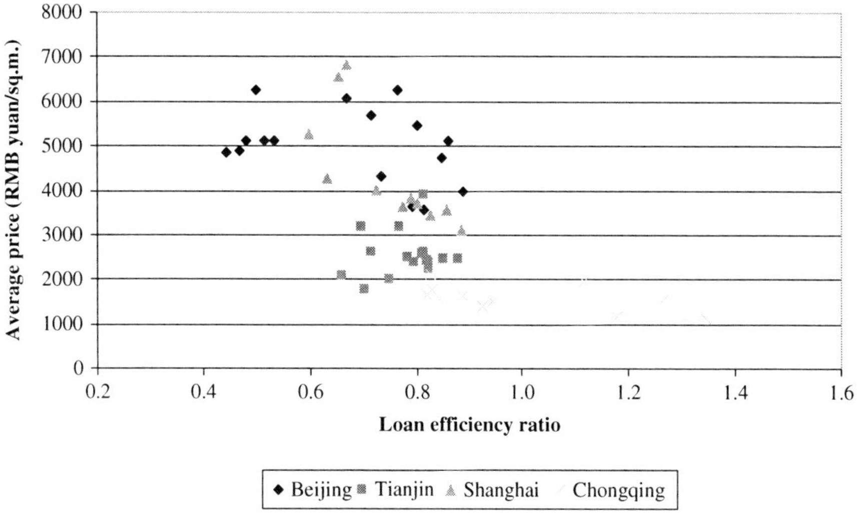

Fig. 5 Average price and loan efficiency ratio in four Chinese municipalities

to improve regional productivity?" have barely been asked. Figure 5 is the scatter-plot of municipality property prices and the loan efficiency ratio. During the last six years in our sample period, Beijing behaved differently from the earlier pattern, registering very low loan efficiency ratio but still maintaining high property prices at the same time.

6 Empirical Results

For the four Chinese municipalities, we estimated in equation (6) a variety of specifications, including average price level, logarithm transformed, and index models. Model I-1 and Model I-2 assume that the housing price could be predicted solely on the past prices. Model I-1 reveals the strong correlation between property price and the lagged price level, which is consistent with prior research (e.g., Case and Shiller, 1990). Model I-2 tries to include a second order of the lagged price, but it is insignificant. Therefore, only the one period lagged price will be used in the following specifications.

Model I-3 to Model I-6 displays several basic regression results relating the changes in price to the economic fundamentals and market conditions. Model I-3 includes only GDP per capita, lagged loan efficiency ratio, and a dummy variable, "After 1998". GDP per capita serves as the proxy of average income level. It is positively related to the local property price level as expected. Loan efficiency ratio is defined as the ratio between municipality GDP and financial institution total outstanding loan amount, serving as the indicator of to what extent the capital investment has been used to improve local productivity. Considering the likely delay in loan efficiency impact, we adopt the lagged loan efficiency ratio. It is negatively significant in determining property price, which means that if the investment loans have not been effectively used to improve local productivity, the non-productive portion may spillover to the asset market and inflate the local property price. The dummy variable "After 1998" represents the market structural change. More affordable housing policies have been introduced[8] and ordinary consumers started entering the market. Some already inflated markets, like Beijing, have been taken into control under a set of central and local government regulations. The observed stabilization in price lasted till around 2003.

Model I-4 addresses the municipalities' distinct characteristics by including the location dummies. Compared to Beijing, all of the other three municipalities have lower average prices. Chongqing has the lowest average property price, followed by Tianjin. Model I-5 addresses the regional effect by explicitly considering the loan efficiency factor for each municipality. This factor turns out to be significant in Tianjin, Chongqing, and Shanghai with negative effect on local

[8] e.g. Economic housing for local homeowners.

average property prices, which is consistent with the explanation of loan efficiency impact above. But it is insignificant in Beijing.

As shown in Fig. 5, the last six years of Beijing in our sample behaved differently from the other years and the general pattern. Hence, we treat Beijing's market with relatively high lagged loan efficiency ratio (>0.6) and with relatively low lagged loan efficiency ratio (≤0.6) separately as in Model I-6.[9]

Model I-7 and Model I-8 are the combinations of autoregressive structure with economic fundamentals and market conditions. Each model contains a one period lag in price changes, which is significant in both specifications. In addition to that, the economic fundamental factor, GDP per capita, is also an important determinant. Market structural changes and the lagged loan efficiency ratio are mostly significant. It reveals that policy intervention has an important impact on regional economic development in China. Efficient utilization of capital investment is a significant factor in determining property price. Also, consistent with previous market studies, it is proper to tread different local markets separately.

Similarly, we ran another set of regressions with logarithm transformed average prices and GDP per capita. Table 3 displays the outputs. Goodness-of-fit is improved after logarithm transformation. The results are consistent with the pre-transformation models. The partial effects of local level lagged loan efficiency ratio are even stronger in this set of results (Model II-7).

Lastly, we indexed the average price level and GDP per capita and reran the regressions. Table 4 shows the output. Previous conclusions still held.

Figures 6 and 7 illustrate the implication of the above models. Figure 6 is based on the logarithm transformed average price models presented in the table. In all the panels, the actual observed average property prices are in the X axis, while the predicted property prices are in the Y axis. Panel (a) uses Model II-1, or the model solely relies on lagged price profile. Panel (b) uses Model II-6, considering lagged price profile, GDP per capita, and the market structure change event. Panel (c) uses Model II-7, besides the factors addressed in Model I-5, also taking the impact of lagged loan efficiency into consideration. The figure shows the improvement in prediction when economic fundamentals, market structural change and policy-related loan efficiency ratios are added into the model specification.

Similarly, Fig. 7 is based on the average price index models presented in Table 4. Panel (a) uses Model III-1, Panel (b) uses Model III-6, and Panel (c) uses Model III-7. The improvements are observable.

Figure 8 is the simulation of year 2006 property price profiles for the four municipalities under different assumption of loan efficiency: base case (using the information as of 2005), 10% more efficient, and 10% less efficient. All of the four municipalities would have lower property price with a more efficient use of the capital and vice versa. On average, the price per square meter will decrease 237 Yuan, 224 Yuan, 332 Yuan, and 83 Yuan separately for Beijing,

---

[9] It is consistent with the split of the Beijing market sample into before 2000 and after 2000, because the low loan efficiency concentrates in the years after 2000.

Table 3 Models of housing price developmentDependent variable: Logarithm of Average Price of Commercial Real Estate (2005 RMB Yuan/sq.m)

	Model						
Variable	II-1	II-2	II-3	II-4	II-5	II-6	II-7
Logarithm of Price (T-1)	0.98					0.84	0.38
	(27.55)					(13.02)	(3.09)
Logarithm of GDP per Capita (2005 RMB Yuan)		0.50	0.48	0.49	0.56	0.11	0.40
		(7.73)	(5.35)	(7.63)	(9.14)	(2.39)	(5.08)
Lagged Loan Efficiency		–0.81					
		(–3.07)					
Tianjin			–0.53				
			(–9.22)				
Chongqing			–0.56				
			(–3.93)				
Shanghai			–0.41				
			(–6.03)				
Tianjin × Lagged Loan Efficiency				–0.62	–0.98		–0.76
				(–3.65)	(–5.31)		(–3.85)
Chongqing × Lagged Loan Efficiency				–0.48	–0.68		–0.46
				(–3.14)	(–4.56)		(–2.81)
Shanghai × Lagged Loan Efficiency				–0.50	–0.93		–0.76
				(–2.93)	(–4.73)		(–3.72)
Beijing × Lagged Loan Efficiency				0.07			
				(0.37)			
Beijing × Lagged Loan Efficiency, if GDP/Lagged Loan Efficiency > 0.6					–0.27		–0.33
					(–1.43)		(–1.76)
Beijing × Lagged Loan Efficiency, if GDP/Lagged Loan Efficiency ≤0.6					–0.80		–0.78
					(–2.68)		(–2.65)
After 1998		–0.27	–0.10	–0.14	–0.18	–0.03	–0.15
		(–3.78)	(–1.41)	(–2.58)	(–3.60)	(–0.83)	(–3.08)
Intercept	0.25	3.92	3.74	3.62	3.30	0.22	1.60
	(0.87)	(4.96)	(4.28)	(5.57)	(5.56)	(0.81)	(2.06)
R square	0.941	0.797	0.932	0.952	0.962	0.947	0.968
No. of observations	50	54	54	54	54	50	50

Table 4 Models of housing price developmentDependent variable: Constant Average Price Index (first year in observation = 100)[11]

Variable	Model III-1	III-2	III-3	III-4	III-5	III-6	III-7
Price Index (T-1)	0.99					0.81	0.46
	(9.08)					(6.55)	(3.62)
Constant GDP per Capita Index		0.21	0.28	0.25	0.30	0.12	0.22
		(3.67)	(4.89)	(4.27)	(6.46)	(2.70)	(4.85)
Lagged Loan Efficiency		−12.81					
		(−0.70)					
Tianjin			−5.91				106.09
			(−0.80)				(1.51)
Chongqing			8.48				55.56
			(1.02)				(1.10)
Shanghai			16.52				137.40
			(2.00)				(2.39)
Tianjin × Lagged Loan Efficiency				−52.60	−146.10		−140.14
				(−1.77)	(−5.23)		(−2.34)
Chongqing × Lagged Loan Efficiency				−27.51	−94.15		−44.11
				(−1.23)	(−4.56)		(−1.61)
Shanghai × Lagged Loan Efficiency				−27.97	−120.31		−160.33
				(−0.91)	(−4.23)		(−2.85)
Beijing × Lagged Loan Efficiency				−45.94			
				(−1.39)			
Beijing × Lagged Loan Efficiency, if GDP/Lagged Loan Efficiency > 0.6					−126.17		7.53
					(−4.37)		(0.12)
Beijing × Lagged Loan Efficiency, if GDP/Lagged Loan Efficiency ≤ 0.6					−253.01		−19.94
					(−5.78)		(−0.21)
After 1998		2.37	−7.03	−8.95	−15.05	−4.94	−12.98
		(0.27)	(−0.77)	(−0.93)	(−2.02)	(−0.75)	(−1.86)
Intercept	8.96	99.61	77.47	119.09	186.22	10.70	34.56
	(0.65)	(4.95)	(8.22)	(4.22)	(7.58)	(0.78)	(0.65)
R square	0.632	0.452	0.520	0.521	0.724	0.690	0.823
No. of observations	50	54	54	54	54	50	50

[11] First year in observations are 1990 for Beijing and Tianjin, 1995 for Shanghai and Chongqing.

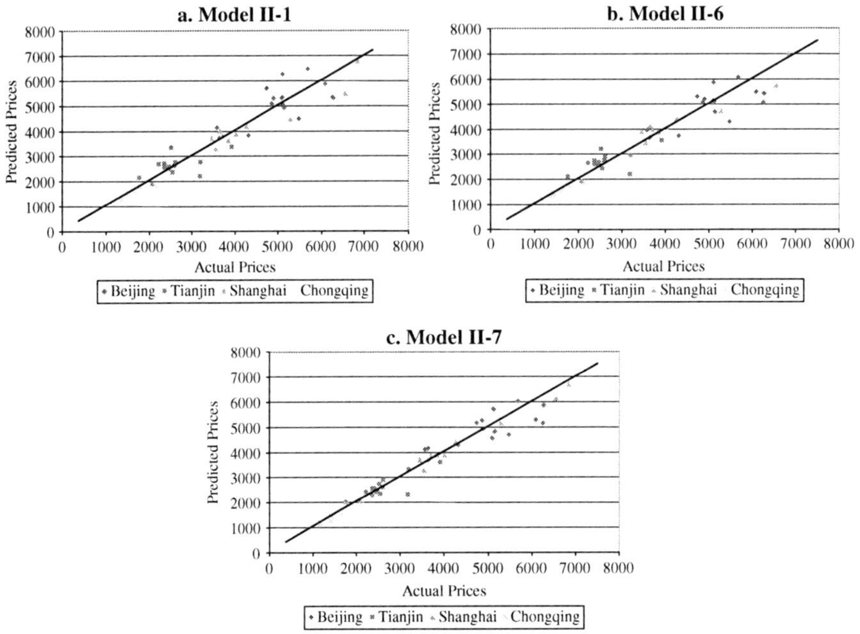

Fig. 6 Implications of logarithmic models in predicting property prices

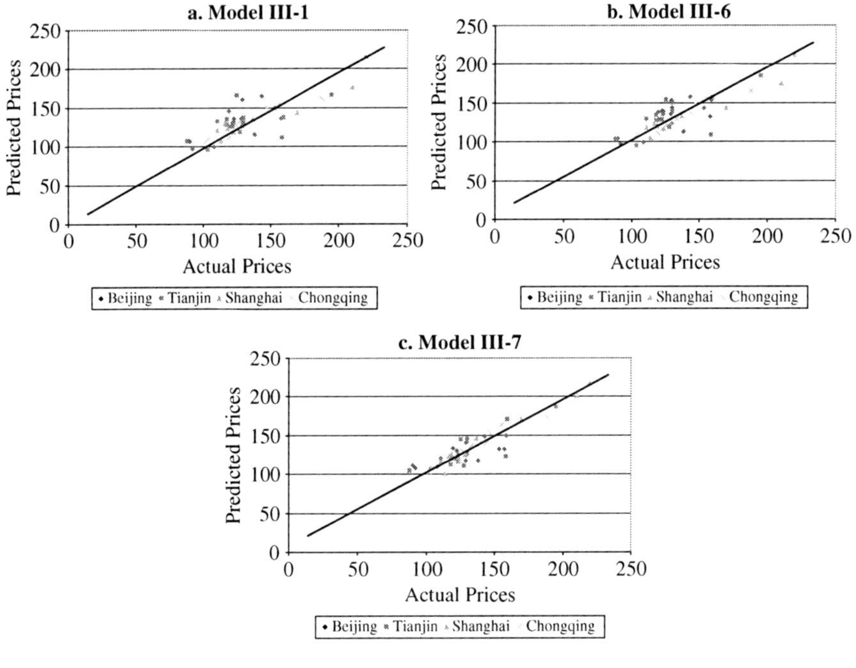

Fig. 7 Implications of index models in predicting property prices

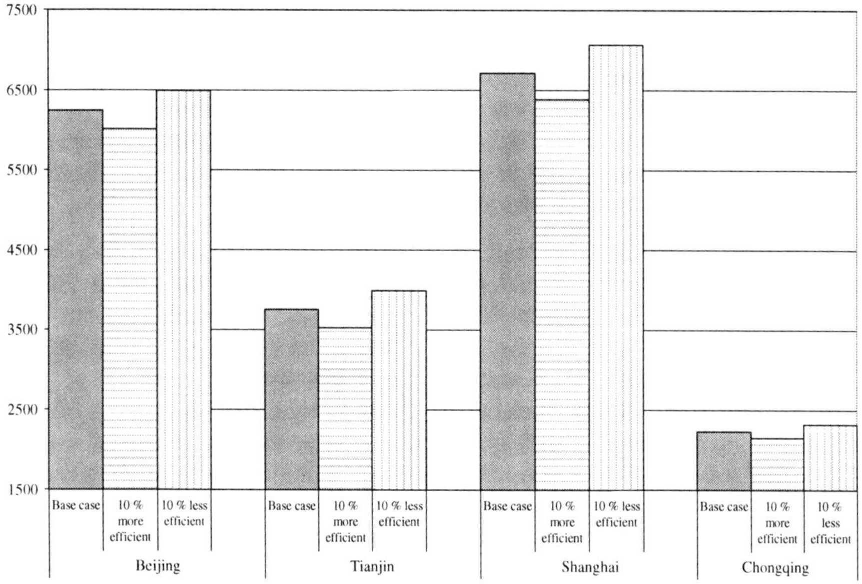

Fig. 8 Comparison of predicted property prices for different loan efficient scenarios

Tianjing, Shanghai, and Chongqing, representing the trimming of price varying from 3.7% to 6%.

7 Conclusion

The relationship between bank lending and property prices has stimulated numerous interesting discussions, especially since the Asian Financial Crisis. Previous research finds a strong correlation between the two. For an emerging economy, it is expected that an increasing level of investment activities and improved regional productivity will raise local asset values, including real estate value. It is widely assumed that strong capital investment is generally associated with higher property prices, which is also confirmed by our study. In addition and more importantly, our study focuses on an often ignored factor that proves to have significant impact on property prices: efficiency of capital utilization. The empirical result indicates that lending efficiency indeed matters in influencing property prices. If the resources a region deploys for its economic development could be efficiently put into productive use, then they should contribute less to asset bubbles, including real estate price bubbles. As a result, any appreciation in property price should reflect the real demand of households. However, when the efficiency of asset utilization is low, it is more likely that extra funds are injected to the real estate market for speculative purposes, contributing to undue inflation in property prices.

China is an emerging market economy where government guidance and intervention play important roles in economic activities. Government policies hence have huge impacts on regional development and property prices. Our findings can shed some light in the policy arena, especially with regard to government-guided investment projects:

1. Government policies can lead to elevated property prices. A large-scale government-planned regional development agenda might unduly inflate local property. Elevations in price in both Beijing and Shanghai from 2000 to 2005 coincided with the greater focus of development policy and capital investment from both the central and local governments.
2. Government should use efficiency measures as a guideline in targeting development, in property as well as industry. A large volume of capital rapidly invested in regional real estate development might be counterproductive.
3. Government targeting development in municipalities can also stimulate speculation among developers since excessive investments will cause property prices to rise. The speculation can further inflate prices on property. A vicious cycle of speculation on property may adversely affect regional resource allocations and hence balanced regional growth. In China's housing market, affordability is still a major policy issue despite all attempts from all levels of government to address it in the last decade.
4. Quality of investment matters. If loans are effectively utilized, fewer government-driven investments will be needed for real estate development. This capital can instead be invested in such a way that a region would attain higher growth through productivity gains.

In this regard, besides policies directly related to the real estate market, other policies regarding regional economic development can also have great, albeit indirect, impacts on the real estate prices. Government policies at different administrative levels can affect capital allocation among different regions and industries. With more efficient use of capital investment, local economies can enjoy healthy growth with low property price inflation and healthy asset appreciation due to productivity gains.

Acknowledgment The authors would like to thank Tong Li for her insightful comments and Brian Vo for editing.

References

Apergis, N. (2003). "Housing Prices and Macroeconomic Factors: Prospects within the European Monetary Union", *International Real Estate Review*, 6(1), 63–74.
BIS (2001). 71st Annual Report.

Borio, C. and Lowe, P. (2002). "Asset Prices, Financial and Monetary Stability: Exploring the Nexus", BIS Working paper No. 114, July 2002.

Case, K.E. and Shiller, R.J. (1990). "Forecasting Prices and Excess Returns in the Housing Market", *Journal of the American Real Estate and Urban Economics Association*, 18(3), 253–273.

Collyns, C. and Senhadji, A. (2002). "Lending Booms, Real Estate Bubbles and the Asian Crisis", IMF Working Paper No. 02/20, February 2002.

Gerlach, S. and Peng, W. (2005). "Bank Lending and Property Prices in Hong Kong", *Journal of Banking and Finance*, Elsevier, 29(2), 461–481.

Goodhart C. (1995). "Price Stability and Financial Fragility", in Sawamoto K., Nakajima Z. and Tagushi. H. (Eds.), *Financial Stability in a Changing Environment*. St. Martin's Press, New York.

Hofmann, B. (2001). "The Determinants of Private Sector Credit in Industrialized Countries: Do Property Prices Matter?" BIS working Paper No. 108.

Hofmann, B. (2003). "Bank Lending and Property Prices: Some International Evidence", the Hong Kong Institute for Monetary Research Working Paper No. 22.

Hook, B. (ed.) (1998). "Beijing and Tianjin: Towards a Millennial Megalopolis", Oxford University Press.

IMF (2000). World Economic Outlook, May 2000.

Kalra, S., Mihaljek, D., and Duenwald, C. (2000). "Property Prices and Speculative Bubbles, Evidence from Hong Kong SAR", IMF Working Paper, WP/00/2.

Le J. (2005). "More than 80 Percent of Newly Issued Bank Credit in Shanghai are Invested into Real Estates", Shanghai Securities. May 31, 2005.

Ng, E.H.K. (1998). "Asymmetric Price Response to Supply: Evidence from Singapore", *Journal of the Asian Real Estate Society*, 15(4), 397–401.

Peng, W. (2002). "What Drives Property Prices in Hong Kong?" *HKMA Quarterly Bulletin*.

Quigley, J.M. (1999). "Real Estate Prices and Economic Cycles", *International Real Estate Review*, 2(1), 1–20.

Combating Financial Exclusion in China: A Banking Regulatory Perspective

Yufeng Gong and Zhongfei Zhou

Abstract The past 10 years have witnessed great achievements made by the Chinese government in enhancing disadvantaged people's access to financial services. Without fundamental regulatory arrangements, however, no sustainable improvement would be achieved in combating financial inclusion in China. A banking regulatory structure being granted operational independence and accountability is helpful to establish an appropriate, facilitative, and incentive-compatible regulatory and legal environment for developing microfinance. In addition to the objectives of banking system stability and depositor protection, promoting financial inclusion should be incorporated into the regulatory objectives of a banking regulator, the result of which is that the banking regulator would more proactively take mandatory measures to fulfill the responsibility in this regard. Although there is debate as regards whether corporate social responsibility of banks is a statutory obligation, the imposition of the duty of increasing financial inclusion on banks in the form of law would contribute greatly to facilitating more access of disadvantaged people to financial services. Bearing in mind the differences between microfinance providers and general commercial banks, the authors argue that prudential regulation aiming at preventing systemic risks and protecting depositors should not be applied to microfinance providers. A tiered, cost-effective regulatory framework taking into account the special features and risk profile of microfinance should be put in place for microfinance providers to balance promotional and prudential objectives.

Keywords Financial exclusion · Financial inclusion · Corporate social responsibility · Regulatory objective · Tiered regulatory framework

---

Y. Gong (✉)
Shanghai University of Finance and Economics, Shanghai, China
e-mail: florayufeng@yahoo.com.cn

J.R. Barth et al. (eds.), *China's Emerging Financial Markets*,
The Milken Institute Series on Financial Innovation and Economic Growth 8,
DOI 10.1007/978-0-387-93769-4_16,

There has not been a nationwide survey on financial exclusion in China's urban and rural areas. In 2006, the China Banking Regulatory Commission (hereinafter CBRC) prepared the Distribution Map of Rural Banking Services of China (hereinafter the Distribution Map), reflecting to some degree how serious financial exclusion is in China. By the end of 2006, there were a total of 197,560 banking branches, among which 111,302 branches were located at the county level or below. According to the Distribution Map, financial resources were imbalanced between rural and urban areas. First, although banking branches at the county level or below accounted for 56% of all the country's banking branches, branches per 10,000 persons in rural areas were 1.26, while the number reached 2 in urban areas. Second, each county had an average of 50 branches; by contrast, each village had less than 3 on average. In other words, more than 30% branches in rural areas were located at the capital of the county. While 3,302 villages had no branch, 8,231 villages had only one branch. Third, all branches in rural areas received deposits of RMB 8.5 trillion, accounting for 26% of the country's whole deposits of banking financial institutions. However, only RMB 1 trillion were loaned to 87 million farmer households.[1] On the other hand, the financial desertification has made it more difficult for people living in disadvantaged areas to have access to financial services. It was reported that over the past few years, the biggest four state-owned banks had closed more than 30,000 branches in disadvantaged areas, and even rural credit operatives did so out of their business concern.[2]

As in other countries, the Chinese government has launched initiatives to improve financial services for low-income and rural people as its whole agenda of reducing poverty over the past decades. With the government's direct involvement or permission, there are six microfinance programs in China: International institution-donated short-term loans, poverty reduction loans subsidized by the government and issued by the Agricultural Bank of China (ABC), farmer household loans with deposits of rural credit cooperatives and re-lendings of the central bank, laid-off people loans operated by urban commercial banks, poverty aid loans operated by rural credit cooperatives, government poverty aid offices and financial agencies, and introduction of new types of microfinance financial institutions.[3] All these programs have made great achievements in enhancing disadvantaged people's access to financial services on the one hand and faced some constraints on the other hand.[4]

[1] CBRC, *Distribution Map*, http://bankmap.cbrc.gov.cn/bank (accessed February 18, 2008).

[2] Wang Zhijun, Financial Exclusion: Britain's Experiences, *Study on World Economy* (2007), vol. 2, at 68.

[3] Du Xiaoshan, The Development and Polices of Microfinance in China (manuscript, March 2006).

[4] The constraints include lack of regulations and rules, government's inconsistent policies, interest rate control, unequal competition between microfinance institutions, and undeveloped credit culture. *See id.*

Authors classified financial exclusion into access exclusion, condition exclusion, price exclusion, marketing exclusion, and self-exclusion.[5] These authors analyze financial exclusion from a perspective of the supplier and demander of financial services. By contrast, this chapter will focus exclusively on the impact of regulation on financial exclusion in the Chinese context. For this purpose, the first four sections will summarize the main regulations and rules with respect to combating financial exclusion. As a matter of fact, in response to the government's initiatives, Chinese financial regulatory agencies have made a sustained effort on financial service access and availability. A number of packages of policies and regulations have been issued, piloted, and implemented. Without these enabling policies and regulations of financial regulatory agencies, no substantial and sustainable improvement would be achieved in combating financial exclusion. Over the past 10 years, the banking regulatory agencies, the People's Bank of China (hereinafter PBOC) and the CBRC, have made great efforts to improve financial service outreach to unbanked people and enterprises. The efforts cover farmer household financial services, small-sized enterprise financial services, reform of rural credit cooperatives, and introduction of new types of microfinance institutions. Section 5 will then discuss how financial inclusion can be increased through improving banking regulation. In this regard, this chapter focuses on a sound banking regulatory system, regulatory objectives of banking regulatory authority, statutory obligations of bank – corporate social responsibility – and tiered regulatory framework for microfinance providers.

1 Farmer Household Financial Services

In April 1999, the POBC, the then banking regulatory agency and the central bank, convened the National Rural Credit Cooperative Conference. At the conference, the PBOC pushed rural credit cooperatives to improve and strengthen support services for rural areas. In parallel to this push, the PBOC issued Temporary Provisions on Uncollateralized Farmer Household Microloans of Rural Credit Cooperatives (hereinafter 1999 Provisions on Farmer Household Micro-loans) in July 1999,[6] under which rural credit cooperatives

---

[5] Access exclusion means the restriction of access through the processes of risk assessment. Condition exclusion means where the conditions attached to financial products make them inappropriate for the needs of some people. Price exclusion means where some people can only gain access to financial products at prices they cannot afford. Marketing exclusion means whereby some people are effectively excluded by target marketing and sales. Self-exclusion means that people may decide that there is little point applying for a financial product because they believe they would be refused. *See* Kenneth M. Amaeshi, Financial Exclusion, Financial Institutions and Corporate Social Responsibility: A Developing Country Perspective (manuscript, 2006), at 4.

[6] The 1999 Provisions on Farmer Household Micro-loans were abolished by the PBOC and CBRC jointly in December 2004.

were required to adopt realistic measures to solve the problem of inaccessibility of farmer households to loans.

Under the 1999 Provisions on Farmer Household Micro-loans, farmer household micro-loan was defined as a small value loan, uncollateralized but guaranteed by the farmer household borrower's reputation, issued by a rural credit cooperative within the predetermined limit and period. Only the farmer household which had good credit reputation, engaged in land farming or other activities consistent with the state's industry policy with reliable income, and had at least a labor force was qualified for applying for the farmer household micro-loan. The maturity of a micro-loan was, in principle, limited to no more than one year, and its interest rate was determined based on the benchmark rate of the central bank.

In December 2001, the PBOC issued the Guidelines on Uncollateralized Farmer Household Micro-loans of Rural Credit Cooperatives (hereinafter 2001 Guidelines on Farmer Household Micro-loans),[7] amending the 1999 Provisions on Farmer Household Micro-loans. Compared with the 1999 Provisions on Farmer Household Micro-loans, the 2001 Guidelines on Farmer Household Micro-loans clearly confirmed that farmer household micro-loan was a credit-based loan without a mortgage or guarantee, issued by a rural credit cooperative. The requirement that a farmer household borrower had at least a labor force was replaced by one that a farmer household borrower had the ability to repay the principal and interest of a loan.

For the purpose of increasing more farmer households' access to micro-loans, the PBOC introduced group-guaranteed loan. In December 2000, the PBOC issued the Guidelines on Farmer Household Group-guaranteed Loans of Rural Credit Cooperatives (hereinafter 2000 Guidelines on Group-guaranteed Loans).[8] Under a group-guaranteed loan, a rural credit cooperative extended the loan to a member of the co-guarantee group which was formed, on a voluntary basis, by farmer households without lineal relatives. A co-guarantee group consisted of 5–10 farmer household borrowers within the jurisdiction of a rural credit cooperative, with members assuming the mutual or co-guarantee responsibility in terms of loan application, use, management, and repayment. A member was jointly and severally liable for a loan of other members. A farmer household borrower deposited no less than 5% of his borrowing with a rural credit cooperative before obtaining a loan. The maturity of a group-guaranteed loan did not in principle exceed one year and its interest rate was negotiated between the borrower and the rural credit cooperative based on the central bank's benchmark rate, deposit rate, cost, and loan risk of the co-guarantee group members.

With the CBRC taking over the banking regulatory power, in 2004 the CBRC replaced the PBOC's 2000 Guidelines on Group-guaranteed Loans with the

[7] The 2001 Guidelines on Farmer Household Micro-loans have been implemented jointly by the PBOC and the CBRC since January 2007.

[8] In July 2007, the CBRC announced that the 2000 Guidelines on Group-guaranteed Loans were not applicable.

Guidance on Farmer Household Group-guaranteed Loans of Rural Credit Cooperatives (hereinafter 2004 Guidance on Group-guaranteed Loans). Under the 2004 Guidance on Group-guaranteed Loans, the basic contents of the 2000 Guidelines on Group-guaranteed Loans remained unchanged with some amendments. The number of the members of a co-guaranteed group was not less than five without the upper limit. Mandatory deposits with the lending rural credit cooperative under the 2000 Guidelines on Group-guaranteed Loans were not needed for a borrower who was only required to open a deposit account with the lender. To establish a co-guaranteed group, all members had to jointly apply to, and sign a co-guarantee group agreement with, a rural credit cooperative.

Regardless of the CBRC's efforts, banks' provisions of rural micro-loans were limited so that financing demands in rural areas were not satisfied because banks still lacked incentives to develop the business. To challenge this situation, the CBRC issued a new more mandatory guidance, Guidance on Increasing Greatly Banks' Provisions of Rural Micro-loans (hereinafter Guidance on Provisions of Rural Micro-loans) in August 2007. Under the Guidance on Provisions of Rural Micro-loans, it is a social responsibility that banking financial institutions, whether large or small, should fulfill to solve the problem of inaccessibility of farmer households to loans. Banks should expand loan coverage from traditional crop farmers and poultry and livestock raisers to individual, industrial, and commercial businesses as well as various micro-economic participants with a view to meet all types of financing needs of farmers. The CBRC permits banks to lift the ceiling of micro-loans to RMB 100,000–300,000 and RMB 10,000–50,000 in developed and undeveloped regions, respectively. For those farmer households and small enterprises with large production scale, good operating profits and sound credit records, the credit ceiling can be raised higher than the above limits. By taking into account the practical needs of the borrowers, banks may extend a loan's maturity for up to 3 years. Banks also have autonomy to fix lending interest rates within a floating range based on the borrower's credit ratings, the amount and maturity of a loan, and risk profiles and management of the borrowers. The loan procedures should be simplified, and a micro-loan to an old borrower should be issued in one day, while a micro-loan to a new borrower or a small enterprise should be issued within one week. In addition, the CBRC requires banks to have in place effective risk management systems regarding rural micro-loans, and banking supervisors at all levels should take incentive-compatible supervision of micro-loan businesses.

2 Small Enterprise Finance Services

For a long time, small enterprises of all types have been an important component of Chinese economy in terms of economic growth, employment increase, and social stability. However, limited access of small enterprises to financial services such as financing, lending, and settlement has seriously restricted the development of small enterprises. To solve the problem, the PBOC issued the

Guidelines on Strengthening and Improving Small Enterprise Financial Services in November 1999 (hereinafter 1999 Guidelines on Small Enterprise Financial Services). Under the 1999 Guidelines on Small Enterprise Financial Services, the PBOC required all banking financial institutions to improve financial services for small enterprises. Urban commercial banks should operate as the main provider of small enterprise financial services while urban and rural credit cooperatives should focus their services on small enterprise shareholders. All financial institutions should set up the credit assessment system for small enterprises, simplify the loan-issuing procedures, and pilot uncollateralized loans. Banking financial institutions should provide loans to small enterprises which were of technology, commerce, foreign trade, or innovation nature, set up for the purpose of recruiting laid-off workers, and provided auxiliary services for large and medium sized enterprises.

However, the PBOC's 1999 Guidelines on Small Enterprise Financial Services did not bring about a positive change in small enterprise financial services because the problem had been a chronic malady. Since 2005, the CBRC has also placed renewed emphasis on small enterprise financial services. In July 2005, the CBRC issued the Guidelines on Small Enterprise Loans of Banks,[9] requiring commercial banks to adopt creative and innovative measures to increase lendings to small enterprises on a commercial basis. All banks should establish special systems suitable for small enterprise loans with respect to lending method, mortgage requirement, risk control, risk pricing, repayment method, performance assessment and accountability. For example, banks should issue a loan based on the cash flow and creditability of the borrower, and simplify the procedures for approving a loan. Consistent with law and regulation, banks should take more flexible forms of guarantee and mortgage, and price lending rates independently. Banks should establish an incentive compatible assessment system for bank staff responsible for small enterprise loans, whose income is determined based on the loan amount, the number of new borrowers, and the ratio of overdue loans and losses.

One year later after the CBRC's Guidelines on Small Enterprise Loans of Banks were issued, no significant changes had taken place in small enterprise lendings. Almost all policies still remained at the level of the CBRC and were not carried out by banks. For this reason, in October 2006, the CBRC issued the Guidance on Duty Fulfillment in Credit Extensions to Small Enterprises, which further required banks to cultivate special credit culture consistent with small enterprise needs, organize a professional team for small enterprise credit extensions, and take practical and flexible measures in extending credits.

The Guidance on Duty Fulfillment in Credit Extensions to Small Enterprises merits attention in the following aspects. First, the procedures for credit extensions to small enterprises should be simplified, and more authorization should

[9] With the implementation of the CBRC's Guidance on Credit Extensions of Banks to Small Enterprises in July 2007, the Guidelines on Small Enterprise Loans of Banks were abolished.

be granted to staff in charge. Second, a flexible customer-oriented mechanism should be established in order to meet the credit needs of a borrower in terms of credit amount, interest rate, and maturity. Third, all banks, whether commercial banks or policy banks, may provide credit businesses (not only limited to loans) to small enterprises. In some cases, banks may issue uncollateralized loans to small enterprises and accept patents, copyrights, and trademark rights as a mortgage or pledge. Fourth, banks should pay attention to collecting non-financial information of a borrower, and a credit extension should be determined not only by financial statements but also by information collected through bank's on-site investigation. Fifth, the "zero risk" rating system should not be applied to banks, and banks should determine reasonable tolerance levels for bad small enterprise loans.

In July 2007, the CBRC issued the Guidance on Credit Extensions of Banks to Small Enterprises which replaced the Guidelines on Small Enterprise Loans of Banks issued by the CBRC in July 2005. The Guidance on Credit Extensions of Banks takes extending credits to small enterprises as a social responsibility of banks. With respect to small enterprise credit extensions, banks should take flexible measures in terms of credit approving procedures, requirements for approving credits, and interest rates, and establish so-called six mechanisms, namely, risk pricing mechanism, independent accounting mechanism, efficient credit approving mechanism, incentive compatible mechanism, professional training mechanism, and default information reporting mechanism.

3 Rural Credit Cooperative Reforms

Rural credit cooperatives were initiated during the rural cooperative movement in the 1950s. During the period, rural credit cooperatives were to a large degree on a membership basis as the capital was contributed by farmers, and credits were mostly extended to the members' production. From 1959 to 1979, rural credit cooperatives were more or less operated by the government. In 1984, the State Council transferred rural credit cooperatives under the administration of the Agricultural Bank of China and tried to turn rural credit cooperatives into a purely cooperative finance organization. Contrary to the State Council's intention, however, rural credit cooperatives became the basic presence of the Agricultural Bank of China, with a large number of loans issuing to township and village enterprises. During the period from 1996 to 2003, the PBOC took the responsibility for regulating rural credit cooperatives which were required to increase farmer household loans. In June 2003, the State Council issued the Pilot Program for Deepening Rural Credit Cooperative Reform to fundamentally restructure rural credit cooperatives. The pilot reform program included the transformation of the administrative responsibility to provincial governments, and the restructuring of rural credit cooperatives in the form of provincial rural credit cooperative union, joint-stock rural commercial bank, or rural cooperative bank.

In addition to the Commercial Banking Law and Banking Supervision Law, the existing regulations specifically applicable to rural credit cooperatives include Provisions on the Administration of Rural Credit Cooperatives (hereinafter Rural Credit Cooperative Provisions), Temporary Provisions on Rural Commercial Banks (hereinafter Rural Commercial Bank Provisions), and Temporary Provisions on Rural Cooperative Banks (hereinafter Rural Cooperative Bank Provisions). The Rural Credit Cooperative Provisions were enacted by the PBOC in 1997 and currently implemented by the CBRC. Under the Rural Credit Cooperative Provisions, a rural credit cooperative is defined to be a rural cooperative financial organization which is formed through the members' contributed capital, is democratically managed by the members, and provides the majority of financial services to the members. Members of a rural credit cooperative include farmer households and rural economic organizations with a legal person status, both of which contribute capital to the rural credit cooperative. One of the basic requirements for establishing a rural credit cooperative is that the number of the members shall not be less than 500. In other words, not all the investors of a rural credit cooperative are members. This judgment can be clarified by the Implementation Measures on Administrative Licensing Items of Cooperative Financial Institutions (hereinafter Measures on Administrative Licensing of Cooperatives) issued by the CBRC in January 2006. To establish a rural credit cooperative, the Measures on Administrative Licensing of Cooperatives requires no less than 500 promoters rather than members.[10] The promoters can be natural persons, domestic non-financial institutions, domestic financial institutions, overseas financial institutions, and others recognized by the CBRC.[11] It is obvious that not all of these types of promoters would be members of a rural credit cooperative, the purpose of which is to increase more funding sources. However, the Rural Credit Cooperative Provisions do not set rural credit cooperative as a cooperative union. A rural credit cooperative may take deposits from the public[12] and issue a maximum of 50% of the whole loans to non-members.[13] This is why over the past years rural credit cooperatives have been operated on a commercial basis and members have had no preference to obtain loans.

In response to the government's pilot reform regarding transforming some of rural credit cooperatives into commercial banks, the CBRC promulgated the Rural Commercial Bank Provisions in 2003. Although the Rural Commercial Bank Provisions require rural commercial banks to focus their financial services

[10] Measures on Administrative Licensing of Cooperatives, art. 6(2).

[11] *Id.* art. 8.

[12] Rural Credit Cooperative Provisions, art. 25(1). As a matter of fact, the Banking Supervision Law regards rural credit cooperative as a financial institution taking deposit from the public. *See* Banking Supervision Law, art. 2.

[13] Rural Credit Cooperative Provisions, art. 27.

on local farmers and rural economic growth,[14] rural commercial banks are operated on a purely commercial basis. Like other commercial banks, rural commercial banks would have no incentives to increase access of rural areas to financial services if no profits could be earned in these areas. For the purpose of increasing financial inclusion in rural areas, it is not workable to restructure rural credit cooperatives into commercial banks.

The rural cooperative bank is a new form of bank, which combines cooperative and joint stock characteristics. Under the Rural Cooperative Bank Provisions issued by the CBRC in 2003, the capital share of a rural cooperative bank involves membership shares and investment shares. With membership share each person is entitled to one vote, i.e. one person-one vote, while each investment share entitles the holder to only one vote. A rural cooperative bank mobilizes deposits, extends loans, and provides other financial services within its jurisdiction with emphasis being putting on farmers who contribute capital shares to the bank.[15] Rural cooperative banks are required to provide some percentages of loans to farmers, agriculture and rural economic development.[16] The CBRC assesses a rural cooperative bank's performance in extending rural loans on a regular basis, the result of which would be a reference used by the CBRC in approving its applications for setting up new branches or opening new businesses.[17] As a matter of fact, the Rural Cooperative Bank Provisions demutualize rural cooperative banks. The mutuality of a rural cooperative bank through a common bond restriction requires it to provide its members with accessible savings, low-cost loans, and other financial services. However, the current regulation does not have a mandate which requires a rural cooperative bank to provide financial services to its members as a legal obligation. Therefore, a rural cooperative bank has strong incentives to prioritize profits over the provision of financial services to its members.

4 Introduction of New Microfinance Vehicles

Given the big gap between huge demands of rural people for financial services and limited providers of financial services, the Chinese government introduces new alternative forms of rural micro-financing, village bank, loan corporation, rural mutual finance society, and small-value loan corporation. Accordingly, in January 2007, the CBRC issued Temporary Provisions on Administration of Village Banks, Temporary Provisions on Administration of Loan Corporations,

---

[14] Rural Commercial Bank Provisions, art. 2.

[15] Rural Cooperative Bank Provisions, art. 48.

[16] *Id.* Under the Measures on Administrative Licensing of Cooperatives, one of the requirements for establishing a rural cooperative bank is that the general shareholder meeting has determined the percentage and size of loans issued to farmers, agriculture and rural economic development. *See* Measures on Administrative Licensing of Cooperatives, art. 54(11).

[17] Rural Cooperative Bank Provisions, art. 48.

and Temporary Provisions on Administration of Rural Mutual Finance Societies. According to the Temporary Provisions on Administration of Village Banks, a village bank is a banking financial institution formed by domestic and foreign financial institutions, domestic non-financial enterprises, and domestic natural persons in rural areas for the purpose of mainly providing financial services to mainly local farmers, agriculture, and rural economic development.[18] Compared to a general commercial bank whose minimum registered capital is RMB 50 million[19] and a rural cooperative bank whose minimum registered capital is RMB 20 million,[20] the minimum registered capital of a village bank is RMB 3 million and RMB 1 million depending on whether its location is in a county or a village.[21] Probably out of concern for prudential operations of a village bank, the CBRC requires that the largest shareholder or sole shareholder of a village bank must be a banking financial institution, and the largest banking financial institution shareholder must hold no less than 20% of the whole equity.[22] This requirement may reduce the number of the investors of a village bank. As a general commercial bank, a village bank may take deposits from the public, issue loans, and conduct other commercial banking businesses. For the purpose of serving local people, however, a village bank shall not issue a loan to people in areas other than its location,[23] and give its priority to rural farmer households, agriculture, and rural economic development within the county region when making loans.[24] According to the basic ideology of strictly regulating village banks, prudential regulations applicable to general commercial banks are equally applied to village banks. Village banks must comply with the requirements for capital adequacy,[25] loan loss provisions,[26] and large exposure control.[27] The CBRC shall take corresponding supervisory measures according to a village bank's capital adequacy and asset quality. For example, a village bank whose capital adequacy ratio is below 8% but above 4% and non-performing loan ratio is below 5% is required to increase its capital adequacy ratio within a specified time frame, receive more frequent on- and off-site examinations, and limit asset growth, distribution of dividends, establishment of branches, and new business commencement.[28]

---

[18] Temporary Provisions on Administration of Village Banks, art. 2.

[19] Commercial Banking Law, art. 13.

[20] Rural Cooperative Bank Provisions, art. 9(3).

[21] Temporary Provisions on Administration of Village Banks, art. 8(3).

[22] *Id.* art 25.

[23] *Id.* art. 5.

[24] *Id.* art. 39.

[25] A village bank's capital adequacy must be not less than 8% at any time. *Id.* art. 42.

[26] The loan loss provisioning ratio of a village bank must be not less than 100%. *Id.*

[27] Loans issued by a village bank to a single borrower must not exceed 5% of the bank's net capital, and credit extensions to a single group borrower must not exceed 10% of the bank's net capital. *Id.* art. 41.

[28] *Id.* art. 51(2).

Under the Temporary Provisions on Administration of Loan Corporations, a loan corporation is a non-banking financial institution which is set up in rural areas by domestic commercial banks or rural cooperative banks for the special purpose of providing lending services to farmers, agriculture and rural economic development within the county region.[29] Only commercial banks or rural cooperative banks whose assets are not less than RMB 5 billion are qualified for setting up a loan corporation.[30] To establish a loan corporation which must operate on a commercial basis, the investors must contribute a minimum of RMB 500,000 capital.[31] Loan corporations are prohibited from taking deposits from the public and have the power to make loans, discount papers, and other approved businesses with their paid-up capital and borrowings from their investors.[32] Like a village bank, a loan corporation must comply with prudential requirements prescribed by the CBRC. Loans to a single borrower and to a single group borrower must not exceed 10% and 15%, respectively, of a loan corporation's net capital.[33] A loan corporation must maintain its capital adequacy ratio of not below 8% and its loan loss provisioning ratio of not below 100%.[34] According to the levels of capital adequacy and of non-performing loans of a loan corporation, the CBRC would take differentiating regulatory measures, including suspension of businesses, capital supplement, and closing the problem loan corporation.[35]

Under the Temporary Provisions on Administration of Rural Mutual Finance Societies, a rural mutual finance society is more like a credit union as it is defined as a community mutual banking financial institution which is formed voluntarily by farmers and rural small enterprises, provides banking businesses to its members,[36] and is managed by members democratically for common interests of the members.[37] To establish a rural mutual finance society, at least 10 qualified promoters are required,[38] with a minimum of RMB 300,000 and RMB 100,000 paid-up capital, respectively, depending on whether it is set up at the level of a town or a village.[39] The funding sources of a rural mutual finance are limited to deposits from members, social donations, and borrowings from other banking financial institutions,[40] the most part of which should be

---

[29] Temporary Provisions on Administration of Loan Corporations, art. 2.

[30] *Id.* art. 9(1).

[31] *See id.* art. 4.

[32] *Id.* arts. 20 & 21.

[33] *Id.* art. 23.

[34] *Id.* art. 25.

[35] *Id.* art. 34.

[36] *See* Temporary Provisions on Administration of Rural Mutual Finance Societies, art. 2.

[37] *Id.* art. 3.

[38] *Id.* art. 9(2).

[39] *Id.* art. 9(3).

[40] *Id.* art. 41.

used to issue loans to its members.[41] In line with the requirements, a rural mutual finance society is prohibited from taking deposits from, issuing loans to, and providing other financial services to, non-members, and providing a guarantee for other institutions and individuals with its own assets.[42] Taken as a banking financial institution, a rural mutual finance society is required by the CBRC to comply with a number of prudential regulations in respect of capital adequacy, risk concentration, and loan loss provisioning.[43]

In May 2008, the CBRC and the PBOC jointly issued the Guidance on Pilot Small-value Loan Corporations in order to direct funds to rural areas and disadvantaged areas. A small-value loan corporation is different from a loan corporation established according to the Temporary Provisions on Administration of Loan Corporations. A small-value loan corporation is set up by natural persons, enterprises, and other social organizations without taking deposits from the public.[44] The registered capital of a small-value loan corporation should not be less than RMB 5 million and RMB 10 million, fully being paid at one time, in the case of a limited liability company and a joint-stock limited company, respectively.[45] Interestingly, a small-value loan corporation is not treated as a financial institution; therefore, applicants for setting up a small-value loan corporation should submit the application to the local branch of the State Administration of Industry and Commerce, with relevant documents being filed with the local branch of the CBRC and PBOC,[46] and it is supervised by the provincial government rather than the local branch of the CBRC or PBOC.[47] Small-value loan corporations make loans with paid-in capital, donated funds, and borrowings from not more than two banking financial institutions.[48] In the case of borrowings from banking financial institutions, the amount should not exceed 50% of its capital net, and the interest rate and maturity can be determined through negotiation between small-value loan corporations and banks.[49] Under the Guidance on Pilot Small-value Loan Corporations, small-value loan corporations have more freedom to determine

---

[41] *Id.* art. 42.

[42] *Id.* art. 45.

[43] A rural finance mutual society's capital adequacy should not be less than 8%. Loans to a single member should not exceed 15% of its net capital while loans to a single enterprise member and connected members not exceeding 20%. Loans to the ten largest borrowers should not exceed 50% of its net capital. Loan loss provisioning ratio should not be less than 100%. *See id.* art. 47.

[44] Guidance on Pilot Small-value Loan Corporations, para. 1.

[45] *Id.* para. 2.

[46] *Id.*

[47] *Id.* para. 4.

[48] *Id.* para. 3.

[49] *Id.*

their lending interest rates ranging from the cap prescribed by the judicial organ to the floor of 90% of the PBOC's benchmark lending rate.[50]

5 Thoughts on Reducing Financial Exclusion from a Regulatory Perspective

There is increasing recognition that financial regulation and supervision have an impact on access to financial services in addition to their importance for financial stability and customer protection.[51] Financial regulation should shift from a sole focus on a prudential objective to one that facilitates more access to disfranchised people. However, without reforming fundamental regulatory systems, financial inclusion regulations, though easily amended and enacted, would not bring about sufficient effects on increasing more access of disadvantaged areas and people to financial services. This means that for the purpose of increasing financial inclusion, fundamental regulatory arrangements should be in place prior to or in parallel with the emergence of new regulations. These arrangements include having sound banking regulatory structure, incorporating promoting financial inclusion into regulatory objectives of a regulatory agency, establishing mandatory obligation of bank corporate social responsibility, and tailoring regulatory framework for micro-finance providers.

5.1 Sound Banking Regulatory Structure

The importance of regulatory structure in the efficiency and effectiveness of banking regulation has been increasingly acknowledged across countries, with emphasis being given to the question of whether and to what extent the achievement of regulatory objectives is influenced by the particular institutional structure within which regulators operate. A number of countries split banking regulatory function from central banking function, and some of them establish a single mega regulator. However, which institutional structure is more efficient and effective is still a vexed issue. In China, it seemed that there had not been too much debate on whether the banking regulatory function should be separated from the PBOC, and the government made quite a straightforward decision on the establishment of the CBRC, which obtained approval of the National People's Congress (hereinafter NPC) at the first session of the 10th NPC on March 5, 2003. According to the explanation made by the State Council to the NPC, the change was intended to enable the PBOC to focus more on monetary policy formulation and implementation and other macro policies, leaving bank regulation to the CBRC as a specialist regulatory agency.[52]

---

50 *Id.* para. 4.

51 United Nations, *Building Inclusive Financial Sectors for Development* (2006), at120.

52 Wang Zhongyu, Explanations on the Restructuring Scheme of the State Council, March 5, 2003.

Following such an institutional restructuring, the NPC grants the CBRC the banking regulatory power through the Banking Supervision Law. Under the Banking Supervision Law, the CBRC is delegated to regulate and supervise banking financial institutions, financial asset management companies, trust and investment companies, finance companies, financial leasing companies, and other financial institutions.[53] Traditionally, banking regulators focus more on soundness of major banking institutions without serious consideration of the role of microfinance providers in mobilizing and intermediating funds in disadvantaged areas and for disadvantaged people. The establishment of the CBRC and the enforcement of the Banking Supervision Law would effectively bring microfinance providers into the scope of regulation and supervision. As a matter of fact, as far as microfinance providers and microfinance services are concerned, an appropriate, facilitative, and incentive-compatible regulatory and legal environment would be more helpful for their development than leaving them outside the scope of regulators.

Under the Core Principles for Effective Banking Supervision, an effective system of banking supervision should grant a banking regulatory authority operational independence and hold it accountable for the discharge of its duties.[54] The Banking Supervision Law provides a basic legal framework for independent and accountable CBRC, which is also a precondition for effectively regulating and supervising microfinance providers and promoting financial inclusion. An independent banking regulator must be free from political interference and from regulatory capture by interest groups as well. The Banking Supervision Law explicitly prohibits local governments, governmental departments of all levels, social organizations, and individuals from interfering with the CBRC's discharge of functions.[55] Moreover, the fit and proper requirements for the regulators of the CBRC can promote to some degree the CBRC's independence.[56] However, as part of the State Council, the CBRC can never be cut off its close relationship with the government. The inseverability between the CBRC and the State Council would no doubt undermine the protection of its independence provided by these legal arrangements.[57]

---

[53] Banking Supervision Law, art. 2.

[54] Core Principles for Effective Banking Supervision, Principle 1(2).

[55] Banking Supervision Law, art. 5.

[56] Under the Banking Supervision Law, the regulators of the CBRC shall have the professional skills and working experiences as required for performing their functions; and shall perform their duties with integrity and in accordance with laws and regulations, and shall not take advantage of their positions to seek inappropriate gains, or concurrently hold a position in enterprises including financial institutions; and shall keep the state secrets and bank secrets for the banks supervised and other parties concerned. *See id.* arts. 9–11.

[57] On a detailed discussion of the problems with CBRC's independence, *see generally* Zhongfei Zhou, On a Legal Framework for Maintaining Banking Regulator Independence, *Chinese Journal of Law*, 174(1), 2008, at 40–50.

It is acknowledged that a well-defined statutory objective against which the agency's performance can be measured is traditionally viewed as a key requirement for holding an independent agency accountable.[58] However, unlike a central bank whose objectives can be measured in the form of an explicit inflation target, the regulatory objectives of a banking regulatory agency are multiple and non-operational and therefore hard to measure.[59] Notwithstanding the difficulty in measuring whether or the extent to which a banking regulator achieves its objectives, the authors argue that the clearly articulated statutory objectives themselves can provide a basis for holding a banking regulator accountable. The lack of measurability in the statutory objectives does not make it entirely impossible to assess a regulator's performance according to the objectives. The statutory objectives stipulated by the Banking Supervision Law expose the CBRC's performance to the checks and balances by its accountors.[60] In addition, the accountability of the CBRC would be heightened by the legal requirements under which the CBRC should make its regulatory and supervisory processes public[61] and be subject to auditing and surveillance by competent authorities.[62]

A sound banking regulatory system means absence of regulatory overlap. However, regulatory overlap seems inevitable when banks face several regulators. In China, even though the CBRC is a specialist banking regulator, the PBOC still performs financial regulatory functions. As a result, the PBOC's and the CBRC's powers overlap to some degree. In the following areas, the CBRC and PBOC power overlap would occur in the regulation of microfinance. First, under the Commercial Banking Law, a bank can conduct the business of settling and selling foreign exchanges subject to the approval of the PBOC and punish a bank conducting such a business without prior approval.[63] This means that it is the PBOC rather than the CBRC that possesses the power to approve the foreign exchange settling and selling business. To be precise, the State Administration of Foreign Exchange (hereinafter SAFE), an independent arm of the PBOC, has been authorized to approve a bank's access to and exit from the foreign exchange settling and selling business, since the establishment

---

[58] Eva Hüpkes, Marc Quintyn & Michael W. Taylor, *The Accountability of Financial Sector Supervisors: Principles and Practice*, IMF Working Paper (WP/05/51, Mar. 2005), at 10.

[59] As regards a discussion on the difficulty in measuring a banking regulator's objectives, *see id.* at 10–15. *See also* Charles Goodhart, *Financial Regulations: Why, How, and Where Now?* (1998), at 61–72 (discussing the difficulty in quantifying the benefits and costs of banking regulation and supervision).

[60] Under the Banking Supervision Law, the regulatory objectives of the CBRC are first to facilitate lawful and sound operations of the banking industry and second to maintain the public's confidence in the banking industry. Banking Supervision Law, art. 3.

[61] Banking Supervision Law, art. 12.

[62] *Id.* art. 14. On a detailed discussion of the problems with CBRC's accountability, *see generally* Zhongfei Zhou, On a Legal Framework for Maintaining Banking Regulator Accountability, *Legal Science*, 308(7), 2007, at 81–90.

[63] Commercial Banking Law, arts. 3 & 76.

of the CBRC. Second, the inter-banking borrowing and lending business, as one of the general activities of a bank, is subject to the approval of the CBRC under the Commercial Banking Law.[64] Meanwhile, the Commercial Banking Law requires a bank to comply with the relevant rules laid down by the PBOC in conducting an inter-bank borrowing and lending business.[65] The Law of People's Bank of China (hereinafter PBOC Law) authorizes the PBOC to regulate and supervise the inter-bank borrowing and lending markets.[66] In common understanding, the PBOC, in addition to laying down the rules governing the inter-bank borrowing and lending markets,[67] is responsible for approving the qualification for a bank to enter an inter-bank borrowing and lending market, while the CBRC is for approving the qualification for a bank to engage in an inter-bank borrowing and lending business. Third, for issuing and trading-in of financial bonds, the approving and regulatory powers are granted to the CBRC under the Commercial Banking Law.[68] Where it issues and trades in financial bonds without the prior approval, a bank would be punished by the CBRC.[69] By contrast, the PBOC's regulatory power in this area is limited to financial bond issuing and trading on an inter-bank bond market. This judgment is concluded from articles 4 (4) and 32 (4) of the PBOC Law which provide that the PBOC performs the function of regulating the inter-bank bond market.[70] Fourth, under the Commercial Banking Law, a commercial bank must obtain approval in accordance with laws and regulations if it borrows money from abroad. As a common practice, borrowing money from abroad falls within the scope of foreign exchange regulation.[71] Apparently, the regulatory agency for borrowing money from abroad is the SAFE, an independent agency affiliated to the PBOC.

---

[64] *Id.* art. 3 (8).

[65] *Id.* art. 46.

[66] PBOC Law, art. 4 (4).

[67] The PBOC has issued several rules in this regard including the Trial Measures on the Administration of Inter-bank Borrowing and Lending, the Provisions on the Administration of Securities Companies' Entrance into Inter-bank Markets, the Provisions on the Administration of Fund Management Companies' Entrance into Inter-bank Markets, and the Provisions on the Administration of Finance Companies' Entrance into Inter-bank Borrowing and Lending Markets and Bond Markets.

[68] Commercial Banking Law, art. 3 (7).

[69] *Id.* art. 74.

[70] A financial institution used to submit its application to the National Center for Inter-bank Borrowing and Lending and the Central Company of Governmental Bond Registration and Settlement separately. After examining the application, the two agencies reported relevant documents to the headquarters of the PBOC for record. Since April 20 2006, the Shanghai headquarters of the PBOC has replaced the Beijing headquarters of the PBOC to assume responsibility for inter-bank bond market and inter-bank borrowing and lending market entry. *See China Business News* (in Chinese), 13 April, 2006, at. B 3.

[71] *See* Regulations on the Administration of Foreign Exchanges, arts. 22 & 44.

5.2 *Promoting Financial Inclusion as a Regulatory Objective*

Up to now, international financial regulatory standards and reforms have been driven and developed by developed countries. Financial reform efforts do not fully consider the actual requirements of economic and social development of disenfranchised populations with respect to the financial sectors.[72] Indeed, virtually all banking laws focus exclusively on safe and sound operations of the banking system and depositor protection without taking financial inclusion into account as one of the responsibilities and objectives. For example, the UK Financial Services and Markets Act provides that the regulatory objectives are market confidence, public awareness, the protection of consumers, and the reduction of financial crime.[73] The UK Financial Services Authority stated that, under the Financial Services and Markets Act, they had no explicit statutory responsibility for financial inclusion; nor was it included in the principles of good regulation as an issue to which they should formally have regard.[74] As with many other banking laws, China's Banking Supervision Law also sets the banking regulatory objectives as facilitating lawful and sound operations of the banking industry and maintaining the public's confidence in the banking industry.[75] With these two regulatory objectives, the CBRC is apparently reluctant to put more regulatory resources to combating financial exclusion, as the reduction of financial exclusion does not mean its successful fulfillment of the statutory objectives and responsibilities.

One of the reasons for rejecting a statutory objective on financial inclusion is that financial inclusion is regarded as the responsibility of the government rather than that of banking regulator. Mr. Tiner, the then Chief Executive of UK's Financial Services Authority, argued that creating social policy was not the responsibility of a regulator – any regulator of appointed people – but is a government responsibility.[76] He concluded that there was an inherent conflict

---

[72] Joseph J. Norton, *Taking Stock of the "First Generation" of Financial Sector Legal Reform* (World Bank Law and Development Working Paper Series, No. 4, 2007), at 16–21 (Professor Norton argues that financial sector reform needs to be part of broader objectives for the sound economic development of a particular developing country and is directed toward broadening the financial system to be more inclusionary).

[73] Financial Services and Markets Act (UK), part. 1, 2(2). Very few banking laws tenuously and indirectly connect banking regulatory responsibilities to financial inclusion. For example, the German Federal Banking Supervisory Office shall counteract undesirable developments in the banking and financial sector which may involve serious disadvantages for the national economy. *See* German Banking Act, Division 2, s.6(2). The Finnish Financial Supervision Authority shall monitor and analyze the availability and pricing of banking services provided by credit institutions. *See* Act on the Financial Supervision Authority of Finland, Section 4(6a).

[74] *See* House of Commons Treasury Committee, *Financial Inclusion: The Roles of the Government, the FSA and Financial Capability*, Nov. 2006, para.39, at 17.

[75] Banking Supervision Law, art. 3.

[76] *See* House of Commons Treasury Committee, *supra* note 75, para. 44, at 18.

between having an objective for financial inclusion and an objective for prudential soundness and market confidence, in that the Financial Service Authority may therefore direct banks to make decisions which were not in their commercial interest.[77] The argument seems unconvincing. In UK, two other statutory regulators, the Office of Gas and Electricity Markets (Ofgem) and the Office of Communications (Ofcom), are required to perform their duties, to have regard to a range of factors, including several relating to vulnerable consumers or other groups who may be disadvantaged under the Communications Act 2003 and the Universal Service Directive.[78] The legislation is based on the basic fact that in modern society telephone has become people's lifeline service. Without telephones people's lives become more difficult. In other words, whether to be offered telephone affects people's life quality and even right to existence. In this case, Parliament may legislate that Ofgem should take into account the interests of vulnerable people in all of its decisions.

By the same token, a bank account and account-based services such as a deposit, cheque, money transmission, micro-credit, and utility services payment are becoming lifeline banking services of people in a modern society. These lifeline banking services are a precondition for running daily life. It is argued that some of the financial services are considered to be services of general interest and can be treated as social rights in the same way as services provided by traditional public utilities.[79] In some countries, the right to a bank account is legally granted to people. Under the French Banking Act of 1984, for example, any person has the right to open an account at the bank. In the event of refusal by the bank, the person may refer to the Banque de France, and the latter shall name a bank for the person.[80] The right to a bank account is a matter of "ordre public" in France, and it is therefore for the state to ensure its efficacy.[81] In our opinion, for matters influencing people's right to existence, legislation should go further with directly spelling out that it is not only government but also the banking regulator that has the responsibility to facilitate access of disadvantaged people and areas to basic banking services.[82] Where a banking law

---

[77] *Id.* at 19.

[78] *See id.* para. 42, at 18.

[79] T. Wilhelmsson, Services of General Interest and European Private Law, in *International Perspectives on Consumers' Access to Justice* (C. Rickett and T. Telfer eds, 2003), at 149, 154. Wilhelmsson argues that services of general interest have the following features: the service fulfils a basic need for its users; there is often not any reasonable alternative to the service; there are few producers of the service; and the service is based on a long-term relationship.

[80] French Banking Act of 1984, art. 58.

[81] Jan Evers & Udo Reifner, *The Social Responsibility of Credit Institutions in the EU: Access, Regulation and New Products* (NOMOS Verlagsgesellschaft, Baden-Baden, 1998), at 46.

[82] *C.f.* Sir Callum McCarthy, who was previously Chairman of Ofgem before becoming Chairman of the FSA, has commented that he was struck by the fact that the FSA had no statutory duty comparable to that placed upon Ofgem to have special regard for those on low incomes—an odd absence given the importance of financial services in our society. *See* House of Commons Treasury Committee, *supra* note 75, para. 43, at 18.

incorporates promoting financial inclusion into the regulatory objectives or responsibilities, banking regulators would have to proactively take more mandatory measures (rather than only in the form of guidance) to require banks to provide more financial services to disfranchised areas and people. Accountors may hold a banking regulator more accountable through assessing whether it achieves the statutory objective or responsibility.

5.3 Corporate Social Responsibility of Banks

Traditionally, the discourse of corporate social responsibility centers on the debate between two influential schools, shareholder benefit school and social public benefit. The shareholder benefit school posits that a corporation owes only a duty to maximize shareholder benefit. On the one hand, the duty could be focused on the maximization of corporate profits. On the other hand, the duty could point to a primary obligation to maximize shareholder wealth.[83] The social public benefit school suggests that the corporation is an economic institution that serves a social purpose as well, reflecting an ideal that the purpose of making all corporations is the accomplishment of some public good.[84] According to this school, corporations might be made to serve other constituencies or might seek to serve such constituencies as corporations are seen as embedded in the social and political fabric of society, in which corporations are expected or permitted to participate.[85]

There is debate as regards whether corporate social responsibility of banks is a statutory obligation. The argument against bank corporation social responsibility is that banks would be acting in the place of the state and be accountable to the political community if banks were to be granted social policy obligations. As a general corporation, bank is a fictitious legal person with two effects: first, it is not a creature of the state, and second, it holds private rights protected legally, often at the expense of the public. However, the argument is under attack by authors who advocate that banks should be positioned to be more socially responsible than ordinary private undertakings in the following aspects.

First, banks are quasi-public organizations as they are chartered and regulated by the state. With the creation of a banking regulatory agency responsible for ensuring the soundness of banks and preventing bank failure, banks are assumed safe. Depositors tend to regard bank regulation and supervision as the government certification of an individual bank's safety.[86] In addition, banks are

---

[83] *See* Larry Catá Backer, Multinational Corporations, Transnational Law: The United Nations' Norms on the Responsibilities of Transnational Corporations as a Harbinger of Corporate Social Responsibility in International Law, *Columbia Human Rights Law Review* (Winter 2006), at 289–299.

[84] *See id.* at 299.

[85] *See id.*

[86] When a regulatory authority is created and establishes regulatory requirements, an implicit contract is perceived as having been created between the user of financial services and the

guaranteed by explicit or implicit deposit insurance scheme and lender of last resort.[87] These features of banks render them quasi-public. Under the Directive relating to the Taking up and Pursuit of the Business of Credit Institutions (2000/12/EC), a host banking licensing authority may stipulate conditions under which such a branch must carry on its activities in the interest of the general good.[88] The European Court has decided that the general good can cover the interests of consumers, the protection of workers, social order, and other matters. Insofar as the interest of the general good may include social responsibility of banks, this EC Directive's provision may be interpreted as an acknowledgment of the appropriateness of such regulation.[89]

Second, financial services provided by banks can be seen as public goods that are essential to enable participation in a modern economy, in an analogous way as is the access to safe water, basic health services, and primary education.[90] In this sense, banks are a legally socially responsible institution providing socially responsible services. Socially responsible services are meant to include services to disadvantaged people and areas for the purpose of fulfilling their commitment to social concerns.

Third, according to the criteria of legitimacy in corporate social responsibility, banks exist because society gives them the right to do so. Thus, a legitimate bank should have an enduring capacity to operate on the basis of civic virtue[91] and is articulated as an active obligation to positively better the environment, to increase the wealth of the inhabitants in places where it operates, and to develop economically depressed neighborhoods.[92] The existence of a bank relies on the public's deposits. It is the public's deposits that create all kinds of bank services. Therefore, there seems some sort of contract of reciprocal rights and obligations between banks and the public depositors, whereby banks have an obligation to provide financial services to the entire communities including low-income and minority communities on a non-discriminatory basis in exchange for the latter's deposits.[93]

---

regulator, i.e., the consumer assumes that, because there is an authorization procedure, specific aspects of regulation are established, the supplier of financial services is authorized and supervised and the institution is therefore safe. *See* Charles Goodhart et al, *Financial Regulation: Why, How and Where Now?* (1998), at 15.

[87] Jan Evers & Udo Reifner, *supra* note 82, at 40.

[88] Directive 2000/12/EC of the European Parliament and of the Council of 20 March 2000 Relating to the Taking up and Pursuit of the Business of Credit Institutions, art. 20(4).

[89] Jan Evers and Udo Reifner, *supra* note 82, at 41.

[90] *See* Thorsten Beck & Augusto de la Torre, *The Basic Analytics of Access to Financial Services* (World Bank Policy Research Working Paper 4026, Oct. 2006), at 2.

[91] Bobby Banerjee, The Problem with Corporate Social Responsibility (manuscript 2005), at 8.

[92] *See* Backer, *supra* note 84, at 301–302.

[93] *See* Jan Evers, A European Regulation for Social Responsibility of Banks? Learning the Lessons from the US Community Reinvestment Act (manuscript, 2000), at 2.

Although the authors agree with the arguments for bank corporate social responsibility, the pros are not more convincing than the cons. It seems to the authors that it is meaningless to spend much time on the reasons why banks should have corporate social responsibility and banks should have an obligation of financial inclusion. In our opinion, for the purpose of economic development, government may call for a legislator or employ its own legislating power to legislate promoting financial inclusion as a bank's statutory obligation. Once the obligation of promoting financial inclusion is translated into law or mandatory regulation, social expectations about responsible bank behavior would be established, around which banks structure their behavior to meet the financial inclusion obligation set out in the law or regulation.[94]

On the one hand, it is inappropriate that banking regulators set detailed financial inclusion targets for banks and punish banks unable to meet the targets as the practice would turn into an intervention into the business operations of banks. On the other hand, such a social responsibility would, even if it is a mandatory one, remain on paper without enforcement measures. This is why the Company Law of 2006 in China, which only simply requires a company to assume social responsibility,[95] and the CBRC's guidelines, under which banks should have corporate social responsibility,[96] do not produce expected results. In our opinion, only imposing financial inclusion on banks as a statutory obligation will not be enough. Some form of mandatory sanction is necessary for banks to fulfill the financial inclusion obligation. That said, the approach taken by the US's Community Reinvestment Act can be first adopted, under which a bank's record of meeting the financial inclusion obligation is rated. In the evaluation of an application for a new charter, establishment of a branch, relocation of a branch, and merger with or acquisition of another bank, the rating is taken into account by banking regulator. Second, for a bank whose financial inclusion rating is below a certain prescribed level, a banking regulator may be authorized by law to set the financial inclusion targets according to the plan submitted by the bank, and impose a penalty on the bank not meeting the targets in a prescribed time period.

5.4 A Tiered Regulatory Framework

A "conventional wisdom" treats microfinance as a risky actor because the micro-credit borrowers normally do not have appropriate collateral, adequate business plans, or other forms of credit enhancement.[97] This results in the

---

[94] *See* Cynthia A. Williams and Ruth V. Aguilera, Corporate Social Responsibility in a Comparative Perspective (manuscript, 2006), at 3–4.

[95] Company Law, art. 5.

[96] *See supra* Sections 1 and 2.

[97] *See* United Nations, *supra* note 52, at 134.

imposition of stricter prudential regulations on microfinance providers.[98] The authors suggest that the differences between microfinance providers and general commercial banks should be borne in mind. Rural credit cooperatives and rural mutual finance societies are mutual institutions owned by members who save with and borrow from them. Loan corporations are credit-only institutions with capital and borrowings from their owners. Although village banks are permitted to take deposits from and issue loans to the public, their businesses are limited to its locality. A recognition of the differences prevents us from treating them as if they are banks for regulatory purposes. The prudential regulation of banks aims to prevent systemic risks and protect depositors. By contrast, the purpose of regulating microfinance providers is to provide banks with the incentives for offering more financial services to disadvantaged areas and people, to which prudential considerations are subordinated. In designing regulatory requirements for microfinance providers, a cost-effective analysis should be taken into account. A prudential requirement may be inappropriate if the regulatory costs including the compliance cost exceed the benefits, i.e. the reduction or prevention of the risk from microfinance services and depositor protection. It is argued that, by imposing the same regulatory requirements on microfinance providers, the potential for them to form and grow is lost, and management is required to focus upon financial targets which are not necessarily consistent with the goals of mutuality and serving poor segments of the population.[99] For these reasons, a tiered or tailored regulatory framework, taking into account the special features and risk profile of microfinance, should be put in place for microfinance institutions to balance promotional and prudential objective.

Market access. The legal status and business powers of special microfinance providers should be prescribed formally by laws. So far, rural credit cooperatives, village banks, loan corporations and rural mutual finance societies are established only based on the ministerial rules.[100] The adverse effect of the low-

---

[98] A number of specific restrictions are listed by the United Nations' document, including (1) entry requirements are onerous, both in terms of minimum capital requirements and licensing procedures; (2) uncollateralized loan portfolios are not allowed or carry excessive provisioning requirements; (3) even where uncollateralized portfolios are allowed for microfinance, the lack of traditional collateral can become a constraint to accessing resources from financial markets, due to legal restrictions or excessive risk weighting of the asset; (4) there is not enough regulatory leeway to introduce new products; (3) the ability to open new branches is restricted and requirements for branches do not correspond to the needs and possibilities of the institutions concerned, particularly in rural areas; (5) reporting requirements, including accounting rules, are ill adapted to the functioning of the institutions concerned; and (6) non-bank financial institutions are excluded from access to the inter-bank market and to the payments system. *See id.*

[99] *See* Nicola Howell and Therese Wilson, Access to Consumer Credit: The Problem of Financial Exclusion in Australia and the Current Regulatory Framework, *Macquarie Law Journal*, 5, 2005, at 141.

[100] Rural credit cooperatives were formed according to the Rural Credit Cooperative Provisions issued originally in 1990 and revised in 1997 by the PBOC, although they existed long before the PBOC's rules. The legal basis of rural credit cooperatives can be dated back to the

level legislation is that the legal status of these microfinance institutions is not guaranteed legally. For example, a rural credit cooperative is in theory a cooperative institution taking deposits from its members and providing finance services to its members. In response to political needs, however, rural credit cooperatives are often changed into quasi-policy banks, profit-orientated financial institutions, or pure commercial banks. In similar vein, it is hard to say that village banks, loan corporations, and rural mutual finance societies would not be changed to meet the government's demands in the future. For this reason, the authors argue that the legal definition, characteristics, and business powers of the microfinance providers should be prescribed through a primary legislation, which is enacted by the NPC or its Standing Committee, ensuring that these specialist microfinance providers focus their services exclusively on members, and disadvantaged areas and people.

To facilitate the entry of more microfinance providers, an incentive-compatible entry policy should be adopted, that is, the entry threshold including capital, fit and proper requirements for shareholders and senior managements should be lowered, and the approval procedures should be simplified. It is understandable that no more institutions are interested in microfinance services if the entry requirements for general commercial banks are equally applied to microfinance providers. In China, the CBRC reduces greatly the registered capital for establishing a village bank, loan corporation, and rural mutual finance society.[101] The requirements for directors and senior management for a village bank are relaxed compared to those for a general commercial bank.[102] Under the Temporary Provisions on Administration of Village Banks and Temporary Provisions on Administration of Loan Corporations, other prudential requirements must be met in setting up a village bank and loan corporation.[103] It is doubtful whether the rule maker knows the true meaning of prudential requirements and how the banking regulator applies prudential requirements. There is indeed a risk that the entry threshold would be raised, if the banking regulator interprets prudential requirements in the sense of limiting the entry of village banks and loan corporations.

Common Program of Chinese Peoples' Political Consultative Conference, the same legislative level as the NPC, in September 1949. Under article 38 of the Common Program of Chinese Peoples' Political Consultative Conference, people in towns and villages are encouraged to form credit cooperatives on a voluntary basis. Although the Banking Supervision Law and Commercial Banking Law mention rural credit cooperatives, they do not prescribe the requirements for setting up a rural credit cooperative and the business powers of a rural credit cooperative. Village banks, loan corporations and rural mutual finance societies are formed, respectively, based on the Temporary Provisions on Administration of Village Banks, Temporary Provisions on Administration of Loan Corporations, and Temporary Provisions on Administration of Rural Mutual Finance Society issued by the CBRC in 2006.

[101] *See supra* notes 22, 32, and 40 and accompanying text.

[102] Temporary Provisions on Administration of Village Banks, art. 13.

[103] *Id.* art. 8(9); Temporary Provisions on Administration of Loan Corporations, art. 9(5).

It may be interesting if we re-consider the "economic needs" issue in the licensing process in the context of discussing microfinance provider entry. The economic needs standard is often invoked to withhold new bank authorizations, even if an applicant fulfills the establishment requirements. Therefore, the standard loses the dimension of encouraging banks to enter but rather is a synonym for an entry barrier. For this reason, the economic needs standard was abolished in some banking laws. For example, as early as the 1970s, the EC attempted to phase out the standard as a precondition for granting a license given that the applicant's head office was located within the EC states.[104] In China, the Commercial Banking Law of 2003 eliminated the requirement of the economic and competition needs in establishing a bank stipulated in the Commercial Banking Law of 1995.[105] In our opinion, the application of the economic needs standard as a bank entry barrier originates from the regulator's deep-rooted philosophy of ensuring the safety and soundness of banks. If financial inclusion is incorporated into the regulatory objectives or responsibilities, the economic needs standard would be interpreted and applied in the sense of increasing bank entry. It is therefore suggested that banking law may re-introduce the economic needs standard as an entry condition for the purpose of promoting financial inclusion.

Prudential requirements. Prudential regulation is mainly aimed at the safety and soundness of the banking system and depositor protection. The liability structure and risk contagion of banks justify prudential regulation. A loan corporation and rural mutual finance society conduct the business activities with their own capital or borrowed funds rather than the public deposits. They are by nature different from general commercial banks which accept deposits from the public. It is therefore unnecessary to apply prudential requirements such as capital adequacy, risk concentration, liquidity adequacy, and loan loss provisioning to loan corporations and rural mutual finance societies. The CBRC's current rules requiring them to comply with prudential requirements as applied to commercial banks[106] would greatly dampen the enthusiasm of microfinance providers.

Even for village banks, light touch prudential regulation should be applied. Although they mobilize deposits from the public, village banks deal in savings and credit transaction with limited areas, and low value, and therefore less risk contagion in relation to the system as a whole. As a result they are unlikely to produce the problem of systemic instability. Inherent in this consideration is the cost-effective test in prudential regulation. With a deposit insurance scheme available, it is sufficient for a village bank to be subject to less stringent

---

[104] First Council Directive 77/780 of 12 December 1977 on the Co-ordination of Laws, Regulations, and Administrative Provisions Relating to the Taking up and Pursuit of the Business of Credit Institutions, art. 3(2)(a).

[105] Commercial Banking Law of 1995, art. 12.

[106] *See supra* notes 34–35 and 44 and accompanying text.

requirements for capital adequacy, risk concentration control, and on- and off-site examination.

For example, it is well known that the risk-weighted capital adequacy requirement is complex and costly. It is more appropriate to apply the leverage ratio rather than the risk-weighted capital adequacy requirement to village banks. The basic function of capital adequacy is to protect depositors and to provide a cushion against the risks (including systemic risk) to which a bank is exposed. Because of the small number of depositors, low value of assets, and limited service areas, village banks would not produce a systemic risk even if they fail, and their depositors can be protected by the deposit insurance scheme or some form of government guarantee. Taking into account this reason, as well as the cost of capital, it is recommended that a lower leverage ratio should be applied to village banks. The leverage ratio serves mainly as the regulatory means by which the banking regulator can restrict unjustified asset expansion of a village bank.[107]

Take risk concentration control for another example, the imposition of a limit on loan size results in diversification of credit risk. In stark contrast to the credit concentration limits typically set for commercial banks which range from 15% to 30% of capital due to the availability of advanced risk measurement and monitoring systems, microfinance institutions are required to employ stricter limits. In Bolivia, the credit concentration limit for private financial funds and regulated credit unions is 1% of the institution's net worth.[108] Under the Temporary Provisions on Administration of Village Banks, loans to a single borrower extended by a village bank shall not exceed 5% of its capital in China.[109] However, the uniform risk concentration limit may restrict the ability of microfinance providers to provide financing to successful borrowers who need slightly larger amounts of credit. For example, a village bank with a capital of RMB 1 million can only extend RMB 50,000 at most to an enterprise, which may not meet the credit needs of the enterprise. This is why the authors suggest that it would be more desirable to adopt flexible risk concentration limits to accommodate different credit needs.[110]

Non-prudential regulation. Given that prudential regulation aiming at protecting the banking system as a whole, as well as protecting depositors, is

---

[107] Some authors argue that microfinance institutions and credit unions should be required to maintain higher capital adequacy ratios than banks because of their governance, diversification, and the volatility of earnings. However, there are not yet sufficient empirical data to firmly conclude that microfinance institutions are, as a general rule, more risky than commercial banks. *See* Tor Jansson, Ramón Rosales, and Glenn D. Westley, *Principles and Practices for Regulating and Supervising Microfinance* (Inter-American Development Bank, Sustainable Development Department, Micro, Small and Medium Enterprise Division, 2004), at 64–65.

[108] *See id.* at 67.

[109] Temporary Provisions on Administration of Village Banks, art. 41.

[110] *See* Tor Jansson, Ramón Rosales, and Glenn D. Westley, *supra* note 108, at 67 (stating that restrictive limits increase diversification and reduce risk but at the same time may prevent the institutions from effectively serving their most successful clients).

generally complex and burdensome, non-prudential regulation should be more applied to microfinance institutions. Non-prudential regulation is designed to enable more financial institutions to provide microfinancial services. Non-prudential regulatory issues relate to conduct of business of microfinance providers such as prevention of financial crimes, information disclosure, consumer protection, credit information collection, and flexible interest rate policy.[111] Even for general commercial banks, regulators tend to gradually shift their focus on the processes of managing risk from observance of prudential ratios. The banking regulator should ensure that the board of directors and senior management of a microfinance institution establish proper risk management, internal control systems, and sound corporate governance and adhere to accounting standards and procedures for internal and external reporting.

Acknowledgments The writing of this chapter was supported by the Program for New Century Excellent Talents in the University of Ministry of Education of China.

[111] *See also* Robert Peck, Christen, Timothy R. Lyman and Richard Rosenberg, *Microfinance Consensus Guidelines: Guiding Principles on Regulation and Supervision of Microfinance* (CGAP, 2003), at 6 (stating that non-prudential regulatory issues include enabling the formation and operation of microlending institutions; protecting consumers; preventing fraud and financial crimes; setting up credit information services; supporting secured transactions; developing policies with respect to interest rates; setting limitations on foreign ownership, management, and sources of capital; identifying tax and accounting issues; plus a variety of cross-cutting issues surrounding transformations from one institutional type to another).

Part IV
The Bond and Equity Market

The Chinese Bond Market: Historical Lessons, Present Challenges, and Future Perspectives

Haizhou Huang and Ning Zhu

Abstract This chapter reviews historical lessons, depicts present challenges, and discusses future perspectives of Chinese bond market. Historical lessons on sovereign right concession and market tumult lead to a quite cautious approach toward the bond market. The legal background and political considerations also played an important role in shaping bond market during the past two decades. Given the increasing demand for financing in China these days, the bond market is expected to enjoy some rapid growth in the coming decade and we discuss some areas with particular potentials and the challenges facing the development.

Keyword China financial markets · Bond market · Fixed income securities · Financial market history · Financial reform · Debt financing

China enjoyed some very impressive economic growth over the past decade. The economic growth generated great wealth to the country and at the same time demands increasing investment and financing for further expansion. Chinese equity market has so far expanded considerably and its high volatility and institutional arrangement[1] have attracted considerable attention. In contrast, the bond market, which is generally believed to be as important to economic growth as the equity market, remained obscure among the general public: Total value of outstanding bonds remain at a relatively low level in light of the total savings in the country; far fewer individual investors actively participate in the bond market than those that trade in the stock market; the

[1] See for research on rights offering and the linkage between Chinese equity market and the transition of state-owned enterprises.

H. Huang (✉)
China International Capital Corporation, Beijing, China
e-mail: huanghz2@cicc.com.cn

J.R. Barth et al. (eds.), *China's Emerging Financial Markets*,
The Milken Institute Series on Financial Innovation and Economic Growth 8,
DOI 10.1007/978-0-387-93769-4_17,

number of bond securities and bond derivatives being offered for trading remains limited; trading activities are light except for some treasury or central-bank bonds.

Bond markets are important to economic growth for the following apparent reasons. From a macroeconomic perspective, the cash flow provided by bond securities correlates well with obligations of many institutional investors (banks, pension funds, insurance companies, etc.) and helps such investors better match the maturity of their assets and liabilities and manage risks. The bond market is particularly important to the transition of the Chinese banking sector, which has been ailing with the problem of non-performing loans. A more developed bond market is useful in helping the banking sector diversify the risk of its holdings and provide much-needed capital to the state-owned enterprises, which used to heavily rely on bank loans.

A microscopic view at the firm level also highlights the importance of bond financing. The pecking order theory in modern corporate finance theory mandates that debt financing is cheaper and therefore more attractive than the alternative way of financing through issuing equities for many companies. Another important feature of the bond market in developed markets is that bond investors play an active role in monitoring and governing corporate managers who tend to waste *free cash flow,* cash flow in excess of that required to fund all projects with positive net present values. It seems that the growth of the bond market can help restore investor trust and confidence in the stock market.

Given its importance, the question seems particularly puzzling as to why the Chinese bond market has not developed at a faster pace. One objective of the chapter is to review the history of the Chinese bond market, outline the current state of the market, discuss the opportunities and challenges that face the market, and offer some guidance for the long-term development of the bond market. By reviewing the history of Chinese bond market, we come to understand that the reservation with the bond market today can partly be traced back to more than a century ago in Qing dynasty. It turns out that the legal background and political considerations from history leave a considerable footprint on the development of the bond market today.

We attempt to understand the legal and political reasons why there was a stark contrast between international and domestic bond financing: while both the government and infrastructure projects relied heavily on foreign bond issuance under the pre-communist governments, there was little activity in the domestic bond issuance. Historical evidence points out that the weak government credibility and lack of contract enforcement was directly responsible for the faltering growth of Chinese domestic bond market in Qing dynasty and Republic of China Regime. Because investors were concerned about the enforceability of the lending contracts, they were unwilling to lend money to people that they did not know and slow in accepting the bond markets.

In contrast, the large-scale foreign borrowing during the same period took place only on the premise that Chinese borrowers, the government or private parties, have to abide by the much stricter Western civil law code in order to obtain bond financing. In order to ensure their investment outcome, foreign investors went to take direct control of Chinese fiscal sources. Although such arrangements temporarily reduce the cost of capital that Chinese borrowers faced, they ended up with exhausting Chinese sovereign income ultimately and caused the fall of the Qing government.

Interestingly, we feel that the bond market's moderate growth during the past two decades since the early 1980s can partly be attributed to reasons quite opposite to those in the history. Years after profound changes have taken place during the economic reforms, the central government still plays a dominant role in allocating credit in the economy, which limits the bond market's role of resource allocation. Bank loans, originating mostly from state-owned banks, lead the financing of most large-scale enterprises. Bond financing, in contrast, is only accessible to companies that are believed to have the highest credit-worthiness and ironclad security, because regulators are concerned about losing control of those companies in the event of default. Given that the government is the debtor for the treasury bond and ultimate debtor for most corporate bonds issued by large state-owned enterprises, the regulators' concerns about credit quality and default risk are not unwarranted and make debt financing somewhat less appealing.

Putting the current Chinese bond market into a historical perspective partly helps justify the moderate growth the bond market lately. Nevertheless, recent economic growth in China and the bond market development around the world both point to a more developed bond market in China in the near future. It is critical that the market plays an increasing role in allocating resources and stimulating sustainable growth. Consistent with such a spirit, we believe that Chinese bond market will witness unprecedented growth in the decades to come. As more companies, including large-scale state-owned enterprises, start financing through domestic and international equity market and instill modern corporate finance and governance, we expect the bond market to play a much more important role as companies become more sensitive to cost of capital and look for alternative ways of financing in the future. As a consequence, we expect a robust growth in Chinese bond market in the coming decades.

The rest of the chapter is organized as follows: Section 1 reviews the history of Chinese bond market till 1949; Section 2 discusses the development of the bond market along with the economic growth under central planning regime and the recent transition to market economy, with a focus on the recent developments of the past few years; Section 3 puts the current development of the bond market into a historical perspective and offers projections about the future development of the bond market; before we conclude in Section 4.

1 History

We will start by reviewing the bond market within two distinct periods: the Qing dynasty before 1911 and the Republic of China regime between 1911 and 1949.

1.1 Qing Dynasty

1.1.1 Government Bonds Issued Overseas

China' access to the bond market can be traced to as early as late Qing dynasty. Provincial government started tapping foreign bond markets during the Taiping rebellion in 1861, and then again in 1862 to control bandits in Fukien and Taiwan. Reliance upon foreign merchants continued in 1867 and 1868 with loans to finance the war against Islamic rebels in western China. Such moves toward foreign financing were primarily motivated by the local governments' desperate need for alternative financing channels, after the central government itself was under great pressure of paying indemnities resulting from a series of wars with the West. Most of such provincial loans were secured on provincial shares of maritime customs, which started the tradition of using maritime customs as collateral for many subsequent foreign bonds issued by various levels of the Qing government.

According to Goetzmann et al. (2005), who compiled and coded all Chinese external loans listed in Kuhlmann (1983) and Stanley (1970), Chinese external loans over the late 19th and early 20th centuries were essentially securitized maritime custom duties. In addition to being one of the largest sources of government revenue, maritime custom duties were particularly attractive to foreigners because they were collected directly by foreign government officials at Chinese ports. By gaining access to the foreign capital market, the imperial government gradually put various sources of its fiscal income into foreigners' hands.

The next waves of government bonds were issued to defend against the Japanese designs on Taiwan in 1874, the war against France in the 1880s, and the 1894/1895 war with Japan. Most of such loans were again secured on the maritime customs. The Boxer Indemnity of £67.5 million, the debt settled on China by the consortium of powers after the Boxer Rebellion (which was divided among 14 powers with roughly 75% going to Russia, Germany, France, and Great Britain), was probably the last foreign issuance that relied on maritime custom as collaterals, before the outstanding loans absorbed the remaining unpledged portion of China's customs revenues and placed her import taxes entirely under foreign control.

With her customs revenues largely pledged after 1900, China had to promise alternative sources of revenue as collateral on major loans. Some of the last obligations of the Chinese Imperial Government such as the 1910 Kiagnan loan issued in France and Belgium were secured by salt taxes. Internal transit taxes, called likin(厘金), which was in existence after the Tai-Ping Rebellion in 1860s, were pledged more commonly as security on Chinese external loans in 1898, 1909, 1911, and in 1912. Goetzmann et al. (2005) report that Chinese foreign bonds during the period were secured on an amazing array of specific government revenues, including salt taxes, internal provincial transfer taxes [likin], mining taxes, alcohol and tobacco taxes, opium revenues, property transfer taxes, and revenues for railways. Of course, verification and collection of these revenues was an important feature of the loan contract. The Qing dynasty lost virtually all of its fiscal income before it collapsed.

1.1.2 Domestic Government Bonds

In contrast to its heavy dependence on foreign bond financing, there has been a very limited number of domestic bond issuances recorded in the Goetzmannn et al. (2005) study. A combination of reasons, including the royal's unwillingness to condescend and borrow from its own citizens, the lack of understanding about modern finance, and insufficient interest in investing in her majesty's government, are all potentially responsible for this contrast.

The question remains as to why China could not develop its own domestic bond market. Although the Qing dynasty was greatly weakened after several rebellions and foreign invasions, it was once very strong and affluent. Although some early forms of banks and savings and loans (S&Ls) came into existence, interest remained limited in having a developed domestic bond market. Several explanations are in place. First of all, the Qing government was not interested in promoting civil commercial activities and did not intend to develop a domestic bond financing market. A related factor is that the lack of a civil law system made it very difficult to enforce contracts at relatively low cost. Finally, with a large fraction of the wealth and the powers of taxing held in the hands of the royal family, they would not condescend to borrow from common people.

It seems that the bond market can develop well when there is a strong enough government which can enforce borrowing contracts, or in some cases, the government itself becomes a major borrower in the market. In addition, it is worth pointing out that the governments, at the same time, have to be willing to abide by the rule of the market and carry out transactions just like any other party in the market. The interesting example of the United Kingdom is that the bond market only started developing robustly after the royal family agreed to borrow from the market using future tax revenues as collateral and to honor the bond contract with the establishment of the Bank of England, a privately owned bank that can enforce the royals' borrowing contract. That is, the royals borrow in just the same fashion as any other market participant does. Such equality in the market ensures the credibility of the government, and at the same time, the market itself. In contrast, the Qing dynasty royal family considered it a disgrace to borrow from the commons and shut the door of domestic government bond financing.

1.1.3 Corporate Bonds

At the same time that government expanded its borrowing from foreign capital markets. A series of large infrastructure and defense projects turned to foreign markets for capital as well. Most significant of all corporate bonds are the bonds issued to raise capital for building railways.

Virtually all of China's railways constructed after 1895 were financed by foreign debt issuances underwritten by European-led investment banking syndicates which obtained right of way, property concessions, and promises of repayment from the Chinese Imperial government.[2] Under the control of the bankers who financed the loans, Chinese railways were constructed, owned, operated, and policed by managers designated by the financial consortium. Foreign debtors enjoy unprecedented protection of their investments at the expense of local residents in the area. For example, the most contentious feature of these loans was their provision for extra-territorial rights, which in essence "means the substitution of the court procedure of a creditor country for the business practices of the debtor country." That is, foreigners enjoy jurisdiction over part of Chinese territory. In retrospect, such concessions clearly indicates that the Qing government was at the mercy of foreign investors and had to give up its sovereignty to raise capital.

For example, the Chinese Eastern Railway reflects many distinct features of the railway built during the era. The Russo-Chinese bank issued a 5 million tael loan in Russia in 1896 to finance the construction of a railway across Manchuria linking the Trans-Siberian Railway to Vladivostok. Russia initiated such a blueprint largely to shorten the travel time from central Russia to its far east territory. Not only did the Qing government grant Russia to build such a railway, but it also agreed to raise capital for the construction for the Russian-backed bank. The railway and its right of way were entirely administered and policed by Russian officials, who controlled the receipts and disbursements. Till the 1920s, over 120,000 Russian citizens lived in Manchuria, accounting for a quarter of the population of the city and over 20,000 Russians worked for the China Eastern Railway. The line even issued its own currency and was in effect a little bit of Russian territory within China's borders.

Such concession of sovereign rights sparked numerous protests, reflecting in part Chinese citizens' request for sovereign rights and also Chinese investors' demand to have the investment opportunities. As some wealthy Chinese individuals realized the lucrative nature of such railway loans, they intended to grab a share of the market for themselves.

The highlight of the clash between foreign and domestic investors, between national and provincial powers, and between Chinese sovereign rights and foreign extra-territorial rights was the struggle over the Hukuang loan, the financing of a railway project that goes through a wealthy central-China area. In 1905, a consortium of Hukuang gentry, officials and businessmen, with the blessing and participation of the provincial governor Chang Chih-Tung, obtained a concession to develop a domestically financed rail line through Hukuang. It came after the successful provincial lobbying for compensated cancellation of the development rights of J.P. Morgan's American China Development Company, which actually fronted for a Belgian rail development

[2] For a specific example of the Chinese Eastern Railway, See Goetzmann et al. 2005

firm seeking to construct a line from Canton (Guangzhou) to Hankow. The line was a key route through Hukuang linking a commercial port to the cross-roads of Chinese rail lines in the interior, and the cancellation of the foreign concession opened the door for domestic development.

After the cancellation of the American concession, the Hukuang gentry took an active role in gaining concessions. For example, the Canton-Hankow line was divided between two domestic concessionaires, one in Kwangtung (Guangdong) and the other in Hunan. The experience of the Kwangtung company illustrates some of the problems of corporate governance experienced in the emerging Chinese legal framework. The firm was among the most successful of Chinese companies at capital subscription. All 4 million Taels was raised, much of it from wealthy overseas Chinese investors.

Unfortunately, the company ran into a series of scandals after a successful start and fell victim to massive embezzlement. Ultimately, the Qing dynasty government granted the issuance rights to the foreign consortium, as a result of diplomacy and political pressure. Such decisions stirred a nationalist movement to regain Chinese rights and overthrow the Manchu governance which coincided with the fall of the regime. Some historians believe that the struggle over the Hukuang loan sparked the 1911 revolution and led to the end of 3,000 years of dynastic rule, epitomizing how mis-handling of financial decisions can have a disastrous shock for the issuing authority.

The Hukuang Railway loan was the last external debt of the Chinese Imperial Government, and it defaulted in the 1920s. China as a nation continued to borrow for railway development until late into the 1930s – rail loans appear in 1934, 1935, 1936, and 1937. The only significant gaps in railroad bond issuance in the database are 1926 and 1927 (coinciding with Chiang Kai-shek (蒋介石)'s northern military campaign to unify China) and the first four years of the Great Depression of the 1930s. With these exceptions, Chinese railway financing and development by foreign investors continued in the face of civil war and eventual foreign occupation.

Lessons from the railway exemplify the potential hazards of bond financing. Creditors had the potential of not only protecting their investment, but overreaching into Chinese territory. Railway construction, which was originally designed to unite the nation, indeed tore it apart for the West. Seemingly economic transactions were unfortunately clouded by political struggles, which left lasting unfavorable memories of bond financing.

One notable pattern about Chinese bonds issued during the period from the Goetzmann et al. (2005) is that the yields of Chinese foreign bonds were strikingly flat, in light of the political and military turmoil of China and the volatile international capital market during the same period. This was not quite due to choice – the stability in Chinese bond prices in the first decade of the twentieth century is almost certainly attributable to the foreign control of Chinese government revenues.

By investigating a couple of political events, the 1894–1895 war with Japan and the funding of the Boxer Indemnities in 1901, the authors point out that new bond issuances secured on alternative fiscal sources had little impact on the pricing of outstanding loans, which were guaranteed by pre-stipulated securities. Such findings may seem odd at first glance because such military and political events should affect the issuing authority, which changes the likelihood of payment of the security. However, if foreign investors believe that their claim protection was ironclad, we would expect to see little price reaction to political events.

In stark contrast with such apparent security in its foreign bonds, holders of Chinese domestic bonds have gone through several defaults and reorganizations and ultimately lost most of their investment as a consequence of the vicious inflation preceding 1949. It seems that the protection of foreign bondholders, who mostly hold senior claim to and direct control over the security, came at least in part at the cost of China's sovereignty and domestic investors.

1.2 1911–1949 – The Period of War Lords and the Republic of China

Paradoxically, the very transparency and accountability of the maritime customs revenues that guaranteed bondholder security in a series of foreign bonds also restricted the ability of the new Republic of China's access to cash when needed. Bond financing may seem to carry a low cost early on but turned out not to be a bargain from a historical perspective. With fluctuating fiscal income and constrained access to future bond financing, the Republic kept running into fiscal problems when wars, infrastructure projects, and natural disaster called for considerable financing. Such fiscal constraints arguably have considerable bearing on the economy, outcomes of wars, and ultimately the fate of the regime.

1.2.1 Government Bonds Issued Overseas

Although the fall of the Qing dynasty in 1911 historically signified the end of imperial governance in China, it did not have much noticeable impact on the foreign bonds issued before the incident. Chinese Republic agreed to honor the debts of the previous government, as a condition upon which it gained the recognition by the great powers.

Following the Qing practice of securing bond issuances with fiscal incomes, the first major loan of the new Republic in 1912 (the 5% Crisp Gold Loan), floated in London, negotiated and approved by the new political leaders Sun Yat-sen 孙逸仙 and Yuan Shi-kai 袁世凯, was backed explicitly by salt revenues. The subsequent loans issued by a variety of Chinese government during the same period in 1911, 1917, 1918, 1922, and 1937 were also secured by salt revenues.

During the period between 1937 and 1949, China went through a series of wars and relied heavily upon foreign aids to balance off its budget. Because of a series of default and reorganization in the 1920–1930s, which hurt the government's credit in repaying its obligations, and the escalating military confrontation during the period, foreign bond issuance was severely interrupted during the period.

1.2.2 Domestic Government Bonds

Although the Imperial government relied almost exclusively on foreign debt, the Republic government started to issue domestic debt immediately after the revolution. Table 2 of Goetzmann et al. (2005) provides a comprehensive summary of domestic government bonds. In 1914, the Republic government established a new agency, Internal Debts Bureau, to overlook the issuance of domestic public debts. One problem with the agency was that most of the high-ranking officers of this bureau were foreigners, although the targeted investors of the bond issues were primarily domestic citizens. The bureau had to cope with the challenge that most Chinese domestic bonds during that time were insufficiently secured – foreign bondholders held senior claim to the security to domestic bondholders. Many domestic debts were secured with the remainder of customs revenues, which were largely pledged to previous foreign debts. Demand for domestic issuance indeed surged in the 1920s, partly due to the financing for the military clashes between the war lords.

Not surprisingly, such extensive borrowing without cash flow backing brought the government to the verge of bankruptcy. In the 1920s, the Republic government defaulted on domestic as well as foreign loans and had to reorganize its debts. After the Nanjing Government took control of most of the country in the late 1920s, it further increased the size of domestic public debt issuance, resulting in another default in 1929. The paper annual yield of most previous public debts was reduced from 7 to 8% down to 6% and the reorganization plan also extended the maturity of the debts to twice as long as originally designed. Shortly after the reorganization, the government picked up the speed of public debt issuance again. The ever-increasing size of public debts put the government into default again in 1935. The government issued 2,082,000,000 Yuan worth of public debts in 1936 to reorganize its debts, which is the largest issuance in a single year till then.

After the Sino-Japanese war broke out in 1937, the Republic issued various domestic bonds during the 8 years of the war. A shift in the issuance process was that such bonds were no longer targeted at individual investors, but at institutions such as banks. Paradoxically, with the weakening of the central government, the banks in Shanghai – China's money center – became relatively strong. While the government defaulted frequently, Chinese banks in this era gained and maintained a sterling reputation. To attract investment from Chinese living overseas, some debts were issued in foreign currencies outside China. In addition to regular debts, the government also issued debt denominated in commodities such as wheat and rice. Because the regular taxes and custom revenues decreased dramatically during the Sino-Japanese War, the public debts issued during that period were at even greater risk of default.

Eventually, inflation solved the government's problems at the expense of domestic bondholders. The inflation of the 1940s decreased the real value of investments by 90%. Finally, the "Currency Reform" of 1948 issued a new currency at a rate of 3,000,000 to 1 to original currencies, wiping out most existing domestic debt.

The development of the domestic bond market during the period should be interpreted as a necessity, instead of initiation from the government. The republic government went into continuous financial distress as a result of disrupted revenue incomes and escalating warfare-related expenses. As the government exhausted its cash flows, the possibility of raising foreign bonds diminished, and the government was forced to raise capital from domestic investors. Unfortunately, due to poor government financing and constant change of powers in the country, the government did not establish itself as a trustworthy borrower. Instead, the government had used its superior power to reset the bond contracts in its own favor, which hurt many domestic investors. Consequently, even if there were more domestic bond issuances and trading than during the Qing dynasty, the quality of the market did not improve much. As a matter of fact, the domestic bond market damaged the image of the bond market in China, and domestic investors became very suspicious of bond financing after suffering steep personal losses.

1.2.3 Corporate Bonds

Possibly as a by-product of the development of the domestic government bond market, the domestic corporate bond market enjoyed some developments during the same period as well. Over 20 enterprises issued bonds in the domestic market. Unfortunately, continuous warfare, unstable governments, and poor contract enforcement led many of the investors to little return for their investment, which further hurt the bond financing's credibility and its long-term development in China.

2 The Present State

A few bonds were issued to assist the economic development and curb the vicious inflation soon after the People's Republic was founded. Most of such bonds were subscribed by patriotic citizens or former "capitalists" under political pressure. These bonds were quite useful in stabilizing the transitory economy and providing the much-needed capital for the new government. There was little trading activities on such bonds, hence little bond market activities.

Not surprisingly, the bond market withered during the next three decades, when the economy was under central planning. The most powerful economic decision-making agency was the State Economic Planning Commission, which allocated credit (often treated as grants for the state-owned enterprises (SOEs)), controlled prices, and managed total supply. The financial system was downgraded to one agency, under the umbrella of the People's Bank of China, which was in fact the central bank as well as the whole banking system, as there were no other banks (aside from small credit unions operating in the rural area), insurance companies, or securities firms. Few bonds were issued except for treasury bonds, which were issued as an alternative form of savings and subscribed as an act of patriotism, rather than as investment.

As the Chinese economy reopened itself to the foreign market and became the focus of the country in the early 1980s, the bond market witnessed resurgence in interest as well. In addition to the more traditional treasury bond issuance (which is often considered a superior way of saving), SOEs started issuing bonds with great enthusiasm during the early 1990s. One needs to be careful, however, in concluding that such sudden growth in the quasi-corporate bond market was a reflection of the maturity of the market or the issuing firms. Quite the contrary, such issuances largely represented distorted incentives facing the large SOEs during the economic transition (see Yi, 1999). Because most of such firms were strictly subsidiaries of various levels of government agencies, they were not financially or legally constrained by bankruptcy prospects, that is, they would face little adverse consequences if there were a debt default or bankruptcy filing. On the other hand, the management had every incentive to borrow at whatever interest rates because such borrowings provided capital for the firms to expand while posing little binding constraints on the SOEs.

As a consequence, SOEs issued excessive corporate obligations in the early 1990s, and many of them ended up in default and resulted as non-performing assets in the balance sheet of the state-owned banks, the major holders of those securities. The State Economic Planning Commission decided to close down the corporate bond market. That ban over a decade ago is still having a major impact on the regulatory sentiment and the structure of corporate bonds in China. As the bond market is considered "risky" compared to commercial bank lending, the latter received more encouragement during the past decade, which further solidifies the main banking system, where banks play the major role of credit allocation. Despite the inefficiency in the main banking system as pointed out by many experts, a financial system based on balanced contributions from and complementary functions between financial markets and banks is still a long way down the road, and the bond market has to develop robustly to assist in such a transition.

2.1 Market Infrastructure

Before discussing the development of each sector of the bond market, as we did with the history of the market, we would like to first offer some overview of the Chinese bond market these days. The total value of outstanding bonds was

CNY 7,831 billion yuans at the end of October, 2006. There are primarily four types of bonds in the Chinese domestic bond market: treasury bonds (2,149 billion yuans, or 27.4% of total outstanding bonds), central bank notes (2,931 billion yuans, or 37.4%), financial bonds (2,097 billion yuans, or 26.8%), and corporate bonds (170 billion yuans, or 2.2%). A closer look at the more dynamic bond issuance during the period January–October 2006 indicates that among treasury bonds (563 billion yuans, or 12.4% of new issuances), central bank notes (3,033 billion yuans, or 67%), financial bonds (584 billion yuans, or 12.9%) and corporate bonds (80 billion yuans, or 1.8%), central bank notes make up two-thirds of the total of 4,526 billion yuan new issuances, while corporate bonds only account for a mere 1.8%.[3]

The primary market of bond issuance is largely completed through syndication. Governmental bonds were mostly underwritten by the four stated-owned banks, while other commercial banks and securities companies play an active role in forming a syndicate to market financial and corporate bonds. Most of the bonds are held by banks, insurance companies, securities firms, and corporations. Mutual funds hold a relatively small fraction of the total outstanding bonds. Starting late 2002, China loosened regulation on foreign investors investing in Treasury bond. The launching of Qualified Foreign Institutional Investor (QFII) offers foreign capital an opportunity to invest in the Chinese bond market. International Finance Corporation (IFC) and Asian Development Bank (ADB) were allowed to issue CNY-denominated bonds in China in 2005.

The secondary bond market is somewhat segmented in a sense that there are three markets: the interbank bond market, the exchange market, and the over-the-counter (OTC) market. The interbank bond market is by far the most active and important one among the three. The interbank bond market relies on the National Inter-bank Funding Center (hereunder referred to as the "interbank center") and the Central T-bond Registration and Settlement Co., Ltd. (hereunder referred to as the "central registration company") and provides a market for the bond transactions and repurchases of commercial banks, rural credit cooperatives, insurance companies, securities firms, and other financial institutions. Most book-entry T-bonds, policy financial bonds are listed and traded in this market. At the end of 2005, there was over 5,000 billion CNY yuan worth bonds deposited at the inter-bond market, over 400 of which were in active trading. Some bonds and bond derivatives started being listed in the Shanghai stock exchanges in the early 2000s, and the OTC market remained moderately active.

Some attempts to launch fixed-income derivatives securities, such as futures and repurchase agreements, were made during the early 1990s. Due to several trading anomalies and scandals, the trading on treasury futures was suspended not too long after the market was born. Starting in early 2000s, some new derivatives products, such as outright repurchase agreement, were introduced.

[3] For insightful discussion on China and Asian regional bond markets development, see, among others, Gynthelberg et al. (2005), Scott and Ho (2004), and Rhee (2000).

The issuance and transactions of Treasury bonds, central bank bills, and various notes are under the respective purview of Ministry of Finance, People's Bank of China, and National Development Reform Commission (NDRC), in accordance with the securities law. The Ministry of finance and Peoples' Bank of China set important guidelines for the quota of bond issuance and China Bank Regulatory Commission oversees the secondary market.

From January 4, 2007, a set of new benchmark interbank market rates, the Shanghai Interbank Offered Rate (Shibor), consisting of overnight rate, 1-week rate, 2-week rate, 1-month rate, 3-month rate, 6-month rate, 9-month rate, and 1-year rate, was established.

2.2 *Government Bonds Issued Overseas*

As of end September, 2006, China's total foreign debt stood at US $305 billion, rising 8.5% from the year-end 2005. The foreign debts were about equally split between long- and medium-term bonds, and short-term bonds, each accounting for 44.7% and 55.3% of the total value. Such an amount of outstanding bond is widely believed to be within the "manageable" range given a much bigger value that China holds in its foreign exchange reserve ($1.066 trillion by end 2006). Bond issuance only accounts for a small fraction of the total amount of foreign debt, which often takes the form of privately negotiated bank loans. In addition to the government, other borrowers also tap the international bond market. By June 2005, debt issued by sovereign government, foreign-invested enterprises, domestic financial institutions, foreign-invested financial institutions, and domestic enterprises each represented 34.4, 23.2, 24, 7.2, 10.7% of the foreign debts.

It is important that the Chinese government seems to display a contrasting attitude toward equity and bond financing. While the government has been encouraging the development of the stock market since its inception in the early 1990s, similar initiatives were lacking in the bond market. Such a contrast can in part be explained by the political and legal consideration outlined earlier in the chapter and illustrated by the history of the bond market.

In contrast to equity financing that gives shareholders a fraction of the residual ownership, creditors holding debt claims could conceivably grab the entire issuing entity, posing unlikely but graver economic consequences to the enterprises than equity financing does. Sovereign bond issuance is tied closely to a government's fiscal and budgetary situation and ability to repay. Default on sovereign bonds can lead to erosion of sovereign and governmental rights, a phenomenon that China has vividly witnessed during its early access to international bond market. A series of foreign bond issuance in late 1800s and early 1900s virtually gave away all Chinese governmental revenues to foreign bondholders, a fact that had profound impact on the path of Chinese history in the following decades. The colonial history of China reminds the current policy makers of the potential hazards of relying heavily on debt financing, especially foreign bond financing. Learning from its historical lessons, the current government manages to vigilantly balance its budget, in both domestic and foreign bond market, which results in conservatism with the bond market and explains the modest pace of the bond market.

In addition to the erosion of sovereign debts, the current policy makers are also aware of the volatile history of bond yields under the China Republic regime before 1949. If bond market were to develop further, it is inevitable that the market will have greater influences over all kinds of interest rates, which ultimately affect the interest rates that banks can charge. Thanks to a series of regulations, the banking sector currently enjoys the monopoly of setting interest rate, which greatly alleviate the nonperforming loan problems and the state-owned enterprises' underfunding crisis. Should the banks and policy makers yield such discretion to the open market, the stability of the bond market and more importantly the entire economy, will be brought under question. Therefore, the government is taking a more conservative approach to the bond market, compared to its attitude toward the stock market.

2.3 Domestic Government Bonds (Treasury Bonds and Central Bank Bills)

Treasury bonds are issued to meet the national government's budgetary needs. Issuance has been fairly limited partly because China's fiscal position has been strong over the last several years (tax revenues increased by over 20% in 2006). Over the last two years, new issuance has been CNY 600bn–700bn a year. Another reason for the moderate T-bond issuances, according to some foreign scholars, was the increasing use of policy financial bonds (not showing up in the national budgetary estimate) by stated-owned and policy banks.[4] With the rapid growth of tax revenues, the total amount of financial bonds (2,097 billion yuans in October 2006) became smaller than that of treasury bonds (2,149 billion yuans).

Before 1993, treasury bonds were issued exclusively as physical printer bonds, with which holders could redeem at maturity. Investors do not have much choice in investing in treasury bonds as there were limited alternative investment opportunities and treasury bond underwriting was completed as part of administrative assignments. After 1993, treasury bonds started being issued as book-entry bonds and certificate bonds. Accordingly, the underwriting of treasury bonds has shifted from administrative assignment to syndication, which most of the time involves the four state-owned banks.

[4] For example, Nicolas Lardy points out in his article that the budget estimate is misleading and the governmental debt is underestimated. China's Worsening Debts, *The Financial Times*, June 22, 2001, Nicholas R. Lardy.

An advantage of the book-entry and certificate bonds is that trading in the secondary market is greatly facilitated. Before 1988, there was hardly a market where treasury bonds could be traded. The preliminary bond market was established in 1988 when treasury bonds could be traded for the first time. After stock exchanges were established in the early 1990s, most of the bonds and bond derivatives (repurchase agreement) were traded at the stock exchanges. In 1997, commercial banks pulled out from the stock exchange and established the interbank bond market, and the over-the-counter (OTC) bond market was started a few years later in 2002. Most recently, the outright repo agreement can be traded both at the stock exchange and in the interbank bond market.

Another form of governmental obligations, the central bank notes is much larger than treasury bonds in issuing size. We may recall that the total amount of newly issued treasury bonds was 563 billion yuans, or 12.4% of new issuances, while central bank notes reached 3,033 billion yuans, or 67% of new issuance in the period January–October 2006, as described above. PBOC, the central bank, started open market operations in late 1990s and used central bank notes as an important tool to adjust money supply and prime interest rate. In recent years, faced with increasing capital inflows and inadequate supply of MoF bonds, PBOC issued more of its own notes to conduct OMOs and "sterilize" the large capital inflows. In 2006, PBOC issued CNY3.03tn yuan notes, mostly in 1-year maturity. Over the period of 2003–2006, PBOC mopped out about CNY3tn yuan liquidity through issuance of central bank notes (see PBoC February 2007).

Currently, Chinese local and municipal governments are not allowed to issue their own bonds, despite the quasi-deficit of local governments and their financing being an important issue.[5,6] Local governments used to rely exclusively on fiscal appropriation from the central government, and thus budgeting and financing used to be an important tool that central government used to keep local government in check. As economy growth spreads to more areas of China, local governments need increasing capital for infrastructure development, and the central government can no longer shoulder the fiscal pressures alone. Consequently, the central government is looking at the possibility of issuing local government bonds. Similar to other forms of governmental financing, municipal bond issuances opens the possibility of excessive borrowing by the local governments, which can jeopardize government sovereignty, increase the financial risks at the national level, and weaken budgetary incentives that the central government can use as discipline tools over local governments.

---

[5] http://english.people.com.cn/200404/15/eng20040415_140484.shtml

[6] Some estimates indicate that the quasi-deficit caused by over borrowing by local governments can be a sizable portion of China's GDP.

2.4 Corporate Bonds and Corporate Short-Term Bills

Corporate bonds market witnessed a tumultuous history during its growth (Zhou, 2005). The market grew slowly in the early 1980s with only a limited number of SOEs being allowed in the market. During the early 1990s, local governments obtained permission to enable local government-owned enterprises to issue bonds and raised considerable amount of capital through the bond market. Many of the issuers defaulted and caused financial instability. Consequently, the central government took steps to separate the securities and banking industry in the mid-1990s, which led the size of the market to fall back to their 1980s level.

The caution exercised with the corporate bond market is in someway similar to that with other forms of the bond market. Bearing in mind that the state owns the majority of large-scale enterprises and financial institutions, one can understand why the government is unwilling to take any chance with potential corporate default and loss of control over the companies. The high hurdle set for corporate bonds can be thought of as a defense mechanism against potential risk of takeover by creditors. Although a large number of SOEs could benefit from bond-financing, there is the risk that state-owned assets may be possessed by creditors, especially foreign ones, like what happened to Chinese railway loans about a century ago. Until very recently, only firms with very sound financial situations were granted access to the bond market, while others in greater need of bond financing were left out of the market.

Corporate bond growth rate increased by over 100% in 2005, but the growth momentum did not last in 2006. A total of CNY101.5bn in corporate bonds was issued in 2006, compared to CNY100.6bn in the first three-quarters of 2005. To avoid the irregularities in the 1990s, the central government takes very cautious steps in developing the corporate bond market. All corporate bond issuance have to be approved by the National Development Reform Commission (NDRC) and must be guaranteed. In addition, only firms of the highest credit ratings can access the corporate bond market. Almost all issuers enjoy the AAA rating. In addition to the limitation in the primary market, the legality of different secondary markets of corporate bonds market remains ambiguous. The two stock exchanges are the only legal exchanges where such bonds can be traded, in the strictest sense, but these two markets only observe modest trading of corporate bond markets. As a result, only about one-half of the corporate bonds are listed and even less are available for trading in the two stock exchanges. Due to the above constraints, the development of long-term corporate bonds has been moderate.

The Administrative Rules for Short-term Financing Bills was published on May 23, 2005 and stimulated the recent growth of the bond market. Short-term corporate bills are issued on the interbank market, which is regulated and supported by PBOC. Such institutional arrangement addresses the problem of the lengthy application process and the needed guarantee, and provides more flexibility to corporate bond issuance. Notwithstanding, issuances are almost restricted only to companies with very good credit ratings, and such short-term financing bills have to mature within 91 days. In 2006, 210 firms issued CNY433.7bn yuan short-term bills.

2.5 *Policy and Financial Bonds*

Policy bond is issued by Chinese policy banks (State Development Bank, China Import and Export Bank, and China Agriculture Development Bank) and often represent subordinated debt. A total of CNY584 billion policy financial bonds were issued during the first 10 months in 2006. Other financial institutions, such as commercial banks, commercial insurance companies, city commercial banks, rural credit cooperatives, and post offices, issue financial bonds, their own subordinated debt, to raise capital. Issuance of policy and financial bonds has to be approved by the State Council and PBOC according to the market issuing mode.

On 27 April 2005, PBOC promulgated the Measures Governing the Issuance of Financial Bonds on the National Inter-bank Bond Market (the Measures). The Measures came into force as of 1 June 2005 and represent a major attempt by China's central bank to standardize the activities of issuing financial bonds on the national interbank bond market. Such measures aim at standardizing the issuance on the national interbank bond market and improve the market-based framework as well as the fairness and effectiveness of market regulation.

The new measures are believed to have a positive impact on the development of the financial bond market and further economic reform. First, a transparent and standard issuance process will encourage more issuers to issue financial bonds. Second, policy/finance bonds enable deposit-taking institutions to better match maturity and reduce financial risks. Banks can take advantage of more policy/financial bonds to improve their balance sheet. Third, the enactment of the Measures will increase the number of issuers from different credit categories. This will increase market competition, enhance pricing efficiency, and attract more investors to participate in the bond market.

On 10 January 2007, the State Council approved a new policy allowing Chinese policy and commercial banks with high credit rating, upon obtaining approval from relevant authorities, to issue CNY denominated bonds in Hong Kong. PBOC will accordingly provide corresponding clearing arrangements for this new business.

In sum, the new measures and new policies permitting CNY denominated bonds to be issued by Chinese financial institution in Hong Kong are largely welcomed by the market because they serve to improve the asset and liability management capacity of financial institutions, expand direct financing, and increase the number of investment portfolios available to investors. It is therefore hoped that the Measures as well as the new policies permitting CNY denominated bonds to be issued in Hong Kong will facilitate the healthy development of the financial bond market in the long run. [7,8]

---

[7] http://www.hg.org/articles/article_787.html

[8] Nonetheless, there is some reservation that the measures will dampen the bond market in the short run due to worries over an excessive supply of bonds.

3 The Future

3.1 Current Challenges

3.1.1 Limited Participation and Lack of Liquidity

Although the size of outstanding bonds does not seem particularly small in light of the size of the Chinese equity market, one consensus among policy makers and practitioners is the lack of participation and the resulting illiquidity in the bond market. Notwithstanding that PBOC has approved many more participants, ranging from insurance companies to corporate pension funds to trade in the interbank bond market over the years (see Table 1), currently banks and

Table 1 Major bond market developments in China

Time	Event
1988	Ministry of Finance began issuing treasury bonds in 61 cities in China as an experiment.
1990 (December)	Establishment of the Shanghai Stock Exchange, which permitted trading of bonds
1994	Short sales of treasury bonds were permitted, raising market risk substantially. T-bond futures contracts were permitted to trade.
1995	Speculation and irregularities in T-bond trading led to the closure of regional T-bond trading centers, e.g., the Wuhan Trading Center, and T-bond features contracts were banned.
1995 (August)	Over-the-counter trading of T-bonds was stopped, and the Shanghai and Shenzhen Stock Exchanges became the only legal trading platforms.
1996	Book-entry bonds were issued on the Shanghai and Shenzhen Stock Exchanges, and the bond trading system was established with the increasing volume in re-purchase transactions.
1998 (May)	PBoC started open-market-operations, which stimulated the development of interbank bond market of bond/notes trading.
1998 (September)	China Development Bank started to issue financial bonds in the interbank bond market.
1998 (October)	PBOC approved insurance companies as members of the interbank bond market.
1999 (October)	A portion of securities firms and all asset management firms became members of the interbank bond market.
2000 (September)	Financial firms were allowed by PBOC to become members of the interbank bond market.
2002 (October)	Non-financial institutions were allowed by PBOC to become members of the interbank bond market.
2005	Short-term corporate notes were allowed to be issued in the interbank bond market.
2007 (January)	The State Council allowed financial institutions to issue CNY-denominated bonds in Hong Kong.
2007 (March)	Corporate pension funds were allowed to trade in the interbank bond market.

insurance companies make up the majority of market participants. As is the case in any other type of securities market, one necessary condition for the development of a market is a broad investor base with different expectation and belief, consumption pattern, and utility functions so that two counter parties can trade with each other. Limiting investors mostly to institutions runs into the dilemma that there are few counterparty traders when the institutions attempt to make certain moves in the bond market. The number of bond mutual funds remains small compared with the number of equity funds and the total number of other participants in the bond market.

3.1.2 Corporate Bond Development

Current regulations on interest rate cap (not more than 40% higher than the prevailing bank lending rate) and minimum credit rating (most issues are AAA rated) limit the corporate bond market to only a handful of companies. In addition, corporate bonds' interest income is subject to a 20% interest tax, which is not assessed on treasury or financial bonds. Such tax treatment almost completely takes away any spread of corporate bonds over competing treasury or financial bonds, confining corporate bond market development. Finally, the trading and clearing of corporate bond in the secondary market remains segmented and lag the development of the primary market.

3.1.3 Competition with the Banking Sector and Equity Market

Under the circumstances of the transitional economy in China, bond market development faces competition from both the equity market and the banking sector. According to the pecking order theory in corporate finance, debt financing should carry lower costs of capital than equity financing. However, many government officials, corporation executives and even private entrepreneurs in China still treat equity financing as the cheaper channel for financing, because the public companies enjoy the right offering, face little governance and regulations, and often do not pay any dividends. Faced with such a challenging environment, regulators need to not only make the bond market available for issuers and investors but also educate the market on the mechanism by which each market operates.

The regulations on interest rate and issuance take away the flexibility of the bond market and many heterogeneous investors. Without a wide range of tradable securities and an active secondary market, bond market cannot fully enjoy its role of price discovery and risk management, which put bond financing into direct competition on interest rate with bank loans, to which many of the high-quality companies already have easy access. Given the much higher administration and transaction costs, bank loans are often times preferred by issuers with access to both markets.

3.2 Future Outlook

There is hardly any doubt that China is trying hard to speed up the development of its domestic bond market. China's regulators, especially the PBOC, suggest that they will fully support the nation's bond market in the coming years, allowing market participants more power to roll out new products, introducing more bond products, improving market infrastructure, and facilitating bond transactions and more sophisticated strategies (Su, 2006; Zhou, 2005). It becomes clear that the bond market development enjoys policy auspice in the near future. A more mature and developed bond market can provide alternative channels for companies that need to raise capital, offer additional opportunities for domestic investors to diversify their portfolio, and help the banking and finance sector to better manage financial risks.

Recent trends in the government policy orientation, as shown in Table 1, highlight the following areas for further bond market development.

3.2.1 Central Government Bonds

Municipal and Local Government Bonds

China has been studying the possibility of allowing its local governments to issue bonds to finance urban infrastructure construction projects. With help from international financial institutions, some local governments, e.g., Jiangmen Municipality in Guangdong Province, have started to issue municipal bonds on an experimental base. The issuance of municipal bonds will give the local governments a new legitimate channel to raise funds, other than Treasury bonds and bank loans, for their massive infrastructure projects.

Municipal will play a key role in raising the huge amount of capital needed for China's urban infrastructure projects as the nation strives to further urbanize itself. Local governments have to undertake infrastructure projects, which may not always be the maximum net-asset-value projects, coveted by private entrepreneurs, and municipal bonds can provide local governments with a strong tool for flexibility in financial management and for reducing the cost of financing. With financing through stocks and corporate bonds today accounting for less than 1% of aggregate urban infrastructure investment, China's fledgling capital market nowadays can hardly handle the volume of such financing, and a new market has to be established.

3.2.2 Corporate Bonds

Several motivations together make the development of the corporate bond market a promising area of the entire bond market. From the issuers' perspective, many corporations and private enterprises with different credit quality are searching for new financing channels. State-owned and commercial banks can no longer come up with enough capital to make the needed loans. Even if they can, banks have to be very conservative in their lending practices, in the face of their own non-performing loan quandary. If companies can issue bonds to targeted investors, with the intermediation of banks and securities companies, the above two problems can be solved at the same time. Although there has been some loosening in the very short-term financial bill issuances, more progress is made on medium- and long-term bonds to satisfy the term structure need of the issuers.

Social security fund and insurance companies, some of the most important institutional investors in China, need fixed-income securities other than the treasury bonds to diversify their portfolios and match cash flow with their obligations. Corporate bonds can bridge this gap by providing higher returns, varying credit grade, and different maturity. In addition, issuing corporate bonds directly to individual investors offer individuals an alternative security class to invest in and channel the over-speculation on stock or the real estate market.

The development of the secondary market is an indispensable element to the above-mentioned proposals. Without an active secondary market, information cannot be effectively communicated, and there will be no liquidity needed to rebalance portfolio and control risks. The short-term bills have set a very good example of being actively traded in the interbank bond market. Now that long-term railway bonds, similar to corporate bond, started being listed in the secondary market, we feel that it will not take too long before all corporate bonds are traded in a unified secondary bond market.

3.2.3 Asset-Backed and Mortgage-Backed Securities

The Administrative Rules for Credit Asset Securitization Pilot Operations were publicized on April 20, 2005, aimed to promote the securitization pilot program. In accordance with the rules, National Development Bank issued some asset-backed securities, and China Construction Bank issued mortgage-backed securities.

Several advantages promised such securities to develop. First, there is a great demand for infrastructure and residential constructions in the coming decades, and securitization has been proved by international practices as an effective way of attracting individual investors and controlling risks. Once the banks successfully securitize their loans, the banking sector can distance itself from the infrastructure loans that they make and reduce the risk of their loan portfolios. The entire banking sector should therefore become stable. Finally, asset-backed securities provide bonds with different levels of credit ratings, which should help investors better understand credit risks and induce the development of credit-rating agencies. Such subordinated securities help market better understand the risks associated with different securities and price such risks accordingly.

3.2.4 Fixed-Income Derivatives

Derivatives are very important securities to risk management and price discovery. As China launches a wide variety of bonds and other fixed-income securities, it is imperative that futures and options have to catch up with the pace of the spot market. In 2004, the outright repurchase agreement started being traded in the interbank bond market and the two stock exchanges. Last year, China introduced and started executing *The Administrative Rules for the Forward Bond Transactions in the National Interbank Bond Market*. It is widely believed that the exchanges have been actively researching the feasibility of starting the option market for fixed-income securities.

One challenge that many derivative market regulators face is the complex nature of derivative products. Many derivative products are treated as off-balance items which can fly under the radar of the regulators. Because derivatives often involve leverage, obsolete price due to illiquidity, and hedging positions, one has to go through many details to obtain an accurate assessment of risks. Given lessons from its own development, Chinese bond market should treat development of derivative products with extra caution and utilize foreign experiences in regulation and risk control.

3.2.5 Open Up Bond Market to Foreign Investors

Although it is understandable that Chinese regulators and investors are both concerned with opening the bond market to foreign investors, given lessons learnt from history, it is important that the opening up of the bond market to foreigners can potentially bring more than just capital. Qualified Foreign Institutional Investors (QFII) and Qualified Domestic Institutional Investors (QDII) not only open up Chinese market to foreign institutional investors but also offer Chinese domestic institutions opportunities to explore foreign bond market. The new policy approved by the State Council that allows CNY denominate bonds to be issued by Chinese financial institutions in Hong Kong, likely in the summer of 2007, is a major step in this direction.

4 Conclusions

We analyze the historical lessons, explain the present challenges, and discuss future perspectives of the Chinese bond market. We believe that this market will grow with great potential in the years to come and outline several particularly exciting areas for future development. Historical lessons so far indicate that legal environment and political considerations have been playing a considerable role in shaping the bond market. Further reforms in the legal and political arenas will likely stimulate the growth of the bond market, and the resulting developed bond market could further fuel future rounds of healthy economic

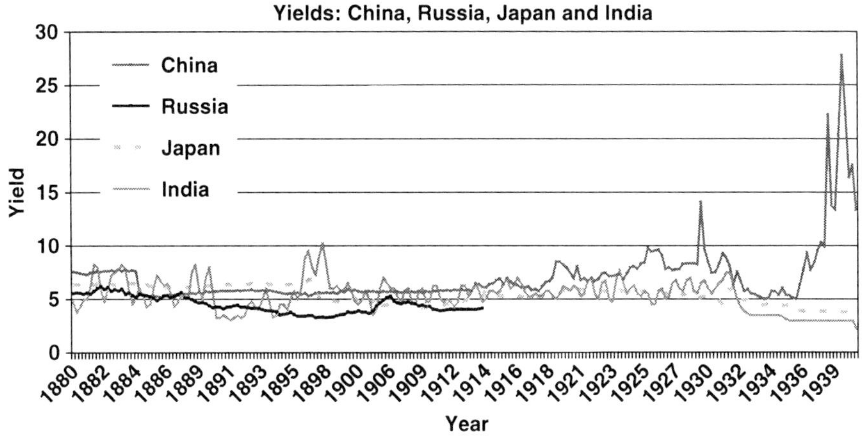

Fig. 1 Yield of China's foreign bonds (1860s–1930s)

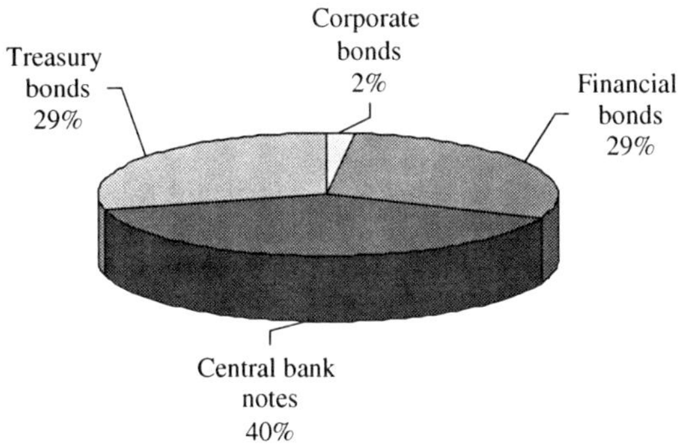

Fig. 2 Breakdown of the Chinese domestic bond market by outstanding bond value, October 2006

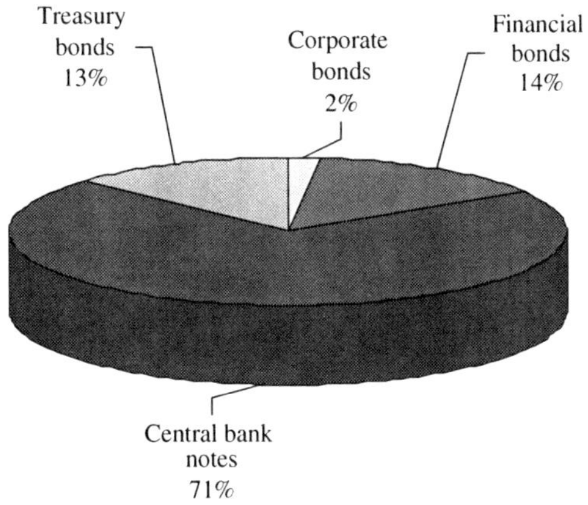

Fig. 3 Breakdown of the Chinese domestic bond market by issuing size, January–October 2006

growth. We expect that market regulators, intermediaries, and investors should pay particular attention to the Chinese bond market in the near future and help the market reach its full potential in the country.

Acknowledgments An earlier draft of the chapter was prepared for the Yale China Conference 2006 and the related book project. The authors benefit from comments from participants at the Yale and BIS-CEPR-HMKA conferences, especially Zhiwu Chen, William Goetzmann (Yale Conference discussant), Fred Hu, and BIS-CEPR-HKMA conference discussants Barry Eichengreen, Guonan Ma, and Richard Portes. Huang is from China International Capital Corporation and can be reached at huanghz2@cicc.com.cn. Zhu is from UC Davis and Lehman Brothers and can be reached at ningzhu@lehman.com. The views as well as errors and mistakes are of the authors.

References

Goetzmann William, Andrey Ukhov, and Ning Zhu, 2005,"China and the world financial markets 1870–1930: Modern lessons from historical globalization," *Economic History Review*, forthcoming.

Gynthelberg Jacob, Guonan Ma and Eli Remolona, 2005, "Developing corporate bond markets in Asia," Background Paper for the BIS Conference on Developing Corporate Bond Markets in Asia. *BIS Papers No. 26*, pp. 13–21.

Kuhlmann Wilhelm, 1983, *China's Foreign Debt*, self-published.

Rhee S. Ghon, 2000, "Regionalized bond market: Are the region's market ready?" Working Paper, University of Hawaii.

Scott David H. and Irene S.M. Ho, 2004, "China's corporate bond market, 2004," The World Bank.

Stanley John C., 1970, *Late Ch'ing Finance: Hu Kuang-Yung as an Innovator,* East Asian Research Center, Harvard University, Cambridge.

Su Ning, 2006, "Actively pushing for China's bond market development with scientific planning and coordinated arrangements," Speech on 26 June. http://www.pbc.gov.cn/detail.asp?col = 4200&ID = 164

Yi Gang, 1999, "Converting debt to equity: at the cross-road of credit economy and default economy," *International Economic Review* (in Chinese) Vol. 5: 9–10.

Zhou Xiaochuan, 2005, "China's corporate bond market development: lessons learned," Speech given on 17–18 November at a BIS conference on Developing Corporate Bond Markets in Asia. *BIS Papers No. 26*, pp. 7–10.

Zhou Xiaochuan, 2004, "Perfecting legal system, and improving financial ecology," Speech Given on 2 December. http://www.pbc.gov.cn/detail.asp?col = 4200&ID = 150

An Update on China's Capital Markets: Focus on China's Securities Industry

Chung-Hsing Chen

Abstracts Despite all the ups and downs, China's capital markets have developed at a very rapid pace over the past 20 years. The market size is growing and systems are gradually being updated. Investors are becoming more mature, and a legal system, regulatory framework, and trading rules have basically been established. Although there is a great deal of room for improvement in China's capital markets, they are playing an increasingly important role in the overall economy. Nevertheless, we should bear in mind that China is still an emerging entity and some issues in the market need to be addressed to achieve greater efficiency. Those issues include an unbalanced financing structure, a lagging fixed income market, an insignificant role played by institutional investors, and the need to improve the quality of information disclosure and drive market innovation. As a key component of China's economy, China's capital markets currently are not functioning efficient enough as a vehicle of capital allocation, with the major reasons being market operational inefficiencies.

Keywords Brokerage industry · Investment banking · Bond markets · Institutional investors · Financial holding companies

1 Introduction

With the successful organization of the 2008 Olympic Games in Beijing, it seems that China has been marching with triumph into the twenty-first century as one of the major powers in the world, not just in sports of course but also politically and economically. But the tasks of transforming this formerly socialist and centrally planned economy into a much more market-orientated economy have been far from over. On the contrary, the tasks ahead are no less challenging. One of the major challenges deals with managing the steady sail of the capital markets through a depressed economic environment, something that the Chinese

C.-H. Chen (✉)
Xinhua Finance, Shanghai, China
e-mail: ch.chen@xinhuafinance.com

J.R. Barth et al. (eds.), *China's Emerging Financial Markets*,
The Milken Institute Series on Financial Innovation and Economic Growth 8,
DOI 10.1007/978-0-387-93769-4_18,

regulators have yet to truly experience. This is particularly important, not only because a healthy capital market is needed to facilitate the further transformation of the state-owned enterprises (SOEs), to finance the much needed infrastructure projects, but, more importantly, to improve the efficiency in allocating capital to the corporate sector during slower economic growth years.

Despite the recognizable success in the developing of China's financial markets, many issues remain. This chapter will try to provide an update on the development of China's capital markets and discuss some of the challenges in the capital market development. To name a few, first of all, the markets are still unable to meet financing needs of different corporate sectors. Listed companies on the Chinese main boards are dominated by large SOEs, with small and medium enterprises (SMEs) and privately owned businesses having limited access to capital market financing. Second, China's capital markets are basically just equity markets, the corporate bond market is negligible. For the fixed income market, problems such as market segmentation, confusing regulatory regimes, and laggard credit rating systems all hinder market development. In addition, the market investors are predominately retail investors, institutional investors who should be the major players in the market are still inadequate, and the structure of institutional investors needs to be improved with the further development of annuity, insurance, and pension investors.

In order for China's capital markets to achieve the goal of efficient capital allocation, there are two prerequisites: one is to be able to achieve a good degree of informational efficiency and the other is to make sure that the market can arrive at a satisfactory level of operational efficiency. In terms of informational efficiency, the regulators have accomplished a lot by establishing a generally well-structured information disclosure system in the capital markets. The task now is to make sure that the system gets executed in a satisfactory fashion. Take the quality of disclosure for example, although corporate issuers are required legally to disclose qualitative information such as forward-looking management's discussion and analysis, the actual disclosure might not be that qualitative. In addition, a well-structured disclosure system should allow regulators to implement "registration system" for offering of shares to the market, but IPOs in China's capital markets are still heavily regulated, a company with a very good disclosure does not necessarily get any benefits in IPO or listing approval process.

With regard to operational efficiency, in addition to the proper functioning of the exchanges and over-the-counter markets, the custodian, the clearing and settlement system, short sells and margin finance, the efficient intermediation of the securities industry all play vital roles in arriving at market operational efficiency. But margin finance and short sales, as well as stock index futures remain on the drawing board despite all the discussions. Although the regulators have a good reason to be heavy handed on market supervision, the fact is, if most of everything that a securities company wanted to do in the market requires prior regulatory approval, this in itself makes the capital markets inefficient.

In addition to those factors derived directly from capital market development, there are few other major developments in the financial markets that might also impact the securities industry. For example, the trend of moving Chinese financial services toward either financial holding companies or universal banking seems inevitable. There is also a debate on whether or not China should have a super-regulatory agency for the entire financial services sector. These developments obviously will impact the future competitiveness of the brokerage industry with another major challenge. This chapter will also touch upon these issues in later discussions.

2 Status of Chinese Capital Markets

2.1 *Equity Market*

In brief, China's equity market has maintained rapid development in recent years. But to understand some of the issues facing the market, it is still worthwhile to have a look at the path of China's market development. In retrospect, China's equity market has experienced three general stages: an embryonic stage (1978–1991), an expansion stage (1992–1998), and a standardized and systematic development stage (1999–2005). There are inevitably certain systematic pitfalls and structural conflicts embedded in China's capital markets due to their early stage of development, and those problems assuredly will come out with the markets' further development, representing valuable opportunities for improvement and reform.

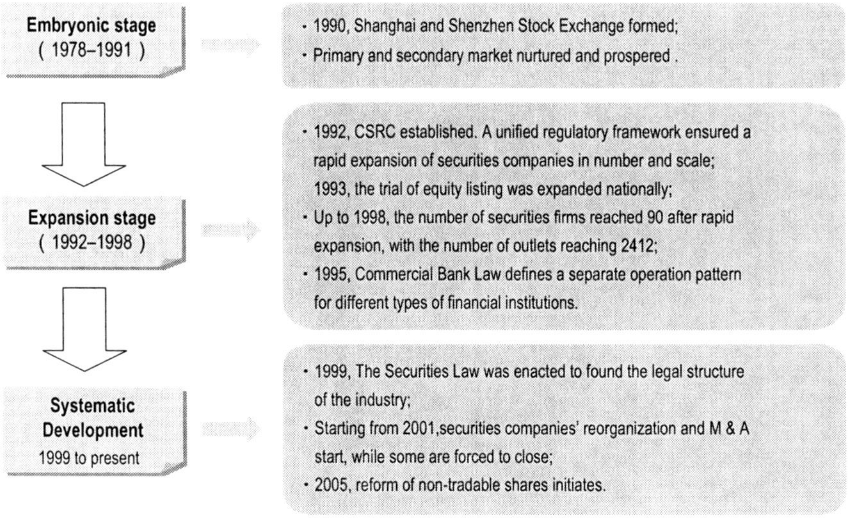

Chart 1 Historical development of China's equity market
Source: Xinhua Far East

For instance, the downturn period for China's stock market since 2001 further indicated the need for necessary reform. That's why the year 2005 saw implementation of the reform of non-tradable shares, which aimed to unify the interests of tradable and non-tradable shareholders and implement fundamental changes in the market. Together with abundant liquidity brought by the rapid development of the Chinese economy and the advance of non-tradable shares reform since 2006, China's stock markets displayed increasing demand and supply and developed an upswing trend, witnessed by record indicator levels such as total trading volume and trading accounts in 2007.

The market has seen dynamic growth driven by the implementation of the reform of non-tradable shares, relatively abundant liquidity and the conversion of H shares into A shares. In 2007, the total amounts of capital raised from the issuance of stock and convertible bonds hit RMB 1.9 trillion. As of year-end 2007, the total number of listed companies was 1550, and total market capitalization reached RMB 32.7 trillion, with the ratio of stock market capitalization to GDP amounting to 133%, an increase of 42% year-on-year and a level comparable to that of developed countries. Considering the low ratio of tradable shares in the current capital markets (tradable shares only account for 28.4% of total shares), the relatively over-valued stocks at the end of 2007, as well as the implicit economic factors in GDP, the real market capitalization to GDP ratio still leaves a great deal of room for improvement.

At least in appearance, the Chinese government appears to adjust supply and demand in the equity markets relatively well. When the domestic capital markets were underdeveloped, large SOEs were allowed to list overseas. When there was abundant liquidity in the country, companies with H shares were encouraged to dual-list in the A share market. When the supply of shares surpassed demand in the market, the government sped up approval of qualified mutual funds. The mentioned actions could be deemed to be market manipulation in Western countries, while for China, as an emerging market, the practices are basically favored. It should be noted, however, that in the very dynamic year of 2008, as of this writing,

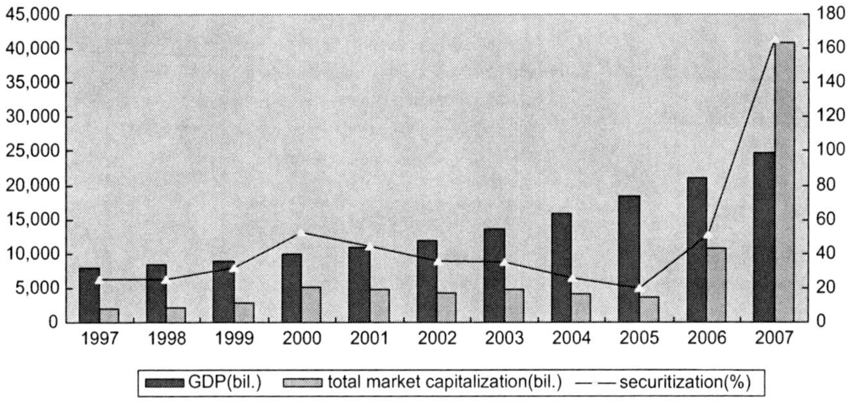

Chart 2 China's GDP and Market Capitalization.
Source: Wind, Xinhua Far East

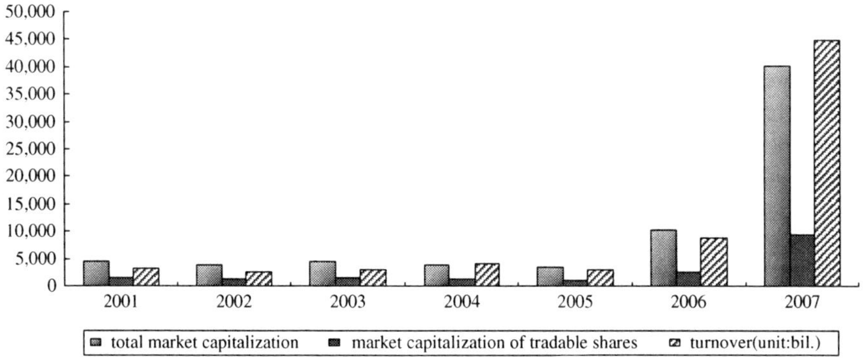

Chart 3 2001–2007 Market Capitalization of Tradable Shares.
Source: Wind, Xinhua Far East

with domestic and international economic environments both under pressure, whether or not China can claim its success in the non-tradable share reform remains to be seen.

The venues for stock trading are primarily the main boards of the Shanghai Stock Exchange (SSE) and Shenzhen Stock Exchange (SZSE), and the SME board of the SZSE. Currently, the main boards dominate the equity market and SOEs in turn dominate the main boards. SMEs and privately owned enterprises find it very difficult to list on the main boards. The SME board is still in its early stage of development characterized by small market capitalization and narrow industry coverage. Moreover, the growth enterprise market (GEM) is still under construction and an over-the-counter (OTC) market is absent. The property rights trading market mainly serves for the transfer of state-owned assets, which is separately supervised by different local governments.

Clearly China's current market system still needs improvement in market depth to meet the financing needs of diversified types of enterprises. On the demand side, China will also need to develop a better institutional investor base. The high volatility of China's equity markets reflect partly the nature of a market dominated by retail investors. Regulatory agencies have taken measures since 2007 to promote the establishment of multi-layer markets, but more actions are also needed to facilitate the participation of institutional investors.

Table 1 China Stock Exchange Market Size and Constituents (Feb 28th, 2008)

Market Type	No. listed Companies		Market Capitalization	
	No.	Proportion	Billion RMB	Proportion
SSE Main Board	861	56%	22,329.90	80%
SZSE Main Board	467	30%	4,408.29	16%
Sum	1328	86%	26,738.19	96%
SZSE SME board	219	14%	1,100.28	4%
Total	1547	100%	27,838.46	100%

Source: www.sse.com.cn, www.szse.com.cn, Xinhua Far East

2.2 Bond Market

The bond markets, as one of the key constituents of capital markets, are still in the early stage of development and lag significantly behind that of the equity markets. When the equity markets encounter a prolonged period of bearish run, the role of fixed income markets in facilitating development of listed companies has become more significant. China's bond markets compared with developed capital markets are far from being able to meet market needs and still have a long way to go in terms of product types, structure, and maturity.

Since the start of 2001, China's bond market has developed steadily with market size gradually increasing. In 2007, the issuance of bonds in the inter-bank market reached RMB 7.98 trillion, a year-on-year increase of 40%. T-bills, T-bonds, and financial debentures are the major types of products in the primary bond market, accounting for over 90% of total issuance. Corporate bonds and commercial paper account for merely 6% of issuance, despite a high growth rate. Although it will take many years before China's bond markets can become an efficient vehicle in capital allocation, there's no doubt that the role is increasingly important and certainly has a good potential if hurdles are managed correctly.

The healthy development of China's bond market will have an important bearing on the revenue of its securities industry. In developed countries, fixed income business accounts for a high proportion of the total revenue of the brokerage industry. Recognizing the needs to boost the bond market development, the government has, since the year 2007, promulgated various regulations paving the way for corporate bond issuance. The successful issuance of the China Yangtze Power corporate bond in October 2007, the first one in China other than enterprise bond, can be deemed a milestone for the market. But, despite efforts by the authorities to expedite the development of corporate bond markets, unless some of the structural problems are resolved, it is unlikely that the corporate bond business can significantly contribute to brokers' revenues over the short term

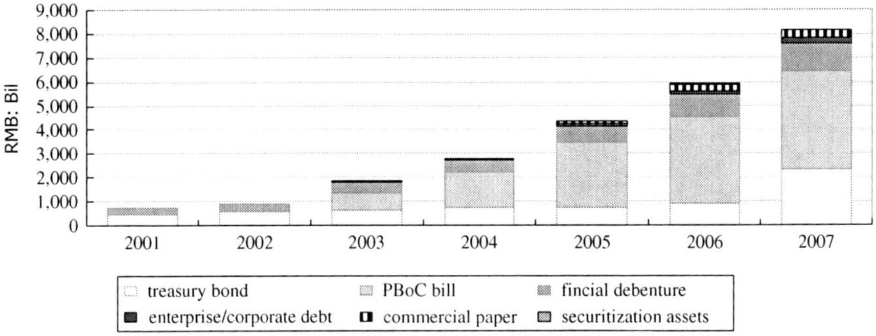

Chart 4 Issuing amount of China's bond market
Source: www.chinabond.com.cn, Xinhua Far East

Chart 5 China's Bond Market Development
Source: Xinhua Far East

The structural problems in China's bond market are many. The most obvious one is the confusion of the market structure and its regulatory regime. For example, China's bond markets consist of the interbank bond market, the exchange-traded bond market, and the OTC market, which are supervised by different regulatory bodies. Due to work division and coordination problems, a confusing regulatory regime exists, resulting in inefficient supervision. Furthermore, the custody of corporate bonds guided by the CSRC is now under the

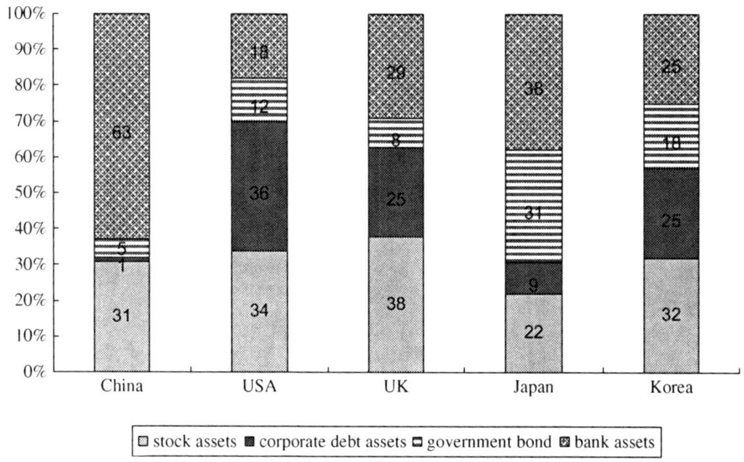

Chart 6 Financial assets structure comparison (as of 2007)
Source: CSRC

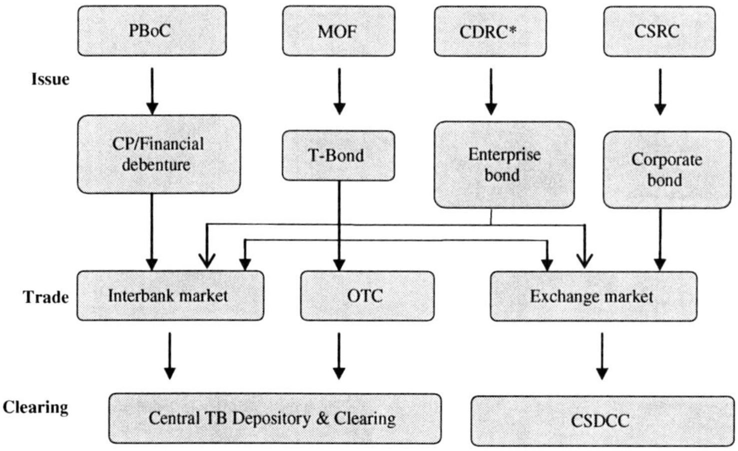

Chart 7 China fixed income market regulatory framework
Source: Xinhua Far East
Note: * The quota of enterprise bond issuance per year was determined by the State Council. The CDRC is in charge of approving the issuance, and the PBoC and CSRC review the coupon rates and underwriter qualifications.

China Securities Depository and Clearing Corporation Ltd. (CSDCC), with the bonds only eligible for trading on the exchange platforms. Separate from the interbank bond market where most institutional investors take more active roles, the issuance of corporate bonds is very low and prospects appear vague. Market segmentation and a confusing regulatory regime hinder the development of the bond market.

Apart from segmentation and a confusing regulatory regime, laggard risk pricing and credit rating systems also impede development of the bond markets to a certain degree. Hindered by limited types of issuers and restrictions on interest rates, risk and credit ratings are irrelevant to the pricing of corporate bonds. Moreover, domestic rating agencies are underdeveloped, lacking recognition and credibility in the market.

2.3 *Increasing Importance of Institutional Investors*

In recent years, institutional investors, especially mutual funds, have been developing at a rapid pace. As of 2007, the total number of fund companies reached 59, managing 364 funds, with assets under management and net asset value reaching 2233.9 billion shares and RMB 3276.2 billion respectively. The market capitalization of mutual funds accounts for 28% of that of the total market. As of 2007, the market value held by institutional investors accounted for 49% of the total, an increase of 30% points compared with that of 2004.

Table 2 China Mutual Fund Market Size and Constituents (Dec 31st, 2007)

Type	Num.	Shares (billion shares)	Net asset value (billion)
Equity funds	171	1307	2,032
Equity-skewed funds	107	749	1,051
Bond funds	31	58	67
Money market funds	51	111	111
Others	5	9	14
total	365	2233	3,276

Source: Wind, Xinhua Far East

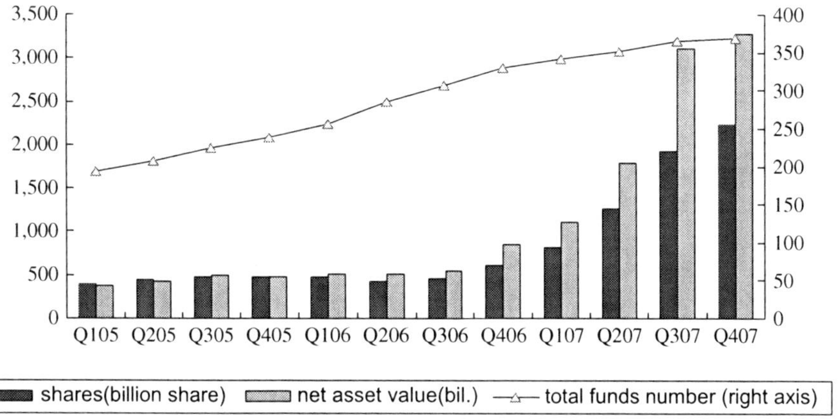

Chart 8 China's mutual fund development 2005–2007
Source: Wind, Xinhua Far East

However, limited by the stage of early development, there is still a large gap between the proportion of China's institutional investors and that of international markets (where institutional investors occupy 60–80% of the market). China's current stock market is still characterized by a high proportion of individual investors, hence exhibits high short-term volatility. Xinhua Far East believes that institutional investors will continue to grow as more individual investors resort to mutual funds as more companies list in the market and industries become more complicated. In addition, institutional investors' structural components need to be further optimized. As of 2007, the market value of shares held by insurance institutions, social security funds, and annuities comprised only 3.34% of all floating shares.

2.4 Disclosure System Is Largely Adequate, but Implementation May Fall Short

In a mature market, market supervision is based on a well-established information disclosure framework, demonstrating the proverb that "Sunshine is said to be the best disinfectant and electricity the best policeman." No matter how powerful

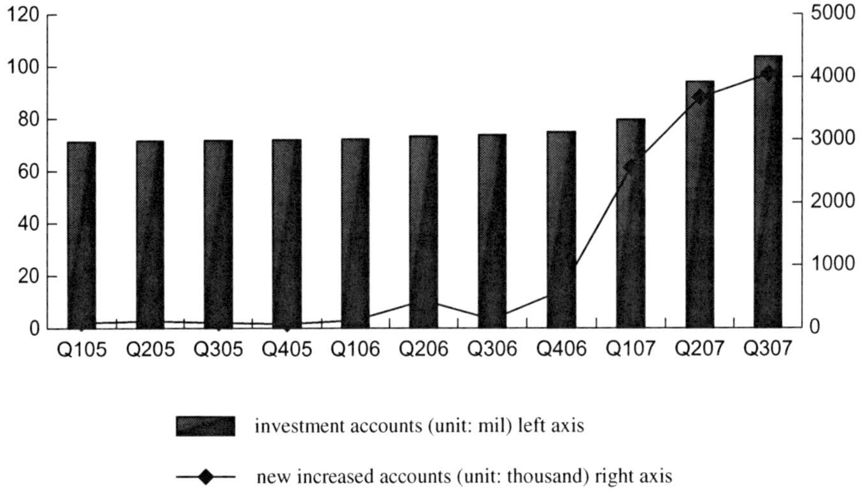

Chart 9 2005–2007 Investment accounts (A&B shares)
Source: Wind, Xinhua Far East

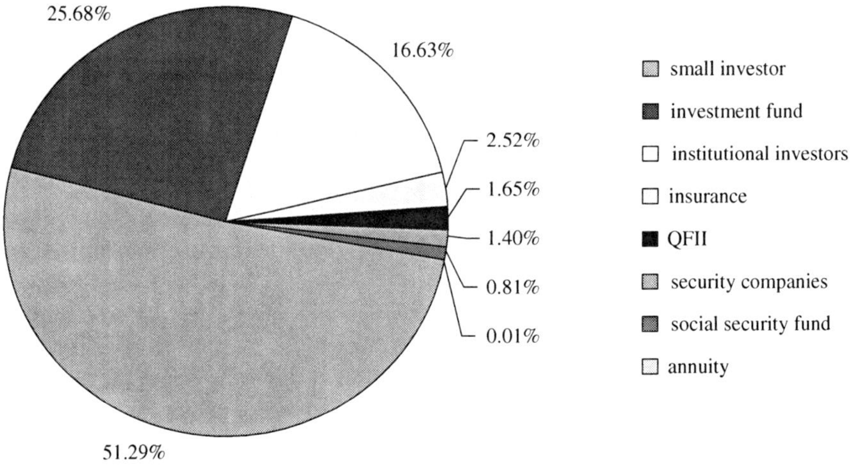

Chart 10 China stock market investors composition (end of 2007)
Source: CSRC

a regulatory institution is, it is incomparable with the surveillance of the entire body of market participants. With the rapid development of listed companies and product types, regulatory institutions are facing a supervision dilemma.

The information disclosure framework of China's capital markets has been adequately established over the past 20 years, with the Company Law, Securities Law and Provisional Regulations on Public Offering and Trading serving as the core of the legal framework, supplemented by other management rules published by the CSRC dictating detailed format and content for listed companies' information disclosure. The initial disclosure (prospectus), periodic reports (semi-annual and annual report) and timely report of material events are key components of information disclosure.

The information disclosure framework for China's capital markets has been well established and the quantity and depth of information disclosure of listed companies are enough, but the actual level of information disclosed is insufficient and the quality needs further improvement. Listed companies do not voluntarily disclose information and tend to adhere to government policies. Management Discussion and Analysis (MD&A) focuses more on current business profitability, lacking prospective views and discussion of strategy and potential risks. The timeliness and truthfulness of information still needs further improvement in order to mitigate issues of false information, insider trading, and malicious price manipulation.

In terms of the detailed reports, there is no systematic consistency between prospectuses, scheduled reports, and provisional reports, which to some degree can be attributed to different methods adopted by different regulatory institutions for each type of information disclosure. Inconsistent regulatory frameworks dampen the effectiveness of regulatory bodies.

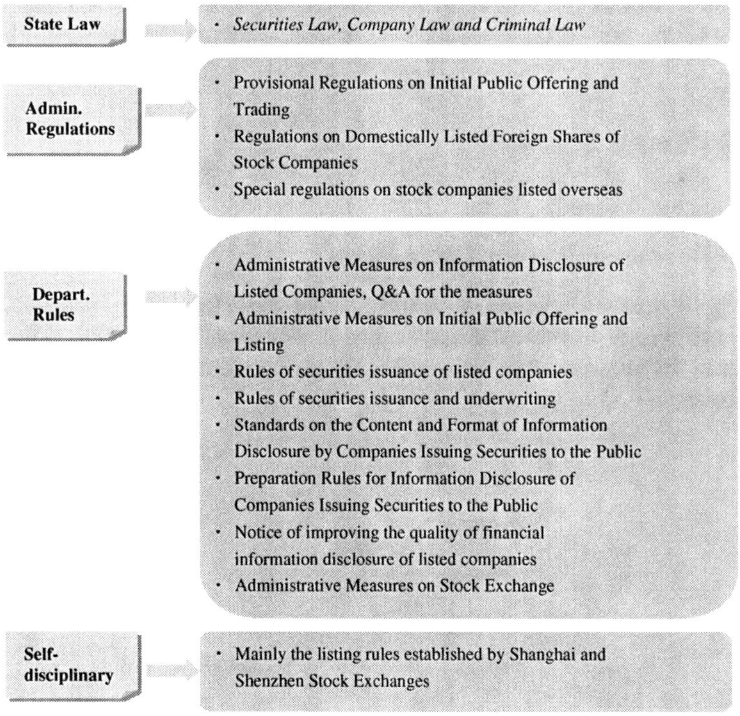

Chart 11 Regulatory framework for information disclosure system
Source: CSRC Complied by Xinhua Far East

Information disclosed in the primary and secondary market should be collected uniformly by regulatory institutions and then provided to market participants. Analysis and comments on the information by institutional investors would assist in the maturation of small investors. For public offering efficiency, a complete and timely information disclosure system would be beneficial in improving the speed and efficiency of administrative approval.

3 Status of the Securities Industry

Due partly to the emerging nature of China's capital markets, and the dynamic regulatory and market environment, the competitive landscape of the securities industry is nothing but certain. Chinese securities firms, in the current environment, do basically trade intermediation. It will take years before local securities firms could transform from the current trade-oriented business model to what most developed markets have, a valued-adding service-oriented business model where wealth management consultancy services could provide the securities firms with more steady and diversified income. Even in this trade-oriented business model, separate approval is required from the CSRC before a securities firm could engage any of the following core businesses: brokerage, investment banking, bonds, proprietary trading, and asset management businesses.

3.1 Brokerage Business

3.1.1 Market Status

Income Depends on Trading Commissions

Trading turnover of A and B shares on the Shanghai and Shenzhen stock exchanges soared from RMB 9trillion to RMB 45trillion in 2007. The active trading in the securities markets pushed up the brokerage business of securities companies.

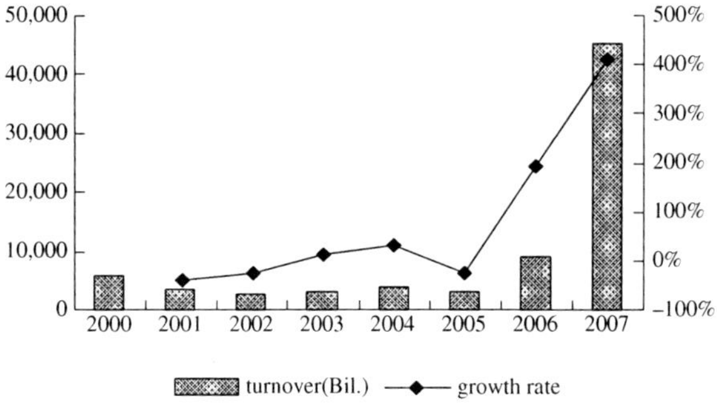

Chart 12 A&B shares trading turnover and growth rate. Data Source: wind

In terms of revenue structure, Chinese brokerage business depends on trading commissions and interest rate spreads. This explains why the brokerage business performance depends heavily on the market environment and is highly volatile. The entire securities industry suffered a loss in 2003, whereas total brokerage income exceeded RMB 100billion in 2007. Moreover, securities companies offer homogeneous channel services, leading to significantly lower commission rates as competition intensified.

Market Structure Is Dispersed

The brokerage business is dispersed. China Yinhe (Galaxy) Securities Co. Ltd holds the largest market share with 6.50% trading volume in the market, whereas the market shares of many small securities companies are very low. The market shares of more than 80% of the securities companies are below 1%.

Market share concentration has been stable over the years.The market shares of the top 10 securities companies has been around 40% over 7 successive years, although it is affected by the market's total turnover. Another factor contributing to changes in market concentration has been M&A in the securities industry, which leads to market consolidation.

Number of Branches Insufficient and Internet Trading Needs Improvement

Relative to China's large population and geographical scale, the number of securities company business outlets is not enough. All in all there are about 3800

Table 3 2007 Total Turnover Ranking (stock, bond, fund, and warrant)

Name	Proportion
China Yinhe Securities	6.50%
Guotai Jun'an	6.15%
Haitong Securities	4.64%
Total of top 10	43.46%
Total of top 20	62.46%
Next approximately 80 companies	37.54%

Source: China Securities Association

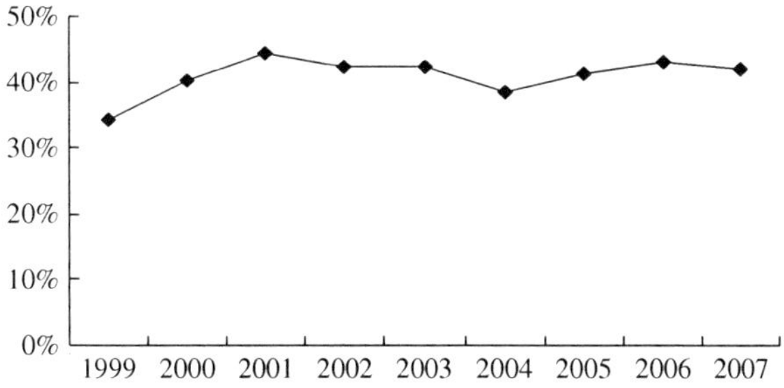

Chart 13 1999–2007 Market Share of Top 10 Securities Companies
Source: Wind

securities outlets in China. China Galaxy Securities sits at the top with 167 outlets, while most securities companies have less than 20 outlets. Moreover, most are located in top tier cities and coastal cities, with few in secondary or third tier cities. Since retail Chinese investors do prefer to trade at the brokerage branches, technically speaking, Chinese securities companies would need to build more branches or trading outlets to meet the need of investors. But the establishment of additional branches will also require the approval from the CSRC. Those firms that have expanded through acquisition prior to the bullish run in 2006 have all benefited from the expansion.

However, securities companies must bear in mind that the costs for operating additional branches will become a burden when the markets experience a prolong downturn. They should adjust the existing practices to having a big outlet to house the investors and accordingly bearing the high fixed investment in outlet construction. Local securities firms should consider building different types of outlets according to the different needs of local investors, and convert the single-function trading lobby into a wealth management center, which would help to reduce outlet cost and enhance profits.

As to Internet trading, the volume has boomed in recent years and reached 60% of total turnover for some of the large securities companies. But there is still plenty of room for Internet trading to grow in the market. Although Internet trading reduces the need for outlets, it still can't cover the needs of all investors, especially since the supervisory institutions require investors to open their accounts on site, and many investors in the secondary and third tier cities are used to trading in the outlet's trading lobby.

Competition Still in a Primary Stage

The brokerage business is still in the primary stage of competition. Competition is based on the branching network as a monopolized source, which is typically represented by trading outlets. There are no distinct differences among most brokerage companies with respect to technologies, services, marketing abilities, and research capabilities. However, some securities companies have begun to adopt differential and brand-cultivating competition models and have made efforts toward serving clients' total financial needs. Although it will take some time before we see the differentiation in the securities industry, it is seemingly on the brink of change.

3.1.2 Main Factors Influencing Future Prospects

Moving forward, there remain lots of certainties that could influence significantly the future prospects of Chinese brokerage industry. To name a few, the challenging economic environment, further capital market reforms, commission deregulation, outlets expansion, and Internet trading. The following factors are also important to the brokerage business operational environment and competitive landscape.

A Trend Moving Toward Financial Holding Companies/Universal Banking

The current trend in China to move toward financial holding companies/universal banking has been evident, some banks and insurance companies have moved to exchange shares, and banks have been operating securities business using subsidiaries. Such strategic cooperation between banks and insurance institutions is penetrating and competing with the businesses of the securities companies in asset management and sales of financial products. By cooperating with each other, developing products that better cater to market needs and then distributing through the banks' powerful distribution channels, financial institutions provide products and services that are much more competitive and that have greater coverage. This cross-industry cooperation has changed the original competitive landscape, presenting at once both opportunities and challenges for securities companies.

There's also an implication for competition in cross sales of financial services. In a mature market, cross selling is an important means of generating additional income for the financial institution. Financial institutions use database and data mining technologies to achieve customer segmentation, and customize products and services to meet the needs for targeted segment. This will allow a financial services firm to better analyze clients' preferences and get a bigger share of a customer's pocket through sales of mutual funds, insurance policy, and other products, thereby increasing their revenue and building up client loyalty. Currently cross-selling by a domestic brokerage firm is limited to selling funds. Regulatory agency will need to consider gradually unlocking the business scope of brokerages to cultivate the securities companies' servicing capability and promote competition with other financial services providers.

Shareholder Base

Shareholder structure could directly influence competitiveness in the new brokerage business model. Under the model of universal banking and cross marketing, securities companies with a banking shareholder base may have broader client resources, and can make use of bank outlets for distribution. If margin trading is permitted, whether or not they have bank support in offering financial services will also greatly influence securities companies' competitive position.

In addition, financial holding companies may share client resources, and offer clients all-embracing services, achieving synergies as a result. Securities companies with shareholders from financial holding companies, such as CITIC Securities, BOC, and Everbright Securities will have more opportunities than competitors. On the other hand, when policies allow, other securities companies are preparing for changes in the market through share investments or strategic alliances with banks, asset management companies, or other financial institutions.

Table 4 Securities companies with banking background

Securities companies	Related banks	Bank net assets (RMB billion)
BOCI	BOC	4,503.39
CITIC Securities	CITIC Bank	81.04
Guangda Securities	Everbright Bank	–
China Merchants Securities	China Merchants Bank	62.95
Minsheng Securities	Minsheng Bank	45.23
Industrial securities	Industrial bank	36.99
Ping An Securities	Ping An Bank	–

Source: Xinhua Far East
Note: Bank net capital data through Sep31,2006

Industry Consolidation of Brokerage Business

When competitive factors transfer from "channel" resource to brand, the competitive landscape of securities companies' brokerage businesses will change: securities companies with powerful brand and leading financial servicing capabilities will continually increase their market share while many small companies will face merger and acquisition. Mergers and acquisitions are important ways to construct big full service securities companies; moreover, the current strict regulation of supervisory institutions on setting up new outlets and requirements that investors open accounts on site also encourage securities companies to enlarge their scale through mergers and acquisitions.

Industry consolidation mainly in the form of mergers, acquisitions and reorganizations is helpful in solving such issues as product homogeneity and over competition; it also allows outstanding securities companies to command more resources and keeps the industry environment dynamically optimized. Securities companies with low market share will probably be merged and acquired during light seasons of the securities market, if there is no segmented market or competitive advantage for them to rely on. However, many securities companies have close relationships with the local government, and acquisition within the industry will likely be hindered by local protectionism.

3.2 Investment Banking Business

3.2.1 Market Status

With the resurgence of securities markets, as well as the return of H shares to the A share market, the securities' underwriting and refinancing business increased rapidly in 2007. The actual annual amount of financing reached RMB786.925 billion, a 199% increase over the same period in 2006. The amount raised by IPO was RMB 438.440 billion and the amount raised by additional stock issue was RMB 325.884 billion, increases of 174% and 218%, respectively, compared to the previous year. However, securities industry prosperity does not lead to

Chart 14 2003–2007 Equity Financing Structure in A-share Market
Source: Wind, Xinhua Far East

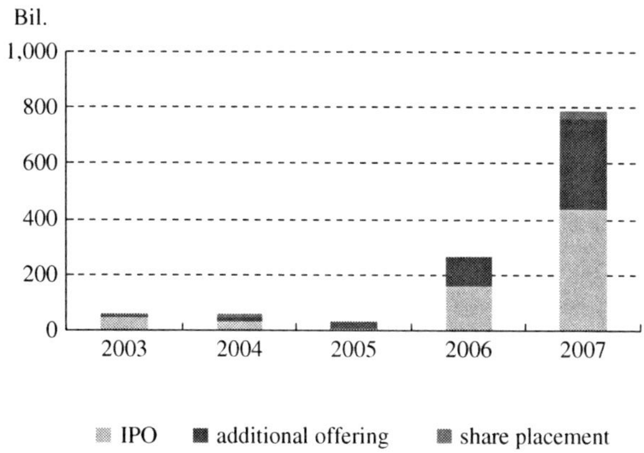

flourishing of securities companies' M&A business; additionally, because of the low consulting fees for M&A, M&A consulting income accounts for only a small proportion of the securities companies' total income and lags far behind international levels.

Underwriting Business

Overall, 121 new stocks were issued in 2007, among which 24 stocks were issued on the main boards and 97 stocks on the SME board. The actual amount of money raised reached RMB 438.440 billion (of which money raised on the SME board was RMB 37.324 billion), bringing a total of RMB8.8 billion in underwriting income for the securities companies. CICC, CITIC Securities, UBS Securities, Galaxy Securities, and BOCI were the top five securities companies in the underwriting business. The positive performance was partly attributed to the resurgence of the market and partly to the return of big red chip stocks represented by China Petroleum, China Shenhua, and China Construction Bank. Seventy-five percent of the total amount raised by IPO in year 2007 was contributed by the return of 7 big state-owned companies' H stocks.

In sharing the profits of China's capital markets, securities companies with foreign investment banks as shareholders are emerging and occupying important positions in the market. Based on the amount of money raised, USB Securities and Goldman Sachs Gao Hua Securities rank No. 3 and No. 7, respectively, posing certain threats to the investment banking business of Chinese securities firms.

The underwriting business of China's A stock market exhibits characteristics of high market concentration, market segmentation, and intense competition.

High Market Concentration: In 2007, the total amount of underwriting by the top five securities companies accounted for 79.8% of the market, and 67% of underwriting revenues, while the amount of underwriting by another 39 companies only accounted for 20.2% of the market. More than half of the

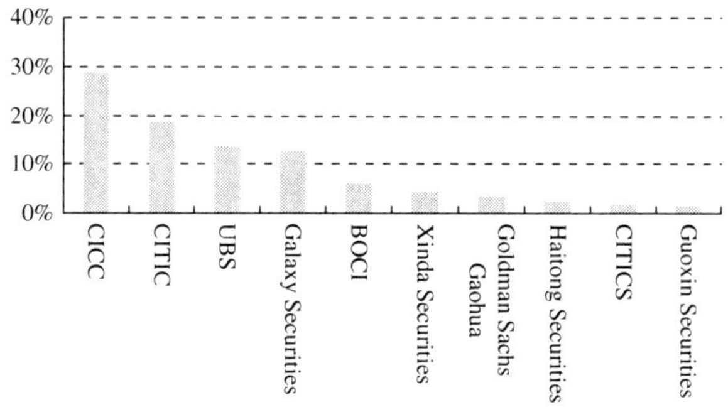

Chart 15 Top 10 securities companies by Underwriting amounts in 2007
Source: Wind, Xinhua Far East (in joint underwriting projects, half-to-half shares of amounts)

securities companies earned nothing from the underwriting market. Large-scale underwriting issues were mostly covered by the top five companies. The underwriting business of China Petroleum, China Shenhua, and China Construction Bank, whose financing sums accounted for 41% of the 2007 total, were, respectively, undertaken by CICC, CITIC Securities, and Galaxy Securities.

Market Segmentation: In underwritings of large-scale issues, powerful shareholder backgrounds, government relations, capital base, the ability to underwrite in both A and H stock markets, as well as market reputation, all awarded competitive advantage to big securities companies such as CICC, CITIC Securities, and Galaxy Securities. For the small and medium sized issues, companies like Guoxin Securities, Ping An Securities, and Guangfa Securities are gradually showing competitive advantages in the niche market in terms of the number of sponsorships and issue amounts. Underwriting fee rates for the SME market are higher than for large-cap stocks.

Intense Competition: Competition in the investment banking business is intensifying. In addition, powerful competition from overseas investment banks pressures domestic players. Goldman Sachs Gao Hua and USB Securities both target the high-end market, especially red chip stocks returning to the A share

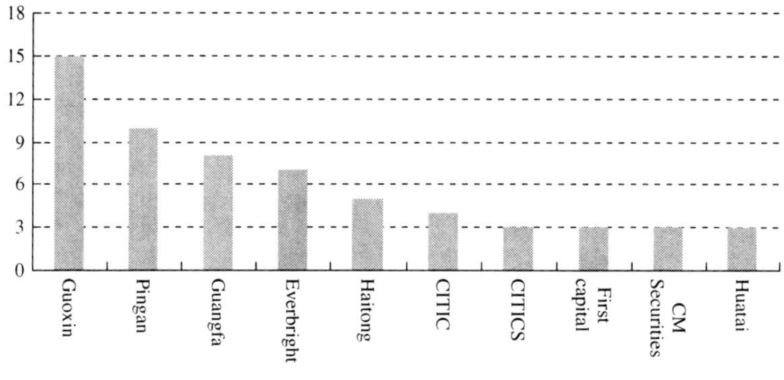

Chart 16 Top 10 Securities Companies in SME Board Underwriting in 2007
Source: Wind, Xinhua Far East

market. After several years of talent acquisition and adaptation to the domestic market, they will have the chance to win in the market and with their international resources and leading technologies pose a significant threat to domestic players.

Additional Share Issuance Business

In 2007, there were a total of 178 additional share issues with the amount of capital raised reaching RMB 325.884 billion, among which private placements accounted for 80.2% of the total. The concentration in the additional share issuance market is also comparatively high, with the top five securities companies holding 46% of the market These include CITIC Securities, CICC, Hua Tai Securities, Dongwu Securities, and Haitong Securities This concentration demonstrates that the additional share issuance business is in fact an extension of the listing services offered by the big securities companies. Of course, there are still exceptions where small companies possess a leading position because they happen to win the opportunity to service a big issue. As an example, Dong Wu Securities held a comparatively large market share in 2007 because of its RMB 25 billion share issuance for CITIC Securities.

Mergers and Acquisitions

The major revenue sources of international investment banks lie in such non-traditional transactions as M&A and financial consulting. In contrast, China's investment bank revenues center on traditional businesses such as brokerage and underwriting, while M&A and financial consulting revenues account for only a very small part of the total. In fact, market demand for M&A in China is tremendous. According to Dealogic, the total amount of M&A transactions completed in China reached RMB 830.4 billion in 2006, among which those undertaken by security companies only accounted for 10% with revenue of

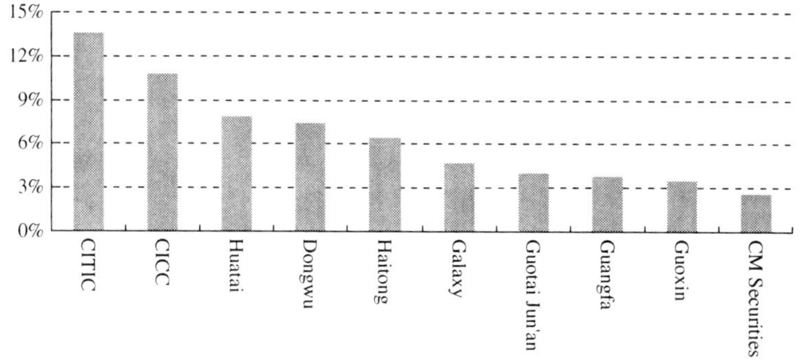

Chart 17 Top 10 Securities Companies in Additional Share Issuance in 2007
Source: Wind, Xinhua Far East

merely RMB 0.6 billion. A large portion of market share was held by accounting firms and consulting companies. Security companies' revenue from the cross-border M&A business, with its higher commissions, was even less.

3.2.2 Main Factors Influencing Future Prospects

Major factors influencing performance of the investment bank business include the building and expansion of multi-layer markets, reforms of the stock issuance system, competition from foreign investment banks, and development of the M&A market. Other than the above, the investment bank business is also affected by securities companies' sales channels, the financial holding companies/universal banking trend, the system of sponsors, and the continuous servicing capabilities of securities companies.

Building and Expansion of Multi-layer Markets

As direct financing plays more important roles in the macroeconomy, future expansion of the main board markets, launching of the growth enterprise market (GEM), and the diversification of re-financing channels will bring great opportunities for securities companies' underwriting business. However, the building of a multi-layer securities market is still in the initial stages: state-owned enterprises account for too large a proportion of the main board markets while the scale of the SME board and OTC transactions is limited. Other problems such as the prolonged IPO cycle and information transparency also hinder development of investment banks.

Future underwriting business on the main boards will be propped up by IPOs in financial sectors such as banks, securities, and insurance companies; the return of red chip stocks composed mainly of telecommunication, real estate and energy companies, as well as H shares; and the listing of overseas companies or multinational corporations in the A share market. The proportion of state-owned companies is expected to increase even further as a result. However, in the primary economy small-and-medium sized private enterprises are on the rise, whose development is restricted by limited financing channels. Hence it is necessary to expand their financing channels in the main board market so that the market is more reflective of the total macroeconomy.

After many years' preparation, the GEM board is going to be launched. At that time, bundles of innovative small-and-medium sized enterprises will be listed. The GEM board will be conducive to expanding financing channels for small-and-medium sized enterprises, promoting economic development, cultivating multi-layer capital markets, and promoting the business of securities companies which target small-and-medium sized companies. Nevertheless, most such enterprises have a short operating history or product life cycle, and are lagging in degree of information disclosure, which will endow the GEM board with certain risks.

Reform of Primary Market: Merits Review vs. Registration Systems

Reform of the stock issuance system will affect not only the pace of initial public offerings, but also the efficiency and cost of underwriting, risk awareness of markets, and investment mentality, thus exerting a great impact on the business of investment banks. As the market matures, the issuance system must undergo reforms to gradually adapt itself to market development demands.

At present, China follows a merits review system for stock IPOs. In comparison to an examination and approval system, the merits review system has made great progress in improving listing companies' quality, protecting investors' interests, and pursuing market fairness, which benefits the healthy development of an emerging securities market. However, the merits review system also has the following major disadvantages. (1) Since the regulator agency's judgment is not 100% accurate, even qualified companies may initially encounter problems issuing stock. (2) Investors become dependent on the regulatory agency to conduct investigations of issuers, thus abandoning their own judgments. (3) Trifling procedures not only increase issuing expenses but also make gaining of approval the main task in issuance rather than considering other important factors such as companies and markets. The issuing time is not optimized as a result and the best opportunities for resource optimization may be missed. Meanwhile, to some extent, fluctuations of the secondary market are also intensified. (4) The scope of profit rent is increased. Considering these negative factors, supervisory institutions are obligated to gradually adjust the examination scope, loosen examination criteria, and transfer the right of valuation and choice to investors, in the end achieving the shift from a merits review system to a registry system.

That said, it is not yet realistic for China to fully adopt a registry system. Implementation of a registration system requires a well developed information disclosure system and a relatively mature securities market. China's securities markets are still in the growth stage, and in the current environment would tend to encounter certain risks under a registration system. It is recommended that China's regulatory authority at the current stage loosen the merits review for additional share issuance. The registration system could be adopted for companies which have been listed for some time (for example, 3 years), whose amount of additional share issuance is within some range, and whose operations are relatively stable. In this way the regulatory authority could be released from trifling examinations for additional share issuance and focus on verifying IPOs, thus shortening the time of the listing examination and accelerating the IPO process.

Competition from Foreign Investment Banks

For large issues in 2007, the proportional amount underwritten by joint venture securities companies reached 52.2% (including that for CICC and BOCI). For some joint venture securities companies, while the stakes held by foreign investment banks appear to be less than 33.33%, they actually control the companies through indirect means, as in the cases of USB SDIC and Goldman Sachs.

Large international investment banks clearly are optimistic regarding hopes of participating in China's securities markets and leveraging their capital strength, market reputation, and leading technologies. In addition, since domestic securities companies' cross-border underwriting is restricted by ability and regulatory authority, the cross-border underwriting business has provided market opportunities for foreign investment banks.

The *Decision about modifying 'Rules of foreign companies holding shares in securities companies' stocks'*, recently announced by the government, restored approval for joint venture securities companies, and may incite interest by foreign investment banks in participating in the domestic securities market. The introduction of foreign investment banks in the domestic market allows domestic securities companies to learn international practices and also cultivates an atmosphere of beneficial competition among securities companies. A firm and orderly opening up policy is of enormous benefit to the development of China's securities industry.

Growth of M&A Business

The present level of Chinese securities companies' M&A business is much lower than the international level. Once all A shares are in circulation and multi-layer capital markets have been established and perfected, companies' M&A and restructuring may flourish. Complete circulation of all A shares will make stock conversion a feasible choice for M&A, as in international markets M&A and restructuring among 80 state-owned enterprises will also provide significant opportunities for investment banks. These three factors will present promising opportunities for security companies in the M&A business and will generate substantial financial consulting revenue. This will be conducive to stabilizing investment banks' income cycle.

However, while M&A provides business opportunities for securities companies, such activities pose new challenges to their operations requiring commitments to honesty & integrity, without which their market reputation will suffer significant damage. Also, foreign securities companies possessing strength in capital, technology and human resources will constitute competition for the financial consulting business of Chinese securities companies. This requires domestic players to begin early preparation for the coming M&A surge through integration of resources from government and corporations, and strengthening their capital and their talent pool.

3.3 Fixed Income Business

3.3.1 Market Status

Development of fixed income business is of great significance to securities companies. It is beneficial in reducing cyclical fluctuation of securities companies' incomes and stabilizing their performance. Securities companies have become fully aware of the importance of fixed income business given the dramatic equity market fluctuations starting from the second half of 2007. However, the Chinese fixed income markets are still at the initial stage in terms of scale and structure, while securities companies' roles in the market lag behind those of other financial institutions such as banks. This has limited the scale of securities companies' fixed income business, which can bring in revenue when the equity market goes south.

Primary Market Experiences Rapid Growth, but Security Companies' Revenue from Credit Products Is Quite Limited

Issuance amount in the bond primary markets has maintained rapid growth in recent years. The years from 2004 to 2007 saw an average annual compound growth rate of 43%, but the overall scale remains small. Moreover, even though the growth rate of true credit products is relatively high, their scale turns out to be very small. In 2007, the underwriting amount for enterprise bonds and commercial paper amounted to only RMB 500 billion or so, and the main underwriters for commercial paper are commercial banks. Hence securities companies have realized little income from underwriting of credit products. Securities companies dealing in T-bills, T-bonds and financial debentures have primarily focused on sales. In this area, securities companies possessing channel advantages have larger market share.

Trading Volume in Secondary Market Is Increasing, but Securities Companies' Market Share Is Relatively Small

In 2007, trade and settlement volume in China's bond markets set new highs with 1.0386 million transactions for the whole year and a settlement amount of RMB 64.88 trillion for a growth rate of 61.43% compared with 2006. Settlement volume in the inter-bank market has increased significantly while the

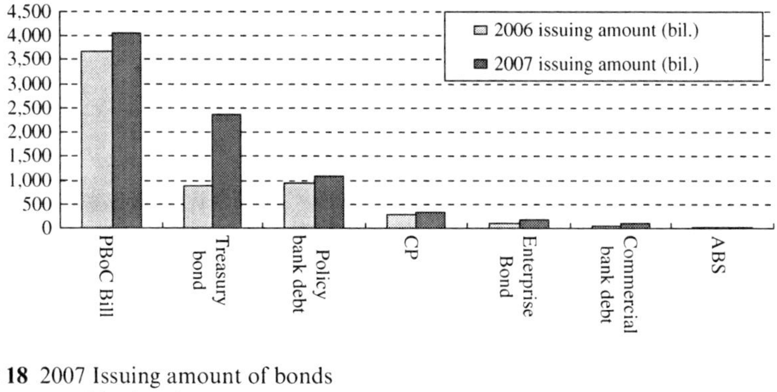

Chart 18 2007 Issuing amount of bonds
Source: www.chinabond.com.cn

Table 5 2007 Bond transactions in all three markets

Trading site		Volume (10,000)	Value (RMB 100 billion)	Percentage (%)
Interbank market		18.86	631273.09	97.31%
Exchange Market	**Shanghai Stock Exchange**	76.62	17457.17	2.68%
	Shenzhen Exchange	3.24	5.08	
Commercial bank OTC		5.14	35.67	0.01%
Total		103.86	648771.01	100%

Source: http://www.chinabond.com.cn http://www.sse..com.cn http://www.szse.com.cn

volumes in the exchange markets and commercial bank OTC market have declined.

In terms of institutional investor structure, commercial banks, insurance, and asset management companies are the major players, holding 67.6% (RMB 8.33 trillion), 7.6% (RMB 0.93 trillion), and 4.2% (RMB 0.52 trillion) of the bond balance respectively. The balance held by securities companies was less than 1% of the market. Among the 29 market makers in the interbank system, there are only 4 securities companies, CICC, CITICS, Guotai Junan, and BOCI.

We believe that securities companies may play a bigger role in the interbank market, expanding market scale and increasing market liquidity through providing services such as bond underwriting and market making. This will in turn bring them new profit-making opportunities.

Securities Companies' Bond Business Is Relatively Concentrated

At present, securities companies' bond business is relatively concentrated. Securities companies possessing competitive strength are mainly those qualified as interbank market makers and those with strong sales channels. The leading market players include BOCI, CICC, CITICS, Guotai Junan, Galaxy and Haitong. Income from their bond business mostly derives from equity sales and trading rather than underwriting.

3.3.2 Main Factors Influencing Future Prospects

To a great extent, securities companies' future bond business is subject to the overall development and reform of the bond markets, such as improvement in the multiple regulators situation, increase in market scale especially in the true credit products, further expansion of the interbank market, etc. At the same time, the bond business will be subject to change in interest rates, stringent credit policy, competition from bank loans and equity markets, establishment of credit rating systems, furthering of guarantee systems, etc.

Change in Interest Rates

Change in interest rates is the predominant factor which will affect the bond market. Although the year 2008 faces expectations of inflation, the frequency of central bank interest rate hikes will slow down compared with 2007 due to pressure from RMB appreciation and economic uncertainties worldwide. Monetary policy will emphasize exchange rates and credit controls, which will have a positive impact on bond markets.

At the same time, it should be recognized that China's interest rates can hardly be described as market-based, which has hindered the development of bond market. Although interest rate reform has made much progress in recent years, due to a great amount of non-market-based elements in the economic system, non-market-based interest rates and many levels of base rates, the interest rate system is quite complicated, and enterprises can hardly establish an effective pricing benchmark during financing. This causes great difficulty in pricing new bond market products. Interest rates have not fully functioned as a market price to control the cost of capital and risk.

Stringent Credit Policy and Competition from Bank Loans

In 2008, a stringent monetary policy will be implemented, and the scale of bank loans will be strictly controlled, highlighting the importance of financing through corporate bond markets. New monetary policy will give priority to credit control. Besides strictly observing quotas for the increasing amount of loans, all commercial banks are obligated to adjust loan amounts on a quarterly basis. If the credit policy is carried out effectively, enterprises' funding chains will be affected, and they will need to seek other channels. Meanwhile, there will be more capital from banks investing in bond markets, increasing the demand for corporate bonds, enterprise bonds, etc.

However, whether the bond market can make use of this opportunity to develop itself is dependent on many factors: the speed of deregulation; the effectiveness of interest rates; whether reputable enterprises will enjoy lower interest rates in bond markets; whether small- and medium-sized enterprises will be able to appeal to investors in bond markets by means of guarantees; and whether small- and medium-sized enterprises will be able to obtain approval to issue bonds.

Cost of Issuing Equity Versus Issuing Bonds

The bond markets and securities companies' bond business is facing strong competition from the equity market. In the presence of a heated equity market, listed companies are not as willing to issue bonds for three reasons. First, companies may raise more funds through the equity market as P/E ratios and other indicators are high. Second, companies face stringent binding clauses when issuing bonds compared with soft binding clauses when issuing equity.

Third, companies in China have insufficient understanding of capital structure issues or have differing viewpoints. Even though companies are functioning well, theoretically speaking ROE will increase with the increasing percentage of debt, companies' willingness to issue debt is weak as the rights of big shareholders and small shareholders are not equal.

From the bond investment perspective, a situation of increasing uncertainties in the equity market will lead some risk averse capital to turn to the bond market, stimulating bond market demand.

Establishment and Development of a Credit Rating System

Little use of credit ratings and risk pricing by the market also constitutes a barrier hindering securities companies' bond business. A bond is a credit product, so credit rating plays an important and unique role in market development. However, in previous years in China, the roles of rating agencies have not been important as the pricing of bonds has little to do with ratings due to restraints on the types of issuers and interest rates. While the market now is attaching increasing importance to ratings, the credit rating system is not fully functional owing to a lack of reputable domestic credit rating agencies, a lack of differentiation in ratings, and the inability of many ratings to reflect companies' real risk profiles.

It should be realized that the success of rating agencies lies in their independence and credibility in the market. A major problem for domestic rating agencies is their lack of independence, which is further compromised due to their small scale and insufficient capital. In this aspect, our suggestion is to moderately open up the rating market and nurture positive competition through introduction of foreign rating agencies. Opening up of the market rather than blind protection is beneficial for market development, enabling domestic players to recognize their own weaknesses and strive to increase their competitiveness. Although it is reasonable and necessary to protect certain domestic industries, protection of the credit rating market is of little importance compared with such macro strategies as developing bond markets and minimizing overall financial risks in the economy.

Guarantees of Corporate and Enterprise Debt

On Nov 11, 2007, the China Bank Regulatory Commission issued *Opinions of effectively mitigating risks related to the guarantees on enterprise bonds* to commercial banks, requiring banks to terminate all guarantees of enterprise bonds based on projects. In the long run, unsecured bonds will play a positive role in the development of the bond market. However, over the short term the bond market is negatively impacted, as interest rates are not decided by market forces and a base for market pricing has not been established. Meanwhile, the China Insurance Regulatory Commission has not allowed insurance institutions to invest in unsecured enterprise bonds. Since enterprise bond maturities are mostly greater than 10 years, insurance institutions are important buyers in the market. Hence their exclusion from the market has an enormous impact on the issuance and trading of enterprise debt.

A guarantee is a type of rating enhancement provided by banks. Banks usually provide guarantees for their customers as they are quite familiar with a customers' financial situation and can provide reliable credit ratings. Through an analysis of the relationship between the equity and bond markets, we see that those companies who can only finance through banks rather than the equity market are more inclined to issue bonds, but they usually require a guarantee to enhance their ratings. Termination of all guarantees prevents some who have needs for issuing bonds from entering the market, and when not accompanied by adjustments to complementary controls, prevents those who would invest in the market from buying. It may be more beneficial to the market if the decision on whether guarantees are allowed is decided by the market itself.

3.4 Proprietary Trading Business

With the comprehensive equity market recovery in 2007, securities companies were able to strengthen their capital base and expand their proprietary trading business significantly. By June 2007, the net value of proprietary trading for 46 large- and medium-sized securities companies amounted to RMB 52.81 billion or so, and income from proprietary trading reached RMB 20.75 billion, accounting for 20% of total revenue. Securities companies' proprietary trading scale and revenue varied significantly, reflecting capital strength, risk preference, and investment capabilities.

The investment style of domestic securities companies varies. Some make long-term investments and pursue relatively stable returns, some are swing traders and employ different investment strategies in different market environments, while others mainly focus on investing in IPO companies or conduct

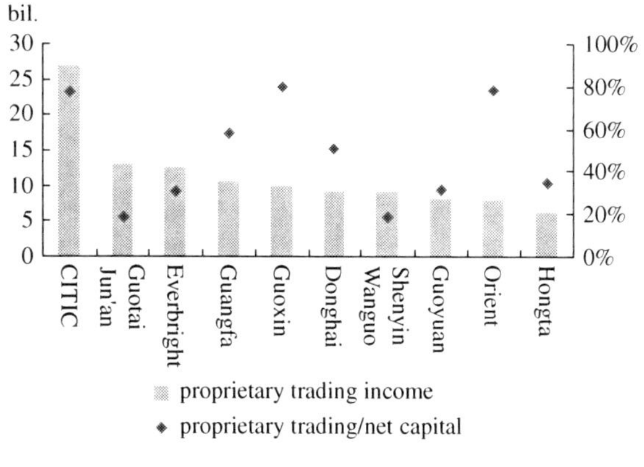

Chart 19 Top 10 Securities Companies in Proprietary Trading Income in 2007
Source: Wind, Xinhua Far East

risk- free arbitrage. In a word, there are a variety of investment styles in the proprietary trading business, and a mature investment style has not yet been formed. While all can benefit in a bull market, some investment strategies will be challenged in a depressed market.

Since funds for proprietary trading come from securities companies' equity, profits and losses directly influence the strength of the securities companies. Proprietary trading is largely subject to market fluctuations and is high risk. As internal control procedures for proprietary trading are currently immature and lacking standards, small blunders can incur great losses. The several securities companies that ran into trouble between 2001 and 2005 due to severe proprietary trading losses serve as examples. Securities companies should enhance their proprietary trading risk management systems and decrease their reliance on proprietary trading by expanding into new business lines.

3.5 Asset Management Business

The asset management business for China's securities companies is small in scale and only accounts for a small proportion of their total revenues. According to published data for 19 securities companies, during the first half of 2007 income from asset management accounted for only 2.6% of total revenues. At present, asset management products are primarily collective products, while specialized and oriented money management products are much less prevalent with few customers. From the pilot collective asset management products at the end of 2004 through the end of 2007, altogether 16 securities companies have issued 33 asset management products. At the end of 2007, there were 29 existing products in the market with total assets under management of RMB 51.65 billion. Due to the surge in equity markets since 2006, the return on collective asset management products soared with the best performer achieving an annual return of 140%. Moreover, due to their distinctive features in seeking absolute returns and operational flexibility (fee structure, product design, and sales channels), their total returns were higher than those of the fund products.

Collective asset management products are limited to innovative securities companies and subject to approval by regulatory authorities. Some securities companies have gradually built up their own brand and unique positioning in the market, leading to a relative concentration of market share. Strict examination and approval procedures and scale limits have turned out to be major barriers to market development. With the completion of third-party custody of clients' deposits and the ending of the comprehensive governance period in the industry, the policy environment will become more relaxed. Moreover, the CSRC issued *Detailed Rules for Securities Companies to Provide Oriented Asset Management Business (trial version)*, which is expected to promote future oriented asset management business.

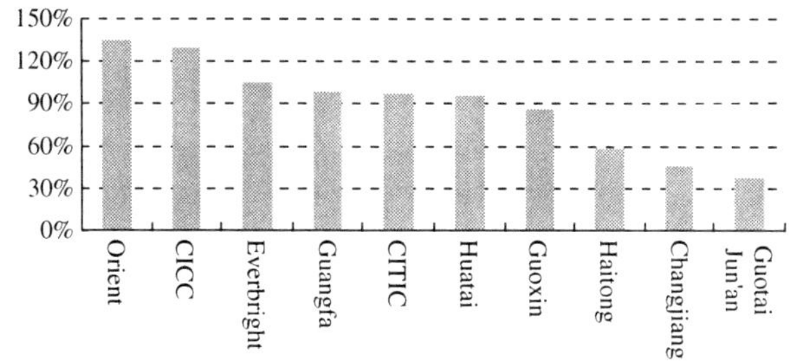

Chart 20 Top 10 securities companies by Average Annualized Returns. Source: Wind, Xinhua Far East
Note: As the launch and withdrawal times for different products do not coincide, data from Jun 30, 2006 through Dec 31, 2007 are taken as a reference sample. Average annualized returns are calculated by averaging the annualized returns of different products for the given securities company.

4 Major Factors Impacting the Development of China's Capital Markets

4.1 Movement Toward Financial Holding Companies and Universal Banking

Since the year 1993, China adopted the principle of separation of financial services and established regulatory agencies, respectively. With the development of China's financial market as well as its overall opening-up to foreign investment, the mode of separation is gradually breaking down with financial holding companies appearing in the market. Various financial institutions, such as banks, insurance companies, and securities firms, have started to penetrate each other's businesses. The most prominent is the across-the-board penetration by commercial banks into the mutual fund, trust, leasing, insurance, and even securities industries. The future emergence of universal banks or financial holding companies will have a fundamental impact on the current competitive landscape of China's financial markets. For securities firms supported by a universal banking firm, it might have greater opportunities to generate revenue, but for those operating pure brokerage business without such support, the pressures of competition is inevitable.

China's individual financial businesses are still in their youth. Many financial institutions like domestic banks, securities firms and insurance companies are still not capable of operating as a financial holding company, with their capabilities restricted in terms of expertise, talent pool, and risk management. Hence any abrupt conversion may increase the operational risk confronted by those institutions.

China's current supervisory framework under Glass-Steagall separation is also hard put to meet the needs of financial holding companies/universal banking.

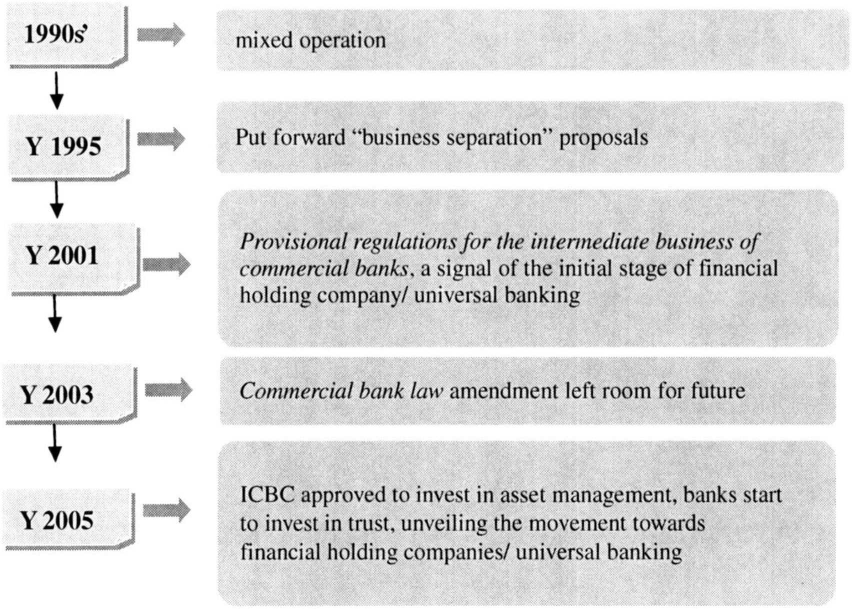

Chart 21 History of financial industry separation and financial holding companies/universal banking in China
Source: Xinhua Far East

Although three-party supervision, joint meeting systems, and periodical information exchange systems have been established among different financial supervisory bodies, coordination efficiency still needs to be improved. Recently, the Chinese government has preliminarily settled on the principle of building up super-ministries to unify government efforts; they have also promoted the conversion of institutional supervision into functional supervision. However, as financial supervisory bodies are lacking in adequate experience and abilities to manage financial holding companies/universal banking, a unified supervisory framework should be put into practice with great care considering the uncertainties it brings to the development of the financial industry. Xinhua Far East believes that the temporarily shelved decision of the central government regarding unified supervision would be beneficial in mitigating the risks faced by the securities industry, and a more efficient supervisory coordination system is of great necessity for the financial market in its current stage.

4.2 Regulatory Regime Maturing But Still Heavily Regulated

The function of the Chinese government has shifted from the previous full-time manager to that of a more commercially oriented supervisor. A regulatory system with government functioning as the supervisor, supplemented by self-discipline of the industry association and market players as well as oversight by the whole of society has been established. In the initial stage of development, moderate government intervention is helpful to cultivate the market, as in the case of China. With the development of the market, the government has gradually changed its supervisory principles and adopted more market-oriented methods. For example, as the listing system has transformed from an examination/approval system into a merits review system and the sponsor system, the pricing of listings is evolving from an approved issuance price to book running. In 2006, publication of the newly amended Company Law and Securities Law demonstrates further steps in the Chinese securities market's movement toward a more legalized framework.

However, the current capital markets in China are still heavily regulated. For instance, there are high regulatory entry barriers for brokerages and asset management companies; the right for initial public offerings is held in the hand of regulatory institutions regarding qualification review, issuance size, time of listing, etc.; enterprise bond issuance still requires waiting for administrative quotas; and new products and businesses cannot be promoted without administrative approval. Overregulation restrains market innovation and further development to some extent. Moreover, the evolvement of regulation policies is not consistent due to lack of mature experience, which further dampens efficient market operation.

Efficient government regulation usually leads to efficient market operation, in which market development will be regulated, risks will be lowered, and the interests of investors will be protected. Chinese regulatory institutions hold one of the most challenging supervisory jobs in the world, engaging in the management of huge amounts of capital and sparing no efforts as well as in nurturing economic development and investment for social security. As the economy and market is in a dynamic mode of change, the prudent regulation manner shows regulators' responsible attitude toward the entire market. But overregulation is detrimental to fair competition and innovation in the market. The current Chinese market is still under the strict control of government institutions and still needs to gradually transform into a more flexible one and rely more on market forces to enhance supervisory efficiency, promoting development of the market and market innovation at the same time.

The principles of government regulation should be in favor of fair competition. The government should relax the stringent approval requirements for traditional business and normal projects, such as establishment of brokerage outlets, IPOs, and asset management products.

Government regulation should also be in favor of market innovation. Current securities firms are limited to traditional businesses such as brokerage, underwriting, and proprietary trading. While access to new products is conducive to diversify market supply, optimize securities firms' income structure, and strengthen their risk bearing capacities, the pace of the relaxation needs to move forward gradually with the maturity of various pre-conditions. In regards to margin trading and short selling, the current market is still immature for their development, and a gradual approach should be adopted considering the huge risks involved.

4.2.1 Development of Multi-layer (Diversified) Capital Markets

The very simple capital markets system is now unable to meet the needs of investors with different levels of scale. The main boards are vital to the development of the overall capital markets and should be assigned priority in the building of more diversified capital markets. To develop the main boards, issues regarding further privatization of SOEs, strengthening of corporate governance, and encouraging foreign enterprises to list in the A share markets need to be addressed.

Sustainable development and healthy structure of the main boards will require reform of the market issuance system, supported by an updated IPO procedure, and the transition from a merits review system to a registry system. The issuance system transformation will in turn rely on an improved information disclosure system.

4.2.2 Increasing Importance of Institutional Investors

Being equipped with strong research capabilities, institutional investors have abundant experience in investment, an incomparable advantage to small investors in terms of information acquisition and analysis. Meanwhile, institutional investors are more rational, and their further development will effectively optimize the investor structure and reduce market volatility. In addition, institutional investors can assist regulatory institutions in strengthening market supervision, promoting information disclosure, while reducing regulation-related expenditures.

Even though institutional investors have been steadily increasing year by year and the makeup of institutional investors is more diversified than before, their proportion is still much lower than that found internationally. Institutional investors are still relatively weak in strength and not yet functioning well in improving market operation efficiency. Hence, the structure of institutional investors and their strength needs further improvement, with more institutional investors such as social security funds, insurance institutions, and annuities expanding their presence in the market.

4.2.3 Foreign Participants in the Capital Markets

China has been making efforts to further open up and attract foreign investment to its capital markets. There is no doubt that more open capital markets is beneficial in creating a just and free competitive environment and promoting healthy market development. The introduction of foreign capital can help domestic securities companies enhance corporate governance and raise management and risk control capacity. Nevertheless, domestic securities companies

Table 6 WTO Entry Commitment of Securities Industry

Service types	Entry commitment
Primary market	Foreign capitals not exceed 33% in joint-venture securities firms; permitted to undertake underwriting of A, B, H shares, T-bonds, and corporate bonds
Secondary market	Direct trading of B shares without agency after joining WTO, qualification of special member seat; permitted to trade B, H shares, T-bond, and corporate bond 3 years after joining WTO.
Asset management	Foreign securities firms can have up to a 49% stake in joint ventures 3 years after joining WTO
Consultancy	Consulting services and other complementary financial services, including credit enquiry and analysis, marketable securities research, M&A
Financial information	Providing financial information, data and consulting services (e.g., Portfolio investment, restructuring)
Capital account	Gradual easing of capital account controls 5 years after joining WTO

Source: Xinhua Far East

will inevitably encounter challenges from foreign companies as their capital strength, internal control systems, and human capital are incomparable with gigantic international peers. Hence, it is possible that the government will provide necessary aid to domestic securities companies along with the opening up of the Chinese securities markets. Allowing foreign investors to enter the Chinese securities markets in a controlled and orderly fashion is conducive to the development of domestic securities companies while cushioning the blow that likely would occur with greater openness.

5 Conclusion

Despite all the ups and downs, China's capital markets have developed at a very rapid pace over the past 20 years. The market size is growing and systems are gradually being updated. Investors are becoming more mature, and a legal system, regulatory framework, and trading rules have basically been established. Although there is a great deal of room for improvement in China's capital markets, they are playing an increasingly important role in the overall economy.

Nevertheless, we should bear in mind that China is still an emerging entity, and some issues in the market need to be addressed to achieve greater efficiency. Those issues include an unbalanced financing structure, a lagging fixed income market, an insignificant role played by institutional investors, and the need to improve the quality of information disclosure and drive market innovation. As a key component of China's economy, China's capital markets currently are not functioning efficient enough as a vehicle of capital allocation, with the major reasons being market operational inefficiencies.

Although securities companies have significantly improved their capital strength and profitability after going through comprehensive governance by regulatory bodies since 2004 and the market boom of the last 2 years, and their management has improved, their business competitiveness has not seen material improvement. As their business lines and product types are strictly regulated by the government, securities companies still lack core competencies and confront high market risks due to their heavy reliance on traditional businesses. This is one of the major factors affecting their credit profiles. Concentration in the brokerage business is moderately low, and more diversified financing channels and industry integration are necessary to improve capital strength and industry concentration. In addition, their risk management skills and abilities are in the early stages of development, and corporate governance also requires further improvement.

Securities companies are currently confronted with market risks, regulatory risks, and strategy risks, as well as operational and credit risks. Market risks are evident as the current macro-economy holds significant uncertainties and securities companies' revenues are not diversified to counter this down-turn market challenges. Overregulation brings securities companies high regulatory risks. Planned-oriented approvals and opaque regulation measures negatively impact in-depth development and structural optimization of the industry. Apart from external factors, major risks facing securities companies internally are their lack of core competitiveness and the possible risks brought on by aggressive expansion, as well as credit and operational risks.

Enhancement of the credit profile of China's securities industry relies to a good degree on gradual and orderly market deregulation. Future development will undoubtedly be affected by the macroeconomic environment and market liquidity. Meanwhile, other factors such as the pace of capital market development, transformation of business models of different financial institutions, perfecting of the regulatory environment, development of multi-layer capital markets, increasing the role of institutional investors, improvement of market information disclosure, and quickening of the opening-up of the market will all fundamentally influence the market.

Privatization in China: Experiences and Lessons

Jie Gan

Abstract This chapter provides a descriptive analysis of China's privatization, by far the largest one in human history. Unlike the mass privatization in other transitional economies, China has adopted multiple approaches to privatizing its state-owned enterprises (SOEs). These approaches included share issue privatization (SIP), joint ventures with foreign firms, management buy-outs (MBO), and sales to outsiders. I examine how these different approaches may affect the incentive and ability of the new owners to restructure the firms and thus influence the outcomes of privatization programs.

Keywords Privatization · Chinese economy · Transition economy Corporate governance

1 Introduction

Privatizing state-owned enterprises (SOEs) is a major step in transforming centralized economies into market economies. Indeed, an important component of the economic transformation in China has been privatization of its SOEs. Unlike the "shock therapies" in transitional economies in Central and Eastern Europe, China took a gradual approach to its enterprise reform. Due to its ideological aversion to capitalism, the government can commit to privatization only after earlier attempts of reforms have failed. Large-scale privatization occurred in the late 1990s. Between 1995 and 2005, close to 100,000 firms with RMB 11.4 trillion worth of assets were privatized, encompassing two-thirds of China's SOEs and state assets and making China's privatization by far the largest in human history.

This "delayed" privatization means that at the time of privatization, most SOEs were losing money and were deep in debt. This posed a significant challenge in restructuring the firms of the SOEs so that they could be sold off.

J. Gan (✉)
Hong Kong University of Science and Technology,
Hong Kong, China
e-mail: jgan@ust.hk

J.R. Barth et al. (eds.), *China's Emerging Financial Markets*,
The Milken Institute Series on Financial Innovation and Economic Growth 8,
DOI 10.1007/978-0-387-93769-4_19, © 2009 by Milken Institute

On the other hand, the market and legal institutional conditions for private ownership were much more developed than those during mass privatization in other transitional economies.

Depending on the ease of restructuring and the incentives and ability of the local governments to bear the social cost of restructuring, China adopted multiple approaches to privatizing its SOEs. These approaches include share issue privatization (SIP), joint ventures with foreign firms, and management buy out (MBO), and sales to outsiders.

Thus China's privatization is of great importance, not only due to its sheer size, but also because of its distinct differences from other privatization programs which can provide valuable insights into privatization designs in general. So far, however, little is known about the full picture of China's privatization. Most of the existing studies are on SIP, where data is available. However, SIP accounts for only a tiny proportion (1%) of the privatization programs in China. For most of the privatization programs, there are no systematic data, since the firms remain private after privatization.

The survey by Gan et al. (2008), GGX survey hereafter, is an important step in filling this gap. The survey was conducted in early 2006 on about 3000 firms, which is based on stratified sampling by region, industry, and sizes. In this article, I draw from the descriptive statistics of the GGX survey as reported in Guo et al. (2008) in my discussion of non-SIP privatization programs.

The rest of this chapter proceeds as follows. Section 2 describes the background of privatization of China's SOEs. Sections 3 and 4 describe the different methods employed in China and key characteristics of firms after privatization. Section 5 presents the effect of China's privatization on the firms' operating performance. Section 6 concludes the chapter.

2 Background of China's Privatization

More than twenty years of reforms in China are marked by the government's piecemeal and gradual approach. The reform of the SOEs is no exception. Instead of outright privatization, China concentrated first on productivity improvement by initiating enterprise governance structures that stressed autonomy and better incentives and then later by adopting long-term managerial contracts with pre-specified financial targets (such as profits and taxes). Instead of introducing markets and liberalizing prices overnight, China first created markets at the margin, parallel to the planned economy, by introducing the "dual-track system" in the state industrial sector and by lowering bureaucratic barriers to entry to the once state-monopolized industries. Admittedly, the reforms brought about fundamental improvements in output and productivity. The marginal productivity of labor increased by 54% and the growth in total factor productivity (TFP) was 4.68-6% per year during 1980–1989 (Li, 1997; Groves et al., 1994).

This gradual reform approach, however, had its limits. When the reforms started in 1979, most SOEs were profitable at least on paper. Since the reforms began, despite significant output expansion and productivity gains, the profitability of the SOEs declined substantially and most of them were losing money in the early 1990s. As a result, many SOEs were deeply in debt and, by 1994, close to half of the SOEs had zero or negative equity. The decline in profitability was due to two reasons. First, without clear allocation of property rights, the SOEs' obligations were on the profit side but not on the loss side, which reduced the SOEs' incentives to improve their operating efficiencies. Second, SOEs operated under unfavorable conditions due to both, their many social responsibilities (e.g., social security, housing, and education) and external price controls imposed by the dual-track system. These policy burdens put the SOEs in a disadvantaged position in their competition with the rapidly growing private sector. Policy burdens also made it difficult for the state to impose hard budget constraints via bankruptcy of money-losing enterprises. Meanwhile, the dual-track system created enormous opportunities for corruption. In the end, the state acted as the residual claimant, absorbing the losses and the consequences of the diversion of state assets. This imposed a severe strain on the country's banking system. With SOEs relying on 70–80% of all bank credit, the banks were saddled with as much as US $200 billion in uncollectible debt, which accounted for, by conservative estimates, a quarter of all outstanding bank loans (USA Today, Sept. 8, 1997).

These problems ushered in a new stage of more fundamental reforms. In 1993, the Third Plenum of the Fourteenth Chinese Communist Party Congress endorsed the creation of a modern enterprise system. In particular, it approved the development of diversified forms of ownership through privatization, which would allow SOEs to compete on equal terms in the marketplace. In 1995, the central government decided on the policy of "retain the large, release the small" (*zhuada fangxiao*). That is, the state was to keep the largest 300 SOEs in strategic industries and allow smaller firms to be leased or sold. The Chinese Communist Party's 15th Congress (1997) gave a green light to privatizing the majority of SOEs nationwide. Regional governments were granted de jure ownership of SOEs within their jurisdictions and were allowed to sell their assets.

Large scale privatization began in the late 1990s. This "delayed" privatization brought about both advantages and difficulties in the designing of privatization programs. On the one hand, the market and legal institutional conditions for private ownership were much more developed than those during mass privatization in other transitional economies. On the other hand, at the time of privatization, most SOEs were losing money and were deep in debt. How to restructure the firms so that they could be sold off and/or how to attract buyers pose a challenge to the Chinese government. Restructuring means laying off excess labor, upgrading of plants and machinery, and injecting new capital, all of which were costly both socially and financially. Thus, depending on the cost of restructuring and the financial resources of the local governments, China adopts multiple methods to privatizing the SOEs. They include both privatization with explicit changes in ownership, such as management buy-outs (MBO) and sales to outsiders, and privatization without explicit changes in ownership, such as share issue privatization (SIP), joint ventures with foreign firms, and leasing. These different methods of privatization are discussed in the following section.

3 Methods of Privatization in China

Under the policy of "retaining the large, releasing the small," various different methods are used in privatizing China's SOEs. Except for SIP, there are no official statistics on the number of firms or the value of the assets that have been

Table 1 Methods of privatization and firm financials prior to privatization This table presents the methods of China's privatization and summary statistics of financial variables prior to privatization. Profits are defined as earnings before interest, tax, and depreciation. Significance levels are all based on on two-tailed tests of differences between MBOs / Selling to Outsiders and the overall sample. Significance at the 1%, 5%, and 10% levels is indicated by ***, **, and *, respectively

Panel A: Methods of privatization

	# of firms	Percentage
Explicit Ownership Change:		
MBO	338	47%
Selling to Outsiders	157	22%
Without Explicit Ownership Change:		
Listed	8	1%
JointVenture	11	2%
Lease	56	8%
Employee Holding	70	10%
Others	77	11%
Total	**717**	**100%**

Panel B: Financial variables by privatization methods

	Privatized SOEs		
	Privatized SOEs	**MBOs**	**Selling to Outsiders**
Asset (in thousands)	260,428	117,114***	119,705***
	(54,685)	(44,237***)	(39,437***)
Sales (in thousands)	155,596	77,595***	71,728**
	(24,662)	(22,121***)	(20,240**)
Leverage	0.143	0.132**	0.118***
	(0.072)	(0.069**)	(0.048***)
Profit/Assets	0.054	0.047**	0.073***
	(0.039)	(0.036)	(0.047***)
Profit/#Employee	10.883	7.901***	12.988***
	(5.230)	(4.449***)	(6.445***)

sold off. In this section, I base my discussions on the large-sample survey of about 3000 firms conducted by Gan et al. (2008), which is based on stratified sampling by region, industry, and sizes.

Table 1 presents the breakdown of different methods of privatization reported in Gan et al. (2008).

3.1 Privatization with Explicit Changes in Ownership

3.1.1 Management Buy-Outs

Management buy-outs (MBOs) are, by far, the most popular method, accounting for about one half (47%) of all privatization programs. In a typical MBO, the manager becomes the largest shareholder, resulting in no separation of ownership and control. Such perfectly aligned incentives can potentially lead to improved efficiency.

Table 1 (Panel B) compares MBOs with non-MBO firms. MBO firms tend to be smaller, slightly less leveraged, and less profitable. There are two possibilities here. One is that these weaker firms and insiders/managers are best able to turn them around. Thus MBOs are rationally chosen to provide the insiders with the right incentives. The second hypothesis is that MBOs are better firms but the managers have deliberately suppressed their earnings prior to privatization so that they could negotiate a better price from the government in the buy-outs, or managers may have private information about the (good) future prospects of the company and thus choose to buy out the better ones. These two possibilities suggest that MBOs are not random and the self-selection needs to be carefully accounted for in the empirical analysis of performance improvement.

3.1.2 Selling to Outsiders

The second most important method is selling to outsiders, which is used in 22% of privatization programs. The buyers include domestic and foreign firms, as well as wealthy individuals. Again as shown in Panel B of Table 1, in this type of privatization, the firms tend to be smaller, less leveraged, and more profitable.

3.2 Privatization Methods Without Explicit Changes in Ownership

3.2.1 Share Issue Privatization (SIP)

SIP is used for large SOEs that the government intends to "retain," under the policy of "retaining the large, releasing the small." Although most of the studies of China's privatization are about SIP, Table 1 shows that this type of privatization is the small proportion (1%) of privatization in China.

The government faced two major challenges during SIP. The first was, due to its ideological aversion to capitalism, how to ensure state control. The government first implemented partial privatization by keeping at least 50% ownership and then declared all state-related shares non-tradable so that control would not be transferred to the private sector through future trading.

The second challenge was how to restructure money-losing SOEs, which is costly both socially and financially. Thus, as reported by Deng et al. (2008), only about one-quarter of the SOEs were fully restructured before going public. For the remaining firms, as a way to avoid costly restructuring, the government organized the SOEs into a parent/subsidiary structure, where the most profitable assets were carved out for public listing while the parent companies became the largest shareholders and kept the excess workers, obsolete plants, and debt burdens.

These two approaches to pre-privatization restructuring created very different incentives for the controlling shareholders. In an economy with very limited legal institutions, the conflicts of interest between large and small shareholders are the main corporate governance concern. In a complete pre-privatization restructuring, the state-owned controlling shares were typically deposited in the State Assets Management Bureau or other SOEs that did not have a close business relationship with the listed company and they tended to be passive shareholders. In contrast, in incomplete restructuring, the state-owned shares are in the hands of the SOE parent company that has strong incentives to expropriate resources from their listed subsidiaries to solve their own problems under state ownership. Moreover, it was common for the parent SOE to send its own managers to be the CEO or chairman of the listed company. Such personnel connections further facilitate the ability of the parent companies to expropriate the minority shareholders.

3.2.2 Leasing, Joint Venture, and Others

There are a variety of other privatization programs that do not impose explicit changes in ownership. These include joint venture (2%), leasing (8%), and employee holding (10%).

4 Characteristics of Firms After Privatization

There are several notable characteristics of China's privatized firms. First, the state still plays an un-negligible role in firm operation: The state retains its influence on daily corporate decision making and good relationships with the government are reported to be important for firm growth. Second, in terms of ownership and control, privatization has created concentrated ownership. Performance-based pay becomes more popular to enhance incentives. Third, firms are moving toward greater level of professionalization by introducing international accounting standards and independent auditors, as well as board of directors.

4.1 The State Influence

A common feature of privatization programs around the world is that they are partial privatization, i.e., the government retains significant ownership in privatized firms (Jones et al., 1999; Gupta, 2005). Among the large SOEs that the government intends to "retain" through SIP, the government explicitly keeps at least 50% ownership so that state control can be ensured. According to Gan et al. (2008), among the smaller firms that are meant to be "released," the average state ownership is close to 20%, which includes both direct government ownership and ownership by another SOE.

In the GGX survey, all firms reported that their relationships with the governments and favorable government policies are important for their development. Fifty-seven per cent of the firms reported no changes in their relationships with the governments, 23% reported closer relationships with the government, and 20% reported more distant relationships with the governments.

Thus either through its ownership or due to the importance of government policies, the government potentially can exert influence on corporate decision making. In the GGX survey, the overall state influence drops from 2.8 to 1.4 after privatization (with 5 being the maximum).[1] State influence, however, is quite important in a significant proportion of firms, with 39% firms having a score above 2 (*Somewhat Important*) and 15% above 3 (*Moderately Important*). Since the state could have political goals that are different from profit-maximization, state control is likely to reduce the effectiveness of privatization.

4.2 Ownership and Incentives

As in many other countries, privatization in China created concentrated ownership (Table 2, Panel A). On average, the largest shareholder in the GGX sample owns 60% and the second/third largest shareholders own 26% of the shares of the privatized firms. Consistent with no-explicit change in ownership, methods other than MBOs and sales to outsiders still have 91% ownership in the hands of the government.

Concentrated ownership has both its advantages and disadvantages. On the one hand, concentrated ownership has the benefit of mitigating the free-rider problem in monitoring managers and, in the case of insider ownership, aligning

---

[1] GGX survey asks about several dimensions of corporate decision making, including the appointment of top managers, employment/layoffs and wages/compensation, corporate financial issues, production, and operations.

Table 2 Ownerships, Incentives, and Professionalization
This table presents basic facts of China's privatization and summary statistics of financial variables used in the empirical analysis. Profits are defined as earnings before interest, tax, and depreciation

Panel A. Ownership of privatized firms

		MBO	Selling to Outsiders	Other	Total
Ownership by the Largest Shareholder	Mean	37%	64%	91%	60%
	Median	(30%)	(70%)	(100%)	(51%)
Ownership by the Second and Third Largest Shareholder	Mean	27%	20%	30%	26%
	Median	(22%)	(15%)	(30%)	(20%)

Panel B. Incentives and professionalization

	Performance-based compensation	Change of core management team	International accounting and independent auditing	Establishing board of directors
MBO	8%	64%	11%	84%
Selling to Outsiders	15%	61%	7%	67%
Other	2%	60%	5%	71%
Whole Sample	7%	62%	8%	76%

managerial interests with those of shareholders. On the other hand, concentrated ownership comes with a well-known cost. That is, a large shareholder can expropriate the outside minority shareholders. This expropriation problem is potentially strongest in countries with weak property rights protection, where much privatization occurs.

Privatized firms have started to adopt equity incentives for top managers (Table 2). Interestingly, probably reflecting already aligned incentives at the MBO firms, they do not have more equity incentives than other firms. Selling to outsiders is twice more likely to have equity incentives than the overall sample. The 7% of firms with equity incentives in the overall sample, however, is a bit low, which makes one wonder if privatized firms without explicit ownership changes can really motivate its managers.

Another factor contributing to enhanced incentives in privatized firms is hardening of soft-budget constraints. The soft-budget constraint is an important reason why the firms had little incentive to improve their efficiency. In the GGX survey, about 18% of the firms experienced financial distress before privatization and 3% of the firms experienced financial distress after privatization. Before privatization, in 27% of the distress cases, the firms gained direct help from the government; more than half obtained bank loans (56%) or loans from other, presumably state-owned, firms (57%). As a result, only 17% were reorganized before privatization despite their financial distress. After privatization, the government, banks, and other SOEs provided help in only 19%, 31%, and 19% of the cases, respectively, and 29% of the firms in financial distress were reorganized.

4.3 *Professionalization*

Privatization is associated with significant personnel changes in firms. Over 62% of the firms changed their core members of the management team after privatization, whereas only 15% of private firms have made similar changes in the GGX survey. Presumably, the new managers are hired based on ability to run the firms, rather than political concerns as in the old SOEs. Thus such top-manager turnover is a step toward professional management in the privatized firms.

About 8% of the firms have adopted international standards, whereas the number is significantly higher among MBOs (11%). Meanwhile, about 76% of firms have established boards of directors and the number, again, is significantly higher among MBOs (84%).

5 Understanding the Efficiency Gain of China's Privatization

It is well known that Chinese SIP does not improve efficiency; rather it reduces operating performance (Sun and Tong, 2003). Deng et al. (2008) point out that the root cause of the failure of SIP is the conflicts of interests between the large shareholders and the minority shareholders. Based on detailed firm-level data on related-party transactions, the authors document two channels through which large shareholders expropriate resources at the expense of minority shareholders. One is through related-party transactions, including transfer pricing of goods and services, assets sales, and extracting trade credits; the other is through dividend policies so that corporate resources are kept in the firm and under their control.[2]

In contrast to SIP, little is known about the outcomes of other methods of privatization, which accounts for 99% of all privatization programs in China, simply because the firms remain private and thus there is not any publicly available data. The existing studies are mainly based on regional data of selected cities/provinces. For example, Li and Rozelle (2000) study 88 privatized township enterprises in Jiangsu and Zhejiang provinces. Song and Yao

[2] There has been a growing literature that examines the relationship between corporate governance and firm performance in China's share issue privatization. For example, Sun and Tong (2003) show that the composition of state-owned shares affects firm performance. Fan et al. (2007) find that CEOs who are former or current government officials are associated with less professionalized boards and worse firm performance. These studies, however, do not speak of the underlying mechanism for how weak corporate governance worsens the performance of China's privatized firms.

(2004) and Garnault et al. (2005) use firm-level data covering 683 firms in 11 cities from 1995 to 2001. The study by Liu and Lu (2005) is based on survey data collected from 451 firms in five cities and four sectors during the 1994–1999. Yusuf et al. (2005) reported on a survey of 736 firms from five cities and seven sectors from 1996 to 2001. All of these papers find that privatization has improved profitability. But the generality of the results are not warranted, nor do these studies speak as to *why* privatization in China has improved efficiency.[3]

The survey by Gan et al. (2008) is an important step to fill the gap. Based on simple summary statistics from the survey, both profitability and productivity have increased. Moreover, among all the privatization methods, only those with explicit ownership change and especially MBOs improve efficiency. These results are strong and robust to endogeneity concerns. Interested readers should refer to Gan et al. (2008) for the details of the analysis.

The success of privatization other than SIP in China is in contrast to the findings in the previous literature that insider privatization does not improve efficiency in Eastern Europe and Russia (Barberis et al., 1996). It is important to point out that there are some key differences between the institutional environment at the time of mass privatization in other transitional economies and that in China. At the time of mass privatization, the countries have not established product markets, labor markets, or financial markets. Private ownership is an unfamiliar phenomenon. Under this situation, managers or private owners may not have sustained interest in running the firms, nor do they have a clear exit strategy. In contrast, when the delayed privatization in China happens, market institutions have developed and, equally importantly, the private sector has become a big part of the economy. Moreover, capital market is developed enough to provide the new owners an exit strategy to fully capitalize the efficiency gains.

6 Conclusion

Privatization in China has greatly changed the landscape of the state-owned firms. In particular, it has created concentrated private ownership and large shareholders essentially control major decision making in their firms. While the control rights of the state has greatly reduced, its policy support is still important to firm growth. Moreover, state influence remains important in a significant portion of firms, which potentially hinders efficiency improvement.

After privatization, soft-budget constraints were substantially hardened and incentives enhanced through equity incentives either as compensation or as

[3] The only work based on the nationwide data is that by Jefferson and Su (2006). However, they did not have direct information about privatization. They inferred that privatization had occurred due to changes in the legal registration of the firms.

ownership. The firms are moving toward greater levels of professionalization by hiring professional managers, introducing international accounting standard, and establishing board of directors.

Privatized firms became more efficient and more profitable based on various measures. Such efficiency gain appears to be most significant among those where incentives are better aligned. Specific mechanisms of improved post-privatization performance are considered in a contemporaneous paper (Gan et al., 2008).

Chinese privatization experience provides several insights on privatization design, in general. First, the Chinese experiences highlights the importance of incentives of large shareholders. Only when the large shareholders' incentives are in place, would the firms undertake fundamental restructuring measures to enhance efficiency. Second, the Chinese experience suggests that postponing privatization to accumulate market institutions increases the effectiveness of privatization. In particular, the privatized firms can benefit from the product and labor markets for expansion and managerial tenant. They also benefit from better developed financial institutions to obtain external financing. Legal institutions protect the property rights of the owners of privatized firms and provide them with incentives to grow their firms (Johnson et al., 2002). Finally, new private owners could use capital market as an exit strategy to capitalize the efficiency gains.

References

Barberis, N., M. Boycko, A. Shleifer, and N. Tsukanova, 1996. "How Does Privatization Work? Evidence from the Russian Shops," *Journal of Political Economy* CIV: 764–790.

Deng, J., J. Gan, and J. He, 2008. "The Dark Side of Concentrated Ownership in Privatization: Evidence from China," *Hong Kong University of Science and Technology Working Paper*.

Fan, J., Wong, T.J., and Zhang, T., 2007. "Politically Connected CEOs, Corporate Governance, and Post-IPO Performance of China's Newly Partly Privatized Firms," *Journal of Financial Economics*, 84 (2), 330–357.

Gan, J., Y. Guo, and C. Xu, 2008. "Privatization of SOEs in China," *Hong Kong University of Science and Technology Working Paper*.

Garnault, R., L. Song, and Y. Yao, 2005. "Impact and Significance of SOE Restructuring in China," *CCER Working Paper Series*, 2005.

Groves, T., Y. Hong, J. McMillan, and B. Naughton. 1994. "Autonomy and incentives in Chinese state enterprises," *Quarterly Journal of Economics*, 109, 183–209.

Guo, Y., J. Gan, and C. Xu, 2008. "A Nationwide Survey of Privatized Firms in China," *Seoul Journal of Economics*, 21, 311–331.

Gupta, N., 2005. "Partial Privatization and Firm Performance." *Journal of Finance* 60, 987–1015.

Jefferson, G and Su, J., 2006. "Privatization and Restructuring in China: Evidence from Shareholding Ownership," *Journal of Comparative Economics*, 34(1), 146–166.

Johnson, S., J. McMillan, and C. Woodruff. 2002. "Property Rights and Finance," *The American Economic Review*, 92(5), December 2002, 1335–1356.

Jones, S.L., W.L. Megginson, R.C. Nash, and J.M. Netter, 1999. "Share Issue Privatizations as Financial Means to Political Ends." *Journal of Financial Economics,* 53, 217–253.
Li, H., and S. Rozelle, 2000. "Savings or Stripping Rural Industry: An Analysis of Privatization and Efficiency in China," *Agricultural Economics*, 23(3), 241–252.
Li, W. 1997. "The Impact of Economic Reform on the Performance of Chinese State Enterprises, 1980–1989," *Journal of Political Economy*, 105, 1080–1106.
Liu, X. and T. Lu, 2005. "Formality of SOEs Transformation Reform and Firms' Performance," (qiye gaizhi moshi he gaizhi jixiao), *Journal of Economic Research (jingji yanjiu)*, 40, 94–103.
Song, L. and Y. Yao, 2004. "Impacts of Privatization on Firm Performance in China,"*CCER Working Paper Series*, No. E2004005, 2004.
Sun, Q. and W. Tong, 2003. "China Share Issue Privatization: The Extent of Its Success." *Journal of Financial Economics*, 70, 183–222.
Yusuf, S., N. Kaoru, and D.H. Perkins. 2005. "Under New Ownership: Privatizing China's State-Owned Enterprises." *Stanford University Press and the World Bank*, 2005.

The Emergence of Shareholder Protection in China

Chen Lin, Clement Chun-Yau Shum, and Sonia Man-Lai Wong

Abstract This chapter seeks to provide an understanding of how legal protection for shareholders gradually emerged in China. Specifically, we trace the underlying forces driving the emergence of legal protection to shareholders to the vested interests of the central government. We show that the evolution of the legal developments is consistent with the government's changing interests in the stock market, with the provision of shareholder protection becoming an increasingly important instrument for the government to serve its interests. To a certain extent, the legal developments in China's stock market show that the country's legal systems still maintain the ancient tradition whereby "[t]he state promulgated laws to make sure its interests were advanced. As this was done, the interests of private individuals or groups of such persons were often protected as indirect results" (Jones 2003, pp. 15–56).

Keywords Legal protections to investors · Stock market development · Political economy of legal development

1 Introduction

The emergence and development of a capital market requires more than the spontaneous actions of fund-seekers and investors. Rules and laws are needed to reduce transaction costs so as to make the market viable (North 1990). Nevertheless, the rules and laws governing the operation of a capital market are not neutral with respect to the interests of fund-seekers and investors, because they define the opportunity sets opened to fund-seekers and investors and change their liability profiles (Shleifer and Vishny 1997). As a result, the nature of the legal coverage for investors has been considered a key determinant of financial market development. The general hypothesis is that in countries

C. Lin (✉)
City University of Hong Kong, Hong Kong, China
e-mail: chenlin@cityu.edu.hk

J.R. Barth et al. (eds.), *China's Emerging Financial Markets*,
The Milken Institute Series on Financial Innovation and Economic Growth 8,
DOI 10.1007/978-0-387-93769-4_20,

where investor rights are better protected, investors are more willing to finance firms, and financial markets in those countries grow more rapidly (La Porta et al. 1997; 1998). While disagreements remain, a large body of empirical studies offer evidence to support the positive links between investor protection and financial market development (La Porta et al. 1997; 1998; 2003; Levin 1998; 1999). These studies raise the important questions of why the level of investor protection in different countries varies so much and why the level of protection within a country changes over time.

This chapter attempts to provide a case study on how legal protection for shareholders has gradually emerged in China. Stock market development in China took off in the early 1990s, when two stock exchanges were established in Shanghai and Shenzhen, respectively. During the early 1990s, China's stock market developed under a weak legal framework that provided little protection for investors (Tenev and Zhang 2002; Allen et al. 2005; Pistor and Xu 2005). Starting from the late 1990s, China's central government began to gradually extend more and more legal protection to shareholders. The most important development was a judicial interpretation issued by the Supreme People's Court (SPC) in January 2001, which stated that cases relating to false information disclosure could be pursued in local courts. This document introduced for the first time civil threats to China's listed companies. The SPC issued another circular in January 2003, which set up some detailed rules for the acceptance and adjudication of private securities litigation (PSL). Furthermore, discussions on amending China's Company Law (1993) and Securities Law (1998) started in 2004 with the aim of increasing the provisions relating to the protection of investors. The amendments to both laws were completed at the end of 2005, and they came into effect on January 1, 2006. Because of the recent developments in legal reforms, more than 2,000 lawsuits have been filed nationwide against some 20 listed companies (Chen 2003). Zou et al. (2008) show that there is a non-negligible perceived securities litigation risk in China, as evidenced by the fact that the listed firms exposed to a high level of litigation risk are more likely to take out directors' and officers' liability insurance.

The previous literature has emphasized the role of a country's legal heritage in influencing the level of legal protection offered to investors. La Porta et al. (1997; 1998) show that differences in legal protection are related to the legal family to which a country belongs: namely, the civil law system seems to grant less protection than common law systems. These authors argue that this finding can be explained by the tradition for common law to protect private property rights relative to the rights of the state. Johnson et al. (2002)1, however, argue that the common law system offers more protection to investors because the judges under it enjoy more discretionary power to detect and punish investor expropriation on a case-by-case basis.

China has a unique legal tradition that is different from both common law and civil systems. A distinctive characteristic of China's legal system is that the courts are not independent of the state administrative system, and the law is an instrument used by the ruling elite to serve their interests (Jones 2003; Chen

2003). As a result, China's legal tradition focuses on administrative and criminal sanctions but not on civil liabilities. Although China's legal system has witnessed significant changes since the introduction of economic reforms in 1978, it still retains its traditional role as an instrument of the ruling class for dealing with problems arising from the economic reform process (Chen 2003). The dominance of the state administration over the courts in China is guaranteed by the fact that the budgets and the appointments of judges in local courts are controlled by the local governments (Hutchens 2003). Furthermore, the local courts are subject to oversight by the Communist Party political-legal committees, which are superimposed on the legal system (Chen 2003).

Under such a unique legal system, the evolution of legal institutions in China is likely to be shaped by the changing interests of the political elite. In this chapter, we trace the underlying forces driving the emergence of shareholder protection to the changing vested interests of the central government in the stock market. We show that the emergence of legal protection to investors is consistent with three major changes in China's financial sector since the late 1990s that have significantly altered the central government's calculations of the costs and benefits involved in providing legal protections to investors. First, there has been a change in the relative importance between the banking sector and the stock market as a venue for the funding of state-owned enterprises (SOEs), with the stock market acquiring an increasingly important role. Secondly, there is a need for the central government to unload its shareholdings in the stock market, which has increasingly tied the government's interests to those of the private minority shareholders. Thirdly, there is a gradual privatization process that lessens the conflict of interests of the government, which has served as a controlling shareholder on one hand and a regulator on the other. We argue that these changes have altered the government's vested interests in the stock market, with the provision of legal protection to shareholders becoming an increasingly desirable prescription for the central government to serve its own interests.

Chen (2003) argues that legal developments in China's stock market have been driven by the emergence of the private investors who are able to form an informal politically powerful constituency because of their increasing size, as well as their common and identifiable economic interests. As we shall show, private investors' efforts to defend their interests, either through voice (demonstrations on the streets, petition to local courts) or exit (selling of stocks), have indeed played an important role in the process of legal development. This chapter, however, emphasizes the direct vested interests of the central government in the stock market and argues that the provision of more and more legal protection to shareholders is also consistent with the changing vested interests of the government. The legal developments in China's stock market have therefore been a consequence of the complex interactions between the government on one hand and private shares on the other. Nevertheless, such interactions were taking place within a one-party authoritarian regime where the government enjoyed the political power to define the rules and law. As such, the interests of the government should play a central role in shaping the course of the development.

The remainder of this chapter is structured as follows. Section 2 briefly reviews the historical development of the stock market and the emergence of investor protection law in China. Section 3 discusses the vested interests of the central government in the stock market and explains how the legal developments are consistent with the changing interests of the government. Section 4 concludes the paper with a discussion of the likely evolution of China's shareholder protection in the future.

2 The Emergence of Investor Protection in China

The rise of the stock market in China's transitional economy has received worldwide attention. For more than 30 years after 1949, China was a centrally planned economy in which virtually all enterprises were state owned or collectively owned. The Central Planning Commission made all the important economic decisions on production and investments, with investments funded by state budgetary grants. In order to ensure effective implementation of production and investment plans and minimal disruptions from the financial system on the operations of the central planning system, China's financial sector was monopolized by only one bank, the People's Bank of China (PBOC).[1] Stock markets, owing to their intrinsic association with private ownership and potential threats posed to the planning system, were viewed as a potent symbol of capitalism. The last stock exchange in pre-reform China was shut down in February 1952, the same year the Central Planning Commission was established.

The stock market re-emerged in China in the mid-1980s out of the initiatives of some local governments, which took over control and cash flow rights of the vast majority of small- and medium-sized collectively owned enterprises in the early 1980s. These governments then experimented with selling the stocks of these enterprises directly to domestic individual investors in order to raise funds to finance the enterprises. Curbed trading of enterprise stocks soon began and was quickly followed by over-the-counter (OTC) trading in more organized but still informal exchanges. In 1991, two stock exchanges, one created by the Shanghai municipal government and the other by the Shenzhen municipal government, were launched with the central government's formal approval (Wong 2006).

Table 1 summarizes the growth of China's stock market since its inception. The market experienced tremendous growth with total (negotiable) market capitalization increasing from 354.15 (86.16) billion yuan at the end of 1993

[1] All state-owned institutions and enterprises were obliged to place all their funds, above a certain cash holding, at the PBOC. The PBOC then provided working capital to enterprises as dictated by central cash and credit plans. Private individuals were not required to place their funds at the PBOC, though saving deposits at the PBOC were their only form of investment allowed. For China's financial system in the pre-reform period, see Xu (1998), pp.8-16.

Table 1 Overview of China's stock market: 1992–2007

	No. of listed enterprises (A,B share)	Total amount of capital raised (RMB billion)	Number of investor accounts (million)	Market capitalization (RMB billion)		Market capitalization to GDP (%)		Trading Volume (RMB billion)	Domestic-raised capital to amount of bank loan (%)
				Total market	Negotiable	Total market	Negotiable		
1992	53	9.41	2.17	104.81	–	3.93	–	68.13	–
1993	183	31.45	8.35	354.15	86.16	10.2	2.39	366.70	4.96
1994	291	13.81	11.08	369.06	96.89	7.89	2.06	812.76	1.91
1995	323	11.89	12.94	347.43	93.82	5.94	1.6	403.65	1.27
1996	530	34.15	24.22	984.24	286.70	14.5	4.22	2,133.22	3.20
1997	745	93.38	34.80	1,752.92	520.44	23.44	6.96	3,072.18	8.72
1998	851	80.36	42.60	1,952.18	574.56	24.52	7.22	2,354.43	6.99
1999	949	89.74	48.11	2,647.12	821.40	31.82	9.87	3,131.96	8.27
2000	1,088	154.10	61.23	4,809.09	1,608.75	53.79	17.99	6,082.67	11.55
2001	1,160	118.21	68.99	4,352.22	1,446.32	45.37	15.08	3,830.52	9.50
2002	1,224	77.98	68.42	3,832.91	1,248.46	37.43	12.19	2,799.05	4.11
2003	1,287	82.31	69.81	4,245.77	1,317.85	36.38	11.29	3,211.53	2.97
2004	1,377	86.27	72.16	3,705.56	1,168.86	23.22	7.32	4,233.39	4.49
2005	1,381	154.44	73.36	3,243.03	1,063.05	17.70	5.80	3,166.48	9.36
2006	1,434	559.43	78.54	8,940.39	2,500.36	42.69	11.94	9046.89	18.29
2007.6	1,477	252.63	107.06	16,623.28	5,557.28	–	–	23718.00	9.90

Sources: China's Securities and Future Yearbook.
GDP for 2006 comes from Wind database; other Data for 2006 and June 2007are obtained from the CSRC website: http://www.csrc.gov.cn and http://www.pbc.gov.cn.

to 8,940.39 (2,500.36) billion yuan at the end of 2006.[2] Total market capitalization relative to the Gross Domestic Product (GDP) increased from 3.93% in 1992 to 53.79% in 2000. Due to weak market conditions in the early 2000s, the total market capitalization-to-GDP ratio slipped to 17.70% in 2005. However, it again ballooned to 42.69% at the end of 2006 after the government introduced a series of policies to boost the stock market. On August 7, 2007, the total market capitalization of the two stock exchanges in China topped the country's GDP in 2006 for the first time when key stock indices hit new record highs.[3] In conjunction with the growth in market capitalization, the market also enjoyed a high level of liquidity, with trading volume increasing from 68.13 billion yuan in 1992 to 9,046.89 billion yuan in 2006.

The development of a stock market needs to be supported by rules and regulations. The rules and regulations would have different implications for the rights enjoyed by shareholders. From the inception of China's stock market in the late 1980s to January 2002, when SPC issued a judicial interpretation that opened the door for private securities litigations, shareholder rights in China were protected through administrative sanctions and criminal punishments (which are determined by the government administration and government-controlled courts) but not private civil actions (Chen 2003; Wong 2006; Howson 2006). Since the early 2000s, significant changes have occurred within the legal frameworks in which private shareholders have been provided with more and more opportunities to use the judicial systems to bring lawsuits against the listed companies (including controlling shareholders, directors, supervisors, and managers). In other words, shareholders in China are granted PSL as a weapon to defend their interests, though their hands are still tied by several impeding legal procedures. Figure 1 provides a brief timeline on the evolution of shareholder protection in China.

Prior to the creation of the two national stock exchanges in 1991, the People's Bank of China (PBOC) acted as China's securities market regulator. As stock issuance and trading were considered politically sensitive "experiments," the PBOC chose to delegate its authority over the regulation of the stock market to its local branches. The earliest regulations over the issuance of stocks in China were therefore promulgated by the PBOC's local branches in areas such as Shanghai Municipality, Beijing Municipality, Guangdong Province, and Xiamen Special Economic Zone. As stock issuance and trading had been banned in China for more than three decades, the primary concern of these early regulations was to make it clear who had the rights to issue and buy stocks.

---

[2] A typical listed firm in China has two types of shares. The first type includes shares issued to state-owned entities which are not allowed to be traded on China's two stock exchanges. The second type includes freely tradable shares issued to private individual investors. Total market capitalization refers to the market value of all shares issued by China's listed firms. Negotiable market capitalization refers to the market value of all shares issued to private individual investors.

[3] Data are obtained from http://www.china.org.cn/english/business/220377.htm

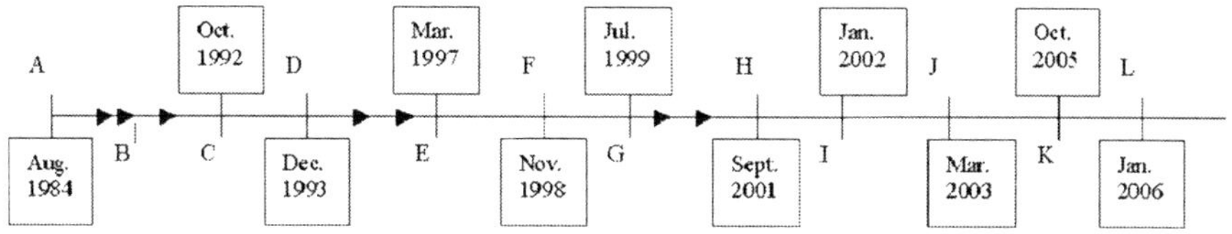

Time Point	Event
A	The local branch of the People's Bank of China (PBOC)in Shanghai issued its first regulation on issuance of stock
B	Regulations on issuance of stocks were promulgated by local branches of PBOC in areas such as Beijing Municipality, Guangdong Province, and Xiamen Special Economics Zone
	The State Council thus issued a regulation in May 1990 to restrict share issuance to SOEs rather than collectively owned enterprises
	State Council then issued another regulation in May 1992 that categorized the shares of a shareholding enterprise into three types: (1) state and legal person shares, (2) A-shares, and (3) B-shares
C	The State Council Securities Commission (SCSC) and China Securities Regulatory Commission (CSRC)
D	China's first *Company Law* was promulgated, which became effective on January 1, 1994
E	The Criminal Law was amended to criminalize securities fraud
F	The first private securities litigation (PSL) case was brought against the *Hongguang Industrial* for false information disclosure
G	China's first *Securities Law* became effective
H	The Supreme People's Court (SPC) issued a temporary ban on accepting PSL cases by local courts
I	CSRC issued "Standard on Corporate Governance for Listed Companies"
	SPC issued a circular that allowed local courts to accept PSL cases relating to information misrepresentation
J	SPC issued detailed rules on handling PSL cases relating to information misrepresentation
K	The revised *Company Law* allows the shareholder to take a derivative action in certain circumstances, and the amended *Securities Law* specifies civil remedies for a number of additional violations such as insider trading
L	The revised *Company Law* and *Securities Law* became effective

Fig. 1 A Timeline on the evolution of shareholder protection in China

The local governments that had spontaneously initiated stock issuance took a cautious approach at the beginning by limiting issuers to only collectively owned enterprises and no SOEs. Shortly afterwards, the central government realized that such a strategy in effect diverted the valuable capital away from SOEs to collectively owned enterprises. The State Council thus issued a regulation in May 1990 to restrict stock issuance to SOEs rather than collectively owned enterprises. As the issuance of stocks to individuals inherently creates private ownership, which could threaten state control over enterprises, the State

Council then issued another regulation in May 1992 that categorized the shares of a shareholding enterprise into three types: (1) state and legal person shares, which are owned either directly or indirectly by the state and which cannot be traded freely on the stock exchanges but can be transferred only with administrative approval; (2) A-shares, which are yuan-denominated and are available for trading by domestic private shareholders on the stock exchanges; and (3) B-shares, which are available for trading by foreign investors in foreign currencies on the stock exchanges. These two regulations served the government's twin objectives of establishing the stock market: reserving for the stock market an exclusive fundraising vehicle for SOEs while maintaining state control over enterprises.

The intent of the early regulations was to authorize stock issuance as a legitimate means of fund-raising in a socialist economy and to restrict the valuable fund-raising opportunities to SOEs. Shareholder rights were not mentioned, except that shareholders were entitled to receive a certain fixed percentage of dividends. Furthermore, there was no regulation aimed at making the market transparent and fair. As a result, the nascent market was plagued by widespread fraud and abuse. In August 1992, a riot broke out in Shenzhen, when roughly a million eager investors became suspicious that corrupt officials had diverted their application forms of a hot IPO. Such incidents indicated that the PBOC was not able to exercise effective control over the newly emerged stock market. In response to this crisis, the central government established the State Council Securities Commission (SCSC) and the China Securities Regulatory Commission (CSRC) in October 1992. While the SCSC was responsible for exercising centralized control over the stock market, the CSRC was the SCSC's executive arm responsible for supervising and regulating the market.

The efforts of private investors to defend their own interests thus led to the establishment of the CSRC as a watchdog on China's stock market. Shortly after its establishment, the CSRC promulgated the *Interim Regulation on the Administration of the Issuing and Trading of Shares* in 1993, which was intended to govern the issuing and trading of stock. In the same year, *the Provisional Measures on Prohibiting Securities Fraud* was also issued. The later regulation detailed different kinds of securities fraud, including insider trading, market manipulation, and false information disclosure. In line with China's legal tradition, penalties for violations were restricted to fines and administrative sanctions but did not include civil remedies. Furthermore, there was no provision allowing private individuals to take their cases to the courts. The intent of these regulations was to crack down on those activities that threatened the functioning of the stock market (Lee 2001). It is true that shareholders' interests were better protected with the introduction of these regulations. However, this was an indirect outcome of the government's attempts to maintain and improve the functioning of its fund-raising vehicle. Without civil remedies and PSL through which aggrieved investors are able to defend their interests and seek remedies directly, shareholders' private right of action was not recognized.

In 1993, the government took another step to promulgate China's first Company Law, which became effective on January 1, 1994. Under the 1994 Company Law, private shareholders were conferred many rights such as the right to seek compensation for damages due to information misrepresentation and market manipulation. On the other hand, directors, managers, and supervisors were required to protect the interests and benefits of the company with loyalty and honesty. Shareholders were, however, not provided the legal procedure to sue them on behalf of the company for their wrongdoing.

On December 29, 1998, the National People's Congress passed the PRC Securities Law, which became effective on July 1, 1999. Similar to the 1993 Company Law, the Securities Law gave considerable power to the government to impose criminal and administrative penalties on wrongdoers. Little attention was paid to civil remedies available to aggrieved investors. The Law contained only one article (Article 63) in which an issuer or underwriter was required to compensate investors for the losses caused by its misrepresentation, misleading statements, or material omissions in prospectuses, financial and accounting reports, and annual reports. Similar to the legal provisions in the Company Law, this clause was not very practicable because of the lack of procedures provided for such litigation. Furthermore, the Securities Law specified no civil liability for insider trading and market manipulation.

During the early 2000s, China's stock market was riddled with outbreaks of corporate scandals. A common feature of these scandals was that the interests of millions of minority shareholders (often individuals) were seriously infringed upon by the controlling shareholders (often a state-owned enterprise (SOE)). Realizing that many of these scandals had stemmed from the poor corporate governance, China launched several corporate governance reforms. One key reform was the introduction of the independent director system under which independent directors are required to express opinions on the fairness of important corporate decisions to minority shareholders; for example, relating to financial reporting, profit distribution, investment plans, and related-party transactions. The independent director system was formalized by the CSRC in 2002 when listed firms were required to have at least one-third of their board members as independent directors by June 30, 2003.

After the promulgation of the Securities Law in late 1998, the CSRC and the two stock exchanges took more aggressive administrative actions to punish corporate misdeeds and securities misfeasance. For the period 1996 to 1998, the regulatory agencies took only 18 administrative actions. However, they imposed 94 administrative sanctions during the period from 1999 to 2001.[4] In 2001, the CSRC declared that year as the "year of market supervision" and commenced a series of investigations into irregularities and illegitimate activities in the stock market. Private shareholders, however, seemed not satisfied

[4] Data on administrative actions taken by the CSRC and the two stock exchanges can be obtained from WIND Information and Technology Ltd.

with the intensified actions from the regulators, probably because they could not recover the financial losses they suffered, though in the absence of a clear legal basis and procedure, some shareholders turned to the local courts to seek remedies. The first reported shareholder lawsuit against a listed firm in China was initiated by an individual shareholder in April 1998 who sued *Hongguang Industrial* company for information misrepresentation. Although the CSRC fined the company for its wrongdoing, a Shanghai local court dismissed the case on the ground that securities disputes should be handled by the CSRC rather than by local courts (Chen 2003).

In late September 2001, the SPC issued a "temporary" ban on accepting private shareholder lawsuits by all the local courts in China, claiming that there were no established legal procedures and a lack of sufficient expertise and knowledge on the part of judges to hear such new and complex cases (Howson 2006). Four months later, the SPC lifted the ban and issued a circular that allowed local courts to accept cases relating to fraudulent and misleading disclosure. The issuance of this circular led to a substantial increase in the number of civil cases brought against listed companies. In 2002 alone, various local courts in China accepted about 900 such cases (Chen 2003; Howson 2006). However, most of the lawsuits against listed firms remained in the courts and were not further handled due to the lack of detailed rules on how these cases should be heard. In January 2003, the SPC eventually issued a judicial interpretation that included detailed rules for handling PSL cases relating to false information disclosure (SPC's 2003 Rule). The interpretation also enabled shareholders to launch collective civil suits in which a number of plaintiffs could gather to sue a listed enterprise through a few representatives.

SPC's 2003 Rule has been regarded as a milestone in the evolution of shareholder rights in China. For the first time, shareholders in China were provided with legal procedures that enabled them to take their cases to the courts. Nevertheless, China's legal tradition of protecting the interests of the ruling class persisted even with this remarkable legal breakthrough. While allowing the possibility of PSL for shareholders, the SPC's 2003 Rule includes several provisions that obviously protect the interests of the government. The most obvious protection is that it requires administrative sanctions by government agencies as a prerequisite for any private securities litigation. In other words, PLS must first be sanctioned by governments. As Hutchens (2003) argues, this requirement effectively puts the "right to sue" in the hand of the governments but not the shareholders. Shareholders in China actually do not enjoy the real "private" litigation rights. Given that many listed companies in China are government-owned, the requirement of enabling government actions in effect provides an effective shield for the government-owned listed firms. Furthermore, the Rule has placed initial jurisdiction with the intermediate-level people's courts where a listed firm defendant is located. Appeals will be made to the higher-level people courts within the same province, which are in fact controlled by the same government. The interests of government-owned firms are therefore further protected. In addition, the Rule explicitly rules out the possibility of class actions that would expose the government-owned listed firms to massive private securities litigation judgments and lead to the formation of politically risky interest groups (Hutchens 2003). Furthermore, the litigation risks faced by the listed firms are further reduced by limiting lawsuits only to cases relating to information misrepresentation but not insider trading, market manipulation, or breaches of fiduciary duties.

Probably due to the above obstacles, the number of cases brought against the listed firms remained small. In the 3 years up to December 2005, though the media revealed cases of securities misfeasance almost every week, there were only 20 listed firm defendants (Howson 2006).

Notwithstanding the obvious reluctance on the part of the SPC to introduce SPL, promising developments occurred in 2004 when discussions on the Company Law and Securities Law were started. The new Company Law and Securities Law, which were adopted in November 2005 and became effective on January 1, 2006, provided expanded rights to shareholders and included many provisions that established a legal basis for shareholders to use the judicial system to defend their interests and recover financial losses. The new Securities Law, which involves amendments to more than 100 articles, contains many detailed provisions regarding the civil liabilities for false corporate disclosure. More importantly, civil liabilities are also established for insider trading and market manipulations.

There are provisions in the new Company Law that are meant to improve corporate governance and give more rights to shareholders. For example, Article 21 prohibits the controlling shareholders, actual controllers, directors, supervisors, and senior management personnel of a company from abusing their positions so as to cause the company to suffer losses, in which case they have to compensate the company. This will catch arrangements such as using company funds to provide guarantee or loan for themselves or their relatives or friends. The difficulty with this provision is who would represent the company in taking the appropriate legal action. According to the revised PRC Civil Procedure Law (adopted on October 28, 2007 by the National People's Congress and effective as of April 1, 2008), a legal person should be represented in litigation by its legal representative (Article 49), but the legal representative may be one of the wrongdoers. A shareholder may apply to the court to have a company resolution rescinded, if it violates the provisions of laws or administrative regulations or the articles of association of the company (Article 22). Shareholders may now require a director, supervisor, or senior management personnel to attend a meeting and answer their queries (Article 151).

Article 148 of the new Company Law provides that directors, supervisors, and senior management personnel shall follow the laws, administrative regulations, and articles of association of the company. They also owe a duty of loyalty and duty of care and diligence to the company. They are not allowed to use their positions to take bribes or other illegal income and seize the company's property. In particular, they are not allowed to (i) misappropriate company funds, (ii) deposit company funds in a bank account opened in their names or in the name of others, (iii) use company funds to make loans to others or provide guarantee for others, (iv) enter into contracts with the company or carry out transactions with the company in violation with the provisions of the articles of association of the company or without the consent of the shareholders' meeting or a shareholders' general meeting, (v) divert commercial opportunities to themselves or others while carrying out their duties, or engage in similar business as the company's in their names or for others without the consent of the shareholders' meeting or a shareholders' general meeting, (vi) pocket the commission for transactions between the company and other parties, (vii) disclose the company secrets, and (viii) do any other act which violates their duty of loyalty to the company (article 149). When they perform their duties not in accordance with the laws, administrative regulations, or the articles of association of the company and cause the company to suffer damages, they shall bear civil compensation liability (Article 150). A shareholder may request the board of directors or supervisors to take legal action against the wrongdoer, and if they refuse the shareholder may file a lawsuit with a people's court directly in his/her own name to protect the interests of the company (Article 152). Article 152 in the new Company Law introduces a new procedure commonly known as derivative action in the common law system under which a shareholder may bring action to the court on behalf of the company against directors or senior management personnel for breach of Article 150. As the right to sue is derived from the company, any damages recovered will belong to the company. But under what circumstances will the shareholder be able to recover his legal cost is not provided in the new Company Law. Derivative action originated in the common law system and both judges and lawyers in China do not have much experience in handling this particular legal procedure. Hence, it is interesting to see how it will be developed in China in the near future.

3 The Central Government's Changing Vested Interests in the Stock Market

At the time that China's stock market took off in the mid-1980s, shareholders in China enjoyed essentially no shareholder rights except for the right to receive dividends. Alongside the growth of China's stock market, shareholders have gained more and more shareholder rights, and eventually gained in 2002 the private right of actions to bring their cases to courts. This is particularly extraordinary given China's legal tradition of deemphasizing civil actions (Chen 2003; Howson 2006). So, how have such significant changes come into being? Chen (2003) emphasizes the role played by private investors who have gradually developed into a politically powerful constituency. Howson (2006), on the other hand, argues that "[i]t is unclear which particular forces in Chinese society were determinative in the Court's lifting of the ban" on the acceptance of lawsuits by the lower courts (p.12), though shareholders, legal professionals, and the media certainly made a great deal of noise when the initial ban was imposed. Our review of the historical development reveals that private shareholders have played important roles in the development process, as shown by the 1982 riot in Shenzhen and their efforts to take their cases to the local courts even before the existence of any juridical procedures issued by the SPC. Nevertheless, shareholders in China were usually less educated people who had never been organized. Although they voiced their anger and demanded compensation when their interests were hurt, they did not have a clear idea or vision of how to defend their rights through legal means. The new provisions in the revised Securities Law and Company Law are certainly not a response of the government to a set of well-articulated demands from shareholders, as many of the provisions (such as cumulative voting, derivative action, and duty of loyalty) are surely beyond the expectations if not the comprehension of many of the shareholders. Media and legal professionals have also exerted some influences by bringing a series of corporate scandals to light and staging debates on how shareholder rights should be protected in China. The voices of the media and legal professionals, however, have never been so overwhelming and embarrassing that the government has had no choice but to compromise. After all, it is not difficult for the government to stop such reports and discussions if it wants to do so. While acknowledging the influences of shareholders, scholars, lawyers, and journalists in shaping the course of development, we try to unveil the direct interests of the central government in the stock market and explain how the provision of legal protection to investors can be a useful instrument of the government for serving its interests.

3.1 The Increasing Importance of the Stock Market Relative to the Banking Sector

Investors will be more willing to finance firms, and financial markets will flourish if investors enjoy better legal protection (La Porta et al. 1997; 1998). The positive relationship between shareholder protection and stock market development suggests that the government's incentive to develop the stock market should be an important determinant of its incentive to provide shareholder protection, with a higher incentive to grant shareholder rights if there is a stronger desire to develop the stock market. As we shall see, China's central government, until the late 1990s, generally favored the state-owned banking system over the stock market as a primary vehicle of financial intermediation in the economy. Given such a preference, the central government simply did not have an incentive to provide more legal protection for investors so as to promote the development of the stock market, provided that the government's reputation as a regulator was not at risk. Nevertheless, China's stock market in the late 1990s took up a role that is unique to a socialist economy – supporting the SOE reforms. Since then, the stock market has played an increasingly important role in the economy. Given the increasing reliance on the stock market for the promotion of economic growth, the government has possessed the incentive to provide more protection to shareholders so as to encourage investors to put their money in the stock market.

When China's stock market emerged in the late 1980s, its financial system was dominated by the state-owned banks, and the stock market was able to assume only a secondary role in the financial sector. Several factors accounted for the central government's preference for a bank-dominated financial system. Initially, the conflict of operating a stock market within the ideological confines of a socialist economy was a huge factor in the central government's decision to minimize its use of the stock market as a financing vehicle before the late 1990s (Jocelyn 1997). The central government's reluctance to expand the role of the stock market was also due in part to opposition from the banking sector. The state-owned banks were the most powerful agencies in the financial arena given their role as the sole supplier of low-cost investment capital. The emergence of the stock market challenged not only the power but also the resource base of the state-owned banks because enterprises now had the option of seeking direct financing, and domestic households likewise had the choice to either invest their savings in the stock market or deposit them in state-owned banks (Wong 2006).

But a more fundamental reason underlying the government's preference for using the banking sector rather than the stock market as the primary financial intermediation vehicle was the central government's need to provide subsidized loans to SOEs. In the early 1990s, SOEs remained the backbone of the Chinese economy in spite of the rise of the collective and private sectors. In 1992, SOEs accounted for 63.16% of those in employment, 51.52% of industrial production, and 66.97% of tax revenue (see Table 2). Furthermore, SOEs were responsible for providing employment and a social safety net to the people.[5] China, like all other socialist economies, did not have independent institutions for social safety in the pre-reform period. In the early 1990s, the central government could not afford to establish such institutions because of its deteriorating fiscal conditions and thus had little choice but to use enterprises to provide the much-needed social safety net including life-long employment, medical care, and a pension. Ensuring an adequate supply of bank loans to finance the investment of SOEs was therefore essential for sustaining healthy economic growth and maintaining social stability.

Consistent with such a strategy, the government introduced a host of measures to limit the growth of the stock market in order to limit the competition for capital between the stock market and the banking sector (Wong 2006). On the supply side, the most important control devices were a set of administrative controls aimed at controlling the amount of shares available to domestic

[5] The burden of excessive employment in SOEs can be revealed by the fact that the percentage of urban labor force employed in SOEs has decreased only marginally from 70.19% in 1985 to 58.98% in 1995, while SOEs' share in industrial production dropped from 64.86% to 33.97% during the same period (see Table 3).

Table 2 The roles of SOEs in the Chinese economy: 1985–2005

	Number of employees in SOE (million)	Employment in SOE to total urban employment (%)	Industrial production of SOE (billion)[a]	Industrial production of SOE to total industrial production (%)	Tax revenue from SOE (billion)	Tax revenue from SOE to total tax revenue (%)
1985	89.90	70.19	630.2	64.86	86.88	72.54
1986	93.33	70.20	697.1	62.27	90.34	70.70
1987	96.54	70.04	825.0	59.73	95.82	69.60
1988	99.83	69.97	1,035.1	56.80	108.20	68.50
1989	101.08	69.97	1,234.3	56.06	127.85	67.95
1990	103.46	70.24	1,306.4	54.61	134.92	68.59
1991	106.64	61.06	1,495.5	56.17	144.70	68.29
1992	108.89	63.16	1,782.4	51.52	155.92	66.97
1993	109.20	62.08	2,272.5	46.95	252.36	63.56
1994	112.14	60.90	2,620.1	37.34	298.10	63.04
1995	112.61	58.98	3,122.0	33.97	329.48	59.74
1996	112.44	56.74	2,836.1	28.48	295.93	54.69
1997	110.44	54.65	2,902.8	25.52	386.50	56.33
1998	90.58	41.90	3,362.10	49.63	467.92	54.05
1999	85.72	38.25	3,557.12	48.92	479.63	49.51
2000	81.02	35.00	4,055.44	47.34	492.04	41.50
2001	76.40	31.91	4,240.85	44.43	536.74	36.00
2002	71.63	28.91	4,517.90	40.78	535.92	32.22
2003	68.76	26.82	5,340.79	37.54	589.09	29.47
2004	67.10	25.34	7,022.90	34.81	685.19	27.20
2005	64.88	23.74	8,375.00	33.28	–	–

Note[a]For industrial production, there is a change in the classification of SOEs in 1998. SOEs include only wholly state-owned enterprises for the years prior to 1998. Since 1998, SOEs include wholly state-owned and state-controlled enterprises.
Sources: China Statistic Yearbook, various years. Tax Yearbook of China, various years.

investors. From 1993 to 1998, the government imposed an explicit annual quota on the total amount of capital that could be raised through IPOs. Similarly, regulations were imposed to restrict the amount of post-IPO issuance, including both secondary and rights offerings. On the demand side, regulations were also imposed to restrict the sources of funds that could be invested in the stock market. While domestic individuals and institutions were prohibited from using bank loans to invest in the stock market, financial institutions and major institutional investors such as insurance funds and pension funds were not permitted to buy shares and could only invest in government bonds and bank deposits (Wong 2006).

The strategy of using bank loans to finance SOEs became no longer viable in the late 1990s when a majority of the SOEs were experiencing financial losses. Table 3 shows the financial conditions of SOEs. In the early 1990s, about one-third of SOEs experienced financial losses while their total profits fell significantly after 1990. From 1994 to 1996, the SOEs experienced total losses of 1,023.3 billion yuan.

Table 3 Financial condition of SOEs: 1985–2005

	Number of state-owned industrial enterprises (10,000)	Total profit (billion)	Number of loss-making enterprises to number of state-owned industrial enterprises (%)	Total profit of profit-making enterprises (billion)	Total losses of loss-making enterprises (billion)
1985	3.92	1,155.28	10.71	1,182.06	26.78
1986	3.85	1,494.59	12.21	1,557.67	63.08
1987	3.80	1,422.31	16.32	1,558.91	136.60
1988	3.78	984.73	31.48	1,270.76	286.03
1989	3.74	1,109.12	29.68	1,419.60	310.48
1990	3.73	1,383.40	24.40	1,672.20	288.80
1991	7.16	780.02	30.31	1,283.51	503.49
1992	7.28	905.44	32.97	1,353.46	448.02
1993	6.86	143.57	33.53	684.18	540.61
1994	6.95	–309.20	37.70	417.49	726.69
1995	6.59	–293.51	39.15	450.93	744.44
1996	6.55	–532.90	41.37	490.40	1,023.30
1997	5.73	115.60	41.36	967.00	851.40
1998	5.40	1,776.16	35.00	2,391.93	615.77
1999	4.76	2,949.80	35.92	3,638.40	688.60
2000	4.27	2,002.90	35.36	2,636.10	633.20
2001	3.66	3,156.70	35.52	3,783.50	626.80
2002	3.18	4,642.40	34.91	5,311.90	669.50
2003	2.92	5,420.70	33.90	6,446.90	1,026.20
2004	3.92	1,155.28	10.71	1,182.06	26.78
2005	3.85	1,494.59	12.21	1,557.67	63.08

Source: A Statistical Survey of China, various years.

The losses of SOEs not only created a burden on the governments' coffers but also led to the accumulation of enormous nonperforming loans (NPLs) in the banking sector. According to Dai Xianglong, governor of the PBOC, the proportion of NPLs as a share of state banks' total loans was 20%. The ratio had increased to 25% at the end of 1997 and then to 35% in 2000 (Tung 2002). The estimates of Western observers are generally higher, putting this ratio as high as 40–50% of loans outstanding (Lardy 1998). The declining asset quality of state-owned banks imposed a heavy tax burden as the government was forced to inject public funds to clean up the banks' balance sheets. Ma (2006) estimates that, up to 2006, the cost of bank restructuring had already reached 22% of the revised 2005 GDP. The bill could eventually exceed 28% after repairing the balance sheets of the Agriculture Bank of China, the three policy banks, city commercial banks, and rural credit cooperatives.

In the late 1990s, China's central government introduced radical reforms in both the SOEs and the state-owned banks by using the strategies of corporatization and public listing. As public listing is an integral part of this reform strategy, China's stock market has since taken on an important role in the economy. Consistent with the changing role of the stock market, the government gradually proceeded to relax the restrictive regulations that had been imposed on both the supply and demand sides of share trading. Of the supply controls, the quota system on IPO issuance was the first to be relaxed in 1999 and eventually replaced by the verification and approval system in 2001, while the requirements for post-IPO issuance were also made less restrictive after 1999. On the demand side, beginning in November 1997 when the first set of rules on securities investment funds was issued, institutional investors, including investment funds, pension funds, foreign institutional investors, and insurance companies, were gradually permitted to invest in the stock market either directly or indirectly through investment vehicles such as investment funds. In December 2002, the A-share market was opened to foreign investors under the scheme of Qualified Foreign Institutional Investors (QFII).

During the three years after the stock market acquired the role of supporting SOEs' reform (1998–2000), there were a total of 343 firms listed on the stock exchanges, and the ratio of the total market capitalization to GDP increased substantially from 24.52% to 53.79% (see Table 1). With its increasing size, the functioning of the stock market was considered by the government as not only a tool for SOEs' reform but also as an important tool for promoting economic growth. In January 2004, the government issued a document to promote the development of the capital markets, which stated that explicitly "developing capital markets is a task of strategic importance linked to the fulfilling of the strategic goal of quadrupling China's GDP within the first two decades of this century."[6] Given the strategic importance of the stock market, the government has the incentive to grant protection to shareholders if the absence of such protection would retard the development of the stock market.

3.2 *The Need to Unload the State Shareholdings*

Legal protection to shareholders helps to reduce corporate misdeeds and thus increase corporate value. This is confirmed by the studies of Claessens et al. (2002) and LLSV (2002) who find that stronger investor protection laws is associated with higher corporate valuations. The provision of shareholder protection is beneficial for shareholders because this will increase their wealth. Since the inception of China's stock market, the government has maintained ownership of about two-thirds of the total equity, either held by government agencies, i.e., the state shares, or held by legal entities (often SOEs), i.e., the legal-person shares. The government, therefore, is the largest shareholder of the listed firms, who are supposed to be benefited from the higher corporate valuations. Nevertheless, the government did not allow the state-owned shares

[6] State Council, 2004. Nine Opinions on the Reform and Development of Capital Market, available at http://www.people.com.cn/GB/jingji/1037/2314920.html

to be traded freely due to the fear of losing state control over the listed firms. The non-tradability of the state-owned shares means that the state shareholders were only fund-seekers but not real shareholders, because they did not have rights to dispose their stocks. This creates a divergence in interests between the state shareholders and the minority shareholders, as state shareholder's interests are not directly affected by fluctuations in market stock prices.

In early 2000, the government decided to sell some of the state-owned stocks in order to raise funds to finance the social security system. Immediately after the beginning of the SOE reforms, the government speeded up the building of an independence social security system. The social security system, however, has been experiencing increasing payment pressure since its establishment. In order to generate income to meet the future obligations, the central government established the National Social Security Fund (NSSF) in 2000 to manage a strategic reserve fund, with its funding sources come from (1) proceeds from selling of state-owned shares; (2) fiscal allocation of the central government; (3) capital raised in other manners with approval of the State Council; and (4) investment returns.[7] Among the four major sources of funding for NSSF, the proceeds from selling off the state-owned stocks and investment returns were derived directly from the stock market.

The selling of state-owned stocks immediately ties the government interests to market prices of stocks and thus aligns the governments' interests to the interests of private minority shareholders. Potential gains from selling of the state-owned stocks represent a significant vested interest of the central government in the stock market. Table 4 shows the percentage and market value of state shares and state legal person shares held by the government during the period of 1992–2006. As we can see, the percentage and the market value of shares have increased over time as more and more SOEs get listed. As at the end of 2006, the total market value of state and state legal person shares reached 3,668.08 and 1,511.41 billion yuan respectively, the total amount was equivalent to 163.65 and 167.81% of the government budgetary and tax revenue in 2005. The government therefore has a strong incentive to develop and maintain a bullish stock market so as to capture more gains from the sell-offs of the state-owned stocks.

The state stock sell-off program would significantly increase the supply of stocks in the A-share market. When the State Council issued a detailed plan of selling state stocks in June 2001,[8] the market responded with a dramatic downturn that marked the beginning of a bear market that eventually lasted for four years. On October 22, the government was forced to announce a

[7] Information on the organization and operation of NSSF can be obtained from http://www.ssf.gov.cn

[8] The specific plan is as follows: when SOEs (including enterprises listed overseas) launched IPOs or issued additional stocks in the secondary market, they were required to sell state stocks at up to 10% of the total value of the offering to replenish the National Social Security Fund.

Table 4 Market value of state-owned shares vs. central government revenue: 1990–2007

	Number of listed firms	State share to total share weighted by market capitalization of each listed firm (%)	State legal person share to total share weighted by market capitalization of each listed firm (%)	Market value of state share (billion)	Market value of state legal person share (billion)	Budgetary revenue (billion)	Tax revenue(billion)
1990	8	57.97	0.59	1.80	0.02	293.71	196.70
1991	12	53.51	1.29	8.47	0.20	314.95	211.89
1992	50	43.55	2.19	49.62	2.49	348.34	232.83
1993	163	42.68	5.87	147.29	20.25	434.90	397.05
1994	269	36.26	9.48	139.76	36.52	521.81	472.87
1995	291	34.05	10.68	126.84	39.78	624.22	551.55
1996	477	27.68	14.84	278.28	149.13	740.80	541.14
1997	676	20.76	23.79	364.04	417.31	865.11	686.12
1998	775	22.07	25.26	389.05	489.85	987.60	865.67
1999	867	18.16	26.97	474.76	704.82	1,144.41	968.79
2000	1006	17.81	26.93	842.51	1,274.22	1,339.52	1,185.58
2001	1071	22.03	25.51	958.93	1,110.59	1,638.60	1,491.07
2002	1153	21.98	26.12	864.74	1,027.29	1,890.36	1,663.30
2003	1121	24.57	25.97	1,077.84	1,139.68	2,171.53	1,999.18
2004	1321	22.79	26.21	878.21	1,010.40	2,639.65	2,518.88
2005	1335	23.79	25.10	804.25	848.66	3,164.93	3,086.58[b]
2006	1400	37.14	15.31	3,668.08	1,511.41	3,937.32[a]	3,763.63[b]
2007.6	1420	28.56	16.89	5,659.47	3,347.40	–	–

Sources:
[a]is obtained from http://business.sohu.com/20070627/n250787225.shtml
[b]is obtained from http://www.chinatax.gov.cn/n480462/n480483/n480549/5099050.html
Other data in Column 7 are obtained from Almanac of China's Finance and Banking 2006
Other data in Column 8 are obtained from Tax Yearbook of China, various years
Shareholding and market capitalization data are obtained from WIND Information and Technology Ltd.

suspension of the sell-off and in June 2002 finally decided to scrap the program altogether. Due to the concerns about the poor corporate governance of the companies and the continued worries about the potential increase in supply of stocks, many investors still have low incentive to participate in the stock market. The composite index of the Shanghai Stock Exchange slid from around 2,250 points in mid-2001 to around 1,300 points in December 2004, a plunge of 42%. In the early 2005, China's stock market remained weak after the central government decided to slash the stamp tax by half in an apparent attempt to boost the falling stock market.

As we have shown in the previous period, the long bear market from mid-2001 to 2005 is the period in which China's government had provided stronger and stronger legal protections to shareholders. Various reasons can be used to explain the timing of the legal changes. For example, it could be caused by China's joining of WTO in December 2001, which required China to gradually open its financial system to foreign investors and thus necessitated the establishment of a more advanced legal frameworks (Wong and Wong 2001). It could be due to the outbreaks of corporate scandals in the late 1990s and early 2000s, which created political pressures on the government (Chen 2003). Nevertheless, the timing is also consistent with the desperately need of the government to restore investors' confidence so as to have a bullish stock market to support the listing of SOEs and the sell-off of state-owned stocks.

3.3 The Gradual Privatization of the Listed Companies

Providing strong legal protection to minority shareholders will increase the risks faced by controlling shareholders when they expropriate the minority shareholders and thus is detrimental to the interests of the controlling shareholders. A fundamental obstacle to the introduction of shareholder protection in China is the fact that, until the late 1990s, most of the controlling shareholders who had expropriated the minority shareholders were enterprises owned by local governments. China's listed companies were mainly spin-offs from SOEs with the parent groups serving as their largest shareholders. When a profitable arm of an SOE was carved out, packaged financially, and floated by the local government, the listed firm was expected to channel funds back to support the parent company's unprofitable business units or non-business units (Tenev et al. 2002). Many controlling shareholders therefore treat the listed company as a vehicle of fund-raising and resource tunneling.

In China, there are two main avenues used by controlling shareholders to expropriate minority shareholders. The first one is false information disclosure by listed companies in relation to equity issues. China has maintained a tight control (via a profitability-oriented screening process) over equity issues since the launch of the stock market. The right to equity financing thus represents a kind of "luxury" that is only available for a small proportion of companies.

Several studies (e.g., Aharony et al. 2000; Yu, Du and Sun 2007) have reported that some Chinese companies engaged in earnings manipulation and false financial disclosure in order to meet the profitability requirements of the CSRC and secure the right to issue shares. False financial disclosure relating to share issues is now a major cause of the pending PSL cases in China.

The second avenue for expropriation is through tunneling related-party transactions (e.g., Cheung et al. 2006; Zou et al. 2008). The documented abuses by controlling shareholders in this respect include obtaining soft loans from the listed companies; using listed companies as guarantors for bank loans; and buying and selling goods, services, and assets at unfair prices. Such tunneling activities by controlling shareholders represent another major cause for PSL cases in China.

The tunneling activities of the government-owned firms mean that it is actually the government who expropriated the minority shareholders. If shareholders are given the legal rights to sue the listed firms, it will be the local governments who are the defendants in lawsuits. It is therefore not difficult to understand why the government has been reluctant and cautious in granting legal protection to shares, as evidenced by the enabling government actions requirement of the SPC's 2003 Rule.

A gradual privatization process, however, has been taking place in China since the mid-1990s, which resulted in a significant reduction in the percentage of listed firms owned by the government. The privatization venue is the one-to-one transfer market where state-owned stocks are transferred to other owners with approval from the government. In the early years, data on the ownership identities of the buyers were not readily available. Green (2004) reported that about 200 to 250 listed firms experienced a change in the largest shareholders from state to private entities from 1996 to the end of 2002. Since 2004, China's listed firms have been required to report the ownership identities of their ultimate controllers. According to the data obtained from the Ultimate Shareholder Database on China's Listed Companies provided by Sinofin, 30.7% of the listed firms in China were privately owned in 2004; the ratio further increased to 31.86% and 37.1% in 2005 and 2006, respectively.

The emergence of more and more private listed firms in the mid-2000s helped to cut the direct links between the government and the listed companies, and lessen the conflicts of interests of the government, which served as the controlling shareholder on the one hand and the regulator on the other. This in turn provided the government with more room to make improvements in the corporate governance of the listed enterprises as well as provide better legal protection for shareholders.

4 Conclusion

This paper seeks to provide an understanding of how legal protection for shareholders gradually emerged in China. Unlike the prior studies that focus on the role of private investors and the media, we trace the underlying forces driving the emergence of legal protection to shareholders to the vested interests of the central government. We show that the evolution of the legal developments is consistent with the government's changing interests in the stock market, with the provision of shareholder protection becoming an increasingly important instrument for the government to serve its interests. To a certain extent, China's legal developments in the stock market show that the legal systems in the country still maintain the ancient tradition whereby "[t]he state promulgated laws to make sure its interests were advanced. As this was done, the interests of private individuals or groups of such persons were often protected as indirect results" (Jones 2003, pp. 15–56).

What will be the future course of legal developments in China's stock market? When will the SPC issue additional interpretations that turn the promises of the recently revised Company Law and Securities Law into practical legal procedures for shareholders? How much legal protection will shareholders in China enjoy in 5 or 10 years? The complexity of China's transitional economy and the inherent chaotic nature of the stock market development make these questions difficult to answer. Assuming the existence of the same political setting such that the government is still in a position to define the rules of the game and is still committed to the goal of promoting economic growth, our analysis of the government's vested interests in the stock market points to a relatively optimistic path.

First, the privatization process will continue on several fronts, which will diminish the government's need to protect its own enterprises. In addition to the one-to-one transfer market where privatization is still on-going, privatization also took place on the two stock exchanges after the government re-introduced the state share reduction program in April 2005. Under this new program, holders of state-owned shares were required to compensate holders of tradable shares as a pre-condition for floating the non-tradable shares on the stock exchanges. By mid-2007, 1,119 listed firms had successfully worked out their compensation schemes with holders of tradable shares.[9] Although it is expected that the government will be unlikely to fully unload its shareholdings while maintaining dominant ownership in large and strategically important listed firms, some of the small and less profitable listed firms will eventually be acquired and controlled by private entities when the government sells off its stakes. Further, more and more private firms have been able to directly get listed on the two stock exchanges since China adopted the verification and approval system in 2001. The Shanghai Stock Exchange also expressed the view that foreign firms will be listed on the exchange in the not very distant future. It is therefore clear that the percentage of government-owned listed firms will become lower and lower. This will help to reduce the political resistance to the introduction of shareholder protection from local governments and clear the obstacles blocking the way for the development of PSL in China.

[9] The data are obtained from WIND Information and Technology Ltd.

Second, the benefits of a well-functioning stock market to promote economic growth will ensure that the government will have a strong incentive to develop and improve the functioning of the stock market. Such an incentive will become stronger and stronger when China has to liberalize its financial sector step-by-step following its entry into the WTO. It is because, in an open financial system, the concern over the possible competition for capital between the banking sector and the stock market – a factor that had constrained the stock market development in China – will no longer be there. With free flows of capital, the problem faced by the government is not the competition of capital between the domestic banking sector and the stock market, but the competition for capital between China and the outside world. Provision of shareholder protection will then become particularly important for stock market development. On the one hand, the removal of capital controls will provide domestic fund suppliers with an exit option to invest in other countries. They will move their money out of China if their investor rights in China are not sufficiently protected. On the other hand, the existence of sufficient shareholder protection is vital in attracting long-term foreign investors rather than speculative hot money. The power of competition will therefore ensure that China will be moving in the direction of providing more legal protection for shareholders, though the speed of change is difficult to predict.

References

Aharony, J., Lee, J., and Wong, T.J. (2000). "Financial packaging of IPO firms in China," *Journal of Accounting Research* 38(1), 103–126.

Allen, F., Qian, J., and Qian, M. J. (2005). Law, finance, and economic growth in China. *Journal of Financial Economics* 77(1), 57–116.

Chen, Z. (2003). Capital markets and legal development: The China case. *China Economic Review* 14, 451–472.

Cheung, Y. L., Jing, L., Rau, P. R., and Stouraitis, A. (2006). How does the grabbing hand grab? Tunneling Assets from Chinese Listed Companies to the State. City University of Hong Kong, Mimeo

Claessens, S., Djankov., Fan, J., and Lang, L. (2002). Expropriation of minority shareholders in East Asia. *Journal of Finance* 57.

Jocelyn, E. G. (1997). Stir-Fired shares: Share dealers, trading places and new options in contemporary Shanghai. *Modern China* 23(2), 181–215

Green, S. (2004). The privatization two-step at China's listed firms. London School of Economics, Chatham House Asia Program China Project Working Paper No. 3.

Howson, N. C. (2006). *Private Securities Litigation in China – Implications for Rule of Law in the People's Republic of China*, University of Michigan School of Law, Mimeo

Holz, C. A. (2001). Economic reforms and state sector bankruptcy in China, *The China Quarterly* 166, 342–367

Hutchens, W. (2003). Private securities litigation in China: Materials disclosure about China's legal system. *24 Pennsylvania Journal of International Economic Law* 599

Johnson, S., McMillan, J., and Woodruff, C. (2002).Property rights and finance. *American Economic Review* 92, 1335–1356

Jones, W. C. (2003). Trying to understand the current Chinese legal system. In C.S. Hsu (Ed.), *Understanding China's Legal System: Essays in Honor of Jerome A. Cohen*. New York University Press, New York and London

North C. D. (1990). Institutions, Institutional Change and Economic Performance, Cambridge University Press, Cambridge

Pistor, K. and Xu, C. G. (2005). Governing stock markets in transition economies lessons from China. *American Law and Economics Review* 7(1), 184–210.

La Porta, R., Lopez-de-Silanes, F., Shleifer, A., and Vishny, R.W. (1997). Legal determinants of external finance. *Journal of Finance* 52, 1131–1150.

La Porta, R., Lopez-de-Silanes, F., Shleifer, A., and Vishny, R.W. (1998). Law and finance. *Journal of Political Economy* 106, 1113–1155

La Porta, R., Lopez-de-Silanes, F., Shleifer, A., and Vishny, R.W. (2000). Agency problems and dividend policies around the world. *Journal of Finance* 55, 1–33.

La Porta, R., Lopez-de-Silanes, F., Shleifer, A., and Vishny, R.W. (2002). Investor protection and corporate valuation, *Journal of Finance* 57, 1147–1170.

La Porta, R., Lopez-de-Silanes, F., Shleifer, A. (2003). What works in securities laws? Harvard University, Mimeo.

Lardy, N. R. (1998). *China's Unfinished Economic Revolution*, Brookings Institution Press, Washington DC

Lee, S. M. (2001). The development of China's securities regulatory framework and the insider trading provisions of the new securities law. *New York International Law Review* 14, 1–42

Levine, R. (1998). The legal environment, banks, and long-run economic growth. *Journal of Money, Credit, and Banking* 30, 596–620.

Levine, R. (1999). Law, finance, and economic growth. *Journal of Financial Intermediation* 8, 36–67.

Ma G. (2006). Sharing China's bank restructuring bill. *China and World Economy* 14, 19–37

Shleifer A. and Vishny, R. W. (1997). The survey of corporate governance. *Journal of Finance* 52(2), 737–783

Tenev, S. and Zhang, C. L. (2002). *Corporate Governance and Enterprise Reform in China: Building the Institution of Modern Market*. World Bank and International Finance Corporation, Washington

Tung, C. Y. (2002). Current problems and reforms of Chinese financial system, *USA-China Business Review* 2–6

Wong, M. L. S. (2006). China's stock market, marriage between capitalism and socialism. *Cato Journal* 26, 389–424

Wong, Y. C. R. and Wong, M. L. S. (2001). Competition in China's domestic banking industry, *Cato Journal* 21, 19–41

Xu X. P. (1998). *China's Financial System under Transition*, Macmillan Press, New York

Yu, Qiao, Bin Du, and Qian Sun (2007). "Earnings management at rights issues thresholds: evidence from China," *Journal of Banking and Finance* 30(12), 3453–3468.

Zou H., Wong, S., Shum, C., Xiong, J., and Yan, J. (2008). Controlling-Minority shareholder incentive conflicts and directors' and officers' liability insurance: Evidence from China. forthcoming in the *Journal of Banking and Finance*

An Appraisal of the Impacts of Non-tradable Shares Reform on Large Shareholders' Behavioral Modes of Listed Companies in the A-Share Market

Honghui Cao and Huazhao Liu

Abstract The non-tradable shares reform has changed the market segmentation problem that has puzzled the Chinese stock market for more than 15 years, because of which large shareholders of listed companies changed their past behaviors, which led to a dramatic improvement in firms' performance. This chapter will appraise such impacts through theoretical and empirical models, indirectly evaluate the effectiveness of the non-tradable shares reform, and provide a guideline for further improvement in the functions of market mechanisms.

Keywords Non-tradable shares reform · Large shareholder · Behavioral mode · Effectiveness evaluation

1 Introduction

Non-tradable shares reform (will be referred to as the reform in the rest of this chapter) transformed the segmented status of equity trading rights since the establishment of the A shares market in the early 1990s. Its impacts on the governance structure are reflected in two aspects: one is direct, where original shareholders of non-tradable shares promise to pay pricing consideration during the reform, which changes the structure of equity ownership; and the other is indirect. Since controlling shareholders (original shareholders of non-tradable shares) is constrained by secondary market behavioral object, stock price enters the objective function of controlling shareholders and changes their old behavioral modes.

The latter impact is more profound. External mechanisms in the governance structure such as merger, acquisition, and the market of control influence controlling shareholders force them to make decisions that improve all shareholders' benefits, including capital budgeting, asset restructuring, financing

H. Cao (✉)
Institute of Finance and Banking, Chinese Academy of Social Sciences, Beijing, China
e-mail: davidcao@163.com

J.R. Barth et al. (eds.), *China's Emerging Financial Markets*,
The Milken Institute Series on Financial Innovation and Economic Growth 8,
DOI 10.1007/978-0-387-93769-4_21,

structure, dividend distribution, etc., and prompt them to reinforce monitoring on managers. On the other hand, creating incentives for managers through equity incentives or stock options, which prompts them to make decisions that benefit all stakeholders, is advantageous for improving operational performance of firms as well. Thanks to the improvement of firms' performance, and a tendency toward consensus of benefit between controlling shareholders and minority shareholders and between shareholders and managers, stocks now have higher investment values, which elevate market efficiency. In terms of impacts on the stock price in the secondary market, higher performance of firms and better market efficiency increase investors' expectation of return, leading to a rise in stock price; and as non-tradable shares flow into the trading market gradually, it generates pressure on stock prices.

The impacts of the reform on stock price depend on the combined effects of the two aspects above. The analytical and structural chart of the transform, corporate governance, and operational performance is as follows:

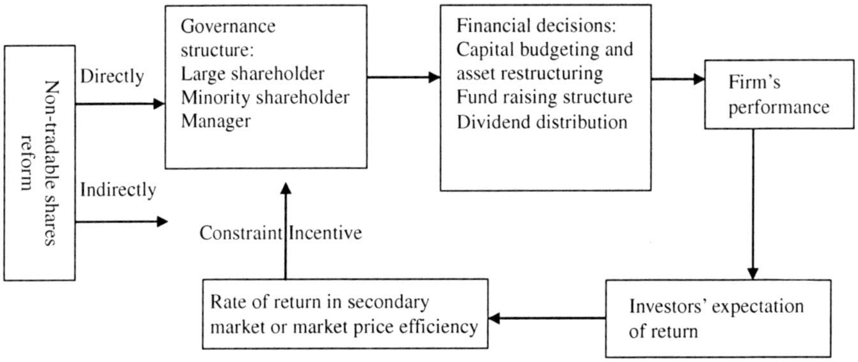

Fig. 1 Evaluation system of the non-tradable shares reform, corporate governance structure, and firms' performance

Because the reform affected the objective function of large shareholders, their behavioral mode was altered, and thereby changed the efficiency evaluation of the whole market. Hence, through analyzing the changes in large shareholders' objective function and behavioral modes, this chapter indirectly evaluates the effectiveness of the reform.

2 Theoretical Model

2.1 Related Literature

The incomplete contract theory believes that corporate agency relationship covers two scenarios, one between shareholders and managers and the other between large shareholders and minority shareholders. Over the recent years, studies of the latter have become a hot topic steadily, which focus on the cost and benefit analysis of large shareholder. Holderness (2003) believes that benefits received by large shareholders consist of shared benefit of control such as increases in the cash flow of all stakeholders and private benefits of control such as excess salaries, corporate expenses, amenity or production synergy, etc. The corresponding costs then include possible loss from forgoing diversified investment and cost arising from acquiring the benefit of control rights such as monitoring, expropriation, lawsuits, etc. These benefits and costs altogether determine the holding motivation of larger shareholders. But Johnson et al. (2000) indicate in "Tunnel Effect" that by asset trading or capital trading that sacrifices the enterprise's own benefit and benefit of minority shareholders, managers or controlling shareholders are able to improve their private benefit or the benefit of their holding firms, which can also be seen as private benefit of control. Porta et al.'s (2002) theoretical model argues that in an equity structure that has only one large shareholder and many small minority shareholders, the holding ratio of the large shareholder and the level of protection for minority shareholders affect the large shareholder's benefit and cost of private control. In his model, the large shareholder's objective function includes net benefit of control and benefit of cash flow. ShouHai (2007) investigates private benefit of control, benefit of cash flow, and benefit of stock cash-out, and he believes that the reform increased the liquidity of large stake ownership, decreased the large shareholder's motivation of expropriation, and increased the value of the firm.

2.2 *Theoretical Model*

In the model of Porta et al. (2002), large shareholders' objective function only considered net private benefit of control and benefit of cash flow but excluded benefit of large stake ownership transfer. Its weakness is that the return of large shareholders is irrelevant to stock price in the secondary market. But ShouHai's (2007) model does not consider the effect of expropriation cost and the consideration paid by large shareholders in the reform. According to the impacts of the transform on large shareholders' objective function, this chapter establishes a model as follows:

Assume the following: 1. The ownership of firm comprises of a single large shareholder and many minority shareholders, there does not exist a relative large shareholder that is able to rival the large shareholder, hence simplifies such gaming relationship between large shareholders. 2. The large shareholder is also an entrepreneur, which means any agency relationship between managers and shareholders does not exist, nor is there the problem of monitoring cost and benefit, hence we concentrate on the agency relationship between the large shareholder and minority shareholders. 3. The large shareholder's holding proportion is an exogenous variable. Demsetz (1985), Stephen (1992), and others believe that the concentration level of equity ownership is endogenous, because it is a result of the optimal selection made by shareholders. But the endogenesis of the concentration level of stake ownership is another problem, hence it will not be considered here. 4. A firm's cash flow income is exogenous, with no production cost involved. 5. It does not consider the acquiring and maintenance cost of the large shareholder's control right.

Assume that the net cash flow of a firm is I, its stock's rate of return is R, and the large shareholder's holding proportion is a prior to the reform. The large shareholder receives private benefit of control in a proportion of s of the firm's profit and pays a cost in a proportion of $c(k, s)$ of firm's profit. Consequently, the benefit of the large shareholder comprises net benefit of control, benefit of cash flow, and benefit of stock cash-out.

Net benefit of control is $sRI - c(k, s)RI$, in which we suppose $c_k(k, s) > 0$, $c_s(k, s) > 0$, $c_{ss}(k, s) > 0$, $c_{sk}(k, s) > 0$. k represents the level of protection for shareholders. This variable is kept in the cost function because at the time of the transform in 2006, the degree of information disclosure about large shareholders of listed firms and their subsidiaries occupying non-operational capital was enhanced, hence k can be used to investigate the impacts of this measure on large shareholders' behavioral modes.

The benefit of cash flow is $a(1 - v)(1 - s)RI$, in which \nu represents the rate of decrease of large shareholders holding proportion due to bonus share, equity reduction of non-tradable shares that are triggered by the reform, in other words, the fall of cash flow right, $v \in (0, 1)$

Benefit of stock cash-out is $a(1 - v)\frac{RI(1-s)}{r}\eta$, in which r represents the required rate of return for all shareholders; assume it is an exogenous variable. η represents the ratio of the transfer price of large stake ownership held by large shareholders to the price of tradable shares on the announcement day, which represents large stake ownership premium (or discount). ShouHai (2007) assumes $\eta \in [0, 1]$, which implies the assumption that large stake ownership is always transferred at discount relative to the price of tradable shares on the announcement day. XinZhong et al. (2006) study a total of 233 non-tradable share transactions that are no less than 3% of total equity among 151 listed companies in A share market between 2002 and 2003 and discover that the ratio of the price of large stake ownership held by large shareholders to the price of tradable shares on the announcement day lies within an interval of 0.05~0.78, with a mean of 0.27 and a mode of 0.26. Their researches also show that the transfer price of non-tradable shares is negatively correlated with the proportion of non-tradable shares and is positively correlated with the ratio of transfer. It seems the assumption of η made by Ding is valid for transactions of large equity ownership prior to the transform. Since transfers of non-tradable shares were usually on a net asset per share pricing basis, and net asset per share is normally below market trading price, before the reform the transfer price of large stake ownership was often at a discount relative to the price of tradable shares. After the transform, however, large stake ownership will be allowed to enter the trading market, and its pricing basis should be stock price in the trading market. Holderness (2003) believes, under a fully liquid market condition, like stock markets in the USA and Italy, large stake ownership is often transferred at a premium, which is because the pricing of large stake ownership takes elements of private benefit of control into account. The authors believe that η lies in the interval of 0~1 before the reform, but the reform alters the pricing basis of large stake ownership, so η could be equal to 1 or even greater than 1 in most cases after the reform . Therefore, we assume $\eta > 0$.

Because the reform has affected large shareholders' objective function through v and η, it follows that, after the transform, the objective function of large shareholders becomes

$$\begin{aligned} &\text{Max}: sRI - c(k,s)RI + a(1-v)(1-s)RI + a(1-v)\frac{RI(1-s)}{r}\eta \\ &\text{F.O.C}: \; c_s(k,s) = 1 - (1+\frac{\eta}{r})a(1-v) \end{aligned} \tag{1}$$

In equilibrium, $s$is a function of a,k,η,v, so comparative static analysis can be performed.

Differentiate equation (1) w.r.t a, obtain:

$$c_{ss}(k,s^*)\frac{\partial s^*}{\partial a} = -(1+\frac{\eta}{r})(1-v)$$

Then obtain:

$$\frac{\partial s^*}{\partial a} = -\frac{(1+\frac{\eta}{r})(1-v)}{c_{ss}(k,s^*)} < 0 \tag{2}$$

Similarly:

$$\frac{\partial s^*}{\partial k} = -\frac{c_{ck}(k,s^*)}{c_{ss}(k,s^*)} < 0, \frac{\partial s^*}{\partial \eta} = -\frac{a(1-v)}{c_{ss}(k,s^*)^r} < 0, \frac{\partial s^*}{\partial v} = \frac{(1+\frac{\eta}{r})^a}{c_{ss}(k,s^*)} > 0,$$

which are indicated by Equations (3), (4), and (5), respectively. Therefore, Equations (2), (3), (4), and (5) show that the expropriation incentive of large shareholders is decreasing functions of large shareholders' holding proportion, level of protection for minority shareholders, and pricing appreciation of large stake ownership and is an increasing function of the consideration paid by large shareholders under the reform scheme.

If using Tobin's q to measure the value of a firm, $q = (1 - s^*)R$, then,

$$\frac{\partial q}{\partial a} = -\frac{\partial s^*}{\partial a}R > 0, \quad \frac{\partial q}{\partial k} = -\frac{\partial s^*}{\partial k}R > 0, \quad \frac{\partial q}{\partial \eta} = -\frac{\partial s^*}{\partial \eta}R > 0, \quad \frac{\partial q}{\partial v} = -\frac{\partial s^*}{\partial v}R < 0,$$

which are indicated by Equations (6), (7), (8), and (9). Equations (8) and (9) illustrate that the reform generates both positive and negative impacts on the objective function of large shareholders: decreases in the holding proportion lead to decreases in benefit of cash flow, which enhance its expropriation incentive and cause the firm's value to fall; but the pricing premium in fact reduces its expropriation incentive, increasing the value of the firm. The net effect of the reform on the firm's value and large shareholders' cost and benefit depends upon the combined effect of these two dimensions.

3 Empirical Study

3.1 Model Parameters

Until now, there is no clear definition regarding private benefit of control; thus, the private benefit of control is usually related to large shareholder expropriation, "Tunnel Effect," etc. This chapter will not distinguish them explicitly. Private benefit of control may be treated as a form of agency cost, and like other agency costs, it can hardly be measured directly. So existing papers rarely calculate the agency cost directly (Ang et al., 2000); for most of the time the existence of private benefit of control is examined indirectly and from different angles. Barclar and Holderness (1989), Dyck (2004), ZongMing and Wei (2002) and others believe that the private benefit of control can be extracted from the difference between the transaction price of large stake ownership and the secondary market price after announcement. Therefore, empirical analysis of the magnitude and influential factors of such transaction price difference can be used to measure the private benefit of control and to reinforce the understanding of these influential factors at the same time. Another method is to use event study to examine the impacts of large shareholders' financial decisions on market value, thereby discussing whether or not expropriation behavior exists (Bae, 2002). This chapter is not going to directly measure large shareholders' private benefit of control, rather test the relationship between the firm's value and two variables: v, the decrease in holding proportion of large shareholder due to the reform, and η, the pricing appreciation multiple of non-tradable shares, thereby analyzing the impacts of the reform on the firm's value and indirectly judge the effects of the transform on large shareholders' cost and benefit.

There are roughly three types of indicators for certifying a firm's value. The first one is based on market value, such as the stock's rate of return and values of Tobin's q, M/B, etc.; stock's rate of return again may be divided into short-term market reaction and long-term performance; the second one is the financial indicators that are based on book value; the third is the economic efficiency indicators based on the angle of production. Since the stock's rate of return reflects market valuation more than the financial indicator does, and is also more realistic, this chapter's empirical test is performed based on the model of Dittmara and Mahrt-Smith (2007), using stock's rate of return of financial years to measure the value of the firm. Since companies listed in A share market normally do not disclose data regarding R&D, nor do they have unified corporate governance indicators, the regression equation of this chapter neglects the effects caused by these two factors and becomes

$$r_{i,t} = \gamma_0 + \gamma_1 \frac{\Delta C_{i,t}}{M_{i,t-1}} + \gamma_2 \frac{\Delta E_{i,t}}{M_{i,t-1}} + \gamma_3 \frac{\Delta NA_{i,t}}{M_{i,t-1}} + \gamma_4 \frac{\Delta I_{i,t}}{M_{i,t-1}} + \gamma_5 \frac{\Delta D_{i,t}}{M_{i,t-1}} + \gamma_6 \frac{C_{i,t-1}}{M_{i,t-1}} + \gamma_7 L_{i,t} + \gamma_8 \frac{NF_{i,t}}{M_{i,t-1}} + \gamma_9 \frac{C_{i,t}}{M_{i,t-1}} \times \frac{\Delta C_{i,t}}{M_{i,t-1}} + \gamma_{10} L_{i,t} \times \frac{\Delta C_{i,t}}{M_{i,t-1}} + \varepsilon_{i,t} \tag{10}$$

in which $r_{i,t}$ is the stock i's rate of return in period t, ΔXrepresents the change of a variable from $t-1$ to t, $M_{i,t}$ is the market value of stock i in period t, $C_{i,t}$ is cash and cash equivalent, $E_{i,t}$ is net profit, $NA_{i,t}$ is net asset, $I_{i,t}$ is interest payment, $D_{i,t}$ is dividend of ordinary shares, $L_{i,t} = Debt_{i,t}/(Debt_{i,t} + M_{i,t})$, $Debt_{i,t}$ is the sum of long-term liability and short-term liability, and $NF_{i,t}$ is net financing which is equal to the sum of net amount financed by equity and liability.

The empirical analysis has two steps. First, whether or not there are significant changes in the value of listed firms after the reform will be tested; if changes are significant, then the second test will be applied, which will examine whether the value of the firm is related to the transform or not, and thereby evaluate the impacts of the transform on the value of firm and the cost and benefit of large shareholders.

First, introduce a dummy variable in Equation (10) to indicate whether or not the transform has started, in order to test whether there is significant difference between firms that have started the transform and those that have not. Divide the sample into test group A and control group B, then use the second difference to see whether the two groups of samples differ significantly, then evaluate the effectiveness of the transform policy. Assume that the regression equation is $y_{i,t} = \beta_0 + \beta_1 diff_{i,t} + \theta_i + r_i + \varepsilon_{i,t}$, in which θ_i is the individual heterogeneity, which does not vary with time, and r_t is the individual effect that varies with time. When individual i is affected by the policy, $diff_{i,t} = 1$, otherwise, $diff_{i,t} = 0$,. It follows that $diff_{A,0} = 0$, $diff_{A,1} = 1$, $diff_{B,0} = 0$, $diff_{B,1} = 0$. Then, the change of each group of sample before and after the reform, is, respectively:

$$E(y_{A,1} - y_{A,0}) = \beta_1(diff_{A,1} - diff_{A,0}) + r_1 - r_0 = \beta_1 + r_1 - r_0 \tag{11}$$

$$E(y_{B,1} - y_{B,0}) = \beta_1(diff_{B,1} - diff_{B,0}) + r_1 - r_0 = r_1 - r_0 \tag{12}$$

The second difference gives the variation between the changes of the two groups:

$$E(y_{A,1} - y_{A,0}) - E(y_{B,1} - Y_{B,0}) = \beta_1 \tag{13}$$

Clearly, β_1 measures the relative change in y of the test group, with respect to the control group after the policy was implemented. Now introduce a dummy variable $diff_{i,t}$ in Equation (10) to indicate whether or not the transform has started; if firm $i$has already started or completed the reform in year t, then $diff_{i,t} = 1$, otherwise $diff_{i,t} = 0$. Therefore, if the regression coefficient of $diff$ is significantly greater than zero, then compare firms which have not started the reform with those firms which have started the reform in that year. By observing whether there is a higher increase or at least a lower decrease in the firm's value that is measured by rate of stock return, one can evaluate whether the reform has generated a fairly good effect.

Afterwards, insert the rate of decrease in holding proportion by a large shareholder v and the pricing appreciation multiple of non-tradable shares η into Equation (10), and examine whether the reform has impact on the value of the firm. By evaluating whether the results deduced from Equations (4) and (5) match the relationship between the value of the firm and v and η, we can indirectly judge whether the relationship between the large shareholder's objective function and $v$and η fit the inferences by Equations (8) and (9).

3.2 Data and Descriptive Statement

This chapter uses all listed companies in A share market at Shanghai and Shenzhen stock exchange as sample and eliminates ST, PT types of stock and stocks in financial sector, because these two types of stocks usually have a heterogeneous rate of return, and operating projects of financial firms are often quite different from ordinary listed firms. All financial data are calculated from Wind database. The annual rates of return are from CCER database, with both dividend and capital gain taken into account. The final effective sample is generated after eliminating missing values. Four-hundred and seventeen firms have started the reform in 2005, accounting for 30.5% of 1367 listed firms in A share market; it was 866 firms in 2006 and accounted for 63.35%. Altogether 1283 firms in two years accounted for 93.38%.

Since the first step requires fixed effect model of balanced panel data, and financial data of A share market firms have only become relatively complete since 1999, the panel data used by this chapter start from 2000. Therefore, the final effective sample of the panel data have 362 firms, in which 54 implemented the reform in 2005, making up 15%; 247 implemented in 2006, making up 68%, and two years altogether account for 83%. In the balanced panel, the weight of the 2005 sample is small relative to the total, the weight 2006 sample is large relative to the total, and the weight of two years sample is close to the total.

The second step of the test applies the cross section of firms that have implemented the reform in 2005 and 2006. Add the rate of decrease in holding proportion by large shareholders v and the premium multiple of non-tradable shares η into Equation (10). In the reform, consideration forms responsible for decreases in holding proportion by non-tradable shareholders are bonus shares transferred from non-tradable shareholders to tradable shareholders involved in the reform, bonus shares to all shareholders, equity reduction of non-tradable shares, put or call warrant, equity incentive programs, etc. Since the impacts of warrants and equity incentive programs on holding proportion of large shareholders are hard to be quantitively measured in the short term, we only consider firms that used bonus shares transferred from non-tradable shareholders to tradable shareholders involved in the reform, bonus shares to all shareholders, equity reduction of non-tradable shares or a mixed form of the three when calculating v. Consideration forms such as cash out, capital injection, liability restructuring, shares exchange, and merger can also be seen as the cost of large shareholders in the reform. However, these forms are difficult to be quantified and do not cause any decreases in large shareholders' holding proportion and benefit of cash flow in the short term, so they are not considered here either. v is the percentage decrease in the proportion of non-tradable shares after the reform, derived from the equity structure of listed firms in Challenger database before and after the reform.

Table 1 2005–2006 weight of firms whose consideration forms were bonus shares to all, bonus shares transferred from non-tradable shareholders to tradable shareholders involved in the reform, equity reduction, and their mixed combination

	2005		2006		2005 and 2006	
Form of consideration	sample	weight%	sample	weight%	sample	weight%
Bonus shares transferred from reserved fund	6	2.79	115	17.01	121	13.58
Bonus shares to all	3	1.40	37	5.47	40	4.49
Bonus shares transferred from non-tradable shareholders to tradable shareholders involved in the reform	203	94.42	521	77.07	724	81.26
Equity reduction	3	1.40	3	0.44	6	0.67
Total	215	100.00	676	100.00	891	100.00
Proportion among all firms started the reform	51.5%		78%		69.4%	

In year 2005, firms whose consideration forms were bonus shares, bonus shares transferred from non-tradable shareholders to tradable shareholders involved in the reform, equity reduction, and its mixed combination make up 51.5% of all firms that implemented the reform in that year; the proportion of non-tradable shares on average fell by 16.59% (measured by mode). In the year 2006, the proportion of firms that used the three forms of consideration above rose to 78%, while the proportion of non-tradable shares fell by 17.3%. For 2005 and 2006, firms using the above forms of consideration had a weight of 69.4% , and non-tradable shares on average fell by 16.9%.

Table 2 Descriptive statement of v

	Sample size	Mode	Mean	Min.	Max.	s.d.
2005	215	16.59%	17.92%	0	51.81%	.0063
2006	676	17.30%	18.25%	0.9%	81.80%	.0069
2005 & 2006	891	16.9%	18.17%	0	81.80%	.0068

Non-tradable shares premium multiple is used specifically for measuring premium benefit, which is the result of the change of pricing basis for large shareholders' share from net asset per share to secondary market price after those shares are allowed to be traded in the market. This chapter uses the ratio of the closing price on the first trading day after the reform to the net asset per share of the year before the reform to calculate η. Net asset per share in the year before the reform is from the CCER database; the daily closing price is also from the CCER database but with negative and missing values eliminated.

Table 3 Descriptive statement of η

	Sample size	Mode	Mean	Min.	Max.	s.d.
2005	413	1.535289	1.858436	.5418604	14.92424	1.892644
2006	786	1.804753	3.438701	.4933586	260	125.5696
2005&2006	1199	1.700284	2.894373	.4933586	260	83.49581

The non-tradable shares premium multiple for firms that implemented the reform in 2005 has a mode of 1.53, a mean of 1.85, and a relatively small standard deviation. For firms reformed in 2006, their premium multiples were higher than those in 2005 from either the mode's or the mean's perspective, with the greatest multiple even reaching 260 and the standard deviation also becoming considerably large. Looking together with the descriptive statistics of v, relative to firms reformed in 2005, those firms that implemented the reform in 2006 experienced a larger decrease in the holding proportion by non-tradable shareholders and higher premium at the same time.

3.2.1 Regression Result and Analysis

In Model 1, if firm i had started the reform in 2005, then $diff_{i,2005} = 1$, otherwise $diff_{i,t} = 0$, $t = 2000, \ldots\ldots, 2005$. In Model 2, if firm i had started the reform in 2005, then $diff_{i,2005} = 1$, and if the firm had started the reform in 2006 (including those already reformed in 2005), then $diff_{i,2006} = 1$, otherwise $diff_{i,t} = 0$,

$t = 2000, \ldots\ldots, 2006$. Model 3 is based on Model 2 but with the sample of the year 2005 removed. p values are in brackets.

Table 4 shows, regardless of the year, compared with those firms that have not reformed, stock's rate of return of those firms that have implemented the reform in 2005 or 2006 has significantly increased. In fact, such difference is especially remarkable in 2006. Clearly, the difference in the stock's rate of return between firms that have reformed and those that have not is widening gradually.

Table 4 Whether the difference in stock's rate of return between reformed and non-reformed firms is significant

	Model 1	Model 2	Model 3
Constant	.1717333 (0.000)	.1762973 (0.000)	.1952162 (0.000)
$\frac{\Delta C}{M}$	2.108159 (0.000)	2.050624 (0.000)	1.921935 (0.000)
$\frac{\Delta E}{M}$	0.9576078 (0.000)	0.7567151 (0.000)	0.6876831 (0.000)
$\frac{\Delta NA}{M}$	−0.2667298 (0.116)	−0.3637785 (0.000)	−0.357685 (0.000)
$\frac{\Delta I}{M}$	7.264815 (0.000)	3.651966 (0.000)	3.488959 (0.001)
$\frac{\Delta D}{M}$	2.097512 (0.001)	0.7653002 (0.126)	1.180542 (0.048)
$\frac{C_{t-1}}{M}$	2.307067 (0.000)	1.572733 (0.000)	1.526204 (0.000)
L	−1.907218 (0.000)	−1.590548 (0.000)	−1.663726 (0.000)
$\frac{NF}{M}$	0.4186805 (0.000)	0.2110416 (0.001)	0.2309897 (0.003)
$\frac{C}{M} \times \frac{\Delta C}{M}$	−1.446902 (0.000)	−0.465498 (0.000)	−0.4511306 (0.000)
$L \times \frac{\Delta C}{M}$	−1.300405 (0.043)	−2.252382 (0.000)	−2.122712 (0.000)
diff	**0.2335396 (0.000)**	**0.4968363 (0.000)**	**0.5623534 (0.000)**
Year	2000–2005	2000–2006	2000–2004, 2006
Sample	2172	2534	2172

Note: Dummy variable $diff_{i,t}$ is added into equation (10) through Model 1 to Model 3, and regression results are obtained by applying the fixed effect model for balanced panel data started from 2000.

For firms reformed in 2005, Model 4 and 5 show that the rate of decrease in the holding proportion by large shareholders is significantly negatively correlated with stock's rate of return, and non-tradable shares' premium multiple has significant positive correlation with stock's rate of return, both of which satisfy the theoretical deduction by Equations (4) and (5); thus, it indirectly supports the inference by Equations (8) and (9) regarding the impacts of the reform on large shareholders' cost and benefit. Model 6 indicates that, when considering both v and η, the negative effect of the rate of decrease in holding proportion by the large shareholder becomes insignificant, and coefficients reduce by more than half, but the positive correlation between the premium multiple and the stock's rate of return still exists. Moreover, using either the mode or the mean of v and η to perform calculation, the positive effect of premium multiple is always greater than

Table 5 Impacts of rate of decrease in holding proportion by the large shareholder v and the premium multiple of non-tradable shares η on stock's rate of return

	Firms reformed in 2005			Firms reformed in 2006			Firms reformed between 2005-2006		
	Model 4	Model 5	Model 6	Model 7	Model 8	Model 9	Model 10	Model 11	Model 12
Constant	–0.0346871 (0.554)	–0.2194765 (0.000)	–0.2229952 (0.001)	0.4751563 (0.000)	0.4646189 (0.000)	0.4387247 (0.000)	0.3886573 (0.000)	0.2703421 (0.000)	0.2407814 (0.000)
$\frac{\Delta C}{M}$	–1.183383 (0.233)	–0.9353994 (0.259)	–1.557551 (0.089)	0.8296615 (0.001)	0.7462536 (0.000)	0.8175329 (0.001)	1.284336 (0.003)	1.148227 (0.000)	1.226407 (0.004)
$\frac{\Delta E}{M}$	1.57324 (0.010)	0.6604733 (0.090)	1.809251 (0.001)	0.1677867 (0.086)	0.2218485 (0.005)	0.1549178 (0.114)	0.4660508 (0.008)	0.5729328 (0.000)	0.4192465 (0.016)
$\frac{\Delta NA}{M}$	1.429086 (0.002)	0.7165212 (0.027)	1.322536 (0.002)	0.1618009 (0.013)	0.1090054 (0.036)	0.1643081 (0.012)	–0.0197622 (0.865)	–0.0655088 (0.473)	–0.0062287 (0.957)
$\frac{\Delta I}{M}$	0.2114456 (0.951)	2.545713 (0.399)	1.871714 (0.554)	2.531545 (0.005)	1.420137 (0.008)	2.481185 (0.006)	3.779776 (0.014)	2.103238 (0.010)	3.704677 (0.015)
$\frac{\Delta D}{M}$	3.08639 (0.002)	2.956713 (0.000)	3.076502 (0.001)	0.0191248 (0.970)	0.105513 (0.780)	–0.0489433 (0.924)	–0.036677 (0.962)	–0.3585412 (0.536)	–0.168703 (0.823)
$\frac{\Delta C_{t-1}}{M}$	0.3963118 (0.018)	0.7959942 (0.000)	0.5347088 (0.001)	0.2611618 (0.000)	0.2732369 (0.000)	0.2683841 (0.000)	0.6765296 (0.000)	0.6533833 (0.000)	0.704638 (0.000)
L	–0.326466 (0.017)	–0.4511105 (0.000)	–0.3032122 (0.016)	–0.3476137 (0.000)	–0.3126284 (0.000)	–0.3263781 (0.000)	–0.7054617 (0.000)	–0.5651289 (0.000)	–0.626618 (0.000)
$\frac{\Delta NF}{M}$	0.0559062 (0.738)	0.2193878 (0.153)	0.1107312 (0.472)	–0.0020486 (0.968)	0.0389549 (0.315)	0.0016414 (0.974)	0.0400361 (0.645)	0.1121517 (0.091)	0.0526832 (0.539)
$\frac{C}{M} \times \frac{\Delta C}{M}$	–0.4411604 (0.493)	–0.642784 (0.279)	–0.3130604 (0.597)	–0.0519807 (0.416)	–0.1093382 (0.001)	–0.0567369 (0.375)	–0.1563153 (0.164)	–0.1960739 (0.000)	–0.1658397 (0.134)
$L \times \frac{\Delta C}{M}$	2.768374 (0.098)	2.581171 (0.069)	3.228649 (0.037)	–1.26362 (0.020)	–1.048691 (0.005)	–1.220947 (0.024)	–1.735182 (0.040)	–1.489922 (0.014)	–1.595573 (0.056)
v	**–0.3361405** **(0.096)**		**–0.154352** **(0.412)**	**0.1199133** **(0.272)**		**0.1551239** **(0.167)**	**–0.1147952** **(0.480)**		**0.0342775** **(0.835)**

Table 5 (continued)

	Firms reformed in 2005			Firms reformed in 2006			Firms reformed between 2005-2006		
	Model 4	Model 5	Model 6	Model 7	Model 8	Model 9	Model 10	Model 11	Model 12
η		**0.0658469**	**0.065743**		**0.0103253**	**0.0092539**		**0.0335893**	**0.0399848**
		(0.000)	**(0.000)**		**(0.012)**	**(0.185)**		**(0.000)**	**(0.000)**
Sample	179	211	179	334	475	334	516	691	516
Adj-R2	0.2964	0.3306	0.4043	0.2313	0.2303	0.2331	0.1861	0.2246	0.2092
mode of v	18.08%		18.08%	18.10%		18.10%	18.08%		18.08%
mode of η		1.400848	1.422414		1.767442	1.692872		1.671218	1.603728
mean of v	19.82%		19.82%	19.06%		19.06%	19.32%		19.32%
mean of η		1.754479	1.76692		2.352429	2.145482		2.168512	2.013391

Note: Holding proportion by large shareholder v or premium multiple of non-tradable shares η is added into Equation (10) through Model 4 to Model 12; regression results are obtained by applying OLS on cross-sectional data of firms that implemented the reform in 2005 or 2006. *p*values in brackets.

the negative effect of rate of decrease in holding proportion; the net effect is 6.56% if calculated using mode, and it is 8.55% if using mean. Clearly, although larger shareholders' holding proportion reduced for firms reformed in 2005, the benefit of premium might exceed the loss due to their reduced benefit of cash flow. Therefore, large shareholders take action that benefits minority shareholders such as reducing private benefit of control, and these are reflected on the positive net effect of the reform on the rate of return of stocks.

In terms of the firms reformed in 2006, Model 8 demonstrates that the premium multiple and the rate of return is still significantly positively correlated; yet Model 7 shows that the rate of decrease in proportion of non-tradable shares and the rate of return of stock turn out to have an insignificant positive relationship. When taking both factors into account, the positive relationship still exists, with greater significance level and larger coefficients. This could be a manifestation of the consensus of benefit between large shareholders and minority shareholders. More than 90% of firms had implemented the reform by the end of 2006; stock price and the stock's rate of return became crucial factors to be considered by large shareholders, and therefore the interest of large shareholders and minority shareholders began to converge. Even sacrificing a large proportional fall in the benefit of cash flow, large shareholders might still take actions that benefit minority shareholders, which illustrates a positive correlation between the rate of decrease in the proportion of non-tradable shares and the stock's rate of return. Although such correlation is not significant at the moment, as the transform continues further, the behavioral mode of large shareholders has already started to change.

When considered aggregately for the time of the transform in 2005 and 2006, Model 10 shows the relationship between the rate of decrease in the proportion of non-tradable shares and the stock's rate of return is negatively correlated and insignificant; Model 11 shows the premium rate of non-tradable shares, and the stock's rate of return is significantly positively correlated, and Model 12 shows that the significant positive correlation between the premium rate of non-tradable shares and the stock's rate of return still exists, but the rate of decrease in the proportion of non-tradable shares and the stock's rate of return are insignificantly positively correlated. This may be explained by the differences in large shareholders' behavioral mode in the 2005 and 2006 samples, and the 2006 sample weighs a lot more.

3.2.2 Test of Stability

For the tests of Models 1–3, we attempt to set year 2001 as the panel's starting year in order to enlarge the sample size, thereby increasing the size of the effective sample to 473 firms, in which the proportion of firms that reformed in 2005 and 2006 is still 15% and 68%, respectively. The regression results of the fixed effect models stay the same as in Table 4, and the regression coefficient of $diff_{i,t}$ is still significantly greater than zero.

In the tests for Models 4–12, the calculation of premium multiple of non-tradable shares is based on market closing price on the first trading day after the reform. This method of calculation reflects market reaction in the short term and short-term premium benefit of large shareholders, but it cannot fully reflect market reactions and premium benefit of large shareholders in the long term. Hence we use STATA application to separately calculate the weighted average of closing price within 30, 100 trading days and half a year after the reform is implemented (use daily trading volume as the weights), then recalculate the relevant premium multiple using these figures, and perform regression on Models 4–12 again. The data of closing price and trading volume are from the CCER database. Coefficients' symbols and their significances are illustrated in Table 6.

Table 6 Summary on regression results of the recalculation for non-tradable shares premium multiple η

		On the first trading day	Within 30 trading days	Within 100 trading days	Within half a year
		Firms reformed in 2005			
Individual regression	v	–, *	–, *	–, *	–, *
	η	+, ***	+, **	+, **	+, ***
Consolidated regression	v	–	–	–	–
	η	+, ***	+, ***	+, ***	+, ***
		Firms reformed in 2006			
Individual regression	v	+	+	+	+
	η	+, **	+	–	+, ***
Consolidated regression	v	+	+	+	+
	η	+	–	–, *	+, *
		Firms reformed between 2005–2006			
Individual regression	v	–	–	–	–
	η	+, ***	+, ***	+, ***	+, ***
Consolidated regression	v	+	–	–	+
	η	+, ***	+, **	+, *	+, ***

Note: Except for the first trading day after the reform, η is the ratio of the weighted average of closing price with daily trading volume as weights for each corresponding period to the net asset per share of the year before the reform. Individual regression represents regressions that are run with v or η added into Equation (10) separately, like Model 4 or Model 5. Consolidated regression represents regressions that are run with v and η added to Equation (10) together, like Model 6. *, **, *** denote that the coefficient of v or η is significant under 0%, 5%, and 1%, respectively.

Table 6 shows that, with respect to firms reformed in 2005, regression results that are obtained after η is recalculated according to different periods, and the results generated from using closing price on the first trading day after the reform to calculate η are roughly the same. Both the correlation relationships of the rate of decrease in proportion of non-tradable shares and the premium multiple with the stock's rate of return agree with the deductions by the theoretical model. For the firms that implemented the reform in 2006, if η is calculated within half a year after the stock resumes normal transaction, the regression results are generally the same as the results generated from using the closing price on the first trading day after-resume to calculate η, but the regression results using 30 and 100 trading days to calculate η are somehow different from the regression results generated from using closing price on the first trading day in terms of the symbol and significance of η. However, all four scenarios show that, using either individual regression or consolidated regression, there indeed exists an insignificant positive correlation between v and the rate of return of stock, which might indicate that there is a stronger trend toward establishing a consensus of benefit between large shareholders and minority shareholders relative to the firms reformed in 2005. The regression results when considering all reformed firms in 2005 and 2006 show that there exists an insignificant negative correlation between v and the stock's rate of return if individual regression is run, but when regressing with adding η together, then the symbol changes; this could be a result of the differences in large shareholders' behavioral modes of those firms reformed in 2005 and 2006. The correlation between η and the stock's rate of return is still positive and significant. Overall, the results of stability test generally bolster the judgments in Tables 4 and 5.

4 Discussion and Conclusion

This chapter applies theoretical models to analyze large shareholder's cost and benefit function, and the authors believe that the reform had impacts on the cost and benefit of large shareholders and on their behavioral modes. Preliminary empirical tests show that relative to firms that have not reformed, those firms that have implemented the reform in 2005 and 2006 experienced an increase in stock's rate of return. And further empirical tests show that large shareholders of firms that reformed in 2005 are indeed affected by the rate of decrease in the proportion of non-tradable shares and the equity ownership premium; moreover, the negative effect of the former is weaker than the positive effect of the latter, thereby resulting in a positive net effect on stock's rate of return. As for the firms that reformed in 2006, however, there is a trend of consensus of benefit between large shareholders and minority shareholders, which is reflected in the insignificant positive correlation between the rate of decrease in the proportion of non-tradable shares and the stock's rate of return. Either according to the positive net effect of the firms reformed in 2005 or looking at the trend of convergence between the benefit of large shareholders and minority shareholders of those firms reformed in 2006, the reform has positively influenced the behavioral mode of large shareholders and the value of firms.

Something to be clarified is that the theoretical deductions of this chapter rely on the models' assumptions; these assumptions are necessarily to be further released. When evaluating the impacts of the reform on large shareholders' cost and benefit function, only two aspects, the rate of decrease in the proportion of non-tradable shares and the equity ownership premium, were considered, especially only the reduced benefit of cash flow due to bonus shares to all shareholders, bonus shares transferred from non-tradable shareholders to tradable shareholders involved in the reform, equity reduction and their combination of consideration were taken into account when measuring their costs and were thus unable to consider other forms of pricing consideration and their impacts. Moreover, in 2005 and 2006, the regulator had enhanced its execution level on minority shareholders' protection, such as requires the controlling shareholder to pay off non-operational occupied capital, but due to the flaws in data disclosure, and the difficulty in quantifing them, this chapter is unable to extract the effect of such action on the value of a firm.

This chapter only measures the value of a firm by its stock's rate of return; thus a more comprehensive analysis requires taking financial indicators, economic efficiency, and others into account. This chapter indirectly evaluates the impacts of the reform on large shareholders' behavioral mode through the analysis of the impacts of the reform on stock's rate of return, but more direct and concrete evaluation methods are yet to be researched. Finally, the reform has a long-lasting effect on the capital market, in which the impact on the cost and benefit and the behavioral mode of large shareholders is particularly essential, but in areas such as investment, capital injection, financing, dividend distribution, etc., whether or not the reform drives the benefit of large shareholders and minority shareholders of a listed firm toward convergence is subject to further investigation and research.

Acknowledgments We thank Quan Wei, Ph.D. candidate at Cornell University, for translation assistance.

References

James S. Ang, Rebel A. Cole, James Wuh Lin, 2000, Agency Costs and Ownership Structure, *The Journal of Finance*, Vol. 55, No. (1), 81∼ –106.

Kee-Hong Bae, Jun-Koo Kang, Jin-Mo Kim, 2002, Tunneling or Value Added? Evidence from Mergers by Korean Business Groups, *The Journal of Finance*, 57(6), 2695–2740.

Michael J. Barclar, Clifford G. Holderness, 1989, Private Benefits from Control of Public Corporations, *Journal of Financial Economics,* 25, 371–395.

Morten Bennedsen, Daniel Wolfenzon, 2000, The Balance of Power in Close Corporations, *Journal of Financial Economics*, 58, 113–139.

Harold Demsetz, Kenneth Lehn, 1985, The Structure of Corporate Ownership: Causes and Consequences, *The Journal of Political Economy*, 93(6), 1155–1177.

Amy Dittmara, Jan Mahrt-Smith, 2007, Corporate Governance and the Value of Cash Holdings, *Journal of Financial Economics*, 83, 599–634.

Alexander Dyck, Luigi Zingales, 2004, Private Benefits of Control: An International Comparison: *The Journal of Finance*,VOL.LIX, 2, 537–600.

Clifford G. Holderness, 2003, A Survey of Blockholders and Corporate Control, *FRBNY Economic Policy Review*, 51–64.

Cao Honghui, 2002, Study on the efficiency of China's capital markets, Economics Sciences Publishing House, Beijing.

Simon Johnson, Rafael La Porta, Florencio Lopez-de-Silanes, Andrei Shleifer, 2000, Tunneling, *The American Economic Review*, 90(2), 22–27.

Rafael La Porta, Florencio Lopez-de-Silanes, Andrei Shleifer, Robert Vishny, 2002, Investor Protection and Corporate Valuation, *The Journal of Finance*, 57(3), 1147–1170.

Stephen D. Prowse, 1992, The Structure of Corporate Ownership in Japan, *The Journal of Finance*, 47(3).

Ding ShouHai, 2007, Positive Analysis of Equity Disparting Reform, *Economic Theory and Economic Management*, 1, 54–59.

Xu XinZhong, Huang Zhang KAI, Liu Yin, Xue Tong, 2006, An Empirical Study on The Pricing of Block Shares in China, *Economic Research*, 1, 101–108.

Tang ZongMing, Jiang Wei, 2002, A Study on the Expropriation Degree of Large Shareholders of China's Listed Companies, *Economic Research*, 4, 44–50.

Jeffrey Zwiebel, 1995, Block Investment and Partial Benefits of Corporate Control, *Review of Economic Studies*, 62(2), 161–185.

Will China Surpass the United States?

John A. Tatom

Abstract Extrapolations of China's growth suggest that China will soon surpass in size and prosperity the leading developed economies, even the United States. China has several advantages that suggest such convergence possibilities, including its land mass, large population, and rapid transformation over nearly three decades. However, there are serious disadvantages that will lessen the pace of convergence in future. This chapter provides several scenarios for the relative size of China's GDP and for convergence of her income per capita. Under plausible assumptions, China will not reach the US standard of living until late in this century, at the earliest. Nonetheless, due to the size of its economy and markets, it will have a relatively large share of production and consumption of most goods and services in a few decades. Experience elsewhere, especially among China's richest neighbors, indicates that convergence is unlikely even by then. China faces four trends that make even this possibility unlikely: urbanization, the transition from state ownership to private sector control of capital, slowing population growth, and rising political risks. The first two forces have been important to China's success but are transitory and will work to reduce growth in the future. The financial sector's development could extend the period of rapid productivity growth in China and could even allow the country to become the financial center of Asia. This would not alter the basic conclusions for the relative size of the economy or its convergence, however.

Keywords Economic growth · Convergence of per capita income · Productivity

---

An earlier version of this chapter was published in *International Economy*, Spring 2007, 38–41. Reprinted with permission.

J.A. Tatom (✉)
Networks Financial Institute, Indiana State University, Indianapolis, IN, USA
e-mail: john.tatom@isunetworks.org

J.R. Barth et al. (eds.), *China's Emerging Financial Markets*,
The Milken Institute Series on Financial Innovation and Economic Growth 8,
DOI 10.1007/978-0-387-93769-4_22,

Reading press reports, one might think that China's economy would soon surpass in size and prosperity that of the world's remaining superpower. There is some basis for this speculation, though it is wildly premature at best, and, at worst, very unlikely for several decades, if ever. The correct factual basis is that China is a very large country with an even larger population. The other correct ingredient in such a story is that, for the past 28 years or so, China has exhibited extremely rapid growth. If its massive population had an average level of productivity for what the IMF calls a "middle income country" or that of some of their wealthier neighbors, China would already have the largest GDP in the world. That is not likely to happen for another 30 years or so, at the earliest. More importantly, even under the best of trends sustained for far longer than is likely, China will not reach the US standard of living, not to mention surpassing it, until mid-century. More likely, even under very optimistic assumptions, China will not reach the US standard of living until late in this century. Nonetheless, due to the size of its economy and markets, it will have a relatively large share of production and consumption of most goods and services in a few decades.

The key facts that determine these possibilities are that China is a country that is almost identically the same size in land area as the United States but has over four times as many people (1.3 billion versus 300 million people). Its output or income has been growing at nearly 10% per year since reforms began in the late 1970s, but earlier the country's economy regressed for several decades due to its political turmoil and exploitation of its people by a political party and class backed by an economically and politically powerful army. Economic reform has allowed the country to climb out of a very deep hole, but it has far to go before reclaiming its earlier relative ranking in the world economy. Fortunately, the notion of convergence means that the further behind a country gets, the more likely it is, if allowed, to grow faster in order to catch up.

To take a long view, consider that in 1820 China produced about 28.7% of the world's GDP with about 35.7% of its population, which implies that it had a productivity level close to 80% of the world average. By 2005, despite incredible growth of nearly 10% per year over the past 28 years, China produced 5% of the world's GDP despite having a smaller, but still world-beating 20.2% of the world's population. By the same standard, China's productivity had fallen to about 25% of the world average. In contrast, the US productivity rose from 1.8% of the world's output with about 0.9% of the world's population (already about twice the world-average GDP per person) to claim almost the same share of output as China had in 1820, 28.1%, with only 4.6% of the world population, or about six times the world-average GDP per person. Had China kept its relative level of productivity, just keeping pace with the world average, its GDP and standard of living would have been over three times higher than it is today, and it would have already had a GDP level in excess of Japan's, or it would have been the second largest in the world, having a standard of living approaching that of Chile instead of Morocco.

The basic facts about China's income and growth are summarized in Table 1. China is classified as a lower middle income country by the International Monetary Fund, but it has grown rapidly in the past 28 years since the transformation from a command to a market economy began, averaging about 9.6% per year from 1980 to 2005. The growth rate data in the table are for the period 1990–2005 and form the "best-case" baseline scenario, where growth rates continue to hold steady. The past period chosen is somewhat arbitrary. The Chinese growth rate used here is a little slower than a shorter period at the end of the interval, but faster than the whole period of reform, which would include some initial years with slower growth and also some years of slow growth that followed a couple of highly inflationary periods. US growth is also faster than in the most recent 5 years at the end of the period, but slightly slower than for the past 25 years.

Table 1 Basic facts of China and US income and growth

	2005 levels		1990–2005 growth rate	
	China	**United States**	**China**	**United States**
GDP ($ billions)	$2278	$12455	9.92%	2.98%
Population (billions)	1.304	0.298	1.08	1.02
GDP per person ($)	1749	41765	8.97	1.93
PPP-based GDP per person	7198	41399	NA	NA

Source: GDP: Economic Insight
Population: Asian Development Bank and UN
PPP-based GDP per capita: International Monetary Fund

1 Best-Case Scenario

In the best-case scenario, China and the United States would continue to grow at the same pace as they did over the 15 years from 1990 to 2005. For China, this is considered the best case because no economy has grown so fast for such a prolonged period over the past 50 years, if ever. Also, the population growth is expected to continue to slow in both countries, more so in China. Finally, the United States is expected to have slowing productivity growth according to the projections of the Social Security Trustees and most experts, and this is even more likely in China as it converges to US productivity levels.

Extrapolating the Chinese and US growth rates shown in Table 1 implies that China will catch up with US GDP in 26 years, or in 2031. The power of compound interest is illustrated by the fact that it would take 18 years to catch up with US GDP in 2005, but within another 8 years China would expand its output enough to match over a quarter century of US growth.

Because of China's population size advantage, its GDP can grow to the same size as that of the US economy with little productivity growth. Just as low productivity holds down output, the expected convergence of productivity, output per worker, means that China's productivity will grow faster than that in the United States, at least until it catches up. Since productivity determines the standard of living, this means that China's standard of living would continue to rise faster than that in the United States, well beyond the period when its GDP catches up with that in the United States.

In the best-case scenario, China's standard of living, measured by its GDP per person, would continue to improve relative to that in the United States well beyond 2031. In 2031, for example, based on the continuation of conditions described in Table 1, China's GDP per capita would be about one-fourth that in the United States, but it would have joined the group of high-income countries, at least based on today's definition. China would converge with the same GDP per capita as that of the United States in 2053, under the "best-case" assumption . The per capita GDP in both countries would be about $105,000 per person, measured in 2005 prices, about 2.5 times the current US level.

Note that the table also provides data on PPP-based GDP per capita. These data are intended by the IMF to better capture comparable measures of the standard of living because they correct for distortions in exchange rates or prices that could bias comparisons based on market prices. These IMF measures suggest a much smaller gap in the current standard of living in China and, together with the "best-case" growth rates, suggest convergence in the standard of living by 2032, about the same time as GDP convergence would occur. In China's case, at least until 2006, there is little reason to believe that these distortions could lead to an understatement of Chinese GDP, not to mention an understatement by a factor of more than three. If they did, however, separate calculations here for GDP and the standard of living would be unnecessary because PPP-based GDP per capita convergence would occur at about the same point as that for actual GDP.

2 Optimistic Case Scenario

China and the United States are not expected to be able to continue the trends of the past 15 years, however. The UN projects that China's population will peak in about 2030 and then decline slightly, averaging about a 0.1% rate from 2005 to 2050. Similarly, US population growth is expected to slow, though not as much, averaging about a 0.6% rate from 2005 to 2050. If these trends are included, both countries' GDPs will grow more slowly. For example, the U.S. Social Security Trustees expect US real GDP to expand at a 2.1% rate from 2005 to 2050, with much of the slowing coming around 2012 and beyond. A slowing in GDP growth in China due to slower growth of the population and labor force, and because of slowing productivity growth as convergence occurs, could easily bring GDP growth to about 8%, still in a very optimistic case. However, since the United States is slowing too, this does not have much effect on the convergence results. China would still, under these optimistic assumptions, reach the same GDP as that of the United States by 2035 and match its GDP per capita by 2057, both only 4 years later than in the "best case."

3 Plausible Case Scenario

Convergence is typically expected to occur primarily because higher rates of return to investment are expected in China than in the United States until convergence occurs, and this in turn is expected to lead to more rapid growth of the capital stock per worker in China. In addition, it occurs because China can take advantage of existing and more productive technologies until the country has exploited all the highest technology available in the world, and it can do so relatively cheaply. Following convergence, however, the possibilities become limited as China's ability to develop new technology through importing it would be virtually eliminated, and the country would have to rely on its own ability to develop its own globally competitive technology. In fact, both processes will slow growth in productivity and GDP well before convergence actually occurs, actually pushing convergence further into the future. Thus, the optimistic case above is just that. Japan's slowing down from the early 1970s to the 1990s is a classic example of this process, as are the more recent experiences of China's Asian Tiger neighbors and its own Special Administrative Region, Hong Kong.

More importantly, China faces four major trends that require close management to avoid major economic and political turmoil. The first is urbanization. Only about 43% of the population currently lives in cities and is part of the modern labor force. Most of the population lives in rural areas where economic opportunities are much more limited. There is strong pressure to move to cities because of huge differences in income possibilities. Second, nearly half of all enterprises are state-owned, and the transition from highly inefficient state-owned firms to profitable ones, or more likely to private firms, results in major disruption and unemployment. Both trends put strong pressure on the central government to slow down these processes and to find other ways to ameliorate the political pressures arising from relative income disparities.

The third trend is the slowing down of population growth which, as noted above, is expected to bring population expansion to a halt around 2030 and then reduce it. At about that time, China is expected to have a median age for its population that is about the same as in the United States, and subsequently its population will continue to age more rapidly. This will create pressures on the social safety net and especially on the retirement system. Fortunately, there will still be ample opportunity to develop both the employment possibilities of the still largely rural population and the productivity of the state industrial sector to continue to boost income growth.

The fourth trend is that such rapid growth in income per person, climbing to at least eight times its 1980 level, today, creates strong demands for political rights as a large middle class begins to emerge. Managing the widening gap between greater economic rights and prosperity and a static political system with few rights and little self-determination will become increasingly difficult over time. There will be growing pressure for political liberalization and openness, but meeting those demands either too rapidly or too slowly is risky for political and economic instability. All of these risks potentially adversely affect GDP growth in China.

Faced with burgeoning risks and blessed by earlier rapid convergence, it is not likely that China will be able to continue the rapid economic growth assumed in the optimistic case. More likely China will begin to slow, like its richer neighbors already have, so that its average growth rate will slow further. A slowing down to 6% real GDP growth over the post-2005 period, mainly achieved by slowing after the next couple of decades, would result in China matching the size of the US economy by mid-century and converging to a similar standard of living by 2080 or so. Only slightly slower growth could push the latter achievement off to the next century. No country in the world has ever achieved a growth rate as rapid as 6% per year over such a long period – in this case for over 75 years. However, though understandable in geopolitical terms, China's growth in the past 28 years defies history by a much greater margin.

References

Barro, Robert J. *Determinants of Economic Growth: A Cross-Country Empirical Study*, MIT Press, 1997.

Barro, Robert J. and Xavier Sala-i-Martin. "Convergence," *Journal of Political Economy*, 100(2), (April, 1992), pp. 223–251.

Fishman, Ted C. *China, Inc.: How the Rise of the Next Superpower Challenges America and the World,* Simon and Schuster, 2005.

Hall, Robert and Charles I. Jones. "Why Do Some Countries Produce So Much More Output per Worker than Others?" *The Quarterly Journal of Economics*, (February, 1999), pp. 83–116.

Kynge James. *China Shakes the World: A Titan's Rise and Troubled Future—and the Challenge for America,* Weidenfeld and Nicolson, 2006.

Maddison Angus. *The World Economy: A Millennial Perspective*, OECD Development Centre Studies, Organization for Economic Cooperation and Development, 2001.

Spence Michael. "Why China Grows So Fast," *Wall Street Journal*, January 23, 2007.

Tatom John A. "Getting to Know China," Networks Financial Institute *NFI Report*, 2007-NFI-01, January 2007.

Trustees of the Social Security and Medicare Trust Funds. *2006 Annual Report of the Trustees of the Social Security and Medicare Trust Funds*, Government Printing Office, 2006.

Index

J.R. Barth et al. (eds.), *China's Emerging Financial Markets*,
The Milken Institute Series on Financial Innovation and Economic Growth 8,
DOI 10.1007/978-0-387-93769-4, © 2009 by Milken Institute

LaVergne, TN USA
02 October 2009
159667LV00001B/8/P